Ego 's

Jameson

7

BOOKMAN
PUBLISHERS

Egon Ronay's Guides
Richbell House
77 St John Street
London EC1M 4AN

Managing Director **Christopher Lewis**
Editorial Director **Erica Brown**
Managing Editor **Angela Nicholson**
Editor **Nigel Edmund-Jones**

Leading Guides Ltd
Part of the Richbell NewMedia Ltd Group of Companies

The contents of this book are believed correct at the time of printing. Nevertheless, the publisher can accept no responsibility for errors or omissions or changes in the details given.

Designed and typeset in Great Britain by Carl Panday for Bookman Projects Ltd. Printed in Italy.

First published 1997 by Bookman Projects Ltd.
Floor 22
1 Canada Square
Canary Wharf
London E14 5AP

Establishments are independently researched or inspected. Inspections are anonymous and carried out by Egon Ronay's Guides' team of professional inspectors. They may reveal their identities at hotels in order to check all the rooms and other facilities. The Guide is independent in its editorial selection and does not accept advertising, payment or hospitality from listed establishments.

Egon Ronay's Guides Ireland Awards

This year's award winners are presented here. Full details of the
recipients can be found on the pages indicated.

14 Kildare Hotel
Straffan
**Hotel of
the Year**

18 Thornton's
Dublin
**Restaurant
of the Year**

22 John Howard
**Chef of
the Year**

40 Connie Aldridge
**Host of
the Year**

Full Contents: Page 4

1997 AWARDS

CONTENTS

Foreword

from the Minister of Tourism and Trade
ENDA KENNY, TD

In tourism today, the demand for an expectation of quality has never been higher. In countries all over the world, wherever tourism is taken seriously, the badges of distinction and excellence are much sought-after, and when won, proudly displayed.

Here in Ireland, we take tourism very seriously indeed. Our third largest industry, supporting over 100,000 jobs and generating over £2b annually, tourism is fast becoming a vital force in the Irish economy. Growing our share of the increasingly-competitive tourism markets means adhering to internationally-recognised codes of excellence. Here, ***Egon Ronay's Jameson Guide 1997 Ireland*** plays a major role.

Branded excellence is what the discerning tourist wants, and it is gratifying to see that large numbers of hotels and restaurants throughout Ireland are being accorded the coveted Egon Ronay's Guides' recommended status. Prospective customers know that in these establishments they will find service and hospitality of the highest international standards.

Branding is now an integral part of international marketing. The tourism industry, from Spain to the Seychelles, is working on brands for tourism that differentiate their product. In Ireland, we have now developed a new brand for tourism that will attract the sophisticated, high-spending visitor, for whom excellence is a priority. I believe that the cachet provided to hotels and restaurants by bodies like Egon Ronay's Guides will be crucial to the success of this brand in this regard.

Egon Ronay's Guides have been providing years of valuable, reliable and useful information on the tourist and hospitality industry. They are to be commended on their very fine work to date, and I wish them every success in this, their 4th all-Ireland edition, and in the years ahead.

Beir bua!

A word of welcome from the distillers of Jameson Irish Whiskey.

Jameson, the world's most popular  Irish Whiskey is part of the renowned welcome and hospitality to be found in Ireland. So it is fitting that Jameson be associated with this Guide.

Whiskey is an intrinsic part of Irish life and whether you are enjoying the warmth of an Irish pub, relaxing in a hotel, or sitting back after a memorable meal, there is always an

John Jameson & Son

occasion to savour a glass of Jameson Irish Whiskey.

We take great pride in the quality of Jameson. From the rich countryside of Ireland come nature's finest barley and crystal clear water. These natural ingredients are carefully distilled three times and then slowly matured for years in oak casks to produce an exceptionally smooth whiskey.

I hope you will enjoy using this Guide as you sample some of the best of Irish hospitality, food and – of course – Whiskey!

Richard Burrows
Chairman
Irish Distillers Group

JAMESON The Spirit of Ireland

Introduction
by Georgina Campbell

Welcome to the fourth annual edition of *Egon Ronay's Jameson Guide* to the best food, drink and accommodation in Ireland – a unique reference source for all travellers in Ireland. The recommendations within this Guide are compiled from the independent assessments of our experienced team of inspectors; they have travelled across the country, from Portmagee on the Ring of Kerry in the south to Portrush near the Giant's Causeway in the north, and from Clifden in Connemara on the west coast to Wicklow, Wexford and Waterford on the east, seeking out Ireland's famous hospitality in hotels, restaurants, bars, pubs and simple snack-stops. The range of establishments covers a wide spectrum, allowing the Guide to be used by business travellers and leisure tourists alike; high or low, all budgets are catered for – from B&B in guest houses to luxurious accommodation in grand castles, and from bar snacks in Ireland's famous pubs to the up-to-the-minute gourmet creations in trend-setting Dublin.

Fine Ingredients
Galway oysters, Cleggan lobsters, Atlantic salmon, Donegal potatoes, Skerries tomatoes, Wexford venison, Mullingar beef, Offaly pork – these and other fine raw ingredients like them are the strong, simple foods that form the building blocks of today's Irish cuisine; at their best they are confidently presented with simplicity, allowing their true characters to speak for themselves. Partner such food with the freshly-baked soda bread (generously spread, of course, with good salty butter) that has become symbolic of Irish food, then add a glass of stout or whiskey and it becomes the stuff of dreams. Except for variety (ever the spice of life – even in Ireland), who needs fashionable fare when the plain, native ingredients are so good?

To complement these natural gifts, Ireland is also fortunate enough to have a growing band of dedicated, outstandingly talented chefs who take great pride in their country and are determined to use its produce with respect and creativity in their cooking. The equation of superb produce, pride and creativity can add up to quite a result, so the traveller who chooses well may indeed have memorable meals in each and every corner of Ireland – a situation that is a far cry from the likely experience of even the best-informed traveller only a decade or two ago. So how has such a miraculous transformation come about – and is there, perhaps, a less pleasing side to this remarkable success story?

Gastronomic Miracles
It is no overstatement to say that Ireland is now a gastronomic destination and much credit must go to pioneers such as Myrtle Allen of *Ballymaloe House* in Shanagarry and her contemporary, the late Theodora FitzGibbon, who wrote appreciatively about the goodness of traditional Irish food at a time when it was deeply unfashionable. Other factors have played their part, too, including timing. The healthy development of all things gastronomic has coincided with the widespread renaissance of interest in Irish regional food and world-wide concern about the integrity of ingredients – covering all farming practices, from animal welfare and fish farming to organic, biodynamic growing methods.

Competition has also played a vital part in the raising of restaurant standards throughout the country. There has been a growing tendency in recent years for restaurants to cluster, providing natural competition (and, ideally, mutual support – as in in The Kinsale Good Food Circle) within the group, helping to develop a reputation for excellence that attracts visitors to the area and creates a healthy, self-perpetuating spiral of competition and achievement. Examples include Kinsale, Kenmare, Dingle, Clifden and the affluent area of North Down between Belfast and Bangor in Northern Ireland; similar developments can be seen in places like Carlingford (Co Louth), Co Wicklow and the Waterford area.

New Irish Cuisine?
However, despite how well the informed traveller can eat in every corner of Ireland, it should not be presumed that such quality is the norm. Alas, this is not the case. Despite the huge improvement overall, bad meals, or perhaps quite good meals that represent bad value, are also all too often encountered. There are still too many Irish chefs – especially those in the city hotels – who have been blindly following food fashions, producing a plethora of menus with so-called world influences. Sadly, despite recent attempts at promoting the concept of a 'New Irish Cuisine', the majority show little interest in

presenting traditional Irish food or developing it to create an identifiably Irish modern cuisine. This is a great shortcoming, especially for visitors who might well eat their way around the country and leave without the slightest idea of what Irish food really comprises. By the same token, the hospitality that is so special to Ireland and can make a visit memorable can also occasionally fail, resulting in a particularly serious sense of disappointment in a country that takes such collective pride in the warmth of its welcome. The best way forward lies in positive interaction between guest and host, so don't be afraid to make your views felt by expressing praise or complaint at the time – and, if possible, writing to us to report on your experiences – good or bad – in order to achieve higher standards.

The perennial problem of service charges in both hotels and restaurants is still a major irritant. Policies vary from 'no service charge' or 'service charge included' in some establishments to 'discretionary' in others and a mandatory charge of 10-15% in many more. A few restaurants have come up with an admirable compromise by charging a mandatory 10% on food orders but not on wine or other drinks. The public is confused and a consistent national policy (or understanding between restaurateurs) would be helpful to all visitors to Ireland. Note that all the hotel and restaurant prices that we quote include a generous amount for service (up to 15% where demanded/expected).

Inconsistent standards in many areas, ranging from quality of food and cooking through to service (particularly regarding training), provoke many complaints where establishments do not consistently reach their recognised potential. This problem is often acute in the accommodation sector and it is ironic that so many hotels are being built at a time when there is such a serious shortage of trained personnel to staff them. As in other years, a disproportionately high percentage of these complaints concerns pubs. Readers should perhaps be more aware that the character of pubs varies considerably according to the time of day, the day of the week and the season. Busy weekend trade may bring poor service, a smoky atmosphere and untidiness in both bar and loos – yes, even in Ireland!

Capital Ideas

If Dublin wants to be acknowledged as one of Europe's 'hot spots', hotel operators really must bear in mind the needs of the travelling businessman. With a plethora of new hotels under construction it is hoped that they will consider the needs of businessmen better than the existing hotels do currently, with the notable exceptions of the *Hotel Conrad*, *Jurys Towers* and *Jurys Custom House Inn* (the latter, newly-built budget hotel wins our Business Hotel of the Year Award this year). While conducting a recent survey we were consistently transferred to a hotel's banqueting department when asking for the hotel's business centre. *The Shelbourne's* business centre was closed at 5pm and practically no hotels offered either fax/modem points in bedrooms, personal computer/Internet access, mobile phone hire or translation services. When asked whether they offered access to an on-line international news and financial information service (eg Reuters), the question was often not understood. So, a clear message for the new hotel builders: build with the technological future in mind if you want to attract business customers from the existing hotels.

Finally, a message of thanks to all our sponsors who have helped to make *Egon Ronay's Jameson Guide Ireland* such a success – you will find their names on the following Sponsored Awards pages. Without their financial support it would be even more difficult to maintain the principles to which we are committed – anonymous inspection, independent assessment and unbiased opinion; these produce a Guide to Ireland that we hope our readers will find indispensable.

How To Use This Guide

This Guide includes not only our recommended establishments but many other interesting features and useful quick reference lists designed to help you select the hotel, restaurant or pub that best suits your requirements. A list of all establishments in county order, with key statistics and prices, lets you see at a glance what is available in the area where you intend to stay or eat. Places of interest are listed under the nearest relevant location throughout the Guide. For details of all listings consult the contents page.

Order of Entries
Republic of Ireland appears first, in alphabetical order by location; Northern Ireland locations come after those in the Republic. See contents page for specific page numbers and the index at the back of the Guide for individual entries by establishment name.

Map References
Map references alongside each hotel, restaurant or pub entry are to the maps at the back of the book. Use this section in conjunction with the county listings to select establishments in areas you wish to visit. Dublin has its own city maps and references alongside Dublin entries refer to those maps. Entries under Blackrock (Dublin not Co Louth), Dun Laoghaire, Monkstown and Stillorgan are also plotted on the Dublin maps.

Accommodation
Hotel entries are identified by the letter **HR**, **H**, **AR** or **A**. The former include several superior guest houses where the public rooms are limited (apart, perhaps, from a drawing room) and the restaurant may only be open to residents; these 'Private House Hotels' are ungraded; you will find a list of them (a useful source of budget accommodation) in the quick reference lists. **HR** and **AR** indicate a hotel with a recommended restaurant open to the public; Private House Hotels that offer good food will still be categorised as **H** if their restaurant is not open to non-residents; the entry will indicate where this is the case. **AR** and **A** entries are not classified by Bord Fáilte (Irish Tourist Board) as 'hotels'.

Accommodation Prices
These are based on current high-season rates at the time of going to press and include VAT, for a *standard double room for two occupants with private bath and two cooked breakfasts*. Wherever possible we have included the service charge that many Irish hotels add on to accommodation as well as food bills; this can be up to 15%.

The Percentage shown on a hotel entry is an individual rating arrived at after careful testing, inspection and calculation according to our unique grading system. **We assess** hotels on 20+ factors, which include the quality of service and the public rooms – their cleanliness, comfort, state of repair and general impression. Bedrooms are looked at for size, comfort, cleanliness and decor. The exterior of the building, efficiency of reception, conduct and appearance of the staff, room service and leisure facilities are among other factors.

The percentage is arrived at by comparing the total marks given for the 23 factors with the maximum the hotel could have achieved.

Percentage ratings

Hotels rating 80% or over are classified 'De Luxe'. A map showing these hotels is on page 13. **The Size** of a hotel and the prices charged are not considered in the grading, but the food is, and **if we recommend meals in a hotel a separate entry is made for its restaurant**.

Lodge-style chain hotels are ungraded and offer cheap, practical accommodation, usually in convenient locations for one-night stop-overs (see Index entries for Forte Travelodge & Holiday Inn Express). Private House Hotels, categorised either as an **A** (if not classified by Bord Fáilte as a 'hotel') or as an ungraded **H** in other cases, are de luxe 'bed and breakfast' establishments offering comfortable (often luxurious) accommodation and personal service. For our purposes an inn (**I** and **IR**) is normally either a pub with hotel-style accommodation or a small hotel with a bar and the atmosphere of a pub. Any hotel undergoing major construction or refurbishment programme at the time of research is also ungraded.

Bargain breaks. Almost all hotels offer bargain breaks of some kind. Specific details regarding the availability and price of such breaks should be checked with individual establishments. In addition to bargain breaks many hotels regularly offer price reductions across their range; seasonal changes, late availability, single rooms, room upgrades - remember the price quoted in this guide is for high season. Phone the hotels in the area you're intending to visit and see what they have to offer.

Restaurants

Restaurants open to the public (as opposed to many of those in private house hotels that are not) are identified by the letter **R**. We award one to three stars ★ for excellence of cooking. One star represents cooking much above average, two outstanding cooking, and three the best in the British Isles. ◼ beside stars indicates a restaurant at the top of its star range; an upward arrow by itself indicates a restaurant approaching star status. A map of Ireland's starred restaurants is on page 13.

The category **RR** denotes a restaurant with rooms, a category based on *restaurants avec chambres* in France. Food is the main attraction, but overnight accommodation is also available. A list of these restaurants appears at the back of the Guide.

We only include restaurants where the cooking comes up to our minimum standards, however attractive the place may be in other respects. We take into account how well the restaurant achieves what it sets out to do as reflected in the menu, decor, prices, publicity, atmosphere – factors that add up to some sort of expectation. Restaurants categorised **JaB** are generally more informal establishments and recommended for eating out on a budget of £15 or less per head.

Symbols

All symbols are judged and awarded by Egon Ronay's Guides' inspection team. Crowns are awarded to restaurants offering a degree of traditional luxury ⚵ or some striking modern features ◼. They have nothing to do with the quality of the cooking.

♔	Awarded a star for **Bar Food** (*not* restaurant)
♫	Good presentation of Irish bread and butter – sponsored by The National Dairy Council
🥖	Good home-made bread
🍷	Outstanding wine list
🍸	Good range of wines served by the glass
🐚	Quality seafood – sponsored by Bord Iascaigh Mhara
🥩	Good Irish meat dishes – sponsored by Bord Bía
🍮	Notable desserts
🧀	Good Irish cheeses – sponsored by The National Dairy Council
V	Vegetarian options on the menu – sponsored by Bord Glas
👪	Family-friendly establishment
☕	Good coffee – sponsored by Robt Roberts

Restaurant prices, correct at the time of going to press, **are for a three-course meal for two including one of the least expensive bottles of wine, coffee, VAT and service**.

Set-price menus. Prices quoted will often not include service and usually exclude wine. They are not necessarily of three courses. Where two prices are given thus – £14.50/£17.75 – it indicates that there is a 2 or 3-course option; prices given thus – £17.95 & £24.95 – indicates that there are two different set-price menus. A growing number of restaurants offer *only* a set-price menu (although this will usually include a choice).

Many restaurants offer at least one main course for vegetarians; tell them your requirements when you book. There are lists of no-smoking restaurants and those offering a serious vegetarian menu in the quick reference list section, as well as those establishments that we consider to be family-friendly.

Pubs

Pubs, identified by the letter **P**, are recommended primarily for their **bar food** and/or atmosphere. They vary from establishments that are more 'Inn' or modest restaurant to much simpler local bars that not only serve a good pint of stout but might also act as the village shop and general meeting place. *Only where bar food is specifically mentioned in the entry (and Bar Food stats given at the end of the entry) is it positively recommended.* Gaming machines are forbidden in pubs by law in the Republic.

De Luxe Hotels

Republic of Ireland

89%	**Cong** Ashford Castle
	Straffan Kildare Hotel
87%	**Kenmare** Park Hotel
	Kenmare Sheen Falls Lodge
84%	**Thomastown** Mount Juliet
81%	**Gorey** Marlfield House
	Newmarket-on-Fergus Dromoland Castle
80%	**Dublin** The Clarence

Map of Ireland showing:

Portrush, Ballybofey, NORTHERN, Bangor, Belfast, Helen's Bay, IRELAND, Blacklion, Castlebaldwin, Cong, REPUBLIC, Dublin, Moycullen, Straffan, Sandycove, Ballyconneely, OF, IRELAND, Newmarket-on-Fergus, Gorey, Adare, Thomastown, Ballingarry, Dingle, Kanturk, Mallow, Killarney, Kenmare, Cork, Shanagarry, Ballycotton, Ahakista

Legend:
- ⊡ 80%+ Hotel and Starred or ↑ Restaurant
- ☐ 80%+ Hotel
- • Starred or ↑ Restaurant

Starred Restaurants

Republic of Ireland

 ★ ↑
Dublin Patrick Guilbaud

★
Ahakista Shiro
Ballyconneely Erriseask House
Castlebaldwin Cromleach Lodge
Cork Arbutus Lodge
Dublin Le Coq Hardi
Dublin Thornton's
Kanturk Assolas Country House
Kenmare Park Hotel
Kenmare Sheen Falls Lodge
Mallow Longueville House
Moycullen Drimcong House
Newmarket-on-Fergus Dromoland Castle
Shanagarry Ballymaloe House
Straffan Kildare Hotel

↑
Adare Wild Geese
Ballingarry Mustard Seed at Echo Lodge
Ballybofey Kee's Hotel
Ballycotton Bayview Hotel
Blacklion Mac Nean House & Bistro
Cong Ashford Castle
Dingle Beginish Restaurant
Dublin The Clarence, Tea Room
Dublin The Commons
Dublin L'Ecrivain
Dublin Peacock Alley
Dublin Roly's Bistro
Dublin La Stampa
Dublin Zen
Killarney Aghadoe Heights Hotel
Sandycove Morels

Northern Ireland

 ★
Bangor Shanks
Belfast Roscoff
Portrush Ramore

 ↑
Helen's Bay Deane's on the Square

Awards

Ireland 1997
Hotel of the Year
Kildare Hotel
Straffan, Co Kildare

The Kildare Hotel has matured gracefully since opening in 1991 and is now known worldwide as 'The K Club', venue for the Smurfit European Open golf championship. Not only is it a fine hotel with splendid facilities and an excellent restaurant, but it portrays a distinct style: grand and dignified, yet without any hint of aloofness

or pomp. It is charmingly Irish, but with an international feel, and the staff go out of their way to make guests feel welcome and comfortable. There are too many grand hotels throughout the world that lack soul or a sense of well-being yet the K Club refreshingly embraces guests with both.

Awards

PAST WINNERS

1996	**Blue Haven Hotel** Kinsale, Co Cork
1995	**Kelly's Resort Hotel** Rosslare, Co Wexford
1994	**Ashford Castle** Cong, Co Mayo

JAMESON

CONGRATULATES THE EGON RONAY'S JAMESON GUIDE
HOTEL OF THE YEAR 1997

KILDARE HOTEL

DRINKING THE BEST OF IRISH

BY JOHN CLEMENT RYAN
AUTHOR OF "IRISH WHISKEY"

Health and long life to you
Land without rent to you
The woman (or man) of your choice to you
A child every year to you
and may you be half an hour in heaven before
the devil knows you're dead!

The art of distilling whisk(e)y has been around almost as long as people have enjoyed fine food, and Irish Whiskey is the world's oldest whisk(e)y

Soldiers of Henry II and Elizabeth I appreciated Irish Whiskey

Finest barley

type. Nobody really knows where the story of whisk(e)y began or who began it. However we do know that the secret of distillation was brought to Ireland, probably from the Middle East, by missionary monks around the 6th century AD. They discovered the *alembic* being used for distilling perfume – they invented *whiskey* and called their version of the alembic a *Pot Still.*

Even the word whiskey comes from the Irish words *Uisce Beatha* (phonetically "isk'ke-ba'ha"). How the name came into the English language was when the soldiers of King Henry II paid what turned out to be the first of several uninvited visits to Ireland in 1170, they found the native Irish consuming their *Uisce Beatha*. Henry's soldiers soon got the hang of it, but never learned to pronounce the word *Uisce Beatha* and so, during the following centuries, the word was gradually anglicised, first to *Uisce*, then to *Fuisce*, and then finally to the word *Whiskey* that we know today.

The Old Bushmills Distillery, the world's oldest licensed whiskey distillery is located in Co. Antrim. They first received their license to distil in 1608 and so have nearly 400 years of tradition behind them. Look for Black Bush as a digestif or with a little plain water, and for Bushmills Malt, the only single malt brand of Irish whiskey.

John Jameson founded his distillery in Dublin in 1780 and Jameson

Purest water

Triple Distillation

soon became the best-known Irish Whiskey in the world, a position it still holds today. A glass of Jameson is particularly appreciated as an aperitif, either on the rocks with a little plain water, and as an accompaniment to a raw or smoked fish dish, and as a digestif try twelve year old *Jameson 1780.*

Matured in Oak Casks

The taste difference between Scotch and Irish is not something that words can convey, and stems largely from the difference in production methods. Both Scotch and Irish are based on barley, part of which is malted, and here comes the first difference: Malt for Irish is dried in a closed kiln, and not over open peat fires which gives the smoky flavour that is typical of Scotch – that smoky flavour is deliberately absent from Irish, and some of the subtleties and delicacies of taste can be appreciated because of the absence of the smoky taste.

John Jameson Distillery, founded in 1780

Secondly, Irish Whiskey is distilled three times in the old-fashioned copper Pot Stills to ensure the maximum purity of the spirit, and no other whisk(e)y category in the world is distilled more than twice.

Finally, Irish is matured in oak casks for a minimum of three years by law, but in practice between five and eight years, and in the case of some of the premium brands ten, and twelve years. As well as the brands from the Jameson and Bushmills stables, other brands that will be encountered are Powers Gold Label, the favourite in Ireland.

If you are travelling around Ireland, be sure to call in to learn the Story of Irish Whiskey. If you are in the North, visit the Bushmills Distillery, located in the village of Bushmills in Co. Antrim. This is open to visitors throughout the year (Mondays to Thursdays 9.00-12.00, 13.30-15.30 and Fridays 9.00-11.45, no reservations necessary). When in Dublin, go to the old Jameson distillery at Bow Street to see the *Irish Whiskey Corner* a museum to the history of Irish Whiskey where visitors are welcome. Here there is a tour daily (Mon-Fri) at 15.30 sharp. Finally *The Jameson Heritage Centre* in Midleton, Co. Cork, just 13 miles east of Cork City, is open to visitors throughout the summer months during each day including weekends from 10.00-16.00. Visitors enjoy a guided tour through the Old Distillery, a whisk(e)y tasting, an audio-visual show, coffee shop, souvenir shop, and craft shops on the site.

After a fine meal, lift your glass of Jameson or Bushmills and wish an old Irish Toast to your companions:

May the road rise to meet you
May the wind be always at your back
May the sun shine warm upon your face
And the rain fall soft upon your fields
And until we meet again
May God hold you in the hollow
of His Hand.

Matured to Perfection

Awards

Ireland 1997
Restaurant of the Year

Thornton's
Dublin 8

Winner of our Chef of the Year last year, Kevin Thornton has consolidated his position at the top of the Dublin culinary scene this year with his eponymous, 40-seat restaurant in a peaceful setting

alongside the Grand Canal in Portobello. His up-to-the-minute cooking of luxury ingredients (lobster, foie gras, caviar, truffle and ostrich are often to be found on the menu) is admirably complemented by elegant dish presentation and impressive service – a marriage that deserves high praise, along with his eye for detail throughout. Style may be an important element in both kitchen and dining-room but it is never allowed to predominate just for its own sake. The decor of the two-roomed restaurant on the first floor is modern and uncluttered, and the open-to-view, ground-floor kitchen is an inspiration for guests who want to sample Kevin's *menu surprise* – a real gastronomic treasure hunt.

Awards

PAST WINNERS

1996 **Cromleach Lodge**
Castlebaldwin, Co Sligo

1995 **La Stampa**
Dublin

ERNEST & JULIO GALLO

CONGRATULATES THE EGON RONAY'S JAMESON GUIDE
RESTAURANT OF THE YEAR 1997

THORNTON'S

The city he loved. The cafe she remembered. California's best loved wi

Memories await. The Wines of Ernest & Julio Gallo, California.

WINE MAKER'S NOTES: Aged in oak, cork matured. Very dry and well balanced. Cla

Across the bay to San Francisco.

...rnet character with hints of berry, plum and spice. Superb with red meat and pasta.

Awards

Ireland 1997
Chef of the Year

John Howard
Le Coq Hardi, Dublin 4

Twenty years on, John's cooking style has changed little: still classically French, though perhaps these days with a nod to new Irish tastes. Last year's fire might have closed the restaurant for a while and destroyed the cellar, but it has not dampened John's enthusiasm. Everything that he and and his wife Catherine have achieved is by dint of hard work and consistent standards, and the Ballsbridge restaurant remains deservedly popular, demonstrating that talented chefs who are true to their roots will be successful in any era. Like John's beloved horses, finishing in front requires good teamwork from behind – and John will be the first to recognise the contribution of his right-hand man James O'Sullivan.

Awards

PAST WINNERS	
1996	**Kevin Thornton** Thornton's, Dublin
1995	**Stefan Matz** Erriseask House, Ballyconneely
1995	**Gerry Galvin** Drimcong House, Moycullen

TIPPERARY

CONGRATULATES THE EGON RONAY'S JAMESON GUIDE
CHEF OF THE YEAR 1997

JOHN HOWARD

TO THE

connoisseur

IT'S THE

purist

WATER

IT'S NOT WHAT IS IN A MINERAL WATER

THAT DETERMINES ITS QUALITY,

IT'S WHAT IS ABSENT. IN THAT RESPECT,

TIPPERARY NATURAL MINERAL WATER

IS OF THE HIGHEST QUALITY.

IT HAS THE LOWEST MINERALISATION

OF ANY IRISH MINERAL WATER

AND A PERFECT PH BALANCE.

═══

FROM THE PUREST ENVIRONMENT,

THE PURIST'S WATER.

THE PURIST'S WATER.

TIPPERARY
═ *Irish* ═
NATURAL
MINERAL WATER

BY APPOINTMENT TO MOTHER NATURE

Ireland
THE FOOD ISLAND

Irish food & drink...

Welcome to the Food Island. With this guide, you will be directed to some of the finest cuisine Ireland has to offer. Bord Bia similarly provides the route guiding Irish companies to place the best of Irish food products on tables around the world.

A Message from

Michael Duffy

Chief Executive,

Irish Food Board,

Bord Bia

Bord Bia is a specialist organisation, founded to promote and develop markets for Irish food and drink. We target overseas markets, acting as a bridge between Irish suppliers and international buyers, and we provide a comprehensive promotional and information service.

But more than that, Bord Bia is a catalyst for innovation and quality in the Irish food industry. As you explore the many establishments recommended by Egon Ronay, you will be struck by the high quality and diversity of our catering sector. The number of restaurants in Ireland has risen by almost 30% in the past five years, and this growth is expected to continue.

Bord Bia plays a key role in supporting these advances by encouraging Irish suppliers to recognise and maximise the potential of the food service sector, and by helping them achieve the high standards required by restaurateurs and consumers alike.

Thus, we are pleased to be associated with, in conjunction with Egon Ronay's Guides, the awards for the hotels and restaurants serving the best Irish food, and for those serving the best beef, lamb or pork. Their use of fine Irish ingredients exemplifies the quality and distinctiveness of Irish food and cuisine.

...naturally good

Whether you live in Ireland, or you are visiting, through this guide you will discover a new map – of the Food Island. But reading the guide is not enough; to really appreciate the sophistication of contemporary Irish cuisine you must experience the hotels and restaurants serving fine Irish food – naturally.

MICHAEL DUFFY,
Chief Executive.

Bord Bia
Irish Food Board

Awards

Ireland 1997
Irish Food Award

O'Callaghan Family, Longueville House
Mallow, Co Cork

Truly a family affair, Longueville House has associations with the
O'Callaghan family that date back a couple of centuries. The imposing,
Georgian house is just the sort of setting where you would hope to find
the vey best that Ireland has to offer, and visitors will not be disappointed.
Michael, Jane and daughter-in-law Aisling offer fine hospitality while
son William presides over the kitchen. Their own farm, river, garden
and vineyard greatly contribute to the tip-top produce on offer – from
gooseberry compote and freshly-pressed apple juice at breakfast to superb
Longueville lamb (a real house speciality), house-smoked Blackwater river

salmon and trout like you've
never tasted before, perhaps
a millefeuille of beef fillet with
herb cake and horseradish sauce,
and loin of Kilbrack farmyard
pork. The past Presidents of
Ireland who gaze down on
diners in the dining-room
see much of which they
can be proud.

Bord Bía
Irish Food Board

Awards

PAST WINNER
1996   **Myrtle Allen** Ballymaloe House, Shanagarry, Co Cork

BORD BIA

CONGRATULATES THE EGON RONAY'S JAMESON GUIDE
IRISH FOOD AWARD WINNER 1997

LONGUEVILLE HOUSE

Awards

Ireland 1997
Irish Lamb Award

Buggy's Glencairn Inn
Lismore, Co Waterford

Ken and Cathleen Buggy's charming new venture (regular readers may remember them from the *Old Presbytery* in Kinsale) is sited in a house that dates back to 1720 and has been an inn for over two hundred years. From the stone-floored bar to the eiderdown warmth of the big brass beds and the table delights of the bountiful River Blackwater, the Glencairn Inn offers the sort of Irish charm that people travel the world

to find. It will probably come as no surprise, then, to find 'traditional Irish stew and soda bread' on the bar menu; however, you won't always find it executed as good as you'll find here. Irish lamb is what makes all the difference, of course – given that you have Ken in the kitchen!

Irish Food Board

Awards

PAST WINNER

1996   Tinakilly House
Rathnew, Co Wicklow

BORD BIA
CONGRATULATES THE EGON RONAY'S JAMESON GUIDE
IRISH LAMB AWARD WINNER 1997
BUGGY'S GLENCAIRN INN

Awards

Ireland 1997
Irish Pork Award
Danette's Feast
Carlow

Danette O'Connell's and David Milne's charming country-house restaurant earns its first entry into the Guide this year. Imagination is a key theme in Danette's kitchen and pork makes regular appearances

on her short menus. Among a selection of five main courses one might find a really good pork dish like soy- and honey-glazed fillet of pork pieces on a rosemary skewer served with an orange and ginger sauce. Attention to detail extends to a choice of home-made breads, well-marinated meats, organic vegetables and fresh flower decorations. Delicious food punctuated by punchy flavourings – excellent all round.

Bord Bía
Irish Food Board

Awards

PAST WINNERS	
1996	**Roly's Bistro** Ballsbridge, Dublin 4
1995	**China-Sichuan Restaurant** Stillorgan, Co Dublin

BORD BIA
CONGRATULATES THE EGON RONAY'S JAMESON GUIDE
IRISH PORK AWARD WINNER 1997
DANETTE'S FEAST

Awards

Ireland 1997
Irish Beef Award
Elephant & Castle
Dublin 2

No fancy cooking wins our Irish Beef Award this year – just good, middle-market food in an informal, buzzy, New York-style restaurant to be found in Dublin's Temple Bar area. The Elephant & Castle offers a choice of a dozen or more hamburgers, all made from fine Irish beef and accurately cooked to order. On the modern brasserie-style menu you might also find beef carpaccio with rocket and shaved parmesan, and popular steaks (grilled fillet with salsa verde and leeks vinaigrette or rare sliced steak with cracked pepper, rocket and ginger vinaigrette). Daily specials might include the likes of stir-fried beef with orange and spinach. Honest cooking using prime ingredients always wins!

Bord Bía

Irish Food Board

Awards

PAST WINNERS	
1996	**Crookedwood House** Mullingar, Co Westmeath
1995	**Rathsallagh House** Dunlavin, Co Wicklow
1994	**Dunraven Arms** Adare, Co Limerick

BORD BIA

CONGRATULATES THE EGON RONAY'S JAMESON GUIDE
IRISH BEEF AWARD WINNER 1997

ELEPHANT & CASTLE

Irish food & drink...
...naturally good

Recipes from some of Ireland's Top Chefs

STARTER

Smoked Eel & Mussel Hotpot
Serves 4

This hot fish broth contains dillisk, a seaweed also known as dulce that is found all round the Irish coast but especially on the western seaboard. It can be used fresh - eaten raw, stewed or fried as a vegetable, or added to fish stews and soups - or more commonly dried and soaked, as here.

50 g (2 oz) dillisk, soaked in cold water
48 plump mussels, scrubbed & de-bearded
Glass white wine
750 ml (1½ pints) fish stock
350 g (12 oz) smoked eel, filleted & cut into small pieces
3 tablesp. chopped sweet cicely
3 tablesp. grated Irish farm cheese
Salt & freshly ground pepper

Soak and shred dillisk. Steam the mussels open with the white wine, then shell them. Bring the fish stock to the boil, add the eel, shelled mussels and shredded dillisk, then simmer for a minute. Divide between six deep plates or bowls and sprinkle sweet cicely and cheese equally over each. Serve with freshly baked soda bread and carrot & dillisk bread.

MAIN COURSE

Spiced Pork Roast, Apple & Thyme Cream Sauce
Serves 4

Belly of pork, also known as "lap" of pork, makes a tender, flavoursome roasting joint; cooked simply on the bone it has the advantage of a large area of skin to make crackling, but here Gerry has his free range pork boned and skinned for stuffing and rolling in this unusual dish.

1 pork belly, about 1½ kg (3 lb)
Stuffing
1 medium onion, finely chopped
3 cloves garlic, crushed
75 g (3 oz) butter
A bunch of mixed fresh herbs, finely chopped

Gerry Galvin of Drimcong House Restaurant, Moycullen, Co Galway, is one of Ireland's culinary pioneers. *He has been outstandingly innovative in his development of original dishes and a consistently dedicated supporter of the best local produce and its suppliers. Always ahead of his time, he has developed some stunningly original concepts in his own restaurant.*

Bord Bía

Irish Food Board

Taken from the Bord Bia booklet **'New Irish Cuisine'**

225 g (8 oz) fine breadcrumbs	
1 egg, beaten	
Salt & freshly ground pepper	
Spicy Paste	
2 tablesp. melted butter	
2 tablesp. chutney	
1 tablesp. lemon juice	
2 cloves garlic, crushed	
2 tablesp. Guinness flavoured mustard	
Sauce	
2 large cooking apples, peeled, cored & chopped	
1 medium onion, peeled & chopped	
2 garlic cloves	
2 sprigs thyme	
125 ml (1/4 pint) medium/sweet white wine	
125 ml (1/4 pint) chicken stock	
250 ml (1/2 pint) cream.	

First prepare the stuffing: Cook the onion and
garlic in butter until soft, then add the herbs
and breadcrumbs. Cool a little before mixing in
the egg and seasoning well with salt and freshly
ground pepper.

Preheat the oven: 300°F/150°C/Gas mark 2.

To prepare the meat: Trim off any excess fat
and prick the centre of the meat with a kitchen
fork, then combine all the Spicy Paste
ingredients together and brush the meat with
half this mixture. Spread the stuffing over the
meat, then roll it up and tie firmly with cotton
string.

To cook: Brown the meat with a little oil in
a hot roasting tin and cook in the preheated
oven, seam side up - preferably on a rack over
the tin - for 3 hours. Halfway through cooking,
remove the joint from the oven and brush
liberally with the remaining Spicy Paste; return
to the oven seam side down and continue
cooking.

To make the sauce: Bring everything to the
boil and simmer for 15 minutes, then discard
the thyme, liquidise the mixture, strain and
season to taste. If it seems too thick, adjust the
texture with extra stock. Serve the sliced meat
on heated plates with its sauce.

To accompany: Mashed potato, pickled carrots
and a seasonal salad.

Tipsy Pudding in Mulled Wine

Serves 6

This light sponge pudding soaked in mulled
wine is an old favourite at Drimcong and has
become something of a signature dish. Its richly
traditional flavouring makes perfect comfort
food in the colder months. It is equally
delicious with a honeyed cream cheese sauce
or home made ice cream.

Pudding
25 g (1 oz) melted butter
4 size 2 eggs, separated
150 g (6 oz) caster sugar
Grated rind of a washed lemon
150 g (6 oz) fine white breadcrumbs
Mulled Wine:
750 ml (1½ pints) red wine
Juice & pared zest of 2 lemons and 1 orange (washed)
100g (4 oz) caster sugar
1 cinnamon stick & 4 cloves
A glass (measure) of whiskey

Preheat a moderate oven, 350°F/ 180°C/
Gas mark 4. Grease six ramekins with melted
butter.

To make the puddings: Beat the egg yolks
with half of the sugar and the lemon rind
until frothy. Whisk the whites, gradually
adding the remaining sugar, until stiff.
Stir a quarter of this mixture into the egg
and lemon froth and fold in the remainder,
then the breadcrumbs. Divide between the
ramekins and bake for about 25 minutes,
then cool and unmould.

To make the mulled wine: Bring everything
except the whiskey up to the boil and simmer
for five minutes, then add the whiskey.
Spoon this mixture over the puddings until
thoroughly soaked, then serve with a bowl
of honeyed cream cheese sauce on the side.

Ireland
THE FOOD ISLAND

Irish food & drink...
...naturally good

Recipes from some of Ireland's Top Chefs

STARTER

Traditional Potato Pancake
with Apple & Ginger Marmalade
Serves 4

Noel eyes the weather anxiously in spring, at potato-planting time - too early and they'll catch the frost, too late and precious days of home-grown crops will be lost. These pancakes are perhaps a little richer than tradition demands, but it is the lightness and piquancy of the accompanying sauce that makes this a thoroughly modern dish, even though all the ingredients have been familiar through many generations

Pancakes

1 kg (2 lb) potatoes
50 g (2 oz) flour
Grated nutmeg, salt & freshly ground pepper
2 eggs
125 ml (¼ pint) cream
125 ml (¼ pint) milk

Sauce

Rind and juice of 1 orange
2 cooking apples, Bramley Seedling
¼ teasp. ground ginger
25 g (1 oz) sugar.

To prepare the pancakes: Peel the potatoes, then boil them until tender; drain and mash.

Add the flour, a grating of nutmeg and seasoning; mix well. Add the eggs, one at a time, then stir in the cream and finally, add the milk slowly until the mixture reaches dropping consistency.

Set aside and leave to rest.

Meanwhile, make the sauce: Wash the orange and, using a vegetable peeler, remove the zest, then cut it into strips and put into boiling water for a couple of minutes to blanch; drain. Peel, core and chop the apples. Combine all ingredients in a saucepan and cook gently until soft.

To cook the pancakes: Heat a heavy frying pan, add a little butter or olive oil, then swirl in a ladleful of the pancake mixture. Cook until set and nicely browned on both sides and serve hot with the sauce.

MAIN COURSE

Knaves of Beef Stuffed
with Wild Mushrooms
Serves 4

Beef olives have been popular in Ireland, under one name or another, for as long as anyone can remember and here again Noel demonstrates his knack of developing a familiar theme to create something quite different and unusual, yet in no way artificial. Field mushrooms and Guinness are simple enough ingredients, but they make a powerful statement.

8 wafer thin slices of round of beef, 50-75 g (2-3 oz) each
A little oil
Stuffing
25 g (1 oz) butter
100 g (4 oz) wild mushrooms, chopped
1 teasp. finely chopped garlic
1 teasp. freshly chopped tarragon
1 cupful breadcrumbs
Salt & black pepper
1 egg, beaten
Sauce
500 ml (1 pint) beef stock
250 ml (½ pint) Guinness

Preheat a moderate oven, 350°F/180°C/Gas mark 4.

First make the stuffing: Melt the butter in a pan and cook the mushrooms and garlic for 2 minutes until softening. Mix in the tarragon and breadcrumbs. Remove from the heat, season with salt and a grinding of pepper and add the beaten egg, mixing well together.

To stuff the meat: Lay the slices of beef out flat, season and place a spoonful of stuffing on each one. Roll up neatly and secure with a wooden cocktail stick.

To cook: Heat a little oil in a heavy pan and add the meat, turning to seal on all side. Place in an ovenproof dish and add the stock and Guinness, which will reduce during cooking. Cook, until the meat is tender, in the preheated oven, occasionally turning the meat in the liquid.

To serve: Check the sauce for seasoning and arrange two pieces of beef and their sauce on hot dinner plates; baked potatoes and crisp green cabbage with bacon make good accompaniments.

Noel Kenny, chef-proprietor of Crookedwood House Restaurant, near Mullingar, is an imaginative yet very down to earth chef, with a sure knowledge of the surrounding countryside, and strongly masculine tastes balanced by a certain delicacy.

DESSERT

Children of Lir
Serves 4

In honour of the local legend, in which the Children of Lir were turned into swans, this fantasy dessert of meringue and chocolate swans swimming across a decorative lake has become a house speciality. It is always on the menu, although it does vary a little occasionally - the swan necks may be piped in meringue instead of chocolate, as given here, for example, or if it is more convenient, the pastry boat can be omitted and the number of swans doubled - and any leftover piping chocolate can be used to draw little "waves" on the lake.

125 ml (¹/₄ pint) cream
1 tablesp. Baileys Cream Liqueur
100 g (4 oz) dark chocolate
6 g (¹/₄ oz) butter
2 tablesp. cocoa powder & icing sugar, sieved together
1 tablesp. golden syrup
2 tablesp. double cream
4 small boat-shaped pastry cases filled with seasonal fruit.
Meringue
2 egg whites
100g (4 oz) caster sugar

First make the meringues: Switch on the oven at its lowest setting. Line a large baking sheet with baking parchment. Whisk the egg whites until stiff, then whisk in the sugar to make a meringue of piping consistency. Pipe sixteen oval shells onto the parchment and dry out in the oven for about an hour. Allow to cool.

Meanwhile, whip the cream, add the Baileys and leave to chill.

To make the swans' necks: Melt 25 g (1 oz) of the chocolate with 6 g (¹/₄ oz) butter and blend in the cocoa and icing sugar to make a smooth consistency, then put into a piping bag fitted with a small plain nozzle and carefully pipe eight curved necks onto parchment paper. Chill for 10 minutes to allow the chocolate to set.

Meanwhile make a light chocolate sauce: Melt the remaining 75 g (3 oz) chocolate, add the golden syrup and whisk in two tablespoons of double cream.

To assemble: Divide the sauce between four large plates. Using the whipped Baileys cream, assemble two swans on each chocolate "lake" - set each meringue shell on a nest of whipped cream and anchor the chocolate necks in the cream. Place a pastry boat filled with fruit on each plate, dust with icing sugar and serve.

Bord Bia
Irish Food Board

Taken from the Bord Bia booklet 'New Irish Cuisine'

Awards

Ireland 1997
Host of the Year

Connie Aldridge
Mount Falcon Castle, Ballina, Co Mayo

Owner and hostess Constance Aldridge has greeted visitors to Mount Falcon for over 60 years and her presence at dinner is an indispensable part of the charm of the 'Castle'. Sitting at the head of the communal dinner table she dispenses lovely home-made soup from an elegant silver tureen, while her staff ensure that the company

is convivial and that all their guests are entertained in a manner that is entirely appropriate to such a welcoming place. Set in a 100-acre estate, the mansion is not only renowned as a fishing and shooting base but also for the watchful, experienced eye of Constance, affectionately known (and never forgotten once met) by all as 'Con'.

Awards

PAST WINNERS	
1996	**Patrick Guilbaud** Restaurant Patrick Guilbaud, Dublin 2
1995	**Mary Bowe** Marlfield House, Gorey
1994	**Francis Brennan** Park Hotel, Kenmare

JAMESON

**CONGRATULATES THE EGON RONAY'S JAMESON GUIDE
HOST OF THE YEAR 1997**

CONNIE ALDRIDGE

"Serve good food,

and your dinner guests will finish

every mouthful.

Open a good brandy and, regrettably,

the same is true."

ARNOLD SORENSON,
VEGAN FOOD CRITIC, CALIFORNIA.

INTRODUCE SOME CALIFORNIAN INTO
THE CONVERSATION.

E&J

SINGLE CASK MATURED BRANDY.

JACOB'S CREEK®

"The wine is loaded with fruit, brilliantly drinkable and so easy to enjoy... This is what food and wine is all about; simple tastes, good quality; and with the wine the Australians tend to do it better than anyone else"

SANDY O'BYRNE
The Irish Times

"The rich chardonnay nose and layers of subtle fruit have a zingy freshness and a complexity that you expect from a much dearer wine. It's a revelation and I would expect it to have the same appeal as the red"

RONAN FARREN
The Sunday Independent

"It is clean, deliciously fruity with lovely tropical fruit nuances and offers remarkable value"

T.P. WHELEHAN
The Sunday Press

DISCOVER AUSTRALIA'S AWARD WINNING WINES

Awards

Ireland 1997
Wine Cellar of the Year
The Wine Vault
Waterford, Co Waterford

Waterford has associations with the wine trade that go back as far as the 13th century, to when King Henry III granted the city a special exemption to only pay half the import duty on wine. David Dennison's bistro, in the oldest part of town, is above the wine shop in the vaults below. Here there are wine tastings and wine courses, but most customers just like browsing around. The wine list comprises some fifty pages, is

clearly laid out and is a good read, presenting wines of supreme quality at very fair prices; around a dozen house wines, all available by the glass, are themselves enough to satisfy most. But delve deeper and you'll find an array of excellent wines from around the world, each carefully and sensibly described; in addition, there are notes on regions, vineyards and growers. The New World fares as well as Europe, and it's noticeable that South Africa features prominently. France and the Irish Wine Geese, of course, are well to the fore, and even Greece and Hungary make token appearances. It's not a huge list, but one which connoisseurs will enjoy, though they will no doubt enjoy the contents of the bottles even more – Slainte!

Awards

Past Winners	
1996	**The Hungry Monk** Greystones, Co Wicklow
1995	**Le Coq Hardi** Dublin
1994	**Arbutus Lodge** Cork

ORLANDO
CONGRATULATES THE EGON RONAY'S JAMESON GUIDE
WINE CELLAR OF THE YEAR 1997
THE WINE VAULT

Orlando. Australia's Award Winning Wines.

In 1847 Johann Gramp, a German immigrant and founder of Orlando Wines, planted his first vineyards at Jacob's Creek in South Australia's Barossa Valley. Within three years Johann had crushed his first grapes and made around eight gallons (36 litres) of white wine.

He later became the Barossa Valley's first commercial winemaker and named the company 'Orlando' a German derivation of the name Roland (now Rowland) Flat, the site of his first winery. Orlando expanded rapidly and by 1971 had become one of the leaders of the Australian wine industry.

Since then Orlando have carefully grown and selected premium grapes from a wide variety of cooler climate vineyard areas throughout South East Australia often many miles from their original vineyards in the Barossa Valley.

These areas such as Coonawarra and Padthaway, south of Adelaide, are becoming internationally famous for the production of some of Australia's finest wines.

BAROSSA VALLEY
EDEN VALLEY
ADELAIDE
SYDNEY
MELBOURNE
COONAWARRA
PADTHAWAY

Carrington.

CARRINGTON EXTRA BRUT AND CARRINGTON ROSÉ

Carrington Extra Brut is produced from early-harvested fruit to ensure delicacy and elegance. A small amount of carefully selected red wine is added to produce the Rosé. Complex in aroma and delicate fruit flavour, extended yeast contact adds richness to these top quality sparkling wines.

ORLANDO "RF" CABERNET SAUVIGNON

An excellent example of a premium, full-flavoured Cabernet Sauvignon. A rich, medium-bodied wine with minty Cabernet characters balanced by integrated soft oak flavours from 12 months maturation in French and American oak.

ORLANDO "RF" CHARDONNAY

This full-flavoured premium white is a complex blend of grapes from a large spectrum of warm and cooler regions. Aged in French and American casks this Chardonnay has distinctive oak character.

JACOB'S CREEK

With its first vintage in 1973 Jacob's Creek broke new ground in establishing a benchmark for quality Australian red wine and became the most popular brand in Australia. With 1992 being celebrated as the twentieth vintage of Jacob's Creek, it is now one of Australia's most successful wine exports being shipped to over forty international markets.

ST. HUGO COONAWARRA CABERNET SAUVIGNON

Coonawarra is regarded as the best region for Australian red wines. St. Hugo is traditionally vinified using selected premium fruit and is matured in oak for up to two years giving depth of colour and excellent fruit structure.

ST. HILARY PADTHAWAY CHARDONNAY

From Padthaway in South Australia, the components are fermented and aged in new and one year old oak for a period of six months. It is a fine elegant Chardonnay with attractive complexity on the nose and rich, round fruit flavours.

Awards

Ireland 1997
Pub of the Year

Mary Ann's Bar & Restaurant
Castletownshend, Co Cork

Fergus and Patricia O'Mahoney's 150-year-old, cosy, low-ceilinged bar is to be found halfway up the steep main street of this picturesque little harbour village. It's a delightful, wonderfully

old-fashioned little place in which to sample a real taste of Ireland. The bar food (particularly the home-made bread) encompasses all the usual Irish favourites like wild smoked salmon, seafood chowder and crab cocktail; upstairs, the pub's small restaurant is a further stage for Patricia to make good use of the best local produce (tip-top seafood, West Cork lamb and farmhouse cheeses among them).

Awards

PAST WINNERS	
1996	**An Poitín Stil** Rathcoole, Co Dublin
1995	**The Hillside** Hillsborough, Lisburn
1994	**Smugglers Creek Inn** Rossnowlagh, Co Donegal

JAMESON
CONGRATULATES THE EGON RONAY'S JAMESON GUIDE
PUB OF THE YEAR 1997
MARY ANN'S BAR & RESTAURANT

Out of Africa...

The Father of South African Wine

Wine making in the Cape began over 350 years ago when, soon after the thirty year war, an expedition under the command of Jan Van Riebeeck (pronounced Ree-bee-ek) ended their four month voyage from Holland to South Africa.

The small fleet of three ships, led by the 200-ton Drommedaris, was sent by the Dutch East India Company to set up a food supplies station and arrived at their destination on 6th April, 1652.

On a four month sea journey at that time, a death rate of up to forty percent was not unusual, but this small fleet had just lost 2 of their company.

The 33 year old Van Riebeeck had been a ship's surgeon and noted that the Portuguese and Spanish losses at sea were less than those of the Dutch. The only difference seemed to be in their diet, the Mediterranean based fleets included wine in their on-board rations.

On arrival, Van Riebeeck quickly determined that the Cape had a Mediterranean climate and soon convinced his council of seventeen back home in Holland to send him some vine cuttings.

There are few countries that have been growing grapes as long as South Africa that can pin-point their exact winemaking beginnings.

Jan Van Riebeeck, however, kept a meticulous diary and on the 2nd of February 1659 he wrote;

"Today, God be Praised, Wine was pressed for the first time from Cape Grapes."

Riebeeck
The New world Wines from the Cape.

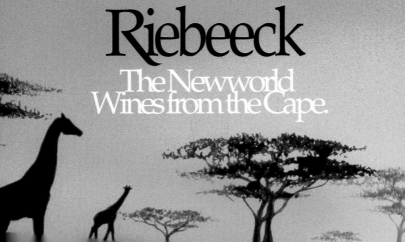

Awards

Ireland 1997
Best Use of Fruit & Vegetables
Katherine Norén
Dunworley Cottage & Kicki's Cabin
Butlerstown & Clonakilty, Co Cork

Katherine Norén's very individual approach to cooking is no secret to Irish food-lovers. Hailing originally from Sweden, she brings to Dunworley an unusual Scandinavian approach combined with a refreshingly straightforward and honest attitude towards cooking. Her pungent nettle soup (made with hand-picked tips of young nettles – a labour of love) had already made its mark by the time she opened *Kicki's Cabin* last year; for her new venture she created a nettle pie – an original, tart-like creation with a distinctive, herby taste. Look out for her home-grown globe artichokes, potato and leek soup, lingonberries served with the local speciality Clonakilty black and white pudding and sherry sauce, mussel soup enhanced with orange juice and fennel, vegetarian gratins, stir-fries (often with ginger and sweet and sour sauce), quiche platters, vegetarian terrines, and wonderful cinnamon-spiced apple strudel and mint mousse among the desserts. Big, colourful organic salads underline the attention to detail that has made both Dunworley and now Kicki's Cabin as popular as they deserve to be.

An Bord Glas
The Horticultural Development Board

Awards

Bord Glas

Congratulates the Egon Ronay's Jameson Guide Best Use of Fruit & Vegetables Winner 1997

Katherine Norén

An apple a

...is a great start!

day

But really we need four or more portions of fruit or vegetables every day to provide a rich natural source of vitamins A, C, E and fibre - as recommended by leading health and nutrition experts. This intake may help to lower the risk of cancer and heart disease as well as diet-related diseases.

Also, to lose weight, it is recommended that we eat more fruit, vegetables and potatoes in our diet and reduce fat intake.

An Bord Glas - the Horticultural Development Board - is dedicated to encouraging the increased consumption of fresh fruit, vegetables and potatoes in our diet as a vital contributor to a healthier lifestyle.

For leaflets, posters or recipes on fresh fruit, vegetables and potatoes please call our information centre at (01) 6614105

An Bord Glas
The Horticultural Development Board

Awards

Ireland 1997
Happy Heart Eat Out Award
The Old Rectory
Wicklow, Co Wicklow

Paul and Linda Saunders' delightful Victorian house is set in Wicklow County, which is renowned as the 'Garden of Ireland' – so where better a retreat to keep both your head and heart happy? Long known as *the* place for health-conscious gourmets, Linda's style of 'green cuisine' is focused on pure wholefoods exquisitely presented with the aid of organically grown herbs and edible flowers. Oil-rich kippers, home-mixed, fibre-rich muesli and home-made bread get

the day off to a good start, with original 'floral cuisine' to look forward to at dinner. Typically, one might find cream cheese-filled kale flowers as canapés, lean meats, sea-fresh fish and shellfish on the menu alongside a floral crepe with stir-fried vegetables and nuts on a red pepper coulis. Interesting salads and lovely, light desserts complete the Old Rectory's picture of health.

Awards

THE IRISH HEART FOUNDATION
CONGRATULATES THE EGON RONAY'S JAMESON GUIDE
HAPPY HEART EAT OUT AWARD WINNER 1997
THE OLD RECTORY

HAPPY
HEART

Eat Out

HEALTH
PROMOTION
UNIT

IRISH
HEART
FOUNDATION

More and more people are interested in healthy eating yet still want to enjoy delicious food, and already many establishments are responding to this challenge.

To help you offer your customers a wider and more creative range of healthy options, the Irish Heart Foundation and the Health Promotion Unit, Department of Health invite you to participate in the 4th annual HAPPY HEART EAT OUT which runs for the month of June 1997.

In line with the national healthy eating campaign for 1997, HAPPY HEART EAT OUT aims to encourage establishments to provide a range of fibre-rich healthy options on menus. Publicity and promotional materials will inform your customers about the campaign.

A recipe booklet including recipes from participating establishments, together with information sheets, promotional table tent cards and posters will be sent to you on request - please telephone the **Irish Heart Foundation at 01 668 5001.**

In association with the Egon Ronay's Jameson Guide, there will be HAPPY HEART EAT OUT AWARD categories for healthy eating in 1998.

Awards

Ireland 1997
Seafood Restaurant of the Year

Gaby's
Killarney, Co Kerry

Though the award goes to Geert and Marie Maes, the success of their restaurant owes as much to the daily landings of the Kerry fishing fleet as to their own dedicated service to the local community

for more than twenty years. Customers come from far and wide – note the Dutch, German and French translations on the menu – to sample fresh seafood at its very best; choose a lobster from the tank, mussels from Kenmare Bay, Atlantic prawns, a rustic fisherman's pie or a simple bowl of seafood cream soup, perhaps accompanied by home-made traditional Irish soda bread, and rest assured that you can depend on the freshness of produce and the warmest of welcomes.

Awards

PAST WINNERS

1996	**Kealys Seafood Bar** Greencastle, Co Donegal
1995	**Red Bank Restaurant** Skerries, Co Dublin
1994	**Chez Youen** Baltimore, Co Cork

BORD IASCAIGH MHARA
CONGRATULATES THE EGON RONAY'S JAMESON GUIDE
SEAFOOD RESTAURANT OF THE YEAR 1997
GABY'S

BIM
An Bord Iascaigh Mhara
Irish Sea Fisheries Board
is responsible for
developing and expanding
markets at home
and abroad
for Irish Seafood

For information contact:

Market Development Division,
BIM/Irish Sea Fisheries Board/
An Bord Iascaigh Mhara,
Crofton Road,
Dun Laoghaire,
Co.Dublin,
Ireland.

Tel: 353 1 2841544
Fax: 353 1 2841123

IRISH SEAFOOD

...Nature's Best

Awards

Ireland 1997
Seafood Dish of the Year

Bon Appétit
Malahide, Co Dublin

Patsy McGuirk's elegant basement restaurant is set in a Georgian terrace and underwent a total transformation last year, producing a more soothing setting with a higher comfort level throughout. The main attraction continues to be excellent fresh fish – from simple Kilmore crab claws in garlic sauce to the more involved 'sole création McGuirk' (boned Dover sole filled with prawns and turbot, served with a beurre blanc). Our 1997 Seafood Dish of the Year is a long-established house speciality: baked hake fillet with a red pepper coulis, garden peas and a creamy herb sauce – a generous square of fillet, served skin side up and set in a pattern reminiscent of the Irish flag. Simple, effective and very tasty.

Awards

Past Winners

1996 **Doyle's Seafood Bar**
Dingle, Co Cork

1995 **King Sitric**
Howth, Co Dublin

1994 **Aherne's Seafood Restaurant**
Youghal, Co Cork

Bord Iascaigh Mhara

Congratulates the Egon Ronay's Jameson Guide
Seafood Dish of the Year 1997

Bon Appétit

IRELAND
A Seafood Isle

We are an island people and much of what made us, including our remotest ancestry came to us from the sea. It has shaped our history; it has found its way into

the lives and minds of the people; it is a source of potential wealth, a source of the most wondrous variety of food - Seafood.

An island with 2,000 miles of beautiful indented coast and surrounded by clear, unpolluted waters on the edge of Europe with the vast Atlantic off the western coast means "Superb Seafood". Its lucrative fishing grounds produce an abundance of fish. Varieties are amazing and amount to 74 in all.

THE CHOICEST FISH

They include cod, haddock, whiting, hake, plaice, sole, brill and turbot. On the menu too you can taste seafish like monkfish, gurnard, John Dory...

Oily fish like herring, mackerel, salmon and trout. Shellfish like prawns, mussels, oysters, lobsters and scallops, so eating should be an ever-changing adventure.

NEW TASTES IN SEAFOOD

At sea the search for new species goes on and BIM's fishing technologists have been successfully pursuing new deepwater species for markets at home and abroad.

Available in the future will be species such as orange roughy, redfish, grenadier, black scabbard, blue ling, siki, shark and argentine.

Aquaculture has made available mussels, oysters, clams, scallops and abalone. Already salmon and trout are our most successful new product developments in the seafood industry and are famous throughout the world. The farming of novel finfish species means that we can choose to eat in the future such delicacies as turbot, arctic char and European eel.

EXPORT MARKETS

Having a small population we export most of our fishing catch to some 30 countries around the globe. The export market is currently valued at £200 million and with consumption increasing in the major markets worldwide this figure is set to grow.

A FEAST OF SEAFOOD

Our visitors perceive Ireland as an island where seafood abounds and so the choice of seafood is favoured by most of them.

If you're looking for seafood in the hotels, restaurants and pubs in Ireland then it's good to know that of late we are acting like an island should. Two thirds of most menus are now seafood and this is probably because seafood cooking is not a popular feature in Irish homes, so people like to eat it when dining out.

Ireland is a perfect island for the traveller who wants to discover countryside and coast in a short time. Discover too that you can eat at least 10 different varieties of oysters from Carlingford to Galway, mussels from Bantry to Lough Foyle, salmon from almost every port and river and fresh catches of fish from just about everywhere!

The fact that seafood is now recognised as a health food, good for the heart and good if you need to keep slim and trim, means it's the 'in' food of the 90's.

If that doesn't tempt you to eat a little more of this food while in Ireland, can I share with you my favourite set of slogans which go - eat fish, live longer, eat clams, last longer, eat oysters, love longer and eat mussels, laugh longer!

Now, how about choosing some of this wonderful food when dining at your favourite table.

Happy eating!

An Bord Iascaigh Mhara
Irish Sea Fisheries Board
*Crofton Road, Dun Laoghaire,
Co. Dublin, Ireland.
Telephone: 353 1 2841544
Fax: 353 1 2841123*

Awards

Ireland 1997
Dessert of the Year

Dromoland Castle
Newmarket-on-Fergus, Co Clare

Elma Campion, chef-patissière, is just champion! The perfect dessert always lingers long in the memory and her 'Assortment Dessert Plate' is no exception. However, be warned! By choosing

it, you will miss out on a hot soufflé (well worth the 20 minutes' wait), perhaps brown bread with sauce anglaise or Guinness with blackcurrant ice cream, not to mention a gratin of rhubarb and strawberry or apple crumble with butterscotch sauce. But back to *that* plate: you'll have to read the restaurant entry for a full description, but it will include chocolate, fruit and ice cream, and no doubt the scent of spirit!

Awards

PAST WINNERS

1996   **Isaacs Restaurant**
Cork, Co Cork

1995   **Cromleach Lodge**
Boyle, Co Sligo

1994   **Mac Nean Bistro**
Blacklion, Co Cavan

WEDGWOOD

CONGRATULATES THE EGON RONAY'S JAMESON GUIDE
DESSERT OF THE YEAR 1997

DROMOLAND CASTLE

LOOKS DESIGNED TO LAST

Wedgwood® tableware is not only beautiful but supremely practical: it is used every day by many of the world's great chefs. Whichever pattern is selected, Wedgwood tableware is designed to last.

for fine Hotels and Restaurants

Wedgwood Hotel and Restaurant Division
Represented by
G. Duke & Co Ltd, Unit K, Greenmount Industrial Estate,
Harolds Cross, Dublin 6.
Telephone: 01-454 7877. Facsimile: 01-454 7879

Geoff Duke
Director

Awards

Ireland 1997
Cheeseboard of the Year

L'Ecrivain
Dublin 2

For the last three years this award has gone to places in Cork, the epicentre of Ireland's superb farmhouse cheese industry. This year we looked for a winning establishment that would ably demonstrate that cheese should always be considered a course in its own right all across the country. At L'Ecrivain you certainly can't ignore or miss it, since the presentation of Irish farmhouse cheeses is a focal display in

the restaurant. Over half a dozen are on display at any one time, ranging from *Durrus*, *Milleens* and *Gubbeen* from Cork to *St Killian* from Wexford, *St Tola* goat's cheese from Clare and *Cashel Blue* from Tipperary. More unusual is Anne Brodie's *Boilie* from Cavan – fresh cheese balls that are marinated in jars of sunflower oil with garden herbs.

The National 🍀 Dairy Council

Awards

PAST WINNERS	
1996	**Lovetts** Cork, Co Cork
1995	**Assolas Country House** Kanturk, Co Cork
1994	**Blairs Cove Restaurant** Durrus, Co Cork

THE NATIONAL DAIRY COUNCIL
CONGRATULATES THE EGON RONAY'S JAMESON GUIDE
CHEESEBOARD OF THE YEAR 1997
L'ECRIVAIN

Farm Made Cheeses From Ireland

IRISH FARMHOUSE CHEESE
IS AS RICHLY VARIED AS THE NATIONAL LANDSCAPE.
IT'S ALSO AS RICH IN TRADITION,
WITH MORE THAN 40 VARIETIES MADE BY FARMERS WHOSE
FAMILIES HAVE LIVED AND WORKED ON THE SAME FARMS FOR
GENERATIONS. TIME-HONOURED METHODS HAVE NOW
COMBINED WITH CONTINENTAL SKILLS TO BRING A FRESH
DIMENSION TO THEIR TRADITIONAL CRAFT. FROM THE
ATLANTIC COASTLINE OF WEST CORK AND KERRY TO THE
LAKELANDS OF COUNTY CAVAN, IRISH FARMHOUSE DAIRIES
PRODUCE A DISTINGUISHED RANGE OF
DELICIOUS HAND-FINISHED CHEESES – BRINGING
CHARACTER TO YOUR CHEESEBOARD.

1. Cooleeney
2. St. Martin's
3. Durrus
4. Coolea
5. Cashel blue
6. Chetwynd
7. Smoked Gubbeen
8. Gubbeen
9. Kerry Farmhouse
10. Cratloe Hills Sheeps' Cheese
11. Ardrahan
12. Knockanore
13. Boilie
14. Liathmore Lite Cream Cheese
15. St. Tola Goats' Cheese
16. Lavistown
17. Carrigaline
18. Glen O Sheen
19. Ryefield
20. Croghan Goats' Cheese
21. Liathmore Full Fat Cream Cheese
22. Milleens
23. Bay Lough
24. Ring
25. Knockalora Sheeps' Cheese
26. Knockanore Smoked
27. St. Brendan Brie
28. Round Tower
29. St. Killian
30. Abbey Blue Brie

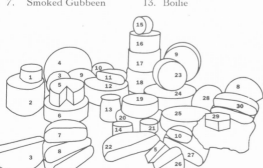

Awards

Ireland 1997
Coffee Award of Excellence
Harvey's Coffee House
Dublin 2

John Harvey's hands-on approach to business set in him in good stead when he decided to set up his own coffee house in 1994. Whether it's a milky *macchiato* with which to start the day or a hit of *doppio espresso* later in the day, Harvey's is *the* place in Dublin

for coffee. Substantial snack accompaniments range from toasted bagels to interesting sandwiches (fancy a 'sea change' with tuna fish and toasted sunflower seeds on wholemeal brown soda bread?), pastries and a brunch on Sundays. Coffee is, however, the main attraction and only the best beans (from Robert Roberts, naturally) are used.

Awards

PAST WINNERS

1996 **Hotel Conrad**
Dublin

1995 **Buzz's Bar**
Carlow, Co Carlow

1994 **The Mustard Seed**
Ballingarry, Co Limerick

ROBT. ROBERTS

CONGRATULATES THE EGON RONAY'S JAMESON GUIDE
COFFEE AWARD OF EXCELLENCE 1997

HARVEY'S COFFEE HOUSE

...OR KENYAN
...OR COLOMBIAN
...OR COSTA RICAN.

Only the best beans, carefully chosen, dried, roasted
and blended to perfection go into
Robt. Roberts fresh, ground coffee. That's why
you'll find it in fine restaurants everywhere.

ROBT.
ROBERTS

TEA & COFFEE

79 Broomhill Road, Tallaght, Dublin 24.
Tel: (01) 4599000. Fax: (01) 4599342.

Awards

Ireland 1997
Oriental Restaurant of the Year

Saagar
Dublin 2

Saagar is situated in the basement of a house once inhabited by Bram Stoker, and Dracula himself would surely have enjoyed

getting his fangs into the authentic Indian dishes served here. It's perhaps an unusual setting for an Indian restaurant, but its hallmark lies in the quality of cooking, whether in a hot and spicy dish such as a traditional Goan curry or a milder prawn balti. The menu forewarns customers as to the spiciness and 'hotness' of dishes, enabling choices to be made without fear of reprisal. If in doubt, the staff will guide you to satisfaction.

Awards

PAST WINNERS

1996 China-Sichuan Restaurant
Stillorgan, Co Dublin

1995 Langkawi Malaysian Restaurant
Dublin

1994 Zen
Dublin

SHARWOOD'S

CONGRATULATES THE EGON RONAY'S JAMESON GUIDE
ORIENTAL RESTAURANT OF THE YEAR 1997

SAAGAR

Sharwood's simple introduction to India will fire your imagination...

BY APPOINTMENT TO H.M. THE QUEEN
MANUFACTURERS OF CHUTNEY & PURVEYORS OF INDIAN
CURRY POWDER J.A. SHARWOOD & CO. LIMITED EGHAM

Sharwoods

To authenticity, Sharwood's add simplicity

...not your palate

Awards

Ireland 1997
Best Pesentation of
Irish Bread & Butter
Mitchell's
Laragh, Co Wicklow

In contrast to the grandeur of last year's winner of this award, Ashford Castle, Mitchell's is on an altogether simpler, more domestic scale, but the sheer wholesomeness of Margaret Mitchell's baking is equally inspiring. Margaret and Jerry Mitchell's delightful cut-stone restaurant with rooms is a haven of tranquillity away from the crowds of nearby Glendalough and those who seek them out will find presentation of traditional Irish bread and butter in a fresh, simple style that is entirely

appropriate to the country atmosphere within. Margaret's everyday baking is wholemeal bread with sunflower seeds that react with bread soda and turn green, creating jewel-like flecks (almost like angelica) running through each loaf; butter is presented in chunky pottery. Baked goods and preserves are made available for sale and displayed on a dresser by the door.

Awards

PAST WINNERS

1996 **Ashford Castle**
Cong, Co Mayo

1995 **The Motte**
(Best Table Presentation)
Inistioge, Co Kilkenny

1994 **Mary Anne's Bar & Restaurant**
(Best Traditional Brown Bread)
Castletownshend, Co Cork

THE NATIONAL DAIRY COUNCIL
CONGRATULATES THE EGON RONAY'S JAMESON GUIDE
BEST PRESENTATION OF IRISH BREAD & BUTTER 1997
MITCHELL'S

taste that will not be overlooked

The natural and appetising appearance of butter complements any table setting, just as its pure, delicious taste enhances any dish. It's always full marks for butter ... for taste.

NATIONAL DAIRY COUNCIL

Butter. Often copied, never equalled.

Awards

Ireland 1997
Business Hotel of the Year
Jurys Custom House Inn
Dublin 1

A budget hotel maybe, but built and designed only last year with business guests very much in mind, including the provision of . fax/modem lines in bedrooms. The business centre (open Mon–Fri 7.30am–7.30pm) meets most business needs, from photocopying to laser printing, faxing and shredding. Additionally, guests have access to E-Mail, a word processor, computer and printer, and secretaries

are always on hand to type, take shorthand or print documents from guests' personal computer discs. Translators can be hired on request and the centre will arrange mobile phone hire.
The hotel offers good conference facilities and adjacent car parking, and occupies a convenient city-centre site beside the International Financial Services Centre, overlooking the River Liffey.

Awards

PAST WINNERS		
1996	**The Towers**	
	Dublin	
1995	**Castletroy Park Hotel**	
	Limerick	
1994	**Hotel Conrad**	
	Dublin	

DHL

CONGRATULATES THE EGON RONAY'S JAMESON GUIDE
BUSINESS HOTEL OF THE YEAR 1997

JURYS CUSTOM HOUSE INN

"IT TAKES *that certain* SPIRIT."

"Wine is passion. Excitement. Sheer poetry. Romance. You have to have a passion about wine – otherwise get out of the business!"

John Gainsford, Director of the Bellingham wine estate clearly loves his job. But he is no mere romantic.

"Wine is my BUSINESS. If you haven't the same passion for your business as I have for mine, I won't work with you. We're PROFESSIONALS and we want to work with professionals."

So when Bellingham distributes its wines around the world, John refuses to compromise:

**"We need crisp, sharp SERVICE, daily. We send to every country in the world. The people at DHL have the same passion as I have, you can see it in their service. They haven't failed me yet. I don't want wine that's due for New York ending up in London. I TRUST DHL that when they undertake a job, they do it. I don't work with amateurs!"

We keep your promises

DRINKING THE BEST OF IRISH

BY JOHN CLEMENT RYAN
AUTHOR OF "IRISH WHISKEY"

Health and long life to you
Land without rent to you
The woman (or man) of your choice to you
A child every year to you
and may you be half an hour in heaven before
the devil knows you're dead!

The art of distilling whisk(e)y has been around almost as long as people have enjoyed fine food, and Irish Whiskey is the world's oldest whisk(e)y

Soldiers of Henry II and Elizabeth I appreciated Irish Whiskey

Finest barley

type. Nobody really knows where the story of whisk(e)y began or who began it. However we do know that the secret of distillation was brought to Ireland, probably from the Middle East, by missionary monks around the 6th century AD. They discovered the *alembic* being used for distilling perfume – they invented *whiskey* and called their version of the alembic a *Pot Still.*

Even the word whiskey comes from the Irish words *Uisce Beatha* (phonetically "isk'ke-ba'ha"). How the name came into the English language was when the soldiers of King Henry II paid what turned out to be the first of several uninvited visits to Ireland in 1170, they found the native Irish consuming their *Uisce Beatha.* Henry's soldiers soon got the hang of it, but never learned to pronounce the word *Uisce Beatha* and so, during the following centuries, the word was gradually anglicised, first to *Uisce*, then to *Fuisce*, and then finally to the word *Whiskey* that we know today.

The Old Bushmills Distillery, the world's oldest licensed whiskey distillery is located in Co. Antrim. They first received their license to distil in 1608 and so have nearly 400 years of tradition behind them. Look for Black Bush as a digestif or with a little plain water, and for Bushmills Malt, the only single malt brand of Irish whiskey.

John Jameson founded his distillery in Dublin in 1780 and Jameson

Purest water

Triple Distillation

soon became the best-known Irish Whiskey in the world, a position it still holds today. A glass of Jameson is particularly appreciated as an aperitif, either on the rocks with a little plain water, and as an accompaniment to a raw or smoked fish dish, and as a digestif try twelve year old *Jameson 1780.*

Matured in Oak Casks

The taste difference between Scotch and Irish is not something that words can convey, and stems largely from the difference in production methods. Both Scotch and Irish are based on barley, part of which is malted, and here comes the first difference: Malt for Irish is dried in a closed kiln, and not over open peat fires which gives the smoky flavour that is typical of Scotch – that smoky flavour is deliberately absent from Irish, and some of the subtleties and delicacies of taste can be appreciated because of the absence of the smoky taste.

Secondly, Irish Whiskey is distilled three times in the old-fashioned copper Pot Stills to ensure the maximum purity of the spirit, and no other whisk(e)y category in the world is distilled more than twice.

Finally, Irish is matured in oak casks for a minimum of three years by law, but in practice between five and eight years, and in the case of some of the premium brands ten, and twelve years. As well as the brands from the Jameson and Bushmills stables, other brands that will be encountered are Powers Gold Label, the favourite in Ireland.

John Jameson Distillery, founded in 1780

If you are travelling around Ireland, be sure to call in to learn the Story of Irish Whiskey. If you are in the North, visit the Bushmills Distillery, located in the village of Bushmills in Co. Antrim. This is open to visitors throughout the year (Mondays to Thursdays 9.00-12.00, 13.30-15.30 and Fridays 9.00-11.45, no reservations necessary). When in Dublin, go to the old Jameson distillery at Bow Street to see the *Irish Whiskey Corner* a museum to the history of Irish Whiskey where visitors are welcome. Here there is a tour daily (Mon-Fri) at 15.30 sharp. Finally *The Jameson Heritage Centre* in Midleton, Co. Cork, just 13 miles east of Cork City, is open to visitors throughout the summer months during each day including weekends from 10.00-16.00. Visitors enjoy a guided tour through the Old Distillery, a whisk(e)y tasting, an audio-visual show, coffee shop, souvenir shop, and craft shops on the site.

After a fine meal, lift your glass of Jameson or Bushmills and wish an old Irish Toast to your companions:

> *May the road rise to meet you*
> *May the wind be always at your back*
> *May the sun shine warm upon your face*
> *And the rain fall soft upon your fields*
> *And until we meet again*
> *May God hold you in the hollow*
> *of His Hand.*

Matured to Perfection

THE IRISH WHISKEY TRAIL

Irish Whiskey is part of the rich heritage of Ireland and its people. Visitors can relive this fascinating story by visiting the historic distilleries that have made Irish Whiskey famous throughout the world.

In Dublin, at the old Jameson distillery at Bow Street, is *The Irish Whiskey Corner*, a museum to the history of Irish Whiskey where visitors are welcome. Here there is a tour daily (Mon to Fri) at 15h30 sharp, and in summer an extra tour at 11h00 May-Oct. There is a charge of £3 per person, and the tour includes an audio-visual film, the opportunity to do a whisk(e)y tasting and to visit the museum. There is a very fine gift shop at the Irish Whiskey Corner, where souvenirs, including bottles of all brands of Irish Whiskey are available for sale. The *Midleton Very Rare* Book which records the name and signature of the owner of each bottle of Ireland's finest whiskey is kept there.

At the Old Distillery in Midleton, Co. Cork, just 13 miles east of Cork City, the buildings on the 10 acre site have been refurbished

and opened as a major new tourist attraction called *The Jameson Heritage Centre.* Here we tell the story of Irish Whiskey to visitors with the aid of some magnificent artefacts, including a 40' Water Wheel, an original stationary Steam Engine, a charming steam-powered fire engine, and best of all the largest Pot Still in the world!

Open every day from 17 March to end October including weekends from 10h00 to 18h00 (last tour commences at 16h00), the entrance fee is £3.50 (£1.50 for children, and group & family rates are also available), which will permit visitors to enjoy an audio-visual show, a guided tour through the Old Distillery, a whisk(e)y tasting, a coffee shop, a large gift shop selling all brands of Irish Whiskey, and craft shops on the site. During winter, groups can visit by prior arrangement.

Bushmills Distillery, located in the village of Bushmills in Co. Antrim, is open to visitors throughout the year on Mondays to Thursdays 9h-12h, 13h30-15h30, and Fridays 9h-11h45, and Friday and Saturday opening 15h in summer (July-Sept), Bushmills is a jewel on the Tourist Trail known as the "Causeway Coast", which includes

the Giant's Causeway, one of the great natural wonders of the world. Visitors are welcome (£2 entry), and have a guided tour of the distillery, a 'dram' of Bushmills, and the opportunity to shop in two delightful souvenir shops, one of which sells whiskey!

L EGEND has it that Irish monks invented whiskey, learning of distillation from the perfumers of the Orient. They called their discovery *Uisce Beatha* (the water of life) and to this day the finest of whiskey is distilled by the Irish.

A visit to the Jameson Heritage Centre in Midleton, Co.

Cork will take you right to the heart of this cherished tradition. You are invited to take a two-hour tour of the Centre – it's a beautifully restored 18th century, self-contained industrial complex, unique in Britain and Ireland. Delight in the fully-operational water wheel and be amazed by the copper pot still of 32,000 gallons, the largest in the world.

An audio-visual presentation, available in six languages, breathes life into the Irish whiskey legend.

After the history comes the tasting. Relax in the atmosphere of a traditional Irish pub and sample Ireland's finest whiskey. *Sláinte.*

Lose yourself in the charm of another age – the Jameson Heritage Centre with its craft and coffee shops is located on the main Cork-Waterford road which links the ferry terminals of Rosslare and Ringaskiddy. We're open from 10.00am to 4.00pm, May to October. Telephone John Callely at 021-613594 or fax 021-613642 for information.

JAMESON The Spirit of Ireland

WHEREVE
BE SURE T
THE BEST F

YOU GO,
O EAT OFF
ASTIC.

THIS PIECE C
OPENS THE D
THE BEST HC

PLASTIC
DORS OF
TEL ROOMS.

MAKING LIFE EASIER

The first whiskey came from Ireland. The smoothest still does.

Before maturing our whiskey for many years, we like to distil it a third time. We think you'll find this rather unique finishing touch gives our whiskey an exceptional smoothness.

JAMESON® The Spirit of Ireland

Republic of
Ireland

ABBEYFEALE   The Cellar

Tel 068 31085   Fax 068 31968   Map 2 B5   **P**
The Square Abbeyfeale Co Limerick

Easily spotted as you drive through Abbeyfeale by the rows of bottles of every shape and size displayed in the end window, Padraig and Mary Fitzgerald's very pleasant "olde-style traditional" pub will not disappoint – the locals are friendly and the open fire and piano are not just for show, so sessions can get going at the drop of a hat (Padraig is a fine musician himself). Traditional Irish music (Thursday nights) is not exclusive, with rock music on Saturday nights and sing-a-long on Sunday nights. The antique decor includes original timber floors and ceiling, stone walls, pub mirrors, gas lamps, church pews, pine dressers and old prints. Snooker and pool room (plus a large-screen TV) on the second storey. Nice walled garden at the back for sheltered summer drinking. *Open 11am-11.30pm, Sun 12.30-2, 4-11.30 (to 11 in winter). No credit cards.*

ABBEYLEIX   Morrissey's

Tel 0502 31233   Fax 0502 31357   Map 2 C4   **P**
Main Street Abbeyleix Co Laois

A discreet black and gold sign singles out Morrissey's from its neighbours in this handsome village; inside the lofty shelf-lined grocery-bar, old-fashioned shades of black and brown predominate, relieved here and there by a little cream. Mundane groceries change hands along with their special blend of tea (packed on the premises) and an unusually wide selection of loose sweets like aniseed balls, pineapple chunks and bull's eyes, kept in rows of big glass jars and sold by the ½ lb in paper pokes. On cold days customers reflect on their pints around an ancient pot-bellied stove while reading the paper or exchanging the news of the day – but card-playing and singing are not allowed. A good place to take a break on the Dublin-Cork road but, although a cup of tea or coffee will be served with charm, don't expect any food, other than a sandwich. The landlord, Paddy Mulhall, is also undertaker, travel agent and newsagent – typically Irish! *Open 10.30am-11.30pm (11pm in summer), Sun 12.30-2, 4-11. No credit cards.*

ABBEYLEIX   Preston House Café   £70

Tel & Fax 0502 31432   Map 2 C4   **RR**
Main Street Abbeyleix Co Laois

An attractive, creeper-clad house a few doors down from *Morrissey's* pub, Michael and Allison Dowling's friendly, informal restaurant with rooms makes a good break on the journey between Cork and Dublin. Country-style decor – deep green walls, pine furniture and lots of well-tended plants – in the main restaurant, a lacy 'front parlour' style in the smaller dining-room (used mainly for residents), friendly staff and enticing aromas from the kitchen all combine to good effect. Allison's home cooking starts off with delicious scones and home-made preserves served with coffee. Lunch is when she really gets into her stride with a short but tempting à la carte with a choice of five in each course: start, perhaps with smoked haddock chowder and lovely Aga-baked brown bread or grilled goat's cheese and side salad, followed by light choices like a warm salad of chicken breast with Abbey Blue cheese, walnuts and croutons, or more substantial fare such as Rudds baked local ham with a wholegrain mustard sauce. Vegetarians can enjoy colourful, zesty dishes such as ratatouille crepe with salad. Delicious desserts range from apple crumble and cream to classics like crème brulée. Dinner offers a more serious, wider choice in the same wholesome style. A first-floor ballroom is currently under renovation and promises to be a remarkable venue; it runs across the whole width of the substantial building, with a library area up a few stairs at one end and a minstrel's gallery at the other. Four tables are set in the garden in summer. *Seats 60. Parties 8. L 12-3 D 6-9 (open for coffee 10-6.30). Closed Mon & 23-30 Dec. MasterCard,* **VISA**

Rooms   £50

Accommodation is available in four large bedrooms, all no-smoking and
interestingly furnished with antiques. En suite facilities are neatly concealed
behind large doors that look like wardrobes but open up to reveal individual
facilities – shower, WC etc. Children over 10 are welcome.

ADARE	Adare Manor	79%	£250

Tel 061 396566   Fax 061 396124   Map 2 B5   **HR**
Adare Co Limerick

After a long drive through some
of the 900 acres of grounds, the
magnificent neo-Gothic mansion,
on the banks of the River Maigue,
will not disappoint, especially at
night when floodlit. Entering the hall
through heavy oak doors and thick
stone walls, you can almost touch
two centuries of the Dunraven family
history – previously it was their
home. Other public areas evoking
eras past are the fine gallery (seating
150 comfortably for a banquet), modelled after the Palace of Versailles, with its
Flemish choir stalls, fine stained-glass windows and hand-carved bookshelves,
the chandeliered drawing-room and the cellar bar, each room featuring antiques
and fine paintings, not to mention the odd welcoming open fire. A grand
staircase leads to the gracious bedrooms in the main house, all with lovely views,
some across the formal box-hedged gardens. They boast individual hand-crafted
fireplaces with dried-flower arrangements, fine locally-made furniture, grand
fabrics and imposing marble bathrooms with large tubs and powerful overhead
showers, bathrobes and good toiletries. Those in the new extension (it's difficult
to see the 'join', so well has the building blended in with the old) are even more
spacious, the best overlooking the river and parts of the golf course (designed by
Robert Trent Jones Sr). A nightly turn-down service is offered; staff are courteous
and correct. Children under 12 are accommodated free in their parents' room.
Tariff indicated is for a de luxe room, standard rooms are less, state rooms more.
Considerable reductions out of season. No dogs. *Rooms 64. Garden, indoor
swimming pool, gym, sauna, beauty/massage therapy, games room, snooker, golf (18),
golf driving range, riding, fishing, clay-pigeon shooting. Amex, Diners, MasterCard,*
VISA

Restaurant   £90

Both the stylish, panelled dining-room and the adjoining glassed-in cloister
(particularly attractive at night when candle-lit) have romantic views. Chef
de Cuisine Gerard Costelloe left briefly for pastures new, but no doubt became
'homesick', so has returned. Menus are now à la carte with quite modern dishes
for such a medieval setting; Americans may love all things historical (and particularly
Irish), but when it comes to eating, their preferences lean towards the lighter
and healthier options offered, as in starters such as braised smoked haddock with
poached egg in a mustard broth served with new potatoes or hot oysters with a
champagne sabayon topped with caviar. Main courses include roast boned-and-
stuffed poussin with brioche dumplings and a truffle and Madeira sauce or confit
of salmon on a bed of asparagus and samphire couscous with a red and yellow
pepper coulis. Few Irish influences here, though no doubt the prime ingredients
are local, and vegetables and herbs come from the estate's own gardens. Staff
are efficient, but perhaps a touch robotic – a little more effervescence would
be welcome. *Seats 70. Parties 40. Private Room 50. L 12.30-2 D 7-9.*

ADARE	Dunraven Arms Hotel	72%	£124

Tel 061 396633 Fax 061 396541   Map 2 B5   **HR**
Adare Co Limerick

Sporting activities, including golf, fishing and especially hunting and all things equestrian, are a particular attraction here at 'the fox-hunting centre of Ireland' but the Dunraven Arms also attracts a wide range of guests, including business clients and many travellers who are tempted by imaginative bar food to break a journey here. Meticulously maintained public areas have a timeless, traditional atmosphere with old furniture lifted by classical colour combinations in the decor everywhere from the busy pubby bar to the peaceful residents' drawing room (known as 'the library'). Bedrooms, including 22 'Executive' rooms and eight suites, are individually furnished to a high standard with excellent bathrooms and antique furniture. 'Standard' rooms attract a lower tariff (£110). No tea/coffee-making facilities – 24hr room service is provided. Frequent functions create a buzz around the hotel, but rooms away from public areas are quiet. Children up to 4 may stay free in their parents' room. Substantial tariff reductions out of high season (Oct-Apr). A new health and leisure centre was completed last year. ***Rooms** 66. Garden, tennis, indoor swimming pool, gym, steam room, games room. Amex, Diners, MasterCard, **VISA***

The Maigue Room   £65

Banqueting and dining are kept separate at the Dunraven Arms and head chef Mark Phelan is building up an excellent reputation for his elegant restaurant, named after the local river. Table d'hote or à la carte menu, the former typically starting with crab claws, whiskey barbecued salmon and smoked trout with pine nut dressing or baked Inagh Farmhouse goat's cheese in an apple and nut croustade with raspberry tagliatelle and strawberry vinaigrette – interesting and unusual fare. Follow with a chilled gazpacho soup or a fresh fruit sorbet, then a pink-roasted wild mallard with caramelised apples and balsamic vinegar or pan-fried River Maigue salmon with basil and leek purée. Local produce is always very much to the fore, including the finest roast prime rib of beef (carved to your liking). Delicious desserts like lightly baked lemon meringue pie served with an orange sauce; lovely brown soda bread and aromatic coffee. A fine setting for Sunday lunch. 12½% service charge is automatically added. ***Seats** 60. Parties 20. Private Room 35. L (Sun only) 12.30-2.30 D 7.30-9.30. Bar Food 12-6pm. Set Sun L £12.95 Set D £22.95. Closed Good Friday.*

ADARE	The Inn Between	£45

Tel 061 396633 Fax 061 396541   Map 2 B5   **R**
Adare Co Limerick

In common ownership with *The Dunraven Arms* (see entry), an informal restaurant in one of the village's old thatched cottages. It retains the original style of the building, although it has been sympathetically renovated and extended to provide extra space. The atmosphere is cheerful (red and white table cloths) and, in contrast to other comparable restaurants nearby, The Inn Between (as its name suggests) aims to provide good, reasonably priced food. An à la carte evening menu offers starters like baked goat's cheese wrapped in filo with a blackcurrant coulis and steamed wild mussels with white wine and garlic and main courses such as pan-fried supreme of ckicken on a bed of oyster mushrooms with yellow mustard seed sauce. Desserts range from the homely (apple pie and cream) to the sophisticated – double chocolate terrine, orange and vanilla sauce. Outside eating area. *Seats 65. Parties 8. L 12.30-2.30 D 6.30-9.30. Closed Tue, Wed & Nov-mid Mar. Amex, Diners, MasterCard, VISA*

ADARE	The Wild Geese	†	£75

Tel & Fax 061 396451   Map 2 B5   **R**
Rose Cottage Adare Co Limerick

Conleth Roche and Serge Coustrain, both formerly of *Dromoland Castle* and, latterly, Limerick's *Castletroy Park Hotel*, took over the former *Mustard Seed* (see now under Ballingary) premises from Dan Mullane in 1996 and renamed it The Wild Geese. They've never looked back since and the cosy cottagey charm of the low-ceilinged two-storey thatched building is as strong as ever. Conleth welcomes and cares for guests with courtesy and charm while Serge's undoubted skills in the kitchen are now given full rein. Carefully constructed menus make the most of his classical French training and take full advantage of the best local produce, in stylish, confident cooking that pleases equally through its broad strokes (where unusual combinations come into play) and its great attention to detail. From the five-course dinner menu you might find a stylish salad with balsamic dressing served with a pan-fried slice of foie gras and black pudding or hot salmon quenelles with medallions of lobster in a herby white wine sauce. A soup course might offer a beef consommé rich with the unmistakable flavour of bone marrow or an unusual polenta soup with a julienne of chicken. Main courses are equally imaginative and well judged, in satisfying yet light combinations such as pan-fried turbot with sautéed beansprouts in a velouté sauce or sole with fennel in a tapénade sauce; more traditional dishes also take their place, like roast fillet of beef with glazed shallots, button mushrooms and lardons in a bordelaise sauce. Delicious desserts include perennial favourites such as crème brulée (served with home-made biscuits) and hot soufflés – chocolate with a vanilla sauce – are a speciality. Or you can round off with good Irish cheeses, aromatic coffee or tea and home-made petits fours. Not suitable for children under 12. *Seats 50. Parties 14. D only 6.30-10.30. Closed Sun, Mon Oct-Apr & 3 weeks Jan. Set D £27. Amex, Diners, MasterCard, VISA*

If you encounter bad service don't wait to write to us but make your feelings known to the management at the time of your visit. Instant compensation can often resolve any problem that might otherwise leave a bad taste.

ADARE	Woodlands House Hotel	60%	£66

Tel 061 396118   Fax 061 396073   Map 2 B5   **H**
Adare Co Limerick

From small beginnings in 1983 the Fitzgerald family have developed their hotel to its present stage, with facilities for weddings, banquets and conferences for up to 350. Roomy public areas include two bars and a strikingly decorated lobby/lounge with comfortable seating and a colourful mural, while both banqueting suites and the restaurant overlook well-maintained gardens and countryside. Bedrooms, including four suites and most with a pleasant outlook, vary in age and amenities but are well maintained. Children under 12 may stay free in parents' room. No dogs. *Rooms 57. Garden. Closed 24 & 25 Dec. Amex, Diners, MasterCard, VISA*

ADARE   Places of Interest
Tourist Information Tel 061 396255

AGHADOE   Killeen House Hotel   64%   £88

Tel 064 31711 Fax 064 31811   Map 2 A5   **HR**
Aghadoe Killarney Co Kerry

This attractively renovated early 19th-century house is self-styled as 'a charming
little hotel' – a description that is perfectly apt. Michael and Geraldine Rosney
have offered a big, friendly welcome here since 1992. Popular with golfers,
holidaymakers and business guests alike, it has a welcoming atmosphere which
is especially noticeable in the recently extended pubby bar, where locals mingle
with residents. Rooms vary somewhat in size but are all en suite and freshly
decorated, with phone, satellite TV and 24hr room service; there's a pretty,
relaxing drawing-room furnished with a mixture of antiques and newer
furniture, with an open fire. Since last year four new 'De luxe' bedrooms
(£106 double) and a private dining-room have been added. Ample parking.
Low season tariffs come down to £55. Ten minutes from Killarney town centre.
Rooms 19. Garden. Closed Jan-Mar. Amex, Diners, MasterCard, **VISA**

Restaurant   £60

Head chef Gillian Kelly's dinner menu is restricted to a choice of just four or so
main courses and starters. The likes of millefeuille of lamb's kidneys with bacon
and mushrooms and port wine sauce, warm tomato and sweet pepper salsa-
topped bruschetta with black olives and mozzarella, marinated leg of Kerry lamb
with creamy garlic potato and a rosemary jus and monkfish with a provençale
crust and fresh tomato sauce show a fine standard of preparation and
presentation. There are always nightly 'specials', a vegetarian option and
a plated selection of Irish cheeses. *Seats 50. Private Room 28. D only 6.30-9.30.
Set D £23.50.*

AHAKISTA   Ahakista Bar

No Telephone   Map 2 A6   **P**
Ahakista nr Bantry Co Cork

Known affectionately as the 'Tin Pub' after the corrugated iron roof it has had
for as long as anyone can remember, it's hard to imagine a stronger contrast
between this laid-back little watering hole and the immaculate precision of the
Shiro 'Japanese Dinner House' just across the road. The bar has been in the same
family for three generations and the current owners, Anthony and Margaret
Whooley, are determined not to allow the passage of time to change anything
about their delightfully simple bar – so no, they will not be getting a telephone
and yes, the rambling, slightly unkempt garden running down to the beach at
the back will be kept as it is and children will be allowed to play around and
make a bit of noise there. *Open Mon-Sat 1-11.30 (3.30-11 in winter), Sun 12.30-2,
4-11 (all year). Garden. Closed Good Friday & 25 Dec. No credit cards.*

AHAKISTA   Hillcrest House   £35

Tel 027 67045   Map 2 A6   **A**
Ahakista Durrus nr Bantry Co Cork

Mrs Agnes Hegarty has won many an award for hospitality at this traditional
farm overlooking Dunmanus Bay. The lovely rural location and good food are
major attractions for some, while those with young children will particularly
appreciate the family-friendly attitude. Rooms are comfortably furnished with en
suite bath or shower, have tea/coffee-making trays and are big enough for an
extra child's bed or cot. Two bedrooms are designated no-smoking and there is
a ground-floor room suitable for less able guests, with parking at the door and
direct access to the dining-room. In addition to the numerous attractions of the

area (including the new 'Sheep's Head Way' 55-mile walk) families are welcome to see what's going on in the farmyard. No dogs. Evening meals (£13.50) by arrangement – not Sat or Sun – plus children's high tea at 6pm. **Rooms 4.** *Garden, terrace, indoor & outdoor play areas, games room. Closed Nov-end Mar. No credit cards.*

AHAKISTA	Shiro	★	£110

Tel 027 67030   Fax 027 67206   Map 2 A6   **R**
Ahakista Durrus nr Bantry Co Cork

Kei and Werner Pilz have been delighting guests at their unique West Cork restaurant since 1983. Firstly, there is the unlikeliness of it: one does not expect to come across a classical Japanese restaurant situated in a lovely, meticulously maintained but remote Georgian house set in wooded gardens overlooking Dunmanus Bay. Then there is the warmth of Werner's welcome and Kei's dedication and talent in the kitchen, which have combined to make a dining experience that is utterly unforgettable. Since the addition of an extension a few years ago there is a reception room where aperitifs are served; the dining area is also more spacious and the arrangement of tables can be more flexible, although the number of seats has only increased very slightly. The biggest plus is that this arrangement allows for a fine view of the bay while dining – an enjoyable bonus to add to the appreciation of Kei's little works of art. The style of food and service is timeless: authentic Japanese dishes are prepared with exquisite precision and beautifully presented, not only individually but also as an arrangement on the table where each item is carefully laid in its allotted place. Although consistent in style the menu changes daily and Werner is always at hand to guide guests through to a happy choice. The meal starts with *zensai* (seasonal appetisers with *azuke-bachi*, egg and sushi snacks) followed by *suimono* (soup served in a traditional lidded bowl topped with a little origami bird). A choice of about seven main courses ranges from popular dishes like *tempura* (seasonal fish and vegetables, lightly battered and deep-fried), quail *yakitori* and and beef *teriyaki* (gently cooked strips of steak, with sake-blended teriyaki sauce and fresh vegetables), through *sashimi* (finely sliced raw fish served with soy sauce and *wasabi*, a very hot green mustard used for dipping) to a combination such as *tempura-sashimi* for the indecisive. Although dishes are not shared in the same way as in other Oriental cuisines, it is most interesting for a group to try as many different dishes as possible to sample the full variety – don't miss the *sushi* (raw fish and vegetables rolled with rice in dried seaweed with *wasabi* and soy sauce for dipping). There is usually at least one choice suitable for vegetarians, but it is wise to mention any special requirements when booking. The meal is rounded off by a selection of home-made ice creams colourfully garnished with fresh fruit and arranged dramatically against black plates, then a choice of teas and coffees. 5% supplement for paying by credit card. No children under 12. Self-catering accommodation is available in a traditional cottage in the grounds (sleeps 2: £50 per night). *Seats 20. Parties 7. Private Room 16. D only 7-9. Set D £45. Closed Jan, Feb & 23-31 Dec. Amex, Diners, MasterCard, VISA*

See the **County Listings** green tinted pages for details of all establishments listed in county order.

ANNAGARY Danny Minnie's Restaurant £60

Tel 075 48201   Map 1 B1   **R**
Annagary The Rosses Co Donegal

This delightful, long-established restaurant has been in the O'Donnell family
since 1980 and first-time visitors may suffer something of a culture shock at the
contrast between the surrounding rugged Donegal landscape and the elegant
interior. It's cool, quite formal and yet intimate with well-appointed tables: crisp
linen, fine glasses, beautiful plates, fresh flowers and candles all set off by a
fascinating collection of objets d'art and pictures. This is a fitting setting for
Michael O'Donnell's stylish food and good but (not over-formal) service under
the watchful eye of his mother, Terri O'Donnell. From a tempting, wide-
ranging à la carte menu, start, perhaps, with creamy seafood chowder, local
mussels with a chive butter sauce, or deep-fried Brie with gooseberry and mint
compote. The choice of local fish main courses leads off with lobster – served
with tomato concassé and fresh basil – and may include fricassé of monkfish and
courgette with a ginger and herb cream; there is also a strong selection of meats
and poultry that includes beef Wellington with a mushroom duxelle and a
Madeira cream sauce. Saucing throughout is creative and well judged. Local
seasonal vegetables are beautifully cooked and generously served and desserts
such as chocolate cup with strawberry mousse with sauce anglaise taste as
dramatic as they look. Light lunches served 12-4 in summer only. No children
under 7 after 7pm. Overnight accommodation is available in three en suite
bedrooms (£50 double – not inspected). *Seats 50 (+ 20 outside on terrace).
Parties 12. Private Room 90. L summer only 12-4 D 6-10. Closed Nov, 1 week
Christmas & Feb. MasterCard, VISA*

ANNASCAUL Dan Foley's

Tel 066 57252   Map 2 A5   **P**
Annascaul Co Kerry

Dan Foley's pub owes its colourful, much-photographed exterior to the
theatrical personality of the man himself – farmer, expert on local history and
magician. Inside, it's a great, unspoilt bar in the rural tradition, made special by
Dan's particular interest in people and chat – and an unexpected collection of
about fifty liqueurs. Food is not the thing here although 'emergency rations' of
sandwiches, sausage rolls, salads and the like will be served (11am-8pm) to those
who resist directions to the proper restaurant next door. Children during
daylight hours only. One of Ireland's most famous pubs where nothing changes
but "we get another year older each year". *Open 11-11 (to 11.30 Mon-Sat in
Summer), Sun 12.30-2.30, 4-11. No credit cards.*

ARDARA Nancy's

Tel 075 41187   Map 1 B2   **A**
Ardara Co Donegal

For seven generations the McHugh family have run this cosy pub, providing yet
another reason to visit the village that is renowned for tweeds and hand-knits.
Nancy's could be the original on which so many modern theme pubs have been
modelled: tiny, cluttered and spread through a series of small, low-ceilinged
rooms culminating in the largest seating at least twelve people and opening on to
a little yard at the back. All around are collections of jugs, of pictures, of all sorts
of bric a brac and a disproportionate amount of tables and chairs. The McHugh
family clearly understand that being seated at a table is a requirement for the
enjoyment of good food. Their staff are friendly, everything is prepared to order
and waiting a few minutes beside the fire is no hardship – the pint is good, too.
Everyone seems to love the soup and no wonder – big bowls of steaming vegetable broth (or a chowder in summer), full of flavour, big bits of vegetable and

lots of barley, are served with a large basket of freshly-baked brown soda bread. Look out for steamed mussels with wine and garlic, oysters (raw or grilled with garlic butter) and smoked salmon as an open sandwich or a Louis Armstrong (topped with grated cheese and grilled); also, spiced prawns or a 'pure and simple' 6oz burger from the local butcher. Vegetarians aren't forgotten either – perhaps ploughman's or vegetarian lasagne – and there's always a home-made apple pie and cream for pudding. Live music is also a feature. *Seats 30. Parties 6. Private Room 12. Bar Food 11-9.30. Closed early Nov-mid Mar. No credit cards.*

ARDEE	Red House	£65

Tel & Fax 041 53523   Map 1 C3   **A**
Ardee Co Louth

Linda Connolly gives guests a warm welcome at her lovely Georgian house, which is impeccably run and furnished to a level that borders on opulence, yet loses none of its rural charm. The huge log fire in the library burns logs from the grounds, and when there are only a few guests Linda sets up a cosy dining table in front of it in preference to the formal dining-room (dinner for residents only, £20), with its long mahogany table. Beautifully furnished bedrooms are very comfortable; although two share a communal bathroom, the corridor is far from draughty; the one en suite bedroom tariff is £80. Delicious breakfasts are served at a bright, colourful table in the morning room; fresh fruits are included along with freshly-baked wheaten brown bread. Small conferences or weddings (30). Not suitable for children except babies under 2. No dogs indoors; kennels provided. *Rooms 3. Garden, tennis, fishing, indoor swimming pool, sauna (summer months only). Closed 20 Dec-1 Jan. MasterCard, VISA*

ARDEE   Places of Interest
Castle Matrix Rathkeale Tel 069 64284
Mellifont Abbey nr Slane Tel 041 26459
Millmount Museum Drogheda Tel 041 33097

ARDMORE	Cliff House Hotel	59%	£80

Tel 024 94106   Fax 024 94496   Map 2 C6   **H**
Ardmore Co Waterford

Eddie and Eileen Irwin run this dramatically situated, unpretentious, family-friendly hotel. Most (15) of the bedrooms are en suite and, along with the restaurant bar and lounge, have lovely sea views. The garden – a lovely spot for afternoon tea – reaches down to the clifftop. Under-3s may share their parents' room free of charge (4 family rooms: two sleeping 4, two sleeping 3); cots, extra beds, high-chairs and early evening meal provided. No dogs. *Rooms 20. Garden. Closed Nov-Mar. Amex, Diners, MasterCard, VISA*

ATHLEAGUE	Gilligan's Olde Worlde Tavern

Tel 0903 63383   Map 1 B3   **P**
Athleague Co Roscommon

Seriously olde-worlde quirky pub, formerly known as *Fitzmaurice's Tavern*, that was renamed in 1995 after Pat and Ed Gilligan took over the premises. What with all the interesting and conversation-commencing country clutter around it could take prizes as an agricultural museum, but it's obviously a good local, judging by the gathering usually found around the open fire on a winter evening. Good beer garden. *Open 10.30-11.30 (to 11 in winter), Sun 12.30-2, 4-11. Garden. No credit cards.*

ATHLEAGUE   Places of Interest
Clonalis House Castlerea Tel 0907 20014 *18 miles*
Old Schoolhouse Museum Ballinstubber Tel 0907 55397 *15 miles*
Strokestown Park House & Famine Museum Strokestown Tel 078 33013 *15 miles*

ATHLONE   Higgins's

Tel 0902 92519   Map 1 C3   **P**
2 Pearce Street Athlone Co Westmeath

West of the river, in the interesting old part of the town near the Norman castle (which has a particularly good visitor's centre for history – siege of Athlone 1691 – and information on the area, including the flora and fauna of the Shannon), the Higginses run a nice hospitable pub with accommodation in four rooms upstairs. Rooms vary from a single to a family room with three single beds (also an extra child's bed available), but all have secondary glazing, neat en suite shower room, television and hairdryer and there are communal tea/coffee-making facilities in the dining-room where breakfast is served. There's also a cosy residents' lounge with television and comfortable armchairs. No evening meals (soup and sandwiches only in the bar). No dogs. *Pub open 10.30am-11pm (to 11.30 in summer), Sun 12.30-2, 4-11. **Accommodation** 4 bedrooms, £32 (single £17). Children under 12 welcome overnight (stay free in parents' room), additional bed & cot supplied. Pub closed Good Friday & 25 Dec; accommodation closed all Dec & Jan. No credit cards.*

ATHLONE   Hodson Bay Hotel   66%   £135

Tel 0902 92444   Fax 0902 92688   Map 1 C3   **H**
Hodson Bay Athlone Co Westmeath

Just three miles outside Athlone town, on the shores of Lough Ree, this large, modern hotel has lovely lake and island views and offers a wide range of leisure activities: boating, fishing, golf (Athlone Golf Club adjoins the grounds) and a fine leisure centre. Spacious public areas include a large foyer with generous lounge space, several function rooms and a bar that enjoys the lake views. Good-sized bedrooms are accessible by lift and are bright and comfortable, with double and single beds in most rooms, quality furnishings and good en suite bathrooms. Banqueting/conferences for 450/700 respectively. Helipad. *Rooms 100. Garden, tennis, bowling, golf (18), pitch & putt, putting green, riding, lake cruiser, fishing, indoor swimming pool, gym, sauna, solarium, sun beds, games room. Amex, Diners, MasterCard, **VISA***

ATHLONE   Left Bank Bistro   £55

Tel 0902 94446   Map 1 C3   **R**
Bastion Street Athlone Co Westmeath

Right in the heart of old Athlone, just behind the castle, this characterful little restaurant looks promising from the street. Within, original stone walls contrast with table settings of oilcloths and paper napkins to create an informal atmos-phere. On the dinner menu starters like potato skins with tomato chili dipping sauce and Left Bank salad (mixed leaves with olives, sun-dried tomatoes, fresh herbs and grated regatto – an Irish hard cheese) rub shoulders with Thai prawn salad, and button mushrooms with pine nuts sautéed in garlic butter. Main courses might include chargrilled steaks, barbecued salmon steak with lime and dill, Thai-spiced chicken breasts and a vegetarian option such as grilled goat's cheese salad with roasted almonds and sun-dried tomatoes. Daily specials often include fish, perhaps Donegal smoked mackerel with a choice of side salad or the day's vegetables. Traditional desserts – cheesecakes, chocolate gateau – are followed by good coffee. Lunch is served from a blackboard menu (focacia bread, chicken tandoori) and is semi self-service. Very unusual bathroom arrangements (beside the upstairs dining-room) warrant a special visit. *Seats 49. Parties 8. Private Room 14. Meals 10.30-5, 5-6 (coffee & desserts only), D 6-10 (till 9.30 in winter). Closed all Sun, Bank Holidays (except Aug), D Mon-Wed mid Sep-Apr, 10 days Christmas. MasterCard, **VISA***

ATHLONE — Restaurant Le Chateau — £55

Tel 0902 94517 Fax 0902 73885
Abbey Lane Athlone Co Westmeath

Map 1 C3

R

Tucked into a laneway close to the castle from which it takes its name, this well-appointed first-floor restaurant is in a characterful old building. Steven and Martina Linehan have run it since the end of 1989 and their consistency is commendable. A typical table d'hote dinner might include a home-made seasonal soup (accompanied by irresistible, dark treacle bread), confit of duck leg with red cabbage and pepper cream and pan-fried stuffed pork fillet wrapped in bacon; à la carte extends to Galway Bay seafood chowder, warm salad of mushroom sausage, medallions of veal fillet with smoked bacon, garlic and herbs, breast of Mayo duck with fresh orange sauce, game in season and turbot with tomato, basil, white wine and cream (accompanied by imaginatively presented vegetables). Round a meal off with a tangy lemon tart and home-made chocolates with the coffee. Reflecting the numbers of Continental visitors holidaying on the Shannon (which is only yards away), Le Chateau also features an unusual 'Euro-Menu' in four languages. An early evening menu offers around five dishes. A dozen or so French house wines, ten or so half bottles and a couple of seriously indulgent champagnes alongside interesting New World choices on the wine list. *Seats 35. D only 6-10.15. Closed Sun (except D Jun-Aug) & 2 weeks Oct. Set D £15 (6-7.15 only) & £21. Amex, Diners, MasterCard,* **VISA**

ATHLONE — Sean's Bar

Tel 0902 92358
13 Main Street Athlone Co Westmeath

Map 1 C3

P

Sean Fitzsimons's seriously historic west bank bar, in the oldest, most characterful part of Athlone, lays claim to being the pub with the longest continuing use in Ireland – quite reasonably, it seems, as all of the owners since 1630 are on record (Sean's been here since 1969). On entering from the street, the sloping floor is the first of many interesting features to strike the first-time visitor; now strikingly covered in bold black and white tiles, it is cleverly constructed to ensure that flood water drains back down to the river as the waters subsides. The pub's a handy watering hole for visitors cruising the Shannon – there's still direct access to the river through the back bar and beer garden – and the bar has some nice old pieces, including a mahogany counter and mirrored mahogany shelving as well as a very large settle bed, which seems particularly appropriate to the soothing, dimly-lit ambience. A glass case containing a section of the original old wattle wall, and a letter about it from the National Museum highlights the age of the bar, but it's far from being a museum piece. Food is restricted to sandwiches and coffee, but the proper priorities are observed and they serve a good pint. Music most nights. *Open Mon-Sat 10.30am-11.30pm, Sun 12.30-2, 4-11. Beer garden. Closed Good Friday & 25 Dec. No credit cards.*

ATHLONE   Places of Interest
Tourist Information & Athlone Castle Tel 0902 94630
Glendeer Pet Farm Drum Tel 0902 37147
Rossana Cruises Tel 0902 92513

ATHY — Tonlegee House — £55

Tel & Fax 0507 31473
Athy Co Kildare

Map 2 C4

RR

Just outside town, Mark and Marjorie Molloy's restored Georgian home offers good cooking, a warm welcome, excellent bedrooms and a favourable price/quality ratio. Dinner is a four-course affair that includes a daily soup – perhaps cream of oyster mushroom with chives – and an inter-course sorbet;

one's main-course choice determines the overall meal price and a selection of Irish farmhouse cheeses (served with a glass of port) is offered for a small supplement. The likes of fresh salmon tartlet with a light tomato sauce and pesto and baked goat's cheese with aubergine and tossed salad may feature among the starters, and roast guinea fowl on a bed of Puy lentils with roast garlic and thyme and beef fillet with creamy Roquefort sauce are typical main-course options. All are prepared with a skill and care that extends to a choice of home-baked breads and desserts like lemon tart and dark chocolate marquise. The day's fish and seasonal game dishes are recited when the menu is offered; venison is particularly popular from October and pheasant from November. Diners and overnight guests share a comfortable period sitting-room. *Seats 40. D only 7-9.30 (to 10.30 Fri & Sat). Closed 1st two weeks Nov, 24-27 Dec & Good Friday. Amex, MasterCard,* **VISA**

Rooms   £60

Nine spacious, antique-furnished bedrooms have been individually decorated with attractive fabrics and offer various homely comforts in addition to remote-control TV, direct-dial telephones and good, large en suite bathrooms. Four of the rooms were refurbished and brought into use last year. Breakfast, using free-range eggs, makes an excellent start to the day.

BAGENALSTOWN	Lorum Old Rectory	£55

Tel 0503 75282   Fax 0503 75455   Map 2 C4   **A**
Bagenalstown Co Carlow

Don and Bobbie Smith have built up a great reputation for good food and hospitality at their delightful Victorian rectory since arriving in 1985. Elegance and comfort receive equal priority in spacious, well-proportioned rooms furnished in period style, including a lovely drawing-room, four thoughtfully furnished, en suite bedrooms (one with a four-poster) and an extra single room which has the use of a big old-fashioned bathroom with generous ball and claw cast-iron bath along the corridor; all rooms are non-smoking. A lovely place for families – there are swings (and a pony to ride under supervision) in the orchard, room for cots and extra beds in parents' rooms, high-chairs, videos and children's teas all available. Bobbie's renowned dinner – for residents only, £20 for five courses – is served communally at a long mahogany table (book by 3pm) and includes a fine selection of Irish cheeses. Private parties for up to 12. No dogs. *Rooms 5. Garden, croquet. Closed Christmas week. MasterCard,* **VISA**

BALLINA	Downhill Hotel	65%	£119*

Tel 096 21033   Fax 096 21338   Map 1 B3   **H**
Ballina Co Mayo

Set in landscaped gardens overlooking the River Brosna, the Downhill offers extensive leisure and conference facilities plus good fishing nearby as major attractions. The purpose-built conference centre and hospitality rooms accommodate groups from 10 to 450 and the newly renovated and refurbished leisure centre has a 50ft oval swimming pool with a children's pool, plunge pool steam room and fully-equipped gym; nightly entertainment in Frog's Pavilion piano bar. Good facilities for families include the provision of a cot, high-chair, a supervised playroom and early suppers. Easy parking for 300. The choice of rooms includes Budget, Standard, Superior and Master Suites; all are to be revamped and sixteen new bedrooms are due to be added during 1997. Room prices are for half-board only, with a reduced tariff Oct-end May. Ask about special salmon fishing arrangements on the River Moy. *Rooms 50. Garden, tennis, indoor swimming pool, children's pool, gym, squash, sauna, steam room, spa bath, sun beds, children's indoor playroom, games room, snooker. Closed 5 days Christmas. Amex, Diners, MasterCard,* **VISA**

BALLINA   Mount Falcon Castle   60%   £98

Tel 096 70811 Fax 096 71517   Map 1 B3   **AR**
Ballina Co Mayo

The 'castle' was built in neo-Gothic style in 1876, and the 100 acres of grounds extend to the banks of the River Moy (fishing is available either here or on Lough Conn). Woodland walks unfold the beauty of the surroundings, while back inside huge log fires and convivial company make for instant relaxation. Simple bedrooms are furnished with period furniture; there are two single rooms and three other levels of tariff for the double rooms (the tariff given here is for the best four rooms at the front of the house with views over the estate). Constance Aldridge, who has owned the 'castle' and greeted visitors for over 60 years, is an indispensible part of the Castle's attraction. Her longevity and warm hospitality win her our 1997 Host of the Year award. *Rooms 10. Garden, tennis, game fishing. Closed Christmas week, Feb & Mar. Amex, Diners, MasterCard,* **VISA**

Dining Room   £55

Local produce, much of it from the estate farm and walled gardens, is the basis of confident, uncomplicated country-house cooking. Guests gather around one table for the set dinner which always features a fine home-made soup like potato and herb, usually served by Constance at the head of the table; this might be preceded by hot cheese soufflé or mussels in wine, and followed by the likes of stuffed loin of pork with apple sauce or leg of lamb with rosemary and garlic. Irish cheeses and a pair of desserts – perhaps apple and cinnamon pie or lemon meringue pie – complete the picture. Lunch available by arrangement. *Seats 28. D only at 8. Set D £20.*

BALLINA   Places of Interest

Tourist Information Tel 096 70848
Mayo North Family History Research & Visitor Centre Castlehill Tel 096 31809

BALLINADEE   Glebe Country House   £50

Tel 021 778294 Fax 021 778456   Map 2 B6   **A**
Ballinadee Bandon Co Cork

A charming, family-run Georgian rectory near Kinsale that has been a restful retreat for guests since 1989. Set in large, well-tended gardens (the source of much that appears on the dinner table), the house has classically-proportioned reception rooms and large, en suite bedrooms that are rather dashingly decorated in an upbeat country-house style. They are comfortably furnished with crisp white bed linen and include tea- and coffee-making trays. Dinner for residents is at 8pm, by arrangement (book by noon; no children under 10 for dinner). Unlicensed, but guests are encouraged to bring their own wine. Several self-catering coach-house apartments are also available. *Rooms 4. Garden, croquet, tennis, children's play area. MasterCard,* **VISA**

BALLINASLOE   Hayden's Hotel   63%   £63

Tel 0905 42347 Fax 0905 42895   Map 2 B4   **H**
Ballinasloe Co Galway

Right on the main street and very much the centre of local activities, this thriving,
bustling hotel makes a good base for touring the Clare/Galway area and is most
notable for its welcoming, informal atmosphere and friendly, helpful staff.
Extensive public areas include the main foyer, a large bar with striking black and
white tiles floor, conservatory seating area, buffet/carvery and a well-appointed
restaurant. Several banqueting and conference rooms include one that overlooks
a courtyard garden and fountain and a smaller one with an unusual skylight
feature providing natural light. Bedrooms vary somewhat in size but are pleasantly
decorated and comfortable, most with both double and single beds (although
there are also some large family rooms and a few singles); all have neat, en suite
bathrooms. Banqueting/conference facilities for 350/400. Ample free parking.
Rooms 48. Garden, coffee shop (8-5). Closed 24-27 Dec. Amex, Diners, MasterCard,
VISA

BALLINGARRY   The Mustard Seed at Echo Lodge   £150

Tel 069 68508   Fax 069 68511   Map 2 B5   **AR**
Ballingarry Co Limerick

Dan Mullane opened his eagerly
anticipated new venture, a country
house and restaurant about 8 miles
from his former home in Adare
village, in the spring of 1996. Echo
Lodge is a delightful, graciously
proportioned period house set on
an elevated site overlooking the
little village of Ballingarry (the seven
acres of grounds already include a
substantial kitchen garden laid out
with fruit trees and many good

things). Emphatically not an hotel, Dan's home bears the marks of the seasoned
traveller with a keen eye for decorative and practical furnishings, and the highly
individual rooms – all with strikingly decorated en suite facilities, some with
shower only – benefit greatly from the collections he has built up over the
years. Fine white cotton on comfortable beds, fresh flowers from the garden,
complimentary mineral water and even a hidden treasure trove of hand-made
chocolates and petits fours are treats in store for the overnight guest – but, while
luxurious peacefulness is the primary characteristic of a stay at Echo Lodge, the
elegantly appointed public areas also promise good company and conviviality.
Two bedrooms are reserved for non-smokers and one room is adapted for
disabled guests. Children up to 3 may stay free in their parents' room.
Banqueting for 70, conferences of up to 20. No dogs. *Rooms 12. Garden,
terrace, patio. Closed mid Jan-Mid Mar & 23-26 Dec. Amex, MasterCard,* **VISA**

Restaurant   [i]   £70

While Echo Lodge itself is a first for Dan Mullane, he brought with him from
Adare a well-loved treasure in The Mustard Seed, the famous restaurant that has
been synonymous with his name since the mid-80s. The two elegant dining-
rooms now offer Dan a larger stage, on which he hosts each evening with
apparent ease – and all his customary panache – backed up by a good front-of-
house team and chef David Norris's skills with local produce in the kitchen.
Attention to detail is evident throughout: drinks, served in the Library, are
accompanied by a tasty amuse-bouche such as crisp little boat-shaped goat's
cheese pastry; flowers, like a tiny pot of soft apricot miniature roses, on simple
but effectively appointed tables echo themes around the room and on the china.

Uncurtained windows frame views of the garden beyond (although window tables can also catch reflections of downlighters on bare glass after dark). Delicious freshly-baked breads are served alongside starters such as herby pork quenelles with a salad from the garden and a creamy, piquant dressing with grainy mustard seeds (what else?), or a crisp-skinned confit of duck on a bed of Oriental vegetables. There follows a soup course (perhaps creamy, well-seasoned leek), a mixed-leaf salad or sorbet. Main courses arrive after a deliberate break – typically a gutsy combination like a pink loin of lamb served with a skewer of liver and kidney on a rosemary jus and garlic cream, or a dish of pan-fried wood pigeon with another Oriental slant: Chinese leaves and a crisp wonton stuffed with the chopped livers sitting jauntily atop sliced breast meat with a sesame and soy sauce dressing. There's a good, plated Irish cheese selection and gorgeous puddings – a warm gratin of strawberries and banana with a contrasting citrus sorbet and caramel sauce, whiskey-flavoured bread-and-butter pudding with a cinnamon anglaise or a delightfully flamboyant ice cream selection with tuile cornets of cream. Coffee and excellent home-made petits fours round the evening off in style. *Seats 65. Parties 8. Private Room 30. D only 7-9.30 (Sun for residents only in winter). Closed mid Jan-mid Mar & 23-26 Dec. Set D £28.*

BALLISODARE   The Thatch

Tel 071 67288
Ballisodare Co Sligo

Map 1 B2

P

This low-ceilinged (and rather tatty-looking) thatched pub just south of Sligo town is very much a local and its open turf fire is as welcoming on a winter evening as the tables outdoors on a fine summer day. Whatever the weather the welcome from Brian and Denise Fitzpatrick (long-standing owners of this family business) is warm and the 'pint' is good. Just soup and sandwiches are served at present, but by the summer more substantial dishes should be available. Traditional music 3 nights a week in winter; every night except Mon and Sat in July and August. *Open 11am-11.30pm (12-11 Oct-Mar), Sun 12.30-2, 4-11. Garden. MasterCard, VISA*

We only recommend the food in hotels categorised as **HR** and **AR**.
However, the food in many **A** establishments throughout
Ireland is often very acceptable
(but the restaurant may not be open to non-residents).

BALLYBOFEY   Kee's Hotel   64%   £72

Tel 074 31018   Fax 074 31917
Stranorlar Ballybofey Co Donegal

Map 1 C2

HR

Centrally located for business and pleasure in Co Donegal, this all-year hotel has always been a coaching inn; it has now been run by Arthur and Claire Kee for 36 years and is noted for the warmth of their hospitality. Bedrooms have all been refurbished recently and the public areas of the hotel are gradually undergoing substantial change – the restaurant has already had a major make-over and Scenes, the traditional bar, is due for something similar before the 1997 season. En suite bedrooms are attractive and comfortable, with fresh flowers and complimentary mineral water as well as above-average amenities. The hotel's excellent leisure facilities are available free to residents who have direct access from their rooms. Children are welcome – cots and high-chairs are available and there's a creche some mornings in the leisure centre. *Rooms 36. Indoor swimming pool, gym, sauna, steam room, spa bath, sunbeds. Amex, Diners, MasterCard, VISA*

See over

The Looking Glass

£55

Recently refurbished in warm tones that complement a striking display of hand-worked tapestries, this fine restaurant is cleverly designed in two main areas, with lots of booths and corners. With the proprietor, Arthur Kee, head chef Frederic Souty has worked wonders since his arrival in 1994 in transforming what was previously a traditional, uninspiring country hotel menu. They have created a promising new style that would be worthy of any capital city. Seasonal menus are augmented by daily specials, especially seafood; five starters on the table d'hote might include fresh Dublin Bay prawns with angel hair pasta and thyme, and warm bacon salad with tomato concassé and garlic croutons; these are followed by a choice of soups, while main courses might include escalope of pork with wholegrain mustard, confit of duck leg with a wild mushroom jus and grilled salmon with green peppercorn sauce. Desserts are shared with the à la carte, which might commence with an amuse-bouche of seared scallop and salmon, and a tempting assortment of freshly-baked breads, following with starters such as warm salad of kidneys and potatoes with blue cheese (a little tower of mixed kidneys, potatoes and cheese topped with greenery) or a soup ('spicy clear fish broth' with salmon, scallop, prawns, white fish, potatoes and croutons, all zipped up with Thai-style spicing). Fish of the day might be lemon sole – three fat fillets folded into a neat tower and served on a wine sauce with garnish of diced pepper; roast rack of Donegal lamb may be served off the bone in slices, with its juices, garnished with baby carrots and whole garlic cloves. Accurately cooked vegetables are kept simple: garlic potato gratin, sautéed potatoes, crisp mangetout and broccoli. To finish, try an artistic 'Tasting Plate' of desserts: a chunk of iced nougat with honey cream on a crisp tuile centrepiece (topped dramatically with spun sugar) and surrounded by mango coulis, a little square each of lemon tart and iced Bailey's soufflé and orange cream, and a wonderfully juicy, crisp-topped crème brulée of pears. Aromatic cafetière coffee and home-made petits fours provide the perfect ending. *Seats 74. Parties 12. Private Rooms 10/60. L (Sun only) 12.30-2.15 D 6.30-9.30 (till 10 Fri & Sat). Set Sun L £10.50 Set D £12.50 & £20*

BALLYBUNION	Marine Links Hotel	60%	£66

Tel 068 27139   Fax 068 27666   Map 2 A5   **H**
Sandhill Road Ballybunion Co Kerry

The Hook and Socket Bar, with its growing collection of golf bag tags from around the world, is the heart of this friendly owner-run hotel close to Ballybunion Golf Club. Cane furniture emphasises the informal holiday atmosphere of the place, both in public areas like the lounge and restaurant, and in the bright, unpretentiously furnished, en suite bedrooms, all of which have sea views across to the cliffs of Clare. *Rooms 10. Closed Nov-mid Mar. Amex, Diners, MasterCard,* **VISA**

BALLYCONNEELY	Erriseask House Hotel	66%	£77

Tel 095 23553   Fax 095 23639   Map 2 A4   **HR**
Ballyconneely Clifden Co Galway

Since 1988 brothers Christian and Stefan Matz have been quietly building up a reputation for excellence at their stunningly located shoreside hotel and restaurant, seven miles south of Clifden. There's a deceptively low-key atmosphere about the place, expecially in the foyer and lounge/bar areas which have a distinctly continental feel with a lot of light wood and (with the notable exception of Gertrude Degenhardt's pictures) a generally understated approach which is also carried through to the original bedrooms – neatly decorated in rather neutral colours with compact shower rooms and tea/coffee trays. The five newest rooms display a different side to the Matz personality with a flamboyance hitherto unsuspected: designed as two-storey suites they have a luxurious ground-floor bedroom and en suite bathroom with romantic spiral staircases leading up to the mezzanine sitting-room, and dramatic drapes, which fall the whole height from ceiling to floor but take nothing from the wild land and seascape beyond. The wildness and raw beauty of the surroundings are perhaps the main strength of the magnet that draws people back to Erriseask, but the hosts' gentle cosseting also plays a major, if discreet, role too. They even lend guests two ever-willing dogs to enhance walks along the white coral strands. Sheer magic. The tariff varies from £60 to £85 (per double room) according to season; particularly good half-board terms (£85-£120). Children under 10 stay free in parents' room. No dogs. **Rooms 13. Garden. Closed Nov-Easter. Amex, Diners, MasterCard, VISA**

Restaurant ★ £65

Well-appointed in every detail, the restaurant provides a fitting backdrop for Stefan Matz's dedicated, passionate cooking – for which he won our Ireland Chef of the Year award in 1995. Four menus are offered: a set 4-course dinner menu, a 3-course residents' dinner (changed daily and the only menu served on Wednesdays) with alternative dishes for each course, short à la carte and Stefan's *pièce de résistance*, a 7-course *menu dégustation*.

Typically, the latter might comprise grilled scallops with marinated scallions, lasagne of sautéed monkfish in a light ginger sauce, fillet of turbot with a herbal potato crust, carrot and yoghurt sorbet, duck with crème de cassis sauce and glazed vegetables, superb Irish and French cheeses, and a blackcurrant soufflé with vanilla ice cream – a masterpiece of flavour balancing, contrasting textures and tip-top ingredients. Even the four-course dinner might offer smoked fillet of black sole with sautéed peppers or cream of curry and courgette soup followed by various fillets of fish and scallops with vegetables in cream sauce or sautéed beef fillet with wild mushrooms in a red wine and shallot sauce, then Explorateur (French farmhouse cheese) or a selection of home-made desserts. Attention to detail encompasses delightful *amuse-bouche*, fine breads – like Stefan's close-textured fruit bread served thinly sliced with the magnificent cheeseboard – and vegetables that are small and carefully judged for colour, flavour and overall balance. A freshly baked Swiss apple pie or parfait of chocolate on a salad of oranges might be a fitting finale for such a fabulous feast. Aromatic black coffee is accompanied by irresistible petits fours. The diner might get lost in admiration of Stefan's skill and precision, the perfectly-judged portions, the balance of imagination and simplicity. Add to this Christian Matz's natural, unassuming hospitality – he pampers without becoming intrusive and excellent service is provided by well-trained local staff – and it becomes clear that this is one of the finest gastronomic destinations in the west of Ireland. A light lunch menu (perhaps monkfish on a bed of lettuce, roast loin of Connemara lamb with fine herbs on sautéed vegetables, Irish farmhouse cheeses or walnut and almond mousse on chocolate sauce) is complemented by a short carte of interesting dishes: seafood salad, home-made noodles with mushroom sauce, grilled turbot with fresh tarragon. A very well-balanced wine list with plenty of half bottles and a dozen available by the glass, though champagnes are perhaps a little scarce; seemingly no vintages on offer. Prices are very fair, considering this is one of the best restaurants in the country. No smoking. Booking advisable. **Seats 36. Parties 6. Private Room 16. L (Fri-Sun only) 1-2 D 6.30-9. Closed L Mon-Thu. Set L £14.90 Set D £18.50/£23.50 & £32.50.**

BALLYCONNELL   Slieve Russell Hotel   71%   £130

Tel 049 26444   Fax 049 26474   Map 1 C3   **H**
Ballyconnell Co Cavan

Named after a nearby mountain, Slieve Rushen, this substantial hotel, golf and country club is set in 300 acres of landscaped gardens and lakes in some of Ireland's finest fishing country. Renowned throughout the country for providing outstanding amenities – it is also a major conference centre – and a high standard of comfort in an area that was until recently relatively unknown, the hotel is now the main social and business focal point of the region. An impressive foyer and lounge area with marbled columns and grand central staircase establish a tone of space and substance that is carried through all the public areas of the hotel, including a large bar and two restaurants and also the adjacent country club, which has a separate entrance but is conceived in the same grand scale. Spacious bedrooms have a pleasant outlook over the grounds and championship golf course and include two equipped for disabled guests; all are comfortably furnished with the amenities expected of a good modern hotel plus extra-large beds and impressive marbled bathrooms. Fine leisure facilities include a 20m pool designed to incorporate a therapeutic whirlpool and massage seats in addition to jacuzzi, steam room and saunas and there's also a gym, squash and all-weather tennis courts. Banqueting/conference facilties can accommodate up to 550/800. Children are welcome (free up to 3 years old in parents' room); there is a supervised creche (10.30am-8pm) plus children's entertainment during school holidays. No dogs. Sean Quinn Group. *Rooms 151. Garden, golf (18), indoor swimming pool, children's pool, gym, spa bath, steam room, snooker, games room, hair & beauty salon, squash, tennis. Amex, Diners, MasterCard, VISA*

BALLYCOTTON   Bayview Hotel   67%   £110

Tel 021 646746 Fax 021 646075   Map 2 B6   **HR**
Ballycotton Co Cork

In an enviable location overlooking Ballycotton harbour, with a private garden leading down to a little beach, this hotel has been in the same ownership since 1974. It was completely re-built a few years ago and now combines all the comforts of a modern building with a discreet design that blends unobtrusively into its setting and gives more than a passing nod to tradition. Stephen Belton (previously at the *Park Hotel Kenmare*), manager since early last year, has a good team that works well together; a high standard of housekeeping and well-trained staff add greatly to the comfort of this well-run hotel. Uninterrupted sea and harbour views are the most striking feature, seen both from the warm and welcoming public areas and all the bedrooms. The latter are of a good size and are well furnished with neat bathrooms and little balconies; two suites occupy corner sites and command particularly good views, while the rooms on the top floor have a cosy, almost 'cottagey' feeling. Children are welcome and may stay free in their parents'

room up to the age of 12 (most rooms have a double and single bed); cots and high-chairs are available, along with high tea at 5.30. Tennis and a putting green are available nearby. No dogs. **Rooms 35.** Garden. Closed early Nov-Easter. Amex, Diners, MasterCard, **VISA**

Restaurant £65

Head chef Ciaran Scully (previously at *The Rectory*, Glandore) recently joined the Bayview team and already has everything running sweetly, making this one of the finest kitchens in the country. The style is modern Irish, a lively reinterpretation of traditional themes with classical and world influences also discernible. The restaurant is elegantly appointed, with well-spaced tables, plenty of alcoves and lovely sea and harbour views. A la carte and dinner menus are equally tempting and, although well balanced, have an understandable leaning towards seafood landed in the harbour below. The dinner menu offers a choice of four dishes for each course; typical offerings might include a medley of crab and smoked mackerel with tossed salad leaves and a lemon and basil sauce (a pretty dish with tomato concassé surrounding a fishy 'cake') or, from the carte, a pastry case of asparagus and smoked salmon with a lemon hollandaise sauce, all served with good home-made breads. Soup – interesting smoked salmon and fennel cream – follows, or perhaps a mixed-leaf salad with fresh herbs. From eight main courses on the carte (including a tempting vegetarian option) roast loin of lamb is typical, served perfectly pink on a little galette of spinach and mushroom with roasted cloves of garlic and shallot in the lamb jus. A choice of four main courses on the dinner menu might include a classically-inspired turbot dish, pan-fried with sautéed summer greens and bacon accompanied by a whole-grain mustard sauce, local new potatoes and a crisp mélange of fresh garden peas, carrots, cauliflower and broccoli. Imaginative desserts could include a dramatic presentation of deep-fried strawberries, tiny balls of mixed ices in a tuile, fresh glazed strawberries and spun sugar. Or there are plated farmhouse cheeses – about five, served with home-made biscuits and a mini-salad – and darkly aromatic cafetière coffee to round off the meal. The wine list deserves study as there are some helpful tasting notes, interesting New World wines and a dozen or so good half bottles. Friendly, efficient service from well-trained, uniformed waitresses. Lunch is served from a daytime bar menu (except on Sunday), available 12.30-6.30. In fine weather light meals may be served in the garden. No children under 4. **Seats 70.** Parties 12. Private Room 20. L (Sun only) 1-2 D 7-9. Set Sun L £13 Set D £25.

The Egon Ronay Guides are completely independent. We do not accept advertising, hospitality or payment from any of the establishments listed in this Guide.

BALLYDEHOB   Annie's Bookshop and Café

Tel 028 37292   Map 2 A6   **JaB**
Main Street Balydehob Co Cork

Just up the street from Annie Barry's famous little evening restaurant, she opened this daytime bookshop and café in 1994 to offer informal daytime food in summer. The atmosphere is lovely – old pine, oilcloths, blackboard menu alongside the books – and prices for undemanding home-cooked snacks (seafood soup with home-baked brown soda bread, fresh crab open sandwich) refreshingly low. Home bakes are tempting: gateau of the day, hot chocolate fudge cake and cream, carrot cake. There's a good choice of teas and coffees too – and home-made scones with butter and jam. **Seats 25.** Open 10am-6pm. Closed Sun & Oct-mid Apr. No credit cards.

BALLYDEHOB   Annie's Restaurant   £60

Tel 028 37292   Map 2 A6   **R**
Main Street Ballydehob Co Cork

Annie Barry's little restaurant just about sums up what people hope for most of all when eating out in Ireland. It's small and intimate, with a slightly eccentric but perfectly practical arrangement with Levis' traditional grocery/bar across the road, which acts as reception for reading the menu and ordering over an aperitif and the natural place to repair to for a little digestif at the end of the meal. What better way to relieve congestion in a tiny restaurant? Once summoned to your table, Dano Barry's talent for doing as little as is necessary with superb ingredients, especially seafood, becomes apparent. Dishes on the menu may have the ring of familiarity – baked avocado with crab meat, grilled mussels stuffed with garlic butter and breadcrumbs, home-made duck liver and bacon paté with Cumberland sauce – but the sheer quality and freshness of ingredients and Dano's talent for simplicity make a meal memorable. Details, like the delicious freshly-baked brown bread, are good and, while seafood usually wins hands down – black sole on the bone is simply superb, also crisp little medallions of monkfish in garlic butter – the menu is well balanced. Free-range duck is a local speciality and not to be missed: Dano cooks it on the bone and serves it tender and juicy but very crisp-skinned, with a Cointreau sauce. All main courses are served with homely vegetables and delicious local spuds. Tempting desserts might include a more-ish roasted almond and Bailey's ice cream and blackberry and apple sponge with traditional custard. Great hospitality, good service. *Seats 24. Parties 8.*
D only 7-9.30. Closed Sun, Mon & all Oct (ring to check opening times in winter). Set D £22. MasterCard, VISA

BALLYDEHOB   Levis Bar

Tel 028 37118   Map 2 A6   **P**
Corner House Main Street Ballydehob Co Cork

A friendly welcome awaits visitors to this veritable institution – a 150-year-old grocery store and bar, run by sisters Julia and Nell Levis for "years and years". The bar is not only host to 'resident' drinkers but also serves as a reception and aperitif area for the tiny *Annie's* restaurant over the road (see entry above). *Open 10.30am-12midnight, Sun 12.30-2, 4-11. No credit cards.*

BALLYFERRITER   Tigh An t-Saorsaigh

Tel 066 56344   Map 2 A5   **P**
Ballyferriter Village Ballyferriter nr Tralee Co Kerry

This colourful little Irish-speaking pub has probably changed little since it first opened in 1854; it has been run by Dermot and Lulu Sears since 1991. A good spot for a quiet pint during the day or for the traditional music sessions that are held nightly in summer. Bar food is served in summer only: typically fish and chips, poached salmon, Irish stew or open crab, prawn and smoked salmon sandwiches. Four bedrooms (£32 double) have en suite showers; children under 12 half-price. No dogs. Formerly known as Long's Pub. *Open 10.30am-11.30pm, Sun 12.30-2, 4-11. Bar Food (May-Aug) 1-8.30. Garden. Amex, Diners, MasterCard, VISA*

BALLYHACK   Neptune Restaurant   £50

Tel & Fax 051 389284   Map 2 C5   **R**
Ballyhack New Ross Co Wexford

Coming off the little Passage East car ferry from Waterford, turn left way from the main road and head instead for Pierce and Valerie McAuliffe's delightful rust-red restaurant just in front of the restored castle. Major changes were afoot in the restaurant as we went to press and the decor promises to be very fresh and quite different for the 1997 season. Changes are due to take place in the kitchen as well, in order to accommodate students in a cookery school (mainly aimed at people running guest houses and doing bar meals) which will be run by the McAuliffes and Martin Dwyer (of *Dwyer's Restaurant* in Waterford city – see entry) from early 1997. Alongside this development Valerie will use her skills as an interior designer to transform the dining areas: the main room, for example, is to be known as The Schoolroom and will be used for teaching classes once again. Diners, however, may be more interested in ensuring that all their old favourites are still available. Rest assured that specialities such as creamy fish soup, mussels and crab claws in garlic butter, fish crumble and, of course, their magnificent hot crab bréhat will still feature on menus that will highlight local seafood; alternatives such as roast rack of lamb with fresh mint, grilled T-bone or fillet steak with whiskey sauce, or a vegetarian special will also be offered. Finish with Valerie's lovely desserts or local cheeses and coffee with mints. Carefully selected short wine list, but BYO also welcomed (corkage £3.50). A telephone call to check opening times is advised. **Seats 36. Parties 6. Private Room 16.** D only 7-9.30. Closed Sun-Wed & mid Dec-mid Jan. Amex, Diners, MasterCard, **VISA**

BALLYLICKEY   Ballylickey Manor House   67%   £154

Tel 027 50071   Fax 027 50124   Map 2 A6   **AR**
Ballylickey Bantry Co Cork

Ballylickey Manor House was built some 300 years ago by Lord Kenmare as a shooting lodge; it has now been the Graves' family home for four generations and the totally restored and refurbished building has been run as a hotel by Mr & Mrs George Graves since 1950. The main house, which is impressively furnished with antiques, has views over Bantry Bay and five spacious suites with well-appointed bathrooms (the tariff given here is for these rooms). Ten acres of formal, park-like gardens afford a splendid setting for an outdoor swimming pool and garden restaurant, in addition to simpler 'rustic' accommodation, including two new suites, in seven chalets (£99-£143), all with en suite rooms; our recommendation is for the main-house rooms. Trout and salmon fishing on the Ouvane river. No dogs. **Rooms** *5 in main house. Garden, croquet, fishing, outdoor swimming pool. Closed Nov-end Mar. Amex, Diners, MasterCard,* **VISA**

Le Rendez-Vous   £75

A daily 'house menu' is available to Manor House residents only, but down beside the heated outdoor swimming pool, *Le Rendez-Vous* restaurant is open to non-residents. The restaurant is small but quite dashing, with a little country house chintz certainly, but strong, warm, plain colours predominating in contrasting cushion covers and table settings in summery blues. It has a certain Continental atmosphere about it – the optimistic location probably has an influence of course, but it's also to do with Gilles Eynaud's stylish (and emphatically French) cooking. Typical starters might include a hearty, strong-textured and well-flavoured *terrine de campagne* served with a well-dressed salad garnish and an *assiette fraicheur*, the kind of melon and raw vegetable salad that only the French seem able to make. Super soups like *velouté d'oseille*, a lovely pale green creamy mixture of sorrel and spinach, or *crème freneuse*, an unusual mixture of baby turnips and carrots, are served with delicous home-baked breads. Seafood always features among the main courses, typically in fillet of turbot with a champagne sauce, and local lamb also makes a regular appearance, perhaps as roast loin with rosemary. Classical puddings – strawberry gratin, crème caramel, chocolate and coffee profiteroles – and local cheeses to finish. But Gilles also has some *plats gourmands* to offer – his own *foie gras*, for example, and grilled prime rib of beef with béarnaise sauce (for two) or, when available, grilled Bantry Bay lobster with brandy butter. No smoking in the dining-room. **Seats 30. Parties 8. L 12.15-2 D 7-9. Set D £25 & £30. Closed Wed & all Dec, Jan. Diners, MasterCard,** **VISA**

BALLYLICKEY   Larchwood House   £60

Tel 027 66181   Map 2 A6   **RR**
Pearsons Bridge Ballylickey Bantry Co Cork

Owner-chef Sheila Vaughan and her husband Aidan have been steadily building
up a reputation for good food and accommodation at Larchwood since they
opened in 1990. Although located in a private home, the restaurant is cleverly
designed to take full advantage of views over garden and river to the mountains
beyond and also to allow maximum privacy in a limited space. Four-course,
fixed-price-only menus offer a wide selection, priced according to the choice
of main course and highlighting fine local produce. A typical menu might offer
chicken liver paté with Cumberland sauce, then seafood and tomato soup, pear
and melon cocktail, black sole with mustard sauce and local farmhouse cheeses
or warm rhubarb and ginger pudding among its offerings. Also warm salads
(perhaps chicken and walnuts or duck with almonds and ginger), venison
with red wine and fillet of hake gratinée. Accommodation is offered in four
comfortable en suite rooms (£44 per room), including two family rooms;
rooms at the back have lovely views. Excellent breakfasts offer an unusual range
of options, including fish choices. No dogs. *Garden, fishing.* **Seats 20.** *Parties 13.*
D only 6.30-10. Set D from £23. Closed Sun & 1 week Christmas. Amex, Diners,
MasterCard, **VISA**

See the **County Listings** green tinted pages for
details of all establishments listed in county order.

BALLYLICKEY   Seaview House Hotel   70%   £90

Tel 027 50462   **Fax 027 51555**   Map 2 A6   **HR**
Ballylickey Bantry Co Cork

Since converting her family home to a hotel in the mid-70s, Kathleen
O'Sullivan has built up an impressive reputation – not only for consistently high
standards of essentials like comfort and housekeeping, but also for her personal
supervision and warmth of welcome. Spacious, well-proportioned public rooms
include a graciously decorated drawing-room, a library and comfortable
television room, while generously-sized bedrooms, including two recently
converted suites/family rooms (under-4s stay free), are all individually decorated
and some have sea views. Family furniture and antiques enhance the hotel
throughout and a ground-floor room has been thoughtfully equipped for
disabled guests. Refurbishment and improvements will continue throughout
1997. **Rooms 17.** *Garden. Closed mid Nov-mid Mar. Amex, Diners, MasterCard,*
VISA

Restaurant   £60

Overlooking the garden, with views over Bantry Bay, several well-appointed
rooms linked by arches and furnished with antiques and fresh flowers combine
to make an elegant restaurant with plenty of privacy. Kathleen's set five-course
dinner menu changes daily and offers a choice of around eight starters and four
meat and four fish main courses, with the emphasis firmly on local produce.
Dishes range from Bantry Bay oysters or roast stuffed quail with port and
almond sauce to fresh Dover sole, monkfish scampi and tartare sauce, veal with
mushroom and Dijon mustard sauce, and roast leg of lamb. Five or so home-
made puds might include hot toffee peaches or strawberry shortcake with a red
fruit coulis; dessert trolley at Sunday lunchtimes. No children under 7 in dining-
room at night; separate arrangements are made for them (high tea served from
6.30 in the library). 10% service is automatically added to menu prices. **Seats 60.**
L (Sun only) 12.45-2 D 7-9.30. Set Sun L £13.50 Set D £23.50.

BALLYMORE EUSTACE Ballymore Inn

Tel 045 864585   Map 2 C4   **P**
Ballymore Eustace Co Kildare

Just a short drive from the south Dublin suburbs, this simple village pub has recently seen some remarkable changes since it was taken over by Barry and Georgina O'Sullivan. Turn left on entering and you will find a typical country bar, but the right-hand door tells a different story. Nothing flashy, but an original hand can be seen at work in the blue- and green-painted furniture in an unusual mixture of designs, the not-too-obviously co-ordinating cushion fabrics, interesting picures and (most strikingly) the generous use of fresh flowers; lovely big lilies (or something equally delightful) are to be found on the bar alongside a simple bowl of lemons and limes, on the mantelpiece and even in the Ladies. The front half of this bar is set up informally with small tables, while the back is more restaurant in style, with larger tables suitable for groups of up to a dozen or so. Whether choosing from the bar menu or rather more extensive Café Bar menu (weekend evenings and Sunday lunch) it all seems more cosmopolitan than country, offering the likes of spicy chicken wings, Caesar salad, roasted vegetables and couscous salad, salmon with watercress and lime sauce; typical accompaniments are mixed salad leaves, stir-fried vegetables or a tomato and black olive salad. Attention to detail is evident from the start, even in the bar, when a cheery waitress lays the table with quality cutlery and glasses, heavy paper napkins, a pottery dish of butter and salt and mix-corn peppermills, and then presents a wonderful choice of freshly-baked breads such as granary brown and white yeast bread with fresh basil. Soup of the day might be luscious, buttery leek and chunky potato served in a beautiful pottery bowl. Steak and rare roast beef sandwiches are a speciality, the former tender, juicy chargrilled steak in warm, crusty French loaf with salad and garlic butter, the latter with superb basil mayonnaise. 'Grilled chicken pesto' is sliced chargrilled breast meat with a lovely 'bitty' pesto drizzled over it and a small salad garnish. A daily special might be bacon and cabbage, a simple 'homely' dish served with fresh parsley sauce and big, floury boiled spuds. Equally more-ish desserts might include a wonderful gooseberry and blackcurrant tart, the juicy fruit topped by a crisp lattice of pastry and served with a ball of beautiful home-made vanilla ice cream. Throughout, chef Martha Ashton's standard of cooking is excellent. All this and good coffee, too... *Seats 32 (+12 in bar). Parties 12.* **Bar Menu** *12.30-9 (till 10 Fri & Sat). D (Fri & Sat only) 7-10. No food Mon evev & all Sun. Bar closed Good Friday & 25 Dec. Amex, MasterCard,* **VISA**

BALLYMOTE Temple House   **£80**

Tel 071 83329 **Fax 071 83808**   Map 1 B3   **A**
Ballymote Co Sligo

Temple House is a magnificent Georgian mansion set in 1000 acres of parkland with terraced gardens, a working farm, walled vegetable garden and a lake well known for the size of its pike. Imposing, even austere externally, Sandy and Deb Perceval's house is warm and welcoming behind its front door, in spite of the grand scale of the outer hall (note the trophies of outdoor pursuits) and the elegant inner hall. There are four centrally-heated double bedrooms – two of them very large, all very comfortable – and a single with shower. Deb Perceval does the cooking, using home-grown or home-reared produce to good effect in her no-choice dinners (residents only, £18). Guests gather for dinner in a cosy sitting room with an open fire, and coffee is served in the drawing-room afterwards. The day starts with the double delight of marvellous views and a super breakfast. High tea for under-5s is served at 6.30 – children's room rates are negotiable. No perfumes or aerosols, please, owing to Mr Perceval's chemical sensitivity. No dogs. *Rooms 5. Garden, croquet, coarse fishing, snooker, lake boats (3). Closed Dec-Easter (except shooting parties Dec & Jan). Amex, MasterCard,* **VISA**

BALLYMURN   Ballinkeele House   £70

Tel 053 38105 Fax 053 38468   Map 2 D5   **A**
Enniscorthy Co Wexford

John and Margaret Maher's substantial early Victorian house has been in the
family since it was built in 1840 and is remarkable because, with the exception
of obvious additions like central heating and en suite bathrooms, so little has
changed. Very much the family centre of a working farm, it is grand in an
unusually matter-of-fact way: large, high-ceilinged rooms are furnished in
style with the original furniture and paintings (the billiards room is especially
impressive), but with no sense of the house being dressed up for guests.
Aside from private bathrooms, the spacious bedrooms (no smoking) are also
remarkable for period pieces and have sweeping country views. ***Rooms** 5.
Garden, croquet, tennis, snooker. Closed 6 Nov-Feb (parties by arrangement in
winter). MasterCard, **VISA***

BALLYNEETY   Croker's Bistro   £55

Tel 061 351881 Fax 061 351384   Map 2 B5   **R**
Limerick County Golf & Country Club Ballyneety Co Limerick

Located in a very pleasing clubhouse at the Golf and Country Club, with
sweeping views over the course and countryside from both bar and dining-room.
Bright and stylishly decorated throughout with colourful quality fabrics and lots
of natural wood, the restaurant is well appointed with soft yellow cloths over
ivory, fine glassware, chunky modern cutlery, smart white china, fresh flowers
and striking modern chairs. Acoustics are surprisingly good (considering the
predominantly hard surfaces), contributing to a very positive atmosphere for
the enjoyment of the confident cooking on offer from new chef Mike Acton.
Country terrine with home-made preserves, baked salmon with fennel and
orange, grilled whitefish with a herb crust and tomato sauce typify the style.
Carvery-style lunch. Excellent service under Daniel Jannier. ***Seats** 60
(+ 40 outside). Parties 12. Private Room 25. Bar Food 12-10. L 12.30-2 D 7-9.30.
Set Sun L £11.50 Set D £17.50. Amex, Diners, MasterCard, **VISA***

BALLYVAUGHAN   An Féar Gorta – The Tea Rooms

Tel 065 77023 Fax 065 77127   Map 2 B4   **JaB**
Ballyvaughan Co Clare

The twin strengths of this charming old harbourside stone building are
Catherine O'Donoghue's skills in the kitchen – particularly baking – and her
lovely garden. Inside, homely groups of mismatched old tables, chairs and sofas
are arranged in front of the black cast-iron range and a display of home-baked
goodies. All kinds of scones, breads, cakes and tarts and home-made preserves
(also to take away) are on offer, along with light savoury specialities such as
salads with baked ham, Irish cheeses, local crab or smoked salmon. Cakes and
desserts are a snip. The *féar gorta* is a kind of fairy grass; if one passes it on the
road it brings pangs of hunger and the limbs refuse to move (so the legend goes)
– but The Tea Rooms are the perfect antidote. No smoking in conservatory.
***Seats** 30 (+20 in conservatory & 16 in garden). Open 11-5.30. Closed Sun & Oct-
end May. No credit cards.*

We do not recommend the food in pubs where
there is no mention of Bar Food in the statistics.
A restaurant within a pub is only specifically recommended
where its separate opening times are given.

BALLYVAUGHAN Gregans Castle Hotel   73%   £120

Tel 065 77005   Fax 065 77111
Ballyvaughan Co Clare

Map 2 B4

HR

Run by the Haden family as a luxurious country house hotel since 1976, Gregans Castle stands in magnificent isolation on the edge of the Burren, at the foot of the aptly-named Corkscrew Hill (which provides the most scenic approach to Ballyvaughan). Changes to the approach made in 1996 have softened the exterior somewhat – the fire officer's request for a convenient source of water has led to the creation of a large ornamental pond (complete with heron and, if they are lucky, goldfish) – and an intriguing new rose garden in the shape of a Celtic Cross has been created near the entrance. But it is still the contrast between the somewhat forbidding grey-stoned exterior and the colour and warmth within that makes this place so special. A welcoming fire in the foyer sets the tone and well-appointed public areas include the characterful Corkscrew Bar (afternoon teas are served here) and a lovely drawing-room, recently refurbished and elegantly furnished with antiques and comfortable sofas. Spacious, individually decorated bedrooms are all furnished to a high standard and have private bathrooms; in addition, there are four magnificent suites, all with wonderful views over the Burren. **Rooms 22.** *Garden, croquet. Closed end Oct-end Mar. MasterCard,* **VISA**

Restaurant   £85

The dining-room, which is under the direction of hotel manager Simon Haden and has views over the new rose garden towards the Burren, has undergone structural changes that have greatly improved it, creating alcoves that allow for more window tables and add to the overall sense of spaciousness. Gentle music has also become a feature – the piano is in regular use and a harpist often plays. Paul Gallagher, appointed head chef early in 1996, is sourcing the best of local ingredients and cooking with confidence and style. An à la carte menu is also available but the six-course dinner menu starts off with a soup – cream of pear and spring onion perhaps, accompanied by exceptionally good breads – before choices such as sliced king scallops in a citrus marinade or slow-roasted tomatoes in fresh herbs and balsamic vinegar with salad and warm goat's cheese. The choice of four main courses will usually include Burren lamb – roast leg, pehaps, on a potato and onion mousseline with rosemary and garlic jus – and a couple of choices based on Galway Bay seafood, as in a pretty, perfectly balanced dish of steamed salmon and monkfish on a tagliatelle of pasta, leek and carrot with a chardonnay and vanilla sauce. Vegetables and salads include organic produce delivered by a local grower when at its peak of perfection. In addition to a fine selection of farmhouse cheeses, desserts will always include some of Gregans' renowned baking, as in pear and almond tart with home-made ice cream or a simple home-made apple pie and cream. Finish with good coffees and an exceptional range of teas with petits fours. Useful tasting notes on the interesting wine list that pretty much scours the globe with the New World well to the fore. Light meals are available all day in the Corkscrew Bar. **Seats 50.** *Private Room 40. D only 7-8.30. Set D £28.*

We publish annually, so make sure you use the current edition
– it's well worth being up-to-date!

BALLYVAUGHAN Hyland's Hotel 65% £64

Tel 065 77037 Fax 065 77131 Map 2 B4 **H**
Ballyvaughan Co Clare

Under the able management of 8th-generation owner Maire Greene since 1965,
family ownership and genuine hospitality is the key to the special atmosphere
at this warm, relaxed hotel in the centre of Ballyvaughan. Attractive, well-
maintained public areas have a sense of country style with comfortable furniture,
thoughtful lighting and open fires – and there is a well-run bar where good
lunches are informally served. The menu encompasses soups, sandwiches, local
mussels, crab claws, Ballyvaughan Bay lobster and beef stir-fry. As we went to
press we heard that the pleasantly furnished bedrooms – all en suite, with phone,
tea/coffee facilities and TV as standard are in such demand that the banqueting
area is to be sacrificed in order to provide more accommodation. *Rooms 20.
Patio. Closed Dec & Jan. Amex, Diners, MasterCard,* **VISA**

BALLYVAUGHAN Monks Bar

Tel & Fax 065 77059 Map 2 B4 **P**
The Quay Ballyvaughan Co Clare

Bernadette and Michael Monks run this away-from-it-all, sensitively modernised
quayside pub which retains a cottagey character and has acquired a reputation
for good, simple bar food, especially local seafood. There are several smallish,
low-ceilinged, white-walled interconnecting rooms with wooden country-
kitchen furniture. Open fires add to the cosy atmosphere. Interest in food is
emphasised by a cluster of sturdy family-sized tables at the far end of the main
bar, and in summer the newly extended patio and adjacent pier provide a sunny
overspill. Everything is home-made by Bernadette, or under her supervision –
and she has the wisdom to keep it simple. Regulars include fishcakes with salad,
mussels steamed with garlic, a big bowl of seafood chowder served with home-
made brown soda bread, poached fresh salmon and a seafood platter which varies
with the catch but might typically include salmon, crab, Dublin Bay prawns,
mussels and oysters; home-made apple pie and rice pudding are always popular.
Open (crab, prawn or smoked salmon) and toasted sandwiches complete the
picture. Baby-changing facilities and a toilet for the disabled. *Open 10.30-11.30
(till 11 in winter), Sun 12.30-2, 4-11.* **Bar Food** *12-9 (till 6 Oct-end Mar). Amex,
MasterCard,* **VISA**

BALLYVAUGHAN Whitethorn Restaurant & Crafts £50

Tel 065 77044 Fax 065 77155 Map 2 B4 **R**
Ballyvaughan Co Clare

In a dramatic location right on the edge of the Galway Bay, this imaginatively
designed, low-level, local stone craft shop/restaurant offers lovely homely fare
through the day – light and airy freshly-baked fruit and brown scones for mid-
morning, then soup of the day (perhaps carrot and parsnip) served with freshly-
baked bread, seafood pie, crab or smoked salmon salad and desserts like apple or
rhubarb pie, pavlova or éclairs. Vegetarian dishes are always available and in the
evening tables are set more formally for dinner, when a lovely summer sunset
can highlight the beauty of the location. A three-course Tourist menu (£14,
served 6.30-9pm only) is offered alongside an à la carte that has helpful wine
to dish matching suggestions from the short, carefully-chosen wine list; six great
choices by the glass for 'dessert drinking' – from a 10-year-old Islay malt to vin
santo and an unctuous Australian muscat. Outdoor eating. *Seats 100. Parties 15.
Private Room 30. Meals 10am-5pm plus D 6.30-9.30 Thu-Sat May-Oct. Closed 28
Oct-17 Mar. MasterCard,* **VISA**

BALLYVAUGHAN   Places of Interest
Tourist Information Tel 065 81171
Aillwee Cave Tel 065 77036
The Burren Centre Kilfenora Tel 0658 80330
Cliffs of Moher Tel 065 81171
Dunguaire Castle Kinvara Tel 091 37108
Thoor Ballylee by Gort. W B Yeats' home. Tel 091 31436

Set menu prices may not include service or wine.
Our guide price for two diners includes wine and service.

BALLYVOURNEY Mills Inn   £44

Tel 026 45237 **Fax 026 45454**   Map 2 B6
Ballyvourney nr Macroom Co Cork

A convenient point for breaking a journey on the N22 between Cork and
Killarney, The Mills Inn is in a Gaeltacht (Irish-speaking) area and one of the
oldest inns in Ireland, dating back to 1755. The bar has olde-worlde charm
(even if log fires have been replaced with the ubiquitous gas) and is popular
with both locals and a steady stream of travellers stopping for sustenance.
The historical interest of the place is taken a step further than usual with a
vintage car and agricultural museum in a courtyard that also provides residents'
parking. Accommodation varies considerably due to the age of the building but
all rooms are comfortably furnished with neat bathrooms, phone, TV, hairdryer
and tea/coffee making facilities; Superior rooms have jacuzzi baths. There is an
exceptionally large, well-planned ground-floor bedroom particularly suitable for
disabled or elderly guests, who can park right at the doo r and come and go as
they wish – or not, as the case may be, as full room service is available for drinks
and meals. Children under 10 half-price if sharing parents' room. *Rooms 12.
Garden, fishing, bicycles. Closed 25 Dec. Amex, Diners, MasterCard,* **VISA**

BALTIMORE   Baltimore Harbour Hotel   64%   £74

Tel 028 20361 **Fax 028 20466**   Map 2 B6
Baltimore Co Cork '

The Cullinane family re-opened this hotel in 1995 after completely refurbishing
it throughout. With its lovely position overlooking Roaring Water Bay, pleasant
modern furnishings (lots of light wood and pastel colours, and a pleasing sense
of space in public areas) and moderate pricing, it has hit the right note. All of
the rooms are comfortably furnished with neat bathrooms, phones, TV and
tea/coffee facilities; most have clear sea views and the 20 larger ones have both
a double and single bed. Public areas include a bar that can be reversed to serve
the Sherkin Room (banqueting/conferences for 130/100) and a bright semi-
conservatory Garden Room for informal meals and drinks. Children are made
most welcome; under-2s stay free, extra beds and cots are available, as well as
a playroom in high season, creche facilities (7.30am–11pm) and high tea from
5.30pm. Deep-sea fishing and visits to neighbouring islands – notably Sherkin,
Hare and Cape Clear – are major attractions, although Baltimore itself is enough
for many visitors. No dogs. *Rooms 35. Garden. Closed Nov-23 Dec, 2 Jan-27 Mar.
Amex, Diners, MasterCard,* **VISA**

If you encounter bad service don't wait to write to us but make
your feelings known to the management at the time of your visit.
Instant compensation can often resolve any problem that
might otherwise leave a bad taste.

BALTIMORE   Bushe's Bar

Tel 028 20125   Map 2 B6   **P**
Baltimore Co Cork

This famous old bar overlooking the harbour is well known for its collection of genuine maritime artefacts such as charts, tide tables, ships' clocks, compasses, lanterns and pennants, all of which make both the local sailing community and visiting sailors feel at home. Equally, it is known for the warm but low-key hospitality of Richard and Eileen Bushe, who have been running the bar since 1973 and creating a 'home from home' for the many who make their annual pilgrimage to Baltimore (it is typical of the Bushes that they have showers available for the use of sailors and fishermen). Yet another attraction is Eileen's homely bar food which starts early in the day with tea and coffee from 9.30, moving on to home-made soups – always a fish one and a vegetable choice – and a range of sandwiches with home-cooked meats (turkey, ham, roast beef), salmon, smoked mackerel or – the most popular by far – Eileen's open crab sandwiches, served with her freshly-baked brown bread. Accommodation is available in three large, comfortable rooms, all with bath/shower, TV and a kitchenette with all that is needed for people to make their own Continental breakfast; there are no phones – 'people come here to get away from them'. No dogs. *Open 9.30am-11pm (till 11.30 in summer), Sun 12.30-2, 4-11.* *Bar Food 9.30am-10pm. Patio, outdoor eating. Closed Good Friday & 25 Dec.* *Accommodation 3 en suite bedrooms, £30. MasterCard,* **VISA**

BALTIMORE   Casey's Cabin

Tel & Fax 028 20197   Map 2 B6   **P**
Baltimore Co Cork

Set high up above Baltimore just off the road in from Skibbereen, and with dramatic views over Roaring Water Bay to the islands beyond, this immaculately maintained pub/bar/seafood restaurant has been run by Michael and Ann Casey for over twenty years. Michael Casey has charge of a splendidly hospitable bar (note the heavy books of local info hanging from the ceiling for visitors' reference) while Anne looks after the front of house and oversees chef Kevin Kiely in the kitchen. You will find everything from open sandwiches (made with home-made brown bread), seafood chowder and oak smoked wild Atlantic salmon to a particularly good range of fish dishes (from hot seafood platter and baked hake with ginger and lemon sauce to scallops from the Bay and lobster). The atmosphere is good, there's room to eat out of doors when the weather is fine (or turf fires to console when it isn't) and traditional music regardless of everything. Facilities for the disabled. Imminent plans extend to building 12 en suite bedrooms for summer 1997. *Open 10.30-11.30 (to 11 in winter), Sun 12.30-2, 4-11.* **Bar Meals** *12-3, 6-9.30). Closed Good Friday & 25 Dec. Amex, Diners, MasterCard,* **VISA**

BALTIMORE   Chez Youen   £70

Tel 028 20136   Map 2 B6   **R**
Baltimore Co Cork

Overlooking Baltimore harbour, an unpretentious Breton establishment where local seafood (notably crustaceans) presented in simple style is the main attraction: shellfish platters and poached lobster are particularly popular. Vegetables are not a big thing here but you might find a pot of local potatoes boiled in their jackets; round off a seafood feast with a plate of French and local Irish cheeses or a tarte tatin. *La Jolie Brise* (see entry) is under the same ownership. *Seats 40. L 12.30-2.30 (Easter-end Sep only) D 6.30-11 (phone ahead to check times of opening in the off-season). Closed Nov & Feb. Set L £12.50 Set D £21.50 & £32. Amex, Diners, MasterCard,* **VISA**

BALTIMORE   La Jolie Brise

Tel 028 20441   Fax 028 20495
The Square Baltimore Co Cork

Map 2 B6   **JaB**

Youen Jacob's latest enterprise is a cheerful, inexpensive Continental-style café that spills out on to the pavement. The day starts with Continental and full Irish breakfasts (look out for kippers, smoked ling and hot smoked salmon among the several fish choices). Pizzas and pastas come on stream a little later and then there is a bistro menu offering the likes of mussels and chips, sirloin steaks, pork chops and a local cheese plate: good, wholesome fare and very reasonably prices. *Seats 50. Meals 8.30am-11pm. Ring ahead to check opening times for off-season.* Amex, Diners, MasterCard, **VISA**

BALTIMORE   The Mews   £55

Tel & Fax 028 20390
Baltimore Co Cork

Map 2 B6   **R**

A well-appointed restaurant located on the ground floor and adjacent conservatory of an attractive stone building. Owner-chef Lucia Carey keeps up to date with the latest food trends in the winter months and the current wave of eclecticism is reflected in her lively menus. A welcoming selection of freshly-baked breads and tapénade is quickly followed by starters chicken satay served with creamy peanut sauce or spicy fresh prawns in garlic and ginger butter. While traditionalists can enjoy a good chowder and perhaps follow it with a fillet steak or rack of lamb with a redcurrant and port sauce, the more adventuorus might relish a well-spiced Thai red curry or a delicious vegetarian dish such as Oriental vegetable parcels with roasted pepper sauce, all served with imaginative and well-cooked vegetables. Tempting desserts might include a trio of home-made ices (rum and raisin, blueberry and vanilla) in a tuile basket or a crisp, light strawberry shortcake; or you could finish with a plate of local cheeses. Good service, too. *Seats 30. Parties 10. Private Room 10. D only 6-10. Closed Mon & Oct-end May (except Bank Holiday weekends & Easter).* MasterCard, **VISA**

BANAGHER   Brosna Lodge Hotel   56%   £52

Tel 0509 51350   Fax 0509 51521
Banagher Co Offaly

Map 2 B4   **H**

A friendly hotel, now under new ownership, offering modest overnight accommodation; some rooms are distinctly cramped, but all have en suite bathroom facilities, TV and direct-dial phones; however, there are two larger rooms for families, sleeping three (plus room for a cot). Cot available free, high-chair and children's early evening meal. Children under 5 may stay free in their parents' room. Banqueting room seating 60. No dogs. *Rooms 14. Garden.* Amex, Diners, MasterCard, **VISA**

BANAGHER   JJ Hough's

Tel 0509 51893
Main Street Banagher Co Offaly

Map 2 B4   **P**

Vines abound in Banagher – in summer the colourful red and white frontage of this atmospheric 250-year-old pub almost disappears behind the luxuriant vine that grows around the door, making it instantly recognisable from anywhere along the main street. Inside, all is dim, especially in the small side and back rooms off the front bar – well-suited to the cheerful eccentricity of the current owner, Michael Hough, and equally well-liked by the locals and groups on cruising holidays, both Irish and visitors, who come up from the harbour for the 'crack' and the traditional Irish music (played nightly). *Open 10.30-11.30 Mon-Sat (to 11 in winter), Sun 12.30-2, 4-11. Closed Good Friday & 25 Dec. No credit cards.*

BANAGHER   The Vine House

Tel & Fax 0509 51463   Map 2 B4   **P**
Westend Banagher Co Offaly

At the bottom of the village in an almost-waterside location, this is a bar with a history; the original restaurant area at Vine House was once Cromwell's refectory – the barracks and a house providing accommodation for his generals are next door – and the bar itself is in the stables. More recently (and in considerable contrast), there is a literary connection – with the Brontë sisters, who also lived here. The interior is very attractive, with indoor vines a major feature, and the current owner – Thomas Barry – continues the Continental feeling through to the menu in authentic renditions of popular pasta dishes like lasagne, tagliatelle napoletana, marinara or bolognese, which take their place quite comfortably alongside favourites such as seafood, Irish stew and steaks. The bistro at the back of the bar is now permanently available for bar food (our specific recommendation here) and the separate restaurant seats 78. *Open 10.30-11 (to 11.30 in summer), Sun 12.30-11. Bar Food 12-2.30, 6.30-10.30. Courtyard, outdoor eating. Closed Good Friday & 25 Dec. MasterCard, **VISA***

BANAGHER   Places of Interest
Cloghan Castle Tel 0509 51650
Clonmacnoise Visitor Centre Tel 0509 74195
Clonmacnoise & West Offaly Railway Tel 0509 74114

BANDON   Munster Arms Hotel   63%   £60

Tel & Fax 023 41562   Map 2 B6   **H**
Oliver Plunkett Street Bandon Co Cork

Well situated for activities such as angling, riding (there is an equestrian centre nearby) or touring the area, this substantial town-centre hotel has spacious public areas and the buzz of a place that is used by the locals. Bedrooms have recently been refurbished to a high standard, providing a commendable level of comfort and amenities at a reasonable rate. All rooms are of a good size, with generous beds and stylish, fully-tiled bathrooms that feature good lighting and toiletries. Banqueting/conference facilities for 250/300. No private parking, but safe street parking is available beside the hotel. *Rooms 34. Closed 24-26 Dec. Amex, Diners, MasterCard, **VISA***

BANTRY   Anchor Tavern

Tel 027 50012   Map 2 A6   **P**
New Street Bantry Co Cork

A town-centre pub with a history going back 130 years, run since 1962 by William E O'Donnell (the third generation of his family to hold the reins) with his son Michael. Pubs are for intelligent conversation and the exchange of ideas, says William, who sees the family's vast collection of mainly nautical memorabilia (including, of course, an old anchor) displayed around the two bars as a talking point more than anything – although he does admit to a special fondness for one item, an original 'croppy pike' from the rising of 1798 which will go with him if he ever leaves. There's also a morning crossword club (dictionaries, atlas and a globe provided) and soup and sandwiches are offered as sustenance throughout opening hours during the summer; recently. Well-behaved children are welcome "if a small bit of control is exercised ... if not we'll help the parents." at reasonable hours. "Old-fashioned in every sense ... everybody who comes into us leaves with a better understanding of Ireland and the Irish." Consult the pub's Red Book for places of local interest. *Open 10.30am-11 (till 11.30pm May-Sep), Sun 12.30-2, 4-11. No credit cards.*

BANTRY — Westlodge Hotel — 66% — £105

Tel 027 50360 Fax 027 50438 — Map 2 A6 — **H**
Bantry Co Cork

Especially suitable for family holidays, the Westlodge Hotel boasts nearby out-door activities including water sports and horse riding plus a a wide range of on-site activities to keep everyone happy if the weather should disappoint. The new health and leisure centre features a 16m swimming pool. Bedrooms have all been recently refurbished and there is 24hr room service. Supervised toddlers' playroom Jun-Sep (10.30-1, 7-10). Banqueting/conference facilities for 300. *Rooms 90. Garden, tennis, pitch & putt, indoor swimming pool, children's splash pool, gym, squash, sauna, steam room, spa bath, sun beds, hair salon, children's playroom & playground, games room, snooker, news kiosk. Closed 24-27 Dec. Amex, Diners, MasterCard,* **VISA**

BANTRY   Places of Interest
Tourist Information Tel 027 50229
1796 Armada Exhibition Centre Tel 027 51796
Bantry House Tel 027 50047

BARNA — Donnelly's of Barna

Tel 091 592487 Fax 091 564379 — Map 2 B4 — **P**
Barna Co Galway

Seafood is the thing at Donnelly's (it's only 100yds from the sea), built as a thatched cottage and extended at the turn of the century. In the cosy, cottagey bar the menu choices run from fresh mussels baked in garlic, seafood crepe and timbale of salmon and crab salad for starters (The Bait) to scallops mornay, pork stroganoff and a festival of seafood and pasta as main courses (The Catch). There are also a few meat dishes and an evening menu (£17.95) in the restaurant at the back: Donnelly seafood chowder, salmon hollandaise, fillet of cod with lovage and bacon sauce. Traditional roast Sunday lunch. *Open 12-11.30 (to 11 in winter), Sun 12.30-2, 4-11. Closed Good Friday, 24 & 25 Dec.* **Bar Food** *12-10 (restaurant 7-10 only). Patio, outdoor eating. Amex, Diners, MasterCard,* **VISA**

BARNA — Ty Ar Mor — £60

Tel 091 592223 Fax 091 590677 — Map 2 B4 — **R**
The Pier Barna Co Galway

Close your eyes and imagine you're in Brittany when you visit this little seafood restaurant, last in a row of cottages on the quay at Barna (*Ty Ar Mor* means The House of the Sea). In summer Hervé Mahé puts a few tables out on the terrace so the guests can enjoy the view; sitting by the cosy turf fire contemplating the pleasures ahead (as read off a large and scrupulously legible blackboard menu) has more appeal on colder days. The place has natural charm with its stone walls, flagstones and narrow winding stairs to an upper room with bigger windows, home-laundered linen and haunting background jazz. All this and good food, too, with starters like grilled Galway Bay oysters with sea spaghetti or warm prawn salad with basil, and, for main course, a fine *plateau de fruits de mer*; lobster is fresh from the sea and cooked to order. Look out for the typically French 'prix-fixe' value in limited-choice three-course menus (perhaps mussels marinière, mignon of pork with sage sauce and corn pancake, crepe Negresse). A wide variety of Breton crepes are a lunchtime speciality – enjoy one with a glass of cider. Short wine list of 30-odd French favourites. *Seats 60. Parties 20. Private Room 30. Open 12.30-11 L 12.30-2.30 D 7-11. Closed 15 Jan-15 Feb & Sun mid Sep-Mar. Set L £8.50 Set D £13.50. Amex, Diners, MasterCard,* **VISA**

BEAUFORT   Hotel Dunloe Castle   72%   £110

Tel 064 44111   Fax 064 44583   Map 2 A5   **H**
Beaufort Killarney Co Kerry

Although somewhat forbidding when seen from the road, close inspection of this large hotel reveals much to charm even the most critical visitor. Like its two sister hotels, the *Hotel Europe* (Killarney) and *Ard-na-Sidhe* (Caragh Lake) the location was selected with devastating accuracy for maximum impact of some of Kerry's finest views, in this case straight through the famous Gap of Dunloe. Although built later and a little less grand in scale (it's a little warmer and more intimate in atmosphere), the interior of Dunloe Castle is strongly reminiscent of the Hotel Europe, not only in general style but, in many cases, because the same materials and even the same furniture have been used – to good effect, it must be said, as all the hotels in this group are remarkable for their quality of workmanship and durability of materials. There is also a generosity of space that is unusual in Ireland – a very large foyer, wide stairs and corridors, bedrooms big enough to include large dining-tables and chairs as part of the normal furnishing. All this, plus excellent amenities inside and out and a caring attitude to service, add up to very good value in a top hotel. The bedrooms (including 20 junior suites) are extremely comfortably furnished with spacious seating areas, excellent bathrooms, views, extra-large beds and TV with video films. Children are welcome – under-3s are free in their parents' rooms and there are family rooms with a division between the main room and an extra single bed. Cots/extra beds, children's high teas and baby-sitting are all available by arrangement. Golf is available very close by and special-rate vouchers may be obtained by guests at the hotel. *Rooms 120. Garden, tennis, jogging track, putting green, fishing, equestrian centre, indoor swimming pool, sauna, children's playground, table tennis. Closed Oct-end Apr. Amex, Diners, MasterCard, VISA*

BELTURBET   International Fishing Centre   £45

Tel & Fax 049 22616   Map 1 C3   **R**
Loughdooley Belturbet Co Cavan

Michel and Yvette Neuville have been running the International Fishing Centre, which provides residential fishing holidays for Continental guests, since 1986, but local interest in the restaurant encouraged them to open the doors to non-residents in 1995. As they have welcoming pontoons at the bottom of the garden, the centre now provides a convenient facility for visitors cruising the waterways as well as land-based diners. The atmosphere is seriously French, with all signage *en français* and a straightforward French menu displayed prominently on the pontoon. The style leans towards Alsace in dishes like *flammekeuche*, a regional speciality rather like a pizza on a bread base with crème fraiche, smoked meat and onion (available as a starter or main course), hearty casseroles such as smoked pork shoulder with prunes and duck leg with turnips. Expect classic desserts such as chocolate mousse and *tarte maison*, a down-to-earth wine selection and a pleasantly modest bill. Six tables are set on the terrace in fine weather. Accommodation (self-catering or otherwise) is sometimes available for overnight guests. *Seats 40. Parties 10. Private Room 40. L (Sun only) 12-2.30 D 6.30-9. Set L £9.50 (children's Sun L £3.50). Closed L Mon-Sat, D Sun, all Dec-Mar. MasterCard, VISA*

BENNETTSBRIDGE — Mosse's Mill Café — £50

Tel 056 27544   Fax 056 27491   Map 2 C5   **R**
Bennettsbridge Co Kilkenny

Just outside Kilkenny, in the 'craft village' of Bennettsbridge, this attractive
informal cafe-restaurant is just beside (and in the ownership of) Mosse's famous
pottery. It overlooks a garden with pond and millstone and is a particularly
pleasant place for lunch or afternoon tea (served in the garden in fine weather).
Recent management changes have not obviously affected the style of the place,
although regular visitors will notice that there is perhaps more emphasis on
Nicholas Mosse's tableware than previously and a new American influence in
the kitchen, where chef Mike Roberts rustles up the likes of Manhattan fish
chowder (tomato-based and finished with fresh thyme) and a range of light,
modern dishes. Daytime menus include open sandwiches – sirloin steak, perhaps,
with home-made tomato chutney or breast of chicken with pesto – and plenty
of choice for vegetarians, typically marinated roast vegetables with melted
mozzarella or goat's cheese and roasted pepper quiche with a leaf salad. While
lunch and dinner menus are more extensive, the style is quite consistent. *Seats 40.
Parties 8. L 12-3 D 6-9.30. Closed Mon & all Feb. Amex, Diners, MasterCard,* **VISA**

BERE ISLAND — Lawrence Cove House — £60

Tel 027 75063   Map 2 A6   **R**
Lawrence Cove Bere Island Co Cork

Fisherman Mike Sullivan and his wife Mary opened their house on Bere Island
as a restaurant in 1995 and, somewhat to their own suprise, found themselves
with a success on their hands, largely down to the quality and freshness of the
seafood they offer guests (Mike supplies some of the finest restaurants in the
country, so he knows a thing or two about seafood for the table). Then there
is Mary's hotel management training and the natural hospitality of the two of
them, plus the fact that they know how to pick a chef – in this case Breton
Gerard Janter, who has been with them for two years. But it's also the romance
of the place: Mike arranges a pick-up time with guests and spirits them over to
the island in his fishing boat (unless, of course, they prefer to take the regular
ferry) and he will return them safely to the pontoon, three miles east of
Castletownbere, after dinner. A short walk up from the harbour brings guests to
the Sullivans' welcoming house and a distinctly professional set-up that includes
not only excellent food but fine service from well-trained staff and surroundings
to match. Menus naturally reflect both the owners' and chef's interest in seafood
and may include some unusual specimens such as the sunfish *conyphere*, baked
and served with a tomato butter sauce. A visit to Bere Island is such an adventure
that we will leave the finer details of its magic to our readers' imagination;
suffice to say, you are unlikely to be disappointed by such a unique operation.
Not suitable for children under 12. *Seats 36. Parties 8. Private Room 16.
D only 6.30-10.30. Closed early Oct-early May. MasterCard,* **VISA**

BIRDHILL   Matt the Thresher

Tel 061 379227   Fax 061 379219   Map 2 B4   **P**
Birdhill Co Tipperary

On the main Dublin road a few miles outside Limerick, this pub has succeeded in becoming one of Ireland's best-known inns since Ted and Kay Moynihan took over in 1987. It's as reliable for its food as for its foolproof location overlooking the Shannon estuary and makes a perfect meeting place. Characterful in the modern mode – red-tiled floors, country-kitchen furniture (including some settles, thankfully cushioned) and bar stools made from old tractor seats – chintzy curtains and gas coal-effect fires introduce a slightly suburban note. But the agricultural theme is developed to its logical conclusion in an unexpected way – home-grown, stone-ground flour is used in all the bread, which is baked on the premises and served with a wide variety of home-made soups (French onion, country vegetable) and bar snacks on the Snug Menu. Seafood is a speciality, with West Cork mussels and crab claws, or salmon from local rivers served hot, or cold in salads (smoked salmon) and open sandwiches, while carnivores may prefer home-baked ham, a good steak, cheese and bacon burger or steak and kidney pie. 10% service charge is added to After Six dishes (served 6-10pm, to 9pm Sun) such as avocado with crab, grilled (or poached) fresh salmon or grilled lamb cutlets with baked potato and a selection of vegetables. A covered patio overlooks the garden; ample parking in the yard, which backs on to a quality craft shop. "Children must remain seated and under parental control at all times." *Open 10am-11.30pm, Sun 12.30-11.* **Bar Food** *11am-10pm (till 10.30 Fri & Sat) Sun 12.30-9. Garden. Amex, MasterCard,* **VISA**

BIRR   Dooly's Hotel   60%   £60

Tel 0509 20032   Fax 0509 21332   Map 2 C4   **H**
Birr Co Offaly

Right on Emmet Square, in the centre of Georgian Birr, this attractively old-fashioned hotel is one of Ireland's oldest coaching inns, dating back to 1747. It's a good holiday centre with plenty to do locally – Birr Castle gardens are very near, also golfing, fishing, riding and river excursions. Public rooms include a characterful bar and a function room; ideal for weddings (220) or conferences (300). Pleasant, modest bedrooms are all en suite; some may be noisy when there's a function in the night-club (open Fri-Sun all year). Children up to 12 share parents' room at no charge. No dogs. *Rooms 18. Garden, coffee shop (8am-9pm), night club. Closed 25 Dec. Amex, Diners, MasterCard,* **VISA**

BIRR   Tullanisk   £90

Tel 0509 20572   Fax 0509 21783   Map 2 C4   **A**
Birr Co Offaly

George and Susie Gossip have run their carefully restored 18th-century Dower House in the demesne of the Earls of Rosse (still resident at Birr Castle) as a delightful country house hotel since 1989. The house is beautiful, interesting and comfortable, the surrounding gardens and parkland lovely and full of wildlife, of which a fair cross-section may make an appearance while you watch from the big mahogany dining table at dinner. George is an excellent chef and enjoys producing memorable no-choice dinners (£22.50 per head for non-residents at 8pm only) and breakfasts live up to the promise of the night before and more. Shooting for groups by arrangement. Reduced tariffs for longer stays. *Rooms 7. Garden, croquet. Closed 8-10 days at Christmas. Amex, MasterCard,* **VISA**

BIRR   Places of Interest
Tourist Information Tel 0509 20110
Birr Castle Tel 0509 20056
Charleville Forest Castle Tullamore Tel 0506 21279 *20 miles*
Slieve Bloom Centre Tel 0509 20029

BLACKLION   Mac Nean House & Bistro   ↑   £60

Tel 072 53022   Fax 072 53404   Map 1 C2   **RR**
Blacklion Co Cavan

Surely qualifying as Ireland's most understated restaurant, MacNean Bistro still retains its modest front-room atmosphere (perhaps a little too low-key to provide an appropriate setting for the quality and finesse of the cooking) but very positive developments have been taking place in several areas of the Maguire family's enterprise in the last two years and it can only be a matter of time before the restaurant is extended and upgraded to match the food. Neven Maguire's inspired cooking skills continue to amaze and delight the growing number of followers beating a path to this little border town. Desserts are still a particular speciality, notably his delicious hazelnut nougat glacé or an iced banana parfait with roast bananas and bitter chocolate sorbet, but greater maturity and experience have produced consistently interesting and skilfully-handled food right across the board. Seasonality is a major feature and, in addition to the well-balanced, fixed-price dinner menu, he offers a special 'Food from the Sea' menu (five set courses, of which three are seafood: typically starting with lobster noodle gratinée on a spice sauce and parsley oil, followed by courgette flower filled with salmon and truffle mousse on a lobster cream, then steamed fillet of turbot with buttered spinach on a basil butter sauce); recently he has also offered a Forest menu specialising in seasonal game (saddle of hare stuffed with chicken and pesto mousse on a parsnip purée and rosemary jus) and wild fungi. Sunday lunch is like no other in the country, with all the traditional options worked into a remarkably inexpensive menu that allows guests to be adventurous if they wish; families are well catered for. Details such as excellent breads (perhaps up to six breads: tomato and chive or pesto and bacon rolls, courgette brioche or wholemeal wheaten bread), fine vegetables and outstanding petits fours are the hallmarks of a chef whose talent is evenly matched by dedication. Weekday lunch parties for ten or over by arrangement. Service, under Neven's father Joe Maguire's direction, is warm and friendly but untrained. *Seats 40. L (Sun only) 12.30 & 3 (two sittings) D 5.30-9 Tue-Sun (winter Thu-Sun only). Closed Mon, 25 & 26 Dec. Set L (Sun) from £12. Set D from £22 (Early Bird 5.30-7 from £12 summer only).* **VISA**

Rooms   £40

Comfortable accommodation is provided in ten attractive, individually decorated rooms; four new bedrooms having come on line at the end of 1996. Although they vary somewhat in size and aspect, all are thoughtfully furnished, have telephones, TV and well-appointed bathrooms. Children are welcome – there's one family room and under-8s may share their parents' room free of charge; an early evening meal can be served on request. Room service is available from 8.30am to 10pm.

BLACKLION   Places of Interest

Enniskillen Keep *10 miles*
Castle Coole Tel 00 44 1365 322690 *15 miles*
Florence Court Tel 00 44 1365 348249 *5 miles*
Marble Arch Caves Tel 00 44 1365 348855 *5 miles*

BLACKROCK   Ayumi-Ya   £40

Tel 01 283 1767   Fax 01 662 0221   Map 2 D4   **R**
Newpark Centre Newtownpark Avenue Blackrock Co Dublin

Situated in a small shopping centre, Ayumi-Ya opened in 1983 and offers a wide range of authentic Japanese dishes. Recently refurbished the restaurant now has a new bar area where light snacks can be ordered. Otherwise, diners are given the choice of western or Japanese-style seating when booking – also the time to opt for a teppanyaki table if you want food cooked in front of you. In addition to the teppanyaki and an à la carte menu there are set menus ranging from 'Early Bird' (£10.95) and vegetarian (£15.95), through the Ayumi-Ya dinner to a special seasonal dinner making the choices easier for newcomers to Japanese cuisine. At the time of going to press a new sushi menu and à la carte menu were about to be introduced. Staff are very ready with advice, and the menu imparts a few tips on how to order and even how to eat ('Japanese customers tend to make noise when sipping soup'). No children after 7.30. 10% service charge. The Dublin *Ayumi-Ya* (*qv*) is slightly more geared to Western tastes.
Seats** 55. Private Room 14. D only 6-11 (Sun 5.30-9.45). Closed 24-26 Dec, Good Friday, 1 Jan. Set D £16.50/£16.95. Amex, Diners, MasterCard, **VISA

BLACKROCK   The Brake Tavern

Tel 042 21393   Map 1 D3   **P**
Main Street Blackrock nr Dundalk Co Louth

A warm, bustling seafront pub with a characterful wooden interior and mountains of fascinating local memorabilia. The bar is broken up into several room-sized areas, with unpretentious but comfortable arrangements of country furniture in welcoming groups and – increasingly unusual these days – a real open fire to settle around. The Brake is especially well known for the quality and variety of food (served evenings only). Seafood is a speciality – Dublin Bay prawns, lobster (as a starter or main course when available), fish platters, fresh sea trout in season, smoked salmon, crab claws in garlic butter – but there's also a good choice for carnivores, including a range of steaks, beef stroganoff, pork à la crème and home-made chicken Kiev. Puddings include fresh fruit pavlova and apple tart. Everything is home-made and very wholesome. No children under 10. *Open 5-11.30, Sat 12.30-11.30 (to 11 in winter), Sun 6-11.*
***Bar Food** 6.30-9.30. MasterCard, Visa*

BLARNEY   Blarney Park Hotel   63%   £80

Tel 021 385281   Fax 021 381506   Map 2 B6   **H**
Blarney Co Cork

About half an hour's drive out of Cork city, this modern, low-rise hotel has good conference and family facilities, including a particularly well-equipped leisure centre with a high and winding 40-metre water slide and an air conditioned gym. Bright, spacious public areas include a lounge area on two levels, each with its own open fire, with a pleasant outlook over extensive grounds at the back of the hotel. Bedrooms are organised along the corridors and are undergoing a programme of refurbishment, with good-sized doubles on one side and smallish twins (especially suitable for children) opposite. Children under one stay free (cot provided), extra beds are available by arrangement; there are fun-packs provided in children's rooms, a supervised playroom operates all year round and children's entertainment can be arranged at any time when five or more children are resident. Conference facilities for 350, with an efficient secretarial service. Paddy Cole's Bar, named after a famous Irish jazz singer, is in pubby style and offers live music nightly (Apr-Sep). Nearby attractions include

Blarney Castle with its famous Blarney Stone, and Blarney Woollen Mills.
24hr room service. No dogs. *Rooms 76. Garden, tennis, indoor swimming pool,
children's splash pool, gym, sauna, steam room, games room, snooker. Amex, Diners,
MasterCard, VISA*

BLARNEY   Places of Interest
Tourist Information Tel 021 381624

BLESSINGTON	**Downshire House**	59%	£77

Tel 045 865199   Fax 045 865335   Map 2 C4   **H**
Downshire House Blessington Co Wicklow

It's difficult not to be charmed by the friendly atmosphere and unpretentious
comfort of this substantial village hotel built in 1800 and run by Rhoda Byrne
since 1959. One enters into the bar-lounge, where all the seats are small
armchairs, before finding the reception desk at the head of a broad flight of stairs
leading down to the function room – a modern addition. Decoratively-modest
bedrooms with plain white walls, pure cotton bedding, candlewick bedspreads
and functional fitted furniture offer modern comforts that include remote-
control TV, hairdryer, direct-dial phone and beverage kit. Bathrooms are a little
dated but, like the whole hotel, are immaculately kept. *Rooms 25. Garden,
croquet, tennis. Closed mid Dec-6 Jan. MasterCard, VISA*

BLESSINGTON   Places of Interest
Russborough Tel 045 865239

BOOTERSTOWN	**La Tavola**		£45

Tel 01 283 5101   Map 2 D4   **R**
114 Rock Road Booterstown Co Dublin

👁 V

Despite its somewhat unlikely location at the bottom of Booterstown Avenue,
right on one of the capital's busiest roads, this friendly, informal, pack-'em-in
little place is quite a gem. The food is varied despite the pages of predictable-
sounding pizza and pasta dishes on the menu; everything is freshly made by
owner-chef Bahaa Jaafi. The choice is wide and includes a range of poultry and
meat dishes (including traditional veal) but, best of all, daily blackboard specials
that are mostly seafood – fresh Dublin Bay prawns, cooked in garlic butter and
served with rice, perhaps, chunks of monkfish tail in a garlicky lemon sauce and
red snapper, with cumin-flavoured yogurt sauce, all served with simple, properly
cooked side vegetables – boiled potatoes and a slection of crisp seasonal vegetables
such as spears of acrrot and crispy mangetout. Finish with desserts from the board,
typically a good baklava, which is also served in little squares with coffee as a
petit four. *Seats 42. Parties 10. D only, 5-11.30. Closed Sun & possibly several days
at Christmas. Amex, Diners, MasterCard, VISA*

BORRISOKANE	**Ballycormac House**		£60

Tel 067 21129   Fax 067 21200   Map 2 B4   **A**
Aglish Borrisokane nr Nenagh Co Tipperary

Country pursuits are the main attraction for most visitors at this cottagey rural
retreat where Americans Herbert and Christine Quigley not only arrange ghillies
for fishing and shooting and hirelings for riding and fox-hunting but, most
importantly, also provide a warm place with plenty of drying space to return to
at the end of the day. All the bedrooms have been upgraded and thoughtfully
refurbished in pretty, country style since the Quigleys came here in 1994; each
of the rooms has its own character – some are on the small side (but no less
charming for that) and all have private or en suite bathrooms with choice of
bath or shower; there is even a romantic ground-floor mini-suite with its own
open fire and a four-poster. Guests conregate around the fire in a cosy sitting-

room before and after dinner. Food is a major interest at Ballcormac: not only is residents' dinner cooked by Christine and served by Herb at a communal dining table in the newly refurbished dining-room (8.30pm, £20/£24, 3-course Sun-Thu, with an extra farmhouse cheese course Fri & Sat), but they've earned a special reputation for their baking, and Herb runs regular bread baking weekends from January to June. Children under 12 may stay free in parents' room; cots and extra beds provided. No dogs. The village of Aglish (not marked on all maps) is about 3 miles from Borrisokane. *Rooms 5. Garden. MasterCard, VISA*

BRAY	Tree of Idleness	£60

Tel 01 286 3498   Map 2 D4   **R**
Seafront Bray Co Wicklow

The exhibition of paintings for sale changes from time to time, but everything else about this well-loved Greek-Cypriot restaurant remains reassuringly constant under the steady managment of Susan Courtellas. Head chef Ismail Basaran, in the kitchen since 1980, continues to delight guests with fresh-flavoured renditions of classsics – in starters like tzatziki (Greek yoghurt with cucumber, mint and garlic), houmus (chick pea, olive oil and garlic dip) and taramasalata (smoked cod's roe dip with lemon and olive oil), for example, and Greek salads with feta cheese and olives and dolmades (vine leaf parcels of minced lamb, tomato and cheese sauce) or fish starters like squid ink ravioli or kalamari, all served with delicious hot pitta bread. Main courses also major on the classics in *souvlaki vodino* (skewered fillet steak, grilled with mushrooms and peppers, then served on rice), moussaka (including a vegetarian version), fish dishes like peppered monkfish in olive oil and – a house speciality – roast suckling pig (boned, stuffed with apple and apricot and served with a wine and apricot sauce). Another speciality is a traditional dessert trolley that groans under the weight of a wide selection of dishes ranging from sticky Middle Eastern pastries with honey, through ices, gateaux and a choice of fresh and poached fruits in season. A very fine wine list indeed with a huge selection of classic clarets (including several from the superlative '82 vintage) and many splendid burgundies. The rest of the world is also well represented and, overall, prices are quite fair for the quality available. Note the Massandra collection from Russia. *Seats 50. Parties 8. D only 7.30-11 (till 10 Sun). Closed Mon, 1 week Christmas & last 2 weeks Aug. Set D £20 (except Sat). Amex, Diners, MasterCard, VISA*

BRAY   Places of Interest
Killruddery House and Gardens Tel 01 286 3405

BRUCKLESS	Bruckless House	£50

Tel 073 37071   Fax 073 37070   Map 1 B2   **A**
Bruckless Co Donegal

Although the family home on a working farm, 'farmhouse' is not the term for Clive and Joan Evans's lovely, classically proportioned 18th-century house. Set in 19 acres of woodland gardens, it overlooks Bruckless Bay through meadows grazed by Irish draught-horses and Connemara ponies. Spacious reception rooms are furnished with an interesting variation on the Irish country house style being enlivened by furnishings and ornaments brought back by the family from Hong Kong. Good-sized, comfortable bedrooms are attractively furnished; those not en suite share a large, well-fitted bathroom. The one en suite room attracts a £10 supplement. No dogs. Self-catering accommodation available all year in a cottage within the grounds. *Rooms 4. Garden, croquet. Closed Oct-end Mar. Amex, MasterCard, VISA*

BUNBEG   Ostan Gweedore   65%   £75

Tel 075 31177   Fax 075 31188   Map 1 B1   **H**
Bunbeg Co Donegal

First-time visitors may be surprised by the appeal of this white, flat-roofed clifftop hotel; despite its unpromising 1960s' blockiness it's a very different world on the inside when looking out on to the ever-changing shoreline backed by the magnificent Atlantic seascape and the grandeur of Mount Errigal dominating the horizon. The hotel was built to make the most of this view and achieves its aim very successfully, with most of the newly refurbished bedrooms and all the public areas (including the restaurant and a very pleasant Library bar – 'the most westerly reading room on the Atlantic seaboard') providing excellent, comfortably furnished vantage points from which to enjoy it to the full. Plans for 1997 include the addition of a further eight bedrooms and a brasserie. Weddings are predictably popular in this romantic setting (banqueting for up to 300, conferences to 400) and it's also ideal for families (children under 5 stay free in parents' room), with good, supervised indoor leisure facilities – there's a 17m swimming pool – for times when outdoor activities on the wonderful beach or a visit to nearby Tory Island fail to tempt. Friendly, down-to-earth staff and 24hr room service. No dogs. *Rooms 39. Terrace, indoor swimming pool, children's splash pool, gym, sauna, steam room, sun bed, pitch & pitt, tennis, children's playroom. Closed 1-28 Dec, 4 Jan-1Feb. Amex, Diners, MasterCard, **VISA***

We endeavour to be as up-to-date as possible but
inevitably some changes to owners, chefs and other
key staff occur after this Guide has gone to press.

BUNCLODY   Clohamon House   £90

Tel 054 77253   Fax 054 77956   Map 2 C5   **A**
Bunclody Co Wexford

Set in 180 acres of rolling farmland in the scenic Slaney valley, with a wonderful view across the River Slaney to Mount Leinster, Sir Richard and Lady Maria Levinge's enchanting 18th-century family home is a haven surrounded by beechwoods and gardens with many rare trees and shrubs. Graciously proportioned rooms are enhanced by family furniture and portraits going back over 250 years creating a lovely family atmosphere as guests gather at the fireside in the chintzy drawing-room for drinks, knowing that Maria is in the kitchen whipping up one of her wonderfully imaginative dinners (if sufficient guests resident, £23.50 – 2-course suppers only Jun-Aug £15), to be served at an elegant, polished table lit by candle. Thoughtfully decorated bedrooms (no smoking) vary, but have a full complement of antiques and characterful bathrooms complete with toiletries; comfortable beds are turned down as you dine and a very good chocolate left on the pillow. In the grounds, Connemara ponies are a major interest – Maria manages an internationally renowned stud – and there is a private stretch of salmon and trout fishing on the Slaney. Self-catering accommodation (available all year) in converted outbuildings, including a barn with facilities for the disabled. Dogs welcome – kennels provided. Busy around the time of the Wexford Opera Festival in late Oct/early Nov. Tariff reductions for longer stays. *Rooms 4. Garden, fishing. Closed mid Nov-end Mar. MasterCard, **VISA***

We only recommend the food in hotels categorised as **HR** and **AR**.
However, the food in many **A** establishments throughout
Ireland is often very acceptable
(but the restaurant may not be open to non-residents).

BUNDORAN   Le Chateaubrianne   £55

Tel & Fax 072 42160   Map 1 B2   **R**
Sligo Road Bundoran Co Donegal

Brian and Anne Loughlin opened their impeccably furnished, warm and
welcoming and family-friendly restaurant in 1993, quickly making an impact
on the north-west dining scene. Well-trained staff ensure that everything runs
smoothly and Anne makes an excellent hostess, keeping a close eye on the
comfort of guests from the moment they are shown into the bar and presented
with the daily-changing menu (priced according to the main-course choice) to
the moment of reluctant departure. Comfortable chairs and well-appointed
tables – white linen over a colourful undercloth, linen napkins, quality cutlery
and fine, plain glasses – provide an appropriate setting for chef Brian Loughlin's
fine food. Typically, terrine of duck and chicken livers with beetroot purée and
Cumberland sauce, or savoury profiteroles filled with ginger-scented crab with
white wine butter sauce could precede roast rack of Donegal lamb with a herb
crust and redcurrant sauce or garlic and herb coated collops of monkfish with
mussels and a lemon and garlic butter sauce. Local ingredients predominate,
cooked with a nicely judged balance of simplicity and imagination. Seafood is
handled with similar flair and imaginatively cooked; plentiful vegetables are left
on the table in their serving dishes. Good desserts such as banana and chocolate
fudge pie, lemon and passion fruit mousse with marinated kiwi and an iced
aniseed parfait with blackberry coulis. Good-value Sunday lunch. Coffee is
served in a cafetière and accompanied by petits fours. No smoking. *Seats 45.
Parties 14. Private Room 16. L Sun only 12.30-3 D 6.30-10. Closed Mon in winter,
3 weeks Nov, 25 & 26 Dec. Set Sun L £12.50 Set D from £20. Amex, MasterCard,* **VISA**

BUNDORAN   Places of Interest
Tourist Information Tel 072 41350

> We do not accept free meals or hospitality – our inspectors pay their
> own bills and **never** book in the name of Egon Ronay's Guides.

BUNRATTY Fitzpatrick Bunratty Shamrock Hotel 63% £121

Tel 061 361177 Fax 061 471252   Map 2 B4   **H**
Bunratty Co Clare

Only four miles from Shannon airport and situated just beside Bunratty Castle,
this low-rise, family-friendly modern hotel is well located for touring County
Clare. With the Bunratty Folk Village next door, up-to-date leisure facilities on
the premises and a new conference centre due to come on stream for 1997, it
has much to offer a wide cross-section of guests. En suite standard bedrooms are
fairly spacious, and 15 superior rooms have the business traveller in mind with
more desk space, fax lines and a turn-down service included in the room
supplement; several (slightly dated) suites are at the quieter end of the hotel.
An excellent new fitness centre opened last year and includes a 20m pool with
separate children's splash pool. Banqueting/conference facilities for 1000/1500.
No dogs. *Rooms 115. Indoor swimming pool, children's splash pool, steam room,
sauna, gym, tennis. Closed 24 & 25 Dec. Amex, Diners, MasterCard,* **VISA**

> We do not recommend the food in pubs where
> there is no mention of Bar Food in the statistics.
> A restaurant within a pub is only specifically recommended
> where its separate opening times are given.

BUNRATTY   Bunratty View   £34

Tel 061 357352   Fax 061 357491   Map 2 B4   **A**
Cratloe Bunratty Co Clare

Joe and Maura Brodie are hospitable hosts at their modern house, providing comfortable, spacious accommodation conveniently close to Bunratty Castle and Shannon Airport. Bedrooms have both double and single beds, phone, tea/coffee facilities, satellite TV, hairdryers; en suite bathrooms vary (some have bath and separate shower, others shower only) but all are fully tiled and well planned. Public rooms include a comfortable residents' lounge with an open fire and a bright dining-room, where good breakfasts are served. Watch carefully for the left turning, signed off the dual carriageway. *Rooms 7. Closed 1 week Christmas.* MasterCard, *VISA*

BUNRATTY   Durty Nelly's

Tel 061 364861   Map 2 B4   **R/P**
Bunratty Co Clare

One of Ireland's most famous olde worlde pubs, Durty Nelly's can easily be spotted from the main road, snuggled in beside the towering presence of Bunratty Castle. It is a complex operation, combining spit 'n' sawdust-style public bars (where music, both organised and spontaneous, is often a feature) and food. Like many places in popular tourist areas, Durty Nelly's has a multi-faceted personality: the quiet charm of an off-season visit is hard to reconcile with the busy, buzzy crush of enthusiastic holiday crowds at the height of summer. Yet, under the management of Gary O'Toole and a team of able assistants, they manage the balancing act remarkably well, providing a genuinely hospitable service with good humour. *Bar open 10.30-11 (Sun 12-2, 4-11), till 11.30 in summer. Closed Good Friday & 25 Dec.*

Restaurants   £60

The food for both restaurants – an all-day restaurant (*The Oyster*) that overlaps with an upstairs evening restaurant (*The Loft*) – is under the supervision of Eugene McNamara, head chef since 1980, who cooks competently for this high-volume operation. The Oyster restaurant offers a carefully judged combination of menus that provides a 3-course dinner for the seriously hungry, a wide range of lighter dishes and an extensive à la carte 'Bill of Fare'. Oysters and smoked salmon jostle for attention alongside stuffed peppers and tagliatelle with vegetables, garlic and pesto, or garlic bread and soups; steaks are a feature, but also roast duckling, scallops mornay, poached salmon and a range of cold plates (including a seafood platter); desserts include home-made ices, cheesecake and chocolate gateau. The Loft is more exclusive and, with its sloping ceiling and open rafters, has plenty of atmosphere. It overlaps with the Oyster for evening meals, offering both similar and a more expensive range of dishes on an à la carte menu. *Seats 65 & 55. Meals 10.30am-10.30pm (Sun 12-10). L 12-4 D 6-10. The Loft is closed Sun & Mon. Closed Good Friday & 25 Dec.* Amex, Diners, MasterCard, *VISA*

BUNRATTY   MacCloskey's Restaurant   £70

Tel 061 364082 Fax 061 364350   Map 2 B4   **R**
Bunratty Mews House Bunratty Co Clare

Shaun and Eileen Smith-Roberts took over this famously atmospheric restaurant in the basement of the 17th-century Bunratty House in September 1995 and it is remarkably unchanged. Not only is the restaurant itself very much the same but – not surprisingly – they have even retained the menu formula that had been so popular under the previous ownership; however, Shaun Smith-Roberts' style is perhaps more sophisticated. A typical five-course dinner menu offers a choice of seven starters – an excellent 'rustic' terrine of rabbit and chicken with home-made piccalilli, full of flavour and texture – followed by soup (roasted tomato and basil 'perfumed' with olive oil), salad (apple and cider with melted goat's cheese dressing) or a granita (elderflower). The eight main courses offer a well-balanced selection, often including beef from the nearby Dromoland Estate, Cratloe lamb (typically with flageolets and seed mustard sauce), Clare pork (imaginatively served with cinnamon-baked pear, perhaps), local Ballyhooly duck and two or three seafood choices. Sometimes the style is quite complex, as in a starter salad incorporating fresh asparagus, artichoke hearts, quail's eggs and more, for example, yet it can also be quite simple, as in fillet of turbot on a bed of braised endive with a light tarragon sauce. Puddings can be disappointing, but they are strong on farmhouse cheeses, which come with full information on their provenance. *Seats 60. Parties 8. Private Room 16. D only 7-9.30. Closed Sun, Mon & all Feb. Set D £28. Amex, Diners, MasterCard, VISA*

BUNRATTY   Places of Interest
Bunratty Castle and Folk Park Tel 061 361511

BUTLERSBRIDGE   Derragarra Inn

Tel & Fax 049 31003   Map 1 C3   **P**
Butlersbridge Co Cavan

A few miles north of Cavan, on the N3, the Derragarra Inn is well situated to break a journey and is easily recognised by its thatched roof and the old agricultural implements and rural artefacts at the door. The agricultural theme is developed inside with items of local interest as well as curiosities from further afield such as a wall covered with bank-notes from various countries. The inn's riverside location means trout will be on the menu, as well as ever-popular seafood like smoked salmon, garlic mussels and fish pie; carnivores are also well catered for with the likes of burgers, dressed pork chop in sweet and sour sauce, steaks, mixed grill, and beef and Guinness casserole. The restaurant menu extends to stuffed whiting, chicken curry and surf'n'turf. Traditional Irish music is a popular attraction on Wednesdays during July and August. *Open 10.30-11.30 (till 11 in winter), Sun 12.30-11. Breakfast 10.30-12 (6 days). **Bar Food** 12 (from 12.30 Sun)-7 (light snacks only after 3pm). **Restaurant Meals** 12.30-3 (Sun only), 7-10. Riverside terrace, outdoor eating. Closed Good Friday & 25 Dec. MasterCard, VISA*

BUTLERSTOWN   Atlantic Sunset   £34

Tel 023 40115   Map 2 B6   **A**
Butlerstown Bandon Co Cork

Mary Holland offers comfortable accommodation and exceptional hospitality in her neat, modern house that lives up to its name – the breakfast room and some bedroom windows have lovely views down to the sea at Dunworley. Two rooms (one double, one twin) have en suite bathrooms and country views; the other two have showers and *the* view. No dogs. *Rooms 4. Garden. Closed Christmas. No credit cards.*

BUTLERSTOWN   Dunworley Cottage   £60

Tel 023 40314
Dunworley Butlerstown nr Clonakilty Co Cork

Map 2 B6   **R**

A renowned yet unpretentious restaurant in a neat assembly of buildings huddled together against the elements on a wild and remote coast; the western aspect can be dramatic at sunset. Guests might be greeted by an extended family of ducks which roam free and contribute to Katherine Norén's organic gardening methods by consuming slugs. The Dunworley Taste Platter is a marvellous way of sampling Katherine's home-made smoked salami, cured wild salmon, marinated herring, wild salmon 'delight' (with mustard sauce and herbs) and smoked mussels; home-made wheat and rye breads (oh, and perhaps a glass of ice-cold akvavit) are the perfect accompaniment. The now-famous nettle soup (or her nearly-famous orange- and fennel-flavoured mussel soup) should definitely be sampled as should the West Cork black and white puddings – a local speciality – served with sherry sauce and lingonberries. Lobster and crayfish should be ordered a few days in advance and only non-farmed fish is served. A typical daily menu might offer crab soup or beer marinated salmon followed by pan-fried monkfish with creamed leeks and a red wine sauce, herb baked sea bass or veal cordon bleu; home-made apple tart to finish. Vegetarians will probably be delighted with stir-fried vegetables with ginger and a sweet and sour sauce, while meat-eaters can tuck into a prime fillet steak. Both a special children's menu (adults can also sample the Swedish meatballs 'by popular demand') and children's portions are available. A loganberry and hazelnut parfait may well feature on the dessert menu alongside home-made ice creams, blackcurrant mousse and local cheeses served with fresh fruit and a glass of port. Big, colourful organic salads underline the attention to detail which makes Dunworley special, and special diets, whether vegetarian, vegan, diabetic, gluten-free, low cholesterol or non-dairy generally present no problem. 10% service charge is added to all menu prices. Take-away meals are also available for self-catering. Winner of our Best Use of Fruit and Vegetable Award for 1997. *Seats* 50. *Private Room* 20. *L 1-5 D 6.30-10. Closed Mon, Tue & Nov-Feb (but open for a few days around Christmas). Set D £21.75. Amex, Diners, MasterCard,* **VISA**

BUTLERSTOWN   O'Neill's

Tel 023 40228
Butlerstown nr Bandon Co Cork

Map 2 B6   **P**

Dermot and Mary O'Neill's nice, old-fashioned pub is on a pretty terrace with views over farmland that slopes away down towards the sea at Dunworley; best enjoyed from the new beer garden. Its gleaming mahogany bar counter and fresh paintwork in pinks and lilacs (somewhat unexpectedly echoing the 'West Cork pastels' exterior theme so familiar throughout the area) create a pleasingly cared-for setting for friendly locals and visitors alike. Children are welcome. *Open 10.30am-11.30pm Mon-Sat (to 11 in winter), Sun 12.30-2, 4-11. Garden. Closed Good Friday & 25 Dec. No credit cards.*

BUTLERSTOWN   Sea Court   £45

Tel 023 40151
Butlerstown nr Bandon Co Cork

Map 2 B6   **A**

Just outside the colourful village of Butlerstown, Americans David and Monica Elder open their 1760 Georgian mansion to guests for the summer months, meanwhile advancing their ambitious restoration programme a little further each year. Expect American priorities tempered by an agreeable element of eccentricity and you will not be disappointed. Large, graciously proportioned rooms are furnished with an eclectic collection of old and antique furniture acquired at auctions but there's a reassuring emphasis on comfort. Bedrooms, which all have private bathrooms of varying vintages (all but one en suite), are in the same style; children under 6 stay free in parents' room. Ask about the Edwardian Ballroom suite. Candlelit dinners (£16.50) are available to residents by reservation (except Sun) and hearty breakfasts feature fresh fruit and David's home-baked fruit and nut scones. The house and surrounding parkland are open to the public, free, during the short summer season. No dogs – kennels provided. Enquiries out of season to the housekeeper, Kathleen McCarthy (Tel 023 40218). *Rooms 6. Garden. Closed 20 Aug-10 Jun. No credit cards.*

CAHERCIVEEN   Brennan's Restaurant   £55

Tel 066 72021   Map 2 A6   **R**
12 Main Street Caherciveen Co Kerry

The Brennans established their stylish restaurant on the main street here in 1993. Interesting daytime food (Irish stew with herbs, open sandwiches on home-made brwon bread, fresh soup) is served as well as owner-chef Conor Brennan's imaginative à la carte menus, which now include a popular Early Dinner menu (served 6-7, popular with walkers) that is exceptionally good value. Creative use of local ingredients remains the hallmark on wide-ranging menus that include dishes like terrine of goose and ripe peach with lemon and blackcurrant dressing, pan-fried Cahirciveen black pudding with salad leaves and balsamic vinegar, roast Barbary duck with honey and lime sauce, and sautéed escalopes of pork with a julienne of red and green peppers. There are always a couple of interesting vegetarian main-course dishes (baked avocado stuffed with ratatouille and wrapped in filo pastry) and a good selection of around six fish dishes, perhaps including pan-fried fillets of John Dory with a basil and lemon butter and baked darne of hake with a lime and chive cream sauce. To finish, good tarts, home-made ices or a plated selection of around four Irish cheeses served with water biscuits. No children after 8pm. *Seats 30. Parties 12. Snacks served 12-3 (except Sun), L 12.30-3 D 6-10. Closed mid Oct-mid Apr (except D 31 Dec). Amex, Diners, MasterCard,* **VISA**

CAHERCIVEEN   Old Schoolhouse Restaurant   £55

Tel 066 73426   Fax 066 72861   Map 2 A6   **R**
Caherciveen Co Kerry

Anne O'Kane's deceptively large restaurant is a good place to stop on the scenic Ring of Kerry. It's open for lunch throughout the tourist season (when limited menus are offered to coaches) as well as for dinner, with a short daily menu inscribed on a blackboard. Start either meal with mussels in garlic butter, half a dozen oysters, an excellent, richly-flavoured seafood chowder or smoked wild salmon, all served with crusty, freshly-baked brown soda scones. Continue with the likes of fillet of turbot beurre blanc, a fresh lobster from the tank, fillet steak with a whiskey sauce or rack of Kerry lamb with redcurrant and ginger sauce. Desserts range from home-made ice creams and Baileys Irish cheesecake to rich chocolate mousse cake with raspberry coulis and Irish farmhouse cheeses at night. *Seats 75. Parties 14. Private Rooms 20 & 50. L 11-3 D 6-9.30. Closed D Sun & mid Nov-mid Mar. Amex, Diners, MasterCard,* **VISA**

CAHERCIVEEN   The Point Bar

Tel & Fax 066 72165   Map 2 A6   **P**
Renard Point Caherciveen Co Kerry

In the same family for ten generations (at least 150 years), this magical little place, at what was until 1960 the final stop on the Great Southern & Western Railway line, overlooks Valentia Island and harbour and has been sympathetically modernised to retain its charm without gimmicks. During the summer Michael and Bridie O'Neill serve ultra-fresh seafood in simple, wholesome dishes ranging from plain and toasted sandwiches to salads made with lobster straight from the pier. Other dishes might include crab au gratin, monkfish Point Special or hake pan-fried with garlic and olive oil. For fine weather there's a very pleasant patio with tubs and tables looking past the old terminal to the sea. Children must be supervised – the bar can get very busy. *Open 10.30-11.30, Sun 4-11.* **Bar Food** *12-9.30 (L 12-3, D 6-9.30) Sun 5-9.30 Apr-end Sep, ring ahead for winter times. Garden. No credit cards.*

CAHERCIVEEN   Places of Interest
Tourist Information Tel 066 72589

CAHERDANIEL Derrynane Hotel	62%	£77

Tel 066 75136   Fax 066 75160   Map 2 A6   **HR**
Caherdaniel Co Kerry

In a spectacular location on the southern stretch of the Ring of Kerry, this unprepossessing 1960s' hotel offers a warm welcome and good facilities for family holidays ("the beautiful Kerry Way, the Mass Path, hills to climb and secluded coves and beaches to visit" – for once the brochure-speak rings true). Accommodation is simple but a high standard of housekeeping, good value for money and lovely sea views ensure satisfaction. Eight family rooms have bunk beds (ask about various rates for children); supervised playroom at weekends (Apr-Jun, Sep-Oct), daily July and August. Good-value terms (half-board only) for stays of two days or more (three days over Bank Holiday weekends). No dogs. **Rooms** *75. Garden, tennis, outdoor swimming pool. Closed mid Oct-mid Apr. Amex, Diners, MasterCard,* **VISA**

Restaurant   £45

The bar and restaurant overlook the open-air swimming pool and are well placed to take advantage of the magnificent sea views. Good, fresh ingredients are used to produce enjoyable home-cooked food and attractive desserts at very reasonable prices. A typical four-course dinner may feature smoked haddock paté with creamed horseradish or vegetable terrine with tomato and herb coulis for starters, followed by seafood chowder and main-courses like baked cod with lobster and tomato sauce, wild salmon with tomato hollandaise, or honey-roast duck with orange sauce. Children's menu; high-chairs provided. No smoking. 10% service charge added to final bill. **Seats** *100. Sun L only, D 7-9. Set D £19.50.*

CAHERDANIEL   Places of Interest
Derrydane National Historic Park Tel 066 75113

CARAGH LAKE Hotel Ard-na-Sidhe	70%	£102

Tel 066 69105   Fax 066 69282   Map 2 A5   **H**
Caragh Lake nr Killorglin Co Kerry

The beautiful lakeside setting and the peace and quiet are major pluses at this splendid Victorian mansion on the edge of Caragh Lake. In the house there are 12 good-sized bedrooms furnished with antiques and a further eight rooms with private patios are available in the garden house; Superior rooms attract a tariff of £118; Junior Suites with a lake view are £132. A full Irish breakfast is served. Sister hotel to *Hotel Europe* (Killarney) and *Dunloe Castle* (Beaufort), whose sporting facilities are available to Ard-na-Sidhe guests. **Rooms** *20. Garden, game fishing. Closed Oct-end Apr. Access, Amex, Diners,* **VISA**

See the **County Listings** green tinted pages for details of all establishments listed in county order.

CARAGH LAKE   Caragh Lodge   65%   £88

Tel 066 69115 Fax 066 69316   Map 2 A5   **A**
Caragh Lake nr Killorglin Co Kerry

Owner (and cook) Mary Gaunt has been in personal charge at this Victorian
country house since 1989 and creates a happy and relaxed atmosphere with a
warm Irish welcome. The lodge stands in delightful gardens on the shore of
unspoilt Caragh Lake; two boats are provided (along with ghillies and permits)
for guests who wish to fish locally. Boating, fishing and swimming are favourite
pastimes, there's a tennis court in the grounds and five championship golf
courses are a short drive away. Peaceful antique-furnished day rooms. Bedrooms
in main house or garden cottages; the former attract a tariff of £104 (including
10% service). Dinner for residents is £24 plus 10% service. Children over 10
are welcome, but not dogs. The gardens are a haven of peace, glorious in full
bloom. Plans are to add six new bedrooms and a suite by May 1997. *Rooms 10.
Garden, sauna, tennis, game fishing, rowing boat, bicycles. Closed 14 Oct-Easter
Amex, MasterCard,* **VISA**

CARAGH LAKE   Places of Interest
Kerry Bog Village Museum

CARLINGFORD   The Anchor Bar

Tel 042 73106   Map 1 D3   **P**
Carlingford Co Louth

As we went to press this famous old bar had just been sold by Maureen O'Hare
(after whose late brother the bar was named). Standing right in the heart of this
picturesque medieval village, it had been in Maureen's family since 1860; she
hoped that the new owners would maintain the unique atmosphere of the bar
that shares the same room as the grocer's shop. It's a favourite spot with the local
sailing community and the walls are covered with items of nautical interest.
The enclosed yard by the bar is a popular summer rendezvous. *Open 10.30am-
11.30pm (Sun 12.30-2, 4-11). No credit cards.*

CARLINGFORD   Carlingford House   £35

Tel 042 73118   Map 1 D3   **A**
Carlingford Co Louth

Hospitable hosts Peter and Irene Finegan provide guests with a real home-from-
home at their lovely old house, conveniently located near the centre of Carlingford
yet backing onto the Mountains of Mourne. Comfortably furnished rooms are
all en suite and children are welcome. One family room has a double and single
bed, and there's a cot and high-chair available. *Rooms 5. Garden. Closed Nov-mid
Mar (unless by arrangement). No credit cards.*

CARLINGFORD   Jordan's Townhouse Restaurant   £60

Tel 042 73223 Fax 042 73827   Map 1 D3   **RR**
Carlingford Co Louth

Harry and Marian Jordan take turns in the kitchen of their warmly decorated
restaurant, but the day always starts with a baking session to produce their
delicious brown soda or walnut and treacle bread and white yeast rolls. Both
table d'hote and à la carte menus are nicely balanced between the traditional and
modern, and local produce is used wherever possible. They grow their own herbs
and even produce their own butter. A typical four-course meal might commence
with pan-fried lamb's kidneys and mushrooms with a red wine and grain mustard
sauce or chicken terrine studded with sun-dried tomatoes and olives and served
with chili oil and apple chutney, followed by a daily home-made soup, then
perhaps confit of duck with an apple and cider sauce, duo of cod and smoked
haddock with pesto and chili oil, or oven baked chicken breast stuffed with crab

and ginger on a bisque sauce and a choice of desserts – dark chocolate parfait with a burnt orange sauce or apple and wild berry brulée – or Irish cheeses. The carte extends to Carlingford oysters served natural or warmed with pesto, lobster, game in season, pan-fried scallops with smoked bacon and provençale sauce, loin of mountain lamb with rosemary and port sauce, and chicken crostini. After your meal why not relax in the sitting room with a 'Carlingford coffee', which is made from Kilbeggan Whiskey distilled on the Cooley Peninsula. Minimum charge of £15 at weekends and holidays. Wines are sensibly priced. A bistro menu is also available in the converted bar where there are a further 18 seats. No smoking in main restaurant (but allowed in bar/bistro area). *Seats 34. Parties 12. Private Room 16. L 12.30-2.30 D 6.30-9.45. Closed L Sat, D Sun Nov-Jan, 24-26 Dec, 3 weeks Jan & Good Friday. Set Sun L £7.50/£10.50 Set D £21. Amex, MasterCard, VISA*

Rooms   £75

A row of old cottages have been recently converted to add five large double bedrooms overlooking the harbour. These are fitted with period-style pine furniture, telephone, TV, trouser press and hairdryer; all have bath and shower en suite. A cot and extra bed can be provided for families; under-4s stay free. Residents' lounge. No dogs. *Tennis.*

We welcome bona fide complaints and recommendations on the tear-out Readers' Comments pages at the back of the Guide. They are followed up by our professional team.

CARLINGFORD	McKevitt's Village Hotel	59%	£60

Tel 042 73116   Fax 042 73144   Map 1 D3   **H**
Carlingford Co Louth

A happy family atmosphere prevails at this bustling establishment and the emphasis is firmly on enjoyment and relaxation for all age groups. Public areas include a comfortable bar and restaurant and a residents' sitting-room is available for quieter moments. Bedrooms vary considerably in size, but all are comfortably furnished and en-suite, with phones and TV. Banqueting/conferences for 120. Children are welcome and under-5s may stay free in their parents' room; cot and high-chair available. Four family rooms hold a double and up to two single beds. *Rooms 13. Closed 24 & 25 Dec. Amex, Diners, MasterCard, VISA*

CARLINGFORD	Magee's Bistro		£35

Tel 042 73751   Map 1 D3   **R**
D'Arcy Magee Centre Carlingford Co Louth

Hugh Finegan and Sheila Keiro's minuscule, tightly-packed restaurant is in a lovely old cut-stone building and looks out on to the foothills of the Mourne mountains – almost reason in itself to visit perhaps, but it's Sheila's wholesome cooking – prepared on site in an open kitchen despite limitations of space – that has attracted a following. Eclectic menus range from classic home-made soups and chicken liver paté through guacomole and corn chips and pineapple coconut cream to main courses like Cajun-style chicken or Mexican hot pot, a range of pasta dishes and vegetarian options like cheese parcels with fresh herbs and tomato or Chinese vegetable curry. Interesting salads are arranged as a buffet, breads are home-baked and you can round off with carrot cake, perhaps, or a juicy apple pie. No smoking. *Seats 26 (+16 in courtyard). D 6.30-9.30 Wed-Sat May-Sept only (may open Fri/Sat in winter – ring to check). Closed Mon, Tue & all Oct-Apr. MasterCard, VISA*

CARLINGFORD   Places of Interest
Carlingford Castle

CARLOW   Barrowville Townhouse   £42

Tel 0503 43324   Fax 0503 41953   Map 2 C4   **A**
Kilkenny Road Carlow Co Carlow

Marie and Randal Dempsey run a tidy ship at this attractive and exceptionally comfortable, antique-furnished Regency guesthouse which is within easy walking distance of the town centre. Public areas include not only a cosy sitting-room with open fire but also a conservatory (complete with vine) and, when weather permits, outdoor seating in a well-kept and secluded back garden. Rooms vary in size and outlook but all are furnished and decorated to a high standard with phone, radio, TV and neat, thoughtfully planned en-suite bath/shower rooms; two rooms have shower only. Delicious breakfasts – served in the delightful conservatory overlooking the garden – include a choice of fresh juices, home-baked croissants and fruit and a buffet with smoked salmon and farmhouse cheeses. No dogs or children under 12 overnight. *Rooms 7. Garden. croquet. MasterCard,* **VISA**

CARLOW   The Beams Restaurant   £60

Tel 0503 31824   Map 2 C4   **R**
59 Dublin Street Carlow Co Carlow

Situated in premises that have held a full licence since 1760, it is appropriate that this restored coaching inn should now be run by Peter O'Gorman, a member of the Guild of Sommeliers. It's a characterful building, notable for the massive wooden beams it is named after, and has a welcoming, cosy atmosphere in the well-appointed dining-room, which has direct access to The Wine Tavern off-licence and specialist food shop (under common ownership) next door. The dinner menu offers some choices more likely to be restricted to the à la carte in other establishments, including game in season and seafood, with sirloin and fillet steaks available at only £1 supplement. Starters may be pleasant rather than inspiring, but French chef Romain Chall gets into his stride with main courses like roast venison grand veneur, fillet of pork with wild mushroom sauce and excellent seafood dishes such as Atlantic salmon with white wine sauce or a hot seafood selection with dill sauce. Finish, perhaps, with an apple and raisin parfait – from a verbally recited list – or a plated selection of farmhouse cheeses. Plenty for everyone on the wine list – lots from France, some from the New World, including the excellent South African Hamilton Russell wines. *Seats 38. Parties 12. D only 7-10. Closed Sun, Mon, Good Friday, 1 week Christmas & Bank Holidays. Set D £16 & £20. MasterCard,* **VISA**

CARLOW   Buzz's Bar

Tel 0503 43307   Map 2 C4   **P**
7 Tullow Street Carlow Co Carlow

With its darkened glass and contemporary lettering Carlow's first café-pub is noticeably different from the rest of the street. This impression is emphasised by a multi-level interior in a mixture of styles – yellow ragged walls and black metal furniture here, tented ceiling and sofas there and a curvaceous bar with wooden stools in the middle. But its real difference runs deep – down to the basement in fact, where the 120-seat Bridewell Lane Theatre (Carlow's only permanent live auditorium) has its home. It's also quieter and attracts a more mature crowd than its sister *Tully's* across the road. Coffee, scones and pastries are served all day, with the likes of a daily soup served with home-made bread and perhaps garlic mushrooms, a salad bar, a carvery roast, and chicken en croute with leek sauce on a lunchtime menu. A recently opened bistro (dinner 6-11, lunch by arrangement) offers various pasta meals, warm salads, roast duck and steaks. *Open 10.30-11.30 (to 11 in winter), Sun 12.30-2, 4-11.* **Bar Food** *12-3. Closed Good Friday & 25 Dec. MasterCard,* **VISA**

CARLOW   Danette's Feast   £65

Tel 0503 40817
Map 2 C4   **R**
Urglin Glebe Bennekerry nr Carlow Co Carlow

A couple of miles outside Carlow town, Danette O'Connell's and David Milne's delightful country-house restaurant is approached by a 'naturalised' (ie with grass down the middle) driveway. There is a warm welcome waiting and a charming set-up that provides a perfect backdrop for Danette's throughly professional skills in the kitchen. Drinks and olives are served in a little drawing-room with deep red walls and an open fire; David takes orders here from four-course menus that are full of promise; guests then move through to one of two well-appointed dining-rooms. Imagination is at work throughout: smoked salmon, for example, is served with marinated cucumber and a crème fraiche and scallion sauce, while a smoked chicken salad comes with fennel and a mint-lemon dressing. A soup like potato, carrot and leek is served with delicious breads, typically a choice of olive or tomato and fennel. Main-course choices include a strong vegetarian option (torte of layered cheeses and roasted vegetables in puff pastry), unusual ways with meat (marinated fillet of pork cooked on a fresh rosemary skewer and served with an orange sauce – winner of our Irish Pork Award for 1997) and fish (monkfish on a bed of stir-fried pak choy with a mustard and yogurt sauce). Delicious organic side dishes like bright red cabbage with cumin, chunky sugar peas and lovely floury potatoes. Tempting desserts could include a luscious caramelised lemon tart – very thin, light pastry, deep, tangy filling, crunchy top – and a hot salad of exotic fruits with amaretti ice cream. Round it all off with freshly-brewed coffee. And, as if good food and delightful service were not enough, musical evenings are another unusual feature of Danette's Feast – ask for details when booking. *Seats 30. Parties 12. Private Rooms 18 & 20. L (Sun only) 1-2.30 D 7-10. Sun L £16.50 D £24. Closed L Mon-Sat, D Sun-Tue & all 24-30 Dec. MasterCard,* **VISA**

CARLOW   Royal Hotel   60%   £58

Tel & Fax 0503 31621
Map 2 C4   **H**
Dublin Street Carlow Co Carlow

Conveniently situated on the main street, this unassuming hotel originated as a coaching inn in the early 18th century and, although the age of the building tends to limit improvements, it has a pleasant atmosphere and helpful staff. Public areas include a thriving, well-run bar and attractive dining-room. Bedrooms, while varying a good deal, all have en suite bath or shower, TV, clock/radio, phone, hairdryer and tea/coffee facilities. On-going refurbishment in recent years has seen standards of most bedrooms improve. Banqueting and conference facilities for 200/300. Children welcome: cot and high-chair available; under-10s stay free in parents' room. 24hr room service. Walled garden. *Rooms 34. Garden. Closed 25 Dec. Amex, Diners, MasterCard,* **VISA**

CARLOW   Tully's

Tel 0503 31862   Map 2 C4   **P**
149 Tullow Street Carlow

They do things differently in Carlow – anywhere else this unspoilt old pub would be likely to provide a serene retreat for mature citizens, but here the young crowd from the Regional Technical College seem to call the shots and the place can be bursting with youth and vigour. Music and atmosphere are the main attraction here. At quieter times Tully's is a nice old-fashioned pub with broader appeal (television is banned from the bar). Light lunchtime snacks like pasta carbonara, lasagne and hot chicken filled baguette with garlic mayonnaise; traditional breakfast with black pudding and home-made brown bread is served from 10.30–12. Plans are to open an evening bistro during 1997. *Open 10.30am-11.30pm (to 11 in winter), Sun 4-11.* **Bar Food** *12-3. Closed L Sun, Good Friday & 25 Dec. No credit cards.*

CARLOW   Places of Interest
Tourist Information Tel 0503 31554

The Egon Ronay Guides are completely independent.
We do not accept advertising, hospitality or payment
from any of the establishments listed in this Guide.

CARNE   Lobster Pot   £50

Tel 053 31110 Fax 053 31401   Map 2 D5   **R/P**
Carne Co Wexford

Ciarán and Anne Hearne's Lobster Pot is a pub, seafood bar and restaurant all rolled into one; they have attracted a loyal clientele here since 1976. In a prime roadside location, the long, low building is typical of traditional houses in the area; inside several small, cosy interconnecting bar areas are furnished in simple, practical style with sturdy furniture designed for comfortable eating – augmented, in fine weather, by an ample supply of picnic tables out at the front. One smallish room is given over to a slightly more formal restaurant area, but the atmosphere throughout is very relaxed and the emphasis is on providing good value and efficient service. The bar menu offers daily home-made soups (perhaps leek and potato and seafood chowder), Wexford mussels in garlic, oven-baked crab mornay, crab claws in garlic and a pasta dish as its hot dishes plus a plethora of cold plates (from egg mayonnaise to generous seafood platters); also sandwiches and a handful of homely puddings (hot apple sponge and cream, Harvey's sherry trifle). More substantial evening-only à la carte offerings in the recommended restaurant might include prawn cocktail, Bannow Bay oysters, wild salmon either smoked, grilled or poached, scallops, grilled black (Dover) sole, seafood mornay, and lobster from the tank (priced per pound). Also a 'landlubber's choice' of chicken Kiev, crispy duckling and various steaks. 4–course Sunday lunch (September-May only) with a reduced rate for children; good-value winter Wednesday evening table d'hote (£14.95). Smoking is discouraged. No children under 10 after 8.30pm. Parents are requested to keep an eye on their children and children are requested to keep an eye on their parents – best behaviour all round! *Open 10.30-11.30 (to 11 in winter) & Sun 12.30-2, 4-11; January bar only open (no food).* **Bar Meals** *(except Jan) 12-10, Sun 12.30-2, 4-10 (winter: to 8 Sun, to 9 Mon-Sat).* **Restaurant Meals** *(except Jan) 6-9 (7 days in summer, Tue-Sat in winter). Kitchen closed all Jan. Paved forecourt with ten tables. Closed Good Friday, 25 & 26 Dec. Amex, MasterCard, **VISA***

CARRICK-ON-SHANNON Hollywell House   £56

Tel & Fax 078 21124   Map 1 B3
Liberty Hill Carrick-on-Shannon Co Leitrim   **A**

Just across the bridge at Carrick-on-Shannon, with lovely views down through the garden to the river, this fine period house offers four comfortable en suite rooms (one with shower only) furnished with antiques (two with river views). Tom and Rosaleen Maher's hospitality makes Hollywell outstanding. Good breakfasts, with home-made bread and preserves, but no evening meals except by special arrangement. No dogs or children under 12. *Rooms 4. Garden, fishing. Closed 20 Dec-1 Jan. MasterCard,* **VISA**

CARRICK-ON-SHANNON   Places of Interest
Tourist Information Tel 078 20170
Lough Rynn Estate and Gardens Mohill Tel 078 31427 *10 miles*
Strokestown Park House Strokestown Tel 078 33013 *12 miles*

We only recommend the food in hotels categorised as **HR** and **AR**. However, the food in many **A** establishments throughout Ireland is often very acceptable (but the restaurant may not be open to non-residents).

CARRICKMACROSS Nuremore Hotel   72%   £120

Tel 042 61438   Fax 042 61853   Map 1 C3
Carrickmacross Co Monaghan   **H**

Just off the N2 south of town, 50 miles north-west of Dublin on the way to Monaghan and Donegal, a modern, low-rise hotel that creates a good impression on arrival. The approach, through 100 acres of golf course and lake-studded parkland ('please drive slowly – look out for ducks'), is pleasant and the exterior of the hotel building not only spick and span but brightened and softened by imaginative planting and generous use of tubs. There's a high standard of furnishing throughout the large, well-appointed public areas and the comfortable, airy bedrooms, many of which overlook the lake. Five family rooms accommodate up to six people; five mini-suites. Banqueting facilities for 200, conferences up to 400. Self-styled as a hotel and country club, the 18-hole golf course (the pavilion offers bistro snacks and there's a resident PGA professional), good leisure club (18m pool and splash pool) and trout fishing on the lake are all major attractions. No dogs. *Rooms 69. Garden, indoor swimming pool, sauna, solarium, spa bath, gym, tennis, squash, games room, golf (18). Access, Amex, Diners,* **VISA**

CARRICKMACROSS   Places of Interest
Carrickmacross Lace Co-op Tel 042 62506
Patrick Kavanagh Musem Inniskeen Tel 042 78104

Many hotels offer reduced rates for weekend or out-of-season bookings. Our guide price indicates high-season rates. Always ask about special deals for longer stays.

CARRIGALINE   Glenwood House   £55

Tel & Fax 021 373878   Map 2 B6   **A**
Ballinrea Road Carrigaline Co Cork

Former hoteliers Robert and Anne McLaughlin provide exceptional purpose-built accommodation at this modern house close to Cork airport and the ferry terminal. Good-sized bedrooms have pleasantly understated decor, twin/double beds, phone, tea/coffee-making facilities, TV, trouser press and neat, tiled bathrooms with quality fittings, heated towel rail, good towels and generous toiletries. Public areas include a spacious foyer/reception room, a large residents' lounge with TV, an open fire and plenty of comfortable seating. In the well-appointed dining-room Anne McLaughlin serves particularly good breakfasts that include a buffet – fresh fruits, farmhouse cheeses and yoghurts – and hot dishes like scrambled eggs with smoked salmon as well as the traditional Irish breakfast, all served with freshly-baked soda bread. Room service from 8am-10pm. No children or dogs. *Rooms 8. Garden. Closed 21 Dec-1 Jan. Diners, MasterCard, VISA*

CARRIGALINE   Gregory's   £50

Tel 021 371512   Map 2 B6   **R**
Main Street Carrigaline Co Cork

Chef Gregory Dawson and partner Rachelle Harley run this buzzy little restaurant. An unpromisingly long, narrow room has been transformed with low key green and cream decor enlivened by some startling modern pictures, providing an appropriate setting for Gregory's imaginative, well-judged cooking. Shortish, keenly-priced à la carte menus (monthly-changing) might typically include steamed mussels with tomato and spices, gateau of Clonakilty black pudding with apple and smoked bacon, rack of lamb with a herb crust and rosemary scented jus, monkfish kebab with dill beurre blanc, pear and almond tart, an Irish cheese plate or hot apple crumpets with vanilla ice cream and butterscotch sauce; ask for the vegetarian menu. Good-value dishes on a weekly-changing light lunch menu. There's a light touch evident throughout, teamed with a clear desire to give value for money. Admirable attention to detail includes lovely breads, good coffee and charming service. *Seats 40. Parties 14. L 12.30-2.30 (till 3.30 Sun) D 6.30-10. Closed L Sat, D Sun, all Mon, 1 week Feb, 2 weeks Nov & Bank Holidays. Set Sun L £10.50. Amex, MasterCard, VISA*

CASHEL   Cashel House   76%   £152

Tel 095 31001   Fax 095 31077   Map 2 A4   **HR**
Cashel Co Galway

Standing in secluded beauty at the head of Cashel Bay, the Victorian house is set in award-winning gardens running down to a private beach. Dermot and Kay McEvilly have been the welcoming, professional hosts since 1967, and their hotel won instant renown a year later when General and Madame de Gaulle stayed for two weeks. Turf and log fires add a cosy glow to the gracious day rooms, where antiques and fresh flowers take the eye. Bedrooms are individually decorated, and the Garden Suite rooms are particularly stylish, with separate seating areas and access to the patio. Service is excellent and breakfast includes a wide range of home-made produce, from good home-made bread and marmalade to black pudding, ham and cheeses. No children under 5. *Rooms 32. Garden, tennis, sea & game fishing, boating, horse riding (inc dressage). Closed 10 Jan-10 Feb. Access, Amex, Diners, VISA*

Restaurant £80

Dermot and his team produce fixed-price four-course dinners; these are served in the sunny restaurant and feature the best of home-grown and local produce prepared without undue elaboration or fuss. On a typical menu you might find a really good choice of main-course fish dishes, from poached fresh brill with yellow pepper and herb sauce or brochette of halibut with basil butter to sautéd mackerel with gooseberry sauce, and a tasting plate of local seafood with saffron sauce. These could be alongside local crab, oysters or smoked chicken salad to start, followed by chilled gazpacho, loin of Connemara lamb with rosemary, sautéed ostrich fillet with thyme sauce, bread-and-butter pudding, warm blackberry and apple tart with Calvados and crème anglaise, Irish cheeses and home-made ice creams. Vegetable quiche with carrot sauce might be the vegetarian option. It would seem entirely appropriate to finish a delightful meal here with a proper Irish coffee. Lunch is served in the bar. 12½% service is added to all menu prices. *Seats 70. Parties 12. Private Room 8. L 1-2 (snacks in the bar) D 7.30-9. Set D £30.*

CASHEL	Zetland House	68%	£118

Tel 095 31111 Fax 095 31117   Map 2 A4   **HR**
Cashel Co Galway

Originally built as a sporting lodge in the early 1800s, Zetland House (named after the Earl of Zetland, a frequent visitor last century) is a comfortable country house set in attractive gardens on the edge of Cashel Bay. Over the past 16 years John and Mona Prendergast have created a welcoming rural retreat, furnishing the smart public areas, including cosy sitting rooms (each with open peat fires) with tasteful fabrics, comfortable soafs, various antiques and other personal objet d'art. Bedrooms are equally well appointed in style and quality of decor and furnishings and most enjoy spectacular views across the Bay; children under 14 half-price if sharing parents' room. All have neatly-fitted en suite bathrooms with good toiletries. Nice touches include tea and home-made biscuits on arrival and a turn down service at night. The hotel is a favoured base for outdoor pursuits, notably fishing and rough shooting. Expect warm hospitality from the ever-present owners and an excellent breakfast to set you up for the day ahead. *Rooms 20. Garden, croquet, tennis, fishing, shooting, snooker. Closed Nov-Easter. Amex, Diners, MasterCard, VISA*

Restaurant £70

Diners lucky enough to be sat by the window in the relaxing and pleasantly furnished dining-room can savour the splendid view across the garden to Cashel Bay, as well as some competently cooked and imaginatively presented food. Both the set dinner and the à la carte menus highlight quality fresh local fish and seafood such as wild smoked salmon roulade with tomato chutney and prawn oil, or oysters served chilled with lemon white wine and herbs for starters. Main-course choices may include baked turbot with orange and fennel, grilled monkfish served on a pool of red capsicum sauces, or shellfish platter. Carnivores may well decide on rack of Connemara lamb on a potato and herb rosti with a rosemary scented jus or confit of duckling with sweet Calvados and apple jus. For dessert try, perhaps, steamed chocolate pudding with apple and blackcurrant topping, raspberry and shortbread millefeuille with summer fruit coulis, or a selection of Irish cheeses. No smoking. Light lunches only (12.30-2pm). 12½% service charge added to final bill. *Seats 45. Parties 15. D 7.30-8.45. Set D £28.50.*

Please note there are two places named **Cashel**, one in Co Galway (see Map 2 A4), the other in Co Tipperary (see Map 2 C5)

CASHEL   Chez Hans   £70

Tel 062 61177   Map 2 C5   **R**
Rockside Cashel Co Tipperary

First-time visitors are amazed by the sheer size and style of Hans–Peter Matthiä's converted Wesleyan chapel which is tucked behind the town right under the Rock of Cashel. The menu is long and strong on seafood, from quenelles of turbot and brill with a white wine and butter sauce, and Rossmore oysters (plain or gartinéed) to Kinsale lobster, seafood cassoulette, and generous, dramatically served fillet of turbot with juicy Dublin Bay prawns and a chive sauce. Parfait of chicken and duck livers, Irish feta cheese with sun-dried tomatoes, olives and fresh pesto, and a trio of soups that includes a classic French consommé show that invention sits happily alongside convention. Carnivores can lick their lips in anticipation of roast guinea fowl with a tarragon and olive jus, and breast of free range chicken with Cashel Blue cheese and a leek sabayonne. Finish, perhaps, with an assorted dessert tasting plate, a selection of continental and Irish farmhouse cheeses, glazed lemon tart or Cointreau soufflé with crème anglaise. *Seats 68. Parties 10. D only 6.30-10. Closed Sun, Mon, 3 weeks Jan, 24-26 Dec & Bank Holidays. MasterCard,* **VISA**

CASHEL   Dowling's

Tel 062 62130   Map 2 C5   **P**
Cashel Co Tipperary

Pat and Helen Dowling's pub stands handily on the main street and its attractions include traditional decor, a cosy open fire and good simple snacks (soup, sandwiches and toasties). Impromptu weekend music sessions. Previously known as *Meaney's. Open 11-11.30 (to 11 in winter), Sun 4-11. Closed L Sun, Good Friday & 25 Dec. No credit cards.*

CASHEL   The Spearman   £50

Tel 062 61143   Map 2 C5   **R**
97 Main Street Cashel Co Tipperary

Tucked in a slip road just off the main thoroughway, the restrained atmosphere of this family-run restaurant belies the hearty wholesomeness of John-David Spearman's food. Swiftly-served lunchtime specials (chicken liver paté with cucumber pickle, steakburger with fries, Irish lamb stew), four-course Sunday lunches and summer Sunday evening pasta nights offer the best value. *Seats 40. L 12-2.30 (to 3 Sun) D 5-9 (to 9.30 Sat), 12-10 Jun-Oct. Closed D Sun (Nov-May), all Mon, 2 weeks Nov, 25-27 Dec. Set Sun L £10.95. Amex, MasterCard,* **VISA**

CASHEL   Places of Interest
Bru Boru Heritage Centre Cashel Tel 062 61122
Cahir Castle Cahir Tel 052 41011
GPA Bolton Library Tel 062 61944
Rock of Cashel Tel 062 61437
Thurles Racecourse Tel 0504 22253 *16 miles*

CASTLEBALDWIN   Cromleach Lodge   78%   £130

Tel 071 65155   Fax 071 65455
Castlebaldwin via Boyle Co Sligo

Map 1 B3   **HR**

The striking style of this purpose-built modern country house is mellowing as the landscaping around it matures, but the passion for the place that inspired Christy and Moira Tighe to design it so that each room (and each table within the restaurant) could take full advantage of its hillside location overlooking the lovely Lough Arrow is clearly as strong as ever. Cromleach is a beacon of excellence, setting high standards that tower over many establishments countrywide which are attempting to offer the same level of hospitality. Christy and Moira Tighe are totally committed, continually stretching themselves to get that little bit closer to perfection and, although the style of decor might be considered a little too 'International' in such a remote location, the warmth of hospitality and impeccable standards of everything from food to housekeeping are never in doubt. Christy makes a solicitous yet discreet host, constantly vigilant of his guests' comfort and providing the perfect back-up for Moira's cooking, which is certainly the main draw. Public areas include an interconnecting drawing room and bar on two levels, one with an open fire and both with groups of comfortable furniture discreetly arranged for quiet privacy and full enjoyment of *that* view. Spacious bedrooms are designed to take full advantage of the setting and are thoughtfully furnished with king-size and single beds, excellent bathrooms (fully serviced while you dine) and almost every comfort that even the most worldly of guests could desire, with all the usual facilities; these include telephone, TV, hairdryer, tea/coffee making and so on, plus a mini-bar (with a little jug of fresh milk in the fridge), complimentary basket of fruit and miniatures of *that* Irish liqueur, Baileys. Families are welcome with extra beds and cots available; under-4s stay free. Five rooms are no-smoking. No dogs – kennels provided. ***Rooms** 10. Garden, game fishing, boating. Closed Nov-Jan. Amex, Diners, MasterCard,* **VISA**

Restaurant   ⭐   £80

👑 /🎵) ☕ 🍽 🍷 🍵 🍶 V 🍵

The beautifully appointed restaurant is broken up into small dining areas for groups of varying sizes, each with its own special view over the lough. Immaculate maintenance and lovely, simple table appointments – crisp linen, modern silver and crystal, fine, understated china with fresh seasonal flowers – provide a delightful setting for the high point of a visit to Cromleach. Moira Tighe has dedication and flair and, with her equally dedicated female kitchen team, she continues to develop her formidable cooking talents with confidence and remarkable modesty. In common with some other self-taught chefs, perhaps, Moira is gifted with endless curiosity and her daily-changing menus provide scope for presenting new dishes to augment the growing number of established specialities that are in regular demand. Two menus are offered each evening, a 5-course table d'hote and a special 8-course gourmet tasting menu for residents, but Christy and his well-trained staff willingly permit guests flexibility between the two. Carefully-sourced local ingredients appear throughout Moira's vibrant interpretations of classic dishes and her passionate touch is always evident, as in a sausage of chicken mousse on a carrot and sauternes sauce, flaked duck confit layered on crispy galette potato, and paupiettes of lemon sole with crabmeat and ginger for starters. Even an oft-maligned sorbet correctly fulfils its refreshing function, while main courses have a real sense of place in dishes like pan-fried escalopes of veal on a grain mustard sauce, or poached John Dory with a julienne of vegetables. A typical gourmet menu might encompass smoked salmon lasagne with tomato and chives, baked mushroom caps filled with smoked chicken and salami mousse, a trio soups, noisettes of venison wrapped in bacon, tossed mixed-leaf salad toasted pine nuts, a superb 'tasting selection' of desserts (perhaps including baked apple soufflé on a cinnamon scented syrup or a pastry barrel of raspberries, strawberries and white chocolate mousse). Cheeses (including Stilton) are served with a glass of port. Details are superb throughout, from the appetisers served with aperitifs in the bar, through the lovely home-made breads, organically-grown vegetables and side salads, to the irresistible plate of petits fours served with fragrant coffee (or a choice of teas) to round off what is likely to be a memorable meal. No smoking and no children under 7 at dinner. Our Ireland Restaurant of the Year last year. *Seats 40. Parties 12. Private Room 20. L by arrangement D 7-9 (Sun 6.30-8). Set D £30.*

CASTLEBALDWIN   Places of Interest
Boyle Tourist Information Tel 079 62145
Boyle Abbey Ruins
Clonalis House Castlerea, Co Roscommon Tel 0907 20014 *15 miles*
King House Boyle Tel 079 63242
Lough Key Forest Park Tel 079 62363

CASTLEBLAYNEY	Glencarn Hotel	62%	£65

Tel 042 46666   Fax 042 46521   Map 1 C2   **H**
Castleblayney Co Monaghan

Situated on the N2, on the edge of Castleblayney, this busy hotel provides a lively centre for the social scene of the area. A popular choice for weddings, the hotel has banqueting/conference facilities catering for up to 500/700 and public rooms that include a large lounge bar where there is entertainment several nights a week (live bands on Fridays). Bedrooms range from quite simple twin rooms to a four-poster bridal suite, but all are en suite. Nearby activities include golf, fishing and horse-riding, and the hotel has an excellent, attractively designed leisure centre with a 21m swimming pool and well-equipped gymnasium. Familes are welcome (children up to 5 may stay free in their parents' room). *Rooms 30. Garden, indoor swimming pool, children's pool, plunge pool, spa bath, steam room, sun bed, gym. Closed 25 Dec. Amex, Diners, MasterCard, **VISA***

CASTLECONNELL	Bradshaw's Bar	

Tel 061 377724   Map 2 B4   **P**
Castleconnell Co Limerick

The Bradshaw family bought this atmospheric 19th-century village pub in the 1920s and since the current owner, Ger Bradshaw, took over in 1992 he has worked hard to make improvements while remaining true to the old traditions – so, although an extra room has been opened up to increase space, it has retained the authentic feeling, with bare floor, fairly spartan furniture and an open fire. Traditional acoustic music midweek. *Open 5-11.30pm (to 11 in winter), Sat & Bank Holidays 10.30am-11.30pm, Sun 12.30-2, 4-11. Closed Good Friday, 25 Dec. Garden. No credit cards.*

CASTLECONNELL	Castle Oaks House Hotel	65%	£99

Tel 061 377666 Fax 061 377717   Map 2 B4   **H**
Castleconnell Co Limerick

In the picturesque waterside village of Castleconnell, six miles from Limerick off the Dublin road, this attractive, well-located hotel makes an excellent venue for local functions, but is of special interest to fisherfolk as it has its own stretch of the River Shannon running beside well-maintained woodland paths in the grounds. Public areas in the hotel are nicely proportioned – notably the pretty blue and yellow dining-room, which can be successfully divided into three without loss of atmosphere. A new wing was added in 1996, providing nine extra rooms, mostly with a double and single bed and neat en suite bathrooms with crisp white suites; one of the new rooms is specially designed for asthmatics, with hard surfaces and specially chosen fabrics. As we went to press a renovation programme had almost been completed and the older rooms should all be refurbished in time for the 1997 season. Nice, helpful staff and a family-friendly attitude make this a pleasant hotel; in the large, wooded grounds there's a well-equipped leisure centre with a 15m pool and also 24 self-catering holiday houses. No dogs. *Rooms 20. Garden, tennis, pitch & putt, fishing, indoor swimming pool, gym, sauna, spa bath, steam room, solarium, games room, snooker. Amex, Diners, MasterCard,* **VISA**

CASTLEDERMOT Kilkea Castle	70%	£203

Tel 0503 45156 Fax 0503 45187
Kilkea Castledermot Co Kildare

Map 2 C4

HR

The oldest inhabited castle in Ireland, Kilkea was built in 1180 by Hugh de Lacy for Walter de Riddlesford. Steeped in history, it has been renovated and converted with skill and sensitivity that allow it to retain its inherent elegance and grandeur. 'De luxe' bedrooms, many with wonderful views over the formal gardens and surrounding countryside, are splendidly furnished to incorporate modern comforts in a manner appropriate to their age and style; a dozen 'standard' rooms attract a lower tariff (£158) and there are six junior suites in addition to the top-of-the-range Conway Suite. The adjoining leisure centre, although architecturally discreet, offers state-of-the-art facilities. Good outdoor sports and fishing on the river Greese that flows through the grounds; the river and two lakes provide natural hazards for the 18-hole championship golf course (par 70). Informal meals are also served in the clubhouse. *Rooms 36. Garden, tennis, golf (18), putting green, riding, fishing, indoor swimming pool, sauna, steam room, spa bath, gym, sun beds, snoooker, clay pigeon shooting, archery. Closed 23-27 Dec. Amex, Diners, MasterCard,* **VISA**

De Lacy's £80

Overlooking formal fruit and vegetable gardens, this grand first-floor restaurant enjoys sweeping views of the surrounding countryside and golf course and has a genuine 'castle' atmosphere. Well-spaced tables are elegantly appointed with crisp linen, cut crystal glasses, fresh flowers and overall attention to detail. George Smith's menus offer four courses at both lunch and dinner, with a wider choice available in the evening and, although it has been modified somewhat of late, the house style is now well-established as intricate, even ornate – perhaps a response to the sense of occasion this beautiful dining-room invariably creates. The best seasonal ingredients are used and the standard of cooking and presentation is high (only spoiled by repetitive garnishing). A choice of five or six starters on a typical summer menu might include a delicate chicken and guinea fowl terrine with mixed leaves, crunchy baby vegetables and red fruit garnish; pan-fried lamb's liver, tender and perfectly cooked, is dressed with a piquant mustard cream and similarly garnished. Freshly-baked bread accompanies a choice of soups (or a sorbet). From a choice of five to seven main courses, local Kildare lamb is a good bet, if embarrassingly generous (a whole roast rack, perhaps, with herb breadcrumb crust and a garlic and rosemary sauce), as is fish (grilled cod fillet served on a bed of lightly-spiced stir-fried root vegetables). Finish with a choice of desserts – chocolate parfait garnished with redcurrants – or plated Continental cheeses (plus Stilton) served with water biscuits and fresh fruit. Good freshly-brewed coffee to finish. *Seats 65. Parties 14. Private Room 40. L 12.30-2.30 D 7-9.30. Set L £15 Set D £28.50.*

CASTLELYONS   Ballyvolane House   £80

Tel 025 36349 Fax 025 36781   Map 2 B5   **A**
Castlelyons Co Cork

This gracious house, set in lovely wooded grounds and surrounded by its own
farmland, dates back to 1728 and was modified to its present Italianate style in
the mid-19th century. The impressive pillared hall with its baby grand piano sets
the tone but, despite the elegance of the house and its period furnishings the
owners, Jeremy and Merrie Green, are well known for their special brand of
informal hospitality. The atmosphere is very relaxed: well-proportioned
reception rooms are warmed by huge log fires, and residents' dinner (£22.50) is
cooked by Merrie and taken communally around a lovely mahogany table, with
stories relating to the house abounding. Bedrooms vary in size, outlook and
tariff (£70-£90) but all are warm and comfortable, furnished with antiques and
with roomy bathrooms en suite – one has an original Edwardian bath reached
by mahogany steps. No dogs. Fishing is offered on the River Blackwater,
20 minutes away, with 16 rods over 10 miles. *Rooms 7. Garden, croquet, fishing.
Closed 23-28 Dec. Amex, Diners, MasterCard, VISA*

CASTLETOWNBERE   MacCarthy's

Tel 027 70014   Map 2 A6   **P**
Town Square Castletownbere Co Cork

One of the first drinking places to be granted a licence in Ireland, MacCarthy's
has been in the same family for 150 years (Adrienne MacCarthy is the fourth
generation). It's not only a pub, but also a grocery which provisions the trawlers
that are based in the harbour. In the front – the grocery section – one of the last
remaining match-making booths (traditionally used by the match-maker and
the bride's and groom's parents to arrange marriage terms) is now used as a snug,
while in the back bar darts and live music make for a very sociable ambience.
*Open 9.30am-11.30pm (till 11 in winter), Sun 12-2, 7-11. Closed Good Friday,
25 Dec. No credit cards.*

CASTLETOWNSHEND   Bow Hall   £60

Tel 028 36114   Map 2 B6   **A**
Castletownshend Co Cork

Americans Barbara and Dick Vickery hace been running this delighful
17th-century house overlooking the anchorage at Castle Haven as a home-from-
home for discerning guests since 1977, but there is no sign of their enthusiasm
flagging and it is not just the high level of comfort but the warmth of their
welcome that makes a visit to their characterful and thoughtfully furnished home
memorable. Barbara is also a dab hand in the kitchen, using produce from their
lovely garden (open to the public once a year) in imaginative dinners for
residents (£20) – and be sure to allow time in the schedule for full enjoyment
of a lengthy breakfast, which includes freshly-baked muffins, pancakes and home-
made sausages. No dogs. *Rooms 3. Garden. Closed for several days at Christmas
(advance bookings only in winter). No credit cards.*

CASTLETOWNSHEND   Mary Ann's Bar & Restaurant   £50

Tel 028 36146 Fax 028 36377   Map 2 B6   **R/P**
Castletownshend nr Skibbereen Co Cork

Halfway up the steep main street of this picturesque and historic village is our
1997 Ireland Pub of the Year. Mary Ann's offers much to please the hungry
sailor in from the sea, from fine foaming pints drawn in the cosy, low-ceilinged
bar and particularly good bar food (including an excellent chowder served with
their famous brown bread) to the leisurely pleasure of a full evening meal
upstairs in the little restaurant. Specialities include an enormous platter of
Castlehaven Bay shellfish and seafood that includes langoustines, crab meat

and claws ('toes'), fresh and smoked salmon plus whatever else the fishermen have brought in on the day – and this is only a starter! Main courses will also depend to some extent on the catch of the day, although local meats are also well represented with good steaks and roasts such as rack of lamb alongside chicken breast stuffed with spinach and served with a herb cream sauce. Tasty vegetables will include generous portions of the delicious local potatoes and perhaps a colourful stir-fry. The best dessert choices after such as feast may be fresh fruit salad or a cooling, home-made ice cream. *Bar open 12-11.30 (11 in winter), Sun 12.30-2, 4-11.* **Bar Food** *12-2.30, 6-9. Bar closed Good Friday & 25 Dec.* **Restaurant Meals** *L (winter Sun only) 12-2 D Tue-Sat 6-9.30. Restaurant closed Mon, Sun (except Christmas period and L Oct-Mar), Good Friday & 25 Dec. Set Sun L £13 Set D £21.95. MasterCard,* **VISA**

CASTLEWARREN   Langton's

Tel 0503 26123
Castlewarren Co Kilkenny

Map 2 C4

P

A bit of a curiosity – not a real pub at all but a relic of what used to be so common in rural Ireland – the kitchen-cum-grocery-cum-bar. A visit here will take the traveller away from main roads through the pleasant countryside of a little-known corner of Ireland and back in time. A row of high stools beside the bacon slicer at the counter and a good shelf of bottles over it are the only real clues to the nature of the premises but, once you're ensconced, Josie Langton, here for over 25 years, will put the world to rights with you and rustle up a bit of a sandwich in the kitchen on demand. *Open 10.30am-11.30pm (to 11 in winter), Sun 12.30-4. Closed Sun eve. Garden. No credit cards.*

CEANANNAS MOR (KELLS)   O'Shaughnessy's

Tel 046 41110
Market Street Ceanannas Mor (Kells) Co Meath

Map 1 C3

P

A reasonably new pub, comfortably and pleasantly decorated on an old-style theme. Unpretentious, fairly-priced bar food is the main attraction – food like Irish stew, chili, grilled lamb cutlets, fresh plaice, quiches and pizzas, but better and cheaper than most. You'll find O'Shaughnessy's just behind St Columba's Church (where a copy of the *Book of Kells* is kept; the original is at Trinity College Library in Dublin). Live music Thu-Sun: traditional Irish music on Thu in summer, more modern Fri-Sun. *Open 10.30-11.30 (till 11 in winter), Sun 12-2, 4-11.* **Bar Food** *12-8, not Sun eve. Closed Good Friday, 25 Dec.*

CHEEKPOINT   McAlpin's Suir Inn

Tel 051 382220
Cheekpoint nr Waterford Co Waterford

Map 2 C5

P

When this tiny black-and-white pub was built in 1750 Cheekpoint was the main port for the boats from England. Today it's a quiet little backwater, although much of the seafood which forms the bulk of the bar menu here is still landed at the quay opposite the inn. Inside, the single bar is as neat as a new pin with old photos and plates decorating the wall, around which are thinly upholstered banquettes and varnished rustic tables. It's truly a happy McAlpin family-run affair: just ask for Dunstan, Mary, Aidan, Marion, Frances or Niall! The menu offers about five starters – seafood vol-au-vent, smoked salmon with salmon mousse – and eight main dishes – perhaps baked cod in Dijon and dill sauce, seafood pie, pan-fried beef fillet with black pepper and mushroom sauce, and vegetable Kiev. There's always a fruit pie along with home-made ice creams, banoffi pie and assorted home-made gateaux. *Open evenings only 6-11.30 (6-11 in winter), Sun 7-11. Closed Mon (except July & Aug), first 3 weeks Jan.* **Bar Food** *6-9.45 Tue-Sat (& Mon in July & Aug). No food Tue Oct-Easter. Amex, Diners, MasterCard,* **VISA**

CLARECASTLE   Carnelly House   £156

Tel 065 28442 Fax 065 29222   Map 2 B4   **A**
Clarecastle Co Clare

Conveniently located close to Shannon airport and nicely positioned for touring
the west of Ireland, this impressive Queen Anne style Georgian residence is set
in 100 acres of farm and woodlands. It offers accommodation to rival the most
luxurious of hotels. Spacious bedrooms, overlooking lawns planted with
spreading trees, are furnished with antiques and individually decorated to the
highest standard, with elegantly draped king-size or twin beds and luxuriously
appointed private bathrooms. Two additional en suite rooms are sometimes
available in the Gate Lodge. Magnificent reception rooms include a beautifully-
proportioned drawing room, with Corinthian pillars, Francini ceiling and grand
piano. Communal dinners (£28 for five courses) are taken in a striking, panelled
dining-room. Hospitality is a priority and the atmosphere at Carnelly is warm
and homely in the true Irish country house tradition. Not suitable for children
or dogs. *Rooms 5. Garden. Closed 22 Dec-early Jan. Amex, MasterCard,* **VISA**

We publish annually, so make sure you use the current edition
– it's well worth being up-to-date!

CLARENBRIDGE   Paddy Burke's

Tel 091 796226 Fax 091 796016   Map 2 B4   **P**
Clarenbridge Co Galway

Synonymous with Clarenbridge, a steady stream of the great and famous have
made their way to Paddy Burke's (The Oyster Inn) – and there's been plenty
of time to do it in, as the history of the pub goes right back to 1650. Especially
famous for their oysters – "The world is your oyster at Paddy Burke's" – they
also offer a wide range of bar food including an excellent Galway Bay chowder,
served with wholemeal bread, poached mussels in white wine, and chicken
supreme; salads (oak smoked Irish salmon, fresh crab) and sandwiches as well.
Lunchtime carvery (12.30-2.30); more formal restaurant meals from a long à la
carte menu are served in the evening. September 1997 sees proprietor Norbert
Fallon's seventh (and the 43rd) oyster festival. This celebrates the beginning of
the new native oyster season; out of season (May-Aug) Pacific oysters are
generally served. Try them American-style with horseradish or with just a
squeeze of lemon and a hint of cayenne; here they are also baked with garlic
and breadcrumbs. *Pub open 10.30am-11.30pm Mon-Sat (to 11 in winter) Sun 12-2,
4-11. Bar Food 10.30am-10.30pm (Sun & Bank Holidays from 12, to 9.30). Garden.
Pub closed Good Friday, 24 & 25 Dec. Amex, Diners, MasterCard,* **VISA**

CLIFDEN   Abbeyglen Castle   60%   £110

Tel 095 21201 Fax 095 21797   Map 1 A3   **H**
Sky Road Clifden Co Galway

Take the N59 from Galway City to Clifden, then Sky Road out of Clifden to
find the hotel, 300 yards on the left in 12 acres of grounds. Owner Paul Hughes
personally welcomes guests, many of whom return year after year, to his
crenellated hotel. Steps lead down from the hotel to landscaped gardens and
an outdoor pool and tennis court. Public areas include a spacious drawing room
for residents and a relaxing pubby bar with open peat fire. Since last year twelve
bedrooms have been converted into six (total nine) de luxe suites, each have
been individually decorated and feature satellite TV among the usual comforts;
refurbishment continues on the remaining bedrooms. No children under 10.
Local fishing facilities are a major attraction. *Rooms 33. Garden, outdoor
swimming pool, sauna, tennis, snooker, table tennis. Closed 10 Jan-1 Feb.
Amex, Diners, MasterCard,* **VISA**

| **CLIFDEN** | **Ardagh Hotel** | 67% | £95 |

Tel 095 21384   Fax 095 21314   Map 1 A3   **HR**
Ballyconneely Road Clifden Co Galway

Although the uncompromisingly blocky 1960s' style of this quiet family-run hotel may be out of vogue, it is quickly forgotten once inside and it certainly doesn't deter the many satisfied visitors who return annually for a reviving dose of its fine hopitality. In strong contrast to first impressions from the road, the interior is warm and stylish – and its large picture windows allow one of the finest views in Ireland to have maximum impact. A personal welcome in the warm-toned foyer, deep-terracotta tiling and rich-hued rugs, open fires, generous seating areas with big, comfortable armchairs and sofas, a grand piano and a man-sized bar – these, plus the generous presence of masses of well-tended plants throughout the hotel, but especially in a delightful sun room on the top floor – are the kind of details that add up to a hotel that guests clearly see as a home from home. Annual redecoration and an ongoing programme of refurbishment ensure a high standard of maintenance and a freshness in the decor throughout. Individually decorated bedrooms vary in size and appointments, but all are en suite (most with full bath and fixed overbath shower, one or two with shower only; decor a little dated in some, but all have quality towels and toiletries) and most have sea views (the four singles do not, but a pleasant hilly outlook instead). A large family room has a partition between the main bedroom and a seating area which includes a child's bed and several other rooms are large enough for an extra bed as well as a double and single. Bedroom furnishing underlines the restful nature of the hotel, with comfortable armchairs provided for quiet reading or just enjoying the view and amenities that make guests feel relaxed and independent. ***Rooms** 21. Terrace. Closed early Nov-late Mar. Amex, Diners, MasterCard,* **VISA**

Restaurant   £67

The restaurant is in two rooms on the first floor with magnificent sea views. It has a light, bright and modern atmosphere, with pale wood replacing the previous traditional dark chairs and a soft creamy yellow the predominant colour, bringing a hint of sunshine on even the greyest of days. This all suitably adds to the enjoyment of Monique Bauvet's flair in the kitchen and her imaginative way with local produce. A typical dinner menu might offer local Salt Lake oysters, a pyramid of avocado, gingered crabmeat and pink grapefruit or home-marinated gravad lax with fresh dill sauce to start, followed by a cream of leek soup, seafood chowder or sorbet, then lobster from their own tank, pot-roasted loin of Connemara lamb coated with a fresh basil pesto crust and a lamb jus, whole black sole grilled with garlic butter or fillet of wild salmon coated in an Oriental glaze on a bed of rocket, spring onions and sesame seeds. $12\frac{1}{2}$% service is added to all menu prices. 60-odd wines on the wine list offer mainly French bottles and just a dozen others. Lighter meals in the bar. ***Seats** 55. Parties 30. D only 7.15-9.30. Set D from £25.*

CLIFDEN — Destry Rides Again — £50

Tel 095 21722   Fax 095 41168   Map 1 A3   **R**
Clifden Co Galway

This entertaining restaurant is in the ownership of Paddy and Julia Foyle – see *The Quay House* in Clifden and *Rosleague Manor* in Letterfrack; it's named after a Marlene Dietrich film and the decor is predictably wacky – an old Georgian fanlight decorates one wall and has a real skull balanced on top, a collection of silver food domes and a variety of 'boys in the backroom' memorabilia all create atmosphere. A recently opened upstairs room overlooks the town square and seats 20. The kitchen is under the direction of Dermot Gannon and he works in a modern Mediterranean style with eclectic offerings; fresh herbs and good olive oils feature in a range of dishes that might include roast tomato, noodle and herb soup, timbale of smoked lamb, quail's eggs and parmesan with garlic and horseradish cream, fresh fish (perhaps monkfish with saffron, lime and orange sauce) and roast venison with cabbage stewed in garlic, smoked bacon and raspberry vinegar. Desserts include good home-made ices and a rich 'Lethal Chocolate Pud', made to a secret recipe. Confident, classy cooking and great fun. Short, user-friendly, keenly-priced wine list. Wheelchair facilities. No children under 5. *Seats 50. Parties 16. D only 6-10. Set D £10.95. Closed Mon & Nov-mid Mar. MasterCard,* **VISA**

CLIFDEN — E J King's

Tel 095 21330   Fax 095 21504   Map 1 A3   **P**
The Square Clifden Co Galway

On the square in the centre of town, a lively old bar on two floors, retaining an essentially traditional character despite modern touches in its atrium and striking primary colour schemes on the upper floors. Menus lean towards local seafood, especially oysters, crab, smoked salmon and seafood chowder but typical blackboard specials might include bacon and cabbage, Irish stew, fish and chips, plus there's a choice of farmhouse cheeses. Trenchermen should head for the fisherman's platter, complete with smoked salmon, prawns, crab, mussels, salmon, cod, smoked trout and mackerel and salad! Live music, mainly traditional folk and ballads, features nightly in season, 2 or 3 times a week in winter. "Nothing changes but the weather round here ..." *Open 10.30am-11.30pm, Sun 12.30-2, 4-11. Bar Food 10.30-9 (from 12.30 Sun). Terrace. Closed 25 & 26 Dec. Amex, Diners, MasterCard,* **VISA**

CLIFDEN — Foyles Hotel — 61% — £68

Tel 095 21801   Fax 095 21458   Map 1 A3   **H**
The Square Clifden Co Galway

Owned by, managed by and home to the Foyle family since 1917, Foyles is run by Edmund Foyle, twin brother of Paddy (see entry for *Quay House*). It's a comfortable, friendly, undemanding, old-fashioned hotel with rather grand corridors and public areas plus rooms that are all en suite but vary considerably in size and appointments; extra beds and cots available for younger guests with under-3s allowed to stay free. The residents' dining-room opens on to a sheltered, private courtyard. Banqueting (80) and conference (70) facilities. Four townhouses adjacent to the hotel have been acquired and will be converted to provide extra accommodation in 1997. *Rooms 30. Garden, gift shop. Closed Nov-Easter. Amex, Diners, MasterCard,* **VISA**

Set menu prices may not include service or wine.
Our guide price for two diners includes wine and service.

CLIFDEN — O'Grady's Seafood Restaurant — £50

Tel 095 21450 Fax 095 21994 Map 1 A3 **R**
Market Street Clifden Co Galway

A traditional seafood restaurant with well-spaced tables, some in alcoves but all with a degree of privacy. Try starting with a speciality like Jack's smoked fish bisque – smooth, creamy and mildly smoky – served with a choice of home-made white yeast or wholemeal soda bread. Sophisticated main courses from a wide choice (predominantly but not exclusively seafood) on the à la carte dinner menu might include grilled fillet of turbot with a compote of rhubarb and champagne butter cream or best end of lamb on a jus of wild mushrooms with a hint of pesto. Lunch offerings are simpler: marinière-style mussels, perhaps, or braised kidneys with a creamy mushroom and pink peppercorn sauce. Follow with 'sinful desserts' or farmhouse cheese. No children under 5 at dinner. Accommodation in eleven en suite bedrooms (£40–£50, Tel 095 21437) is available in nearby Sunnybank House; there are gardens, an outdoor swimming pool, sauna and tennis. *Seats 50. Parties 21. Private Room 12. L 12.30-2.30 D 6.30-10. Closed Sun (mid Mar-Jun), Nov-mid Mar. Set L £10.95. Amex, MasterCard,* **VISA**

CLIFDEN — The Quay House — £80

Tel 095 21369 Fax 095 21608 Map 1 A3 **AR**
Beach Road Clifden Co Galway

Significant changes have been taking place at Paddy and Julia Foyle's harbourside establishment. The restaurant has been reduced to about half its original capacity and moved sideways, so that it now occupies the conservatory and the previous residents' sitting-room alongside it. The old restaurant, meanwhile, has now been completely changed, to make a sitting-room and an extra (wheelchair-friendly) ground-floor bedroom. The growing number of rooms – there is also another new one, at the top of the house – means that the accommodation at Quay House is now the key element but, despite all the re-allocation of space, the atmosphere remains reassuringly constant and the whole thing has been done with the Foyles' customary flair. Paddy's collection of animal prints, real and otherwise, in the new sitting-room, deserves especially close inspection and the rooms, which are all en suite, are comfortable with a good dash of flamboyance. *Rooms 10. Garden. Closed Nov-mid Mar. MasterCard,* **VISA**

Restaurant — £55

Peter McMahon (previously working with Dermot Gannon, who has moved back up to *Destry Rides Again* – see entry above) is now in charge of the kitchen at the Quay House but, as the two worked as a team for some time, there has been no noticeable change of style. Paddy Foyle is a charming and thoughtful host, as ever, and Peter produces delicious home-baked bread from the Aga to go with the likes of lentil and smoked salmon chowder and modern dishes like crab and spinach millefeuille with apple and apricot chutney and tagliatelle of smoked salmon with chorizo. Local seafood takes centre stage in main courses such as baked halibut in filo pastry with cardamom, orange and basil vinaigrette, but Connemara lamb always features as well and there will often be a less predictable choice such as roast venison. However, the smaller restaurant means the emphasis has shifted from restaurant with rooms towards meals mainly for residents. Although changes had not been completely finalised when we went to press, it was anticipated that bookings will only be accepted from non-residents if tables are available in 1997. A phone call to check the situation is advised. *Seats 35. Parties 8. Private Room 10. D 7-9.30. Set D £23. Closed Sun & Nov-mid Mar.*

We only recommend the food in hotels categorised as **HR** and **AR**.

| CLIFDEN | **Rock Glen Manor** | 67% | £110 |

Tel 095 21035   Fax 095 21737   Map 1 A3   **HR**
Ballyconneely Road Clifden Co Galway

A mile and a half from Clifden on the Ballyconneely road, this lovely, restful 19th-century shooting lodge is tucked away over a secluded anchorage in what must surely be one of the most beautiful hotel locations in Ireland. John and Evangeline Roche, who have owned Rock Glen since 1973, describe it as "an oasis of tranquillity" and they are right. Comfortable, chintz-covered sofas and chairs in front of a welcoming turf fire tempt guests into a drawing room which, along with the bar and conservatory area beside it, enjoys lovely hill and sea views. Fourteen of the bedrooms are on the ground floor and the standard of comfort is high throughout. Golf, horse riding, fishing, mountain climbing and beaches are all available nearby. Children welcome "if well behaved". No dogs. **Rooms** 29. *Garden, croquet, tennis, putting green. Closed Nov-mid Mar. Amex, Diners, MasterCard,* **VISA**

Restaurant £60

Clever use of mirrors creates a feeling of spaciousness in this pleasant, traditionally decorated room with round mahognay tables, and uniformed staff move swiftly to ensure that every comfort has been anticipated. Meanwhile, John Roche prepares local produce in starters such as Salt Lake oysters grilled with tomatoes, capers, spring onions and parmesan cheese, timbale of crab with cucumber, radish and tomato salad in a balsamic dressing, and guinea fowl consommé with poached quail's egg and tarragon. Enticing main courses such as roast Connemara lamb with a parsley and basil crust, parsnip purée and rosemary sauce, pan-fried sea bass with saffron potatoes and a light Dijon mustard cream sauce, and crispy half duckling with honey-glazed pears, potato stuffing and a thyme duck jus. Finish off with peach and apple fritters with cinnamon ice cream and gingered caramel sauce, home-made ice creams in an almond and pistachio wafer basket and a chocolate fudge sauce or a plate of farmhouse cheeses. Next morning's breakfast sees the room transformed, with fresh juice and freshly-baked brown bread on the table and a very fine breakfast menu to choose from, including a selection of fish and vegetarian options. Informal bar snacks served from 12 to 5. No smoking. 12% service charge is added to the final bill. **Seats** 60. *Parties 10. D only 7-9. Set D £23.*

CLIFDEN   Places of Interest
Tourist Information Tel 095 21163
Connemara National Park Tel 095 41054
Dan O'Hara's Homestead Farm Lettershea Tel 095 21246

| CLONAKILTY | **An Súgán** | £50 |

Tel 023 33498   Map 2 B6   **R/P**
41 Strand Road Clonakilty Co Cork

On a corner site, reassuringly easy to find on the way into town after leaving the N71, a colourful, characterful pub that sums up everything that now makes Clonakilty such a delightful place to visit. Above the famous bar (where there's fine bar food, seafood being the main attraction alongside traditional dishes on a daily blackboard menu) there's a more formal restaurant – adorned with pictorial tributes to many of the musical greats of Ireland's past – that provides a fine setting for Brenda O'Crowley's hearty fare, especially local seafood in fresh-flavoured renderings of popular dishes including starters such as seafood chowder, smoked salmon and seafood mousse and fresh oysters, typically followed by hake in prawn and butter sauce, John Dory with a tarragon and cream sauce, and fresh lobster in a brandy cream and tomato sauce. Steaks and roast rack of lamb with rosemary and garlic are on offer for carnivores, with generosity the keyword throughout. " 'S é an t-ocras an t-anlann is fearr" (hunger is the best sauce). *Seats 45. L (Sun only) 12.30-2.30 D 7-9.45. Set Sun L £9.50 Set D £19.50. Bar open 10.30-11.30 (to 11 in winter), Sun 12.30-2, 4-11.* **Bar Food** *12-9.30. Closed Good Friday, 25 Dec. MasterCard,* **VISA**

CLONAKILTY   **Fionnuala's**   **£35**

Tel 023 34355   Map 2 B6   **R**
30 Ashe Street Clonakilty Co Cork

Known affectionately as 'Fionnuala's little Italian Restaurant', this laid-back place charms with its mis-matched chairs, tables and cloths in warm colours, walls covered with pictures and personal memorablia. At present evening meals are served in the soothingly dim atmosphere on the ground floor and in the summer, and winter weekends, in a characterful upstairs room, but during 1997 the whole restaurant will be relocated to the ground floor (to be enlarged) to make way for further alterations upstairs. Menus offer zappy colourful food with bags of flavour: nutty brown soda bread, memorable soups, pasta with piquant, spicy sauces richly flavoured with olive oil and colourful salads, and popular garlic bread served with a basil-flavoured hot cheese dip; nightly specials such as mozzarella, tomato, garlic and fresh basil and chicken cacciatora (with red wine, garlic, fresh herbs and tomatoes). Snazzy snacks include half a pizza of your choice and vegetarian choices like hummus with garlic bread and spinach and cream cheese lasagne. Finish, perhaps, with a rich chocolate pot laced with brandy, or home-made ice cream with butterscotch sauce. *Seats 40. Parties 14. Private Room 20. D only 5-10 (May-mid Sep) 7-9.30 (mid Sep-Apr). Closed Mon mid Sep-Apr, 24-26 Dec. MasterCard,* **VISA**

If you encounter bad service don't wait to write to us but make your feelings known to the management at the time of your visit. Instant compensation can often resolve any problem that might otherwise leave a bad taste.

CLONAKILTY   **Kicki's Cabin**   **£35**

Tel 023 33384   Map 2 B6   **R**
53 Pearse Street Clonakilty Co Cork

Little sister of the famous *Dunworley Cottage* out on the cliffs near Butlerstown (see entry), this charming town-centre restaurant brings the seaside to the busy street scene with lots of summer blue in the decor and seashells in glass jars instead of flowers on the table. Katherine Norén somehow manages to be in both places at once and producing her usual delicious dishes – lovely fish soups served with freshly-baked bread, more-ish Clonakilty black and white pudding (made just down the road at Edward Twomey's) served with a sherry sauce and shellfish gratins of crab or mussels. Main courses may include a choice of fresh fish, perfectly and simply cooked with classic accompaniments like parsley butter or butter sauce. Demand for the famous Dunworley nettle soup has prompted Katherine to develop a similar speciality for Kicki – nettle pie, a vegetarian starter or main course which has gone down a treat. Katherine Norén wins our 1997 Best Use of Fruit and Vegetable Award for both *Kicki's Cabin* and *Dunworley Cottage. Seats 35. Parties 12. Private Room 12. L 12.30-2.30 D 7-9.30. Closed L Sat & all Sun. MasterCard,* **VISA**

CLONAKILTY   Strand House   £40

Tel 023 34719   Map 2 B6   **A**
Sand Quay Clonakilty Co Cork

In the same ownership as *An Súgán* pub next door, this attractive, well-proportioned house is pleasingly decorated in a colour scheme of green/rusty red with blues/yellows, and furnished with antiques. Comfortable rooms are spacious and finished to a high standard with TV and tea/coffee-making facilities (but not phones). Bathrooms are not quite up to the standard of the rooms: all are en suite but most are with shower only, although there is also a communal bathroom available. Breakfast is served in an elegant dining-room on the ground floor. *Rooms 7. Closed 25 Dec. MasterCard,* **VISA**

CLONAKILTY   Places of Interest
Tourist Information Tel 023 33226
West Cork Model Railway Village Tel 023 33224

CLONDALKIN   Kingswood Country House   £60

Tel & Fax 01 459 2428   Map 2 D4   **RR**
Old Kingswood Naas Road Clondalkin Dublin 22

Within its old stone-walled garden and surrounded by mature trees, a remarkable country house atmosphere prevails at Kingswood, despite its location within the city limits and just yards from the Naas dual carriageway. The restaurant is divided between a series of rooms of pleasingly domestic proportions, one with an open fire and all overlooking the garden and, although the welcome is warm, service is uniformed and efficient, befitting chef Jaswant Samra's delicious, well-balanced fixed-price-only meals. Start, perhaps, with a vegetable and chicken broth, then roast black pudding and smoked bacon with apple purée or grilled Irish seafood with a lemon and mussel butter; typical main courses might be roast rack of Wicklow lamb with minted ratatouille, medallions of spiced monkfish with caper and sweetcorn relish, or baked chicken breast with braised red cabbage and raisins. Good desserts include white chocolate marquise with a rich chocolate and hazelnut sauce and an iced apricot brandy parfait with mango coulis. 12½% service charge is added to all menu prices. *Seats 60. Private Room 30. L 12.30-2.30 (till 3 Sun) D 6.30-10.30. Closed L Sat, D Sun, Good Friday, 25-27 Dec. Set L £13.95 (Sun L £12.95, children £5.50) Set D £21.95. Amex, Diners, MasterCard,* **VISA**

Rooms   £80
Seven comfortable, en suite rooms are individually decorated to a high standard. 24hr room service. Tariff reductions at weekends. No dogs.

CLONES   Hilton Park   £135

Tel 047 56007   Fax 047 56033   Map 1 C3   **A**
Scotshouse Clones Co Monaghan

Set in 600 acres of parkland in wonderful wooded countryside studded with lakes and islands, Hilton Park is a gem. Now in the hands of Johnny Madden, the eighth generation in the Madden family, this magnificent mansion is one of Ireland's finest country houses, offering luxurious accommodation in a family setting, with warm hospitality and excellent food to match. Immense outer and inner halls set the tone in a house that is very grand yet surprisingly informal. The drawing and dining-rooms are impressive, with lovely views of the recently renovated formal gardens and lake, while the elegant bedrooms are all gloriously different. Three have four-poster or half-tester beds, some have dressing rooms, all have private bathrooms (of which three are en suite). First-time visitors will be rewarded with a sense of discovery as this region is wonderful but largely overlooked; it is at the head of the Lough Erne basin, a fine but relatively little known waterway stretching 70 miles across the country to Donegal Bay on the

Atantic Coast. Lucy Madden's cooking (four-course dinner £25) is another joy to discover. Now that she has personally taken over the mainly organic kitchen garden, guests have the pleasure of enjoying the fruits of her handiwork both outside and in the kitchen. The style of cooking and service is 'country house' – imaginative dinner party fare with no menu; everyone sits down (but not necessarily at a communal table) at 8 o'clock. Local produce, Lucy's own herbs, vegetables and fruit, farmhouse cheeses and great baking are the hallmarks and breakfast in the semi-basement Green Room is a special high point. Aside from the house itself, the area around it has much to offer – cruisers can be hired, the fishing is superb and riding can be arranged at a nearby equestrian centre with a cross-country course in a beautiful setting. Off-season house parties (all year, for up to five couples) and shooting parties (Nov-Jan) by arrangement. Banqueting/small conferences for 30/50. No dogs. **Rooms 6. Garden.** *Closed Oct-end Mar. MasterCard,* **VISA**

CLONMEL	Clonmel Arms Hotel	61%	£85

Tel 052 21233   Fax 052 21526
Sarsfield Street Conmel Co Tipperary

Map 2 C5

H

Some of the bedrooms at the town-centre Clonmel Arms, owner-managed by Brendan Pettit, are suitable for family occupation, and children under 10 can stay free in their parents' room. Fifteen of the rooms cherry wood furniture and colourful fabrics. Plans are to add a further 30 bedrooms and a leisure centre in the near future. There are extensive banqueting and conference facilities (for up to 600), two bars and an all-day buttery/coffee shop. No dogs. **Rooms 31. Patio,** *coffee shop (9-6). Closed 25 Dec. Amex, Diners, MasterCard,* **VISA**

CLONMEL	Knocklofty House	67%	£120

Tel 052 38353   Fax 052 38300
Knocklofty Clonmel Co Tipperary

Map 2 C5

HR

Formerly the country residence of the Earls of Donoughmore, Bill and Marie Mulshaw's beautifully located, impressive period house is set in 35 acres of gardens and extensive rolling parkland. Graciously proportioned, high-ceilinged rooms have fine period detail and the scale throughout is quite grand, yet without solemnity. Sunny, south-facing front rooms include an unusual two-storey galleried library (light meals served here 11-5.30) with a finely decorated Georgian ceiling (and plenty of real books) and spacious bedrooms; the latter are all individually decorated in period style, their old-time elegance balanced by the convenience of en suite bathrooms, phone, TV and hospitality trays. Children are most welcome; under-6s can stay free, 6-15s half-price. The recently refurbished leisure complex now houses a sauna. **Rooms 14. Garden,** *indoor swimming pool, spa bath, sauna, sun bed, gym, tennis, croquet, fishing. Closed 26 & 26 Dec. MasterCard,* **VISA**

Restaurant

£60

In the corridor beside the dining-room door there is a framed photograph of Her Majesty The Queen together with a dinner menu which, as it turns out, Bill Mulshaw cooked for the Queen and Prince Philip's Ruby Wedding, no less, while he was employed as a private chef at *Luton Hoo* in Bedfordshire. Once past the regal photograph, guests can fully appreciate the elegantly-appointed, panelled dining-room, which enjoys sweeping views over a private stretch of the River Suir to the Comeragh and Knockmealdown mountains. Despite (or, perhaps, because of) Bill's rarefied culinary background, menus are tempting without over-sophistication; local produce stars and vegetables and herbs are mostly grown on the premises. Typical starters on the dinner menu might include smoked salmon and mackerel roulade with a chive and dill cream dressing, seafood hors d'oeuvres or warm mussels in a ginger and lemon sauce served in a millefeuille case. A soup like cream of celery with Cashel Blue cheese might be balanced with unusually tempting sorbets – orange or lemon and fennel – and followed by pan-fried venison with a pink peppercorn and gin sauce or salmon with an almond and sweet herb crust and a sorrel and white wine sauce. You might even find blue shark, caught off the Irish coast, alongside good poultry, seafood from Dunmore East and river fish dishes. Classic desserts might include chilled lime and lemon soufflé or strawberry and port wine jellied dome with fresh raspberry coulis; Irish cheeses are served with grapes and home-made biscuits. *Seats 48 (+ 20 on terrace). Parties 30. Private Room 12. L 12.30-2.30 D 7-9.30 (Fri & Sat to 10, Sun to 8.30). Set L £13.50 Set D £24.*

CLONMEL   Places of Interest
Tourist Information Tel 052 22960
Cahir Tourist Information Tel 052 41453
Clonmel Racecourse Powerstown Park Tel 052 22611
Ormond Castle Carrick-on-Suir Tel 051 40787
Michelstown Cave
Michelstown Castle Gardens

COBH	Mansworth's	

Tel 021 811965   Map 2 B6   **P**
Midleton Street Cobh Co Cork

Well up the hill, a hundred yards from St Colman's Cathedral, Mansworth's is Cobh's oldest-established pub and has been run by the same family for over 100 years now. It's been a pub since 1857 and the great grand-aunt of the current owner, John Mansworth, purchased it in 1895. A warm, welcoming place by any standards, an the unspoilt, traditional bar is especially worth visiting for its fascinating collection of memorabilia connected with the naval history of the port, both past and present; apparently there were 104 pubs in Cobh when the British fleet were based here, but nowadays there are 'only' 28 left! Many of the more recent photographs feature the landlord, who is an enthusiastic promoter of Cobh (now an important Heritage Town) in general and its maritime characteristics in particular. There's an unusually good choice of non-alcoholic drinks, including wines. *Open 10.30am-11.30pm Mon-Sat (to 11pm in winter), Sun 12.30-2, 4-11. Closed Good Friday, 25 Dec. No credit cards.*

COLLON	Forge Gallery Restaurant	£65

Tel 041 26272 Fax 041 26584   Map 1 D3   **R**
Collon Co Louth

This stylish, meticulously appointed two-storey restaurant – the upper half is an elegant galleried bar/reception area overlooking the dining-room below – provides a fitting setting for Des Carroll's bounteous fare and Conor Phelan's hospitality. A patio area is a pleasant setting for pre-prandial drinks in fine weather. Frequently-changed à la carte and fixed-price menus feature local seasonal produce – seafood, game in season, vegetables, fruit – in first courses such as braised ox tongue with mustard sauce or Annagassan smokie with Welsh rarebit, then often a choice of three soups (perhaps carrot and courgette or smoked ham and cabbage), followed by braised pigeon wrapped in Chinese leaves with Madeira sauce or chicken breast with smoked cheese and lemon sauce; home-made breads – white yeast bread, scones or brown bread with thyme – are served to mop up the juices. Outstanding vegetables – a plentiful selection of about five, imaginatively presented – and lovely seasonal desserts such as a apple and sultana strudel or chocolate and orange cheesecake. Round it all off with freshly-brewed coffee or tea (including herbal teas) and petits fours. *Seats 50. Parties 10. D only 7-9.30. Closed Sun, Mon, 3 days Christmas, 2 weeks in Jan & Bank Holidays. Set D £25. Amex, Diners, MasterCard, VISA*

COLLOONEY   Glebe House   £45

Tel 071 67787 Fax 071 30438   Map 1 B2   **RR**
Collooney Co Sligo

Marc and Brid Torrades opened Glebe House as a restaurant in 1990 and their
warmth of hospitality and willingness to please win the hearts of many a guest.
Chef Brid makes good use of the best local produce on both table d'hote and à
la carte menus; the former offers a good choice with, perhaps, roulade of plaice
with smoked salmon mousse followed by cream of summer vegetable soup, then
baked herb-crusted cod with hollandaise. The carte extends to more hearty,
generous dishes such as duck liver paté with mixed fruit jelly, seafood chowder,
daily fresh seafood dishes (monkfish tossed in garlic butter), a couple of
vegetarian options (baked pepper stuffed with lentils and pilau rice) and sautéed
fillet of beef with wild mushrooms. Good vegetables are served up in dishes
left on the table for guests to help themselves. Classic desserts include a surprise
dessert plate and a tray with ten or so Irish farmhouse cheeses. Informal eating
(oysters, seafood chowder, steak sandwich, Irish cheeses) in The Coach House
wine bar, open 7 days in the summer months from 1-9pm. Good wheelchair
access. *Seats 40. Private Room 30. L by arrangement D 6.30-9.30. Set D £17.95.
Closed Sun & Mon in winter (except Bank Holiday weekends), 25 & 26 Dec.
Amex, Diners, MasterCard, **VISA***

Rooms   £42
Accommodation is available in five spacious, individually-decorated rooms,
all en suite, two with baths (those with shower are £37). *Garden.*

COLLOONEY   Markree Castle   66%   £108

Tel 071 67800 Fax 071 67840   Map 1 B2   **HR**
Collooney Co Sligo

Sligo's oldest inhabited castle, Markree has been the home of the Cooper family
since 1640 and, overlooking the magnificent main staircase, features a stained-
glass window which purportedly traces the family tree back to the time of King
John of England. Currently in the energetic 10th generation ownership of
Charles Cooper, who has gradually been restoring the castle over the last decade
or so, returning guests find something new to marvel at on each visit – most
recently the triumphant opening of the top floor (which included the installation
of a lift, for which guests are given a key) and a new bar at the front of the
building. Everything is on an appropriately over-sized scale throughout – arriving
guests enter via a covered portico and ascend a flight of stone steps to reach the
enormous hall, where a welcoming log fire always burns. Lofty reception rooms
include a spacious, comfortably furnished drawing room (where excellent afternoon teas are served) running the full depth of the castle. Despite its grandeur
of scale, the atmosphere at Markree is always friendly and relaxed, very much
a family home. Bedrooms vary in size and outlook, but all have pleasant views
over the castle grounds and are individually furnished, with good bathrooms,
phone and TV; like the rest of the castle, they are well heated. Banqueting for
100, small conferences for up to 50 delegates. ***Rooms** 30. Garden, terrace, patio,
croquet, riding, fishing, shooting. Closed 24-27 Dec. Amex, Diners, MasterCard,
VISA*

Restaurant   £55

Overlooking formal gardens and woodlands at the back of the castle, this
beautiful restaurant is in two interconnecting dining-rooms with spectacular
Louis-Philippe style plasterwork created by Italian craftsmen in 1845. Yet,
despite the elegance of the surroundings, the atmosphere is pleasantly informal
largely due to the personality of Charles Cooper, who keeps a close eye on his
team of friendly local waitresses and makes sure everyone is happy. Tom Joyce,

head chef since 1993, creates well-balanced menus which nicely combine a certain sophistication demanded by the surroundings and an admirable simplicity. From a choice of five starters, seasonal dinner menus might include home-cured gravad lax with mustard and honey sauce and a warm salad of chicken and sweet peppers, followed by a choice of soups and sorbet; five main-course choices will usually include steak – perhaps pan-fried with leek and Pommery mustard sauce – and lamb (roast rack with herb and peppercorn jus) as well as one or two fish dishes (baked seabass with lemon and dill sauce) and poultry or game in season. Classic desserts could include chocolate and hazelnut tart, peach and plum brulée and a Bailey's cheesecake – or Irish farmhouse cheeses. Sunday lunch menus are on the same lines, although with a couple of traditional roasts included (leg of lamb with rosemary, sirloin with Yorkshire pudding) and a hearty day-time selection of vegetables on the side. *Seats 70. Parties 12. Private Room 30. L 1-2.30 (Sun only) D 7-9.30. Set Sun L £13.50 Set D £20.50 & £25.95. Closed L Mon-Sat (bar meals 10-6 daily, L 1-2.30).*

We do not accept free meals or hospitality – our inspectors pay their own bills and **never** book in the name of Egon Ronay's Guides.

CONG	Ashford Castle	89%	£275

Tel 092 46003 Fax 092 46260   Map 1 B3   **HR**
Cong Co Mayo

With its origins dating back to the early 13th century and set amid 350 acres of magnificent parkland (including a golf course) on the northern shores of Lough Corrib, this splendid castle has been lovingly restored – its recent history is depicted for all to see by photographic and written memorabilia displayed in various parts of the building. Throughout, there's rich panelling, intricately carved balustrades, suits of armour and fine paintings. Whether you wish to relax in the elegant drawing room, wander around the halls and galleries, or retire to the Dungeon Bar after dinner and listen to the delightful Annette Griffin singing traditional Irish folk songs and playing the harp to the accompaniment of Carol Coleman's piano, there's a unique atmosphere throughout. Managing Director Rory Murphy has been in situ for over 20 years and, with the assistance of William (Bill) Buckley, runs a truly fine hotel, backed up by excellent professional and committed staff. Spacious bedrooms (including several suites) offer attractive views and every conceivable luxury, from flowers and fresh fruit on arrival to slippers, bathrobes and Molton Brown toiletries in the splendid bathrooms; throughout the rooms you'll find period furniture, fine fabrics and superb housekeeping that includes a turn-down service. Discreet conference facilities (several EEC ministerial conferences have been held here) accommodate up to 140 theatre-style and 150 for banquets. The hotel is committed to excellence, in standards of both service and ambience. An elegant Health Centre features a fully-equipped gym, spa bath, sauna and steam room (but there's still no swimming pool!); it's stylishly decorated with Italian tiles and hand-painted murals. Bright lounge areas and balconies have commanding views of the estate and a conservatory overlooks Lough Corrib. No dogs. *Dromoland Castle* in Newmarket-on-Fergus (see entry) is Ashford Castle's sister hotel. ***Rooms** 83. Health centre, garden, golf (9), tennis, clay pigeon shooting, archery, equestrian centre, jaunting-car, fishing, lake cruising, bicycles, boutique, beauty salon, hair salon, snooker. Amex, Diners, MasterCard, VISA*

Connaught Room   £110

Part of the original Georgian House built in 1715, the handsome, panelled dining-room with chandeliers and vast windows is only open at night and is sometimes used for theme evenings. Executive chef Denis Lenihan presides over both restaurants (see George V below) and here presents an à la carte menu with supplementary daily specials. Meat and poultry are sourced from local farms, so you can rely on the quality of raw materials, and fish comes only from the 'clear waters of the West Coast'. The rather grand carte sets out dishes in French with English translations: from wonton soup infused with oysters or foie gras layered with a mousse of green pulses and surrounded by broad bean and truffle oil dressing to whole duckling, carved at your table, on a bed of citrus chicory with lime and honey sauce, accompanied by a timbale of kohlrabi, carrot and mooli. Free-range poussins stuffed with tripe and leeks and served on a prune and port sauce, or Cleggan lobster tail in a ginger fish consommé with tomato and leek and a little bavarois of the claws show that the style is involved and sophisticated. Fine cheeses, a plate of assorted chocolate desserts and good coffee might be the perfect end to a meal in grand style. Service is both caring and supremely professional. No children under 12. There are a few French wines quite reasonably priced for a hotel of this class, though look outside France for the best value. **Seats** 40. D only 7-9.30. Open May-end Oct only.

George V Room   £100

Part of the original Georgian House built in 1715, the handsome, panelled

A much larger room, also with handsome panelling and chandeliers. Service is again outstanding, and here daily-changing fixed-price menus with several choices at each stage are offered. Dinner is usually a four-course affair: start, perhaps, with native Galway oysters served warm with strands of cucumber and butter sauce, then cream of champ or broccoli and almond soup, following with roast sirloin of beef on a crab and lime sauce and traditional potato cakes or pan-fried supreme of salmon with a champagne sauce and black pasta. Finish with local farmhouse cheeses or a lightly frozen prune and armagnac soufflé from a choice of desserts. 15% service is added to all prices. No children under 12. Snack lunches (perhaps local smoked salmon with horseradish cream, a chicken stir-fry or a toasted BLT with pickles) are served in the Sun Lounge. **Seats** 135. Parties 12. L 1-2.15 D 7-9.30. Set L £17/£23 Set D £29/£35.

Cong   Places of Interest

Ballinrobe Racecourse Tel 092 41052
Ballintubber Abbey 10 miles
Cong Abbey
Moore Hall nr Claremorris 20 miles
Ross Abbey Headford

CORK   An Spailpín Fánac

Tel 021 277949   Map 2 B6   **P**
28/29 South Main Street Cork Co Cork

Food at John and Deirdre O'Connor's pleasant pub is of the simple, wholesome variety: freshly-cut sandwiches, toasted Kiev and doorstep special with fries, chicken curry, lamb cutlets, bacon and cabbage, Irish stew, minced beef and onion pie, T-bone steak, a fish special. Low ceilings, open brickwork, soft natural colours, a simple wooden bar with rush-seated stools and dim natural light create a soothing atmosphere emphasised by the friendliness of the proprietor; a growing collection of postcards from regulars bears witness to the local popularity of the premises. The name of the pub (pronounced 'an spawlpeen fawnoc') translates roughly as 'the jobbing traveller', recalling a once-familiar Irish character who used to keep on the move around the country in search of work. No children after 6.30pm, but they are welcome during the day. The Beamish brewery is opposite the pub and the River Lee is 40 yards away. Traditional, folky music five nights a week Jun-Sept (not Fri & Sat); plus possibly Mon from Oct-end May. An extension to the building, almost doubling the capacity of the place, was due to be completed in December 1996. *Open 12-11 (to 11.30 in summer), Sun 12.30-2, 4-11. Bar Food 12-3. Closed Good Friday, 25 Dec. No credit cards.*

| **CORK** | **Arbutus Lodge** | **70%** | **£90** |

Tel 021 501237   Fax 021 502893   Map 2 B6   **HR**
Montenotte Cork Co Cork

Former home of a Lord Mayor of Cork, high above the city with views of the River Lee and the surrounding hills. The hotel gets its name from the Arbutus tree, one of the many rare trees and shrubs growing in the spectacular terraced gardens. The house is full of genuine antique furniture (note the four-poster in the Blue Room) and some marvellous art, both old and new, the modern paintings by Irish artists much in demand by galleries and museums. Declan and Patsy Ryan, here since 1962, extend a warm welcome to all their guests, ably backed up by charming staff. Whether you choose to relax in the cosy lounge or the panoramic bar with its own terrace, you'll feel at home, and the cleverly designed and smartly decorated bedrooms provide both comfort and tranquillity. Bathrooms boast quality towels, bathrobes and toiletries and you'll start the day with as good a breakfast as you'll encounter anywhere. Four suites are in a mansion directly across from the hotel; each is quite grand, with its own kitchen, videos and faxes. 24hr room service. Conference facilities for up to 180. No dogs. *Rooms 20. Garden, tennis. Closed 24-26 Dec. Amex, Diners, MasterCard, VISA*

Restaurant   ★   **£80**

Declan Ryan has moulded together an enthusiastic young team that remains loyal to its roots – no slavish copying of French trends but a reliance on local produce including herbs and soft fruit from the hotel's own garden and traditional Cork dishes. Game in season and the freshest of fish feature (inspect the seafood tank in the bar) and the nightly-changing, seven-course tasting menu, prepared by new head chef Kevin Arundel (ex *Marlfield House*, Gorey), is a fine example of the kitchen's style. No mini-portions, but enough to satisfy the hungriest of souls – typically, this might commence with galette of foie gras with black pudding, then potage of shellfish and chives, pan-fried turbot with gazpacho sauce, orange and mint sorbet, loin of veal with ballotine of potato and bacon with red wine jus, Irish farmhouse cheeses in tip-top condition, sweets from a trolley that will tempt even those beginning to flag by now, and home-made petits fours with coffee to finish! A la carte you may find hot oysters with samphire and herb sauce, and warm salad of wood pigeon with blackcurrants alongside brill with a ragout of clams and beef fillet with confit of garlic, basil pesto and red wine essence. Service is as caring and professional as you'll find anywhere. One of the country's great wine lists, cleverly presented in three parts, including a section with around twenty wines under £17. Several grand wines from France, but equally, the New World is well-represented. Prices are fair throughout: even a glass of marque champagne is well under £6. A variety of breads (courgette and chive, walnut and saffron) is baked on the premises daily. Bar food (lunchtime only, except Sunday) offers traditional Irish dishes like tripe with onions or drisheen, Irish stew or spiced beef with home-made chutney. *Seats 50. Parties 12. Private Room 30. L 1-2 D 7-9.30. Closed Sun, 1 week Christmas. Set L £14.50 Set D £23.50 & £28.95.*

See the **County Listings** green tinted pages for details of all establishments listed in county order.

CORK	Bully's	£25

Tel 021 273555   Fax 021 273427   Map 2 B6   **R**
40 Paul Street Cork Co Cork

Pizzas from the wood-burning oven are one of the specialities of Eugene Buckley's popular little place. They come in a dozen varieties, top of the range being *calzone* and Bully's special – a half-folded version with bolognese sauce, ham, onion and mushrooms. Also on the menu are home-made pasta, grills, omelettes and seafood dishes. Also at Douglas (Tel 021 892415) and Bishopstown (Tel 021 546838). *Seats 40. Parties 20. Meals 12-11.30, Sun 1-11. Closed 25 & 26 Dec. No credit cards.*

CORK	Crawford Gallery Café	£45

Tel 021 274415   Map 2 B6   **R**
Emmet Place Cork Co Cork

On the ground floor of the Crawford Municipal Art Gallery (in the city centre next to the Opera House), an offshoot of the renowned *Ballymaloe House* at Shanagarry. Snackier items include spinach and mushroom pancake, 'tartine of the day' and open sandwiches but one can easily push the boat out and enjoy the day's fish catch from Ballycotton or chicken breast with chive and cherry tomato butter sauce, followed by strawberry meringue roulade or rhubarb fool. *Seats 70. Private Function Room 200. Meals 9-5 (till 4.30 Sat). Set L £10. Closed Sun, Good Friday, Bank Holidays, 1 week Christmas. MasterCard, VISA*

CORK	Dan Lowrey's	

Tel 021 505071   Map 2 B6   **P**
13 MacCurtain Street Cork Co Cork

A delightfully old-fashioned, small pub with two interconnecting rooms (the one in the back with an open fire), named after a much-lamented local theatre. The pub's history goes back to 1875 and many of the original tavern features have been retained, including the wooden floor and a remarkable mahogany bar unit with unusual shelving and antique bevelled mirrors. The stained-glass windows on the street are also of special interest, as they came from Kilkenny Cathedral. Since arriving here in 1995 Anthony and Catherine O'Riordan have introduced hot lunches and evening meals. Directly opposite *Isaacs* restaurant. *Open 10.30am-11.30pm (till 11 in winter), Sun 12.30-2, 4-11. Closed Good Friday, 25 Dec. No credit cards.*

Entries categorised as **JaB** are recommended for 'Just a Bite'.

CORK	Farmgate Café	

Tel 021 278134   Fax 021 632771   Map 2 B6   **JaB**
Old English Market Princes Street Cork Co Cork

Kay Harte and Maróg O'Brien's thriving café is located above the English market, from where much of the produce used in their cooking is drawn, notably fresh fish and traditional dishes like tripe and drisheen. Full Irish breakfast is available until 11am when the lunch menu comes on stream offering the likes of seafood chowder, chargrilled lamb burger, Mediterranean salad, catch of the day (John Dory, plaice, cod or tuna pan-fried with herb butter), a daily tart (perhaps blue cheese and smoked bacon), smoked salmon open sandwiches and freshly-filled baguettes. Tarte tatin or créme caramel to finish; afternoon teas with home-made scones and jam from 4pm. High-chairs provided. *Seats 40 (plus 50 outside on the heated balcony). Meals 8.30-5.30 L 12-4. Closed Sun, Bank Holidays, Good Friday & 25 Dec. No credit cards.*

CORK   Fitzpatrick Silver Springs   65%   £112

Tel 021 507533   Fax 021 507641   Map 2 B6   **H**
Tivoli Cork Co Cork

On the side of a steep hill overlooking the river and the main Dublin road, about 2 miles out of town, the modern Silver Springs is also a major convention centre with a large, up-to-date facility built in 1990 a little further up the hill above the hotel (banqueting for 750, conferences up to 850). Even further up the hill are an extensive leisure centre and nine-hole golf course. Within, the hotel public areas are spacious and include a large public bar with live music from Thursday to Sunday evenings. Bedrooms are all double-glazed, have lightwood fitted furniture, good easy chairs and practical bathrooms. 'Club' rooms are larger and there are two 'full' and three 'junior' antique-furnished suites. 24hr room service. Children under 5 share their parents' room at no charge – 5-12s £5. No dogs. *Rooms 109. Garden, indoor swimming pool, gym, aerobic studio, solarium, sauna, spa bath, steam room, golf (9), squash, indoor & outdoor tennis, snooker, courtesy coach, creche, indoor children's play area. Closed 25 Dec. Amex, Diners, MasterCard, VISA*

We do not recommend the food in pubs where
there is no mention of Bar Food in the statistics.
A restaurant within a pub is only specifically recommended
where its separate opening times are given.

CORK   Flemings   £55

Tel 021 821621   Fax 021 821800   Map 2 B6   **RR**
Silver Grange House Tivoli Cork Co Cork

Just a short drive from Cork on the Dublin road, Flemings is a large Georgian family house standing in five acres of gardens overlooking the commercial harbour at Tivoli. Those acres include a kitchen garden which provides much of the fruit, vegetables and herbs needed in the restaurant, a light, handsome double room with marble fireplaces, gilty overmantel mirrors, elegant drapes, comfortably upholstered chairs and well-dressed waiters. Michael Fleming's cooking is French, his menus written in French with English translations; the à la carte encompasses smoked salmon, crab gateau and a warm seafood tartlet in champagne sauce, warm smoked duck breast and confit with raspberry vinegar dressing, lobster bisque with lobster raviolis, roast loin of lamb baked in pastry with a tarragon and tomato jus, and black sole on the bone with herb butter. The menu du chef table d'hote offers just alternatives for each course – perhaps a warm tomato tart with herbs, smoked bacon, mozzarella and fresh tomato coulis, then wild salmon pan-fried with hazelnuts and sesame oil served with a filo pastry and nut crust, and poached garden fruits and vanilla meringue with a fruit coulis to finish. There's always a roast at Sunday lunchtime. The decent wine list veers not unreasonably towards France, given the style of cooking. However, the New World is represented, Australia fairly, the rest patchily. *Seats 50. Parties 22. Private Room 36. L 12.30-2.30 D 6.30-10.30. Set L £13.50 Set D £21. Closed 24-26 Dec. Amex, Diners, MasterCard, VISA*

Rooms   £85
Accommodation is currently available in four spacious en suite rooms, all comfortably furnished in a style appropriate to the age and graciousness of the house. However, by April 1997 a further 18 bedrooms are due to come on line, in conjunction with major refurbishment to public areas, a new bar and patio, and further development to the extensive gardens. No dogs. *Garden.*

CORK — The Gingerbread House

Tel & Fax 021 276411
Paul Street Plaza Cork Co Cork

Map 2 B6   **JaB**

Barnaby Blacker's Gingerbread House is ideally situated for taking a break from a hectic day's shopping. The menu offers good daytime snacking with good breakfasts (8.15-12), home-baked cakes like carrot, French chocolate, praline and lemon, sausage rolls, soup, quiche and Cornish pasties (baked fresh every morning with puff pastry and an Irish stew filling). Home-made jams and preserves to take away. Good cafetière coffee. A short, regularly-changing, reasonably priced evening menu (lasagne with garlic bread, baked pork steak with fresh sage stuffing and apple purée) is served from 6-10.30pm. *Seats 100. Parties 20. Open 8.15-9.30 (till 10.30 Thu-Sat). Closed Sun (except before Christmas), 25 & 26 Dec, Bank Holidays. Amex, Diners, MasterCard,* **VISA**

CORK — Harolds Restaurant   £55

Tel 021 361613
Douglas Village East Cork Co Cork

Map 2 B6   **R**

Chef Harold Lynch and front-of-house partner Beth Haughton run this stylish little place just off the busiest shopping area of Douglas. The interesting, modern interior features unusual paintings by local artist Carol Hodder, clever lighting, striking mirrors, arty floral arrangements and well-furnished tables with cloths, fine glasses, pottery butter dishes, bentwood chairs and fashionably paper napkins – setting just the right tone for Harold's lively mix of modern food. On a sensibly limited, moderately priced à la carte menu you'll find the likes of bruschetta of smoked bacon, aubergine, sweet peppers and mozzarella, spinach roulade with tomato and marjoram sauce, or Provençal soup with pesto to start, following with chicken breast wrapped in Parma ham with fresh herb stuffing, seafood casserole with cream, white wine and saffron, steaks, a daily fish dish (pan-fried brill on a bed of caramelised onions with ginger butter sauce) and Malay curry. chocolate terrine with crème anglaise, peach crumble with raspberry cream and Irish farmhouse cheeses to finish. Delicious brown soda bread, good coffee by the cup. *Seats 50. L Sun only (Sep-end Apr only) 12.30-2.30 £10.95 D 6-10. Closed D Sun (winter), all Sun (summer), Mon, 25 Dec. MasterCard,* **VISA**

CORK — Hayfield Manor Hotel   75%   £175

Tel 021 315600 Fax 021 316839
Perrott Avenue Cork Co Cork

Map 2 B6   **H**

Discreetly situated in landscaped grounds just behind University College Cork, this luxurious new hotel opened in spring 1996 and has been planned with meticulous care to look (and feel) like a large period house – an impression that is reinforced by many small details, including the mingling of antiques with new furnishings throughout and the skilful use of occasional pieces that have not been recently refurbished and take the 'new' feel off the overall decorative scheme. A large entrance hall with impressive staircase and welcoming open fire sets the tone; to one side is a large club-like bar (where weekday lunches are served) plus an elegantly appointed dining-room and country-house style drawing-room, both overlooking a walled garden at the back – which can be used for drinks and afternoon teas and also has access to a particularly pretty swimming pool. Conference rooms of varying sizes include a library/boardroom beside the drawing-room that doubles as a private dining-room. Spacious bedrooms vary in decor, are beautifully furnished to a high standard with antiques and have generous, marbled bathrooms with individual tiling styles, heated towel rails and good toiletries. The range of bedrooms includes include two suites, six junior suites, two rooms designed for disabled guests and a further two ground-floor rooms that are wheelchair-friendly. Conference facilities for up to 210 delegates. Beauty and massage therapies by arrangement. *Rooms 53. Garden, indoor swimming pool, gym, steam room, spa bath. Closed 24-27 Dec. Amex, Diners, MasterCard, VISA*

| CORK | Holiday Inn Express | £57 |

Tel 021 354354 Fax 021 354202   Map 2 B6   **L**
Lee Tunnel Roundabout Dunkettle Cork Co Cork

Newly-built budget hotel offering straightforward, comfortable accommodation. Modern facilities include queen-sized beds, computer phone points, voice-mail telephone system and 'double double bed' family rooms. The room price quoted includes two cooked Irish breakfasts; the room price with Continental breakfast is £45 (£40 Jan-Apr and Nov-Dec). Five bedrooms are equipped for disabled guests. No dogs. East of the city, by the Dunkettle Lee Tunnel roundabout. See also entry under Galway. Toll-free central reservations 0800 897121 UK. *Rooms 100. Closed 1 week Christmas. Amex, Diners, MasterCard, VISA*

| CORK | Imperial Hotel | 66% | £110 |

Tel 021 274040   Fax 021 275375   Map 2 B6   **H**
South Mall Cork Co Cork

The Imperial is on the main commercial and banking street of town and its neo-classical facade conceals something of a mixture of styles. The marble-floored lobby and some of the bedroom corridors, which feature a number of fine antiques, retain their original 19th-century grandeur (with nightly pianist) and restaurant have been given a 1930s' theme and the public bar remembers Cork's history as a shipbuilding centre. Bedrooms, apart from a few that are furnished with antiques in traditional style, are determinedly modern with white fitted units, glass and chrome coffee tables and contemporary lights. About half the rooms have novel wall-mounted 'clothes grooming cabinets' that are designed to deodorise and dewrinkle garments. 12 of the bathrooms have shower and WC only. Room service is available but not advertised. Secure covered parking for about 80 cars, three minutes' walk from the hotel. Reduced winter tariff (double £99). *Rooms 100. Closed 25 Dec-3 Jan. Amex, Diners, MasterCard, VISA*

| CORK | Isaacs | £40 |

Tel 021 503805   Fax 021 551348   Map 2 B6   **R**
48 MacCurtain Street Cork Co Cork

An 18th-century warehouse has been carefully adapted into a fine restaurant serving an interesting menu conceived by chef Canice Sharkey. A few snacky items (chargrilled burger with fries, bruschetta with roast peppers, olives, goat's cheese and pesto) are added at lunchtime to further all-day eclectic options: seafood chowder, salmon and potato fishcakes with herb mayonnaise, Moroccan lamb kebabs, pasta dishes (tagliatelle with wild mushrooms, smoked bacon, parmesan and cream) and enticing desserts such as crème brulée, pressed chocolate cake with strawberry sauce, or a plate of Irish cheeses. Additional daily specials may feature carrot and tarragon soup, hot buttered crab toes with garlic, and grilled salmon with chive champ. Vegetarians who like fashionable Mediterranean ingredients should be particularly well satisfied. *Seats 100. Parties 30. Open 10am-10.30pm (till 9 Sun), L 12-2.30, D 6.30-10.30 (till 9 Sun). Closed L Sun, 5 days Christmas. Amex, Diners, MasterCard, VISA*

CORK | Ivory Tower Restaurant | £65

Tel 021 274665 Fax 021 277750   Map 2 B6   **R**
35 Princes Street Cork Co Cork

Situated in the first-floor front of a period office building just off one of Cork's main shopping streets. The atmosphere is friendly and informal – bare-board floor, unclothed tables, work of local artists on the walls – and chef/patron Seamus O'Connell's cooking is certainly individualistic. Try peppered lamb's liver on celeriac and onion confit with saffron apple sauce or organic courgette and fennel soup to start and Cajun blackened swordfish with banana ketchup, whole turbot braised with tarragon and smoked chicken, or lamb shank osso buco for main course. There are always several vegetarian options – aubergine and chocolate chili bean chimichanga. Lunch prices are lower than in the evening. Two or three home-made breads vary from day to day. *Seats 35.* *L 12-4 D 6.30-11. Set D £17.50 Tue-Thu. Closed Sun & Mon, 25 Dec & 1 Jan.* *MasterCard,* **VISA**

CORK | Jacques | £55

Tel 021 277387 Fax 021 270634   Map 2 B6   **R**
9 Phoenix Street Cork Co Cork

Jacqueline and Eithne Barry's city-centre bistro has been an integral part of Cork life for 17 years now, whether for a reviving bite during a day's shopping or a more leisurely meal in the evening, when crisp linen and lowered lights create a more formal ambience. Warm and vibrant decor in deep pumpkin and sunny yellows works equally well at any time of day and, although they see their style as modern Irish, there's no denying the influence of sunnier climes on the plate as much as the surroundings. Jacqueline Barry creates tempting menus, with salads a particular strength – typically with rocket salad with Caesar dressing and shavings of parmesan, chicken with crispy bacon, hazelnuts and tomato vinaigrette or a warm salad of spiced lamb fillet with green beans, feta cheese and parsley potato – available as starter portions or main courses at lunch. Strong vegetarian options might tempt the most determined carnivore – feta cheese with grilled red pepper, croutons and black olives, grilled polenta and parmesan with field mushrooms and chili jam, red pepper and tomato tart – although local seafood is also a major feature in unusual dishes like fresh scallops with a piquant sauce, deep-fried leeks and bacon. This imaginative cook is not afraid to try novel ingredients either, typically in ostrich served with tomato and caper sauce and battered onions. Delicious desserts range from homely blackberry and apple pie through luscious cakes like sachertorte and a superb classic lemon tart. Good coffee to round it all off. *Seats 58. Parties 14. L 12-3 D 6-10.30. Set L £9.90/£12.90. Set D £9.90 (6-7 pm only) & £19.50. Closed Sun, Bank Holidays & 4 days at Christmas.* *Amex, MasterCard,* **VISA**

| CORK | Jurys Cork Inn | 60% | £65 |

Tel 021 276444   Fax 021 276144   Map 2 B6   **H**
Anderson's Quay Cork Co Cork

A newly-built Jurys budget hotel in a central riverside site. Like the other Jurys Inns, room prices include accommodation for up to four (including a sofa bed) and there is space for a car. Although there are no frills, simple design and good quality furnishings combine to provide maximum comfort at the minimum price: not only ample open wardrobe and writing/dressing space, well-placed mirrors and lighting but also phone, TV, cleverly designed built-in tea/coffee facilities and neat well-lit bathrooms with full (if unusually small) bath, overbath shower and the necessary toiletries. Cot, extra bed and high-chair available by arrangement. Seven rooms are equipped for disabled guests. No dogs. Limited parking (27 spaces), plus arrangement with a nearby car park. Considerable seasonal tariff reductions. Café open for breakfast and dinner. **Rooms 133.** *Closed 24-26 Dec. Amex, Diners, MasterCard,* **VISA**

| CORK | Jurys Hotel | 66% | £152 |

Tel 021 276622   Fax 021 274477   Map 2 B6   **H**
Western Road Cork Co Cork

Modern low-rise riverside hotel about half a mile from the centre of town on the Killarney road. Public areas include a choice of two bars, both with live music nightly: the convivial, pubby Corks Bar that is popular with locals and a cocktail bar with waterfall feature in the open-plan, split-level restaurant area. Decor in the well-kept bedrooms is gradually being changed from abstract to more appealing floral patterns with matching curtains and quilted bedcovers. TVs are multi-channel with the remote-controls rather annoyingly wired to the bedside units. Extras include fruit and mineral water. Good, well-lit bathrooms all have vanity units, sometimes in white marble, offering good shelf space. Children are very welcome; creche facilities are provided (summer only), as are extra beds and cots, with under-12s free if staying in parents' room. Room service is 24hr and beds are turned down at night. Conference and banqueting facilities for 700/520. No dogs. **Rooms 185.** *Garden, indoor & outdoor swimming pool, gym, sauna, spa bath, squash, outdoor play area. Coffee shop (7am-11pm, Sun 10pm). Closed 24-27 Dec. Amex, Diners, MasterCard,* **VISA**

| CORK | Lotamore House | 60% | £50 |

Tel 021 822344   Fax 021 822219   Map 2 B6   **A**
Tivoli Cork Co Cork

Once the home of the Cudmore family, a large house only a few minutes' drive from the city centre; set in four acres of mature gardens which soften the view over what is now a commercial harbour. Although not grand, the house was built on a large scale with airy bedrooms that have slightly dated but well-maintained bathrooms and are comfortably furnished to sleep three, with room for an extra bed or cot (no extra charge). A large drawing room has plenty of armchairs and an open fire and, although only breakfast and light meals are offered, *Flemings* restaurant (see entry) is next door. Conference facilities for up to 20. **Rooms 21.** *Garden. Closed 2 weeks Christmas. Amex, MasterCard,* **VISA**

We only recommend the food in hotels categorised as **HR** and **AR**.
However, the food in many **A** establishments throughout
Ireland is often very acceptable
(but the restaurant may not be open to non-residents).

CORK   Lovetts   £72

Tel 021 294909 Fax 021 508568   Map 2 B6   **R**
Churchyard Lane off Well Road Douglas Cork

♔ 》) ☕ ● ✍ ▯ V ♡

Dermod Lovett continues to make guests feel welcome in the cosy bar and
reception area of this well-established restaurant and to keep a close eye on
proceedings throughout. Margaret Lovett and Marie Harding's extensive and
carefully sourced menus for the main restaurant include a fixed-price dinner
which might offer hot black and white pudding terrine with onion and raisin
confit, a daily home-made soup (perhaps apple and pimpkin), then noisettes
of pork with rosemary and served with bread stuffing and a choice of dessert
(crème brulée, terrine of sorbets). A la carte might offer a warm salad of crispy
duck, Berehaven squid simmered in olive oil and garlic and served with garlic
soda bread, mussel and mushroom soup to start, following with breast of Barbary
duck served rare with spiced mulled pear sauce and fresh fish specialities like
kebab of monkfish with mushrooms and peppers and pan-fried salmon with
lemon sauce. The lunchtime fixed-price menu is particularly good value.
Separate vegetarian menu (£12 for two courses). Char-grills are the speciality in
the brasserie (open for dinner only), with limited but carefully selected regulars –
chicken, gammon, steak and salmon – cooked in front of diners and served with
salad and potatoes; limited starters/soups and desserts, plus a keen pricing policy
complete the formula. All the bread (wholemeal and traditional soda), tagliatelle
and chutneys are home-made and the use of home-grown herbs and unusual
vegetables like sea kale, kohlrabi and artichokes is commendable. Lighter snacks
served in the bar Mon-Fri at lunchtime only (soups, pasta, stir-fries, quiches,
casseroles). *Seats 45. Parties 14. Private Room 25. L 12.30-2 D 7-10. Closed L Sat,
all Sun, Bank Holidays, 1 week Christmas. Set L £14.50 Set D £24. Amex, Diners,
MasterCard,* **VISA**

CORK   Metropole Hotel   60%   £95

Tel 021 508122 Fax 021 506450   Map 2 B6   **H**
MacCurtain Street Cork Co Cork

On-going investment and refurbishment has given the 100-year-old 'Met' a
new lease of life. That the hotel is the epicentre of Cork's annual jazz festival is
reflected in the numerous photos and sketches of the stars who have performed
here displayed in the bar. By April 1997 all of the bedrooms will have been
completely refurbished, partly with dark-stained pine furniture (some retain the
old units revamped); they all have good bathrooms that are given a period feel
by the tiling, wood-panelled tub and generously sized, chunky wash basins.
Bedroom size and shape varies considerably and the view from some is a bit
grim. The best have views over the River Lee as it flows through the centre
of town. 24hr room service. Banqueting for 320, conference facilities for 500.
The Waterside Café has views over the swimming pool (part of the smart Leeside
leisure centre) and offers all-day snacks. No dogs. *Rooms 108. Indoor swimming
pool, splash pool, gym, sauna, solarium, steam room, beauty salon, creche. Amex,
Diners, MasterCard,* **VISA**

CORK   Morrisons Island Hotel   68%   £110

Tel 021 275858 Fax 021 275833   Map 2 B6   **H**
Morrisons Quay Cork Co Cork

Overlooking the River Lee, in Cork's business district, this 'all-suite' hotel –
in France it would be called a *hotel résidence* – is designed for the business person
with each suite having a separate lounge (with kitchenette): ideal for meetings
or entertaining. Actually four are junior suites (large rooms with separate sitting
area) without the kitchenette and there are four larger penthouse suites with
balconies and completely separate kitchens, two with two bedrooms. Decorwise

it's fairly simple with lightwood units in the bedrooms and darkwood in the sitting rooms with tweedy soft furnishings. Ten rooms are specially adapted for disabled guests. Downstairs there's a smart marble-floored lobby and cosy bar that with several sofas doubles as a lounge area. Room service is 24hr, as is porterage, and there is free secure parking. No dogs – kennels are provided. *Rooms 40. Closed 4 days at Christmas. Amex, Diners, MasterCard, **VISA***

CORK	Proby's Bistro	£40

Tel 021 316531 Fax 021 316523   Map 2 B6   **RR**
Proby's Quay Crosses Green Cork Co Cork

Quietly situated near St Finbarr's cathedral and the river, yet only a short walk from the main shopping area, this informal restaurant offers much to please, including patio tables with umbrellas for sunny days. Inside, a large space is divided between a gallery (which can be used for private parties) and the main ground-floor restaurant which has a feature fireplace, oil-clothed tables and bright Mediterranean-inspired decor, which suits the modern Italian-style food very well. Bruschetta, polenta, mixed-leaf salad with flavoured oils are typical dishes, with 'world' influences (houmus, satay) creeping in alongside the risottos and flat breads. Tasty fare, served with charm. *Seats 120. Parties 20. Private Room 25. Meals served 8am-10.30pm summer, 12-10 in winter (till 11 Fri & Sat all year). L 12-3 D 6-10. Closed 24-26 Dec. MasterCard, **VISA***

Rooms   **£40**
Deans Hall, next door to Proby's, is a student hall during the academic year but available for B&B or self-catering in summer. Units of various sizes (3-5 bedrooms) include a high proportion of single rooms; while quite simple, accommodation is in good order and each unit has a well-equipped, fitted kitchen. There's also a shared laundry facility, residents' sitting-room, bar and shop/deli on site. Breakfast is available at Proby's. Car parking (50 spaces). *Open mid Jun-mid Sep only.*

We publish annually, so make sure you use the current edition
– it's well worth being up-to-date!

CORK	Quay Co-op	

Tel 021 317026   Fax 021 317660   Map 2 B6   **JaB**
24 Sullivan's Quay Cork Co Cork

A former priest house by the River Lee near the city centre, this vegetarian restaurant occupies several period rooms on the two floors above a wholefood shop – the stairway walls acting as a notice-board for events and organisations in the city. Work by local artists features on the peach-coloured walls and there are bare board floors. From opening there's tea, coffee (including espresso), cakes and croissants until 12 noon when the self-service lunch counter opens. This features a selection of soups (perhaps cabbage, leek and almond or carrot and leek) served with organic wholemeal bread, pizzas, spinach, corn and pepper lasagne and daily specials like cashew nut and vegetable paella or baked aubergine fritters. For the sweet-toothed there's carrot cake, coffee almond cake and the like. From 7pm the mood changes and there is table service from a printed menu – Greek salad, vegetable curry, broccoli roulade and Caribbean casserole demonstrate the range. Children can have smaller portions at reduced prices; two high-chairs are provided for very junior diners. About a dozen wines are offered or you can bring your own for a £2 corkage charge. Two of the three rooms are no-smoking. *Seats 80. Parties 20. Open 9.30am-10.30pm (L 12-6 D 7-10.30). Closed Sun, 25 & 26 Dec, Good Friday, Easter Monday. MasterCard, **VISA***

CORK   Reidy's Wine Vaults

Tel 021 275751   Map 2 B6   **P**
Lancaster Quay Western Road Cork Co Cork

Imaginatively converted from a wine warehouse (and conveniently situated just opposite the entrance to *Jurys Hotel*), Reidy's is quite large and stylish, with vaulted ceilings, a minstrel's gallery housing country antiques, dark green and terracotta paintwork, traditional black-and-white tiles and a pleasing mixture of old and new furnishings. The focal point is the main bar fixture – a massive mahogany piece, complete with a London clock, bevelled mirrors, stained glass and all the original Victorian details. Bar food is prepared to a high standard by Noelle Reidy, starting with wholemeal brown bread and quiches baked on the premises in the early morning and with choices noted on the blackboard as the day progresses. The menu dishes might typically include fresh salmon, Irish stew, chicken curry, steak and kidney pie or lasagne, savoury pancakes (perhaps chicken and mushroom) and seafood platter. Sandwiches and home-made soup (vegetable made with a beefy stock) also available. *Open 10.30am-11.30pm (winter to 11), Sun 12.30-2, 4-11. **Bar Food** 10.30am-10pm. Closed Good Friday, 25 Dec. Amex, Diners, MasterCard,* **VISA**

CORK   Rochestown Park Hotel   67%   £101

Tel 021 892233   Fax 021 892178   Map 2 B6   **H**
Rochestown Road Douglas Cork Co Cork

Take the south ring road to Douglas and keep a sharp lookout for the hotel's signs (they're small and brown) to find the bright yellow building. Public rooms are in the original Georgian house, formerly a seminary for trainee priests and once home to the Lord Mayors of Cork, with bedrooms in modern extensions. Standard bedrooms have been designed with the business person very much in mind and have practical fitted furniture including a well-lit desk with a second phone. Extras include mineral water, bowl of fruit, mints and towelling robes in bathrooms that all boast bidets. 20 Executive rooms are very large and have spa baths. Public areas include comfortable sitting areas off the marble-floored lobby, a bar with rattan-furnished conservatory and a snug residents' bar for late-night drinkers. The hotel's pride and joy is a most impressive leisure centre that features a curving Romanesque swimming pool, a gym with high-tech exercise machines and a Thalassotherapy Centre using the sea's virtues 'to restore health and vitality'. Such is the demand among the corporate sector in Cork for good business facilities that the hotel is embarking on an £8 million expansion programme to be completed by July 1997. Rochestown Park will then boast a further 51 air-conditioned bedrooms (including a Presidential suite), and an 800-delegate international conference centre, complete with syndicate rooms, translation and audio-visual facilities. Seven acres of mature gardens are open to residents. Good weekend tariff reductions (£31 B&B per person). Children under 4 may share their parents' room at no charge (meals charged as taken). No dogs. ***Rooms** 63. Garden, fishing, indoor swimming pool, children's splash pool, gym, solarium, sauna, spa bath, steam room, hydro-massage pool, aerobics studio, thalassotherapy clinic. Amex, Diners, MasterCard,* **VISA**

CORK   Seven North Mall   £60

Tel 021 397191   Fax 021 300811   Map 2 B6   **A**
7 North Mall Cork Co Cork

This elegant house dating from 1750 belongs to the family of Cork city architect Neil Hegarty and is run by his wife, Angela, who offers guests tea on arrival. It's centrally situated on a tree-lined south-facing mall overlooking the River Lee. Rooms are all spacious, individually furnished in a pleasingly restrained style in keeping with the house itself and with bathrooms cleverly added to look as if they have always been there. Some rooms have river views and there is a ground-floor room especially designed for disabled guests. An additional three en suite rooms are due to be ready for the 1997 season. Excellent breakfasts. A nice touch is the personalised map of the city centre given to guests, which shows clearly restaurants, pubs, museums, galleries and theatres, mostly reassuringly near. No dogs and no under-12s overnight. *Rooms 5. Garden. Closed 18 Dec-6 Jan. MasterCard,* **VISA**

CORK	Travelodge	£48

Tel 021 310722 Fax 021 310707   Map 2 B6   **L**
Cork Co Cork

Spacious accommodation for two adequate space for a family of five at a room rate of £36.50 (£29.95 Nov-Apr) 1½ miles south of Cork city centre on the main airport road and 1 mile from it. Well-maintained, scrupulously clean pre-paid rooms (one equipped for the disabled) have neat bathrooms, tea/coffee making facilities, TV, radio/alarm. Pay phones in foyer and breakfast available in the adjacent Little Chef. *Rooms 40. Amex, Diners, MasterCard,* **VISA**

CORK   Places of Interest
Tourist Information Tel 021 273251
Church of St Francis Liberty Street Tel 021 270302
Cork City Gaol Tel 021 305022
Cork Heritage Centre Tel 021 358854
Cork Airport Tourist Information Freephone at Airport Terminal
Crawford School of Art and Gallery Emmet Place Tel 021 966777
Everyman Palace MacCurtain Street Tel 021 501673
GAA Athletic Grounds Pairc Chaoimh Tel 021 963311
Jameson Heritage Centre Midleton Tel 021 613594
Opera House Emmet Place Tel 021 270022
The Queenstown Story Cobh Tel 021 813591/5
Royal Gunpowder Mills Ballincolig Tel 021 874430
St Finbarre's Cathedral Sharman Crawford Street Tel 021 963387
St Colman's Cathedral Cobh Tel 021 813222
Triskell Arts Centre off South Main Street Tel 021 272022
University College Walking Tours Tel 021 276871

Historic Houses, Castles and Gardens
Blarney Castle, House and Gardens Tel 021 385252
Dunkathel Glanmire Tel 021 821014 *4 miles*
Riverstown House Glanmire Tel 021 821205 *4 miles*
Fota Wildlife Park Carrigtwohill nr Cobh Tel 021 812678

COURTMACSHERRY	Courtmacsherry Hotel	60%	£63

Tel 023 46198 Fax 023 46137   Map 2 B6   **H**
Courtmacsherry Co Cork

Family-run by Terry and Carole Adams since 1974, this unpretentious, homely hotel, formerly the summer residence of the Earl of Shannon, offers simple comfort and a relaxed atmosphere right by the side of Courtmacsherry Bay. Public areas are quite spacious, if a little dated and, although on the small side, all bedrooms have TV and direct-dial phones and most are now en suite. Traditional family holiday activities are well catered for, with boats and bikes available nearby, lawn tennis in the grounds and also Carole Adams' riding school where many children happily spend most of their holiday time. Accommodation is also available in eight self-catering modern, two-storey 'cottages', furnished to a high standard. *Rooms 11. Garden, riding, tennis. Closed Oct-Easter. MasterCard,* **VISA**

CRINKLE   The Thatch   £50

Tel 0509 20682 Fax 0509 21847
Crinkle Birr Co Offaly

Map 2 C4   **R/P**

Just outside Birr in the village of Crinkle, this characterful little thatched pub and restaurant is well worth seeking out. Under the energetic management of owner Des Connole since 1991, the restaurant was cleverly added a couple of years ago and head chef James McDonnell has succeeded in drawing eager diners from a wide area. Five-course dinner menus are changed weekly but might include starters such as a hearty country terrine of wild rabbit with a fruit compote, imaginative soups (beetroot) served with home-baked bread – and main courses like poached salmon on a bed of creamed cabbage with smoked salmon, cassoulet of lamb with summer vegetables, or a simple sirloin steak. Vegetables are bountiful, desserts wholesome. There's also an à la carte menu and a tempting bar food menu. Sunday lunch is a speciality, attracting two sittings. *Seats 40. Parties 24.* **Bar Meals** *12.30-2.30 Mon-Sat & 4-7 Tue-Sat. L (Sun only) 12.30 & 2.30 D Tue-Sat 6.30-9. Set Sun L £10.50 Set D £17.95. Closed Good Friday & 25 Dec. Restaurant closed D Sun & Mon (& Tue Oct-May). Diners, MasterCard,* **VISA**

CROOKHAVEN   Journey's End   £70

Tel 028 35183
Crookhaven Co Cork

Map 2 A6   **R**

Ina Manahan has been running this tiny waterside cottage restaurant for 21 summers now -and, like the swallow, invariably turns tail and heads for warmer climes at the end of August. A cosy sitting-room with an open fire welcomes arriving guests, who then squeeze past the kitchen to the attractive little dining-room and conservatory with sea views. Seafood is the order of the day, with a sprinkling of local cheese dishes – warm goat's cheese grilled with pesto or deep-fried Brie with kiwi fruit and Cumberland sauce – and maybe a duck confit salad. Seafood specialities include a superb pale, home-made gravad lax cut into big, thin slices, and main courses like wild Crookhaven salmon wrapped in sorrel leaves, monkfish medallions with a lobster sauce; other, simpler dishes such as black sole on the bone or plainly cooked fillet of turbot are successful due to the tip-top quality of the ingredients. Also look out for a lovely beef dish of fillet steak marinated in teriyaki sauce then chargrilled. Imaginative side dishes might include red cabbage with cumin and mixed-leaf and fresh herb salads brightened with nasturtium flowers. Good desserts (loganberry pavlova, perhaps, or ice cream terrine), a well-balanced cheese plate or freshly-brewed cafetière coffee to finish. Service (under the management of Peter Manford for the last fifteen years) runs smoothly. *Seats 26. Parties 8. Private Room 8. D only 7-9. Closed Sun & Sep-end May. MasterCard,* **VISA**

CROOKHAVEN   O'Sullivan's

Tel 028 35200
Crookhaven Co Cork

Map 2 A6   **P**

One of the most popular traditional pubs in Ireland, sited beside the delightful little sandy-beached harbour at 'Crook'. O'Sullivan's has been family-run for 20 years and nowadays it's run by Billy and Angela O'Sullivan, who somehow successfully combines the function of providing a proper local for the lobster fishermen and the kind of pub dreams are made of for families on holiday. The stone-flagged bar is practical for sandy feet and parents can easily keep an eye on castle-builders when the tide is right. Angela looks after the food herself, making soups and chowders (perhaps chicken and vegetable or seafood chowder), bread and good, simple dishes based on local seafood – fresh and smoked salmon, smoked mackerel, crab or shrimp – toasted ham sandwiches and more-ish home-made ices, apple and rhubarb crumble or chocolate biscuit cake. Six tables are almost on the water's edge. Live music most nights in summer. Next door, the Welcome Inn (028 35319) is under the same ownership (but leased out) and has a restaurant in summer (June, July & August) plus two self-contained apartments to let (not inspected). *Open 10.30-11.30 (to 11 in winter), Sun 12.30-2, 4-11.* **Bar Food** *10.30-9 (Sun 12-2 & 4-9). Closed Monday afternoons in winter (Nov-Apr). No credit cards.*

CROOKHAVEN   Places of Interest
Mizen Head Signal Station Visitor Centre Goleen Tel 028 35225

CROOM	The Mill Race	£50

Tel 061 397130 Fax 061 397199   Map 2 B5   **R**
Croom Mills Croom Co Limerick

A few miles outside Limerick on the N20 to Cork, Croom Mills demonstrates vividly the life story of a country watermill and the community it served, but, whether or not you have time to visit the exhibition, the Mill Race Restaurant is worthy of a special stop. Wholesome home-cooked food is the order of the day, an array of salads, cold meats, quiches, freshly-baked breads and desserts all laid out in a self-service, daytime display cabinet. In the evening, three days a week all year round, Mary Hayes subtly changes the atmosphere of the warm-toned, wood-filled room to provide a slightly more formal setting for chef Patrick Rahilly's short à la carte and 'flavour of Ireland' three-course dinner menus, with starters like Clonakilty black pudding with raspberry and clove sauce, followed by Irish stew, with 'baker's bread' and croutons, then a rich porter cake with Guinness and fudge sauce. The carte perhaps offers a more sophisticated choice, but real home-cooked food is what it's all about and baking is a particular strength. **Seats 65. Meals served 8am-6pm. L 12.30-2.30 D (Thu-Sat only) 7.30-9.30. Closed D Sun-Wed, Good Friday & 25 Dec-2 Jan. Set L £13.95/£15.95 (Sun £8.50). MasterCard, VISA**

CROSSHAVEN	Cronin's Bar	

Tel 021 831829 Fax 021 832243   Map 2 B6   **P**
Crosshaven Co Cork

'The lovely pub that's full of nautical stuff' is how people tend to describe Cronin's – and so it is. Situated at the far end of the village, beside the boatyard, Cronin's has been in the family for a quarter of a century and has been run by Sean Cronin and his wife Thecla since 1980. It's a traditional, welcoming, cosy kind of place – ideal for tucking into some of Thecla's good home cooking in the bar or, perhaps, in the little back room which is sometimes set up more like a dining-room. Plans for this 'restaurant' side of things were under review at the time of going to press, but you can be sure of good, wholesome food one way or another. *Open 10-30am-11.30pm (till 11 in winter), Sun 12.30-2, 4-11.* **Bar Food** *12-7 (no food Sun). Closed Good Friday & 25 Dec. MasterCard, VISA*

CROSSMOLINA	Enniscoe House	£96

Tel 096 31112   Fax 096 31773   Map 3 B3   **A**
Castlehill nr Crossmolina Ballina Co Mayo

Generations of the same family have lived here at this Georgian mansion – 'the last great house of North Mayo' – on the shores of Lough Conn. The mature woodland, antique furniture and family portraits all contribute to today's enjoyment of Irish hospitality and country house life. The current owner, Susan Kellett, has established a Research and Heritage Centre in converted yard buildings behind the house. One service offered by the Centre is tracing family histories. The main bedrooms have four-posters or canopied beds, private bathrooms and fine views of parkland and lake. Standard rooms are £84 in low season and de luxe rooms £108 in high season. An organic market garden supplies all the vegetables to the house; dinner is available to non-residents (£25). No dogs. Lough Conn is renowned for good brown trout fishing (Feb–Sep) and spring salmon fishing; the hotel has its own landing stage, boats and Ghillies. *Rooms 6. Garden, game fishing. Closed 14 Oct–end Mar. Amex, MasterCard,* **VISA**

CULDAFF   McGuinness's

Tel 077 79116
Culdaff Inishowen Co Donegal

Map 1 C1

P

Just the kind of place the traveller might hope to happen upon, this traditional country pub has been in the McGuinness family for generations (albeit some under different names) and always has a welcoming turf fire burning in the public bar. This is simply furnished in a pleasant way with plain furniture, old prints, plates and notices of local interest. Next door, a comfortable lounge bar has great appeal, with homely chintzy sofas, cushioned chairs and a nice old-fashioned conservatory on the back of the pub with a few more tables leading on to the small back garden. Food requirements other than very simple snacks are dealt with in a practical way – by telephoning orders to the village restaurant, which is under the same ownership. The bar also acts as an off-licence, so a variety of wines can be served by the glass. Well-behaved children are welcome during the day, but they "must be kept under control". *Open 10.30-11.30 (from 1pm Sep-Easter, till 11 in winter), Sun 12.30-2, 4-11. Closed Good Friday, 25 Dec. Garden. No credit cards.*

DALKEY   The Queens

Tel 01 285 4569   Fax 01 285 8345
Castle Street Dalkey Co Dublin

Map 2 D4

P

One of South Dublin's most famous pubs, The Queens is a characterful and extremely professionally-run operation, with open fires, old pine and whiskey jars creating atmosphere and friendly, efficient staff dispensing the good food and drink which has earned it so many awards. The bar menu features sandwiches (closed or open), ploughman's salads, paté and a very popular seafood chowder and garlicky mussels. Sunday brunch fry-up. There's also an Italian restaurant, *La Romana* (and a sister pub in Budapest!). *Open 12-11.30 (to 11 in winter), Sun 12-11. Bar Food 12-6 (Sun brunch menu 12-3). Restaurant Meals 5.30-11.30 (11 in winter), 5-10 Sun. Front and back patios. Closed Good Friday, 25 Dec. Amex, Diners, MasterCard,* **VISA**

DELGANY   Delgany Inn   £50

Tel & Fax 01 287 5701
Delgany Co Wicklow

Map 2 D4

IR

Very pleasing inn with two comfortable bars each side of the front door (one, with a gas coal-effect fire, is more of a lounge than the other) and, behind them, a simply-furnished but stylish modern restaurant decorated with warm Mediterranean colours. This leads into a bright semi-conservatory; a barbecue area and garden are accessible from both the bar and restaurant, with ample sturdy tables and seating. Modest, comfortable accommodation is offered in two styles of well-equipped bedrooms (phone, TV, tea/coffee facilities). Front rooms are quite spacious with both a double and single bed, attractively decorated with old-style furniture and en suite bathroom; those rooms at the back include two good-sized family rooms with a cot and have simple, modern furniture and showers. *Rooms 12. Garden. Closed 24 & 25 Dec. Access,* **VISA**

See over

Restaurant at the Inn   £40

Both restaurant and bar food are based firmly around good local ingredients, typically in a speciality starter such as smoked loin of Wicklow lamb (from a traditional butcher and cold-smoked) or fish fresh from Greystones harbour – perhaps grilled ray with caper butter – or, just like real home-cooking, chicken breast with a herb stuffing and a red wine gravy. Vegetables are simple and perfectly cooked, and there are good, classic desserts. The hallmarks are simple, creative cooking with refreshingly direct flavours. *Seats 60. Parties 12. Private Room 40. L 12.30-3 D 7-10. Closed D Mon (all year) & Tue (winter).*

DELGANY	Glenview Hotel	65%	£125

Tel 01 287 3399   Fax 01 287 7511   Map 2 D4   **H**
Glen o' the Downs Delgany Co Wicklow

Nestling beneath Sugarloaf Mountain, with 30 acres of gardens and dramatic views of the Glen o' the Downs, the Glenview is certainly benefitting from the major on-going refurbishment programme. The building encompasses a conference area with state-of-the-art facilities (catering for up to 200) at one end and extra bedrooms at the other (future plans include building a further 30 bedrooms). Well-equipped bedrooms come in two styles of decor: mahogany and pastel shades or pine with floral patterns. All rooms have tea/coffee-making facilities, hairdryer and trouser press as standard; 24hr room service. Children under 3 stay free in parents' room. Top of the range are two suites and a further two mini-suites. The leisure centre now boasts a children's splash pool beside the 18m swimming pool, an 'underwater air lounge' with a sofa that has massaging jets and makes good use of the scenic views. Upstairs you can work out in the gym while also taking in the splendour of the Glen. No dogs *Actons Hotel* in Kinsale, Co Cork is a sister hotel. *Rooms 43. Garden, indoor swimming pool, children's splash pool, sauna, steam room, spa bath, solarium, gym, games room, children's indoor playroom, aerobics studio. Closed 25 Dec. Amex, Diners, MasterCard, VISA*

We endeavour to be as up-to-date as possible but inevitably some changes to owners, chefs and other key staff occur after this Guide has gone to press.

DINGLE	Bambury's Guest House	£40

Tel 066 51244   Fax 066 51786   Map 2 A5   **A**
Mail Road Dingle Co Kerry

This highly-regarded, purpose-built guesthouse is easily spotted on the way into Dingle and only a couple of minutes' walk from the town centre. Spick and span from top to bottom, the bedrooms are both spacious – six with both double and single beds (plus room for an extra one if required) – and comfortable, with phone, satellite TV, hairdryer and neat en suite bathrooms. Bernie Bambury cooks a mean breakfast – griddle cakes with fresh fruit and honey are a speciality and vegetarian breakfasts are offered by arrangement. It's one of the few guest houses to remain open all year, including Christmas. Children welcome: under-5s may stay free in their parents' room; no cot provided. No dogs. *Rooms 12. Garden. MasterCard, VISA*

Set menu prices may not include service or wine.
Our guide price for two diners includes wine and service.

DINGLE   Beginish Restaurant   †   £58

Tel 066 51588   Fax 066 51591   Map 2 A5   **R**
Green Street Dingle Co Kerry

John and Pat Moore's airy, high-ceilinged restaurant takes its name from one of the nearby Blanket Islands and is elegantly appointed, with two main rooms leading into a conservatory that overlooks a lovely garden, floodlit at night. The most striking decorative feature of the restaurant is a large oil painting in an unusual gilt frame (thereby hangs a tale which John is happy to recount), but the main attraction is definitely Pat's talent and dedication in the kitchen. Seafood stars on the à la carte menu: in starters like a Cromane mussels with creamy garlic sauce, fish chowder or feuillete of smoked haddock; and in main courses such as steamed cod with herbs, spicy tomato and ravioli, medallions of monkfish with a herb crust and provençale sauce, or lobster, proudly proffered before cooking, perfectly cooked and served, perhaps, in a cognac, cream and herb sauce. There's a wider choice of meat and fowl than found in many seafood restaurants – perhaps loin of lamb with rosemary and garlic jus and fillet of beef with pepper sauce, rösti and onion purée, and a daily vegetarian special. Bread and vegetables are outstanding; an aromatic dish of no less than seven vegetables stir-fried in sesame oil is a harmonious mix of singingly fresh ingredients and sound cooking. Desserts have always been a great strength, too, notably chocolate roulade with fruit coulis, sticky toffee puddingwith butterscotch sauce, and a selection of home-made ices in a particularly good tuile. Irish and French farmhouse cheeses, served plated, and excellent coffee, tea or herbal infusions to round off a meal that features some of the country's best cooking. *Seats 50. Private Room 18. D 6-10.*
Closed Mon & mid Nov-Mar. Amex, Diners, MasterCard, **VISA**

DINGLE   Cleevaun Country House   £43

Tel & Fax 066 51108   Map 2 A5   **A**
Lady's Cross Milltown Dingle Co Kerry

Charlotte and Sean Cluskey provide excellent accommodation and hospitality at their modern house, which is just outside the town on the Slea Head road, with views over Dingle Bay. Good-sized, comfortably-furnished bedrooms have orthopaedic beds, telephone, hairdryer, satellite TV, clock/radio, fruit bowl and stylish bathrooms. Shared tea/coffee-making facilities are provided in the hall and there's access to the garden. Guests can relax in a comfortable sitting-room. Charlotte's famous breakfasts, served in a bright, south-facing dining-room, include pancakes, muffins, farmhouse cheese and fruit as well as the traditional cooked breakfast. Not suitable for children under 10 except for under-3s who may share their parents' room free of charge in the cot provided. No dogs.
Rooms 9. Garden. Closed mid Nov-mid Mar. MasterCard, **VISA**

DINGLE   Dick Mack's

Tel 066 51960   Map 2 A5   **P**
Green Lane Dingle Co Kerry

Amazingly unspoilt shop-bar, once a cobbler's, now selling modern leather items and wellington boots. Run by Dick's son Oliver J MacDonnell, the bar is basic with bench seating, bar stools and no pretensions – it's a wonderful part of all that Dingle has to offer. The cashier's booth remains as a very snug 'snug' and all is as it should be. *Open 10.30-11.30 (till 11 in winter) Sun 12-2.30, 4-11. Closed Good Friday & 25 Dec. No credit cards.*

| DINGLE | Dingle Skellig Hotel | 61% | £115 |

Tel 066 5114 Fax 066 51501   Map 2 A5   **H**
Dingle Co Kerry

Pleasant, practical and comfortable behind its unprepossessing 60s' facade, the
Dingle Skellig is a popular place with families on holiday. Children are very
well looked after, and there's also plenty to keep grown-ups active and amused.
The sea views are quite a feature, and there's special anti-glare glass in the
conservatory restaurant. Bedrooms are of a reasonable size, with several designated
for family occupation. On-going refurbishment has seen 32 bedrooms upgraded
in the past year with a further 40 rooms to be revamped for Spring 1997 (also
the completion date for the new conference (200)/leisure centre). 24hr room
service. No dogs. *Rooms 115. Garden, indoor swimming pool, children's splash pool,
tennis, gym, steam room, solarium, beauty salon, outdoor play area, games room,
snooker, deep-sea fishing. Closed mid Nov-mid Mar. Amex, Diners, MasterCard,*
VISA

We welcome bona fide complaints and recommendations on
the tear-out Readers' Comments pages at the back of the Guide.
They are followed up by our professional team.

| DINGLE | Doyle's Seafood Bar | | £65 |

Tel 066 51174 Fax 066 51816   Map 2 A5   **RR**
4 John Street Dingle Co Kerry

A leading restaurant in the area for a long time now, John and Stella Doyle
established their charming, informal seafood restaurant in the 70s and, despite
the introduction of strong local competition in recent years, they still retain a
special niche. On entering, there's a proper little bar with high stools (and many
interesting bottles on the shelves), low-ceilinged cottagey rooms with stone-
flagged floors and sugan chairs creating a cosy, easy-going atmosphere which is
nicely-balanced by a bright 'indoor garden' feature at the back. Stella's overall
approach in the kitchen is fairly classical with familiar starters such as hot
haddock smokies and seafood sausage with honey mustard sauce on Puy lentils
regularly featuring. While all are good, one or two specialities seem to leap off
the plate with their freshness and exuberance; one such dish is the millefeuille
of warm oysters with Guinness sauce (winner of our Seafood Dish of the Year
award last year): a perfectly concocted dish of gently heated oysters in a
wonderfully silky, yeasty-toned sauce, topped by a featherlight wisp of pastry –
enough to win over the most reluctant oyster-taster). Main courses (all seafood
except for a token rack of Kerry lamb) are deliberately understated, depending
for their success on the sheer quality and freshness of the fish; typical dishes
might include roast fillet of turbot with red onion marmalade, grilled raywing
with a warm coriander vinaigrette, and baked lemon sole with lobster sauce.
Lovely desserts include baked chocolate and vanilla cheesecake, vanilla terrine
with berries, or a selection of Irish farmhouse cheeses. Good-value early evening
3-course menu (£14.50). Delicious home-made breads. An Irish coffee might
just top a quintessential Irish seafood informal dining experience. 10% service
charge is added to the final bill. *Seats 50. Parties 8. D only 6-9. Closed Sun &
mid Nov-mid Mar. Set D (6-7pm) £14.50. Diners, MasterCard, VISA*

Rooms   **£72**

Accommodation is offered in eight generously-sized bedrooms that are
comfortably furnished, some with a sofa bed for a third person, all with phone,
TV and en suite bathroom facilities. Extra beds and cots available for children;
under-4s stay free. No dogs.

DINGLE — Greenmount House — £60

Tel 066 51414   Fax 066 51974   Map 2 A5   **A**
Gortonora Dingle Co Kerry

Convenient to Dingle yet high enough to command lovely views of the harbour and across the bay to the mountains beyond, John and Mary Curran's meticulously-maintained modern guesthouse makes an exceptional base from which to visit the area. Spacious, imaginatively designed mini-suites added last year have their own entrance/balcony and are well designed for comfort with generous seating areas and good amenities that include fridges, although bathrooms are relatively small and cramped. Public areas include a comfortable residents' sitting-room and a conservatory where guests can take in the view while enjoying the excellent breakfasts for which the Currans are renowned. At the time of going to press it was anticipated that some of the older rooms (which are smaller and attract a lower tariff) would be upgraded for the 1997 season. Room service available for breakfast (8-9). No children under 8. No dogs. *Rooms 12. Garden. Closed 22-27 Dec. MasterCard,* **VISA**

DINGLE — The Half Door — £55

Tel 066 51600   Fax 066 51883   Map 2 A5   **R**
John Street Dingle Co Kerry

Cosy and welcoming, with a genuine cottage atmosphere enhanced by exposed stone walls, copper pots and original white tiles around the chimney breast. There's a sunny conservatory area to the rear. Denis O'Connor's menu majors on seafood, so the choice varies with the season and the catch. Shellfish cocktail, steamed mussels, or sautéed oysters masked with a chive sauce could be your starter, followed perhaps by grilled brill, boiled lobster or fillet of plaice with mustard sauce. Good, simple sweets. Early Bird menu (6-6.30pm) offering choice of six starters, five main courses and four desserts is good value at £15.50. *Seats 50. Parties 14. Private Room 20. L 12.30-2.30 D 6-10. Closed Tue & early Nov-early Mar. Amex, Diners, MasterCard,* **VISA**

DINGLE — James Flahive

Tel 066 51634   Map 2 A5   **P**
The Quay Dingle Co Kerry

Down by the harbour near the marina, this comfortable, welcoming and most friendly of pubs has been run by James and Peggy Flahive for 30 years. It dates back to the 1890s when it opened as a tailor's shop and has long been a great favourite of sailing people. Photographs of distinguished visitors adorn the walls but none is more proudly displayed than that of Dingle Bay's best-loved resident, Fungie the dolphin. No food, but you're assured of a good pint of Guinness. The loo is in the back yard. *Open 10.30am-11.30pm (to 11 in winter), Sun 12-2 & 4-11. No credit cards.*

DINGLE — Lord Baker's Bar & Restaurant — £65

Tel 066 51277   Fax 066 521174   Map 2 A5   **R/P**
Main Street Dingle Co Kerry

Tom Baker — businessman, councillor, auctioneer, poet and director of the Tralee-Dingle railway (and affectionately known as Lord Baker) — acquired these premises in 1890 and traded as a general supplier and function caterer; it has developed into a popular and thriving restaurant and bar, now run by John Moriarty. Locally-made tapestries are an eye-catching display in the main eating area, beyond which is a conservatory extension leading into the garden. The full restaurant menu and the less formal bar menu offer similar choices, with particularly good seafood. On the bar menu one can sample home-made seafood soup, Kerry oysters with a glass of Guinness, Dingle Bay smoked salmon and capers, crab claws in garlic butter; more elaborate restaurant dishes might include baked hot crab au gratin, pan-fried lemon sole with lemon butter, wild salmon with hollandaise, loin of lamb with rosemary, and prime steaks. Sunday lunch (£12) is always popular. *Seats 65. Parties 20. L 12.30-2.30 D 6-9.30. Closed 24 & 25 Dec. Set D £18.90 (+£15 in summer). Amex, Diners, MasterCard,* **VISA**

DINGLE   Milltown House   £60

Tel 066 51372   Fax 066 51095   Map 2 A5   **A**
Dingle Co Kerry

In a unique waterside location on the western edge of Dingle, with views of the harbour framed by distant mountains and lawns sweeping down to the shore, John and Angela Gill's attractive guesthouse understandably attracts a high proportion of returning guests. Public areas include an informal reception room, a comfortably furnished sitting-room with plenty of armchairs and also a breakfast room, which includes a conservatory that is considerately reserved for guests who do not have views from their bedrooms. Breakfast is quite a feature and daily specials such as omelettes or kedgeree are always offered. Rooms vary somewhat in size and outlook, but include two with private patios and one designed for wheelchair-users; all are comfortable and prettily furnished to a high standard and attention to detail includes individual decor based around Angela's growing collection of patchwork quilts. Bathrooms also vary, but are thoughtfully planned with differing tiling schemes. Room service available for breakfast (8.30-9.30). There are horse stables on site and riding holidays are popular. *Rooms 10. Garden, equestrian centre, small gift shop. Closed mid Nov-mid Mar. MasterCard,* **VISA**

DINGLE   O'Flaherty's

Tel 066 51983   Map 2 A5   **P**
Bridge Street Dingle Co Kerry

Large square room, high-ceilinged, with flagstones, a stove, barrel tables, an old piano and masses of old shelving for a collection of antique signs, advertisements, poetry and local bric-a-brac. Traditional Irish music is the main attraction, with regular sessions in summer (nightly May-Sep), other impromptu sessions and occasional bursts from multi-instrumentalist landlord Fergus O'Flaherty. Access to the harbour from the back of the bar. No food. *Open 10.30am-11.30pm, Sun 12-2, 4-11. Closed Good Friday, 25 Dec. No credit cards.*

DINGLE   The Old Merchant

Tel 066 51458   Map 2 A5   **JaB**
The Harbour Dingle Co Kerry

Right down beside the marina, John and Pauline Dillon's jaunty little restaurant offers lively fresh flavours in informal surroundings. Starters might include fresh Atlantic seafood salad with sweet pepper dressing, or sautéed garlic mushrooms with herb mayonnaise, while main courses have a choice of five sauces with freshly-made pasta, also suggested 'simply natural with virgin olive oil and parmesan', home-made pizza or a fresh fish dish of the day. Tempting sweets tend towards the bawdy in 'The Merchant's Tart' and a 'chocolate fetishist's fantasy cake'! High-chair provided for little ones. The more formal *Waterside Restaurant* (066 51458 – also in Dingle) is under the same ownership. *Seats 40. Parties 8. Open 10.30-10 (L 11.45-3.30, D 6-10). Closed Oct-Apr. MasterCard,* **VISA**

DINGLE — Tigh Mhaire de Barra

Tel 066 51215
The Pier Head Dingle Co Kerry

Map 2 A5

P

Since 1989, when Dubliners Mhaire de Barra and Pat Leahy opted out of the rat race for the "easy" life in Dingle, they've hardly had a day off between them, but have built up a great reputation for this harbourside pub (its name translates as 'the house of Mary'). Unpretentiously comfortable, without the olde-world charm of some other establishments in the area but, instead, the solid attractions of real hospitality, good food and music – music sessions nightly in Jun–Oct (Wed, Fri & Sat in winter) may curtail food service. Dingle Bay chowder with freshly-baked bread, local seafood specials, traditional dishes like Irish stew and shepherd's pie are typical lunchtime fare, while evening meals include a further range of hot main courses, including, cod, monkfish and T-bone steaks. Visit off-season if you can – once the tourists start to disappear, the famous Dingle mutton pies (made with suet pastry to an old recipe) return to the menu, much to the delight of hungry locals. *Open 10.30-11.30 (to 11 in winter), Sun 12-2.30, 4-11.* **Bar Food** *10.30-11 (L 12.30-3.30 D 6.30-9.30. Closed Good Friday, 25 Dec. No credit cards.*

If you encounter bad service don't wait to write to us but make your feelings known to the management at the time of your visit. Instant compensation can often resolve any problem that might otherwise leave a bad taste.

DINGLE — The Waterside

£60

Tel 066 51458
Dingle Co Kerry

Map 2 A5

R

On the harbour, just beside the entrance to the marina, John and Pauline Dillon's friendly restaurant starts off each day (from 10am) with a dashing array of cakes, pastries and freshly-baked scones that can be enjoyed in the conservatory area overlooking the harbour. By lunchtime the repertoire has extended to include a good selection of savoury dishes like home-made soups served with freshly-baked brown bread, chicken liver paté with home-made pickles and salad, dressed crab, smoked salmon and salad platters or a warm salad of poached salmon, followed by Irish cheeses and home-made ices. John's kitchen is in full swing for dinner when you might find classic Caesar salad or roast duck confit served with a small, gingered orange salad, pot-roast pork on a cassolette of pulses with a whiskey sauce or steamed monkfish and mussels with Thai spices and crispy vegetables. Puddings (also served with morning coffee) include specialities such as sticky toffee pudding and a truly wicked 'chocolate cake', a many-layered confection of different chocolate styles and textures. Four tables are set on a patio in fine weather. The informal restaurant, *The Old Merchant* (just in front of The Waterside) is under the same ownership (see entry). **Seats** *45. Parties 8. Private Room 16. Open 10-5.30 L 12.30-3 (Sun to 4) D 6.30-10.30. Closed Tue & Oct-Mar. Set D £23.*

DINGLE   Places of Interest
Tourist Information Tel 066 51188
Great Blasket Island Heritage Centre Tel 066 56444/6

DOOLIN	Aran View House Hotel	60%	£70

Tel 065 74061   Fax 065 74540   Map 2 B4   **H**
Doolin Co Clare

Just outside Doolin and, true to its name, with dramatic sea views across to the
Aran islands, this neat hotel has been run by the Linnane family for 20 years and
provides a good base for a family holiday (it's only a mile to a good beach),
sea-angling, golf (7 miles) or touring. Comfortable public rooms include a bar
that provides for all weathers, with both the view and an open fire. Bedrooms
vary considerably in size and outlook due to the age and nature of the building;
recently refurbished rooms at the front are the most desirable (several at the back
have no view but are otherwise pleasant), nevertheless, all have phone, TV and
private bath and/or shower – some have a shower only, with a wash-basin in the
room. No dogs indoors, but kennels provided. *Rooms 19. Garden. Closed*
Nov-mid Mar. Amex, Diners, MasterCard, **VISA**

DOOLIN	The Lazy Lobster	£45

Tel 065 74390   Map 2 B4   **R**
Doolin Co Clare

Just on the edge of Doolin village, Anne Hughes's pretty, unpretentious little
cottage restaurant has cheerful oilcloth-covered tables in two rooms – an inner
one with an old range and a bright, semi-conservatory area for non-smokers.
The simple menu includes a few daily specials (leek and potato soup, for
instance, served with freshly-baked bread and little pottery dishes of butter), a
vegetarian dish of the day, a chicken dish and pan-fried steak. However, it is
seafood that is the main attraction – notably lobster (a blackboard in the hall lists
those available, with their exact weights), of course, cooked to order and served
simply with a choice of garlic or herb butters, delicious local spuds and a choice
of hot vegetables or a really good side salad. Tempting desserts include specialities like irresistible cappuccino meringues served with a chocolate sauce.
Children welcome, high-chairs available. *Seats 38. Parties 10. Private Room 18.*
D only 6-9.30. Closed Sun during Apr, May & Oct, all Nov-Mar. MasterCard, **VISA**

DOOLIN	O'Connor's Pub

Tel 065 74168   Fax 065 74668   Map 2 B4   **P**
Doolin Co Clare

Right down in Doolin village, near the harbour (where ferries leave for the
Aran island, but it is not scenic), O'Connor's pub is the main reason many people
visit Doolin. Traditional music sessions are held every night from 9 o'clock, but
it's a pleasant pub in the daytime, too, with helpful staff, interesting local memorabilia and good home-cooked food to offset the vagaries of an Irish summer.
Expect simple soups (chowder, mixed vegetable) and local mussels served with
crusty home-baked soda bread, main courses such as beef in Guinness, wild
Doolin salmon or pan-fried breast of chicken and then a slice of apple pie or a
mug of freshly-brewed coffee to finish. They also have B&B accommodation in
Daly's House just up behind the pub: it's simple, but comfortable and inexpensive,
with en suite showers, hairdryers, TV room and a warm welcome. *Open 10-11.30*
7 days. **Bar Food** *12-9.30 7 days.* **Accommodation** *4 bedrooms, £34 double.*
Closed Good Friday & 25 Dec. No credit cards.

DONEGAL   St Ernan's House Hotel   70%   £124

Tel 073 21065   Fax 073 22098   Map 1 B2   **HR**
Donegal Town Co Donegal

Utter tranquillity is the main attraction of Brian and Carmel O'Dowd's secluded hotel on its own wooded tidal island across a causeway just two miles from Donegal Town. Arriving up the covered stone entrance steps, with original Victorian glazing and lots of pot plants, is rather like going through a time capsule – once inside the foyer at the top, the pressures of modern life fall away and the deep peacefulness of the island and the gentle hospitality of its owners begins to work its magic. Well-proportioned rooms have log fires and antique furniture and each of the spacious, individually decorated bedrooms has telephone, television and an en suite bathroom (all with showers) while most also have beautiful views of the sea and surrounding countryside. Not suitable for children under six. No dogs. Low season tariff starts at £110; high season tariff for seven 'superior' rooms is £144. An optional service charge is added to the bill. *Rooms 12. Garden, woodland walks. Closed Nov-Easter. MasterCard,* **VISA**

Restaurant   £65

Although mainly intended for resident guests, Gabrielle Doyle's 5-course country house style dinner menu is available to non-residents if there is room in the no-smoking dining-room. Local produce is used to good effect on well-balanced menus that offer the likes of hot baked goat's cheese in filo with blackberry coulis, celery and blue cheese soup, roast guinea fowl with toasted shallots and hazelnut sauce, and an iced chestnut parfait with passion fruit coulis (or Irish cheeses); vegetarian dishes on request. *Seats 24. Parties 6. D only 6.30-8.30. Set D £26.*

DONEGAL   Places of Interest
Tourist Information Tel 073 21148

DONEGAL TOWN   Ardnamona House   £90

Tel 073 22650   Fax 073 22819   Map 1 B2   **A**
Lough Eske Donegal Town Co Donegal

Beautifully situated in outstanding gardens overlooking Lough Eske, the secluded position of this attractive, rambling house belies its close proximity to Donegal Town. Front bedrooms are en suite and most desirable, with lovely views over the lough to the mountains beyond. Two rooms have their own private bathrooms (not en suite)and attract a tariff of £70. All rooms are individually decorated with private bathrooms; they have a peaceful outlook through rhododendrons and azaleas which have received international acclaim (the garden is now designated a National Heritage Garden). It is truly a gardener's paradise (with a garden trail, guide leaflet and all plants labelled) with miles of serene walks through ancient oak forests full of mosses and ferns; in addition fishing is available on a lake (by permit only). No smoking. No dogs. *Rooms 5. Garden. Closed end Oct-early Feb. MasterCard,* **VISA**

DONEGAL TOWN   Harvey's Point Country Hotel   63%   £99

Tel 073 22208   Fax 073 22352   Map 1 B2   **HR**
Lough Eske Donegal Town Co Donegal

Situated in a marvellous location close to Donegal Town on the shores of Lough Eske at the foot of the Blue Stack mountains, Jody Gysling's low-rise, purpose-built hotel has a unique Swiss-German atmosphere. The chalet-style buildings make good use of wood, with pergolas and covered walkways joining the residential area to the main bars and restaurants. Views over the lough are lovely and the waterside location brings an atmosphere of serenity which is emphasised by the good nature of everybody involved in this family-run business, ranging from the host himself down to his trusty dogs. Continental-style rooms, all on the ground floor with direct access to verandah and gardens, are well equipped with satellite TV, video and mini-bars as well as direct-dial phones, hairdryers, tea/coffee facilities and, in Executive rooms, four-poster beds and trouser presses. Banqueting and conference facilities for 200/300. No children under 10. Ask about trips on their horse-drawn wagon 'Harvey's Jarvey'. Easy parking.
Rooms *20. Garden, tennis, rowing boats. Closed Nov-end Mar (except weekends and Christmas). Amex, Diners, MasterCard,* **VISA**

Restaurant   £60

The alpine atmosphere of the hotel is continued through to an elegantly appointed dining-room beside the bar, where orders are taken. Original paintings by a talented family member add greatly to the feeling of personal care taken in the decor, the view is truly lovely and table settings are most promising – crisp linen, simple silver cutlery, fresh flowers and plain modern crystal – all of which, with the lively buzz that has been evident on our recent visits (even at Saturday lunch), gets things off to a good start. Marc Gysling's well-balanced menus offer a good range of choices appropriate to the time and season, in a classical style based on Swiss training but tempered by years of cooking in Ireland. Typically, starters might include a warm quail salad with Donegal Bay prawns and a curry sour cream dressing or crab ravioli with melted tomato, both accompanied by a choice of freshly-baked breads. Main courses, accompanied by perfectly-cooked vegetables, might include fresh king scallops with black noodles and a brandy cream sauce and loin of lamb with shallots and thyme. Plated farmhouse cheese are served with a delicious home-made nut bread instead of biscuits and well-presented desserts include specialities like Swiss chocolate mousse and lighter options such as a pretty tuile basket of seasonal fruits with home-made ice cream. Attentive, thoughtful service, and good coffee to round it all off. ***Seats*** *70. L 12-2.30 D 6.30-9.30. Closed Mon-Fri Nov-end Mar. Set L £9.50/£12.50 Set D £22.50.*

DROGHEDA   Boyne Valley Hotel   65%   £84

Tel 041 37737   Fax 041 39188   Map 1 D3   **H**
Drogheda Co Louth

In the ownership of Michael and Rosemary McNamara since 1992, this family-run hotel -and now country club – just on the south side of Drogheda town has been developed around a 19th century mansion set in 16 acres of gardens and woodland. Spacious public areas include well-proportioned period rooms in the older part of the hotel, with some fine plasterwork, fireplaces and pillars in ground-floor rooms which include a daytime dining-room (evening meals are served in an atmospheric cellar restaurant) and a modern curvilinear conservatory bar overlooking mature trees and gardens. Rooms vary somewhat due to the nature of the building, but include eight no-smoking and eight suitable for dis-abled guests; all have the facilities expected of a modern hotel and are more characterful than most hotel rooms. En suite facilities have slightly dated decor, but are functional and comfortable with bath and shower plus thoughtful extras including stools as well as toiletries. Families are welcome and children up to 6 may stay free in their parents' room. Excellent new leisure facilties added in

1996 include an impressive Romanesque 20m swimming pool, state-of-the-art gymnasium and outdoor 'cushioned' tennis courts. Banqueting/conference facilities for up to 280/400. No dogs. *Rooms 38. Garden, tennis, pitch & putt, leisure centre, beauty salon. Amex, Diners, MasterCard,* **VISA**

DROMAHAIR   Stanford's Village Inn

Tel 071 64140   Fax 071 64770   Map 1 B2
Dromahair Co Leitrim

Situated just south of Lough Gill (eleven miles from Sligo) on the ever beautiful Yeats country route, Stanford's has been in the McGowan family for five generations and the front bar remains as a testament to the Irish country pub of yesteryear – not a sentimental reconstruction, but the real thing. Elsewhere in this fisherman's hideaway, there are comfortable bars with fires and good, simple fare (home-made soup with freshly-baked soda bread, Irish stew, salads, sandwiches) and a 36-seat restaurant (straightforward 3-course lunches – £7, 4-course dinners – £14) for those who prefer to sit at a table. Sunday lunch (£7.50). Impromptu live music during summer. Children are welcome throughout; a high-chair can be provided. Straightforward accommodation is also offered in five rooms (£30, one family room £45, but not inspected, but Bord Fáilte Irish Tourist Board approved and due to be upgraded). No dogs. *Open 10.30-11.30 (to 11 in winter), Sun 12.30-2, 4-11. Bar Food 11am-9pm, Sun 12.30-2, 4-9. Restaurant Meals 1-2.30, 7-9 (Sun 12.30-9). Garden, outdoor eating, private fishing. Closed 25 Dec, bar closed Good Friday. MasterCard,* **VISA**

DRUMCLIFF   Yeats Tavern Restaurant & Davis's Pub

Tel 071 63117   Fax 071 63993   Map 1 B2
Drumcliff Co Sligo

Sympathetically modernised Yeats country pub beside Drumcliffe river, efficiently run by Mary, Damian, Angela and Jacqueline Davis – a family affair if ever there was one! The extensive menu, served throughout the bars and 80-seat restaurant, holds few surprises, but there's plenty of variety, from vegetable soup, garlic mushrooms and barbecue ribs to home-made burgers, omelettes, chicken every which way, salads and omelettes; poached salmon hollandaise, bacon and cabbage and braised steak might also be on offer. Seafood is now a strength, with a variety that covers oysters (try them baked with smoked salmon and cornmeal or sesame seeds), cod with white wine sauce, dressed garlic mussels and crab salad. Also snacks of sandwiches and filled baked potatoes. Children's menu. Country and Western music every weekend and other nights in summer. *Open 10.30-11.30 (till 11 in winter), Sun 12-11. Bar Food 12.30-10, Sun 12.30-2, 4-10. Closed Good Friday, 25 Dec. Amex, MasterCard,* **VISA**

DUBLIN   Aberdeen Lodge   £83

Tel 01 283 8155 Fax 01 283 7877   Map 4 C2
53 Park Avenue off Ailesbury Road Dublin 4

Located in a smart, peaceful south Dublin suburb, Aberdeen Lodge stands on an avenue lined with well-established trees. The Halpins have converted two substantial Edwardian properties to create a discreet, comfortable private hotel. There's a simple lounge on the ground floor along with an attractive and spacious breakfast/dining-room (dinner is available to residents by prior arrangement). Bedrooms, their windows double-glazed, are identically furnished, each with custom-built modern pieces; rear ones overlook a cricket and rugby ground. The usual comforts like trouser presses and hairdryers are provided and bathrooms have full facilities, showers being quite powerful. Enjoyable breakfasts include the likes of scrambled eggs and smoked salmon. Sister hotel to *Halpin's Hotel* in Kilkee, Co Clare (see entry). No dogs. *Rooms 16. Gym, spa bath. Amex, Diners, MasterCard,* **VISA**

DUBLIN   Adams Trinity Hotel   62%   £120

Tel 01 670 7100   Fax 01 670 7101   Map 5 F3   **H**
28 Dame Street Dublin 2

Although the busy Dame Street frontage, shared with The Mercantile Bar, is most obvious, the main Trinity Hotel entrance is from Dame Court, a less crowded approach and handier to the multi-storey car park used by guests (overnight rate £5). The small but cosy foyer provides a foretaste of priorities in the accommodation areas, where space is at a premium but the standard of furnishing is high. There is a lift and bedrooms include two designed for disabled guests; all the rooms are individually decorated in a pleasing old-world 'domestic' style with a mixture of new and old furniture, including queen-size half-tester beds, and fax/computer points and safes. Double-glazing effectively reduces traffic noise and neat en suite bathrooms are well planned, with plenty of shelf space, toiletries and quality towels. Dining facilities are available in the mezzanine restaurant overlooking The Mercantile Bar & Grill (see entry) and also all day in the Mercantile Café. 24hr room service. *Rooms 28. Closed 24 & 25 Dec. Amex, Diners, MasterCard,* **VISA**

DUBLIN   Albany House   £90

Tel 01475 1092   Fax 01475 1093   Map 5 F2   **A**
84 Harcourt Street Dublin 2

The Corcorans' fine 18th-century residence, tastefully converted into a pleasant guest house, is conveniently sited just south of St Stephen's Green and ideal for centre-of-town shopping. The entrance hall has a very welcoming ambience with its blazing log fire, comfortable settees and period furniture. Bedrooms are simply appointed, mostly with antiques and have neat, modern shower or bath rooms. Continental breakfast is served either in the bedroom or in the recently-added breakfast lounge. Free parking. *Rooms 29. Closed 1 week Christmas. Amex, Diners, MasterCard,* **VISA**

DUBLIN   Anglesea Town House   £90

Tel 01 668 3877   Fax 01 668 3461   Map 3 B2   **A**
63 Anglesea Road Dublin 4

A fine, creeper-clad south Dublin Edwardian residence run with enormous dedication and flair by Helen Kirrane with the help of her charming daughters. The minute you enter, the heady perfume of pot pourri greets and all around are beautiful ornaments and furnishings. The drawing-room is the epitome of cosy homeliness with its fine, comfortable seating and numerous books and yet more tasteful ornaments. Bedrooms feature lacework, heavy drapes and a comforting, motherly decor. Bathrooms, some with shower only, are spotless, like the rest of the house. Bedding has a wonderful 'all-through' freshly laundered smell. In the mornings guests are treated to what is without doubt the most stunning breakfast in the British Isles. To begin, a large bowl of fresh fruit salad is brought, then a bowl of dried fruit compote and one of baked fruit in creamy yoghurt. Next comes a bowl of warm baked cereal (oats, fruits, nuts soaked in orange juice overnight then freshly baked with cream). You help yourself to all these along with a glass of freshly-squeezed orange juice. The main course follows – specialities are kedgeree and Anglesea omelette (a soufflé omelette with smoked salmon and three different cheeses). Other options include kidneys, sole, plaice and salmon or trout as well as more usual offerings. To accompany, hot buttered toast, home-baked breads and limitless amounts of good tea or coffee. To finish, a selection of small dainty cakes such as a moist frangipane tart. A quite extraordinary place. No dogs. *Rooms 7. Garden. Closed 22 Dec-4 Jan. Amex, Diners, MasterCard,* **VISA**

DUBLIN   Ariel House   £99

Tel 01 668 5512   Fax 01 668 5845   Map 6 H2
52 Lansdowne Road Ballsbridge Dublin 4   **A**

This substantial, listed Victorian mansion, built in 1850, has for the past 35 years been home to the O'Brien family. It has also been one of Dublin's most charming private house hotels. Unusually for such premises there's a cosy 'wine bar' close to the reception desk where a selection of wines can be enjoyed. The drawing room, in the original house, is furnished with beautiful pieces of Victorian furniture. The main-house bedrooms are spacious and well equipped and each has its own character. There is, however, a wing of ten standard bedrooms at the rear which are more functional in style and overlook the neat, well-tended garden; some tariff reductions are available here. All bedrooms have a trouser press with iron and board, a hairdryer and an array of useful extras plus both tub and shower in their en suite bathrooms. Breakfast is served on highly-polished mahogany tables in a pretty conservatory. Smoking is discouraged. Free parking. No dogs. *Rooms 28. Closed 22 Dec-1 Jan. Amex, MasterCard,* **VISA**

DUBLIN   Ashtons

Tel 01 283 0045   Fax 01 260 0399   Map 3 B2
Clonskeagh Dublin 6   **P**

Behind a frontage which can only be described as a cross between those old country garages with facades disguising Nissen huts and a glossy Chinese restaurant (all shiny marble, black and gold), lies one of Dublin's most surprising pubs. A large, multi-level establishment it descends down to the River Dodder and as many tables as possible are positioned to take advantage of the river view with its ducks and waterfowl, the occasional swan foraging among the reeds and locals pottering along the banks. Inexpensive bar snacks include excellent home-made soups and brown bread with walnuts and hazelnuts, but it is the lunchtime buffet for which they are famous. There's always a roast joint and a selection of hot dishes (stuffed trout with scallop and monkfish, stuffed aubergine) plus an imaginative cold buffet and salad bar, where a whole salmon takes pride of place surrounded by dressed crab, crab claws, prawns and other freshly-cooked seafood as available. After the lunchtime buffet is cleared a separate bar snack menu operates until 8.30pm: burgers, minute steaks, crab claws, open sandwiches. A full à la carte dinner is served downstairs in the restaurant. *Open 10.30-11.30, Sun 12.30-2.30, 4-11.* **Bar Meals** *lunch 12.30-2.30, snacks 2.30-9. Restaurant 6-11 (Sun till 9.30). Closed 24-26 Dec. Amex, Diners, MasterCard,* **VISA**

DUBLIN   Ayumi-Ya Japanese Steakhouse   £40

Tel 01 662 2233   Fax 01 662 0221   Map 6 G2
132 Lower Baggot Street Dublin 2   **R**

Slightly more geared to Western tastes than its parent restaurant in Blackrock. One section of the lunch menu at this informal basement restaurant comprises the popular 'bento boxes', which consist of a main dish of choice and three selected accompaniments in a single four-section dish, with complimentary miso soup served alongside. Other favourites include boiled rice 'donburis' with a selection of lightly seasoned toppings and the mild Japanese-style curries with meat, seafood or vegetables. The evening selection is more extensive, with a new sushi menu, a lengthy à la carte, teppanyaki steaks and a gourmet Japanese tasting menu (£13.95); Japanese-style seating is available on request. There are also early- and late-evening supper specials. No children after 7.30pm. *Seats 45. L 12.30-2.30 D 6-11.30. Closed Sun, Good Friday, 24-26 Dec & 1 Jan. Set L £6.50/9.95 Set D from £10.95. Amex, Diners, MasterCard,* **VISA**

DUBLIN   Bats Restaurant   £45

Tel 01 660 0363   Map 6 G1   **R**
10 Baggot Lane Dublin 4

Located at the Eastmoreland Place end of Baggot Lane, opposite the AIB drive-in bank, Leonie Guy (previously at Tinakilly House, Rathnew with John Moloney) has established a warm, welcoming ambience at Bats; the tone is set at the entrance, where shelves groan under the weight of her home-made preserves for sale. The restaurant itself is simple enough – tiled floor, plain darkwood furniture – but a combination of fresh, homely food cooked to order and reasonable prices is likely to win many friends. Lunch menus offer a home-made soup – perhaps cream of winter vegetable – served with freshly-baked bread, plus several tempting starters and a good range of light, wholesome main courses including an imaginative vegetarian option such as vegetable strudel served with a side salad and tomato and basil coulis. Evening menus are more elaborate but have the same wholesome appeal -start with baked goat's cheese on a bed of leaves with home-made tomato chutney, perhaps, followed by mustard-crusted fillet of pork with savoury profiteroles and a redcurrant jus, fillet steak with a red onion confit or fish of the day. Tempting deserts might include a prune and brandy parfait and almond tart, or finish with Irish cheeses. Herbal teas are offered as well as tea and coffee. *Seats 60. Parties 8. Private Room 30. L 12.30-2.30 D 6-10. Closed D Sun, Bank Holidays & 1 week Christmas. Set D £7.95 (6-7.30 only). Diners, MasterCard, **VISA***

DUBLIN   Berkeley Court   76%   £235

Tel 01 660 1711   Fax 01 660 2365   Map 6 H1   **H**
Lansdowne Road Dublin 4

The flagship of the Doyle Hotel Group, the luxurious Berkeley Court has an impressively large split-level lobby-lounge with mirrored columns, brass-potted parlour palms and reproduction furniture in a mixture of styles. There are two bars – the Royal Court and the popular Conservatory – and two restaurants. The Court Lounge is a civilised spot for afternoon tea. Ballroom, boardroom and several suites provide function facilities for up to 300 (banquet) and 400 (conference) people. The spacious Executive and De Luxe suites with classic furnishings and a sumptuously appointed Penthouse Suite come at a commensurately higher tariff than the standard rooms. One floor of rooms (29) is designated non-smoking. Children under 8 stay free in parents' room. As we went to press Tom O'Connell (previously at *The Ritz* in London) had just taken over as General Manager. *Rooms 188. Keep-fit equipment, hair salon, news kiosk, boutique. Amex, Diners, MasterCard, **VISA***

DUBLIN   Bewley's Hotel at Newland's Cross   60%   £57

Tel 01 464 0140   Fax 01 464 0900   Map 2 D4   **H**
Newland's Cross Dublin 24

One of the latest additions to budget accommodation on the Dublin hotel scene, Bewley's charges for room only (£49) – breakfast is an optional extra and, except for limited service of Continental breakfast in rooms (7-9.30am) is served in Bewley's Café, off the foyer. The decor in public areas is unusual, featuring collectable pieces of modern furniture and original flower arrangements – and there is a stylish residents' sitting-room. Accommodation is all in family-sized en suite rooms, with a sofa bed in addition to double and single beds in all rooms; facilities include tea/coffee-making, multi-channel TV, direct-dial phone and hairdryer. Café open 7am-10pm. No dogs. *Rooms 126. Garden. Amex, Diners, MasterCard, **VISA***

DUBLIN   Bistro Vino   £45

Tel 01 497 1566
1 Upper Rathmines Road Dublin 6

Map 3 B2

R

Younger sister to Dermot Baker's thriving neighbourhood restaurant in
Sandycove (Glasthule), this dashing new two-storey affair has retained the
striking Italianate decor of the previous owner but transferred the menu and
cooking practice lock, stock and barrel from the Sandycove role model (see entry).
Expect informal fare such as garlic mussels, roast Mediterranean vegetables,
pan-fried fresh prawns, lots of pasta main dishes, steaks and some veal or
seafood main courses. *Seats 95. Parties 12. Private Room 40. D only 5-11.
Closed Good Friday & 25 Dec. Amex, Diners, MasterCard,* **VISA**

DUBLIN   The Bleeding Horse

Tel 01 475 2705
24 Upper Camden Street Dublin 2

Map 5 F1

P

Family-owned and partly family-run, on sound, traditional principles of service
and efficiency, the Bleeding Horse is lofty and impressive, with vast dark timbers
and a huge fireplace in the smaller bar. A balcony runs right around, giving an
almost medieval feel. There's a simple selection of bar food served at lunchtime
when daily soups and sandwiches made with home-made bread take pride of
place alongside salads and toasties; leave room, too, for home-made desserts like
lemon cheesecake, bread-and-butter pudding and banoffi pie. A la carte dining
in the first-floor restaurant; live music on Saturday nights. *Open 12-11.30 (Thu &
Fri till 1.30, Sat till 12.30), Sun 4-11.* **Bar Food** *(Mon-Sat) 12-3. No credit cards.*

DUBLIN   Blooms Hotel   60%   £87

Tel 01 671 5622   Fax 01 671 5997
6 Anglesea Street Temple Bar Dublin 2

Map 5 F3

H

Close to the city centre, near Trinity College and Dublin Castle, Blooms is
named after James Joyce's hero of Ulysses. Bedrooms are pleasant and well kept
with triple-glazed windows and extras like a complimentary quarter bottle of
wine and evening newspaper; a further twelve rooms have been added this year.
Bathrooms are generally of a good size and quite adequate; all have low stools
and telephone extensions and some have bidets. The pubby bar and picturesque
drinks terrace are a popular early evening meeting place. No dogs. *Rooms 97.
Night club. Closed 24, 25 & 26 Dec. Amex, Diners, MasterCard,* **VISA**

DUBLIN   The Brazen Head

Tel 01 677 9549
20 Lower Bridge Street Dublin 8

Map 5 E3

P

Dublin's oldest pub is worth a visit out of curiosity alone (and was a real
curiosity until a few years ago when they finally got electricity) but, although it
is undoubtedly ancient, with a series of thick-walled, low-ceilinged, rather dark
rooms, it isn't caught in a time-warp and does a thriving trade with locals as well
as visitors. Handy for the law courts just across the bridge and a lot of offices
around Christchurch, so the lunchtime carvery is especially popular (latecomers
must expect to queue). But it's a pleasant place for a quiet drink at other times,
either beside the fire in the back bar in winter, or in the yard on a fine summer
day. The essence of what makes a real Dublin pub is to be found here – look
out for Phil O'Soffer and other drinkers with writing problems sorting out the
world over a pint or two of stout! *Open 10.30-11 (Sun 12-11).* **Bar Food** *Carvery
Mon-Fri 12.30-2.30, bar menu till 7 (Sun till 5.45). Closed Good Friday & 25 Dec.
MasterCard,* **VISA**

| DUBLIN | **Burlington Hotel** | 70% | £177 |

Tel 01 660 5222   Fax 01 660 8496   Map 6 G1   **H**
Upper Leeson Street Dublin 4

Part of the Doyle Hotel Group, the Burlington always bustles with commercial business. Public rooms are on a grand scale, with large chandeliers in the main lobby and lounges, while a diverse choice of nightlife is offered by the Diplomat bar, Annabel's disco and the renowned traditional Irish cabaret. Bedrooms are well equipped and thoughtfully designed, with good working space for the business guest, and neat, tiled bathrooms with ample shelf space and bathrobes. Conference facilities for up to 1000. Residents enjoy use of the affiliated Riverview Healthclub nearby (5 minutes by taxi). Ireland's largest hotel may incorporate even further bedroom extensions in 1997. No dogs. *Rooms 450. Hair salon, kiosk, boutique. Access, Amex, Diners,* **VISA**

We do not accept free meals or hospitality – our inspectors pay their own bills and **never** book in the name of Egon Ronay's Guides.

| DUBLIN | **Le Café** | | £35 |

Tel 01 855 2424   Map 5 F4   **R**
5 Beresford Place Dublin 1

Situated close to Busaras, Connolly Station and the Financial Services Centre, Le Café is in a dream location for passing trade and invariably busy. The decor is stylish – lovely warm orange-washed walls covered with all sorts of ethereal pictures, gilded cherubs and a large gilt mirror reflecting light back into the room, which is topped with a 'sky' blue ceiling complete with scudding clouds. Waitresses in black jeans and T-shirts welcome arrivals with charm, presenting the large and informative menu promptly. The menu kicks off with 'substantial nibbles' like hot salsa dip, crunchy, deep-fried mozzarella fingers served with a small salad garnish of slivered cucumber and red onion. Next comes a choice of bangers 'n' mash, 'mussel mania' (eight styles – mussels Dublin-style, for example, is a clever variation on the classic moules marinière with chopped onions, carrot, garlic and thyme and stout replacing white wine in the sauce) or a whole page of 'Heavenly' burgers. Puddings are seriously wicked things, mostly chocolate. Short, exceptionally keenly priced wine list. 12 tables outside. Previously known as *Hamburger Heaven. Seats 80. Parties 16. Private Room 25. Meals 12 noon-11pm. L 12-6 D 6-11. Set L £5 Set D £7.50. Closed Good Friday & 25 Dec. MasterCard,* **VISA**

| DUBLIN | **Café en Seine** | | |

Tel 01 677 4369   Map 5 F2   **P**
40 Dawson Street Dublin 2

A seriously trendy, high-ceilinged European café-style bar (and pub of sorts) whose long, narrow copper-topped bar is reminiscent of La Stampa just a few doors away at number 35. Bottled lagers, cappuccino and people-watching are the order of the day and in summer the fashionable clientele spill out on to the pavement under its distinctive green awning. Food is of secondary importance to the craic (the 'crack'). *Open 10.30-11.30pm, Sun 12-11. Closed Good Friday & 25 Dec. Amex, MasterCard,* **VISA**

We do not recommend the food in pubs where there is no mention of Bar Food in the statistics. A restaurant within a pub is only specifically recommended where its separate opening times are given.

DUBLIN — Canaletto's — £35

Tel 01 678 5084   Fax 01 628 1120   Map 6 G1   **R**
69 Mespil Road Dublin 4

Just beside the canal near Baggot Street Bridge, this atmospheric little restaurant lives a double life. By day its a bright self-service affair with breakfasts, cakes and Danish to which at lunchtime is added soup, sandwiches (including chicken and beef 'subs'), lasagne, a potato and bacon dish and always various things such as goat's cheese wrapped in filo pastry. At night the lights are dimmed, candles lit and a printed à la carte menu gives chef Terry Sheeran a chance to show off his zesty style with his own 'unique' garlic bread with sun-dried tomatoes or chopped olives and basil, and dishes like poached egg salad with smoked bacon lardons and spicy fried spaghetti, salmon croquette with tomato and basil sauce and rigatoni pasta with chicken, lemon and mangetout in a rich cream sauce. Vegetarians are well catered for with dishes like tortelloni with mascarpone, sugar-snap peas and toasted cashew nuts or oven-baked bruschetta of mozzarella, tomato, olives, basil and artichoke heart. A brunch menu takes over on Sundays and Bank Holidays. *Seats 65. Parties 8. Meals served 7.30-5, 7-11 (Sat 9-4, 7-11.30, Sun & Bank Holidays 10.30-4). Closed Good Friday & 3 days Christmas. Amex, Diners, MasterCard,* **VISA**

DUBLIN — Central Hotel — 57% £140

Tel 01 679 7302   Fax 01 679 7303   Map 5 F3   **H**
1 Exchequer Street Dublin 2

Aptly-named for its proximity to Dublin Castle and Trinity College, this privately-owned hotel's other plus points include nightly live music in the Tavern, the owner's collection of contemporary Irish art around the walls and free use of a nearby office car park overnight (7.30pm-8.30am) and at weekends. Bedrooms vary widely in size and shape but all are furnished in similar style with functional lightwood units. About half the bathrooms have shower and WC only. Conference/banqueting facilities for up to 80. Children under 12 stay free in parents' room. No dogs. *Rooms 70. Closed 24-26 Dec. Amex, Diners, MasterCard,* **VISA**

DUBLIN — The Chameleon — £45

Tel 01 671 0362   Map 5 F3   **R**
1 Fownes Street Lower Temple Bar Dublin 2

Down near the river Liffey, Carol Walsh and Vincent Vis's unassuming little two-storey restaurant offers traditional Indonesian dishes through a selection of rijsttafel menus augmented by à la carte choices. The ground floor is quite tiny, with space for just a few tables (and the kitchen); steep stairs lead up to a slightly larger, mirrored room and a third-floor room with low, opium-table seating. The decor is warm and cheerful, with pumpkin tones, paper lanterns and stark table settings softened by candlelight. The food is simple but tasty, with honest flavours; coconut and peanut are dominant while many of the rijsttafel's true flavours are augmented by the genuine spices collected on holiday trips to Indonesia. A typical selection might include satay ayam (chicken satay with peanut sauce), ikan bumbu Bali (Balinese-style spiced fish), sambal goreng kook (fried peppered cabbage in coconut milk), nasi goreng (Indonesian omelette over spicy fried rice with ham, pork, chicken or shrimps) and a selection of accompaniments such as boiled rice, prawn crackers, roast grated coconut, fried peanuts and sambal, a hot chili chutney mixture. Minimum charge £8.50 (+ 10% service charge). *Seats 60. D only 5-11 (Sun till 10). Closed Mon, Tue, (Oct, Nov & Jan-Jun), Bank Holidays, 10 days Nov, 1 week Christmas & 25, 26 Dec. MasterCard,* **VISA**

DUBLIN | Chapter One | £70

Tel 01 873 2266   Fax 01 873 2330   Map 5 F4   **R**
18/19 Parnell Square Dublin 1

The setting, a vaulted cellar beneath the Dublin Writers Museum, speaks of soliciting and tradition but the menu is bang up-to-date in taking its inspiration from around the world. Chef/proprietor Ross Lewis gives his whole life to the business, and his creative menus are based on the best ingredients he can find locally: fresh crab and smoked haddock blinis, Dublin Bay prawns with garlicky lemon butter, calf's liver with roast apple and Clonakilty black and white pudding. Desserts are no less intriguing: bread-and-butter pudding with a liquid chocolate centre and roasted pear with pecan toffee ice cream. Lunch is a fixed-price affair (five or six choices at each stage), while dinner offers both à la carte and fixed-price options. Good pastry dishes among the desserts. Concise wine list. The Museum Coffee Shop, upstairs, serves more informal food all day. *Seats 80. Private Rooms 20/12. L 12-3 D 6-11. Closed D Mon, all Sun & Bank Holidays (except coffee shop). Set L £13.50 Set D £13.50 (6-7 only) & £19.50. Amex, Diners, MasterCard,* **VISA**

DUBLIN | Charleville Lodge | £65

Tel 01 838 6633   Fax 01 838 5854   Map 3 A4   **A**
268/272 North Circular Road Dublin 7

Situated close to the city centre and Phoenix Park, this comfortable guest house has been created from an elegant terrace of Victorian houses. Homely, interconnecting lounges are neatly furnished and sport open fires, relaxing armchairs, magazines and a TV. Pleasantly decorated bedrooms vary in size and offer direct-dial telephones, TVs and most have en suite shower rooms. Two family rooms with extra beds; under-4s stay free, 4-12s half-price. Ground-floor dining-room serving good Irish breakfasts. Secure parking. No dogs. *Rooms 22. Closed 1 week Christmas. Amex, Diners, MasterCard,* **VISA**

DUBLIN | Chicago Pizza Pie Factory

Tel 01 478 1233   Fax 01 478 1550   Map 5 F2   **JaB**
St Stephen's Green Centre Dublin 2

In a busy basement with deep red walls, Chicago-related memorabilia create an entertaining backdrop while waiting for the delivery of your chosen deep-pan or thin-crust pizza, burger, chili, lasagne, salad or other fast-cooked food. The service is cheerful and the whole operation should not be taken too seriously. Special value weekday lunch menus and family entertainment on Sundays with balloons, face-painting and a magician. *Seats 90. Meals 12-11.30 (Sun from 12.30). Closed Good Friday & 25, 26 Dec. Amex, MasterCard,* **VISA**

DUBLIN | The Chili Club | £45

Tel 01 677 3721   Fax 01 493 8284   Map 5 F2   **R**
1 Anne's Lane South Anne Street Dublin 2

Just off bustling South Anne Street, in Dublin's most fashionable shopping area, this intimate, low-ceilinged restaurant is an oasis of peace. The chili club promotes the hot and spicy food of Thailand 'as traditionally as the market will allow'. Satays, sweet and sours and even most of the curries are easy on the palate, but the soups have the expected Thai kick. A good-value Early Bird Dinner is offered from 6-7pm. *Seats 42. Parties 30. Private Room 20. L 12.30-2.30 D 6-11 (Thu-Sat till 11.30). Closed L Sun & Bank Holidays, Good Friday & 25, 26 Dec. Set L £9.95 Set D £17.50. Amex, Diners, MasterCard,* **VISA**

DUBLIN   The Clarence   80%   £191

Tel 01 670 9000   Fax 01 670 7800   Map 5 E3
6-8 Wellington Quay Dublin 2   **HR**

Following a lengthy refurbishment programme, the hotel re-opened in mid-1996. On the banks of the River Liffey in the city's Temple Bar district, The Clarence first opened its doors over 140 years ago and many of the old property's best and original features have been retained to blend in with today's contemporary design and modern technology, resulting in an intimate, luxurious and smart interior. Each of the individually designed and double-glazed bedrooms (all with king-size double beds; three rooms suitable for disabled guests) is decorated with American oak furniture, leather chairs, wrought-iron bedside lamps, nickel-plated desk lamps and candle sconces; colours are 'holy' (harking back to the days when the hotel was popular with the clergy): rich purple, deep brown and gold. Amenities include remote-control satellite TV with VCR, mini-bar, private safe, PC/fax connections and temperature control panels. Modern white-tiled bathrooms offer large bathrobes and good toiletries; housekeeping is immaculate and a full turn-down service (note the pristine white bed linen with gold borders) is offered at night. Public areas, with original oak panelling, include The Study, featuring an open fire, and The Octagon Bar, with several alcoves. The self-contained two-storey Penthouse suite, overlooking Dublin's rooftops, is a fantastic setting for business meetings and small private functions; larger ones (banqueting 80/conferences 40) can be accommodated in bright rooms overlooking the river. General Manager Claire O'Reilly leads by example; courteous staff are right on the ball. Valet parking. No dogs. *Rooms 50. Amex, Diners, MasterCard, VISA*

The Tea Room   £75

The original dining-room, on two levels, is now a light and spacious room with a coved ceiling, a mosaic and marble bar, and its own entrance on Essex Street. Chef Michael Martin trained in some of the most illustrious London restaurants and has brought all his considerable knowledge and experience to bear here, presenting modern dishes with both Irish and eclectic influences. A good start is that the bread (buttermilk, walnut) is baked on the premises, and that there are several choices on the à la carte and a few on the fixed-price lunch menu. Start with caramelised mango served with sautéed foie gras, an interesting innovation (it works!), a soufflé of Swiss cheeses or a tian of crab and tomato with a parmesan crust; follow, perhaps, with a fillet of hake served with basil mash and red pepper jus, roast fillet of lamb with spiced couscous or roast corn-fed chicken in a bacon and cabbage broth. Desserts are equally enticing: a trio of chocolate, warm apple tarte tatin, or a pyramid of sesame seed and white chocolate with a saffron sauce. If you can't make up your mind, the assiette gourmande offers little tastes of everything; alternatively, try the plated selection of Irish farmhouse cheeses. Cheerful service zips along with panache. The modish and sensible wine list is not at all expensive, with an excellent choice under £25. *Seats 85. L 12-2.30 D 6.30-10.45 (Sun till 10). Closed L Sat & Sun. Set L £13.50 & £17.*

We only recommend the food in hotels categorised as **HR** and **AR**.
However, the food in many **A** establishments throughout
Ireland is often very acceptable
(but the restaurant may not be open to non-residents).

DUBLIN   The Commons Restaurant   ↑   £90

Tel 01 478 0530   Fax 01 478 0551   Map 5 F2   **R**
Newman House 85/86 St Stephen's Green Dublin 2

Prestigiously located in the basement of Newman House, one of Dublin's most historic buildings, this airy restaurant has French doors opening on to a spacious paved courtyard and striking decoration in elegant, modern cream and deep blue. Thick Oriental rugs, fashionable flower arrangements and a growing collection of specially commissioned modern paintings grace the interior. Immaculately presented tables, comfortably upholstered chairs, heavy linen and fine glasses complete the scene. The standard of cooking has reached new heights since the arrival of the current head chef, Leslie Malone, towards the end of 1995. Two dinner menus are offered, the simpler one being similar to lunch: a choice of three starters might include a creamy, well-flavoured wild mushroom soup or a wonderful salad of asparagus and chicory arrestingly presented in a star shape. Excellent, freshly-baked breads (tomato and chive is particularly irresistible) are handed regularly and close attention is paid to details such as butter, wine and water. A choice of about four well-conceived main courses follows: perhaps baked cod in a fresh green herb crust (typically served with little aubergine chips and encircled with brilliant red, diced beetroot) or fillet of lamb, cooked perfectly pink, sliced on the diagonal and presented insouciantly in an informal stack, surrounded by little 'boats' of halved new potatoes topped with a garlic cream and whole roasted garlic cloves. Side vegetables are likely to be simple but perfectly cooked: little chunks of crisp 'rustic' potatoes, cauliflower and red cabbage. The £42 dinner menu is much more extensive (and more sophisticated), with a choice of seven starters and ten main courses. Typical first courses, for example, range from an oxtail broth with a morel parcel, or a mosaic of baby leek and rabbit with black truffle dressing, through to a dramatic galantine of foie gras and black pudding with a herb Chablis jelly and mango and black pepper caramel, all presented with panache. A similar style is developed in main courses that include a stunning vegetarian option like tarte tatin of aubergine, spinach and ricotta cheese with a cucumber salsa; in addition to several fine fish dishes there may be an exotic ingredient such as grilled ostrich with lyonnaise potatoes and creative meat dishes typical of the 'New Irish Cuisine' such as cannelloni of crubeens with a cider sauce. An Irish cheeseboard could follow, or intriguing desserts such as a simple-sounding 'selection of sorbets with a banana and pear compote' (a trio of well-made sorbets atop a crisp spun sugar disc, set on a banana and pear compote –an engineering masterpiece) and 'warm crepe with kumquats, apricots and vanilla ice cream' (a modish stack of mini crepes deliciously layered with a juicy mixture of fresh kumquats and dried apricots, with a ball of creamy vanilla ice cream on the side); all are beautifully, but not ostentatiously, presented. The wine list is presented by grape variety, each with brief tasting notes, but hardly user-friendly. Aromatic coffee and wonderful home-made petits fours round off one of Dublin's finest dining experiences. A mandatory 15% service charge is added to the bill; howver, service under the personal supervision of the proprietor, Michael Fitzgerald, is flawless. *Seats 60. Parties 12. Private Rooms 20/60. L 12.30-2.15 D 7-10.15. Closed L Sat, all Sun, Bank Holidays & 2 weeks Christmas. Set L £18 Set D £32 & £42. Amex, Diners, MasterCard,* **VISA**

Many hotels offer reduced rates for weekend or out-of-season bookings. Our guide price indicates high-season rates. Always ask about special deals for longer stays.

DUBLIN Conrad International 78% £259

Tel 01 676 5555 Fax 01 676 5424 Map 5 F2 **H**
Earlsfort Terrace Dublin 2

Perfectly located in the city's business district, opposite the National Concert Hall, yet just a short walk away from fashionable Grafton Street for shopping and St Stephen's Green for a stroll in the park, the hotel is blessed with wonderful staff, who are courteous, friendly, efficient and professional, an important asset to a hotel of distinction. Indeed, it has an impressive array of facilities and a staffed business centre, and thus caters largely to a corporate clientele, though at weekends, when very attractive rates are available, it serves as a good base to explore the delights of Dublin. Public areas are contemporary in style, though you'll find all the atmosphere of a traditional pub in Alfie Byrne's. Well-planned bedrooms are models of good taste and offer all the necessary comforts, from large beds and easy chairs to plenty of work space and good lighting, as well as air-conditioning. There are three telephones in the room (one in the bathroom), a fax socket, remote-control satellite TV, and mini-bar, while the bathrooms have large tubs and good showers, decent toiletries and towelling, and generously-sized bathrobes. At night there's a full turn-down service with a bottle of mineral water and hand-made Irish chocolate left beside the bed. Full 24hr room service. Lounge service until 2am. Wake up in the morning to a fine breakfast served in the Plurabelle Brasserie. Free valet parking. Banqueting for 260, conference facilities for 350. No dogs. ***Rooms 191.*** *Patio, beauty/hair salon, gift shop/news kiosk, brasserie (7am-11.30pm). Amex, Diners, MasterCard, **VISA***

DUBLIN Cooke's Café £70

Tel 01 679 0536 Fax 01 679 0546 Map 5 F3 **R**
14 South William Street Dublin 2

Johnny Cooke's fashionable city-centre restaurant has its main dining area on the ground floor. Much of the original, 'distressed' classical Italianate style has been retained and the open kitchen is still a major feature. Apart from a brilliantly coloured mosaic floor in the reception area, the first thing that meets arriving diners is Johnny and his dedicated team hard at work on the meal ahead. The menu describes itself as 'new age – new style' despite a number of Italian influences, typically beginning with crostini with artichoke paste, Serrano ham, peppers and olives, fried calamari with garlic, aïoli and roasted red chili, or crab salad with papaya, avocado, salad leaves and hazelnut dressing – to which Cooke's home-made bread selection and olive oil dip are ideal accompaniments. Similarly diverse main courses range from fettuccine with chorizo sausage, pimentoes, tomato, chili and parmesan cheese, coriander-crusted swordfish with lemon, capers and croutons, and, in season, perhaps a warm game salad of mallard and teal with white asparagus, figs, fried celeriac and fondant potato. Desserts include good home-made ice creams and the likes of banana parfait and raspberry and chocolate crème brulée, but pride of place goes to the baked goods, particularly Cooke's chocolate cake, that come from their own bakery in Dawson Street; a choice of coffees and herb teas completes the picture. Recently expanded upwards and outwards to create a spacious café, Upstairs at Cooke's serves teas, coffees and light snacks during the day and plans are now afoot to add full bar facilities and a grill room; outside, a wide awning over the pavement shades a handful of tables which are particularly popular in fine weather.
Seats *Restaurant 50. Upstairs at Cooke's 55. Parties 12. Private Room 50. L 12.30-4 (Sun till 3.30) & 6-11 (till 11.30 Fri & Sat, till 10 Sun). Upstairs at Cooke's 12-12. Set L & D £14.95. Closed Bank Holidays. Amex, Diners, MasterCard, **VISA***

| DUBLIN | Le Coq Hardi | ★ | £100 |

Tel 01 668 9070   Fax 01 668 9887   Map 6 H1   **R**
35 Pembroke Road Ballsbridge Dublin 4

Located in a classic end-of-terrace Georgian building and consistently popular with the business community, John and Catherine Howard's renowned Ballsbridge restaurant was completely refurbished in the first quarter of 1996 after an almost disastrous fire. The style now is lighter and brighter, but the discreet elegance of the new furnishings is still very definitely 'Coq Hardi'. Much rosewood furniture, gilt-framed pictures and mirrors, Irish linen, Newbridge silver and Rosenthal china are all still there to create this restaurant's unique, reassuringly club-like atmosphere. The cooking is as good as ever and the most remarkable aspect of it all is still John Howard's trueness of purpose, his absolute refusal to be swayed by fashion – in fact, fashion has simply come around full circle to recognise the wisdom of his ways. For his steadfastness and reliability John wins our Ireland Chef of the Year Award for 1997. The house style, shared by John and his trusty right-hand man James O'Sullivan, is classical French, with some concessions to modern tastes in the choice and presentation of vegetables; there are a significant number of dishes on the menu which might now be classed as New Irish Cuisine, with a lightness of touch and style of presentation that are essentially modern, yet clearly showing the influence of traditional Irish cooking. Specialities which have stood the test of time include 'smokies', an appetizer made with smoked haddock, marbled with tomato, double cream and Irish cheese and baked en cocotte, and Coq Hardi, which is chicken filled with potatoes, mushrooms and herbs, wrapped in bacon, oven-baked, and finished with Irish whiskey – although on the menu long before the term was coined, this is in essence New Irish Cuisine, in which traditional combinations are adapted to make more sophisticated dishes pleasing to present-day tastes. Traditional Irish classics also appear in more recent additions to the menu: Clonakilty black pudding served with a traditional potato cake and apple sauce, and baked fish (typically cod or hake) served with bacon and cabbage with a whiskey cream sauce. Strongly influenced by the seasons, table d'hote menus include many of the best choices from the carte, reducing the temptation to stray, and John's lunches, in particular, offer some of the best value in town. Seafood, including lobster from Howth or the west coast, is always well represented and game in season is a particular strength – not just the usual pheasant and venison, but rarer treats such as partridge (pot-roasted, perhaps, with wild mushrooms and winter berries), appear on John's menus whenever possible. Luscious desserts include many a treat (including, even, a return to the dramatic art of flambéeing, in classic crepes Suzette) and there's always a fine choice of Irish farmhouse cheeses kept in good condition. Finish with aromatic coffee and wonderful petits fours and life will seem pretty good. While the fire caused great losses in John Howard's outstanding wine list, he has taken to building up new stocks with predictable verve and enthusiasm and, although many of the classic vintages are irreplaceable, his love of the great wines of Bordeaux, Burgundy, Loire and Champagne is sure to bear fruit; however, there are very few selections under £20. *Seats 50. Parties 20. Private Room 35. L 12-2.30 D 7-11. Closed L Sat, all Sun, Bank Holidays, 2 weeks Aug & 10 days Christmas. Set L £18 Set D £33. Amex, Diners, MasterCard,* **VISA**

DUBLIN · The Courtyard · £45

Tel 01 283 8815 Fax 01 260 2797   Map 3 B2

Belmont Court 1 Belmont Avenue Donnybrook Dublin 4

R

Owned by Tom Williams, The Courtyard is a model of what a succesful middle-market restaurant can be. Built around an attractively planted courtyard with decorative pool and pleasant seating area, its size is deceptive, being broken up into quite intimate sections, including a separate bar. There's a no-bookings policy which appears to work well without undue delay and is especially appropriate for the popular carvery lunch which operates every day except Sunday. The table d'hote lunch menu (also available early evenings) and the fixed-price dinner produce unpretentious food, well cooked and based on good ingredients: seafood bisque, Cajun chicken poppadums, Caesar salad, pepper steak, chicken en croute, tomato and spinach roulade, apple crumble, raspberry charlotte. A la carte choices are heavier on meat and poultry and a bistro selection offers omelettes and burgers. Service by well-trained and well-informed staff is invariably courteous and helpful. Patio seating for 50. **Seats** 200. L 12-3 (Sun till 3.30) D 5-11 (Sat till 12, Sun till 10). Closed 25 & 26 Dec. Set L £7/£8.95 (Sun £9.95) Set D £16 (5-7 £9.95). Amex, Diners, MasterCard, **VISA**

> If you encounter bad service don't wait to write to us but make your feelings known to the management at the time of your visit. Instant compensation can often resolve any problem that might otherwise leave a bad taste.

DUBLIN · The Davenport Hotel · 76% · £201

Tel 01 661 6800 Fax 01 661 5663   Map 6 G3

Merrion Square Dublin 2

H

The original, imposing neo-classical facade of architect Alfred G Jones's Merrion Hall fronts one of Dublin's most elegant hotels, younger sister to the Mont Clare (qv). Only a stone's throw from Trinity College and the National Gallery, the impressive exterior of The Davenport is matched by the marble-pillared lobby, an atrium encircled by Georgian windows which soar up through six storeys to the domed roof and cupola. Rooms beyond are on a more human scale, with relatively low ceilings creating an unexpectedly intimate atmosphere. Colour schemes tend to be bold, giving each area a specific character – the Presidents Bar is masculine and club-like, the restaurant lighter and more feminine – and stylish drapes and quality materials, notably marble and a variety of woods, are used throughout. Although not individually decorated there is considerable variety among the bedrooms (some Lady Executive designated), which tend to have a homely, almost country atmosphere which is emphasised by the irregular shape of some rooms and bathrooms. Nice touches include a safe as well as trouser press, air-conditioning, good American over-bath showers, bath robes, turn-down service and an attractive Irish-made range of toiletries. 24hr room service. The ten junior suites also contain an extra modem line, dedicated fax machine and printer. Banqueting and conference facilities for 400/500. Guests have use of the private Riverview Racquets and Fitness Club at members' rates. No dogs. Valet parking (100 cars). **Rooms** 116. Amex, Diners, MasterCard, **VISA**

DUBLIN   Davy Byrnes

Tel 01 677 5217   Fax 01 677 5849   Map 5 F3   **P**
21 Duke Street Dublin 2

At the heart of Dublin life (and immortalised in James Joyce's Ulysses), Davy
Byrnes is not only a mecca for literary-minded tourists, but also a pleasant,
well-run and conveniently central place well used by Dubliners in town
on business, shopping in nearby Grafton Street or simply having a day out.
Decor-wise, it is in a 1920s' time-warp but for such a famous pub, it is
remarkably unselfconscious. They take pride in seafood, particularly, with fresh
crab or king prawn open sandwiches featuring among the lunchtime dishes,
and poached salmon steak with hollandaise appearing among additional hot
dishes in the evening and pride of place going to the mixed seafood platter
which includes 'a little bit of everything'. Quick and inexpensive hot dishes such
as spaghetti bolognese, chicken and mushroom pie and minute steak with onions
feature on the lunchtime blackboard, with oysters (in season), pasta carbonara
and traditional Irish stew supplementing the steaks, salads and open sandwiches
on offer at night. Irish cheeses and apple or almond tart complete the picture.
Sunday brunch. No children under 7. *Open 10.30-11.30, Sun 12.30-2, 4-11.*
Bar Food 12-10 (Sun 12-3, 4-10), till 9pm in winter. Minimum charge £3.50
12.30-2.30pm. Closed Good Friday & 25, 26 Dec. MasterCard, **VISA**

DUBLIN   Dobbins Wine Bistro   £75

Tel 01 661 3321   Fax 01 661 3331   Map 6 G2   **R**
15 Stephen's Lane Dublin 2

Probably best visited in a group, this clubby, city-centre, air-conditioned
'Nissen-hut' operates well under the close supervision of owner John O'Byrne.
There's a dark, curved ceiling (offset somewhat by the bright conservatory area
at the far end, which is very popular in summer), sawdust-strewn floor and a
series of tables in intimate booths along the wall; low lighting and an abundance
of bottles add to an away-from-it-all atmosphere (which means this is a place to
approach with caution if you have to go back to work after lunch). Chef Gary
Flynn's tempting menus might include starters such as tagliatelle of lobster and
crab or paté of chicken and foie gras on toasted brioche, followed by crispy fried
fillets of brill with tartare and chili jam or loin of wild venison with shallot,
apple, port and juniperberry sauce. Attention to detail is good: generous, plain
wine glasses, lovely home-baked brown bread and white rolls and lightly cooked
vegetables. Interesting desserts and particularly creamy, flavoursome ice cream
served with a brandy snap; good, freshly-brewed coffee. Ten tables on a patio
for summer eating. *Seats 80. Parties 12. Private Room 40. L 12.30-3 D 7.30-11.30.*
Closed D Mon, L Sat, all Sun, Bank Holidays & 1 week Christmas. Set L £15.50
Set D £25. Amex, Diners, MasterCard, **VISA**

DUBLIN   Doheny & Nesbitt

Tel 01 676 2945   Fax 01 676 0655   Map 6 G2   **P**
5 Lower Baggot Street Dublin 2

Only a stone's throw across the road from Toners, Doheny & Nesbitt is another
great Dublin institution, but the similarity ends. Just around the corner
from the Irish parliament, this solid Victorian pub has traditionally attracted a
wide spectrum of Dublin society – politicians, economists, lawyers, business
names, political and financial journalists – all with a view to get across, or some
scandal to divulge, so a visit here can often be unexpectedly rewarding. Like
the Shelbourne Meridien hotel down the road, which has a similar reputation
and shares the clientele, half the fun of drinking at Nesbitt's is anticipation
of 'someone' arriving or 'something' happening, both more likely than not.

Apart from that it is an unspoilt, very professionally run bar with an attractive Victorian ambiance and a traditional emphasis on drinking. Traditional Irish music on Sunday nights. *Open 10.30-11.30 (winter to 11), Sun 12.30-2, 4-11. Amex, Diners, MasterCard,* **VISA**

DUBLIN	Doyle Montrose Hotel	65%	£133

Tel 01 269 3311   Fax 01 269 1164   Map 4 C2   **H**
Stillorgan Road Dublin 4

A hotel of smart, modern appearance located alongside the N11 a few miles south of the city centre. The Montrose also has an attractive 'old Ireland' themed pub with its own entrance. Spacious public areas include a large open-plan bar and lounge. Bedrooms are furnished in an identical smart, contemporary style with Executive rooms differing only in being larger. A good selection of amenities includes an iron and ironing board. Breakfasts are cooked to order – a commendable rarity in a hotel of this size. *Rooms 179. Beauty salon, hair salon, news kiosk/shop. Amex, Diners, MasterCard,* **VISA**

DUBLIN	Doyle Tara Hotel	61%	£133

Tel 01 269 4666   Fax 01 269 1027   Map 4 C2   **H**
Merrion Road Dublin 4

Formerly the Tara Tower, the hotel has undergone major changes under the Doyle banner, with the bar and restaurant the latest to reap the benefit of extensive remodelling. At the rear there are 32 splendid Executive rooms decorated in a smart, modern style and well worth the supplementary room charge (£10). All standard rooms have the same amenities but those at the front enjoy the best views over Dublin Bay. The hotel is very convenient for the Dun Laoghaire ferry. *Rooms 114. News kiosk/shop. Amex, Diners, MasterCard,* **VISA**

DUBLIN	Eamonn Doran		

Tel 01 679 9114   Fax 01 679 2692   Map 5 F3   **P**
3a Crown Alley Temple Bar Dublin 2

This Dublin cousin of a well-known trio of New York bars serves some of the best steaks in town. Operating as a pub, bar and restaurant all rolled into one, there are bar snacks (till 2am) and a multiplicity of menu choices, from traditional Irish (corned beef and cheese omelette) and vegetarian (Oriental pancakes) through to à la carte dishes such as fruits de mer in wine and cream sauce and the '32nd Street' Gaelic sirloin. There is also an Early Bird menu between 6 and 8 (£7.95) and daily table d'hote (£12.50) offering 3 courses and coffee. *Seats 100. Parties 10. Private Room 30/40. Bar open 10.30-2am (Sun from 12.30). L 12-2.30 D 5-12.30. Closed Good Friday & 25 Dec. Amex, Diners, MasterCard,* **VISA**

DUBLIN   Eastern Tandoori   £60

Tel 01 671 0428   Map 5 F3   **R**
34 South William Street Dublin 2

Larger and more elegant premises than the off-shoot at Malahide (see entry),
the restaurant has wood panelling where windows might be, creating a dark
and intimate interior which is lit by large, ornate brass lanterns. The heady
perfume of incense strikes one upon entering and there's a small, comfortable
bar area set aside for pre-dinner drinks. A short flight of stairs leads up to the
smartly-appointed dining area. The menu features a good selection of familiar
dishes and tandoori specialities such as moghul kebab and marinated quail, mildly
spiced kormas of chicken or lamb are among recommended dishes; spicier
alternatives include salman masala and beef jalfrezi. The food is highly enjoyable
and staff couldn't be friendlier or more helpful. Branches also in Blackrock (Old
Parish Hall, Kill Lane, Deansgrange Tel 01 289 2856) and Cork (Emmet Place
Tel 021 272 020). *Seats 72. Parties 40. L 12-2.30 D 6-11.30. Set L & D from
£17.50 (+12½ % service). Closed L Sun, Good Friday & 25, 26 Dec. Amex, Diners,
MasterCard,* **VISA**

DUBLIN   L'Ecrivain   †   £80

Tel 01 661 1919   Fax 01 661 0617   Map 6 G2   **R**
109a Lower Baggot Street Dublin 2

Now in their second year at this address, Derry and Sallyanne Clarke have taken
to the larger premises like ducks to water and the whole operation is blossoming,
both in the kitchen and front of house. The place has a sense of space and style,
a warm, welcoming atmosphere that is immediately striking as guests hurry into
the ground-floor bar/reception area where aperitifs are served beside the gas fire.
Upstairs, the restaurant is in an airy, high-ceilinged (and air-conditioned) room
that opens on to a little terrace where tables are set up in fine summer weather;
the room is boldly decorated in strong colours and good pictures provide
contrasting interest. A thoughtful and practical chef, Derry has evolved a range
of menus that take in both traditional Irish and modern international influences,
which he interprets in his own style – leaning towards 'New Irish Cuisine' –
and, whenever possible, through the best of Irish produce. Dinner menus include
an early evening budget menu, a five-course table d'hote (offering a choice of
four starters, five main courses and the full range of around six desserts), a short
à la carte with starters and main courses each priced at a flat rate and a vegetarian
set menu. A typical autumn menu might start with dishes that owe a debt to
Irish tradition like baked rock oysters with cabbage and bacon and a Guinness
sabayon or a colourful modern dish like baked goat's cheese on chargrilled
vegetables with roasted red peppers. Main courses, which include a good choice
of game in season, could include crisp confit of duck leg with honeyed chicory
and a red wine fumet, simple black sole on the bone ('meunière') and an
interesting dish of boned saddle of rabbit with black and white pudding, onion
relish and vegetable frites – a creative, well-balanced dish inspired by more than
one tradition. Presentation throughout is on over-sized plates and is stylish
without dominating the food. Desserts will usually include classics that have
been given a bit of a twist – crème brulée with prunes and armagnac, for
example – and the problem of how to present cheese (trolley, board or plated)
is neatly solved: a dramatic display of Irish farmhouse cheeses makes a focal point
in the restaurant and, from it, a plated selection is cut as required and presented
with fresh fruit – perhaps a bunch of green and black grapes – and water
biscuits; winner of our 1997 Irish Cheeseboard of the Year Award. Lunch
is extremely good value and there's a great buzz; service, under the direction
of Sallyanne Clarke, is surprisingly swift and efficient, bearing in mind that
everything is cooked to order (it can be slower in the evening). L'Ecrivain has

found its niche and is operating with confidence. 10% service charge is added to all food bills (except the early dinner menu) but there is no service charge on wine or drinks. *Seats 54. Private Room 10. L 12.30-2.15 D 7-11. Closed L Sat, all Sun & Bank Holidays. Set L £11.50/£14.50 Set D £16.95 (inc service 6.30-7.30 Mon-Thur) & £27.50 (Veg £23.50). Amex, Diners, MasterCard,* **VISA**

DUBLIN   **Elephant & Castle**   **£50**

Tel 01 679 3121   Fax 01 679 1366   Map 5 F3
18 Temple Bar Dublin 2   **R**

In a prime location in Dublin's 'Left Bank', this busy, buzzy New York-style restaurant specialises in informal food: pasta dishes (fettuccine, perhaps, with shrimp, sun-dried tomatoes and saffron), big, healthy salads served in huge glass bowls (their special Caesar salad is legendary), daily specials such as Thai curried chicken or beef stir-fry with orange and spinach, New York sandwiches and hamburgers all kinds of ways. It's noisy and full of life; first come, first served – so be prepared to wait. Winner of our Irish Beef Award for 1997. *Seats 89. Parties 10. Meals 8am-11.30pm (Fri till 12), Sat 10.30-12, Sun 12-11.30. Closed Good Friday & 25, 26 Dec. Amex, Diners, MasterCard,* **VISA**

DUBLIN   **Ernie's**   **£80**

Tel 01 269 3260   Fax 01 269 3969   Map 3 B2
Mulberry Gardens Donnybrook Dublin 4   **R**

The Evans family has owned this elegant south-city restaurant since 1984 and its most remarkable feature is the late Ernie Evans's personal collection of paintings (mostly of Irish interest and many of his beloved Kerry), which take up every available inch of wall space There is also a pretty little central courtyard garden which makes an especially attractive feature when floodlit at night. Chef Sandra Earl is very much in control in the kitchen, producing refreshingly updated versions of the classics on the fixed-price lunch and two extensive dinner menus. The former might include grilled salmon cake with chive mayonnaise and confit of duck in filo with black olive and tarragon jus. A la carte, warm crostini of sardines with tomato and basil, scallops on a broad bean and tarragon risotto, and rack of Wicklow lamb with tomato sauce and black olives are all typical of her style; desserts might include strawberry and mango tartlet with passion fruit sorbet and rhubarb and ginger ice cream with 'Japonaise meringue'. *Seats 60. L 12.30-2.30 D 7.30-10.15. Closed L Sat, all Sun, Mon & 1 week Christmas. Set L £13.95 Set D £25. Amex, Diners, MasterCard,* **VISA**

DUBLIN   **Fitzers Café Ballsbridge**   **£65**

Tel 01 667 1301   Fax 01 667 1303   Map 3 B2
RDS Merrion Road Dublin 4   **R**

The dashing neo-classical interior in warm, bold colours makes the most of Fitzers location in the members' annexe of the Regency-style Royal Dublin Society building – sculptures and old paintings from the RDS archives look wonderful against deep orange walls. A modish new menu from William Fitzgerald typically offers starters of crab salad with coriander, chili and ginger, and chargrilled focaccia, broccoli, capers and marinated turnips, followed by smoked haddock, mustard mash and béarnaise and saddle of rabbit with black pudding and parsley juices, plus desserts such as hazelnut tart with honey ice cream and chocolate marquise with burnt orange jus. There is a large, elegant and comfortably furnished bar/reception area at one end of the main dining area, where the Café Orchestra plays on occasion. Disabled facilities. Private parking. *Seats 120. Parties 15. Private Room 30. L 12-3 D 6-11.30. Closed Good Friday & 25-28 Dec. Set L £10.95. Amex, Diners, MasterCard,* **VISA**

DUBLIN   Les Frères Jacques   £80

Tel 01 679 4555   Fax 01 679 4725   Map 5 E3   R
74 Dame Street Dublin 2

Situated opposite Dublin Castle, a stone's throw from Trinity College, this discreet two-storey French restaurant has dark green and cream decor, Parisian prints, pristine white table linen and fine glassware. Fish and seafood specialities, purchased according to market availability and much of it stored in their own tank, vie for prominence on weekly-changing menus that are uncompromisingly French: les croustillants d'escargots de Bourgogne au beurre d'ail; medaillons de veau farcis aux épinards et ricotta sauce au marsala; feuillantine de mascarpone parfumée à l'amaretto et purée de fruits. Appended to each day's menu at supplementary prices are the pick of the fish and seafood selections: sautéed monkfish tournedos with cider and braised onion; supreme of Atlantic turbot with freshwater crayfish. Desserts are decidedly sophisticated (with fine French and Irish cheeses as the alternative), various coffees come with home-made petits fours and the special house recommendations on the wine list are good value. *Seats 65. Parties 12. Private Rooms 15 (downstairs)/40 (upstairs). L 12.30-2.30 D 7.30-10.30 (till 11 Fri & Sat). Closed L Sat, all Sun, Bank Holidays & 25-31 Dec. Set L £13.50 Set D £20. Amex, Diners, MasterCard, VISA*

> We endeavour to be as up-to-date as possible but inevitably some changes to owners, chefs and other key staff occur after this Guide has gone to press.

DUBLIN   Furama Chinese Restaurant   £60

Tel 01 283 0522   Fax 01 668 7623   Map 3 B2   R
Eirpage House Donnybrook Main Road Donnybrook Dublin 4

Like eating inside a gleaming black lacquered box, with the dining area reached via a small wooden bridge over an ornamental pool with goldfish, Furama offers a selection of familiar Cantonese as well as a few Szechuan dishes, capably cooked and served by hardworking, very pleasant staff. Special seafood dishes such as black sole, squid and lobster (from a tank) are available steamed with garlic and black bean sauce, with ginger and scallions or in the traditional 'drunken style'. Sweets – like much of the menu – are aimed at Western palates with banana fritters about the only alternative to the ice cream selection. *Seats 100. Parties 25. L 12.30-2 D 6-11.30 (till 12 Fri & Sat, Sun 1.30-11). Set L £8.50/£9.50 (Sun £10.50) Set D £13.50/£15/£20. Closed L Sat, Good Friday & 24-26 Dec. Amex, Diners, MasterCard, VISA*

DUBLIN   George's Bistro & Piano Bar   £70

Tel 01 679 7000   Map 5 F3   R
29 South Frederick Street Dublin 2

In a side street between the Dail and Trinity College, this basement bistro is popular with the post-theatre crowd who obviously enjoy the live music (piano with female vocal), which tends to inhibit conversation but fuels the late-night buzz. A straightforward menu keys in with prawn bisque, mushrooms in Guinness batter and duck liver parfait, modulating into red meat, fish and vegetarian dishes (rack of lamb, beef stroganoff, sautéed monkfish, steamed brill and wild mushroom and ricotta cannelloni), which are generally in tune with the times. *Seats 60. Parties 16. D only 7-12 (till 1 Fri & Sat). Closed Sun, Bank Holidays & 24-26 Dec. Set D £18.50. Amex, Diners, MasterCard, VISA*

DUBLIN   Georgian House   56%   £88

Tel 01 661 8832   Fax 01 661 8834   Map 6 G2   **H**
18 Lower Baggot Street Dublin 2

Bedrooms in the original Georgian houses (two of which connect and accommodate their own pub, Maguire's, on their ground floors – a third is one door along) have character and charm, while those in the recently built bedroom annex to the rear are more modern and functional. Conveniently located for the city centre. Children up to 4 stay free in parents' room. 24hr room-service. No dogs. Free valet parking. **Rooms** 47. Closed 24 & 25 Dec. Amex, Diners, MasterCard, **VISA**

DUBLIN   Girolles   £60

Tel 01 679 7699   Map 5 F3   **R**
64 South William Street Dublin 2

Gary Morris, previously at L'Ecrivain with Derry Clarke, opened here late in 1995, with Helen Morris managing the front of house. Together they have established a niche in the somewhat heady gastronomic atmosphere of South William Street, where Gary's progressive Irish cooking and comparatively moderate prices have assured a good following. The place is quite tiny, with a minuscule no-smoking area at the kitchen end where non-indulgers can watch the full range of dishes going out to other tables: starters like warm rillettes of rabbit with rösti potatoes and hot and sour red onions or an authentic risotto with mushrooms and two cheeses. Tempting main courses might include strips of beef fillet with oyster mushrooms and green peppercorns or baked cod with courgettes, lemon and thyme; pastry is good – in both desserts and vegetarian dishes such as a gorgeous onion tart with tossed leaves and roasted peppers. **Seats** 38. Parties 10. 12.30-2.15 & 6-11. Set L £12.50 Set D £9.95 (pre-theatre only 6-7.15). Closed L Sun, all Mon, Good Friday & 25 Dec. Amex, Diners, MasterCard, **VISA**

DUBLIN   Glenveagh Town House   £80

Tel 01 668 4612   Fax 01 668 4559   Map 6 H2   **A**
31 Northumberland Road Ballsbridge Dublin 4

A large Georgian house within comfortable walking distance of the city centre. Single, twin and family bedrooms are all pleasantly decorated and sport duvets, remote-control TVs and bathrooms with excellent showers. Breakfasts, available from 7.30am (though earlier meals can be arranged), include black and white pudding among the options. There's a comfortable drawing room at the front. Friendly, caring staff. Private parking for 10 cars. No dogs. **Rooms** 10. Closed 1 week Christmas. MasterCard, **VISA**

DUBLIN   The Goat

Tel 01 298 4145   Fax 01 298 4687   Map 3 B1   **P**
Goatstown Dublin 14

'Dublin's Sporting Pub' is a real city landmark: big, with an even bigger car park (complete with house mini-bus to ferry customers home safely) and its own unmissable clock tower. Inside, despite its size, it is a friendly sort of place where families are made especially welcome. The lounge menu offers sandwiches, omelettes, steaks and salads, and a popular Sunday lunch menu served till 4pm. The adjacent restaurant, rather more formal in style, is now called 'Stirrups' (our recommendation is currently for bar food only). Children are allowed in the bar to eat until 7pm and there's a children's menu provided. Open 10.30-12 (Sun 12-11). **Bar Food** 12.30-11 (Sun till 9). Garden, patio. Amex, Diners, MasterCard, **VISA**

DUBLIN   Good World   £40

Tel 01 677 5373   Map 5 F3   **R**
18 South Great George's Street Dublin 2

V

A city-centre restaurant much favoured by Dublin's Chinese community for its excellent selection of carefully prepared dim sum (served daily until 6pm). These come in steamer baskets of stainless steel rather than bamboo but this is no way affects their quality. Mixed meat dumplings and char siu buns are noteworthy, as are the long, slippery rice-flour envelopes of the various cheung funs. The regular menu features a standard selection of classic Cantonese dishes. 2- and 3-course business lunches are served till 2.15pm on Mondays to Fridays, and there's an array of set meals – but it's the dim sum that are primarily of interest here. *Seats 95. Parties 40. Private Room 20. Meals 12.30pm-3am. Closed 25 & 26 Dec. Set L £6/£7.50 Set D £15/£21/£29.50. Amex, Diners, MasterCard,* **VISA**

DUBLIN   Gotham Café   £45

Tel 01 679 5266   Fax 01 679 5280   Map 5 F3   **R**
8 South Anne Street Dublin 2

Right in the heart of the city, off Grafton Street, Gotham Café is bright and buzzy. Walls are lined with framed Rolling Stone magazine covers and the menu features 'American-Italian' pizza and pasta cooking. Not for the foolhardy, Gotham's gourmet pizzas echo to New York scene from Harlem to Broadway; the 'Chinatown' unusually features barbecued Peking duck with hoisin and in the 'Wall Street' you'll get four quarters for your dollar. Other main dishes mix pasta (linguine served with pesto whose flavour varies daily!) with a wide range of salads and grills that has been further extended this year – flame-grilled tuna steak, chicken with lime and coriander salsa. Extensive variations on the espresso to finish. *Seats 65. Parties 8. Meals 12-12 (Sun till 10.30). Closed Good Friday & 25, 26 Dec. MasterCard,* **VISA**

DUBLIN   Grafton Plaza Hotel   64%   £110

Tel 01 475 0888   Fax 01 475 0908   Map 5 F2   **H**
Johnsons Place Dublin 2

Modern, well-designed and not without a certain style, the Grafton Plaza is located by Grafton Street and St Stephen's Green, putting shopping areas, parks, museums and theatres all within easy walking distance. Decor is bright and stylish in the day rooms which include a recently added resident's lounge. Bedrooms are of various sizes and are well appointed with Irish-made carpets and furniture (except for some antiques) also of Irish origin. Hairdryers, multi-channel TVs, tea-makers, quality toiletries and good shelf space in the bathrooms. No private parking, but there's a nearby multi-storey park. No dogs. *Rooms 75. Closed 24-26 Dec. Amex, Diners, MasterCard,* **VISA**

DUBLIN   Gresham Hotel   64%   £236

Tel 01 874 6881   Fax 01 878 7175   Map 5 F4   **H**
Upper O'Connell Street Dublin 1

A prime position on Upper O'Connell Street and free, secure valet parking are major attractions of this famous north-city hotel. The comfortably furnished, chandelier-lit lobby/lounge is a popular meeting place, especially for morning coffee and afternoon tea, and Toddy's Bar (named after an illustrious former manager) is an all-day eating spot. Front bedrooms are best, with smart modern bathrooms, and there are six full suites. Banqueting/conference facilities for 250/350 include a business centre with secretarial support. 50 standard rooms have a tariff of £202. Construction of a 100-bedroom extension and additional parking will occupy most of the coming year, but with minimal disruption to guests' services promised. Ryan Hotels. *Rooms 202. Amex, Diners, MasterCard,* **VISA**

DUBLIN   Grey Door   £65

Tel 01 676 3286   Fax 01 676 3287   Map 5 F2   **RR**
22 Upper Pembroke Street Dublin 2

The Grey Door has completely abandoned the luxurious surroundings and
Russian/Scandinavian cuisine which has characterised it for the last 20 years
and gone for a new cool look that is nothing less than a celebration of Irish
craftmanship – everything, right down to the specially commissioned tableware
has been handcrafted to order. Now, instead of 'the food of the Czars' on which
their reputation was founded, head chef Michael Durkin has turned his hand to
the contemporary re-working of traditional Irish themes in dishes that are typical
of the current move towards a 'New Irish Cuisine'. Typical starters might now
include a delectable dish of pan-fried slices of black and white pudding with
apple and red onion – several slices of each pudding, perfectly complemented
by lovely juicy little wedges of apple and slivers of red onion, served with
crisply-baked breads. Main courses not only offer a full range of Irish meats,
poultry and seafood (especially salmon and crab) but also particularly good
vegetarian main courses such as light and luscious seasonal vegetables wrapped
in crispy pastry and red pepper dressing. Round off, perhaps, with fresh
strawberries and home-made shortbread biscuit or an aptly-named 'tangy lemon
cream'. Interesting wine list with an interesting selection of bottles at £10 and
others arranged in price order. Admirable service, too, under restaurant manager
Fintan Lynch. In the basement, Pier 32 (see separate entry) offers pub fare
(12.30-2.15, 6-11) and live music nightly. *Seats 60. Parties 12. Private Room 70.
L 12.30-2.15 D 6-11. Set L £14.50 Set D £20. Closed L Sat & Sun, L on Bank
Holidays, 4 days at Christmas. Amex, Diners, MasterCard,* **VISA**

Rooms   £104

Seven spacious, well-appointed bedrooms are comfortably furnished with
mahogany furniture, quality fabrics and thoughtfully-appointed bathrooms.
There is a drawing-room for residents' use and a studio suite available at
a small extra charge. The room-only price is £90. Street parking (metered).
Staff are friendly and helpful. No dogs.

See the **County Listings** green tinted pages for
details of all establishments listed in county order.

DUBLIN   Halfway House

Tel 01 838 3218   Map 2 D4   **P**
Ashtown Dublin 7

A big, well-run pub/restaurant just off the new West-Link motorway providing
decent, middle-of-the-road fare from a carvery and hot and cold buffet that caters
admirably for the crowds. The large, 600-seater floor area is divided into fairly
intimate sections, some with coal-effect gas fires to give a cosy atmosphere, and
there's an area beside the buffet with oil-clothed tables (and plenty of high-chairs)
for families. Twelve tables are set outside on a patio for good-weather drinking.
*Open 10.30am-11pm. **Meals** (hot and cold carvery) 12-8 (bar snacks till 11).
Closed Good Friday & 25 Dec. Amex, Diners, MasterCard,* **VISA**

We do not recommend the food in pubs where
there is no mention of Bar Food in the statistics.
A restaurant within a pub is only specifically recommended
where its separate opening times are given.

DUBLIN   The Harbourmaster

Tel 01 670 1688   Fax 01 671 2672   Map 6 G4   **JaB**
Custom House Docks Dublin 1

Right in the heart of Dublin's new financial services centre, this old Dock
Offices building was sensitively converted and opened as a pub/bar in 1994.
The building retains an unusual amount of genuine character and the two-storey
hall once used to auction goods impounded for non-payment of taxes is now
the main bar area. Upstairs, a little look-out corner where the Dock Manager
used to keep an eye on things is reached by a balcony overlooking the bar, now
all set up with tables. Although there is still a very pleasant bar, the food operation
has grown to such an extent that it is now more restaurant than pub at meal
times. All available space is used simply but quite stylishly for eating and most
tables have an interesting (and increasingly attractive) view of the development
outside, which is now reaching its final stages. A short written menu is
augmented by daily blackboard specials and emphatically eclectic: Cajun chicken
wings rub shoulders with moules à la marinière, while Spanish tortilla sits
alongside a Greek parcel, and Thai-style chicken stir-fry wrests the eye from
beef in Guinness. While not exactly gourmet fare it is cheerfully appropriate to
the surroundings and some thought has gone into the planning – soup of the day
is made with vegetable stock, for instance, and there's a fair range of vegetarian
dishes on the menu – and service, under the direction of manager John Duff,
is friendly and efficient. Under the same ownership as *Thomas Read* (see entry).
Meals 12-10. Closed Good Friday & 25 Dec. Amex, Diners, MasterCard, **VISA**

DUBLIN   Harding Hotel   £61

Tel 01 679 6500   Fax 01 679 6504   Map 5 E3   **A**
Copper Alley Fishamble Street Christchurch Dublin 2

New, purpose-built hotel conveniently located in the heart of the city within
Temple Bar, Dublin's thriving 'Left Bank'. The prime central position and
the competitive room prices (£40 single, £50 double/triple exc breakfast) are
proving popular with business people and tourists (especially families) visiting
Dublin on a limited budget. Compact bedrooms, most with attractive views of
Christchurch Cathedral opposite, are clean and functional, with pine furnishings,
bold fabrics, open wardrobes and en suite shower /WC (the handbasin is in the
room). Those wishing to linger in their room will find a telephone, TV and
tea-making facilities. No lounge, but one can relax in the Viking-themed
Wood Quay Bar or in Fitzers Café, also the venue for breakfast (charged extra).
No dogs. *Rooms 53. Closed 23-27 Dec. MasterCard,* **VISA**

DUBLIN   Harvey's Coffee House

Tel 01 677 1060   Map 5 F3   **JaB**
14/15 Trinity Street Dublin 2

John Harvey's bustling corner café does a number of things very well. For
instance, they lay on a very tasty breakfast which, on Sundays (when there
is space to set up tables on the pavement) develops into brunch: toast, bagels,
scones, croissants, toasted bacon sandwiches and even porridge with cinnamon,
honey and cream. Later, the choice widens when the home-made soup comes
on stream alongside more substantial fare like the Trinity Special (focaccia bread
with traditional baked ham and melted mozzarella topped with fresh basil,
pepperoni and toasted sunflower seeds) and Vegetarian Delight (avocado, salted
peanuts, tomato, grated carrot and curly endive on rye and walnut bread). Bagels
by the bagful, sandwiches, pastries and desserts – Harvey's does them all very
well. But what they do best is coffee: ristretto, espresso, doppio espresso,

cappuccino, latte, machiato, espresso con panna, ciocolatta, American and mocha are all served here – and how! No wonder it's sometimes so hard to get into this magic coffee house ... and it's no wonder that Harvey's wins our Coffee Award of Excellence for 1997. *Seats 50. Parties 6. Open Mon-Sat 7.45-7 (Sat to 6), Sun 9.30-5. Closed 25 & 26 Dec. No credit cards.*

DUBLIN   P Hedigan: The Brian Boru

Tel 01 830 8514   Fax 01 860 0242   Map 3 A4   **P**
5 Prospect Road Glasnevin Dublin 9

Named after an 11th-century High King of Ireland, this smartly maintained pub is also known as Hedigan's after owner Peter Hedigan. Original Victorian themes – mahogany, stained glass and, especially, very fine tiling – have been carried through faithfully as alterations have been made through the years, everything is neat and clean and the eye is drawn past an abundance of strong tables and seating, to a patio/beer garden at the back, also furnished with comfortable eating in mind. It comes as no surprise that the Brian Boru has been in the same family since 1904. Bar food is best described as traditional: soup of the day, ever-popular roast prime rib of beef, Irish stew or Baileys gateau on the lunchtime carvery, followed by an evening menu with garlic mushrooms, melon, chicken Kiev, steaks and home-made apple pie. *Open 10.30-11.30, Sun 12.30-2, 4-11. Bar Food (carvery) 12-3 (Sun 12.30-2.30), 3-9 (Sun 4-7). Garden, outdoor eating. MasterCard, VISA*

We publish annually, so make sure you use the current edition
– it's well worth being up-to-date!

DUBLIN   Hibernian Hotel   70%   £145

Tel 01 668 7666   Fax 01 660 2655   Map 6 G1   **HR**
Eastmoreland Place Ballsbridge Dublin 4

This magnificent Victorian redbrick building, once a nurses' home and tucked away in a quiet residential area, is handy for the centre of Dublin as it's just off Upper Baggot Street. The public areas, including two reception lounges, can double up to receive small conferences/receptions; they are cosy, with open fireplaces and well furnished with decent pictures and plenty of comfortable seating as well as pretty floral arrangements; the perfect spot for afternoon tea. The hotel's trademark is a huge glass bowl of liquorice allsorts and jelly babies on the reception counter, a theme carried through to the bedrooms, where it becomes a novel alternative to fresh fruit. Bedrooms, by no means lavish but quite adequately furnished, offer remote-control TV, trouser press, hairdryer, bathrobe and slippers. Quality Crabtree & Evelyn toiletries (plus emergency shaving and dental kit) are to be found in the compact bathrooms. A further nine bedrooms (described as junior suites and priced accordingly – £180) opened last year. Super-friendly staff provide just the right level of service, which includes a bed turn-down service. No children under 12. Under the same ownership as Grey Door (see entry). A boardroom seats 18. Secure parking. *Rooms 40. Patio garden. Closed 25 & 26 Dec. Amex, Diners, MasterCard, VISA*

See over

Restaurant   £70

Relaxing dining in an elegantly appointed room decorated in deep terracotta, dark green and cream or under stylish cream parasols on the terrace – an oasis of tranquillity in the city. Chef David Foley produces a seasonally-changing à la carte, from which roast quail with fettuccine of vegetables and green peppercorn jus, millefeuille of salmon and codling with cabbage leaves and caviar cream, and warm blueberry pancake soufflé with cardamom ice cream are typical choices. A simpler weekly table d'hote might offer cream of lentil and smoked bacon soup, pan-fried skate wings with aubergine caviar and cinnamon and rum savarin with summer fruits. No children under 12. *Seats 40. Parties 15. Private Room 25. L 12.30-2.30 D 6.30-10 (Sun 7-9). Set L £13.95. Set D £19.95/£24.50. Closed L Sat, all Good Friday & 25, 26 Dec. Amex, Diners, MasterCard, VISA*

DUBLIN	Imperial Chinese Restaurant	£40

Tel & Fax 01 677 2580   Map 5 F3   **R**
13 Wicklow Street Dublin 2

This smartly decorated Chinese restaurant with pink and gold marble-effect walls and much polished brass has a distinctly upmarket interior complete with an ornamental pool stocked with golden carp (not on the menu!). The regular carte features a familiar selection of mainly Cantonese dishes. On Sundays (especially) there's a good selection of dim sum available till 5.30pm, supplemented Mondays to Saturdays by good-value businessmen's lunches. Standards of service are usually excellent. *Seats 180. Parties 50. Private Room 70. Meals 12.30pm-11.45pm (till 12.45 Fri & Sat). Closed 25 Dec. Set L £7 Set D from £17. Amex, MasterCard, VISA*

DUBLIN	Ivy Court	£55

Tel 01 492 0633   Fax 01 492 0634   Map 3 A2   **R**
88 Rathgar Road Dublin 6

Swiss chef Josef Frei cooks an eclectic and imaginative range of dishes in his delightful restaurant almost due south of the city centre. Walls have large Breughel-inspired murals while the menu offers such varied starters as squid ribbons with garlic and chili, wild mushroom feuilleté with cream sauce and traditional black and white pudding with onion marmalade. Main courses include enjoyable pasta and stir-fry dishes as well as Swiss-style veal liver with rösti potatoes, seafood medley in a brandy bisque sauce and fillet steak topped with tiger shrimp and Provençal sauce. Out at the front there's an attractive courtyard that is used for fine-weather dining. No smoking in downstairs dining-room. Children welcome before 8pm. Early Bird set dinner (5.30-7, £11.25) Mon-Fri. *Seats 80. Parties 12. Private Room 34. D only 5.30-11.30. Closed Sun, Good Friday & 24-27 Dec. Diners, MasterCard, VISA*

DUBLIN	Jurys Christchurch Inn	60%	£67

Tel 01 454 0000   Fax 01 454 0012   Map 5 E3   **H**
Christchurch Place Dublin 8

Budget hotel within walking distance of the city centre run on the same lines as its sister hotels in Cork and Galway (see entries). Spacious rooms, some with views over Christchurch cathedral and its environs, accommodate up to four people for a flat-rate room tariff. Basic requirements are well provided for, with good-sized beds, neat bathrooms with over-bath showers, decent towels and toiletries, direct-dial phone and colour TV. One floor of rooms is designated non-smoking. Children up to 14 stay free in parents' room. No room service. No dogs. Multi-storey car park nearby. *Rooms 182. Closed 24-26 Dec. Amex, Diners, MasterCard, VISA*

DUBLIN   Jurys Custom House Inn   60%   £55

Tel 01 607 5000   Fax 01 829 0400   Map 6 G4   **H**
Custom House Quay Dublin 1

The latest (and largest) Jurys Inn opened last year on a remarkable site beside the financial services centre, overlooking the River Liffey and close to train and bus stations. The requirements of business guests are met in better facilities than normally expected in budget hotels; large bedrooms can sleep up to four and have all the usual facilities, plus fax/modem lines and a higher standard of finish than earlier sister hotels. Fabrics and fittings are of a better quality and neat bathrooms are more thoughtfully designed, with more generous shelf space but tiny bath tubs. Large bar, restaurant, conference facilities in four rooms (seating up to 100 theatre-style) and a business centre staffed from 7.30am-7.30pm. No room service. A 400-space multi-storey car park is adjacent to the hotel. No dogs. *Rooms 234. Mini-gym, news kiosk. Closed 24-26 Dec. Amex, Diners, MasterCard,* **VISA**

DUBLIN   Jurys Hotel Dublin   69%   £178

Tel 01 660 5000   Fax 01 660 5540   Map 6 H1   **H**
Pembroke Road Ballsbridge Dublin 4

With its close proximity to the Lansdowne Road (rugby and soccer) ground, the main hotel can get seriously busy on match days with fans clamouring to gain access to the bars. The traditional Dubliner Pub, to the right of the bright and airy foyer, has a comfortable raised seating area, while the other, the Pavilion Lounge, is to the rear under a glass pyramid with rockery, greenery and trickling water. In addition there's a long-hours coffee shop, and from May-October 2_ hours of sparkling Irish cabaret. Most of the bedrooms have undergone recent refurbishment and provide decent comfort and facilities, with plenty of workspace for the business executive, bright marble-tiled bathrooms and comprehensive 24hr room service. Children under 14 stay free in their parents' room. Sharing the same site and many of the same facilities, the adjacent Jurys Towers hotel now has its own access and reception on Landsdowne Road and is listed this year as a separate entity (see entry for details). Extensive banqueting (600) and conference (850) facilities. Ample parking. No dogs. *Rooms 290. Garden, indoor & outdoor swimming pools, spa bath, beauty & hair salons, masseuse, shop, airline desk, coffee shop (6am-4.30am, Sun till 10.30pm). Amex, Diners, MasterCard,* **VISA**

DUBLIN   Kapriol   £65

Tel 01 475 1235   Map 5 F1   **R**
45 Lower Camden Street Dublin 2

A popular Italian restaurant near the famous Bleeding Horse pub and within walking distance of many of the main hotels. Egidia and Giuseppe Peruzzi provide a warm greeting, a very friendly atmosphere and a menu of traditional Italian dishes which has barely changed in 20 years. Pasta is all home-made, and main-course specialities include baked salmon with prawns and cream, chicken involtini, veal Marsala and beef steaks either plainly grilled or alla pizzaiola. *Seats 30. D only 7-12. Closed Sun, Bank Holidays & first 3 weeks Aug. Amex, Diners, MasterCard,* **VISA**

DUBLIN   Kavanagh's

No Telephone   Map 3 A4   **P**
Prospect Square Glasnevin Dublin 9

An entertaining, unselfconscious pub that's been in the Kavanagh family since 1833. It's known locally as the 'Gravediggers Arms' because of its location at the back of Dublin's largest cemetery. It's a small place, with a stone floor, rather rickety woodwork breaking up the bar, and fittings and decorations which are simple, original and authentic. Pints of Guinness are, naturally, the main liquid sustenance. *Open 10.30-11.30 (Sun 12-2, 4-11). Closed Good Friday & 25, 26 Dec. No credit cards.*

DUBLIN   Kielys

Tel 01 283 0209   Map 3 B2   **P**
22/24 Donnybrook Road Donnybrook Dublin 4

Kielys is a Donnybrook landmark with its long, impressive frontage. Inside, where art nouveau decorations writhe around the mirrors (especially at the impressive mahogany bar area), there's an unexpectedly fin de siècle atmosphere; reinforced by the use of traditional mahogany tables on curvaceous wrought-iron bases, stained-glass windows at the back and a semi-snug, the size of a domestic sitting room, which creates the feeling of a club within the pub. The lunchtime carvery (£4.95) has a choice of four hot dishes including a daily roast and the likes of beef and Guinness casserole, haddock mornay and vegetable lasagne. From 3pm a bar menu of basket meals takes over. Another surprise awaits the curious – at the back there is another pub, Ciss Madden's, a very traditional old Dublin spit 'n' sawdust kind of a place; it has a separate entrance but can also be reached through Kielys bar. Furthermore, there's an Italian restaurant, *La Finezza*, upstairs (Tel 01 283 7166, open from 5pm, bar and restaurant menus). *Pub open 10.30-11.30, Sun 12.30-2, 4-11.* **Bar Food** *12.30-10.30 (Sun 12.30-2, 4-10). Children allowed in the bar to eat till 7. Closed Good Friday & 25 Dec.* Amex, MasterCard, **VISA**

If you encounter bad service don't wait to write to us but make your feelings known to the management at the time of your visit. Instant compensation can often resolve any problem that might otherwise leave a bad taste.

DUBLIN   Kilkenny Kitchen

Tel 01 677 7066   Map 5 F3   **JaB**
Nassau Street Dublin 2

Situated on the first floor over the famous Kilkenny Shop with its Irish crafts and Blarney woollens, this self-service restaurant is a favourite spot for local workers and shoppers alike, thanks to its wholesome, inexpensive all-day food. Although the menu is quite wide-ranging (it includes a good choice of hot and cold lunch dishes – spinach and nutmeg soup, good fresh pasta, salmon and potato fish cakes with sour cream, chicken and basil lasagne with pesto bread), it is for refreshing salads (to eat in or take home) and, even more, their home-made, gluten-free baking (scones, lemon cake) and own-label preserves and dressings (marmalades, pesto etc) that the Kilkenny Kitchen is best known. Increased demand has led to a recent restaurant extension, and the best tables overlook Trinity college playing fields. *Seats 250. Open 9-5 Mon-Sat (lunch dishes served 12-4). Closed Sun (Oct, Nov & Jan-Apr), Winter Bank Holidays & 25-27 Dec.* Amex, Diners, MasterCard, **VISA**

DUBLIN   Kitty O'Shea's Bar

Tel 01 660 8050   Fax 01 668 3979
23/25 Upper Grand Canal Street Dublin 4   Map 6 G2   **P**

One of Dublin's best-known and best-loved pubs, a favourite meeting place before or after a rugby match at Lansdowne Road and a popular spot for a snack or a meal. Typical dishes on the luncheon menu include chicken liver paté, prawn cocktail, Irish stew, Connemara spring lamb and beef and Guinness casserole, with, to follow, a trolley laden with desserts. Evening à la carte items include fried Ballycastle crab claws, fresh River Moy salmon and Kitty's home-made beefburgers topped with Charleville cheddar. Tour groups over 35 are offered fixed-price menus (from £14.50), which include the live traditional Irish music staged every night. Saturday and Sunday brunch (12-3). Branches in Paris, Brussels and Barcelona. *Open 10.30-11.30 (winter till 11, Fri/Sat till 12.30), Sun 12.30-11.* **Bar Food** *12-10. Beer garden, outdoor eating. Closed Good Friday & 25, 26 Dec. Amex, MasterCard,* **VISA**

We welcome bona fide complaints and recommendations on the tear-out Readers' Comments pages at the back of the Guide. They are followed up by our professional team.

DUBLIN   Langkawi Malaysian Restaurant   £40

Tel 01 668 2760   Map 6 G1   **R**
46 Upper Baggot Street Dublin 4

Decorated throughout with a batik theme, Langkawi offers a selection of Far Eastern dishes with Malay, Chinese and Indian influences. Chef Alexander Hosey brings street credibility to his mee goreng 'hawker-style' – the type of popular food sold cheaply in outdoor markets in Malaysia and Singapore – as well as subtlety to some of his more exotic dishes. Most of the spices he uses are mixed in Malaysia by his mother, from whom are obtained such essentials as dried anchovies, salt fish, prawn paste, banana leaves and tamarind as well as much of the inspiration for his impressive array of authentic dishes. The choice ranges from mild satay to 'devil's curries' (for fireproof palates) and all are enlivened by his faultless sambals, rendangs and ackar pickle. *Seats 60. L 12.30-2 D 6-11.45. Closed L Sat & Sun, Good Friday & 24-27 Dec. Amex, MasterCard, Diners,* **VISA**

DUBLIN   Little Caesar's Pizza

Tel 01 671 8714   Map 5 F2   **JaB**
5 Chatham House Balfe Street Dublin 2

Right opposite the entrance to the Westbury Hotel, this great meeting place occupies a buzzy little ground-floor and basement premises with considerable chic – mirrors and murals work miracles in minuscule spaces. The menu may hold no surprises but it is honest fare, cooked to order before your very eyes, and its popularity bears witness to a high level of consistency. Go for the rich, thick minestrone served with crisp garlic bread, the thin-crusted pizzas (either medium or large – easily enough for two) topped with bubbling-hot mozzarella, spaghetti del marinara with Sicilian-style salad (heady with olive oil) or the ever-reliable 'Caesar's Favourites' – pollo alla diavolo and charcoal grilled steak alla pizzaiola. *Seats 90. Meals Noon-12.30am (Sun 1-12). Closed Good Friday & 25, 26 Dec. Amex, Diners, MasterCard,* **VISA**

DUBLIN — Lobster Pot — £70

Tel & Fax 01 668 0025
Map 6 H1
R
9 Ballsbridge Terrace Dublin 4

A welcoming and comfortable first-floor dining-room with a cosy ambience and very genial, long-serving staff. A tray of the day's fresh fish is brought to the table with Galway oysters, mussels, Dublin Bay prawns, plaice, monkfish, black sole and lobster invariably among the selection. Soundly classical, traditional cooking delivers extremely enjoyable main dishes such as sole bonne femme, poached turbot, prawns mornay and fruits de mer à la crème. Despite the predominance of fish they also have a good choice of meat dishes that includes peppered entrecote and steak tartare, both prepared at the table. Dessert trolley offerings are supplemented by meringue glacé (with that Irish cream liqueur) and crepes Suzette for two. *Seats 40. L 12.30-2.30 D 6.30-10.30. Closed L Sat, all Sun, Bank Holidays & 24 Dec-2 Jan. Amex, Diners, MasterCard,* **VISA**

DUBLIN — Locks Restaurant — £85

Tel 01 454 3391
Map 5 E1
R
1 Windsor Terrace Portobello Dublin 8

Claire Douglas's relaxing canal-side restaurant is full of charm with antiques, interesting pictures, crisp linen, fine glasses and delightfully mis-matched old plates on which Brian Buckley's appealing dishes are served. Locks fish soup, spicy crab cakes with pineapple salsa, and goat's cheese with pesto crust and a beetroot and rocket salad might precede more-ish main courses such as feuilleté of salmon, asparagus and mussels with tarragon sauce or medallions of venison with lentils on a balsamic vinegar sauce. Desserts are confidently presented on extra-large plates, or there is a selection of Irish farmhouse cheeses. *Seats 47. Parties 16. Private Room 35. L 12.30-2 D 7.15-11. Closed L Sat, all Sun, Bank Holiday Mondays, 1 week Christmas & 2 weeks Jul/Aug. Set L £14.95 Set D £23.50 (+12_% service charge). Amex, Diners, MasterCard,* **VISA**

DUBLIN — Longfield's Hotel — 61% — £123

Tel 01 676 1367   Fax 01 676 1542
Map 6 G2
HR
Fitzwilliam Street Lower Dublin 2

Charming, antique-furnished hotel right in the heart of Georgian Dublin and with the intimate atmosphere of a graciously proportioned and beautifully furnished private house. Public areas are comfortable and bedrooms are individually furnished, but do vary considerably in size. All rooms are en suite but only three have bathtubs, the remainder have shower and WC only. Friendly staff and 24-hour room service. Morning coffee and afternoon tea are served in the drawing-room. Limited private parking (6 spaces). Children welcome: under-12s stay free in parents' room, with cots and high-chairs provided. *Rooms 26. Closed 24-27 Dec. Amex, Diners, MasterCard,* **VISA**

No 10 Restaurant   £65

In the basement, with direct access from the hotel or the street, this attractive restaurant uses space with ingenuity (aperitifs are served in what was once the coal bunker, now cleverly transformed with trompe l'oeil) and, although tables are rather tightly packed, it is a popular venue. Tommy Donovan's imaginative menus strike a balance between traditional Irish fare (such as smoked salmon with lemon and capers or rack of lamb with garlic potoates and tomato jus) and fashionable, Mediterranean-influenced alternatives: spiced beef salad with basil oil, black olives and aged parmesan, a fish soup 'typical of south-east France', grilled salmon fillet with red pepper and basil pommes purées and confit of duck leg with green peppercorns and Grand Marnier. French and Irish cheeses are offered as an alternative to desserts such as rich chocolate terrine with a coffee bean sauce. *Seats 40. Parties 10. Private Room 20. L 12.30-2.30 D 6.30-10 (Fri/Sat 7-11, Sun to 9). Closed L Sat & Sun, 24 Dec-2 Jan. Set D £24.95.*

DUBLIN   **The Lord Edward**   **£60**

Tel & Fax 01 454 2420   Map 5 E3   **R**
23 Christchurch Place Dublin 8

Billed as Dublin's oldest seafood restaurant, The Lord Edward occupies three floors of a tall, narrow and appropriately ancient building overlooking Christchurch cathedral. The style is club-like, traditional, downright old-fashioned in fact – which appears to be just the way the loyal local following like it. Kilcolgan oysters (hot or cold) and smoked salmon, eel and trout dominate hors d'oeuvre selections, following which are a dozen ways with sole (from plain grilled to véronique) and lobster, scallops and prawns in multitudinous variations. Concessions to meat eaters are minimal – chicken breast, grilled steak and veal Holstein –with vegetarian dishes on request. *Seats 40. Parties 8. L 12-5 D 6-11.45. Closed L Sat, all Sun, 24 Dec-2 Jan & Bank Holidays. Set L from £11.95 Set D £20. Amex, Diners, MasterCard,* **VISA**

DUBLIN   **Marine Hotel**   **64%**   **£120**

Tel 01 839 0000   Fax 01 839 0442   Map 4 C4   **H**
Sutton Cross Dublin 13

Standing right at Sutton Cross at the isthmus of Howth some 10kms from the city centre, the Marine has a large car park at the front while at the rear lawns lead right down to the waters of Dublin Bay. Public rooms include a delightful sun lounge overlooking the lawns and the popular Schooner Bar. Bedroom decor is appealing with richly coloured floral fabrics and smart darkwood furniture. All are well equipped (hairdryer, trouser press, remote TV). Bathrooms are neat, all with showers, some with shower and WC only. Conference/function facilities (max 200). Friendly and helpful staff. No dogs. *Rooms 26. Garden, indoor swimming pool, sauna, steam room. Closed 24-26 Dec. Amex, Diners, MasterCard,* **VISA**

DUBLIN   **Marrakesh Restaurant**   **£60**

Tel 01 660 5539   Map 6 H1   **R**
11 Ballsbridge Terrace Dublin 4

V

Chef Fethi Kartas is delighting a growing number of discerning guests with his authentic north African flavours at this tiny, atmospheric first-floor restaurant overlooking the bridge. The à la carte offers a wide range of traditional dishes, including classic starters like tabouleh (cracked wheat salad with tomatoes, scallions, mint, parsley, lemon juice and olive oil), briouat (deep-fried pastries filled with prawn, chicken or lamb) and mezze (selection of deep-fried prawns, vine leaves, felafel, houmus and chicken wings, served with savoury dips). Main courses are divided into styles of cooking: tagine (named after the pottery dishes in which these stews are simmered), couscous (the most famous Morrocan dish, based on steamed wheat and served with a variety of soupy vegetable, meat or fish dishes) and dolmas (vegetables or leaves stuffed with rice tomatoes and fresh herbs, served separately or as a selection). Typical desserts include excellent honeyed Moroccan pastries and fruit dishes such as a salad of fresh oranges scented with rose water. Best value on a first visit is probably the set menu for two, which offers a good selection of dishes and mint tea or coffee to finish. *Seats 25. Parties 6. D only 6-11 (Fri & Sat to 11.30). Closed 24-27 Dec. Set D £40 for two. Amex, Diners, MasterCard,* **VISA**

DUBLIN   McCormack's Merrion Inn

Tel 01 269 3816   Fax 01 269 6877   Map 4 C2   **P**
188 Merrion Road Dublin 4

They take their lunch and its comfortable consumption seriously at this
well-established pub. Despite its considerable age – and more than a passing
nod to tradition where serious matters such as service, friendliness and efficiency
are concerned – a modern hand has been at work with the decor, but the
unexpectedly bright colours work surprisingly well to create a cheerful atmosphere,
with various styles of seating and a generous distribution of tables and bar space
to enjoy food and drink in comfort. Soup and sandwiches are available at the bar
and there is a hot and cold buffet at the back. Choices on the blackboard change
daily, but there is always a roast, typically beef with roast potatoes and a selection
of five vegetables, a traditional casserole such as beef and Guinness. Evening
offerings include steamed mussels (as a starter or main dish), chargrilled chicken
on an open sandwich with a variety of spicings (fresh ginger and orange, lemon
and rosemary, spicy tandoori) and a range of Spanish-style omelettes; there's also
a range of salads and good desserts like pear and chocolate tart or banoffi pie.
Sunday brunch is the works (including black pudding). Children 'under control'
are welcome at lunchtimes and until 6pm on Sunday. No parking, use the
hospital's car park over the road. *Open 10.30am-11pm (Fri/Sat to 12.30am).*
Bar Food 12-3, 4-10 (Sat & Sun 12-10). Garden, outdoor eating.
Closed Good Friday & 25, 26 Dec. Amex, Diners, MasterCard, **VISA**

DUBLIN   The Mercantile Bar & Grill

Tel 01 679 0522   Map 5 F3   **P**
27-28 Dame Street Dublin 2

Transformed from its previous incarnations as a dreary old bank, the new
owners retained its architectural gems after a fashion, completely renovating and
remodelling it in a totally over-the-top style – mosaic floors, pillars, wrought
iron, plenty of colour. Though this possibly may not please architectural purists,
it certainly makes an impact, and the ground-floor bar is a useful meeting place,
handy for Trinity College, theatres and Temple Bar. Part of the Adams Trinity
Hotel (see entry), it also incorporates a 120-seat grill restaurant at mezzanine
level. *Bar Food 12-3. Closed Good Friday & 25 Dec. Amex, Diners, MasterCard,*
VISA

DUBLIN   La Mère Zou   £45

Tel & Fax 01 661 6669   Map 5 F2   **R**
22 St Stephen's Green Dublin 2

Eric Tydgadt and his wife Isabelle concentrate on providing real French country
cooking, at surprisingly reasonable prices. At lunchtime choose between the
three-course prix-fixe, the day's suggestion (individually priced) or their novel
Big Plates on which a salad starter and hot main dish are served together –
La Provençale: lettuce, tuna fish, anchovy and olive salad plus chargrilled lamb
brochette with Provençal sauce and baked potato; L'Océan, which twins
pan-fried Atlantic salmon in chive butter sauce with a mixed salad of peppered
mackerel and smoked trout. At night there's a four-course Early Bird menu
(till 7.30) plus an à la carte with the likes of Mediterranean fish soup with
rouille, roast magret of duck, Atlantic fish bouillabaisse and daily-changing fish
and meat suggestions according to the market. Finish off with French cheeses
or classic desserts like poire belle Hélène and Belgian chocolate mousse. *Seats 55.*
L 12.30-2.30 D 6-11. Closed L Sat & Sun, all Good Friday, 25, 26 Dec & 1-10 Jan.
Set L £9.50 Set D £12.50 (6-7.30)/£18.50. Amex, Diners, MasterCard, **VISA**

DUBLIN   Mermaid Café   £55

Tel 01 670 8236   Fax 01 670 8205   Map 5 E3   **R**
69/70 Dame Street Dublin 2

Owner-chef Benedict Gorman and his front-of-house partner Mark Harrell brought their East Coast American cuisine to town with a bang late in 1995 and their small restaurant on the edge of Temple Bar is already well established. Decor is quite simple, although the chunky furniture has a hint of 'designer' about it; every inch of space is utilised, with banquettes along the wall and an open kitchen at the back. An à la carte offering about half a dozen choices on each course is augmented by a short blackboard lunch menu, changed daily. Either menu might include starters like New England crab cakes with piquant mayonnaise and smoked mackerel rillettes with scallion and tomato salad, while typical autumn main courses could range from a strong vegetarian choice like savoury pumpkin and red onion tart with cumin and parmesan, through home-made venison and port sausage with celeriac and elderberry gravy to a 'giant Atlantic seafood casserole'. Paired Irish cheeses are imaginatively served – perhaps with apricot chutney and celery biscuits – and desserts may include a hot steamed pudding like blueberry with custard and an ice cream of the day served with home-made tuile. Espresso and cappuccino come with crystallised pecan nuts. All wines on the list are imported privately and are exclusive to the restaurant. Not suitable for children under 15 after 9pm. *Seats 55. Parties 10. Private Room 24. L 12-3 D 6.30-11. Closed Sun & Mon. Set L £11.25.* MasterCard, **VISA**

DUBLIN   Merrion Hall   £65

Tel 01 668 1426   Fax 01 668 4280   Map 3 B3   **A**
56 Merrion Road Ballsbridge Dublin 4

The adjacent properties of this charming, immaculately maintained, family-run guesthouse stand by the main ferry road just south of the city centre. The main sitting-room is very comfortable, encapsulating perfectly the friendly and homely ambience generated by the Sheeran family. Bedrooms are pretty and well equipped. Four are triple rooms while a further four have both a double and a single bed. The excellent breakfast features a self-service buffet that includes home-made yoghurt, poached fruits, fresh fruit salad and a cheeseboard. New extensions housing a further eight bedrooms were scheduled for completion in early 1997. No dogs. Private parking. *Rooms 15. Garden. Closed 2 weeks from 17 Dec.* MasterCard, **VISA**

DUBLIN   Mespil Hotel   65%   £86

Tel 01 667 1222   Fax 01 667 1244   Map 6 G1   **H**
Mespil Road Dublin 4

Overlooking Dublin's Grand Canal, the Mespil Hotel has been a welcome new addition to the Dublin hotel scene. Transformed from a former Government building into one offering stylish and modern accommodation, it enjoys a lovely location close to Baggot Street Bridge – only a short distance from the city centre. The foyer is splendidly fitted with floors tiled with Kirkstone, contrasting beech and mahogany woodwork, comfortable charcoal-grey leather settees and armorite walls; the latter are in deep blue and burnt orange, adding to the visual appeal of the decor. Bedrooms are of a good size and the best of them overlooking the canal; all are well equipped with hairdryer and multi-channel TVs as well as well co-ordinated colour schemes – bottle green in some, burgundy in others. Executive rooms have a trouser press and scales in the bathroom. Some bedrooms sleep three and nine rooms have facilities for less able-bodied guests. Limited room service. Conference facilities for 60. Secure car parking. No dogs. Sister hotel to the Sligo Park Hotel in Sligo (see entry). *Rooms 153. Closed 24-26 Dec.* Amex, Diners, MasterCard, **VISA**

DUBLIN   Mitchell's Cellars   £35

Tel 01 662 4724   Map 5 F2   **R**
21 Kildare Street Dublin 2

Situated in the arched cellars under the famous Mitchell's wine merchants, and in common ownership, little seems to have changed since this daytime restaurant first opened in the mid-70s (though their stylish lunches have happily moved with the times). Dependable home cooking is the order of the day: duck liver paté, avocado and crab salad, asparagus quiche, spiced chicken with basmati rice, raspberry frangipane, mocca meringue and a commendable Irish cheeseboard. Expect to queue – however, waiting in the bar is no hardship as the wines are worth spending some time on. No reservations. *Seats 70. L only 12.15-2.30. Closed Sun (also Sat Jun-Sep), Bank Holidays, Easter Tuesday & 24-28 Dec. Amex, Diners, MasterCard,* **VISA**

DUBLIN   Mont Clare Hotel   66%   £172

Tel 01 661 6799   Fax 01 661 5663   Map 6 G3   **H**
Merrion Square Dublin 2

Sister hotel to The Davenport (qv) across the road and with a similar clubby feel, although a little less grand and a bit more intimate in style. The bar is a fine example of a traditional Dublin pub complete with bare-board floor, enough mahogany to stock a rain forest and lots of atmosphere. The only other sitting area is a small but snug library off the smart, marble-floored lobby. Bedrooms are generally not large but have warm decor in stylish dark reds and blues with darkwood furniture, air-conditioning and telephones at both desk and bedside with a third in the good marble bathrooms. Guests have use of the private Riverview Racquets and Fitness Club at members' rates. Banqueting/conference facilities 120/150. Free valet parking. No dogs. *Rooms 74. Amex, Diners, MasterCard,* **VISA**

We only recommend the food in hotels categorised as **HR** and **AR**.
However, the food in many **A** establishments throughout
Ireland is often very acceptable
(but the restaurant may not be open to non-residents).

DUBLIN   National Museum Café

Tel 01 662 1269   Map 5 F2   **JaB**
Kildare Street Dublin 2

Before or after a stroll around the exhibits of Ireland's heritage, the café offers a counter-service selection of savoury and sweet foods. The setting is a grand one – a fine mosaic floor with a beautiful crystal chandelier overhead. Tables are of pink granite and the range of food encompasses light snacks such as home-baked scones, biscuits and banana bread. Daily-changing hot specials served between 12.30 and 3 include soup served with a scone, good-value main dishes like poached haddock in dill sauce and roast loin of pork with potatoes and vegetables for under £5. Cold fare and vegetarian dishes, too, plus a good choice for the sweet-toothed that includes a highly popular cheesecake. *Seats 70. Meals 10-5 (Sun 2-5). Closed Mon, Good Friday & 25 Dec. Amex, Diners, MasterCard,* **VISA**

DUBLIN · Number 31 · £75

Tel 01 676 5011   Fax 01 676 2929   Map 5 F1   **A**
31 Leeson Close off Lower Leeson Street Dublin 2

Brian and Mary Bennett have now purchased the Georgian building on Fitzwilliam Place, which backs on to their exisiting mews house, thus increasing (no-smoking) bedroom capacity. Accessible via the garden, the newly acquired house includes three very large bedrooms (suitable for families) decorated in the same bright and homely style as the others (one with its own patio). In essence, this is exclusive bed-and-breakfast accommodation, with the emphasis very much on Mary's breakfasts, taken at two upstairs refectory tables or in the conservatory, overlooking the kitchen, during summer months. She daily bakes the bread (perhaps brown soda, banana or nut) and scones to go alongside home-made jams, freshly-squeezed juices, Irish farmhouse cheeses, fry-ups and vegetarian options. The mews house once belonged to architect Sam Stephenson; it's mostly in white, with lots of artwork on the walls, the centrepiece being the lounge with a sunken black leather seating area. Secure, locked parking available. Not really suitable for children under 10, but on a recent visit we encountered a babe in arms, so ask! No dogs. *Rooms 18. Garden, sauna. Closed 1 week at Christmas (open New Year's Eve). Amex, MasterCard, VISA*

DUBLIN · No 88 · £72

Tel 01 660 0277   Fax 01 660 0291   Map 6 H1   **A**
88 Pembroke Road Ballsbridge Dublin 4

The recent sympathetic conversion of three Georgian town houses has retained many of the original features at this smart Ballsbridge address adjacent to the American embassy. Day rooms include a comfortable day lounge and a boardroom. Generally spacious bedrooms are fairly uniform with modern lightwood furniture, good firm beds and power showers. Some family rooms have an adjoining double and single; the lower level rear rooms, however, suffer from noise and the lack of a view. Private parking. *Rooms 50. Patio. Amex, Diners, MasterCard, VISA*

DUBLIN · O'Donohue's

Tel 01 676 2807   Map 5 F2   **P**
15 Merrion Row Dublin 2

One of Dublin's foremost traditional music pubs and a family-owned establishment, this is where The Dubliners first came to fame. It was rebuilt after a major fire in the 80s, though the dark wood panelled walls and heavily smoke-stained paintwork give the impression that the place is really rather ancient. As well as the usual pub mirrors and pictures, the walls of the larger, smoky back music room are hung with large portraits of many of the other famous musicians who have appeared here. Arrive early for a seat at weekends. *Open 10-11 (music from 9pm as well as Sat and Sun afternoons). Closed 25 Dec. No credit cards.*

DUBLIN · O'Dwyer's

Tel 01 676 3574   Fax 01 676 2281   Map 6 G2   **P**
Mount Street Dublin 2

This large, bustling pub always has a good buzz and is well supported both at lunchtime and in early evening by the thriving local business and professional community. Later, a night club attracts a younger crowd who are especially appreciative of the renowned O'Dwyer's pizzas. Professionally run, cheerful and central. *Open 11-11.30 (Sat from 6, Sun from 5). Closed Good Friday & 25 Dec. Amex, Diners, MasterCard, VISA*

DUBLIN   Old Dublin Restaurant   £65

Tel 01 454 2028   Fax 01 454 1406   Map 5 E3   **R**
90/91 Francis Street Dublin 8

Situated right in the old Viking area of the city in a street that has become
legendary for its antique shops, Eamonn Walsh's oasis of civilised dining is one
of Dublin's longest-established fine restaurants. Although completely refurbished
in 1996 (everything right down to the menu covers came in for a change),
the restaurant has retained all its charm and, perhaps because the dining area
is broken up into several domestic-sized rooms with special features – a marble
fireplace here, some very good pictures there – it still has a cosy, old-world
atmosphere. While most famous for its Russian and Scandinavian specialities like
blinis (buckwheat pancake with cured salmon, prawns and herrings) and planked
sirloin Hussar, which still feature strongly on the à la carte menu, head chef Neil
McFadden has broadened the appeal of his menus considerably. Now, alongside
the lime-cured gravlax served with warm dill potato and forsmak (a tasty 'sausage'
of lamb, herrings, potato, garlic and onions, served with creamed potato and
beetroot with soured cream), you can expect to find starters like grilled goat's
cheese with pressed red pepper and basil on toasted brioche, or even a salad
of candied aubergine with vine tomato, rocket and parmesan crackling. Main
courses often include Errigal lamb from Donegal (roast loin with shiitake and
basil) and wild Greencastle salmon (roast fillet served with lemon and balsamic
oil); a vegetarian menu is also offered. Tasty desserts include good home-made
ice creams. *Seats 65. Parties 28. Private Room 16. L 12.30-2.30 D 6-11.
Closed L Sat, all Sun, Bank Holidays, 25 & 26 Dec. Set L £12.50 Set D £10
(2-course Early Bird 6-7pm) & £21. Amex, Diners, MasterCard,* **VISA**

DUBLIN   The Old Stand

Tel 01 677 7220   Fax 01 677 5849   Map 5 F3   **P**
37 Exchequer Street Dublin 2

A sister pub to Davy Byrnes (see entry), The Old Stand is a comfortable,
old-fashioned place, attractive in a strong, sensible way with black paint outside
and dark mahogany inside, good detail behind the bar and a loyal local
following. The food is simple but good – they are famous for their sirloin steaks,
both 6oz and 12oz. Daily specials are keenly priced and always popular: be they
roast lamb with fresh vegetables, roast stuffed chicken leg or baked cod with
parsley sauce, you'll have change from £5. Omelettes, salads and open
sandwiches (smoked salmon or prawn) and many more grills fill out the menu
further at night. A well-run, gimmick-free pub. *Open 10.30-11.30, Sun 12.30-3,
4-11. Bar Food 12.30-9, Sun 12.30-3, 4-8. Closed Good Friday, 25 & 26 Dec.
MasterCard,* **VISA**

DUBLIN   101 Talbot   £30

Tel & Fax 01 874 5011   Map 5 F4   **R**
101 Talbot Street Dublin 1

Upstairs in a busy shopping street, close to O'Connell Street and the Abbey
and Gate Theatres, this bright, airy restaurant has a rather arty cheap and
cheerful atmosphere which harmonises well with the wholesome Mediterranean-
influenced and spicy Eastern food. Pasta, vegetarian, fish and meat dishes all
appear on the menu: spiced Mexican vegetable casserole with tomato risotto
and lamb mousaka with rosemary pesto for a good-value lunch, and only slightly
higher-priced evening offerings such as Cajun-style monkfish tails with lime
butter sauce, Moroccan aubergines stuffed with couscous, dried fruit and

vegetables in spicy tomato sauce and beef fillet medallions in garlic butter. Open all day for tea, coffee, soup, pasta and snacks (£3.50 minimum charge at peak times). *Seats 90. L 12-3 D 6-11 (light meals 10am-11pm). Closed D Mon, all Sun, Bank Holidays & 1 week Christmas. Amex, Diners, MasterCard,* **VISA**

DUBLIN   Pasta Fresca

Tel 01 679 2402
2-4 Chatham Street Dublin 2   Map 5 F2   **JaB**

Bustling Italian restaurant/wine bar/deli just off the smart Grafton Street shopping area. Friendly waiting staff serve an all-day selection of straightforward food starting with full Irish breakfast at £2.95. The usual pasta, pizza, salads and burgers are supplemented by hot lunch dishes which might be of chicken or fish, while grilled steaks and chicken Kiev help fill out the evening menu. *Seats 85. Meals 7.30am-12pm (Sun 12-9). Closed Good Friday, 25 & 26 Dec. Set L £6.95 Set D from £12.75. Diners, MasterCard,* **VISA**

> If you encounter bad service don't wait to write to us but make your feelings known to the management at the time of your visit. Instant compensation can often resolve any problem that might otherwise leave a bad taste.

DUBLIN   Patrick Guilbaud   ★↑   £115

Tel 01 676 4192   Fax 01 661 0052   Map 6 G2   **R**
46 James Place off Lower Baggot Street Dublin 2 – *see story*

This rather anonymous building, tucked away in a mews-like street behind Baggot Street to the east of St Stephens Green, is the somewhat modest address of one of Dublin's leading restaurants – however, as we went to press we were advised that the restaurant was moving to 21, Upper Merrion Street, Dublin 2 in August 1997. The air-conditioned interior, however, is far from modest, with a smart reception area leading on to the restaurant proper with its high, atrium-like ceiling, abundance of greenery and abstract art work around the walls. Patrick Guilbaud himself is always very much in evidence, presiding over his creation with urbanity and Gallic charm while his well-drilled team ensure the smooth progress of your meal. The cooking, in the safe hands of head chef Guillaume Le Brun, is as sophisticated as the surroundings, consistent (if a shade unvarying) in his signature dishes: pan-fried duck foie gras with peaches and gewürztraminer sauce, lobster ravioli with curried olive oil dressing, and roast Challans duck (for two) with peach and green peppercorn sauce all appear as redactions of previous à la carte specialities. The best of Irish ingredients also retain their prominence in dishes like Connemara lobster (with baby fennel and lemon balm), Bantry Bay king scallops (seared and served with watercress and deep-fried leeks) and crubeens (braised pig's trotters with wild mushroom pudding and rosemary sauce). As much thought goes into the well-balanced dessert list: hot croustillant of apples, summer pudding with home-made vanilla ice cream, a light red fruit cheesecake or lemon mousse with sablé biscuit and strawberry sorbet. In addition, there are French cheeses from Philippe Olivier (and particularly good home-baked breads, too). The wine list is largely French with reasonable prices; look to the Specialist Cellar list for the 'classic' bottles. *Seats 60. Private Room 28. L 12.30-2.15 D 7.30-10. Closed Sun, Mon & Bank Holidays. Set L £22.50 Set D £35 & £60. Amex, Diners, MasterCard,* **VISA**

DUBLIN   Peacock Alley   †   £90

Tel 01 662 0760   Fax 01 662 0776   Map 5 F3   **R**
47 South William Street Dublin 2

Conrad Gallagher's move from small basement premises on Baggot Street to a bright, spacious restaurant in the city's premier dining area has allowed this talented, energetic and genial young chef to indulge his sense of drama and create more appropriate surroundings to frame his culinary works of art. Strong background colours – blue in one room, green in the other – show off striking modern paintings, statuary and generous use of plants, all contrasting effectively with classic, white-clothed tables. A reception area/bar with comfortable seating shortens the long, narrow dining area, while a large skylight towards the back of the restaurant brightens and broadens it. Well-spaced tables and carefully contrived extra corners allow a fair degree of privacy. Gallagher has worked hard over the last year to establish a reputation as the enfant terrible of the Dublin restaurant world, providing a slick package for people who see food as entertainment and like to be right where the buzz is. Expect skilful cooking and high-fashion presentation based on an extraordinary range of fresh ingredients; the house style involves a vast amount of preparation, design and skilled assembly work – as far from home cooking as it is possible to get. Also be prepared for noticeable delays between courses (a note on the menu warns 'Please allow sufficient time as everything is cooked to order. If you are in a particular hurry, please let us know'). The choice of menus includes a 3-course lunch menu (with numerous supplements, including all side dishes), an à la carte and a dégustation menu. A 'little appetiser', compliments of the chef' and half a dozen choices of bread – along with butter presented in a pretty pear shape on a pool of extra-virgin olive oil (it's a pity to spoil it – a feeling created by the visual impact of almost everything here) – are offered by smiling waiters, creating a good first impression. Dishes are generally dramatic and complicated, with at least three or four elements in each – an understatement in most cases. Starters tend to be generous to a fault, the wild greens in a 'salad of wild greens with pumpkin seeds, baked tomato and baby asparagus' may be cultivated but are nevertheless delicious and pretty much as expected from the menu, while 'crab meat salad with a confit lemon and coriander with marinated beetroot and curried crème fraiche' is presented as a little tower set amid a complicated array dominated by diced marinated beetroot. The same style of presentation runs through the main courses – a 'daube of beef with caramelised onions, root vegetables and rosemary mashed potatoes' has a deep-fried 'bird's nest' vegetable garnish on top like a miniature lighthouse within a sea of accompaniments, while 'fillet of lamb with purée squash, herbed risotto and ratatouille' is a bonfire of a dish piled up on a base of herbed risotto. Seriously impressive presentation – the many, complex elements are constructed to create a colourful and dramatic effect, but so much detail clamours for attention that the taste buds may be inclined to acquire amnesia. An admirable cheese selection lists six French and six Irish speciality cheeses (with useful descriptions) while a choice of seven desserts might include some welcome (and unexpected) simplicity in the likes of a delicious 'hot and cold vanilla and pear' – a little crème brulée with tender pear slices and not too much else. Good choice of teas and coffees to finish. *Seats 65. Parties 10. L 12.30-2.15 D 6.30-11. Set L £16.95. Closed all Sun & Mon, Bank Holidays & a few days at Christmas.* Amex, Diners, MasterCard, **VISA**

DUBLIN   Periwinkle Seafood Bar

Tel 01 679 4203   Map 5 F3   **JaB**
Unit 18 Powerscourt Townhouse Centre South William Street Dublin 2

Established 15 years ago in a ground-floor corner of a colourful, bustling 'arty crafty' shopping mall, Phena O'Boyle's and Anne Green's Periwinkle goes from strength to strength. It has the simplest of decors – split-level quarry-tiled floors, varnished pine tables and counters with low or high stools depending on where you choose to sit, and blackboard menus proclaim the day's offerings. The most popular item remains the thick seafood chowder served with freshly-baked Irish brown bread; in addition, there's a fish dish of the day, perhaps cod provençale, and perennial favourites that run from marinated mussels and smoked salmon bagels through popular crab and prawn salads to a 'Periwinkle Platter' – a selection of everything on the cold table, sufficient for two. Hot food items such as baked oysters and toasted crab claws are promptly available at 11.30am and continue until closing time. *Seats 55. Meals 10.30-5. Closed Sun & Bank Holidays. No credit cards.*

DUBLIN   Pier 32   £55

Tel 01 676 1494   Fax 01 676 3287   Map 5 F2   **R**
23 Upper Pembroke Street Dublin 2

In the basement of the Grey Door (see entry), Pier 32 resembles a sort of West of Ireland pub-restaurant, with the emphasis on Atlantic seafood and live traditional or contemporary Irish music nightly. Typical fare might include grilled oysters with garlic cream and cheese, Dublin Bay prawn and scallop bake, roast rack of Wicklow lamb and mushroom pancake with stir-fried vegetables alongside the Pier 32 seafood platter for which they say 'you'd better be hungry'. Set lunch and early evening menus. *Seats 75. Parties 20. L 12.30-2.15 D 6-11.30. Set L £10. Set D £10 (2-course Early Bird till 7pm). Closed L Sat & Sun, Bank Holidays. Amex, Diners, MasterCard, VISA*

DUBLIN   Pierre's   £30

Tel 01 671 1248   Fax 01 671 1249   Map 5 F3   **R**
2 Crow Street Temple Bar Dublin 2

There are now four Dublin outposts of the growing British franchise chain (generally called Pierre Victoire) whose hallmarks are simple decor and keen prices. Tomato and lemon grass soup and steamed mussels in orange, ginger and honey followed by baked fillet of cod with herb and lemon butter and a trio of fillet of beef, lamb cutlet and pork fillet served with a light mushroom sauce typify both the à la carte and fixed-price options at this budget-conscious Temple Bar restaurant. *Seats 55. Parties 12. L 12-3 D 6-11 (Sun 1-4, 6-10). Closed 24-26 Dec, 1 & 2 Jan. Set L £5.90 Set D £9.90. Amex, Diners, MasterCard, VISA*

DUBLIN   Popjoys   £45

Tel 01 492 9346   Map 3 A2   **R**
4 Rathfarnham Road Terenure Dublin 6

Previously at Roly's Bistro, Warren Massey opened here in partnership with
restaurant manager John Coleman towards the end of last year. An attractive
shopfront bodes well and the interior is fitted throughout to a high standard.
Warm tones, high-back chairs and classic table settings with promising modern
wine glasses provide a comfortably undemanding background for Warren's
progressive cooking and there's a nice little seating area to use for aperitifs.
A choice of eight starters on an early autmn menu offered potato and watercress
soup, pan-fried scallops with lemon and garlic and a particularly enjoyable warm
pigeon salad – juicy, tender pink pigeon breasts served as a warm salad with
mixed leaves, bacon and toasted almonds. Eight main courses ranged from
tomato and mozzarella tart with pesto to fillet of beef with mushroom purée and
fried potatoes, pan-fried skate wing with black butter and capers and old-style
rabbit and prune pie (a house speciality). Interesting vegetables like mashed
potatoes with garlic and braised leeks with Chinese leaf. Young staff are keen to
please and service is very prompt. Finish with simple desserts or a plated trio of
Irish farmhouse cheeses and good cafetière coffee. *Seats 70. Parties 10. Private
Room 35. L 12.30-3 (Sun to 6) D 6.30-10.30. Set L £11.95. Closed L Sat, D Sun,
Good Friday, 25 & 26 Dec. Amex, Diners, MasterCard,* **VISA**

Set menu prices may not include service or wine.
Our guide price for two diners includes wine and service.

DUBLIN   The Porter House

Tel 01 679 8847/50   Fax 01 670 9605   Map 5 E3   **P**
16-18 Parliament Street Dublin 2

Hailed as 'Dublin's second biggest brewery' when it opened in May 1996,
The Porter House is (more importantly) the city's first microbrewery. A fine,
imaginatively restored five-storey building, the decor throughout features
salavaged pitch pine, with beer bottles from all over the world in glass display
cabinets around the walls. Other nice touches include a specially commissioned
ceramic-topped bar and glasss-topped tables containing decorative displays
related to brewing. Eight beers produced on the premises include three stouts
(one actually made with oysters), two ales and three lagers, and there's a sample
tray offered with a glass of each laid out on an information sheet giving details
of all the beers and the brewing process. Although the microbrewery is the heart
of the operation, good food was in the plan from the start (just as well, since the
beers go up to 7% abv!). Generous, stylish and comfortable seating is provided
throughout the building, both at bars and tables, with slightly more formal tables
set in the upper regions, known as The Cookhouse. Wholesome home-cooked
food ranges from popular bar snacks – chicken wings, nachos, spare ribs and so
on – to an excellent carvery lunch, while the Cookhouse menu offers the snacks
as starters, plus a further range of dishes especially strong on chargrills, notably
steaks and chicken (cooked over a wood-burning grill) and so-called global
cuisine. In practice, bar and Cookhouse menus overlap considerably and,
although in the early stages of development, the food operation is promising.
*Seats 150. Parties 15. Food 12-11, L 12-3 D 5-11 (Thur & Fri to 1am). Closed 25 Dec
& Good Friday. MasterCard,* **VISA**

See the **County Listings** green tinted pages for
details of all establishments listed in county order.

DUBLIN   Il Primo   £45

Tel 01 478 3373   Map 5 F2   **R**
16 Montague Street Dublin 2

Simply appointed little Italian restaurant opposite the Children's Hospital
(Harcourt Street). Pasta, pizzas and salads predominate on a wordy menu which
extends itself little beyond bruschetta with roasted peppers, tomatoes and olives,
gnocchi with tomato, spinach and ricotta, and insalata caprese with buffalo
mozzarella and pesto. 52 Italian red wines but only one French! *Seats 44.
Parties 30. L 12-3 D 6-11 (Fri & Sat till 11.30). Closed Sun, 25-28 Dec & Bank
Holidays.* Amex, Diners, MasterCard, **VISA**

DUBLIN   Raglan Lodge   £80

Tel 01 660 6697   Fax 01 660 6781   Map 6 H1   **A**
10 Raglan Road Ballsbridge Dublin 4

Helen Moran has created a charming and hospitable environment within this
grand Victorian town-house set in a select tree-lined avenue off one of the main
routes to the city centre. Thirteen white granite steps lead up to the main door,
painted a distinctive and cheering sunshine yellow. There's a lounge on the
lower ground floor, though it is little used, while on the ground floor there's
a fine breakfast room wherein to enjoy the likes of slices of smoked salmon
bordered by soft scrambled eggs. The seven high-ceilinged bedrooms are
spotlessly maintained and feature creature comforts like thick towels, good
soaps and crystal-clear reception of all the major television channels. No dogs.
Rooms 7. Garden. Closed 22 Dec-6 Jan. Amex, MasterCard, **VISA**

DUBLIN   Rajdoot   £50

Tel & Fax 01 679 4274   Map 5 F3   **R**
26 Clarendon Street Westbury Centre Dublin 2

Part of a small UK chain (and one on the Costa del Sol) of reliable restaurants
specialising in tandoori and North Indian Moghlai cooking. The latter tends to
produce mild and subtly spiced dishes like chicken pasanda – the breast stuffed
with flaked almonds, mint and cherries with a sauce of cashew nuts and almonds
– and Kashmiri fish – more highly-spiced with red dry chilis. Luxurious,
somewhat exotic decor. *Seats 92. L 12-2.30 D 6.30-11.30. Set L from £6.95
Set D from £17.50. Closed Sun, L Bank Holidays, all Good Friday, 25, 26 Dec
& 1 Jan.* Amex, Diners, MasterCard, **VISA**

DUBLIN   Roly's Bistro   ↑   £50

Tel 01 668 2611   Fax 01 660 8535   Map 6 H1   **R**
7 Ballsbridge Terrace Ballsbridge Dublin 4

A restaurant on two-floors – bistro-ish upstairs, a bit
more sedate on the ground floor – where restaurateur
Rory Saul and chef Colin O'Daly have proved a
winning combination. First comes an excellent variety
of breads, followed by an eclectic selection of dishes
from Clonakilty black pudding and herb sausage or
Dublin Bay prawns Newburg (as a starter or main
course) to pan-fried ray wing with celeriac and caper
butter, lamb's liver with creamed cabbage and Madeira
jus or loin of pork with Guinness and caraway sauce.
Good accompanying salads and vegetables as well as
the puddings and super Irish cheeses. Inexpensive wines
– with a dozen house selections under £10 and as many again at less than £16.
An excellent value lunch menu offers three courses for £10.50 (cheese course
£2 extra). *Seats 120. Parties 12. Private Room 65. L 12-2.45 D 6-10 (Sun till 9.45).
Closed Good Friday & 25, 26 Dec. Set L £10.50.* Amex, Diners, MasterCard, **VISA**

DUBLIN   Royal Dublin Hotel   63%   £120

Tel 01 873 3666   Fax 01 873 3120   Map 5 F4
40 Upper O'Connell Street Dublin 1

A modern hotel, on Dublin's most famous street, with practical overnight accommodation, traditionally-styled bar, an all-day brasserie and a business centre. 24hr room service and secure parking for 35 cars in a basement garage. Conferences/banqueting 200/230. Children stay free in their parents' room (breakfast £6). A 30-bedroom extension is planned for 1997. *Rooms 117. Brasserie (7am-midnight). Closed 24 & 25 Dec. Amex, Diners, MasterCard,* **VISA**

DUBLIN   Ryans of Parkgate Street

Tel 01 671 9352   Fax 01 671 3590   Map 3 A4   **P**
28 Parkgate Street Dublin 8

The professionally-run, well-appointed little restaurant over the famous pub is popular with locals and, as it is handy for Heuston station just across the bridge, a visit can be a treat before or after a journey. Downstairs, one of Dublin's finest Victorian pubs is a reconstruction dating from 1896 and retains many original features, including two snugs at the back, a magnificent carved oak and mahogany central bar (its centrepiece a double-faced mechanical clock), brass gas lamps and an outstanding collection of antique mirrors. Bar fare runs from soups and simple light snacks to traditional hot dishes; slightly more variety in the evening. No under-12s after 9pm. Pub telephone: 01 677 6097. *Restaurant: Seats 32. L 12.30-2.30 D 7-10.30. Closed L Sat, all Sun, D Mon, Bank Holidays & 1st week Jan. Set L £13. Pub: Open 10.30-11.30, Sun 12.30-2, 4-11. Bar Food 12.30-2.30 & 5-9 (Sun sandwiches only). Amex, MasterCard,* **VISA**

> Many hotels offer reduced rates for weekend or out-of-season bookings. Our guide price indicates high-season rates. Always ask about special deals for longer stays.

DUBLIN   Saagar   £50

Tel 01 475 5060   Map 5 F2   **R**
16 Harcourt Street Dublin 2

An unusual cellar setting for an Indian restaurant – it is located in the basement of a house once inhabited by Bram Stoker (creator of Dracula) and still contains the old black range once used in his kitchen. But this is no ordinary tandoori joint, more a superior and quite sophisticated restaurant serving authentic Indian dishes, some of which are quite hot and spicy. Not so the aloo papri chaat, a mixture of crisp bread, chick peas and potatoes, topped with yoghurt and tamarind chutney, nor the kebabs, though the prawn puri in a hot, sweet and sour sauce might burn the roof of your mouth! However, both the chicken chetinad, cooked in pepper sauce with green herbs, and the chicken vindaloo, a traditional hot Goan curry, will certainly tickle the taste buds, as will the black peppered lamb curry from Madras. Gentler are the rogan josh and prawn balti, and some of the vegetarian dishes such as vegetables makhanwala (cooked with mild spices in a creamy sauce) and dal tarka (lentils with cumin seeds). There are, of course, several tandoori and biriyani dishes, the usual rice side orders and assorted breads, and for those unable to make a choice, some suggested set meals. Service is very efficient, and all in all this is a welcome addition to the Dublin scene – and a worthy winner of our Oriental Restaurant of the Year award. Owners Mr and Mrs Sunil Kumar also have Little India, a tandoori and take-away restaurant at 2 Dublin Bridge, Mullingar, Co Westmeath (Tel 044 40911). *Seats 60. Parties 20. Private Room 100. L 12.30-3 D 6-11.30. Closed L Sat & Sun. Set menus from £16. Amex, Diners, MasterCard,* **VISA**

DUBLIN — Sachs Hotel — 62% — £118

Tel 01 668 0995   Fax 01 668 6147   Map 3 B2   **H**
19-29 Morehampton Road Donnybrook Dublin 4

The night club at this small hotel in a Georgian terrace is a popular attraction, and a different kind of exercise is available (free to residents) at a leisure centre a short drive away. Bedrooms are individually appointed in period style, and double-glazing at the front keeps things peaceful. Conference/function facilities for up to 200. **Rooms 20.** Closed 24 & 25 Dec. Amex, Diners, MasterCard, **VISA**

DUBLIN — Señor Sassi's — £60

Tel & Fax 01 668 4544   Map 6 G1   **R**
146 Upper Leeson Street Dublin 4

Busy, bustling restaurant, with densely packed marble-topped tables where chef David McCelland creates fashionable Mediterranean/Californian style dishes; include imaginative pasta dishes and a Mediterranean fish chowder that comes as both starter and main-course portions. Alternatively, start with warm smoked chicken and roast pepper salad or filo-baked avocado with gorgonzola and follow with the likes of pan-seared salmon with bok choi (Chinese mustard greens), chili and lemon broth and chargrilled lamb with tomato couscous, smoked lentils and coriander-scented yoghurt. There's always a vegetarian option offered with side orders such as roast tomatoes with garlic and herb crust and pan-fried spinach with pine kernels. A set lunch menu offers three courses for £10.50. **Seats 65.** Private Room 35. L 12-3 D 6-11.30 (Fri & Sat 7-12, Sun 6.30-10.30). Set L £10.50. Closed L Sat & Sun, Good Friday, 25, 26 Dec & 1 Jan. Amex, Diners, MasterCard, **VISA**

DUBLIN — Shalimar — £50

Tel 01 671 0738   Fax 01 677 3478   Map 5 F3   **R**
17 South Great George's Street Dublin 2

Smart, comfortable restaurant opposite the Central Hotel serving standard Indian fare in friendly fashion. Numerous Balti dishes may be mixed and matched to individual requirements; wide-ranging alternatives include tandoori specialities and assorted seafood, vegetarian and basmati presentations. **Seats 100.** L 12-2.30 D 6-1. Closed 24-26 Dec & Good Friday. Set L from £6.95 Set D from £14.95. Diners, MasterCard, **VISA**

DUBLIN — Shelbourne Meridien — 74% — £240

Tel 01 676 6471   Fax 01 661 6006   Map 5 F2   **HR**
St Stephen's Green Dublin 2

Situated on St Stephen's Green, Europe's largest garden square, the Shelbourne has been at the centre of Dublin life since opening its doors early in the 19th century. The Irish Constitution was drafted in what is now one of the many function rooms. The hotel has retained much of its original grandeur, with a magnificent faux-marble entrance hall and a sumptuous lounge where morning coffee and afternoon tea are taken. The famous Horseshoe Bar and the newer Shelbourne Bar are among the favourite gathering places for Dubliners, especially on a Friday night, and many a scandal has originated from within their walls. Spacious, elegantly furnished

Superior and De Luxe rooms and suites have traditional polished wood furniture and impressive drapes, while Standard rooms in a newer wing are smaller. All rooms are well appointed, with bathrobes, mini-bars and three telephones as standard. As celebrated by Henry James, the 'hour dedicated to the ceremony known as afternoon tea' is nowhere more agreeably spent than in the Lord Mayor's lounge: dainty tea sandwiches, home-baked scones with whipped cream and assorted fancy cakes and pastries can all be expected. Valet parking. The largest of 12 function rooms can cater for up to 400. Children up to 16 stay free in parents' room. *Rooms 164. Beauty salon, gents' hairdressing, news kiosk. Amex, Diners, MasterCard,* **VISA**

The Side Door   £55
Opened in the autumn of 1996, this stylish, ultra-modern restaurant next to the hotel's Kildare Street bar is an innovative, design-conscious departure for Dublin's most traditional hotel, and accessible from the hotel through the bar, or directly from the street. So cool one wonders if this can really be Dublin, never mind The Shelbourne, the decor is all pale woods and metallics, with light blue and mauve Cal-Ital menus to match the minimalist surroundings. A la carte lunch and dinner menus are similar, but with more choice (and higher prices) in the evenings. Starters range from simple focaccia bread with tapénade, through the likes of baked blue cheese with plum and pear chutney and crispy croutons to a Thai soup, which sounds promising ('light spiced vegetables with fresh chili, ginger and coconut') but turns out to be a disappointing puréed vegetable soup flavoured mainly with salt. Main courses start with pizzas and farinaceous dishes (including an above-average risotto) and progress to the likes of baked cod, chargrilled 'rib-eye of beef' and brochette of spicy lamb with a coriander pesto. Vegetables and side salads are given as side orders and charged accordingly. Desserts include a calorific hot and cold chocolate plate known as a Side Door Dessert Special. Although the kitchen had clearly not settled as we went to press, this adventure by The Shelbourne has promise. Note that 15% service charge is added to all bills. *Seats 68. Parties 12. L 12-5 D 5-11. Closed 25 Dec. Amex, Diners, MasterCard,* **VISA**

DUBLIN   **The Stag's Head**

Tel 01 679 3701   Map 5 F3   P
1 Dame Court Dublin 2

Although small by comparison with the vast drinking emporiums being built today, The Stag's Head remains one of Dublin's most impressive old pubs – a lofty, spacious bar and one of the few with its original late-Victorian decor more or less untouched. Sit at the long granite bar and regret the absence of hand pumps which used to grace it, but enjoy the acres of original mahogany and admire its hand-worked detail. Some of it frames the marvellous bevelled mirrors that soar up to finish in curvaceous arches over the panelling and original fittings behind the bar. *Open 10.30am-11.30pm (Sun & Bank Holidays 7-11 only). Closed Good Friday & 25 Dec. No credit cards.*

DUBLIN La Stampa † £60

Tel 01 677 8611 Fax 01 677 3336 Map 5 F2
35 Dawson Street Dublin 2 **H**

Big and bold, lively and fun – a place where the food really does complement the surroundings. And what a room, high-ceilinged, huge mirrors adorning the walls with shelves at either end of the dining hall (indeed it is more hall than room) interspaced by candelabra, lamps, urns, plants and the odd bust. The plain wood floor emphasises the clatter and bustle, and (if you can hear it above the din) the music is often loud. Comfortable banquettes, marble-topped tables, lots of art – a mixture of old and new – and terrific staff all add to the sense of occasion. Nibble the decent bread (perhaps brown soda or focaccia) while scrutinising Paul Flynn's monthly-changing menu that takes its inspiration from around the world: bouillon of prawn with crab ravioli, coriander and ginger; chicken liver, bacon and brioche pie with grain mustard sauce; baked sea bass with creamed tomatoes and basil mash; escalope of veal with buttered spinach and a ragout of field mushrooms. Afters appreciated on a recent visit included a crème caramel with poached peaches and schnapps, and a stunning warm chocolate fondant with mint gravita. Good Irish cheeses such as Abbey Blue, Cooleeney and Gubbeen, plus excellent coffee. The wine list is both inexpensive and cheerful. Downstairs, the bistro serves a slightly different and shorter menu. *Seats 200. Parties 14. Private room 50. L 12.30-2.30 D 6.30-11.15 (11.45 Fri & Sat). Closed L Sat & Sun, L Bank Holidays, all 25, 26 Dec & 1 Jan. Set L £10.50. Amex, Diners, MasterCard,* **VISA**

DUBLIN The Station House

Tel 01 831 3772 Map 4 C4
3-5 Station Road Raheny Dublin 5 **P**

Outside may be deceptively like any other fairly traditional Dublin pub, but inside, the Station House has surprising Spanish-style decor – heavy, rustic furniture upholstered in warm, 'aged' tapestry and carpet-bagging fabrics sit comfortably around tile-topped tables on hard wooden floors enlivened by the occasional trompe l'oeil 'rug' strategically placed to trip the unwary. Traditional bar food from the carvery is freshly cooked and wholesome: roast rib of beef, soup, plaice and chips, vegetable stir-fry, steaks; also sandwiches and salads. During the afternoons and evenings the menu offers steaks, burgers and 'make your own' omelettes with Station House fries and the odd children's favourite. Staff are friendly and helpful and there's a walled garden at the back. Barbecues most weekends (weather permitting) in the garden which has its own bar. *Open 10.30-11.30, Sun 12.30-2, 4-11. Bar Food & Meals carvery 12-2.30 (Sun 12.30-2), à la carte 2.30-9 (Sun 4-8). Children allowed to eat in the lounge until 6.30, children's menu. Garden, outdoor eating. Closed Good Friday & 25 Dec. MasterCard,* **VISA**

DUBLIN Stauntons on the Green £94

Tel 01 478 2300 Fax 01 478 2263 Map 5 F2
83 St Stephen's Green South Dublin 2 **A**

Bedrooms at the front of this hotel, formed out of three town-houses in a Georgian terrace, overlook St Stephen's Green while those at the back have views of the hotel's own garden and the Victorian Iveagh Gardens beyond. Fitted with simple units, they have tea/coffee facilities and remote-control TVs. Bathrooms, about half with shower and WC only, have good toiletries. No dogs. *Rooms 33. Garden. Closed 24-26 Dec. Amex, Diners, MasterCard,* **VISA**

DUBLIN   Stephen's Hall Hotel   65%   £157

Tel 01 661 0585   Fax 01 661 0606   Map 5 F2   **HR**
Earlsfort Centre 14/17 Lower Leeson Street Dublin 2

Situated in a thriving business and tourist area just off St Stephen's Green, Stephen's Hall is an all-suite hotel. Each suite has its own lobby and kitchenette in addition to a dining area and sitting room. Suite types range from studios (double bed, kitchen, bathroom) to three townhouses each with one double and two single bedrooms, two bathrooms, sitting room, kitchen, dining-room, balcony and private entrance to the street. All are well furnished in a pleasingly understated modern Irish style, with thoughtfully planned bathrooms and well-designed furniture. In addition to full room service and 24hr porterage, a special shopping service is available for guests who wish to cook in their suite; all meals, including breakfast, can also be taken in the restaurant. Free, secure parking. *Rooms 37. Garden. Closed 24 Dec-2 Jan. Amex, Diners, Mastercard,* **VISA**

Morels Bistro at Stephen's Hall   £60
Tel 01 662 2480   Fax 01 662 8595

Alan O'Reilly (see entry for Morels in Sandycove) has just recently opened here, bringing his successful formula to the city centre. The decor embraces the same vibrant Mediterranean theme – summer blues, sunflower yellows and rich reds – and features work by young Irish artists, while the food (at least initially) is under the direction of John Dunne, executive chef in the parent restaurant. Typical starters could include angel hair pasta with spiced chorizo sausage and plum tomato coulis, crab cake with coriander, sesame seeds and lime, and baked goat's cheese with pine nuts and basil oil. To follow, perhaps spiced Thai chicken with sesame and chili aïoli, tempura monkfish with lime and coriander dressing or heartier choices like braised beef with root vegetables and a red wine sauce. Desserts include a tempting dark chocolate terrine with espresso sauce, or you can finish with an Irish farmhouse cheese plate along with a choice of coffees. Cheerful service from young, designer-uniformed staff. *Seats 60. Parties 10. Private Room 30. L 12.30-2 D 6-10.15. Closed L Sat, all Sun, Bank Holidays & 24-31 Dec. Set L £12.50 Set D £12.50 (6-7.30 only). Amex, Diners, MasterCard,* **VISA**

We do not recommend the food in pubs where
there is no mention of Bar Food in the statistics.
A restaurant within a pub is only specifically recommended
where its separate opening times are given.

DUBLIN   Ta Se Mohogani Gaspipes   £45

Tel 01 679 8138   Map 3 A4   **R**
17 Manor Street Stoneybatter Dublin 7

A nonsense name for a stylish little American restaurant featuring live jazz on Friday and Saturday. Lunchtime brings pasta, omelettes, burgers and Oriental specialities such as Chinese chicken or vegetable fried rice while in the evening there's pasta plus specialities like Beijing pork, glazed pork calvados and teriyaki steak. Also daily fish, international and dessert specials ('your waitperson will inform you') and live jazz every Friday and Saturday evening. *Seats 47. Parties 16. L 12-3 D 7-11.30 (Fri & Sat to 1.30am), Sun 1-4 (brunch menu). Closed D Sun, all Mon, Bank Holidays, Good Friday & 25, 26 Dec. Diners, MasterCard,* **VISA**

DUBLIN   Temple Bar Hotel   66%   £120

Tel 01 677 3333   Fax 01 677 3088   Map 5 F3   **H**
Temple Bar Dublin 2

Set in former bank premises, this hotel is well-located in Dublin's 'Left Bank' area. Everything of interest on both sides of the river that divides the city centre is within easy walking distance and the hotel itself has a pleasant atmosphere, starting with the spacious reception/lounge area and adjacent cocktail bar, through the bright and airy, all-day Terrace Café through to 'Buskers', a lively Irish-theme bar. Bedrooms (two equipped for disabled guests) are soberly decorated in deep shades, generally larger than average, and almost all have a double and single bed plus TV, phone, tea/coffee-making, hairdryer and trouser press as standard. Neat, well-lit bathrooms have over-bath showers and marble wash basin units, all identical except for variations in size. Toilets equipped for disabled guests. No private parking. Conference facilities for 35. *Rooms 108. Closed 23-28 Dec. Amex, Diners, MasterCard,* **VISA**

DUBLIN   Thomas Read Café/Bar

Tel 01 677 1487   Fax 01 671 2672   Map 5 E3   **P**
Parliament Street Dublin 2

Opposite the entrance to Dublin Castle and next door to the long-established cutlers from which it gains its name, the gleaming curved glass frontage and enticing lights within encourage the curious to venture into this dashing example of the new breed of café-bar (more bar in the evenings) – and, true to its Continental origins perhaps, this one seems to be attracting literary types from nearby newspapers and Trinity College. Live music in the cellars at weekends. In the same ownership as The Harbourmaster (see entry) in Custom House Docks. *Open 10-11.30 (till 11 in winter, Thu & Fri to 3am, Sat to midnight, Sun 11-11). Closed Good Friday & 25, 26 Dec. Amex, MasterCard,* **VISA**

DUBLIN   Thornton's   ★   £90

Tel 01 454 9067   Fax 01 454 9067   Map 5 E1   **R**
1 Portobello Road Dublin 8

Standing on a corner site alongside the Grand Canal, Kevin Thornton's eponymous restaurant has a brightly-lit exterior – a guiding light to some of Dublin's most successfully inventive, modern cooking. The tiny bar shares the ground floor with the kitchens, which are visible from outside on the canal. Upstairs, there are two quite simply furnished, informal dining areas with cream and cinnamon swathes of muslin draped over poles above the windows and doorways. These are almost the only decorative flourishes apart from matching designer-chipped tiles arranged in small groups just above the charcoal-grey dado. Kevin cooks with a passion and evidently will not compromise on quality; the intricacy of the amuse-gueule and his exceptional home-baked breads give an early indication of a menu style that consists of thoughtful and innovative marriages of flavours and textures. From a short and carefully balanced list of no more than seven choices at each stage diners are faced with an enviable choice, perhaps between sautéed foie gras with scallops and black truffle (served with a warm brioche), roast squab pigeon with cabbage and millefeuille of aubergine and lobster with rösti potato and lobster coral sauce to start. Main courses are equally innovative in concept and intricate in execution: fillet of sea bass with squid ink and star anise, puréed potatoes and red peppers; partridge with tarte tatin of shallots, foie gras and cep mushroom sauce; loin of sikka deer with roasted salsify and trompettes de mort. In a separate, tiny copper saucepan might come really delicious buttered potatoes simply dressed with fresh tarragon and coarse salt. Desserts like warm plum tartlet with Valrhona ice cream and lemon verbena sauce or fresh fig millefeuille with fig ice cream and damson jus epitomise the classiness of production from start to finish. Were this not enough, a six-course surprise menu is also available when ordered by an entire table party. Kevin Thornton clearly has a superb palate and he supervises every detail personally: there's no repetition in accompaniments or garnishes and his presentation, especially of the desserts, deserves high praise. This scrupulous eye for detail is carried through to the very end when coffee and tisanes come with an immaculate plate of petits fours. The wine list is short but carefully chosen and includes a smattering of New World wines. Friendly, attentive staff and reasonably sensible prices both help to further enhance the enjoyment of seeking out 'perfection on a plate'. 10% service charge is added to all menu prices. Thornton's wins our Restaurant of the Year Award for 1997. *Seats 40. Parties 20. Private Room 20. D only 7-10.30. Closed Sun, Mon, Bank Holidays & 10 days Christmas. Set D (surprise) £45. Amex, Diners, MasterCard, VISA*

We only recommend the food in hotels categorised as **HR** and **AR**.

DUBLIN   **Toners Pub**

Tel 01 676 3090   Fax 01 676 2617   Map 6 G2   **P**
139 Lower Baggot Street Dublin 2

Situated only a few hundred yards from the Shelbourne Hotel and St Stephen's Green, this rare survivor of a style of pub which has all but disappeared in Dublin is fiercely resistant to change. Owners, regulars and visitors alike blossom in its dimly-lit interior, where pints are drunk in the hard-benched little snug, or on high wooden stools at the bar with its rackety old combed-wood divisions. Journalists from offices across the road discuss the issues of the day, actors on location in the city come to share the buzz and everyone enjoys the genuine charm of Toners. Totally Irish, great crack ... 'you couldn't change this place'. *Open 10.30-11.30 (Sun 12.30-2, 4-11). Closed Bank Holidays. MasterCard, VISA*

DUBLIN   **Tosca**

Tel 01 679 6744   Fax 01 677 4804   Map 5 F3   **JaB**
20 Suffolk Street Dublin 2

The blackened hull of a ship (wrought out of papier maché but authentic-looking with rivets and portholes) with a gleaming espresso machine in the middle is the striking centrepiece of this stylishly modern Italian restaurant. The à la carte features such main courses as pasta (various shapes served with a variety of sauces – dried pimento, field mushrooms in cream, fillet of chili beef), seafood (smoked fish hot pot, baked ray wings, mussel stew) and specialities like braised lamb shank with herby roast potatoes, wood pigeon salad basket and chicken pot au feu with garlic sausages. From 5.30-7pm you can play 'Beat the Clock' with selected dishes for which you pay according to the time you place your order (eg order at 5.36pm and pay £5.36). At lunchtime there's an additional menu that includes pizzas and bocadillos (grilled-bread open sandwiches) plus a short Tosca Pronto menu – 'on the table within 12 minutes (parties of 6 or less) or it's free'. Note the nine different home-baked breads on offer. *Seats 70. Parties 15. Private Room 15. Meals 12-3.30, 5.30-12 (Thu-Sat till 1am). Closed Good Friday & 25, 26 Dec. Amex, Diners, MasterCard, VISA*

Entries categorised as **JaB** are recommended for 'Just a Bite'.

DUBLIN   The Towers at Lansdowne Road   76%   £240

Tel 01 667 0633   Fax 01 660 5324   Map 6 H1

Lansdowne Road Dublin 4   **H**

Flagship of the Jurys hotel group and away from the hustle and bustle of its sister hotel, Jurys in Ballsbridge Road (qv), the Towers has its own private entrance more in keeping with the quiet elegance of Landsdowne Road. The unexpected intimacy of the Hospitality Lounge, private reading room and boardroom are indicative of the sophistication of its interior where service matches up with complimentary hot beverages round the clock, an evening cocktail and Continental breakfast all provided. Bedrooms are equally superior both in size (currently the most spacious in Dublin) and furnishings which include king-sized beds, sofas and rocking armchairs as well as marble-clad bathrooms and walk-in dressing rooms. There are automatic mini-bars, several telephone extensions with fax and modem capability and comprehensive services including nightly turn-down, 24hr room service and express check-in and check-out. Four Executive and Presidential suites also have private dining areas and whirlpool baths. Not unsurprisingly, perhaps, The Towers won our Ireland Business Hotel of the Year last year. When livelier company is called for the full facilities of the adjoining Jurys with its busy bars, restaurants and coffee shop are just a short stroll away across the garden. Valet parking. No children. No dogs. **Rooms 104.** *Garden, indoor and outdoor swimming pools, spa bath, sauna, beauty and hair salons, masseuse, shop, airline desk, coffee shop (6am-4.30am, Sun till 10.30). Amex, Diners, MasterCard,* **VISA**

DUBLIN   The Westbury   79%   £226

Tel 01 679 1122   Fax 01 679 7078   Map 5 F3

Off Grafton Street Dublin 2   **HR**

Part of the Doyle Hotel Group since 1985, the Westbury is located within walking distance of many Dublin landmarks. The major shops are also close at hand, and the hotel has its own shopping mall. Among the day rooms are the Terrace Bar and the Sandbank Seafood Bar. Pinks and blues are key colours in the bedrooms, which offer a high standard of comfort and accessories; they range from singles to luxury penthouse suites. Business gatherings and banquets (to a maximum of 200) are accommodated in elegantly furnished boardrooms and function suites. Legions of staff provide good levels of service. **Rooms 203.** *Gym, spa bath, beauty & hair salon, news kiosk, coffee shop (10am-10pm). Amex, Diners, MasterCard,* **VISA**

Russell Room   £90

A classic French carte, suitably matched to the stylish surroundings and service, measures up with some soundly-cooked dishes but few surprises; eggs Benedict or bisque de langoustines followed by a 'rendezvous' of seafood and shellfish with basil sauce, or (for two) le chateaubriand béarnaise typify the style. More modish main dishes from the table d'hote lunch and dinner menus might include fillet of brill with smoked salmon and lamb noisettes with thyme and rosemary. There's a separate vegetarian menu (£11.50) but it only offers a choice at the starter stage. **Seats 96.** L 12.30-2.30 D 6.30-10.30.
Set L £14.50/£16.50 Set D £25 (+15% service charge).

DUBLIN — Wong's — £60

Tel 01 833 4400
436 Clontarf Road Dublin 3

Map 4 C4

R

Black marble gleams invitingly at this well-established northside Chinese restaurant, featuring the cuisines of Peking, Shanghai, Szechuan and Canton, and a loyal local following continues to appreciate the high standard of service and easy-going attitude as much as the consistent excellence of the food. From a lively à la carte, which also forms the basis of the set dinners for a given number of diners, start perhaps with an authentic rendition of Peking duck, or meat sung, a delicious mixture of minced pork, roast duck and crunchy vegetables on a bed of crispy rice noodles. To follow, a typical Cantonese speciality might be fillet steak with garlic and black bean sauce, served of a sizzling hot plate or, from Shanghai, hot peppery chicken, sliced and stir-fried with herbs and spices, or Szechuan chicken, stir-fried with celery and spicy garlic sauce. *Seats 120. Parties 10. Private Room 40. L 12.30-2.30 (1-23 Dec only) D 6-12. Set L from £10 Set D from £18.50. Closed Good Friday & 24-26 Dec. Amex, Diners, MasterCard,* **VISA**

DUBLIN — Yellow House

Tel 01 493 2994   **Fax 01 494 2441**
Willbrook Road Rathfarnham Dublin 14

Map 3 A1

P

Named after the unusual shade of the bricks with which it is built, the Yellow House is the landmark pub of Rathfarnham. It makes a perfect rendezvous, with no chance of confusion. Tall and rather forbidding from the outside, the warmth of the interior comes as a pleasant surprise and pictures and old decorative items of local historical interest repay closer examination. Daily lunchtime carvery in the lounge bar; basket snacks and straightforward dishes like chicken kiev, minute steak, crab claws and lasagne in the evening. Evening à la carte (and Sunday lunch) in the restaurant upstairs (no young children after 7pm) – but our recommendation is for the bar food. *Open 10.30-11.30 (Sun 12.30-2, 4-11).* **Bar Food** *Mon-Fri 12.30-2.30, 5-8 (Sat 12-8). Carvery Mon-Sat 12.30-2.30. Closed Good Friday & 25, 26 Dec. Amex, Diners, MasterCard,* **VISA**

DUBLIN — Zen — £50

Tel 01 497 9428
89 Upper Rathmines Road Dublin 6

Map 3 B2

R

An unusual Chinese restaurant in many respects, not least that the south-city premises occupy what was once a Church of England meeting hall which features a lofty hammer-beam roof. Irish owner Dennis O'Connor doesn't speak a word of Chinese yet he sources his chefs and staff directly from Beijing. The cooking is mainly Szechuan with the particularly hot and spicy dishes, such as the hot (in both senses) appetizer of dumplings in a ginger, garlic and chili sauce asterisked on the menu. For the less adventurous there are more conventional starters: sesame prawn toast, crispy spring rolls and orange-flavoured sliced beef. Succulent and carefully prepared prawns (fried with cashew nuts or in a garlic sauce), steamed whole black sole in ginger sauce and various sizzling meats are perennial favourites. Aromatic duckling is also popular and, as part of a feast for two (£45), you could give a day's notice and order crispy Beijing duck – roasted whole, its skin and meat mixed with spring onions and bean paste, then rolled in wheat pancakes. For those undecided there are several set dinners from which to choose, or else one can ask for a cross-section of specialities; incidentally, the house white wine goes extremely well with the style of cooking. *Seats 95. L 12.30-2.45 (Sun 12-3) D 6-11.30. Closed L Mon-Wed & Sat, all Good Friday & 25, 26 Dec. Set L £10. D from £16. Amex, Diners, MasterCard, **VISA***

DUBLIN AIRPORT   Forte Posthouse   57%   £135

Tel 01 844 4211   Fax 01 844 6002   Map 3 B4   **H**
Dublin Airport Co Dublin

Conference facilities for 160, 10 meeting rooms, ample car parking and 24hr room service in a modern hotel within the airport complex. Some non-smoking rooms, some of family size (children up to 14 stay free in parents' room). There is a Chinese restaurant, Sampans, within the hotel. Planned extensions will add 60 more bedrooms, larger conference facilities and a health club. Formerly the *Forte Crest*. **Rooms 189.** *Closed 24 & 25 Dec. Amex, Diners, MasterCard, **VISA***

DUBLIN   Places of Interest

British Embassy Merrion Road Tel 01 269 5211
Tourist Information Tel 01 550 2233
Dublin Airport Tel 01 844 5387
Dublin Bus 01 873 4222 Closed Sun & BH
Bus Eireann (Irish Buses) Booking Information Tel 01 836 6111
Automobile Association Tel 01 283 3555
Bank of Ireland College Green Tel 01 661 5933
Croke Park Football Ground Hurling and Gaelic Football Tel 01 836 3222
Fairyhouse Racecourse Ratoath Tel 01 825 6167
Irish Rugby Union Tel 01 668 4601
Lansdowne Road Rugby Ground Baub Bridge Tel 01 668 4601
Leopardstown Racecourse Fox Rock Tel 01 289 3607
The Curragh Co Kildare

Theatres and Concert Halls

Abbey and Peacock Theatres Lower Abbey Street Tel 01 878 7222
Andrew's Lane Theatre Exchequer Street Tel 01 679 5720
Gaiety Theatre South King Street Tel 01 677 1717
Gate Theatre Cavendish Row Tel 01 874 4045
Irish Film Centre Eustace Street Tel 01 679 3477
National Concert Hall Earlsfort Terrace Tel 01 671 1888
Olympia Theatre Dame Street Tel 01 677 7744
The Point (Exhibitions and Concerts) North Wall Quay Tel 01 836 3633
Tivoli Theatre Francis Street Tel 01 454 4472

Museums, Art Galleries, Other Attractions

Chester Beatty Library and Gallery of Oriental Art Shrewsbury Road Tel 01 269 2386
Civic Museum South William Street Tel 01 679 4260
Dublin Writers' Museum Parnell Square North Tel 01 872 2077
Dublinia Christchurch Tel 01 679 4611
Fry Model Railway Museum Malahide Castle Tel 01 846 3779
Guinness Hopstore Tour James's Gate Tel 01 453 6700 ext 5155
Hugh Lane Municipal Gallery of Modern Art Parnell Square Tel 01 874 1903
Irish Museum of Modern Art Royal Hospital Kilmainham Tel 01 671 8666
Irish Whiskey Corner Bow Street Distillery Tel 01 872 5566 ext 2375
National Wax Museum Granby Row, Parnell Square Tel 01 872 6340
National Gallery of Ireland Merrion Square West Tel 01 661 5133
National Museum of Ireland Kildare Street Tel 01 677 7444
Natural History Museum Merrion Street Tel 01 677 7444
Trinity College: Book of Kells & Dublin Experience Univ. of Dublin Tel 01 608 2308/1833

Houses, Castles and Gardens

Ashtown Castle Phoenix Park Tel 01 677 0095
Drimnach Castle Longmile Road Tel 01 450 2530 4 miles
Dublin Castle Dame Street Tel 01 677 7129
Dublin Zoo Phoenix Park Tel 01 677 1425
George Bernard Shaw House Tel 01 475 0854 May-Oct
James Joyce Museum Joyce Tower, Sandycove Tel 01 280 9265
Kilmainham Gaol Kilmainham Tel 01 453 5984
Malahide Castle Malahide Tel 01 846 2516
Marsh's Library St Patrick's Close Tel 01 454 3511
National Botanic Gardens Glasnevin Tel 01 837 7596
Newbridge House Donabate Tel 01 843 6534
Newman House St Stephen's Green Tel 01 475 7255
Number Twenty Nine Lower Fitzwilliam Street Tel 01 702 6165
Powerscourt Townhouse South William Street Tel 01 679 4144

Cathedrals & Churches

Christ Church Cathedral Christ Church Place Tel 01 677 8099
St Patrick's Cathedral Patrick's Close Tel 01 475 4817
Whitefriar Street Carmelite Church Aungier Street Tel 01 475 8821

DUGORT   Gray's Guest House   £40

Tel 098 43244   Map 1 A3   **A**
Dugort Achill Island Co Mayo

Vi McDowell runs this legendary guesthouse which is renowed for its relaxing properties and gentle hospitality; it occupies a series of houses in the attractive village of Dugort, each with a slightly different atmosphere especially appropriate to particular age groups. Public areas include a large comfortably furnished sitting-room with an open fire and several conservatories for quiet reading. Rooms and bathrooms vary considerably due to the age and nature of the premises, but the emphasis is on old-fashioned comfort and there are extra shared bathrooms in addition to en suite facilities. Children are welcome (free in parents' room up to 4, under-12s 50%), cot provided at no extra charge, high-chair, children's early evening meal (6pm); four family rooms each sleep three. There's an indoor play room and safe outdoor play area, also pool and table tennis for older children. Small conference facilities (25-30 delegates). ***Rooms 15. Garden, croquet.***
No credit cards.

DUN LAOGHAIRE Brasserie na Mara   £50

Tel 01 280 6767 Fax 01 284 4649   Map 4 D1   **R**
1 Harbour Road Dun Laoghaire Co Dublin

Railway buffs will be fascinated by this elegant harbourside restaurant located in the old Kingstown terminal building and owned by Irish Rail Catering Services. In 1970 a preservation order was issued by the local authority. The interior has been totally refurbished in the past year, with a modern style of decor replacing the classical look of before. French-influenced menus (changed seasonally) are a mixture of traditional and modern styles, with a strong emphasis on seafood in dishes like seafood chowder, Thai-crusted cod fillet with buttered tagliatelle and coriander cream, and peppered monkfish with fried artichoke, orange cous cous and balsamic butter sauce. Menus may also encompass chicken and mushroom terrine, baked breast of wigeon with leg confit and raspberry sauce, or, for vegetarians, tianne of vegetables with braised lentils and tomato coulis. Breads are baked daily (brioche, onion bread and soda bread) and ice creams and sorbets are also home-made. Well-chosen wines (mostly French) at fair prices, with some helpful notes; several good champagnes. ***Seats 75. Private Room 50. L 12.30-2.30 D 6.30-10. Closed Sun, Good Friday, Bank Holidays (winter), 1 week Christmas. Set L £9.90 Set D £29 (for two). Amex, Diners, MasterCard, VISA***

DUN LAOGHAIRE   Chestnut Lodge   £60

Tel 01 280 7860 Fax 01 280 1466   Map 4 D1   **A**
2 Vesey Place Monkstown Dun Laoghaire Co Dublin

Built in 1844, the building is a very fine example of classical Regency architecture. From its position almost at the end of a row of similar houses on a hillside, there are glimpses of the sea visible through chestnut trees planted in a small park across the road at the front. This is very much a family home with breakfast taken communally at a beautiful highly polished mahogany dining table in the drawing-room. Here, after a very comfortable night's sleep in one of the spacious, warm and well-appointed bedrooms, you can enjoy freshly squeezed orange juice, a choice of fresh fruit salad, yoghurts, stewed fruits and cereals before tucking into a delicious traditional Irish cooked breakfast finished off by oven-warmed croissants and home-made preserves. Very usefully located close to the Dun Laoghaire/Holyhead ferry terminal. No dogs. *Rooms 4. Garden. MasterCard, VISA*

DUN LAOGHAIRE   de Selby's   £45

Tel 01 284 1761 Fax 01 280 7089   Map 2 D4   **R**
17/18 Patrick Street Dun Laoghaire Co Dublin

Centrally located and handy to the shopping centre and the station, John MacManus's family restaurant is named after a famous Irish literary character and offers a blend of informality and class that makes a visit of appeal to all generations. The style is light and bright yet full of personality, the large room divided into more intimate areas by the clever use of plants and an evocative *currach* centrepiece; John's ever-growing collection of interesting pictures (as well as nautical bric-a-brac and memorabilia) make good use of wall space alongside a blackboard that proclaims specials of the day and well-selected wine offers. The compact, well-planned menu offers a carefully balanced selection of trusty old friends and contemporary favourites: chicken and ham terrine with Cumberland sauce, Irish stew,, chicken, leek and mushroom pie, a strong fish selection (from crispy fish and chips to a mixed fish grill), rack of lamb with rosemary and honey. Specialities include home-made burgers, imaginative vegetarian dishes and dessert pancakes. No children after 8pm. *Seats 105 (+ 50 in garden). Parties 15. L (Sun & Bank Holidays only) 12-10pm D 5.30-11 (to 10 Mon-Thu). Closed Good Friday & 3 days Christmas. Set D (early bird) mid-week £10.45. Amex, Diners, MasterCard, VISA*

> We endeavour to be as up-to-date as possible but inevitably some changes to owners, chefs and other key staff occur after this Guide has gone to press.

DUN LAOGHAIRE   Royal Marine Hotel   64%   £135

Tel 01 280 1911 Fax 01 280 1089   Map 4 D1   **H**
Marine Road Dun Laoghaire Co Dublin

Imposing Victorian hotel set in four acres of grounds overlooking the ferry port yet just moments from the main street of town. Grand day rooms (recently refurbished) feature faux-marble columns, high ceilings and elaborate coving. Upstairs, it's a hotel of two halves with the best rooms, off broad chandelier-lit corridors in the original building, having nice lightwood furniture and smart bathrooms; eight of the rooms here are particularly large, with four-poster beds, antique furniture and spacious bathrooms boasting chunky Victorian-style fittings. The remaining bedrooms are in the 1960s' Marine Wing and offer ageing shelf-type fitted units and a textured finish to the walls; 24hr room servce. Substantial cooked breakfast. Complimentary secure parking. No dogs. Ryan Hotels. *Rooms 104. Garden. Amex, Diners, MasterCard, VISA*

DUN LAOGHAIRE   The South Bank   £50

Tel 01 280 8788   Fax 01 280 5990   Map 4 D1   **R**
1 Martello Terrace Dun Laoghaire Co Dublin

A solitary survivor on a seafront once renowned for its fine restaurants, the South Bank has been run by David and Deirdre Byrne since 1986. It's a neat, slightly formal place in a cosy semi-basement safe from the onshore winds which sometimes lash across the seafront here, but a piano and photographs recording high-profile visits indicate that any formality may melt away as the evening progresses and a friendly waitress eases guests through quieter times. Food tends to be fairly traditional, as in duck liver and brandy paté enlivened by a home-made fruit chutney and freshly-baked wholemeal bread; soup might be a pleasingly smoky bacon and spinach. There's no hint of special preferences in the wide-ranging main courses (lamb cutlets with a white port and onion sauce, roast Monaghan duckling with redcurrant and Cointreau sauce), but although there is always a choice of fish – typically poached salmon with a light lemon and sorrel sauce – vegetarian options (plus any other dietary requirements) should be arranged when booking. Good homely desserts – baked lemon cheesecake, fruit salad – or Irish cheeseboard. Unlimited, freshly-brewed coffee. *Seats 50. L by arrangement D 6.45-10.45. Closed Good Friday, 23-27 Dec. Set D £16/£18.50. Amex, Diners, MasterCard, VISA*

DUN LAOGHAIRE   Places of Interest
Tourist Information Tel 01 284 4768
James Joyce Tower Sandycove Tel 01 280 9265
National Maritime Museum Haigh Terrace Tel 01 280 0969
Stena Sealink Ferry information Tel 01 280 4193

We publish annually, so make sure you use the current edition
– it's well worth being up-to-date!

DUNDALK   Ballymascanlon House   62%   £80

Tel 042 71124   Fax 042 71598   Map 1 D3   **H**
Ballymascanlon Dundalk Co Louth

Set in acres of parkland 2 miles on the Belfast side of Dundalk, this Victorian mansion makes a comfortable and characterful hotel with plenty of space for guests to relax and friendly, helpful staff. Bedrooms vary considerably in size but all are en suite and, although some small singles have shower only, most have bath and over-bath shower. Four Executive rooms (that attract only a small supplement) are larger rooms in the original part of the house; an additional wing of 20 new bedrooms opened in October 1996. 24hr room service. Banqueting/conferences for 250/300. Children under 2 may stay free in their parents' room; outdoor & indoor play room; cot, high-chairs available. Three interconnecting family rooms can sleep up to seven. In the past year the old leisure complex has been completely updated and the golf course extended to 18 holes. No dogs. *Rooms 55. Garden, golf (18), tennis, indoor swimming pool, gym, sauna, steam room, spa bath, outdoor play area. Closed 24-26 Dec. Amex, Diners, MasterCard, VISA*

If you encounter bad service don't wait to write to us but make
your feelings known to the management at the time of your visit.
Instant compensation can often resolve any problem that
might otherwise leave a bad taste.

DUNDALK — Quaglino's — £60

Tel 042 38567 Fax 042 28598
88 Clanbrassil Street Dundalk Co Louth

Map 1 D3   **R**

An extensive, well-appointed first-floor restaurant (totally refurbished recently with the addition of air conditioning), where comfort is a high priority and good service, under the watchful eye of restaurant manager Pat Smyth, ensures maximum enjoyment of the confident cooking. Separate à la carte and table d'hote menus are offered. Snails, smoked salmon, chowder and Carlingford oysters baked in garlic, Dover sole, chateaubriand, steak Diane and crepes Suzette cover the traditional angle of the menu (which rather endearingly says: 'this menu is intended only as a guide'). Brown bread is home-baked, presentation is careful and vegetables are imaginatively prepared. Desserts might include lemon tart, apple brulée or chocolate and hazelnut steamed pudding with bitter chocolate sauce. Good cafetière coffee. *Seats 50. D only 6.30-11. Closed Sun (except Mother's Day), 3 days at Christmas. Set D £19.50/£23.50. Amex, Diners, MasterCard,* **VISA**

DUNDALK   Places of Interest
Tourist Information Tel 042 35484
Basement Gallery Town Hall Tel 042 32276
Dundalk Racecourse Dowdallshill Tel 042 34800
Kilnasaggart Pillar Stone on the Armagh/ Louth border
Moyry Castle between Newry and Dundalk

DUNDRUM — DUNDRUM HOUSE — 66% — £97

Tel 062 71116 Fax 062 71366
Dundrum Co Tipperary

Map 2 B5   **H**

Austin and Mary Crowe take great pride in their hotel, a large Georgian house set in 150 acres through which a trout-filled river runs. Public rooms include a lofty reception hall, a comfortable drawing room furnished with wing chairs and, in the old chapel, a bar with live music every night in summer. Spacious en suite bedrooms, including the five new rooms added last year, are furnished with antiques. Children under 12 may share parents' room free of charge. The 150-acre County Tipperary Golf and Country Club is incorporated within the extensive grounds. *Rooms 60. Garden, tennis, golf (18), fishing, snooker. Amex, Diners, MasterCard,* **VISA**

DUNDRUM   Places of Interest
Holy Cross Abbey Tel 0504 43241

DUNKERRIN — Dunkerrin Arms

Tel 0505 45377/45399
Dunkerrin Birr Co Offaly

Map 2 C4   **P**

Set well back from the road but clearly visible, the Fogarty family's pristine pink-washed pub makes a good place for a break on the Limerick-Dublin road, even for early morning travellers as hearty breakfasts are served from 7.30am. Wholesome food is served all day from a menu that encompasses a daily home-made soup, salads, grills (steaks, mixed grill, beefburger), salmon, plaice fillets and children's favourites. There are six en suite rooms (three with bath, three with shower) and a new conservatory-style self-service restaurant with function facilities was due to open in early 1997. Toilets equipped for the disabled. *Open 7.30am-11.30pm (to 11 in winter), Sun 8am-11pm. Bar Food 7.30am-10pm to 11 in summer). Closed Good Friday & 25 Dec. Amex, MasterCard,* **VISA**

DUNKERRIN   Places of Interest
Roscrea Castle Roscrea Tel 0505 21850

DUNKINEELY   Castle Murray House   64%   £68

Tel 073 37022   Fax 073 37330   Map 1 B2   **HR**
Dunkineely Co Donegal

A cool reception may surprise guests accustomed to warm Irish hospitality, but Thierry and Clare Duclos' small hotel has much to recommend it. In a stunningly beautiful location with wonderful sea and coastal views over the ruined castle from which it gets its name, it has now grown considerably since they opened in 1991. The latest addition – a large verandah with boldly striped awning – is admittedly seasonal, but it seats 25 for private parties, or dinner on warm summer evenings, and neatly balances other recent improvements like the cosy bar and residents' sitting-room, both just off a pleasant plant-filled semi-conservatory along the front of the building – a lovely place to have aperitifs while enjoying the view. Bedrooms are all en suite, quite large and fairly comfortably furnished with a mixture of utilitarian modern units and a sprinkling of antiques; all have a double and single bed, phone, TV and tea/coffee-making facilities, most have sea views and there are extra beds and cots available for families if required. Good breakfasts are served in bedrooms or the restaurant.
Rooms 10. Garden, beach. Closed end Jan-end Feb. MasterCard, **VISA**

Restaurant   £55

The restaurant's corner location maximises the dramatic seascapes and views of the ruined castle, which is floodlit and spectral after dark and charming by day with its own flock of waddling geese. Within, all is warmth and light, with tweed curtains and an open fire (raised well up the wall for the benfit of all) ensuring a cosy ambience even on the most blustery night. Owner-chef Thierry Duclos' multi-choice menus (basically three courses plus options of soup and sorbet) are sensibly priced according to the choice of main course. Although there's a wide selection of meat, poultry and daily vegetarian options, most guests come for the fish and shellfish that are the specialities of the house in the summer months. Typical examples from an early autumn menu might include starters such as prawns and monkfish in garlic butter – a speciality of the house that is cooked in dimpled 'snail' dishes, topped with grated cheese and finished under the grill – and a large crab salad, attractively presented on a triangular plate. Main courses might include John Dory with ginger and lime (rather fussily presented but with fine flavours and texture) and, perhaps, a marinated kebab of chicken with prawns set on a dark, richly-flavoured sauce. Vegetables – a cheesey potato gratin, perhaps, and colourful seasonal choices, such as turned carrots and crisp mangetout – may be a better choice than an unimaginative side salad. Finish off, perhaps, with a tasting plate of desserts, or a selection of Continental cheeses (spoilt on our last visit by poor presentation, packet butter and ordinary cream cracker biscuits). 25 seats on teh verandah in summer.
Seats 45 (+ 25 on verandah in summer). Parties 8. Private Room 25 (summer only). L (Sun only) 3-8 D 7-9 (till 9.30/10 at weekends). Closed L Mon-Sat.

DUNLAVIN   Rathsallagh House   72%   £140

Tel 045 403112 **Fax 045 403343**   Map 2 C4   **AR**
Dunlavin Co Wicklow

'Not a Hotel' proclaims the colourful brochure of Joe and Kay O'Flynn's delightful, rambling country house built in the former stables of a Queen Anne house that burned down in 1798. 32 miles from Dublin city centre, Rathsallagh House is set in 530 acres of mature parkland, now surrounded by an elegantly rolling 18-hole championship golf course. Fishing, archery, clay pigeon shooting and deer-stalking are easily arranged (also hunting in season) or simply catch up with your reading by the fireside in one of the delightful drawing-rooms. Bedrooms are generally spacious and quite luxurious in an understated way, with lovely country views; some smaller, simpler rooms in the stable yard have a special cottagey charm. There is a completely separate private conference facility for up to 50 theatre-style (25 boardroom-style) in a courtyard conversion at the back. Outstanding breakfasts are served in the traditional way from a huge sideboard. No children under 12 and no dogs. *Rooms 17. Garden, croquet, indoor swimming pool, sauna, tennis, golf (18), snooker, helipad. Closed 3 days Christmas. Amex, Diners, MasterCard,* **VISA**

Restaurant   £70

Take in the easy-going atmosphere in the old kitchen bar while reading the menu, then settle down in the dining-room. Traditional in style it is a fine setting in which to enjoy the evening shadows falling on parkland and the hills beyond. Good home cooking is the order of the day, allowing the freshness and quality of prime local produce to come through. Typical offerings on the limited choice four-course menu might include warm salad of haddock and white cabbage with lemon dressing, then spinach and sorrel soup, followed by gigot of monkfish wrapped in bacon and garlic cream or roast guinea fowl with mushroom sauce. Roast local beef and Wicklow lamb are specialities. Leave some room for a tempting dessert from the trolley, or some Irish farmhouse cheese. Snacks are also served all day in the bar. *Seats 100. Private Room 50. L by arrangement for groups only (not Sun). D 7.30-9. Closed 3 days Christmas. Set D from £30.*

DUNMORE EAST   The Ship

Tel 051 383144   Map 2 C5   **P/R**
Dunmore East Co Waterford

This well-located roadside bar/restaurant is situated high up over the bay, but is more remarkable for its atmosphere than a sea view. The solidly-built house dates back to Victorian times and enjoys a good reputation for local seafood served in pleasantly informal surroundings. The bar area near the entrance develops gradually into a dining area, with unusual, sturdy furniture made from old barrels, darkwood walls and a strongly nautical theme – the interior is dimly atmospheric in contrast to the bright roadside patio area used for casual summer eating. Fresh local fish and shellfish (vichyssoise of smoked mussels, oysters, seafood pie, oak smoked salmon) is definitely the main attraction and very good it is too – perhaps at its very best when served simply on the fortnightly-changing menus. Popular, good-value lunches, including Sundays when a fixed-price menu is offered. Sophisticated evening menus encompass roulade of Dover sole filled with saffron mousse, baked monkfish wrapped in Bayonne ham with mussel butter sauce, fillet steak with confit of roasted shallots and garlic and peppercorn sauce, Irish farmhouse cheeses and crème brulée with fruit tartlets. *Open May-Oct 7 days 12.30-2, 7-10, Nov-Apr Tue-Sat 7-10 only.* **Bar Food** *12.30-2 7-10. Closed Mon & Sun Nov-Apr, Good Friday & 25 Dec. Set Sun L £11.50. Amex, MasterCard,* **VISA**

DURRUS	Blairs Cove House Restaurant	£65

Tel 027 61127   Map 2 A6
Blairs Cove Durrus nr Bantry Co Cork

Converted from the characterful outbuildings of the 17th-century Blairs Cove House, in a lovely waterside location overlooking Dunmanus Bay, Sabine and Philippe de Mey's restaurant has been delighting guests with its unique style since 1981. The renowned buffet groans under an abundance of starters (local seafood, patés and salads), then a wide range of main courses that includes locally caught fish – blue shark with bean and tomato salsa perhaps, or roasted monkfish with beurre blanc and marinated peppers – and specialities like grilled rib of beef with béarnaise. To finish, irresistible desserts and local farmhouse cheeses are dramatically displayed on top of the grand piano. The loos are up a long flight of stairs. Well-equipped, self-catering accommodation (daily B&B or weekly terms) is available on the premises and nearby. Look for the blue entrance gate, 1½ miles outside Durrus, on the Goleen/Barley Cove road. *Seats 70. D only 7.30-9.30. Closed Sun (& Mon Sep-Jun), & Nov-mid March. Set D £27.50. Amex, Diners MasterCard,* **VISA**

We do not accept free meals or hospitality – our inspectors pay their own bills and **never** book in the name of Egon Ronay's Guides.

EAST FERRY	The Marlogue Inn	

Tel 021 813390 Fax 021 811342   Map 2 B6
East Ferry Marina Cobh Co Cork

Despite the name, which somehow conveys the impression of an old-established hostelry, this beautifully located little waterside pub only opened in 1992 and features a riverside patio/barbecue area. Bar food covers a range from rolls, sandwiches, salads and creamy mushrooms to fish pie, poached or grilled salmon, steaks, a daily pie and fruit tart. Children under 12 welcome until 7pm. *Open 12-11.30 (to 11 in winter), Sun 12-11.* **Bar Food** *12-8.30. Garden, outdoor eating. Closed Good Friday, 25 Dec. MasterCard,* **VISA**

ENNIS	Auburn Lodge Hotel	64%	£80

Tel 065 21247 Fax 065 21202   Map 2 B4
Galway Road Ennis Co Clare

Although just off a busy road (the N17, 20 minutes from Shannon airport), the peaceful atmosphere of this modern, low-rise hotel is quite striking, possibly because the soothing influence of its central courtyard garden permeates right through the building. A programme of redevelopment and refurbishment has been taking place over a number of years and now seems more or less complete. Public areas, including the bar ('Tailor Quigley's pub') and dining-room, are spick and span and, in the latest phase, the foyer was completely redesigned. All rooms are now of a similar standard, mostly quite spacious with pleasantly warm decor; all have neat en suite bathrooms with over-bath showers and TV/video, phone, hairdryer and tea/coffee-making facilities. Executive suites (and a pretty bridal suite) are similar in design and decor but larger and more flamboyant. Banqueting/conferences for up to 400/650. No dogs. *Rooms 100. Garden. Amex, Diners, MasterCard,* **VISA**

ENNIS   The Cloister

Tel 065 29521
Abbey Street Ennis Co Clare

Map 2 B4

P

Built right in the walls and garden of a 13th-century Franciscan abbey, Jim and Annette Brindley's famous pub is steeped in history and the back windows of its cosy low-ceilinged rooms overlook the friary and its brilliant emerald-green grass surrounds. The main restaurant incorporates rooms from the original abbey kitchen and the bar's patio has now been converted into a conservatory for enjoying the good bar food. In winter, fires create a sense of cheer and, in the event of fine summer weather, an attractive patio garden provides an escape from the unseasonable dimness of the bar. A compact, well-balanced à la carte restaurant menu and a three-course table d'hote (£20) offer a good choice – the later perhaps offering a pasta bake of clams, crab and mussels mornay to a medley of seafood with Noilly Prat sauce and poached pear compote with sablé biscuit, butterscotch sauce and pistachio ice cream. The bar menu sees a daily fresh soup (or seafood chowder), toasted sandwiches, tossed tomato salad with Cashel blue cheese dressing, baked Inagh goat's cheese with a port wine sauce, crab claws in garlic butter, home-made pizza with Parma ham, sun-dried tomato and olives, alongside the more substantial dishes like traditional Irish stew and Atlantic seafood pie. 12½% service is added to all menu prices. *Open 12-11.30 (to 11 in winter), Sun 12-11.* **Bar Food** *12-3, 6-9.30. Closed Sun Nov-Easter. Amex, MasterCard,* **VISA**

ENNIS   Cruise's Pub

Tel 065 41800
Abbey Street Ennis Co Clare

Map 2 B4

P

Dating from 1658, Cruise's pub is beside the ruins of the Ennis Friary; a laneway running between them gives access to Cruise's and its neat courtyard/barbecue area. There is a real sense of history about the place and the front bar – which also has direct access from the street – is in old-fashioned 'spit 'n' sawdust' style and, although recently renovated, still more or less original. Behind it (and with separate access from the laneway) there's a 'country kitchen' with traditional red- and black-tiled floor, pine tables and chairs; traditional music sessions are held nightly. In addition, there's a medieval theme room, 'The Sanctuary', available for folklore evenings or private functions for up to 200 guests. *Open 10am-11.30pm 7 days. Closed Good Friday & 25 Dec. Amex, Diners, MasterCard,* **VISA**

ENNIS   Old Ground Hotel   £108

Tel 065 28127   Fax 065 28112
Ennis Co Clare

Map 2 B4

H

One of Ireland's best-loved hotels, The Old Ground was sold by Forte in 1995 and, now in the caring ownership of the Flynn family, is partway through an extensive redevelopment programme which so far seems to be creditably sensitive to the age and unusual character of the building. Major surgery was successfully undertaken (on walls several feet thick) to improve exisiting banqueting/conference facilities last year and, although less drastic improvements are taking place throughout the hotel, another bold move was due to take place as we went to press – by the 1997 season it is most likely that the whole building will have an extra storey of new rooms on top and, if sympathetically designed, this could well be an improvement once the famous ivy-clad frontage has had time to grow in again. Meanwhile, existing rooms throughout the hotel have already been significantly improved. Banqueting/conferences for up to 250/300. No dogs. Graded at 67% in last year's Guide. *Rooms 82. Garden, gift shop. Closed 24-26 Dec. Amex, Diners, MasterCard,* **VISA**

ENNIS	Temple Gate Hotel	64%	£70

Tel 065 23300   Fax 065 23322   Map 2 B4   **H**
The Square Ennis Co Clare

Right in the middle of Ennis, this imaginatively designed hotel is surprisingly quietly situated, with a pedestrian area on one side and a large public car park (including spaces reserved for residents) at the main entrance. The bar, known as McAuley's, was originally a church and retains many interesting features like the soaring ceiling and open beams; this has provided inspiration for the Gothic theme that recurs throughout the hotel. Ingenious 'cloister'-style glassed-in walkways join the various parts of this unusual building, and the new accommodation wing, although clearly built to a budget, has many quality features like specially made bedheads and mirror frames reflecting the Gothic theme. Rooms are of a comfortable size and well thought-out, with phone, TV and modern bathrooms. Although we quote a B&B price for two guests, the hotel quotes a room price without breakfast. No dogs. *Rooms 34. Amex, Diners, MasterCard,* **VISA**

ENNIS	West County Hotel	66%	£100

Tel 065 28421   Fax 065 28801   Map 2 B4   **H**
Clare Road Ennis Co Clare

Well situated for touring County Clare and with excellent facilities for business guests, this friendly modern hotel on the outskirts of Ennis has undergone major changes recently, especially in the public areas. Exceptional conference facilities provide state-of-the-art audio-visual equipment for anything from a small meeting to a convention of 1200 delegates, video-conferencing (global communication) and a business centre for the use of all guests. A fine new leisure centre (including three swimming pools, up-tp-date gym and an imaginatively furnished, professionally staffed children's playroom) was opened in the summer of 1996. Bedrooms, which include ten no-smoking rooms and four equipped for disabled guests, have all been recently refurbished. Families are well catered for, with complimentary use of the leisure centre (which includes a splash pool), children's entertainment and high teas all laid on; children up to 13 may stay free in their parents' room. At the time of going to press further structural changes were due to take place in the bar and the main road frontage of the hotel. No dogs. Lynch Family Hotels. *Rooms 110. Terrace, tennis, indoor swimming pools, children's splash pool, sauna, steam room, solarium, spa bath, gym, beauty salon, children's playroom, games room, snooker. Amex, Diners, MasterCard,* **VISA**

ENNIS   Places of Interest

Tourist Information Tel 065 28366
Bus Eireann Tel 065 24177
Ennis Friary Tel 065 29100
Graggaunowen Bronze Age Project Quin Tel 061 367178
Knappogue Castle Quin Tel 061 361511

ENNISKERRY	Enniscree Lodge Hotel	59%	£80

Tel 01 286 3542   Fax 01 286 6037   Map 2 D4   **HR**
Enniskerry Co Wicklow

Acquired in January 1996 by Raymond and Josephine Power, Enniscree Lodge is a beautifully located inn/hotel high up on the sunny side of Glencree valley. The comfortable bedrooms have been the first to benefit from the new owners' attention and they have all been redecorated, now featuring good linen and towelling; most rooms have lovely views. Bathrooms are still rather poor but may have been improved by the time this Guide is published. A very friendly and relaxed atmosphere is a major attraction along with informal bar meals, a cosy bar with an open log fire in winter and a south-facing terrace for warmer days. A residents' sitting-room doubles as a small function room. Children under 5 free when sharing parents' room. No dogs. **Rooms 10. Closed Mon-Wed in Jan & Feb. Access, Amex, Diners, MasterCard, VISA**

Restaurant   £60

☺ ⓘ ● ⓖ ⓒ ⓞ ⓤ V

Glorious, sweeping views across Glencree provide a fitting setting for Paul Moroney's imaginative, confident combination of traditional and contemporary cuisine. Dishes enjoyed on a recent visit included melon, strawberry and mango with banana liqueur, a salad of crisp leaves with hazelnut dressing and bacon, and mixed fish with beurre blanc and filo vegetable parcels; good carrots, new potatoes and broccoli accompanied the main course. Good home-made bread, luscious desserts (like a rich chocolate parfait) and first-rate farmhouse Irish cheeses (Gubbeen, Milleens and Cashel Blue) to finish. Lighter meals are also served in the bar. **Seats 40. Parties 8. L 12.30-3 D 7.30-9.30 (Sun to 9). Closed 25 Dec, Mon & Tue in Nov, Jan & Feb. Set L £14.50 Set D £21.**

ENNISKERRY   Places of Interest
Fernhill Gardens Sandyford Tel 01 295 6000 *3 miles*
Powerscourt Gardens and Waterfall Tel 01 286 7676

FAHAN	**Restaurant St John's**	**£55**

Tel 077 60289   Map 1 C1   **R**
Fahan Inishowen Co Donegal

🎵 ☺ ⓘ ● ⓖ ⓒ ⓞ ⓤ

In a substantial period house overlooking Lough Swilly, Reg Ryan's warm welcome is underlined by a glowing open fire in the bar area and the decor throughout is comfortably unassertive, leaving the mind clear to enjoy Philomena McAfee's confident cooking to the full. Both a five-course table d'hote dinner menu and a short à la carte are offered. A table d'hote menu might start with smoked haddock tartlets with tomato crème fraiche, then seafood chowder, roast duckling with redcurrant and Dubonnet sauce, and crème caramel or home-made ice cream. A la carte brings daily fresh fish dishes like goujons of monkfish with tartare sauce, baked fillet of pollack with tomato and basil sauce; in addition, you might find fresh crab and prawn salad. baked parmesan chicken with lemon and tarragon cream and fillet of beef with armagnac and mushroom sauce. Details – delicious home-baked bread, imaginative vegetables, Irish cheeses, desserts with the emphasis on flavour rather than show (such as peaches in brandy with vanilla ice cream) and wonderful choux petits fours with spun sugar served with freshly brewed coffee – all add up to a great dining experience. There's a good selection of half bottles and New World wines on the comprehensive wine list, all at friendly prices. No smoking. 10% service is added to all menu prices. Early 1997 will see the addition of a new dining area and accommodation. **Seats 40. Private Room 10. D only 7-9.30. Closed Sun-Tue, Good Friday, 3 days Christmas. Set D £20. Diners, MasterCard, VISA**

FENIT	**The Tankard Restaurant**	**£65**

Tel 066 36164   Fax 066 36516   Map 2 A5   **R**
Kilfenora Fenit nr Tralee Co Kerry

🎵 ☺ ⓘ ● ⓖ ⓤ V

Easily identified by its striking yellow ochre exterior, The Tankard is situated between the road and the sea. While the focal point in the cosy, newly refurbished bar is a welcome glass-doored fire, the restaurant enjoys dramatic views across the water to the mountains beyond; the interior echoes the exterior yellow theme with dashing tartan drapes and upholstery. Local seafood and steaks are the specialities on a fairly traditional menu cooked in a strong, simple style. Typical dishes from a choice of a dozen soups and starters might include a creamy, well-flavoured seafood chowder with plenty of fish, local oysters with a squeese of lemon, or chicken liver paté with Cumberland sauce; all dishes are served with moist, freshly-baked brown bread. Typical main courses include seafood symphony (various seafoods served hot with a white wine sauce) and rack of Kerry lamb with a honey and rosemary sauce. There are farmhouse cheeses or classic desserts that include a very correct crème caramel and juicy apple pie made with light, crisp pastry decorated with pastry hearts. Solicitous service throughout. A winter visit will be rewarding as shellfish is at its best then. Bar food is served daily during pub hours. *Seats 70 (+ 40 on patio). Parties 20. L 12-2.30 D 6-10.30. Closed Mon (Jan & Feb), Set L Sun £8.95. Good Friday, 24 & 25 Dec. Amex, Diners, MasterCard,* **VISA**

FERRYCARRIG BRIDGE	Ferrycarrig Hotel	61%	£100

Tel 053 20999   Fax 053 20982   Map 2 D5   **HR**
Ferrycarrig Bridge nr Wexford Co Wexford

All bedrooms in this well-run modern waterside hotel overlook the Slaney estuary and there is a path leading to Ferrycarrig Castle. Comfortably furnished public rooms include the Dry Dock bar and two restaurants, all enjoying the views. Stylish bedrooms have well-equipped bathrooms with plenty of shelf space; 24hr room service. There's conference space for up to 400, ample free parking and the hotel is part owner of the cliff-top 18-hole St Helen's Bay golf course at Rosslare Harbour, 15 minutes' drive away. No dogs. Guests should have use of a new leisure complex, including a swimming pool, and the choice of 51 extra bedrooms when work is completed in April 1997. *Rooms 40. Garden, gym, sauna, steam room, solarium. Amex, Diners, MasterCard,* **VISA**

The Conservatory   £65

The Conservatory restaurant is a pleasant spot beside a paved garden and makes good use of the waterside location. Perhaps best known for Sunday lunch, the kitchen (under head chef Mairead Kennedy) is at its best when stretched on the à la carte. Local produce is highlighted in, for example, in a starter like fresh Duncannon mussels steamed in white wine and served with a roast garlic butter sauce; this might be followed by cream of celery and lovage soup, then a choice of local beef, pork or seafood and a more unusual choice such as supreme of chicken filled with French goat's cheese and served with salsa verde. Desserts range from key lime pie with mango coulis to tulipe marble (black and white chocolate with chocolate sauce); there's always a farmhouse cheeseboard. The Boathouse bistro is open for à la carte D only (6.30-9.30, seats 60). *Seats 90. Parties 20. L 12.30-2.15 D 7-9.15. Set Sun L £10.95 Set D £25. Closed D Sun- D Tue Nov-Mar (except Christmas & New Year). Amex, Diners, MasterCard,* **VISA**

> We only recommend the food in hotels categorised as **HR** and **AR**.

FIGHTING COCKS	Fighting Cocks

Tel 0503 48744   Map 2 C4   **P**
Fighting Cocks Co Carlow

Tim Radford's attractive, well-run crossroads pub is a real local, with open fire, snooker and darts plus traditional Irish music every Thursday, Saturday and Sunday night, all year. Although visually striking, with a collection of agricultural and rural artefacts displayed to advantage around the lofty main bar area, this seems more a fair reflection of bygone ways of country life in the area than just another theme pub. A hot toddy (warm brandy,whiskey or port) is just the thing to keep out the cold during the winter months. No food. *Open 1-11.30 (to 11 in winter) Sun 12.30-2, 4-11. Garden. Closed Good Friday, 25 Dec. No credit cards.*

FOULKSMILLS — Horetown House — £50

Tel 051 565771 Fax 051 555633
Foulksmills Co Wexford

Map 2 C5

R

Horetown House is best known as a residential equestrian centre with a relaxed country atmosphere. Residents generally use the dining-room in the main house (where a hearty farmhouse family dinner is offered as an alternative to the more formal table d'hôte). Alternatively, the Cellar Restaurant, which is cosy and atmospheric, with an open fire, whitewashed arches and sturdy country furniture, is open to non-residents, especially for Sunday lunch (2 sittings at 12.30 & 2.30). Proprietor Ivor Young and his head chef David Cronin can be relied on to produce meals based on quality ingredients, including local salmon, wild Wicklow venison and other game in season. Try also Tuskar Rock mussels, pot roast duckling with orange and Grand Marnier sauce, roast rack of lamb with rosemary, or the chef's special dessert tasting plate. A mid-week farmhouse special (6.30-7.30 £16.50) four-course menu offers a good choice. *Seats 40. Private Room 25. L 12.30 & 2.30 (Sun only, other days by arrangement only for parties of 15+) D 6.30-9.30. Set Sun L £11.95 Set D from £20.50. Closed D Sun, all Mon (except Bank Holidays) & 3 days Christmas. Amex, Diners, MasterCard,* **VISA**

We welcome bona fide complaints and recommendations on the tear-out Readers' Comments pages at the back of the Guide. They are followed up by our professional team.

FURBO — Connemara Coast Hotel — 71% — £135

Tel 091 592108 Fax 091 592065
Furbo Co Galway

Map 2 B4

H

Snuggled down into rocks between Barna and Spiddal, on the sea side of the road, this pleasingly unobtrusive, low-rise modern hotel has been developed with an environmentally considerate design policy already successfully applied at the sister hotel, *Connemara Gateway*, at Oughterard. Spacious public areas include an impressive foyer/lounge area, large restaurant and banqueting and conference rooms (capacity up to 450/500) overlooking the sea and a well-equipped leisure centre. Most bedrooms have views across Galway Bay and are comfortably furnished with neat en suite bathrooms. Twenty were completely refurbished last year and the on-going upgrading programme should see more bedrooms revamped during 1997. Executive suites (£185) are also available, along with a considerably reduced tariff between October and the end of April. 24hr room service. Good family facilities include six interconnecting rooms, a playroom (evenings and weekends), high tea and a children's entertainment programme in high season. However, the hotel stresses that they make great efforts not to let children dominate the atmosphere. Adults can enjoy the massage/therapy room and the cottage-style Irish pub (Sín Scéal Eilé – That's Another Story). No dogs. **Rooms 112.** *Garden, tennis, indoor swimming pool, gym, sun beds, sauna, steam room, beauty salon, children's indoor playroom, games room. Closed 25-27 Dec. Amex, Diners, MasterCard,* **VISA**

GALWAY   Ardilaun House   66%   £110

Tel 091 521433   Fax 091 521546   Map 2 B4   **H**
Taylors Hill Galway Co Galway

Taking its name from the Irish Ard Oilean (High Island), a picturesque island
on nearby Lough Corrib, the house was originally built in 1840 and contains
handsomely proportioned day rooms looking out over the attractive grounds.
Sympathetic extensions have been added over the past 30 years or so, providing
unpretentious, traditionally furnished bedrooms of various sizes, and a modern
conference facility for up to 400 delegates. Considerable tariff reductions out
of high season; children under 4 share parents' room free of charge. Friendly,
helpful staff. No dogs. Tennis, squash and badminton facilities are available
at Galway Lawn Tennis Club for hotel guests. *Rooms 89. Garden, gym, sauna,
steam room, solarium, snooker. Closed 4 days at Christmas. Amex, Diners,
MasterCard,* **VISA**

GALWAY   Brennans Yard   64%   £95

Tel 091 568166   Fax 091 568262   Map 2 B4   **H**
Lower Merchants Road Galway Co Galway

An unusual hotel created from stylishly converted old warehousing in Galway
city's 'Left Bank' area, adjacent to the historic Spanish Arch and only a stone's
throw away from the shopping and business areas. Public rooms include a
pleasantly bright if smallish dining-room and, at the back, the striking Oyster
Bar for informal meals, especially local seafood. Individually decorated bedrooms
make up in style what is lacking in space – well-planned, clean-lined rooms have
old stripped-pine pieces, locally-made pottery and neat, functional bathrooms;
three rooms have both a double and single bed; family facilities are provided.
Direct-dial phones, radio and TV, tea/coffee-making facilities, hairdryer and
toiletries included as standard. Children under 12 share parents' room free
of charge. No dogs (except Guide Dogs. *Rooms 24. Closed 25 & 26 Dec.
Amex, Diners, MasterCard,* **VISA**

We only recommend the food in hotels categorised as **HR** and **AR**.
However, the food in many **A** establishments throughout
Ireland is often very acceptable
(but the restaurant may not be open to non-residents).

GALWAY   Bridge Mills Restaurant

Tel 091 566231   Fax 091 563393   Map 2 B4   **JaB**
O'Briens Bridge Galway Co Galway

Just beside O'Brien's Bridge, overlooking the turbulent Corrib river, this informal
restaurant is snugly situated in the recently renovated old mills, now used as an
educational and arts and crafts centre. The structure of the building divides the
restaurant area up naturally into a series of 'rooms' around the recently restored
16th-century waterwheel, some of which have fine views down river, allowing
convenient arrangement of non-smoking areas. Vegetarians are well catered for
as specialities include the Bridge Mills omelette, available with a wide choice of
fillings, as well as a vegetarian dish of the day and a variety of salads. Good for
morning coffee or afternoon tea with home-made scones or cakes, and for a
relaxing Sunday brunch. Although our specific recommendation is for daytime
snacks, the restaurant is also open for dinner from 6 to 10.30 (mid Jun-Sep only).
Children's menu. Eight tables on a balcony. *Seats 80. Parties 20. Open 9-6 7 days.
Closed 25-27 Dec & 1 Jan. Amex, MasterCard,* **VISA**

GALWAY   Corrib Great Southern Hotel   68%   £142

Tel 091 755281   Fax 091 751390   Map 2 B4   **H**
Dublin Road Galway Co Galway

Overlooking Galway Bay, a large, modern hotel on the edge of the city, offering a wide range of facilities for both business guests and family holidays. Bedrooms vary considerably; spacious 'superior' rooms are well planned with good attention to detail and stylish bathrooms. Children under 2 stay free in parents' room, £25 per night for 2-12s, children's early supper 5-6pm. The (smallish) swimming pool has a lifeguard at all times and, in summer only, children's entertainment and a creche are provided. A state-of-the-art business/convention centre has a variety of suites with facilities for conference groups of 8 to 850 and banqueting for up to 550. Public areas include a cosy residents' lounge and O'Malleys Pub, a big, lively bar with sea views. Ask about two-night stay rates and special Sunday rates. Special green fees at the 18-hole Christy O'Connor Jnr Galway Bay Golf Club, 5 miles away. *Rooms 180. Indoor swimming pool, steam room, spa bath, snooker, helipad. Closed 24-26 Dec. Amex, Diners, MasterCard,* **VISA**

GALWAY   Galway Ryan Hotel   63%   £136

Tel 091 753181   Fax 091 753187   Map 2 B4   **H**
Dublin Road Galway Co Galway

A useful business base, 2 kilometres from the city centre, with an excellent leisure centre which, although having a private membership, is also open to all hotel guests and offers a deck-level swimming pool, sports hall (for badminton, indoor football and the like), gym, aerobics studio, sauna, steam room, jacuzzi and games room. Conference facilities for 80, theatre-style. Children are well catered for; extra beds and cots are provided (under-2s stay free), high teas in season and play facility provided weekends and during July and August. Reduced tariff Jan-20 Jul. Ryan Hotels. *Rooms 96. Patio, tennis, indoor swimming pool, leisure centre. Closed 25 Dec. Amex, Diners, MasterCard,* **VISA**

GALWAY   Glenlo Abbey Hotel   75%   £175

Tel 091 526666   Fax 091 527800   Map 2 B4   **HR**
Bushy Park Galway Co Galway

Formerly the ancestral home of the Ffrench and Blake familes (two of the fourteen tribes who ruled over Galway for centuries), this impressive, privately-owned hotel opened in 1992, having been lovingly created around an abbey conversion and the beautifully restored 18th-century original house. Situated on a 137-acre estate, 4km from Galway City along the N59, it commands splendid views across Lough Corrib and has an 800-metre frontage on to the River Corrib, beyond the 18-hole golf course, putting green and floodlit driving range. As well as a keen golfing clientele, the hotel attracts good corporate business with its various meeting and seminar rooms (80), notably those in the converted abbey, and the fully serviced business centre. All the clean, spacious and well-appointed bedrooms have king-size beds, attractive fabrics, personal safes, trouser presses, satellite TV and well-designed marbled bathrooms with good towels and toiletries, bathrobes and telephone; top-of-the-range bedrooms include six suites with whirlpool baths; 24hr room service. Children are welcome; under-3s stay free and babysitting is available on request. The Pavilion clubhouse houses the business centre and all day bar and brasserie; the convivial Oak Cellar Bar (informal bar meals) and Kentfield Bar (afternoon teas) are both ideal for pre- or post-dinner drinks. Fishing, shooting and riding can be arranged. No dogs. *Rooms 45. Garden, golf (18), putting green, driving range, private jetty. Amex, Diners, MasterCard,* **VISA**

See over

Ffrench Room Restaurant   £70

A relaxed atmosphere prevails in this elegantly appointed dining-room, decorated in green with attractive plasterwork and furnished with antiques, while quality linen and china grace neat, well-spaced tables. Creative Irish and International cooking from head chef Elliot Fox highlights the imaginative set dinner menu that changes every two weeks. Fresh local seafood features well in starters such as pressed monkfish and pimento terrine with green peppercorn dressing, spinach and lobster ravioli served in a creamy bisque sauce, or spicy mussel soup, followed by main-course options like grilled supreme of turbot with carrot and ginger coulis or baked fillet of salmon (fresh from The Weir in Galway) topped with onion glaze with a truffle dressing. Quality Irish meat may appear in the form of pan-fried cannon of lamb coated in cracked black pepper with cabbage dumplings and a rich red wine sauce. Finish off with warm rhubarb tart with lemon sabayon and home-made brown bread ice cream, or a plate of farmhouse cheeses. Friendly and efficient service. The comprehensive wine list has pretty stiff claret prices – better value in the New World (Cloudy Bay excepted). *Seats* 40. *Private Room 28. L 12.30-2.30 D 6.30-9.30 (till 8.30 Sun). Set L £14 D £19/£24/£28.*

Entries categorised as **JaB** are recommended for 'Just a Bite'.

| GALWAY | **Great Southern** | 69% | £155 |

Tel 091 564041 Fax 091 566704   Map 2 B4   **H**
Eyre Square Galway Co Galway

Overlooking Eyre Square right in the heart of Galway, this historic railway hotel (built in 1845) has retained many of its original features, and old-world charm mixes easily with modern facilities. Public rooms are quite grand and include a cocktail lounge and O'Flahertys Pub bar decorated with railway memorabilia. Bedrooms are undergoing an upgrade (30 completed to date) and are generally spacious and traditionally furnished with dark mahogany units, brass light fittings and smart fabrics. Various rooms offer conference facilities for up to 300 (banquets 250). Roof-top swimming pool with magnificent views over the city. Ask about two-night stay rates and special Sunday rates. No dogs. *Rooms 114. Indoor swimming pool, sauna, steam room. Closed 24-26 Dec. Amex, Diners, MasterCard,* **VISA**

| GALWAY | **Holiday Inn Express** | | £62 |

Tel 091 771166 Fax 091 771646   Map 2 B4   **L**
Headford Road Galway Co Galway

Newly-built budget hotel offering straightforward, comfortable accommodation. Modern facilities include queen-sized beds, computer phone points, voice-mail telephone system and 'double double bed' family rooms. The room price quoted includes two cooked Irish breakfasts; the room price with Continental breakfast is £50 (£40 Jan-Apr and Nov-Dec). Five bedrooms are equipped for disabled guests. No dogs. East of the city, towards the airport. See also entry under Cork. Toll-free central reservations 0800 897121 (U.K.). *Rooms 100. Closed 1 week Christmas. Amex, Diners, MasterCard,* **VISA**

Many hotels offer reduced rates for weekend or out-of-season bookings. Our guide price indicates high-season rates. Always ask about special deals for longer stays.

GALWAY — Hooker Jimmy's Steak & Seafood Bar

Tel 091 568351   Fax 091 568352   Map 2 B4   **JaB**
The Fishmarket Spanish Arch Galway Co Galway

John, Margaret and James Glanville run this determinedly middle-market steak and seafood bar near *Jurys Inn* (see entry below). Decor has been transplanted from their old premises, with dark green paintwork and soft-toned upholstery, lots of divisions making private corners and, in summer, the recently enlarged terrace overlooking the river seats a further 70. Good value is the keynote and, whether it's a quick steak served as you like it with baked potato and stir-fry vegetables, half-a-dozen oysters baked in herb and garlic butter, or seafood chowder served with dark, moist home-made bread, good value is what you will get. A family-owned trawler ensures that all the seafood from Galway Bay is as fresh as it can be – lobster being a particular favourite. 'Diaper deck' provided for baby-changing in the disabled toilet; high-chairs provided. *Seats 96. Parties 20. Terrace. Open 12-10.30. Closed 25 & 26 Dec. Amex, Diners, MasterCard,* **VISA**

GALWAY — Jurys Galway Inn   60%   £56

Tel 091 566444   Fax 091 568415   Map 2 B4   **H**
Quay Street Galway Co Galway

The emphasis at the Galway Inn is firmly on value for money; run on the same lines as the *Jurys Christchurch Inn* in Dublin, this 'inn' offers a good standard of basic accommodation without frills. Rooms, almost all with river views, are large (sleeping up to four people) with everything required for basic comfort and convenience – neat en suite bathroom, TV, phone – but no extras. Beds are generous, with good-quality bedding, but wardrobes are open; don't expect tea/coffee-making facilities or room service, either. Public areas include an impressive, well-designed foyer with seating areas, a pubby bar with a good atmosphere and a self-service informal restaurant. Obviously a good place for family accommodation (extra beds and cots available) and budget-conscious travellers; booking some way ahead is advised. Conference facility for 40. No dogs. *Rooms 128. Garden. Closed 24-28 Dec. Amex, Diners, MasterCard,* **VISA**

GALWAY — McDonagh's   £35

Tel 091 565001   Fax 091 562246   Map 2 B4   **R**
22 Quay Street Galway Co Galway

This chameleon-like establishment starts the day as a wet fish shop, then starts a roaring trade as an informal restaurant from 12 noon, serving as many as 18-20 varieties of fish at the front of the shop along with traditional fish and chips, chowder with home-baked bread and much more. The right-hand side of the premises provides slightly more formal dining space – for meals rather than quick snacks – where a lunch menu of fine local seafood kicks off with oysters from nearby Clarenbridge, ranges through a wide selection of seafood (including a large bowl of about 3lb wild mussels steamed in wine and garlic, served with salad and garlic bread) to conclude with an Irish farmhouse cheese selection. At dinner the choice widens yet again, to include specialities such as McDonagh's shellfish plattter – half a lobster, scallops, mussels, crab claws and prawns, served with garlic butter and wine sauce – lobster grilled in garlic butter and a wide range of barbecued or chargrilled fish. For the 1997 season there should be more space, with additional seating outside in the rear courtyard. *Seats 100. Meals 12-5, D 5-10 (till 9 Sun). Closed L Sun & 24-26 Dec. Amex, Diners, MasterCard,* **VISA**

GALWAY Hotel Spanish Arch 65% £150

Tel 091 569600 Fax 091 569191 Map 2 B4 **H**
Quay Street Galway Co Galway

Next to its large bar, which also has independent access from the street, a discreet entrance leads to a small foyer with minuscule seating area and desk, then a lift whisks surprised first-time guests up to rooms which are furnished with a medieval theme. Heavy tapestries and rich velvets are used to good effect in drapes, bedcovers, upholstery and cushions, all fitting in well with the age and location of this ancient building. Bedrooms are not especially large, wardrobes are small and there is very little space for luggage. Bathrooms are good-sized, however, and have full-size tubs with over-bath showers, generous marbled shelf space and toiletries, good lighting, mist-free mirrors and plenty of warm towels. Informal dining space at the back of the bar leads out to a patio area. No-smoking and wheelchair-friendly rooms are available. Banqueting/conferences for 100/120. Parking is available in the multi-storey car park next door; overnight vouchers are arranged at a special rate. Check-out time is 11am. *Rooms 20. Terrace. Closed 25 & 26 Dec. MasterCard, Amex,* **VISA**

GALWAY Tigh Neachtain

Tel 091 568820 Map 2 B4 **P**
Cross Street Galway Co Galway

One of Galway's most relaxed and unspoilt pubs, Tigh Neachtain has great charm and a friendly atmosphere – the mysterious, dark interior (almost unchanged since 1894) reflects the medieval origins of the building, which has been in the same family for a century now, but it's not a bit precious. The pint is good and there's usually bar food but perhaps the nicest thing of all is the way an impromptu traditional music session can get going at the drop of a hat. As we went to press there were plans to re-launch the tiny restaurant upstairs as a seafood bar. *Open 10.30am-11.30pm (to 11pm in winter), Sun 4-11.* **Bar Food** *12.30-2 (not Sat & Sun). No credit cards.*

GALWAY Westwood Bistro £60

Tel 091 521442 Fax 091 521400 Map 2 B4 **R**
Dangan Upper Newcastle Galway Co Galway

Bernie and Mary Casey have been running this popular eating place since 1982 and the long, low building houses a number of recently revamped bars and restaurant areas to suit various occasions. An evening in the main restaurant starts in the new private bar for diners, where orders are taken before you settle into a comfortable carver or banquette at a well-appointed table to enjoy son John Casey's sound cooking; there's no doubting John's commitment or his imaginative flair in the kitchen. His menus offer a wide choice, including several daily specials, and might feature cassolette of mussels with a rissotto of squid, roast wood pigeon on a ragout of lentils with mead sauce or fishcakes in a creamy tarragon sauce to start, followed by venison and cranberry pie, fillet of Cajun monkfish with a red pepper and sun-dried tomato jus, or medallions of pork stuffed with black pudding on a bed of colcannon and a spicy apple jus. A set lunch is offered on Sundays. Vegetables are imaginative, desserts unusual and prettily presented and home-made petits fours are served with coffee. Low-cholesterol and vegetarian dishes available. Private dining-room upstairs. *Seats 60. L 12.30-2.15 D 6.30-9.45. Closed Good Friday, 5 days Christmas. Set Sun L £11.95. Amex, MasterCard,* **VISA**

Set menu prices may not include service or wine.
Our guide price for two diners includes wine and service.

GALWAY   Places of Interest
Tourist Information Tel 091 563081
Bus Eireann Tel 091 562000
Arts Festival (July) Tel 091 583800
Oyster Festival (September) Tel 091 522066
Aran Ferries Tel 091 568903
Aran Islands Tourist Office Tel 099 561263 *May-Sep*
Athenry Castle Athenry Tel 091 844797 *Summer Season only*
Coole Park Gort Tel 091 31804 *Nature Reserve*
Galway Racecourse Ballybrit Tel 091 53870
Island Ferries Teo Tel 091 561767
Leisureland Salthill Tel 091 521455
Nora Barnacle House Museum Tel 091 564743
Siamsa an Taibhdearc Theatre Tel 091 562024
Thoor Ballylee Gort Tel 091 31436
W B Yeats's home

GLANDORE   Hayes' Bar

Tel 028 33214
Glandore Co Cork   Map 2 B6   **P**

The beautifully situated village of Glandore boasts a surprising number of
excellent hostelries, each with its own particular character and most with
pavement tables and lovely harbour views, but when choices have to be made
Hayes' Bar has a powerful attraction in Ada Hayes' famous bar food. Sensible
tables and chairs, the right height for comfortable consumption, provide the first
promising hint of priorities, then there's an unusual emphasis on wine, both
decorative and actual: clearly this is not your average Irish bar. The menu is short
and inscrutable – chicken and vegetable soup, sandwiches, a few 'specials' like
paté on toast or prawn salad (the house speciality) – but the soup reminds you of
the kind your granny used to make and the sandwiches (perhaps tuna and corn,
garlic sausage, Westphalian salami or egg and chive) are nothing short of a new
culinary art form. A 'prawn special' sandwich, for example, is made with lovely
fresh brown bread stuffed with masses of freshly cooked prawns in home–made
mayonnaise, quartered and prettily served with thinly-sliced fruit – apple, plum,
orange – and a cocktail stick kebab of cherry tomatoes, olives and cucumber,
then garnished with a mixed–leaf salad. Everything is served on different plates
(Ada is a collector and never returns from her frequent travels without a new
batch of ware) and attention to detail is outstanding, even for something as simple
as a cup of coffee: a little tray is laid with an individual cafetière, a large French
cup and saucer with matching tiny jug of cream and bowl of sugar, a biscuit and
a chocolate. Spiced beef, too often restricted to the role of Christmas fare, is a
speciality here and makes excellent sandwiches and the (farmhouse) cheese and
(home-made) chutney is an unusually good vegetarian alternative. *Open 12-
11.30pm (to 11pm in winter), Sun 12.30-2, 4-11pm: Jun-end Aug, Christmas, Easter
& all weekends.* **Bar Food** *all day. Closed weekdays Sep-Jun except Christmas &
Easter. No credit cards.*

| GLANDORE | **Marine Hotel** | 60% | £64 |

Tel 028 33366   Fax 028 33600   Map 2 B6   **H**
Glandore Co Cork

This friendly family hotel is right down beside the harbour, with most of
the family rooms in an attractive ivy-clad annexe in a converted stable block
alongside a courtyard car park. Rooms in the main hotel are on the small side
and simply furnished, without phones, but all are en-suite and some have
harbour views. Public areas include two bars where bar menus, including
children's early evening meals, are served. *Rooms 16. Closed Nov-end Feb (unless
by arrangement). Amex, Diners, MasterCard,* **VISA**

| GLANDORE | **Pier House Bistro** | £50 |

Tel 028 33079   Fax 028 33880   Map 2 B6   **R**
Glandore Co Cork

Tucked into a corner beside the harbour, the Pier House Bistro lives up to its
promise of lively, keenly priced evening fare with a full vegetarian menu offering
a choice of two or three dishes for each course. Regular evening menus offer
starters like crab (or sometimes even lobster) salad, alongside oysters, guacamole
or home-made soup such as carrot and coriander, followed perhaps by fillet
steaks, spinach and ricotta in filo pastry and a good choice of fish (John Dory,
skate wing in lemon butter sauce or moules marinière. Homely desserts – lemon
cheesecake, baked bananas, pavlova, honey and orange ice cream – and freshly-
brewed coffee. White rolls are baked every evening using organic, unbleached
flour. *Seats 32. D 7-9.30. Closed mid Sep-Easter. MasterCard,* **VISA**

| GLANDORE | **The Rectory** | £70 |

Tel 028 33072   Fax 028 33600   Map 2 B6   **R**
Glandore Co Cork

This fine Georgian residence is in a prime location, set in wooded gardens
looking down Glandore harbour towards the islands of Adam and Eve.
Indications of a courageous hand at work are seen in the bold use of colour
throughout the reception and dining areas where strong background colours –
blue in one area, green in another – are picked up in generous drapes and other
soft furnishings; thsi is most notable in the reception/bar area where aperitifs are
served and orders taken. Tables are clothed in classic white with crisp napkins,
gleaming silver and glasses and fresh flowers, with comfortable chairs. Window
tables are particularly desirable, but most are agreeably positioned even if not
blessed with a long view. So the scene is set for an enjoyable meal. There have
been changes in the kitchen recently and, although the style has not undergone
fundamental changes, the confident sense of direction previously so striking now
seems less sure – some inconsistency in standards of dishes was noted on a recent
visit – and there are also problems with service, not all new but unresolved after
a long 'running-in' time. Short-staffing seems to be a problem: at any restaurant,
particularly a restaurant of this calibre, guests expect to be properly greeted, but
there does not appear to be a restaurant manager to do this, or indeed to supervise
waiting staff during service (even the menu was dog-eared). The food was
uneven, although it did include some very good dishes: a millefeuille of chicken
livers served with black and white pudding and bacon and garnished with a
small leaf salad was perfectly cooked with a jaunty little square of crisp golden
pastry on top – as tasty a starter as anyone could wish for; a dish of scallops, just
seared and tossed through a big mixed-leaf salad, was also excellent. Yet a huge,
coarse main-course lobster failed to be the treat that any diner is entitled to
expect and an otherwise well-conceived turbot dish was unexpectedly served

without asparagus, a component advertised on the menu. On the same occasion, blackberry fool with hazelnut wafers made a very nice dessert but several of the plated cheeses were wrongly named by the waitress – hardly inspiring. *Seats 70. Parties 10. Private Room 40. D only 7-9. Closed Sun-Wed (except high season) & Nov-Apr. Set D £24.50. Amex, Diners, MasterCard,* **VISA**

GLANMIRE   The Barn Restaurant   £60

Tel & Fax 021 866211
Glanmire nr Cork Co Cork   Map 2 B6   **R**

Long established as a popular neighbourhood restaurant, this discreetly-located place deserves a wider audience. Situated on the 'old Youghal road', from which it is cleverly screened by judicious planting, it is in fact very close to the big roundabout on the main road into the north side of Cork city and accommodation in the Tivoli area. The restaurant is comfortable in a cosy, slightly old-fashioned way and, appropriately enough, provides the similarly 'old-fashioned' pleasures of willing service by uniformed waiters and food with a real home-cooked flavour. The four-course dinner menu offers a wide choice for all courses – perhaps including a green salad with slivers of duck and a plum sauce, or baked mushroom caps with herb-flavoured cream cheese among the starters. From a wide choice of main courses you might choose roast fillet of local salmon with sorrel sauce, roast pork steak with the chef's special stuffing and a wholegrain mustard sauce, or free-range chicken breast in filo with 'Barn garden' herb mousse and tarragon sauce. Accompaniments are also carefully selected and there's a full vegetarian menu (£13.50), all followed by Irish cheeses or treats from a traditional dessert trolley. Sunday lunch menus, although simpler, are in the same general style; children are welcome for Sunday lunch. Six tables are set on a patio in fine weather. Car parking behind the restaurant. *Seats 60. Parties 12. L 12.30-2.30 (Sun only) D 6.30-10. Set Sun L £11 Set D £22.50. Closed Ash Wednesday, Good Friday & 26 Dec. Amex, Diners, MasterCard,* **VISA**

If you encounter bad service don't wait to write to us but make your feelings known to the management at the time of your visit. Instant compensation can often resolve any problem that might otherwise leave a bad taste.

GLASSON   Glasson Village Restaurant   £50

Tel 0902 85001
Glasson Athlone Co Westmeath   Map 1 C3   **R**

An attractive stone building (once a barracks) in a pretty village off the main road in Goldsmith country. The atmosphere is friendly and the place really bustles at Sunday lunchtime. Owner-chef Michael Brooks is something of a seafood specialist – choose lobster or oysters fresh from the tank or, from the dinner menu, perhaps salmon stuffed with prawns with a dill and pink peppercorn sauce, pan-fried Lough Lee eels with capers and black butter, sautéed scallops with fennel, Vermouth and cream, or the fresh fish dish of the day. Other choices could include a julienne of chicken tandoori style with coconut sauce, medallions of pork with sage and Parma ham on a bed of rösti with mustard seed vinaigrette and roast venison with juniper and game sauce. Particularly good value, weekly-changing four-course table d'hote includes a choice of soups. *Seats 55 (+ 14 in garden). Parties 14 Private Room 12. L 12.30-2.30 D 7-10.15. Closed D Sun, D Mon (except Bank Holidays), 3 weeks from mid Oct & 24-26 Dec. Set Sun L £11.25 Set D £17.95. Amex, Diners, MasterCard,* **VISA**

GLASSON — Grogan's & Nannie Murph's

Tel 0902 85158   Map 1 C3   **P**
Glasson nr Athlone Co Westmeath

"Established 1750", Grogan's is a delightfully quaint, family-run pub in the pretty and accessible village of Glasson, six miles north of Athlone. The cosy, low-ceilinged front bar is divided in the traditional manner, with an open fire at one end along with flagstones and a mix of wood and brass furnishings. Thérèse Gilsenan runs the food operation under a menu entitled 'Nannie Murph's Seafood & Steak Bar', providing a good choice of bar food that encompasses steamed Galway Bay mussels with garlic bread, traditional Irish stew, fresh fish and chips, toasted sandwiches and a smoked bacon and black pudding baguette with mustard mayonnaise. More substantial meals could range from rack of lamb with a honey, lemon and thyme sauce to seared fillet of wild salmon with Thérèse's special salsa. Leave room for meringues and cream with Baileys Irish cream sauce or a strawberry coulis, or Hazel's favourite chocolate truffle cake. There's a large back bar and a beer garden where summer barbecues are held. Traditional music every Wed and Sun night. *Open 10.30-11.30 (to 11 in winter), Sun 4-11.* **Bar Food** *12-9 (D 5.30-9), Sun 4-8. Garden. Closed L Sun, 3 weeks Jan, Good Friday & 25 Dec. MasterCard,* **VISA**

GLASSON — Wineport Restaurant — £55

Tel 0902 85466 Fax 0902 85471   Map 1 C3   **R**
Glasson nr Athlone Co Westmeath

This delightful waterside restaurant, just outside Athlone on Lough Ree, continues to charm on all fronts – the location is idyllic, Ray Byrne and Jane English are outstanding hosts and they head up an excellent team that includes head chef Noel Ryan. The restaurant is quite informal, yet somehow manages to create a sense of occasion; the view alone would do this, perhaps, but Ray and Jane have put a lot of their personalities as well as hard work into the place, making it both cosy – reading the papers in front of the fire before and after Sunday lunch is a real treat – and characterful, with lots of nautical memorabilia in the decor balanced by Jane's growing 'cat' collection. Noel uses good local ingredients in an enticing repertoire of dishes that combine simplicity and imagination. Lively first courses might include choices as varied as deep-fried Irish Brie with rhubarb sauce, home-made soup with freshly-baked bread, and smoked Lough Ree eel and mackerel paté served on ripe avocado. Well-balanced main courses might range from deep-fried casseroled rabbit with a rich meat jus through steamed king prawn tails with white wine, garlic, herbs and cream to a 'healthy options' (vegetarian) menu offering roast courgette filled with mixed nuts and savoury vegetables with a chive and mustard sauce. Seasonal desserts (lemon tart with passion fruit crème anglaise) are always unusual and tempting. Innovative ideas include Noel's Game Tasting Menu (£16), in season (quail, pigeon, eel, smoked pike, pheasant etc as available), a wine selection in three price bands (guests choose their bottles from the rack rather than a list) and a free local taxi service. Early Tee-Bird menu £13.95/£15.95 served 5-7pm daily. Children are 'always welcome' and are offered their own little menu. *Seats 65 (+ 25 0n terrace). Parties 12. Private Room 50. Meals Jul & Aug 4-10 L (Sun only) 12-4 D 5-10. Closed L Mon-Sat (except Jul & Aug), 25 & 26 Dec & 1 Jan. Set Sun L £13.95 Set D £20. Amex, Diners, MasterCard,* **VISA**

See the **County Listings** green tinted pages for
details of all establishments listed in county order.

GLEN OF AHERLOW   Aherlow House Hotel   63%   £70

Tel 062 56153   Fax 062 56212   Map 2 B5   **H**
Glen of Aherlow nr Tipperary Co Tipperary

Set in a wonderful wooded hillside location with panoramic views, this small, romantic hotel has a charming country-house atmosphere; pastel colour schemes provide the perfect background for well-chosen antiques and a delicious smell of wood smoke gently wafts its way around beamed rooms. Originally a hunting lodge, much is usually made of the building's Tudor style and Alpine atmosphere, but the first-time visitor is more likely to be struck by its general air of elegance and the warm welcome extended by the staff. Bedrooms vary somewhat in size (due to the nature of the building), but all are spacious, well appointed and individually decorated in appropriate country-house style with good, en suite bathrooms. Twenty new bedrooms in a recent extension offer multi-channel TVs, views of the Galtee Mountains and good family accommodation; under-5s may stay free in their parentsl room. A large sunny terrace commands views over the glen. Banqueting/conference facilities for 230. No dogs. *Rooms 30. Garden. Closed 6 Jan-17 Mar. Amex, Diners, MasterCard,* **VISA**

GLEN OF AHERLOW   Places of Interest
Tipperary Racecourse Tel 062 51357

GLENCAR   Climbers' Inn   £46

Tel 066 60101   Fax 066 60104   Map 2 A5   **I**
Glencar Killarney Co Kerry

Most people arrive at the renowned Climbers' Inn on foot but, whether coming up from Killarney via the secret pot-holed roads that wind past Caragh Lake or by the equally tortuous southern pass from Sneem, it also happens to be on one of Ireland's wildest, most memorable and (providing you meet no other traffic) thrillingly enjoyable drives. (Let us pray that plans currently afoot to make it an official 'Half Ring of Kerry' come to nothing, or its unique, wild beauty is doomed to disappear.) The inn, which has been in the current family for 35 years, came into the energetic young ownership of Johnny and Anne Walsh in 1993 and they have set themselves about getting it in order. Accommodation – both budget (hostel) and B&B (rooms with en suite showers) – has all been completely refurbished. Rooms, with strong slatted-base pine beds/bunks, cheerful duvet covers and tea/coffee-making trays (but no extras such as phones or TV), have simple en suite facilities with power showers as the main feature. The atmosphere is robust, no-nonsense, cheerful – and everything is spotlessly clean. Good home-cooked food is served in the bar, which is somewhat surprisingly furnished with old church furniture (complete with a pulpit and lectern) but it's strong, serviceable and slightly reminiscent of Alpine inns. Menus are written on a blackboard: hearty soups are served with home-baked brown bread and main courses will include Kerry mountain lamb in the likes of Highland stew (Irish stew with carrots – winner of our Irish Lamb Award for 1997) along with wild venison and salmon, all served with simple, wholesome vegetables. Breakfast, served in a separate room that is also used for group dining, is a more pedestrian affair. There is also a shop and post office on the premises. *Bar open 11-11.30 (till in winter). **Bar Food** served all day from late April to mid-September. Meals L 12.30-2.30 D 6.45-9. **Rooms** 8. Closed Mon-Thu Nov-mid Mar (ring for weekend walking tours with guides). Amex, MasterCard,* **VISA**

We publish annually, so make sure you use the current edition
– it's well worth being up-to-date!

GLENCULLEN   Johnnie Fox's Pub

Tel 01 295 5647   Fax 01 295 8911   Map 2 D4   **P**
Glencullen Co Dublin

"Eat fish – live longer; eat oysters – love longer; eat mussels – last longer; eat from the sea to see your way back to Fox's Famous Seafood Pub!" One of the best-known pubs in the south Dublin area, Tony and Geraldine McMahon's pub is situated in a hamlet in the Dublin mountains and claims (albeit along with numerous other pubs around the country) to be the highest licensed premises in Ireland. Purists may wince a little at the inevitable sawdust strewn on the stone floor and the somewhat contrived collection of bric-a-brac and old country furniture, but it's a friendly, entertaining place and the open fires have real warmth. Famous for traditional Irish music since the 1950s when RTE broadcast regular Sunday night sessions from here on the wireless, and, more recently, for 'Fox's Seafood Kitchen', an extensive choice of home-cooked seafood in the bar. Galway Bay rock oysters, seafood chowder, tagliatelle with smoked salmon and cream, 1lb lobster with a creamy saffron sauce, dressed crab salad, and even Beluga caviar with blinis; open sandwiches for the smaller pockets and appetites! A wooden inscription on the wall reads: "There are no strangers here, only friends who have never met". Winner of our Ireland Bar Food of the Year Award last year. *Open 10.30-11.30 Mon-Sat (to 11 winter), Sun 12-2, 4-11.* **Bar Food** *12-10 (Sun 4-10). No bar food Sun lunchtime. Closed Good Friday & 25 Dec. Amex, Diners, MasterCard,* **VISA**

GLENGARRIFF   The Blue Loo

Tel 027 63167   Map 2 A6   **P**
Main Street Glengarriff Co Cork

Philip Harrington's unusually named pub may well inspire a first visit out of curiosity alone, but its friendliness will ensure a return. Spick and span, with a choice of sitting indoors in a pleasant traditional country atmosphere or at roadside tables and benches out in the sun, it is a pleasingly simple place, with food (May-Oct) to match – fresh crab and fresh or smoked wild salmon are the specialities, served in open or closed sandwiches. Only simple snacks in winter. *Open 10.30am-11.30pm, Sun 12.30-2, 4-11.* **Bar Food** *12-8. Closed Good Friday & 25 Dec. No credit cards.*

GLENGARRIFF   Places of Interest
Tourist Information Tel 027 63084

GLIN   Glin Castle   £210

Tel 068 34173   Fax 068 34364   Map 2 B5   **A**
Glin Co Limerick

Home for 700 years of the Fitzgerald family, hereditary Knights of Glin, Glin Castle – described by the present Knight with magnificent understatement as "basically a plain Georgian house with later castellations and many windows" – is now the home of Desmond Fitzgerald, the 29th Knight of Glin, and his wife Madam Olda Fitzgerald who are continuing restoration work, which was mainly completed in the 1950s, and welcome guests. The interior is breathtakingly impressive, but mercifully devoid of the museum-like atmosphere such grandeur normally entails – in fact it has an astonishingly real, matter-of-fact feeling about it and everything is kept just the same as usual for guests. Accommodation is all in suites, some even grander than others and a set dinner (£25) is served communally in the beautiful dining-room. Children may stay in their parents' suite without extra charge up to the age of 8. Both the garden and house are open to non-residents at certain times. No dogs in bedrooms – kennels provided. **Rooms** *6 (all suites). Garden, croquet, shooting, tennis. Amex, MasterCard,* **VISA**

GOLEEN   The Heron's Cove   £45

Tel 028 35225   Fax 028 35422   Map 2 A6   **RR**
Harbour Road Goleen nr Skibbereen Co Cork

Sue Hill admits that after she got over the loss of fire-damaged treasures in the winter of 1994/5 she realised that the reconstruction of Heron's Cove was an improvement. The dining-room seems much the same to the casual observer – indeed, looking around and admiring the enormous collection of (over 50) china cheese dishes and other antiques and curios around the restaurant, it is hard to credit that anything has changed. It is still a very relaxed place, pleasing but not too posh and ideally suited for the changing requirements of serving meals at different times of day. Inexpensive daytime food – which may be taken on a balcony overlooking the harbour in fine weather – includes hearty soups served with home-baked bread, home-cooked ham, farmhouse cheeses and multitudinous seafood specials, while dessert treats like Sue's tangy lemon tart or a more-ish chocolate gateau can also be taken with afternoon tea. The structure of dinner menus was under review at the time of going to press, but the style will be true to the Heron's Cove philosophy of using only the best of fresh, local ingredients – typically in wholesome starters like Caesar salad and confit of duck, followed by local seafood and roast rack of lamb with a port and redcurrant sauce. Lobster and Rossmore oysters are available fresh from a tank and prices are refreshingly reasonable. Children are welcome (high-chair, booster seat and children's menu are all provided). *Seats 30. Parties 16. L 12-6.30 D 6.30-9.45. Set Sun L (£8.95) served 1.30-3 only Set menu £16.50 (exc service). Closed Nov-mid Mar. Amex, Diners, MasterCard, VISA*

Rooms   £37

The five en suite rooms are now more spacious and better equipped, with modern bathrooms, satellite TV and phones. The three double rooms have private balconies with sea views and two smaller rooms have a woodland view. Open for B&B all year except Christmas week, but it is always advisable to book, especially when the restaurant is closed. No children overnight. *Waterside terrace, garden, antique shop.*

GOLEEN   Places of Interest
Mizen Head Signal Station Visitor Centre Goleen Tel 028 28350
Open Apr-Oct daily, Nov-Mar weekends

| GOREY | **Marlfield House** | 81% | £160 |

Tel 055 21124   Fax 055 21572   Map 2 D5   **HR**
Gorey Co Wexford

Built in 1820 and standing in lovely gardens and woodland, the stately mansion has been owned and run by the Bowe family since 1978. Mary Bowe is a wonderful host and won our Host of the Year in 1995. There are fine beaches and many tourist spots within walking distance or a short drive, but it's equally pleasant to 'stay put' and relax in the sumptuous, stylish day rooms. These include a semi-circular hall (note the splendid 18th-century marble fireplace) and an elegant lounge. Bedrooms are individually decorated and vary from charming smaller rooms at the top of the house – some with four-posters and all with good facilities and beautiful bedding including fine, broderie anglaise-trimmed, cotton sheets – to a very grand series of six luxurious 'State Rooms' (£195-£400) on the ground floor, each different but all with elaborate use of exclusive fabrics, carefully chosen antiques and pictures and appropriately large, well-appointed marble bathrooms. Colours throughout the house are rich and subtle and beautiful fresh flowers abound. The garden is a restful oasis with well-kept lawns and rose beds contrasting with tall trees; to the rear of the house is a large pond where birds retreat to an island. *Rooms 19. Garden, croquet, sauna, tennis, helipad. Closed mid Dec-end Jan. Amex, Diners, MasterCard,* **VISA**

Restaurant   **£80**

👑 ⛄ 🍽 🥘 🍴 📖 V 👐

In one of the loveliest formal dining-rooms of any Irish country house, trompe l'oeil greenery leads effortlessly into a conservatory richly hung with well-maintained plants and through to the garden with its immaculate lawns and borders backed by mature trees. New head chef Jason Matthia (ex-*Chez Hans*, Cashel) works closely with the owner Mary Bowe, producing sophisticated seasonal menus firmly based on local produce, much of it grown under Ray Bowe's supervision in a delightful kitchen garden almost within sight of the dining-room window. Local game features in season, and the area is famous for its soft fruit, especially the strawberries that take pride of place on high summer dessert menus; there is always fresh fish straight from Courtown harbour and also mussels from Wexford in season. A typical dinner might start with parfait of chicken livers and foie gras with plum chutney toasted brioche, followed by langoustine soup with Pernod and tarragon cream and roast rib of lamb with minted pea purée amd thyme jus. Garden vegetables are just that, appearing in side dishes and imaginative vegetarian alternatives. Tempting desserts like dark chocolate tart and terrine of raspberry sorbet on a compote of citrus fruits. Irish farmhouse cheeses include one of the longest-established and best, locally-made St Killian Brie from Carrigbyrne. Formal luncheon is available in the dining-room and, in addition, a library snack menu offers superior bar food. The wine list is long on French classics (with notes on Bordeaux and Burgundy vintages) but short on half bottles. No children under 12. 10% service is added to all menu prices. *Seats 60. Private Room 20. L 12.30-2 D 7-9. Set L £18.50 Set D £30.*

GOREY   Places of Interest
Tourist Information Tel 055 21248

We only recommend the food in hotels categorised as **HR** and **AR**.

GOUGANE BARRA   Gougane Barra Hotel   60%   £66

Tel 026 47069   Fax 026 47226
Gougane Barra Ballingeary Co Cork

Map 2 A6

H

Overlooking Gougane Barra Lake, famous for its monastic settlements, this delightfully old-fashioned, family-run hotel – which has been in the Lucey family since 1937 – offers simple, comfortable accommodation in one of the most beautiful locations in Ireland. Set in a Forest Park it makes a quiet, restful base for walking holidays – there are no weddings or functions of any kind to spoil the peace. Rooms are comfortable but not over-modernised, with en suite facilities and phone but no TV ('people come here to read' – although it can be provided on request). All rooms have a pleasing outlook of the lake or mountains. Breakfast is served in the lakeside dining-room. *Rooms 27. Garden, gift shop. Closed early Oct-mid Apr. Amex, Diners, MasterCard,* **VISA**

The Egon Ronay Guides are completely independent.
We do not accept advertising, hospitality or payment
from any of the establishments listed in this Guide.

GREENCASTLE   Kealys Seafood Bar   £50

Tel & Fax 077 81010
The Harbour Greencastle Co Donegal

Map 1 C1

R

The progress of James and Tricia Kealy's excellent seafood restaurant is a heartening success story and proof, if it were needed, that fancy trappings are in no way essential to the provision (or enjoyable consumption) of extremely good food. The premises has virtually doubled in size since its first entry in this guide but, although there is now more space between the tables and it is attractive in an informal way, the Kealys have had the good sense not to change the essential character of the place, especially the bar that is at its heart. Everything from the table settings to the loos have been upgraded, but nothing is too fancy, so the sheer quality and generosity of James Kealy's cooking is allowed to take centre stage. Although limited in choice, daytime menus will delight casual visitors with the same high standard of cooking and attention to detail expected of the dinner and à la carte menus; James handles it all well with his own special blend of skill and simplicity. A bowl of Greencastle chowder, for example, makes the perfect ambassador for the fishing fleet that unloads just yards from the door; based on the freshest of ingredients according to daily availability, this is a chowder unlike any other, deeply flavoursome and chock-a-block with a perfectly balanced mixture of fish and shellfish. Something as simple as a grilled fillet of plaice or cod is not just vibrantly fresh and perfectly cooked, but comes with a choice of anchovy, garlic or a delicious lime and dill butter, crisp golden chips and a pretty side salad. Although more sophisticated in execution, evening meals retain the same essential directness. A wide choice of hot and cold starters includes baked stuffed mussels, half a dozen oysters as well as baked smoked haddock florentine, or temptations like tempura of squid on a seasonal green salad. Typical main courses also offer pan-fried monkfish Mediterranean-style alongside combinations like poached fillet of John Dory with anchovy butter or halibut steak with lemon butter, parsley and capers. Limited meat dishes include steaks and duck; some vegetables are organically grown, and delicious desserts such as passion fruit bavarois with raspberry coulis. No children after 8pm. Winner of our Seafood Restaurant of the Year Award last year. *Seats 60. Parties 15. L 12.30-3 (from 1 Sun) D 7-9.30. Bar 12.30-12 (to 11.30 in winter), Sun 12.30-11. Bar Food 3-5. Set D £19.50. Closed Mon (Sep, Oct & Mar-May), Mon-Wed (Nov-Feb – except Christmas week), 1 week Nov & Mar, Good Friday & 25 Dec. Amex, Diners, MasterCard,* **VISA**

GREYSTONES   The Hungry Monk   £60

Tel 01 287 5759   Map 2 D4   **R**
Greystones Co Wicklow

On the first floor, over a building society, Pat Keown's characterful little
restaurant is unassuming from the street and the contrast inside is remarkable: a
glowing fire and candlelight – even at Sunday lunch, now sensibly extended to
make a very Irish lunch (with last orders at 8pm!) – add to the warm welcome.
Well-appointed tables with fresh flowers, delicious home-baked bread, serious
wine glasses and, of course, a plethora of monk-related pictures and bric-a-brac
complete the picture. Menus change seasonally (emphasis on game in winter)
and are carefully hand-scripted and enhanced by witty illustrations; in addition
there are always daily blackboard fish specials 'according to the luck of the local
fishermen'. A typical winter à la carte might offer lamb's kidneys dijonnaise or
marinated breast of wood pigeon in puff pastry with wild mushrooms, game
soup, Woodenbridge pheasant Normandy, rack of Aughrim lamb with
redcurrant jus, or a massive 28oz T-bone steak. The mid-week table d'hote is
particularly good value and follows exactly the same style. All main courses are
served with vegetables and colcannon. Value for money is a priority here and
the size of the bill is often a welcome surprise. The wine list (The Thirsty
Monk!), last year's winning cellar, is a model for others to follow. Regularly
updated – note the 'game season' reds when available – it is both thoroughly
comprehensive and fairly priced, as well as being cleverly laid out. France, of
course, is well represented, equally so: Spain, Italy, the Americas and Australia.
But really, you can't go wrong wherever you look. If you've got a few quid,
try the Rhone selection, not usually seen elsewhere. 10% service is added to
all menu prices. *Seats 40. Parties 20. L (Sun only) 12.30-8 D 7-11. Closed D Sun,
all Mon & Tue, Good Friday & 25 Dec. Set L Sun £11.95 Set D (Wed-Fri) £17.95.
Amex, Diners, MasterCard, VISA*

HOWTH   Abbey Tavern

Tel 01 839 0307   Fax 01 839 0284   Map 2 D4   **P**
Abbey Street Howth Co Dublin

Situated next door to Howth Abbey and its 12th-century Chapter House,
halfway up a hill above the picturesque harbour, the Abbey Tavern has all the
hallmarks of a cosy, convivial pub. Blazing turf fires warm the two rooms, which
are characterised by thick stone walls, flagstone floors with converted church
pews, gas lamps and polished darkwood furniture adding flavours to a venue that
is popular with locals as well as visitors from the Dublin area. The Irish evenings
of music and song (held here most nights in a separate entertainment room
holding up to 200) are a major attraction and booking is required. "Old-world
charm, authenticity and simplicity (no gimmicks)" in the bar contrasts with the
organised group entertainment. *Open 12.30-11.30 (to 11 in winter), Sun 12.30-2,
4-11. Closed Good Friday & 25 Dec. Amex, Diners, MasterCard, VISA*

HOWTH   Adrian's   £50

Tel 01 839 1696   Fax 01 839 0231   Map 2 D4   **R**
3 Abbey Street Howth Co Dublin

Adrian Holden and his daughter Catriona run the kitchen of this small, family-
run restaurant. The à la carte menu changes little but offers interest, variety and
careful use of fresh produce. Crudités and a tasty dip are on the table to
welcome new arrivals and a basket of home-made breads, warm from the oven,
follows very shortly afterwards. Typical dishes might include a confit of duck
with green lentils, crab toes in chili oil, a variety of pasta and sauces, spicy local

fish and shellfish with couscous (considered a speciality), game in season, and
a trio of desserts (or an Irish cheese platter). Children are not encouraged.
*Seats 33. Parties 16. Private Room 15. L 12.30-6 (Fri & Sat to 2.30), D 6-9.30
(Sun to 8). Closed Good Friday, 25 & 26 Dec. Amex, Diners, MasterCard, VISA*

HOWTH   Casa Pasta

Tel 01 839 3823   Map 2 D4   **JaB**
12 Harbour Road Howth Co Dublin

Tiny, buzzy little first-floor restaurant overlooking the harbour. Atmosphere
is the main attraction along with Mediterranean food that ranges from bresaola,
houmus and pitta bread and anti pasto misto to a long list of pasta dishes and
salads. Tiramisu and banoffi pie to finish. Live music most nights. Booking
recommended. Three high-chairs provided. Plenty of parking on the seafront.
Also at 55 Clontarf Road, Dublin 3. Tel & Fax 01 833 1402. *Seats 40.
Open 6-12pm Mon-Sat, 1pm until late Sun. Closed Good Friday, 25 & 26 Dec.
Amex, Diners, MasterCard, VISA*

> We endeavour to be as up-to-date as possible but
> inevitably some changes to owners, chefs and other
> key staff occur after this Guide has gone to press.

HOWTH   Deer Park Hotel   64%   £96

Tel 01 832 2624 Fax 01 839 2405   Map 2 D4   **HR**
Howth Co Dublin

Built high up on Howth demesne, surrounded by 12 acres of parkland and golf
courses and with sea views over Ireland's Eye and Lambay, this hotel started
modestly in the 1970s but has gradually increased in size and comfort over the
years. Golfing holidays are a speciality and public areas, including a large lounge
bar and a coffee shop, tend to have the informality expected of a sporting environment. Rooms are spacious with extra-large beds, TV and phone and all are
en suite (some bathrooms are somewhat dated); the best rooms have sea views
and kitchenettes with fridge and toaster as well as tea/coffee-making facilities.
Two rooms are equipped for disabled guests. The first-floor sitting-room
has a terrace for residents to enjoy in fine weather; rhododendron gardens
(unfortunatly now somewhat neglected but still of interest) behind the hotel
are in bloom in late spring and early summer. A leisure centre was under
construction at the time of going to press and a new range of facilities, including
an indoor swimming pool, should be available for the 1997 season. Ask about
special golf holiday rates. No dogs. *Rooms 51. Garden, golf. Closed 24-27 Dec.
Amex, Diners, MasterCard, VISA*

Restaurant   £50

On the sea side of the hotel (although only a few window tables have views),
the restaurant is comfortably furnished and concentrates on unpretentious menus
offering good value in straightforward dishes that sound somewhat ordinary but
are redeemed by their admirable simplicity and use of good-quality ingredients.
Expect starters like cream of broccoli soup or shrimp salad with garlic mayonnaise,
main courses such as entrecote steak with a bordelaise sauce, fillet of cod
véronique and supreme of chicken with tarragon and garlic or a vegetarian
option like fresh spinach and ricotta tortelloni. Everything is freshly cooked
and wholesome. Popular desserts, like apple pie and cream or profiteroles and
chocolate sauce, are followed by tea/coffee and mints. Air-conditioning;
disabled toilets. *Seats 60. L 12.30-2.30 D 6-9.15. Set L (Sun only) £8.50 Set D £15.*

HOWTH   Howth Lodge Hotel   65%   £95

Tel 01 832 1010   Fax 01 832 2268   Map 2 D4   **HR**
Howth Co Dublin

Built 175 years ago and since considerably enlarged (but keeping the original
style), with the whole frontage painted a distinctive black and white, Howth
Lodge offers good standards of accommodation as well as a very fine leisure
centre across the car park. On the ground floor, public areas are open-plan,
featuring a spacious lounge with bamboo furniture that leads to a cosy, beamed
bar with stripped bare floorboards at the rear. There are 13 older bedrooms
in the original building, but the majority are in a purpose-built modern block;
children under 5 stay free in parents' room, 5-12s £12. All bedrooms are well
equipped, double-glazed and offer at least a partial view of the sea. Newer
bedrooms are excellent – of good size and very prettily decorated. Front rooms
have traditional-style darkwood furniture, while the rear rooms have lightwood
pieces. Bathrooms are bright and clean; six have bidets. No dogs. *Rooms 46.*
Garden, indoor swimming pool, plunge pool, gym, beauty salon, solarium, sauna,
spa bath, steam room. Closed 24-28 Dec. Amex, Diners, MasterCard, **VISA**

Restaurant   £55

On the front of the hotel, with sea views from window tables and a bank of
greenery dividing the bar/reception area from diners, both the atmosphere and
imaginative food here are more typical of an independent restaurant than hotel
dining-rooom. From a wide selection on well-balanced dinner and à la carte
menus, one might choose filo-wrapped Brie parcels with raspberry coulis or
smoked chicken salad served with pink grapefruit an mustard sauce, followed by
really good fish (monkfish, sole sea bass with basilbutter, baked red mullet, fresh
prawns and king scallops), chargrilled meats (veal steak, tender Irish beef steaks)
or perhaps Gaelic chicken in a mushroom and Irish whiskey sauce. Look out
for good oeufs à la neige or plated farmhouse cheeses. Service charge is not
included. *Seats 68. L (Sun only) 12-2 D 7-9.30. Closed L Mon-Sat, D Sun, 24-28*
Dec. Set Sun L £12.50 Set D £18.50/£20.

The Lodge Bistro   £45

An informal restaurant in the French style: dark wood, deep green and red
colour scheme (lightened by primrose paper cloths over dark green undercloths)
and a tiled fireplace with mirrored overmantle and prints of old Howth. The
menu (à la carte only in the evening) is fairly long, with a wide choice of starters
(including an authentic French onion soup) and main courses (tyically chargrilled
lamb and Cajun chicken) plus a selection of pasta dishes and side orders.
Home-baked brown and crisp French breads are handed separately. Puddings
do not seem to be a forte, but good cafetière coffee and tea plus a resasonable
bill rounds a meal off quite well. *Seats 50. D only 5.30-10.30 Mon-Sat, 3.30-9 Sun.*

HOWTH   King Sitric   £70

Tel 01 832 6729/5235   Fax 01 839 2442   Map 2 D4   **R**
East Pier Harbour Road Howth Co Dublin

Aidan and Joan MacManus's fine seafood restaurant is perfectly placed on the
harbour front – overlooking the yacht marina and Balscadden Bay beyond – to
receive the very freshest of supplies from Ireland's largest fishing fleet. Smoked
salmon is smoked to their own specification on the West Pier, lobster and crab
come directly from the bay, mussels from Killary Harbour in Co Mayo, and
oysters from Ballyvaughan in Co Clare. A typical table d'hote might offer a
aubergine mousse with tomato coulis, poached ray with capers and black butter,
strawberry romanoff and petits fours with coffee. A la carte holds much interest,

from marinated monkfish with lime and ginger, crab and coriander parcel and, of course, Dublin Bay prawns to turbot with bacon stuffed cabbage and caviar cream sauce, scallop and prawn thermidor and black sole with whiskey and orange sauce – the choice is mouthwatering. Visitors will also find helpful translations of popular fish names into five languages, including Japanese. Meringue Sitric, home-made ice creams and a fresh fruit plate plate among the desserts. Excellent home-made brown bread and first-class Irish farmhouse cheeses. A more modest, but certainly appealing and excellent value for money, lunch menu is served in the Seafood & Oyster Bar (only) from Jun-Sep, from which there are great views. Joan MacManus runs front-of-house with a charming efficiency. King Sitric is not only an outstanding seafood restaurant but boasts one of the finest wine lists in Ireland with excellent house recommendations (superb matches for seafood), an especially splendid selection of over 36 Chablis and Alsace, plus a comprehensive choice of magnificent white burgundies and other interesting New World wines. Incidentally, the restaurant is named after King Sitric, a Norse King of Dublin in the 11th century who had a close association with Howth and who was a son-in-law of the famous Irish King, Brian Boru. *Seats 70. Private Room 45. L in Seafood & Oyster Bar only 12-3 Mon-Sat Mon-Sep (Jun-Sep only) D 6.30-11. Closed Sun, Bank Holidays & 2 weeks Jan. Set D £26. Amex, Diners, MasterCard,* **VISA**

HOWTH   Places of Interest
Howth Castle Gardens Tel 01 832 2624

INISHBOFIN ISLAND   Day's Bar

Tel 095 45829
Inishbofin Island Co Galway

Map 1 A3   **P**

Conveniently situated close to the ferry, a very pleasant family-friendly bar run by John and Olive Day, with Olive's good home cooking on offer seven days a week in high season. After that it's a matter of pot luck, although winter visitors only have to ask: 'Nobody need go hungry', says John. Given the location, seafood is unsurprisingly popular, typically in scallops mornay, garlic prawns or scampi, but steaks are also in great demand and Olive often does roasts of lamb, pork or beef. Vegetarians can choose from a selection of omelettes or a special salad and there's a short children's menu as well as half portions. No special facilities for children but they're happy playing on the beach in front of the bar. *Open 10.30am-11.30pm Mon-Sat (to 11 in winter), Sun 12.30-2, 4-11. Bar Food 12-5, 7-10 Jun-mid Sep. Closed Good Friday & 25 Dec. MasterCard,* **VISA**

INISHBOFIN ISLAND   Day's Hotel   61%   £55

Tel 095 45809
Connemara Co Galway

Map 1 A3   **H**

Just beside the harbour, close to the landing place for ferries from the mainland six miles away (boats leave Cleggan 11.30am, 2pm and 6.30pm daily, weather permitting), this unpretentious hotel has been in the Day family since 1918 and still offers the same warm welcome and genuine hospitality today. Families thrive on the away-from-it-all atmosphere and Mary Day's good home cooking (visitors out for the day can organise a lobster lunch by phoning the night before). Three family rooms sleep up to five (plus a baby in a cot). *Rooms 14 (8 en suite). Patio. Closed Oct-end Mar (ring to check). Amex, MasterCard,* **VISA**

INISTIOGE   The Motte   £60

Tel 056 58655   Map 2 C5   **R**
Plas Newydd Lodge Inistioge Co Kilkenny

The Motte is located in a lodge in one of Ireland's prettiest villages and everything about Tom Reade Duncan and Alan Walton's intimate, characterful little restaurant is just right, from the antiques and the artistic candle-lit table settings to the warm, welcoming atmosphere. Chef Alan changes his menu with the seasons according to availability of produce and sensibly limits the choice to about six dishes for each course. Start, perhaps, with Toulouse sausage with pickled cabbage salad, white gazpacho with smoked salmon, chicken and pork paté with spicy grape chutney, followed by horseradish-crusted roast cod with garlic and pepper sauce or sirloin steak with onion marmalade. Details are excellent: three kinds of olives to nibble over aperitifs, three kinds of bread served with nice little chunks of butter in a pottery bowl, a good choice of imaginatively presented vegetables, an Irish farmhouse cheese selection, delicious gimmick-free desserts and lovely aromatic coffee. No children under 12.
*Seats 30. Parties 10. D only 7-9.30. Set D £21. Closed Sun (except Bank Holidays), Mon, Good Friday & Christmas week. MasterCard, **VISA***

INNISHANNON   Innishannon House Hotel   63%   £110

Tel 021 775121   Fax 021 775609   Map 2 B6   **H**
Innishannon Co Cork

Self-styled as 'the most romantic hotel in Ireland', Conal and Vera O'Sullivan's Inishannon House Hotel was built in 1720 for a wealthy farmer and it does indeed enjoy a romantic setting in gardens and parkland right on the banks of the River Bandon (fishing available). The house is furnished throughout with Conal's splendid art collection. Bedrooms, all en suite, are individual in their size, shape and furnishings; some overlook the river, others the gardens. Superior (£125) and De Luxe (£150) rooms are larger and have seating areas; the best three De Luxe rooms all have river views. The airy Garden Suite (£250 for two, £10 per extra person) features a period bathroom and sleeps a family of up to six. There's a cosy residents' lounge and a snug bar where snacks are served all day; afternoon teas are also served all year to non-residents. We have received good reports about the cooking of chef Philippe Chicois; he offers both à la carte and table d'hote (L from £12.50, D £24.75) menus and his speciality is seafood.
*Rooms 14. Garden, fishing, boating. Closed mid Jan-mid Mar. Amex, Diners, MasterCard, **VISA***

INNISHANNON   Places of Interest
Timoleague Castle Gardens Tel 023 46116 *10 miles*

We welcome bona fide complaints and recommendations on the tear-out Readers' Comments pages at the back of the Guide. They are followed up by our professional team.

KANTURK   Alley Bar

Tel 029 50171   Map 2 B5   **P**
Strand Street Kanturk Co Cork

A little gem of a drinking pub (no food is served), in the same family ownership for several decades and now run by Eilish and John D O'Connor. It's opposite the creamery and tucked away behind a modest grocery which is stocked with some items not held by many more glamorous shops. Look out for 'The Ballad of Ned Jones's Toyota', a true story in verse. *Open 10.30-11.30 (to 11 in winter), Sun 12.30-2.30, 4-11. No credit cards.*

KANTURK — Assolas Country House — 72% — £120

Tel 029 50015   Fax 029 50795   Map 2 B5   **AR**
Kanturk Co Cork

Only an hour from Cork city, Assolas is well situated as a base for visiting West Cork and Kerry. The charming creeper-clad house goes back to the 17th century and is currently home to three generations of Bourkes, including the manager, Joe, and his wife Hazel, a very talented chef. An exceptional welcome is backed up by open log fires, elegant furnishings and antiques, excellent housekeeping and a high level of comfort throughout. Of the nine bedrooms, three in the main house are designated 'Superior' (£160) and are large, with the finest views over the grounds; three are in a restored old stone building in the courtyard. Despite its undeniable elegance, Assolas has all the warmth and hospitality of a family home – best summed up, perhaps, by the collection of wellington boots in the hall for anyone who feels like seeking out the otters along the riverbank. No dogs in the house. Considerable tariff reductions in April. **Rooms** 9. *Garden, croquet, tennis, fishing. Closed Nov-end March. Amex, Diners, MasterCard,* **VISA**

Restaurant   ★   £75

Deep red walls, polished antique furniture and neatly uniformed staff provide a fitting background for Hazel Bourke's wonderful food. Herbs, vegetables and soft fruit are produced in their own beautifully maintained walled kitchen garden and trusted suppliers produce tip-top local produce. Both a short seasonal menu and a table d'hote are offered daily and diners are invited to choose from a combination of both menus. A typical table d'hote might offer a home-made pasta with West Cork mussels and prawns, followed by cream of spinach soup, oven-baked fillet of brill with a basil butter sauce (accompanied by sautéed leeks, gratin of tomatoes and pesto and pan haggerty), and a choice of desserts and Irish cheeses, both from trolleys. Additional dishes might include roulade of aubergine and roasted peppers with creamed goat's cheese, roast breast of hand-reared duck with marianted pear, or free range chicken breast cooked French-style with a courgette and cream cheese stuffing. There's always a vegetarian option, perhaps vegetarian strudel of garden spinach and vegetables. Simplest desserts are sometimes the best: superb blackcurrant ice cream or a shimmering jewel-like compote of garden fruits. Freshly-ground Java coffee and petits fours are served beside the fire in the drawing room. No children in restaurant; early supper served from 5pm. No service charge is applied and 'tipping is not expected'. **Seats** 25. *Private Room 20. D only 7-8.30. Set D £30.*

KANTURK — The Vintage

Tel 029 50549   Fax 029 51209   Map 2 B5   **P**
O'Brien Street Kanturk Co Cork

Stephen Bowles has owned this pleasant, well-run riverside pub since 1985 and it is well worth a visit, whether for a quiet pint or a bite to eat. The interior is pleasingly traditional and comfortably furnished. Suitable for just a quick snack or a complete meal; choose from traditional dishes like bacon and cabbage or Irish stew, T-bone steak or a traditional roast on Sundays. Daily-changing blackboard specials always include a vegetarian main dish. *Open 10.30am-11.30pm (to 11 in winter), Sun 12.30-2, 4-11.* **Bar Food** *12.30-9.30, Sun 12.30-2, 6-9.30. MasterCard,* **VISA**

KEEL   The Beehive

Tel 098 43134
Keel Achill Island Co Mayo

Map 1 A3   **JaB**

Husband and wife team Patricia and Michael Joyce opened this attractive craft shop and informal restaurant in 1991 and it has now become a regular stop for visitors to the island, whether for a light bite (daily choice of soups – nettle, seafood chowder – served with home-baked wholemeal brown bread, tea/coffee, toasted sandwiches, freshly-baked scones with home-made jam – perhaps damson or blackberry – and cream) or a full meal (moules marinière, local wild salmon salad, a daily lunchtime hot dish, lemon gateau, blueberry and apple pie and cream). *Seats 100 (+ 20 on terrace). Open 9.30-6.30. Closed Nov-Easter. MasterCard,* **VISA**

Set menu prices may not include service or wine.
Our guide price for two diners includes wine and service.

KENMARE   d'Arcy's   £60

Tel 064 41589   Fax 064 41589
Main Street Kenmare Co Kerry

Map 2 A6   **R**

Matthew and Aileen d'Arcy provided a warm welcome at this converted bank (previously known as *The Old Bank House)*. There's a real fire glowing where the main banking hall used to be and the vault at the back is opened up on busy nights. Staff are informal and friendly and the menu longish and ambitious. Cream of seafood soup or lobster terrine with chive sauce could start your meal, with pan-fried fillet of Kerry lamb served with tomatos, garlic and shallots, or wild salmon topped with horseradish cream and smoked salmon roasted in filo pastry to follow. Desserts include warm apple tartlet with vanilla sauce. No babies (under-2s) after 7.30pm. *Seats 35. Private Room 25. D 6-10.30. Set D £18/£22. Closed Mon in winter, 24-26 Dec & 2 weeks Jan. Amex, MasterCard,* **VISA**

KENMARE   Dromquinna Manor Hotel   60%   £90

Tel 064 41657   Fax 064 41791
Blackwater Bridge nr Kenmare Co Kerry

Map 2 A6   **H**

About three miles out of town and beautifully situated in extensive grounds leading down to the private foreshore and a little quay and marina (the setting for their informal summer Boathouse Bistro: open May-Sep, live jazz and barbecue every Sun). This Victorian manor boasts a most unusual tree-house apartment (£150, sleeps four) and a Great Hall with original oak panelling. Generously proportioned bedrooms are individually decorated and all have en suite facilities; five rooms have four-poster beds (£95-£100) and there are five suites (£120-£130). A function suite, doubles up as a breakfast room in summer. Banqueting (110) and conference (80) facilities. A generally relaxed atmosphere pervades the hotel. *Rooms 28. Garden, croquet, games room, tennis, mooring, fishing. Amex, Diners, MasterCard,* **VISA**

We do not recommend the food in pubs where
there is no mention of Bar Food in the statistics.
A restaurant within a pub is only specifically recommended
where its separate opening times are given.

KENMARE — The Horseshoe — £45

Tel 064 41553
3 Main Street Kenmare Co Kerry

Map 2 A6

R

Behind its unassuming exterior The Horseshoe hides a pleasantly rustic old-fashioned bar. Behind this again, there's a cosy, informal restaurant with open fire, oil-clothed tables, (real) cattle stall divisions and an unpretentious menu backed up by owner-chef Irma Weeland's simple, wholesome food. Old favourites like seafood cocktail take on a new lease of life in Irma's hands, and, while steaks and fish are reliable, a vegetarian main course such as aubergine vegetable bake can be memorable. A daily specials board might offer monkfish with a creamy tomato sauce and spicy rice, crab Breton (baked crab, apple, celery and onion topped with cheese and breadcrumbs), chargrilled steaks and beef and Guinness stew. To finish, perhaps lemon tart, banoffi pie and home-made ice cream with hot chocolate sauce. No children after 8pm. Tables outside in summer. *Bar open 12-11.30 (to 11 in winter), Sun 6.30-11. **Seats** 35. Restaurant Meals 12-9.30, Sun 6.30-9.30 (to 10 in summer). Closed Tue Nov-May, Good Friday & 25 Dec. MasterCard,* **VISA**

KENMARE — The Lime Tree — £58

Tel 064 41225   Fax 064 41402
Shelburne Street Kenmare Co Kerry

Map 2 A6

R

An informal restaurant in an attractive stone building next to the *Park Hotel*, run by Tony and Alex Daly. The predominant colour within is a cheering Mediterranean yellow and there are big mirrors, modern paintings from local artists and dashingly artistic still life arrangements setting the scene for chef Michael Casey's zesty food. Menus balance both modern and traditional influences; thus, steamed mussels with cilantro sit happily alongside broth of Irish stew, and goat's cheese and olive potato cake baked with tomato sauce and served with a balsamic vinegar dressing sits beside roast herb-crusted Kerry lamb, medallions of Irish beef with colcannon and port wine jus, and Dover sole with leek compote and a lime beurre blanc. Try a glass of Chateau Fayau dessert wine with super sweets like warm chocolate sponge pudding with orange caramel sauce, and strawberry crème brulée. *Seats* 75. *Parties* 10. *Private Room* 30. *D only 6.30-9.30. Closed Nov-Easter. MasterCard,* **VISA**

KENMARE — Packie's — £50

Tel 064 41508
Henry Street Kenmare Co Kerry

Map 2 A6

R

Owner-chef Maura O'Connell Foley packs in the crowds with cooking that's short on pretension and long on flavour. The sunny menu offers a long choice that covers everything from potato pancakes to lobsters live from a tank. In between you might find cheese soufflé with hazelnut dressing, wild smoked salmon with red onion salsa, chicken in coriander and lime, rack of lamb with redcurrant and mint sauce, and Dover sole stuffed with mushrooms and spinach with a vermouth sauce. Among the desserts there may be walnut tart with rum custard, chocolate pot or Irish coffee meringue gateau. The short, interesting wine list is carefully chosen and sensibly priced, with ten particularly good value house wines. Maura also runs a local guest house with six bedrooms: see entry below for *Shelburne Lodge*. *The Purple Heather* (see entry below) is under the same ownership (and open for lunch). *Seats* 35. *D only 5.30-10. Closed Sun & Nov-Easter. MasterCard,* **VISA**

KENMARE   Park Hotel Kenmare   87%   £230

Tel 064 41200 Fax 064 41402   Map 2 A6   **HR**
Kenmare Co Kerry

In late Victorian times the gentry travelled from various parts of the country by train, stopping at Kenmare, and the hotel was built in 1897 by the Great Southern and Western Railway Company for passengers to stay overnight, before continuing their journey the next day. The company sold the hotel in the late 70s, and since then, under the direction of Francis Brennan, it has enjoyed an enviable reputation – indeed, it was our Hotel of the Year in 1988. Set in eleven acres of unspoilt gardens on the shores of Kenmare Bay, and yet only a short walk from town, the hotel is particularly renowned for its fine antiques, stained-glass windows, marvellous paintings, attention to detail (an expert Dutch gilder spends the entire off-season painstakingly restoring every crevice in the ornate plasterwork and cornices), comfortable and elegant day rooms, and beautiful flower arrangements. On a cold day one can relax in front of a crackling log fire, or in summer and autumn take a stroll in the grounds and admire the changing colours. Guests sleep both soundly and in supreme comfort – the nine suites (£398) and most of the rooms are very spacious indeed with wonderful views, and offer every conceivable luxury, from bathrobes, slippers and exquisite toiletries in the marble bathrooms to fresh fruit, mineral water and books. Quality bed linen, good furniture, fine fabrics and excellent towels, backed up by superb housekeeping, complete the picture. Superior double rooms are £276. Breakfast is quite wonderful experience, including a 'healthy' alternative prepared in accordance with the recommendations of the world's heart associations. Special 'programmes' for Christmas and New Year – ask for their brochure. Banqueting for 80, conference facilities for 60. No dogs. **Rooms 49.** *Garden, croquet, tennis, golf (18), keep-fit equipment. Closed Nov-23 Dec & early Jan-mid Apr. Amex, Diners, MasterCard,* **VISA**

Restaurant   ★   £100

The Park's warm welcome and special magic continue right from the ever-burning fire in the hall through to the beautifully appointed, yet surprisingly relaxed, high-ceilinged dining-room with its wonderful views. Formal touches such as antiques are amusingly offset by quirks of personal taste – no designer co-ordinations here. Enjoy an aperitif in the bar, where the door opens to give a view of the mountains beyond, framed by palm trees stirring in the wind. If you're lucky enough to sit at a window table the view broadens to include the upper reaches of the estuary and hotel lawn. A daily-changing four-course table d'hote menu and carte are available, the former offering a choice of three dishes at each stage, the latter tempting with dishes described in refreshingly plain English on a menu that uses a watercolour of Kenmare's rich scenery as a backdrop. Chef Bruno Schmidt now heads a confident kitchen team that revels in producing dishes that are often breathtakingly presented, yet letting natural flavours and textures speak for themselves. Typically, a table d'hote dinner doesn't stint on the involved nature of dishes, starting with pearls of marinated duck and pistachio nuts with wild mushrooms, asparagus and a whiskey vinaigrette, followed by cream of potato annd leek soup with lavender cream, then beef fillet on a caramelised chicory cake with a ginger scented demi-glaze, with banana fritters on a lime syrup with basil flavoured ice cream to finish. The carte might offer rabbit cassoulet with sautéed vegetables and deep-fried won-ton leaves, seafood (including lobster) from Kenmare Bay, crepinette of squab pigeon and a sage scented mousse with braised cabbage and vanilla game jus and half a dozen or so tempting desserts (white chocolate parfait in a dark vahlrona chocolate cage with a compote of red berries). A selection of Irish cheeses is served with home-made walnut bread and a glass of port – a very civilised way to end an enjoyable meal in such a delightful setting. Service under Jim McCarthy mirrors the balance shown in the kitchen – superbly professional complemented by the right amount of friendliness. The exceptional wine list offers several French classics of different vintages, as well as a comprehensive Californian section of over 30 bins; the Australian, Italian and Spanish sections present perhaps the best value. Lunches are no longer served; lounge service of light snacks is offered from 10 to 6. **Seats 80. Private Room 30. D only 7-8.45. Set D £39.**

KENMARE   The Purple Heather

Tel 064 41016
Henry Street Kenmare Co Kerry   Map 2 A6   **P**

One of those delightful Kerry establishments which begins as a bar near the door and goes on to declare its real interest in food with tables and chairs properly set up for comfortable eating towards the back, the Purple Heather began serving good, simple food long before it was fashionable in these parts, in 1975. Gutsy home-made soups served with home-made, crusty wholemeal brown bread, wild smoked salmon with salad, home-made chicken liver terrine with Cumberland sauce, omelettes and a wide range of sandwiches – regular, open and toasted – are typical savoury offerings, followed by irresistible desserts like wholemeal fruit crumble or coffee and walnut cake, served with fresh cream. *Open 10.45-7pm.* **Bar Food 11-6.30.** *Closed Sun, Good Friday & Christmas Week. No credit cards.*

KENMARE   Sallyport House   £70

Tel 064 42066   Fax 064 42067
Kenmare Co Kerry   Map 2 A6   **A**

Exceptionally well-appointed accommodation in a recently renovated country house on the edge of Kenmare town, in a quiet and convenient location overlooking the harbour and with views over an orchard towards mountains at the back. A large entrance hall with welcoming fire sets the tone: spacious rooms are individually furnished with a mixture of antique and good reproduction furniture, orthopaedic beds, well-placed lights and mirrors, TV and phone. Practical, well-lit, fully-tiled bathrooms have good over-bath showers and built-in hairdryers. Delicious breakfasts are served in a sunny dining-room overlooking the garden. Ample parking. No dogs. Not suitable for children under 12. **Rooms 5. Garden.** *Closed Nov-Easter. No credit cards.*

KENMARE   Sheen Falls Lodge   87%   £266

Tel 064 41600   Fax 064 41386   Map 2 A6   **HR**
Kenmare Co Kerry

In a spectacular setting overlooking Kenmare Bay, the hotel is based round a 17th-century house and a country estate that dates back to the 1600s. Other buildings have been added to blend in with the beautiful surroundings – over 300 acres of grounds featuring manicured lawns, semi-tropical gardens, tranquil woodland walks, and, of course, the cascading waters from the Sheen River after which the hotel is named.

Inside, all is modern: there's a spacious foyer featuring marbled columns, lounges with welcoming fires, a mahogany-panelled library, a sophisticated bar and a snooker room with arguably the finest views to put you off your stroke! Very spacious bedrooms have natural wood and fine fabrics, and all enjoy fantastic views of Kenmare Bay and/or the Falls. Standard amenities include remote-control satellite TV, VCR, personal safe and three telephones (bedside, desk, bathroom), with trouser press, iron and board all concealed in a wardrobe. Additionally, there's a self-contained apartment and several suites (one suitable for disabled guests). In the marble bathrooms you'll find his and hers washbasins, bathrobes, slippers, excellent toiletries and towelling, and, naturally, while you're dining there's a nightly turn-down service. In fact, housekeeping is immaculate, as is the service from all the staff under the direction of new General Manager Adriaan Bartels. The state-of-the-art William Petty Conference Centre, named after the original landowner, can accommodate up to 120 delegates and lies in the basement, almost undetected and unnoticed by other guests, alongside the superbly equipped leisure facilities. Breakfast is well worth getting up for! At the time of going to press planning permission was in place for an indoor swimming pool; construction of an additional 20 bedrooms had already commenced. Children under 12 free in parents' room. 24hr room service. No dogs in bedrooms – kennels provided. ***Rooms 40***. *Garden, croquet, golf (18), gym, sauna, spa bath, plunge pool, steam room, solarium, beautician, tennis, riding, bicycles, clay-pigeon shooting, coarse and game fishing, games room, snooker, boutique, vintage Buick car for hire. Closed 1-23 Dec, 2 Jan-7 Feb. Amex, Diners, MasterCard, **VISA**

La Cascade   ★   £100

Not only is this one of the most attractive dining-rooms in the country, but Fergus Moore has consistently proved that he's one of the best chefs in Ireland. The views from the split-level room are of course fabulous, the pianist is talented and not too intrusive, service is on the ball, and, most importantly, the menu positively bristles with enticing dishes in a modern Irish style. Dinner is now a fixed-price affair, offering four courses (two for the less hearty) with several choices, though the second course is either a soup (cream of parsnip and turmeric, fennel and leek, spiced plum tomato and coriander) or a salad (perhaps mixed leaves with hazelnut oil dressing). Start with roast breast of squab pigeon with braised red cabbage and caraway essence, terrine of chicken and foie gras with a sweet mustard dressing or fresh scallops wrapped in smoked bacon on a ragout of lentils and split peas. For a main course, try the pan-fried fillet of brill on a truffle-scented celeriac purée with lobster cream or grilled sirloin of beef with honey-glazed shallots, parsley pesto and red wine essence. Desserts include warm baked pear and almond frangipane with caramel cream, vanilla custard with macerated strawberries or iced redcurrant and passion fruit parfait with a compote of raspberries. Alternatively, there's a good selection of Irish farmhouse cheeses served with parmesan biscuits. Mark-ups on the wine list are generally high – entry price for champagne is a staggering £45 and there's not a red burgundy under £32! The list is predominantly French and includes some very grand names and growers (though no 1982 Bordeaux), but the New World is only patchily represented. Incidentally, you should ask to visit the marvellous cellar, which is often used for tastings and small private parties. No children under 7. Sunday is the only lunchtime opening in the restaurant, but the bar lounge serves snacks all day every day. *Seats 120 (+16 on terrace). Parties 12. Private Room 24. L Sun only 1-2 D 7.15-9.30. Set Sun L £17.50 Set D £29.50 & £37.50.*

KENMARE	**Shelburne Lodge**	£70

Tel 064 41013   Fax 064 42135   Map 2 A6

Killowen Cork Road Kenmare Co Kerry   **A**

Eagerly-awaited by the many fans of their dashing restaurant, *Packie's* (see entry), Tom and Maura Foley's recent venture into accommodation at the oldest house in Kenmare has won them many new followers, as the visitors' book will bear witness to; many guests clearly felt that they had found heaven in Kenmare. Since acquiring the house in 1991 the Foleys have invested time, talent and very considerable resources to good effect. The place has all the style that would be expected by anyone familiar with *Packie's*; add to this gracious proportions and the unusual character and quality of Shelburne Lodge become clear. Spacious rooms include an elegant drawing-room and have a charming mixture of old and new furnishings, with admirable attention to quality in choice of essentials (especially beds and bedding); individual decoration extends to bathrooms that would cheer the most weary traveller: all have a bath except the more formal conversion at the back of the house (suitable for families; children under 6 stay free in parents' room) which have neat shower rooms. A superb kitchen provides the special breakfasts that are served in a lovely dining-room. No dogs. *Rooms 7. Garden, tennis. Closed early Oct-end Mar. MasterCard, **VISA***

KENMARE   Places of Interest

Tourist Information & Heritage Centre Tel 064 41233
Seafari Tel 064 83171

KESHCARRIGAN	**Canal View House**	£40

Tel 078 42056   Map 1 C3

Keshcarrigan nr Carrick-on-Shannon Co Leitrim   **AR**

Jeanette Conefry makes a caring hostess at this immaculate guesthouse and restaurant overlooking the Shannon-Erne Waterway. A welcoming cup of tea with home-baked scones or biscuits is served in a comfortable residents' lounge with a turf fire and views of the cruisers passing by. Bedrooms have a pleasant outlook (some with water views) and are individually furnished to a high standard; all have neat, en suite shower rooms and in addition there is a large bathroom for anyone who prefers a bath. Peace and quiet are an attraction here, but TVs are available in bedrooms on request. Family rooms, cots, high-chairs and a children's menu are all available, along with an enclosed garden. *Rooms 6. MasterCard, **VISA***

Restaurant   £55

Jeanette and Gerard Conefry opened their restaurant in 1992 to coincide with the opening of the new waterway. Jeanette's table d'hote and à la carte menus are based on the best local produce; herbs come from her own herb garden and a wide range of carefully sourced supplies include Keshcarrigan venison, locally-grown organic vegetables, fish from Killybegs and ostrich meat from Sligo.

See over

Popular dishes – egg mayonnaise, prawn cocktail, chicken Maryland and steaks – are lifted out of the ordinary by the quality and freshness of ingredients and attention to detail in the cooking and presentation. Good soups (broccoli and Stilton) are accompanied by home-baked breads, griddled veal steak might come with an Irish whiskey sauce and three types of peppercorn, and John Dory fillets could be topped with an orange butter sauce. The dessert menu offers a choice of five or six dishes, perhaps including Grand Marnier or Bailey's soufflé, poached peaches in a caramel-orange sauce or red wine syrup and home-made ice cream with fresh fruit. *Seats 40. Parties 9. Private Room 12. L 1-3 D 6.30-9. Set Sun L £10 Set D £18.95.*

KILBRITTAIN   Casino House   £50

Tel 023 49944   Fax 023 49945   Map 2 B6   **R**
Kilbrittain nr Kinsale Co Cork

A few miles west of Kinsale, this immaculately restored old house has been run as a restaurant by Kerrin and Michael Relja since the summer of 1995. The whole place has great style, including a charming patio furnished with heavy teak tables and chairs – snacks and lunches are served here in fine weather. Indoors, there is a lovely reception/sitting-room where aperitifs and after-dinner coffee are served and, beside it, the restaurant proper which shares the same lively decor, with a judicious mixture of the best of old and new that gives the place a distinctly Continental feeling. Tableware is quality modern (chunky stainless cutlery, simple glasses and crisp cotton napkins) reflecting the style of food and service to be expected. Michael cooks with verve and confidence; delicious freshly-baked breads are served with saffron-scented fish soup with aïoli (or fresh tomato soup given a zip with the addition of a dash of gin) and starters like gnocchi with an interesting lemon and oregano sauce, garlic prawns on a mixed-leaf salad or risotto of lobster. Well-balanced main-course choices (fillet steak with a burgundy sauce, saddle of lamb with rosemary jus or spicy pork kebabs with pesto noodles) include local seafood (cod in a sesame crust on creamed spinach and classic grilled salmon steak with sauce hollandaise) and are all served with their own vegetable garnish and seasonal side vegetables. Excellent desserts might include a gorgeous chocolate and hazelnut torte and Bakewell tart; these are also available with afternoon tea. Kerrin makes a charming hostess and the standard of service matches the food. *Seats 27. Parties 8. Private Room 18. Food Served 1-6 (Jul/Aug only), L 1-4 (Sun to 3) D 7-9. Closed Wed Mar-Oct & Mon-Thur Nov-Feb, 2 weeks Feb.* MasterCard, **VISA**

KILCOLGAN   *Moran's Oyster Cottage*

Tel 091 796113   Fax 091 796503   Map 2 B4   **P**
The Weir Kilcolgan Co Galway

Willie Moran, champion of all things oyster-wise, is the sixth generation of Morans to run this immaculate old thatched cottage pub, whose bar looks out on to the pier. Gigas oysters are available all year round, the more flavoursome native oysters only from September to April. Alternatives include crab and smoked salmon (platters or sandwiches), mussels, seafood chowder, seafood cocktail and egg mayonnaise. All dishes are served with home-made wholemeal brown bread. "What we do, we do well" – which is true, and one of the reasons why Moran's reputation spreads worldwide; another, of course, is that the Moran family own their own oyster beds. *Open 10.30am-11.30pm (to 11 in winter), Sun 12-2.30, 4-11.* **Bar Food** *served all day. Terrace, outdoor eating. Closed Good Friday, 24 & 25 Dec.* Amex, MasterCard. **VISA**

KILCOLGAN   Places of Interest
Dunguaire Castle Tel 091 37108

KILCULLEN · Berney's Bar & Restaurant · £60

Tel 045 481260 Fax 045 481063   Map 2 C4   **R**
Main Street Kilcullen Co Kildare

On the main street of this attractive little town, Paul and Freda Mullen's place is a welcoming bar with plenty of character, a beer garden for summer and a cosy corner with a log fire for colder days. Freda (ex-*Longueville House*, Mallow – see entry) is in charge of the kitchen and, not surprisingly, food is a priority; she operates a short bar menu of 2-3 soups, hot dishes and puddings, all changed daily. Typical dishes might include a distinctively home-made mushroom soup with freshly-baked home-made bread, a fish dish such as cod au gratin and a substantial meat dish like chicken à la crème, all rounded off by home-made strawberry pavlova or bread-and-butter pudding. The restaurant, a large L-shaped room with warm red walls and interesting pictures, is beside the bar and takes over the service of hot meals during the evening; here you will find a good choice of seafood and vegetarian dishes as well as popular fare like steaks done in a variety of ways, roast venison and duck. Limited bar food (sandwiches and salads) is available through to 11pm. *Bar open 10.30-11pm. Closed Good Friday & 25 Dec. Restaurant: Seats 85. Parties 25. Private Room 90. D 7-10 (from 6 Sun). Closed Good Friday, 24-26 & 31 Dec. Amex, Diners, MasterCard, VISA*

KILFENORA · Vaughan's Pub

Tel 065 88004   Map 2 B4   **P**
Kilfenora Co Clare

In the Vaughan family for 250 years, traditional Irish music and (increasingly, as the craze grows and grows) set dancing are the big attractions at this attractive old pub and thatched barn but, although it's the music that draws the crowds, Kay Vaughan makes sure visitors will be well fed as well as entertained. The L-shaped bar is quite traditional, with an open fire at one end and, at the other, access to a large back garden set up with tables. Food is what Kay calls 'traditional Irish' which means the likes of chowder or wild mussels with brown soda bread, smoked salmon, North Clare cheese salads, Kay's baked crab and a range of daily blackboard specials such as bacon and cabbage or Irish Stew. Simple desserts include home-made ices and the ever-popular apple pie. A fancier dinner menu is served from 6 in the evening. Well-behaved children are welcome. *Open 10.30-11 (till 11.30 in summer). Bar Food 12-9. Closed Good Friday & 25 Dec. MasterCard, VISA*

KILKEE · Halpin's Hotel · 63% · £75

Tel 065 56032 Fax 065 56317   Map 2 A4   **H**
Erin Street Kilkee Co Clare

In common ownership with *Aberdeen Lodge* in Dublin and operated with the same attention to personal supervision, this renovated Victorian hotel has been in the Halpin family since the '70s. Architectural limitations mean that the bedrooms tend to be rather small; however, they are neat and comfortable, with phone, TV, hairdryer and en suite bathrooms. Rooms at the top have windows in their sloping ceilings to give sea views; four rooms are for non-smokers. Public areas include a popular basement bar with open fire, where the many visiting golfers get together at night. 24hr room service. No dogs. *Rooms 12. Garden. Closed 15 Nov-15 Mar. Amex, Diners, MasterCard, VISA*

KILKEE   Places of Interest
Tourist Information Tel 065 56112

KILKENNY   An Caisléan Uí Cuain

Tel 056 65406   Map 2 C5   **P**
2 High Street Kilkenny Co Kilkenny

Eccentric, perhaps, but popular nonetheless, this tall, narrow pub on three floors is situated on a prominent corner in the city centre and is striking, both inside and out. The interior is a mix of simple modern and traditional, with lots of aged wood and a good scattering of original posters. It has a relaxed, friendly and comfortable atmosphere and attracts a youngish, cosmopolitan crowd; writers, artists and musicians tend to congregate here due to the bar's reputation for lively discussion in Irish and for their live music. Officially, all year round, Monday night is traditional Irish music night but, in practice, an impromptu session can take off without warning at any time, to the great delight of all. Thursday and Sunday nights may also see organised blues and folk music. Food varies according to seasonal demand and, in addition to conventional bar fare there's now an à la carte restaurant at the top of the pub. *Open 11am-11.30pm, Sun 12-11. **Bar Food** 12.30-3, 5.30-9.30 (12.30-9.30 summer). MasterCard,* **VISA**

KILKENNY   Café Sol   £50

Tel 056 64987   Map 2 C5   **R**
William Street Kilkenny Co Kilkenny

Well known from a previous enterprise, the *Millstone Café* in Bennettsbridge, Gail Johnson and Eavan Kenny now run this little place just off the main street, opposite the town hall in central Kilkenny. It's a jolly, cheap and cheerful kind of place with oil-cloths, venetian blinds and bright overhead lighting during the day, when snacks and light meals (including some tempting vegetarian main dishes) are served. Good home baking is quite a feature for morning coffee and afternoon tea when freshly-baked scones are served with home-made jam, and one can choose between a healthy banana and carrot cake, home-made biscuits, a classic jam and cream sponge or a light, moist coffee cake. After a short break the mood changes for dinner, when gentler background lamps and candles on the tables provide a softer setting for short à la carte menus that are typical of the familiar Millstone style: starters like crab cakes with tomato and coriander salsa rub shoulders with warm salads (quail and bacon) and gazpacho with 'all the bits', then main courses ranging from good steaks, with garlic butter or grainy mustard, through fresh pasta dishes – with lemon chicken, perhaps, or tomato, smoky bacon and mushrooms – to fish of the day. Finish with classic desserts – gooseberry and elderflower fool with home-baked biscuits, Normandy pear tart – or a plate of four or so local cheeses and freshly-brewed tea/coffee. *Seats 60. Parties 8. Morning coffee 10-12. L 12-5.30 D 7-10 (Sun 12-5 only). Closed D Sun-Tue, Good Friday & 25-29 Dec. MasterCard,* **VISA**

KILKENNY   Kilkenny Kitchen

Tel 056 22118   Fax 056 65905   Map 2 C5   **JaB**
Kilkenny Design Centre Castle Yard Kilkenny Co Kilkenny

Situated in the Design Centre, a collection of craft shops and studios in the beautifully built outbuildings opposite the Castle, the Kilkenny Kitchen offers good home cooking that includes crusty home-made breads and delicious cakes to take away. Both hot and cold meals are much admired for their variety and general wholesomeness. A typical daily lunch menu might offer spicy parsnip and apple soup or tomato, leek and fresh basil soup served with cheese and garlic bread, following with beef in Kilkenny beer or baked cod topped wuth mussels, herbs and cheese, then pear and almond tart, Irish whiskey and coffee cake or Irish farmhouse cheeses. Freshly-ground coffee to finish. Afternoon tea is also offered. *Seats 170. Light meals 9-5 (from 10 Sun, L 12-5). Closed Sun Jan-Easter, Good Friday & Christmas. Amex, Diners, MasterCard,* **VISA**

KILKENNY   Lacken House   £65

Tel 056 61085   Fax 056 62435   Map 2 C5   **RR**
Dublin Road Kilkenny Co Kilkenny

Eugene and Breda McSweeney's Lacken House, just on the edge of Kilkenny and still very much the leading restaurant in the area, is running sweetly with well-trained, efficient teams operating in the kitchen and, under Breda's watchful eye, also front of house. Aperitifs are served and orders taken in front of the fire in the drawing-room/bar, then guests descend to the elegantly appointed, air-conditioned cellar restaurant. Eugene takes pride in using the best of local produce in a fine four-course table-d'hote menu as well as a wide-ranging à la carte, which features many of the specialities that have won awards and become an essential ingredient in the repertoire – starters like baked crab gateau, grilled goat's cheese on toasted tomato soda bread, Clonakilty black pudding with an onion marmalade and wholegrain mustard sauce. Main courses might include roast crispy duckling, served off the bone with a port and orange sauce or stuffed black sole and superb fillet steak, presented on a rösti potato cake and served with a meltingly piquant Cashel Blue cheese sauce. Well-balanced, thoughtfully constructed menus are designed around the seasons, with game available in winter, and always include strong vegetarian main courses – typically a parcel of ratatouille with ginger butter sauce – and individual organic vegetable garnishes for each dish. Desserts include old favourites – like a tuile basket of brown-bread ice cream with butterscotch sauce – luscious hot fruit puddings such as a poached pear sabayon and an unusual hot chocolate fondue with assorted fruit dip, or there are Irish farmhouse cheeses from the trolley, served with home-made biscuits. Short, rather top-heavy (yet interesting) wine list. Banqueting/conferences by arrangement for up to 30/10 guests. *Seats 30. Parties 12. Private Room 15. D only 7-10.30. Set D £23. Closed Sun, Mon & 2 weeks at Christmas. Amex, Diners, MasterCard,* **VISA**

Rooms   £60

Nine guest bedrooms are available, varying in size and outlook; the decor is perhaps a little dated, but all are en suite with phone, TV, tea/coffee-making trays in all rooms and hairdryer and ironing board available on request. Excellent breakfasts, including freshly-baked bread, fresh fruit and juice, and choices that include fresh fish of the day, devilled kidneys on toast, scrambled eggs with smoked salmon or an Irish farmhouse cheese plate in addition to the usual full Irish breakfast.

KILKENNY   Langton's

Tel 056 65133   Fax 056 63693   Map 2 C5   **P**
69 John Street Kilkenny Co Kilkenny

One of the best-known (and most praised) pubs in the country, run by Edward Langton since 1978 when he took over from his father. Edward has made a point of adding an extension or opening up a new area every year, so the huge premises are now a series of bars, each with its own individual style but all furnished to the highest standards in durable materials. Open fires with attractive basket grates are generously distributed through the various seating areas, all equally comfortable but with different attractions – one low-ceilinged area has a clubby atmosphere with buttoned leather wing chairs and banquette seating, while the next features an atrium, with walls of hanging plants and a genteel 'afternoon hotel tea' sort of atmosphere. Well-trained staff in black-and-white uniforms are helpful and efficient and bar menus offer food appropriate to the time of day – lunchtime sees a long list of sensibly-priced dishes (from chicken, honey and almond salad or fresh soup to smoked cod with egg and caper sauce, oyster-cut bacon and cabbage), through to a greater choice of dishes (like egg and Kilkenny ham mayonnaise, brunch, mussels farci, chicken curry and a daily special) in the afternoon and evening. Leave room for the likes of strawberry millefeuille and pear and chocolate trifle. Both fixed-price and à la carte menus are offered in the restaurant. Dancing Tue & Sat eves. Accommodation is available next door to the pub in ten rooms (£90), all furnished and decorated to an exceptionally high standard with luxurious en suite bathrooms. *Open 10-11 (Sun 12-11).* **Bar Food** *all day.* **Restaurant Meals** *12-3, 5.30-10.30. Garden. Outdoor eating. Closed Good Friday & 25 Dec. Amex, Diners, MasterCard,* **VISA**

KILKENNY   Newpark Hotel   58%   £102

Tel 056 22122   Fax 056 61111   Map 2 C5   **H**
Castlecomer Road Kilkenny Co Kilkenny

Set in 40 acres of parkland by the N77, this 60s' hotel sports a leisure centre with a good-sized pool and a gym with an array of exercise machines. The Ebony Bar is a pleasant spot for a drink while a piano plays away in the background. There is also a new residents' lounge and an extended restaurant. Children under 3 share parents' room free; 3-12s 50% of tariff. Conference facilities for up to 600 delegates. No dogs. *Rooms 84. Garden, indoor swimming pool, plunge pool, children's pool, gym, sauna, spa bath, steam room, solarium, tennis, table tennis, outdoor children's play area. Amex, Diners, MasterCard,* **VISA**

KILKENNY   Shem's

Tel 056 21543   Map 2 C5   **P**
61 John Street Kilkenny Co Kilkenny

Pleasantly unfussy, clean-lined premises run along the lines of the simple old country pub by Shem and Julie Lawlor. Lots of wood and, in winter, generosity with the heating, make this a warm and welcoming place and its relative simplicity and small size will please those who find larger premises somewhat overpowering. Julie looks after the cooking herself and takes pride in preparing simple food well – all-day home-made daily soups (chicken and sweetcorn, French onion), lunchtime main courses such as home-made beef burger with black pepper sauce, Lancashire hotpot, sweet and sour chicken, daily pasta dishes, plus the likes of bread-and-butter pudding and gateau Diane to finish. Sandwiches (open, closed, toasted) on the all-day bar snack menu. Evening 'tourist' menu (May-Sep only). *Open 10.30-11.30, Sun 12-2, 4-11.* **Bar Food** *L 12-4, snacks 4-9.30 (snacks only on Sun). Closed Good Friday & 25 Dec. MasterCard,* **VISA**

KILKENNY   Tynan's Bridge House Bar

Tel 056 61828   Map 2 C5   **P**
Bridge House 2 Johns Bridge Kilkenny Co Kilkenny

One of the most genuine and interesting of Kilkenny's old pubs, Tynan's has had the same landlord for over 50 years – Michael Tynan, and his father was here before him. The spotless little bar features a marble counter, an old chiming clock, gas lamps, lots of mahogany and a charming tapestry on a wall. No children after 7pm. No food – "just talk". *Open 10.30-12 (to 11.30 in winter), Sun 12.30-2, 4-11.30. Closed Good Friday & 25 Dec. No credit cards.*

KILKENNY   Places of Interest

Tourist Information Tel 056 21755
Dunmore Cave Tel 056 67726
Gowran Park Racecourse Tel 056 26120
Irish National Design Centre Tel 056 22118
Jerpoint Abbey Tel 056 24623
Kilkenny Castle Tel 056 21450
Rothe House Parliament Street Tel 056 22893
Shee Alms House Tel 056 51500

KILLALOE   Goosers

Tel 061 376792
Killaloe Ballina Co Tipperary

Map 2 B4   **P**

This delightful pub, in a quiet situation just across the road from the lake, has built up a formidable reputation for its double act of good food and characterful ambience. Settle into your choice of several intimate bar areas, each with its own fireplace and simply but comfortably furnished with country furniture and a finely-judged selection of decorative rustic bric-a-brac, and enjoy anything from a quick snack to a 3-course meal from the blackboard menu. Seafood is the star among the bar food, including oysters, crab, mussels and scallops. Sandwiches and salads provide satisfying snacks, and larger appetites will be allayed by bacon and cabbage, Irish stew or a steak. Good bread comes from a local bakery. *Open 10.30-11, Sun 12.30-10.30.* **Bar Food** *10.30-10.30 (Sun from 12.30). Closed Good Friday & 25 Dec. MasterCard,* **VISA**

KILLALOE   Kincora Hall   60%   £80

Tel 061 376000 Fax 061 376665
Newtown Killaloe Co Clare

Map 2 B4   **HR**

First-time visitors who have read the brochure may be suprised by the newness of this old-sounding establishment overlooking the Shannon to Killaloe but, although their 'private marina' may not be immediately obvious, the outlook over an old stone harbour is pleasant enough and it has the comforts expected of a modern hotel. Public areas are in olde worlde style – in the foyer a large fireplace of baronial dimensions houses a welcoming gas fire – but spacious bedrooms are more straightforward with fairly neutral modern decor, king-size beds, cable TV and above-average bathrooms as standard. One bedroom is equipped for disabled guests. The bar commands a fine river view and has access to a terrace in fine weather. Banqueting/conferences for up to 200/250. No dogs. **Rooms** *25. Garden, fishing. Closed 4 days Christmas. Amex, Diners, MasterCard,* **VISA**

Thomond Room   £60

The attractive dining-room adjoins the bar and shares the same view (and also noise from the bar on busy nights, as the unusual design of the building features dividers between some rooms rather than full walls). Competently cooked à la carte menu with a well-balanced choice of 6-8 dishes for each course. Service is friendly and helpful. **Seats** *55. L 12.30-3 D 7-9.30. Closed Mon-Thu in winter & 4 days at Christmas.*

KILLALOE   Places of Interest
Tourist Information & Heritage Centre Tel 061 376866

KILLARNEY   Aghadoe Heights Hotel   70%   £155

Tel 064 31766 Fax 064 31345
Aghadoe Killarney Co Kerry

Map 2 A5   **HR**

Low-rise concrete and glass hotel of 1960s' origin refurbished in varying styles but to a generally high standard in public areas. The panorama over Lake Killarney and the mountains beyond is stunning, especially when viewed from the elegantly appointed dining-room. Leisure facilities, although conspicuous from the road, do not intrude; the curving pool is simply delightful and takes in all the views. Bedrooms and bathrooms are neat, although not large; suites are from £215 (£165 in low season). 24hr room service. No dogs. Conference/banqueting facilities for 80/70. Considerably lower tariff (£115) from Jan-Apr and Oct-Dec. The hotel overlooks Killarney's two 18-hole championship golf courses; salmon and trout fishing 12km from the hotel.

See over

Sister hotel to *Fredrick's* in Maidenhead, England. *Rooms 60. Garden, indoor swimming pool, plunge pool, mini-gym, sauna, steam room, solarium, massage/beauty treatment rooms, tennis, fishing.* Amex, Diners, MasterCard, **VISA**

Fredrick's Restaurant   £100

A luxuriously appointed first-floor dining-room with dramatic (probably unrivalled) views over the Lakes of Killarney. Chef Robin Suter runs a very fine kitchen, with dinner menus changing daily and lunch menus every week. The style is formal, imaginative, distinctly French and based on top-quality produce – everything positively zings with freshness and portions are unexpectedly generous. Both à la carte and a table d'hote are offered. The latter might include chicken terrine with leek on bell pepper dressing to start, followed by passion fruit sorbet (or cream of fennel soup), then baked medallions of monkfish with a herb and garlic crust and and a home-made dessert or Irish cheeses at dinner. A la carte extends the choice to such inviting dishes as marinated scallops and sea trout with mustard and dill sauce, chicken consomme with fresh tortellini, a magret and confit of duck with Bramley apples and black cherries, or John Dory with fresh clams in Pernod. An exceptional selection of freshly-baked breads will undoubtedly prove irresistible as will the imaginative vegetable selection. Fritters are a favourite dessert, mixed fruit perhaps, very light and crisp, followed by fragrant cafetière coffee and delicious home-made petits fours. Lively Sunday lunch with a buffet (£21.50) and a jazz band. An interesting wine list includes some selected for exceptional value, a collection of 'Wild Geese' wines from Irish-connected families, and a good selection of half bottles. *Seats 120 (+ 35 on terrace). Parties 14. Private Room 70. L 12.15-2 D 7-9.30. Set L £19.50 D £31.50.*

KILLARNEY	Beaufield House	£42

Tel 064 34440   Fax 064 34663   Map 2 A5   **A**
Cork Road Killarney Co Kerry

Former hotel owners Danny and Moya Bowe have run their purpose-built guest house on the edge of Killarney since 1991. Bedrooms are identically decorated in a fairly neutral style; all have neat, en suite shower rooms and direct-dial telephones; most have both a double and single bed. Children under six may share their parents' room free of charge (6-12s £12) and a cot or extra bed can be provided on request. There's a large comfortably furnished residents' sitting/television room and a pleasant breakfast room overlooking the back garden. No dogs. *Rooms 14. Garden. Closed 15-28 Dec.* Amex, Diners, MasterCard, **VISA**

KILLARNEY	Cahernane Hotel	65%	£130

Tel 064 31895   Fax 064 34340   Map 2 A5   **HR**
Muckross Road Killarney Co Kerry

The location – close to the town of Killarney yet with views over unspoilt meadows to the mountains beyond – is the greatest strength of this long-established hotel. Add to this the charm of a country residence which, although now somewhat swamped by a large modern wing added about a decade ago, still has the power to please: the aroma of an open fire in the delightfully old-fashioned foyer creates a genuinely warm welcome, complemented by the friendly and helpful staff. Both public areas and bedrooms in the old house are well proportioned and appropriately furnished with antiques. The main first-floor bedrooms are spacious, with seating areas from which to enjoy the long mountain views; bathrooms vary and tend to be a little dated, with coloured suites, but are otherwise fine. The new wing –designed to be sympathetic to the main house and built behind established trees – is rather cleverly joined to the old by a glassed-in area furnished with cane seating, with a golf shop under-neath. Although the newer rooms lack the country feel of the original ones and (as victims of their era) are furnished with 1980s' modern black furniture, they are of a fairly good size, quite comfortable and have the compensation of more recent bathrooms. No TVs in the bedrooms, but there is a comfortable television lounge downstairs. Children are welcome (under-4s may stay free in their parents' room). *Rooms 48. Garden, croquet, tennis, shop, currency exchange. Closed mid Nov-end Mar. Amex, Diners, MasterCard, VISA*

Herbert Room Restaurant £80

In the smart Herbert Room chef Eddie Hayes offers a choice of menus for dinner – four courses with coffee and petits fours on the table d'hote, or a wide-ranging à la carte. Dishes on the former are unusually good: perhaps local oysters with balsamic vinegar and red onions or seared tuna fish with cherry tomato gazpacho, beef consommé with herb pancake, noisettes of Kerry lamb with courgette tagliatelle and port sauce, and gratin of nectarine with muscat sabayon. Alongside these tempting dishes the large carte's additional offerings make choosing even more difficult: ravioli of lobster and artichokes, squid-ink pasta with monkfish and prawns, a spiced-up vegetarian couscous dish, roast duckling with black olive sauce, flambé dishes and tempting desserts. The menu spelling is eccentric but the cooking is more mainstream! The comprehensive wine list features lots of half bottles, reasonable prices and includes an extensive Spanish section along with, rather unusually, wines from Romania and Mexico; the New World is generally very well represented. Light lunches are served in the lounge. No smoking. *Seats 90. Parties 30. Private Room 14. D 7-9.30. Set D £27.50.*

KILLARNEY	Castlerosse Hotel	63%	£106

Tel 064 31144   Fax 064 31031   Map 2 A5   **H**
Killarney Co Kerry

A low-rise modern hotel under the same ownership since 1987, with an impressive new leisure centre. The accommodation has been significantly improved recently with the addition of a well-appointed new bedroom wing and refurbishment and upgrading of older rooms to match the higher standard set by those in the new wing. The back of the hotel, including a large dining-room and banqueting room (capacity 240) on the first floor, enjoys wonderful lake and mountain views and there is easy access to well-maintained grounds from all rooms. Long corridors run down the side of this pleasant but sprawling design; however, it is worth noting that luggage can be delivered to back rooms by car. Bedrooms include a few for non-smokers, two specially designed for disabled guests and family rooms (one sleeps up to five, five others sleep up to four); children under-five may stay free in their parents' room and an extra bed or cot is available on request. *Rooms 110. Garden, indoor swimming pool, children's splash pool, gym, sauna, steam room, snooker. Closed Dec-Mar. Amex, Diners, MasterCard, VISA*

KILLARNEY	Dingles Restaurant		£55

Tel 064 31079   Map 2 A5   **R**
40 New Street Killarney Co Kerry

Genuine hospitality and congenial surroundings are the keynotes at Gerry and Marion Cunningham's relaxed restaurant and it is obviously a favourite rendezvous for locals who appreciate Gerry's easy welcome as much as Marion's excellent uncomplicated food, which is based on the best ingredients and delivered with admirable simplicity. Open fires, ecclesiastical furniture and old plates on the walls create a characterful ambience in which to enjoy starters like oysters, mussels in wine and cream, or seafood pancake, followed by Irish stew, beef stroganoff or Dingles seafood plate (lobster, scallops, prawns and crab) Round off with bread-and-butter pudding or chocolate mousse. *Seats 45. D only 6-10.30. Closed Sun (except Bank Holiday weekends) & Nov-end Mar. Amex, Diners, MasterCard, VISA*

KILLARNEY   Earls Court Guesthouse   £60

Tel 064 34009 Fax 064 34366   Map 2 A5   **A**
Woodlawn Junction Muckross Road Killarney Co Kerry

Ray and Emer Moynihan opened their purpose-built guesthouse quite near
to the town centre early last year, aiming to provide owner-run hotel-type
accommodation at a moderate price. Bedrooms – all are designated no-smoking
and the eight largest ones have private balconies – have double and single beds,
integrated storage for suitcases in an open-plan wardrobe, phone and satellite
TV; no tea/coffee-making facilities are provided, but guests are offered tea
and scones on arrival and it can be served in rooms on request (otherwise room
service is limited to breakfast 8–10am). Thoughtfully planned bathrooms have
cast-iron baths with over-bath shower, good shelf space, lighting and extraction
and 'no-mist' mirrors. Downstairs, there is a pleasant breakfast room and
comfortable seating in the foyer, where ice and glasses can be provided for
guests' own drinks. No dogs. ***Rooms** 11. Terrace, children's playground.*
Amex, MasterCard.

KILLARNEY   Hotel Europe   74%   £110

Tel 064 31900 Fax 064 32118   Map 2 A5   **H**
Killorglin Road Fossa Killarney Co Kerry

Although situated in one of the most
spectacularly beautiful locations in
Ireland, the Europe is well named.
Not only is the hotel itself clearly
Germanic in influence, but the view
of the lakes and mountains to the
rear – especially when seen past a
bank of balconies complete with
sunbeds – is particularly 'European'.
The style and scale of the interior
is also outstanding – a magnificent
foyer with soaring pillars, marbled

floor and luxurious seating areas sets the tone for a building where it is clear no
expense was spared. Spacious, well-appointed rooms have every comfort (phone,
radio, satellite TV, videos, mini-bars), most have balconies and all have excellent
bathrooms that have been thoughtfully fitted out. 24hr room service. No dogs.
The health and fitness centre is now over 20 years old and includes a 25m pool
which was so well planned (and built with such good-quality materials) that it
can still outshine many a new one. The hotel caters equally well for private
guests and conference delegates (up to 500 theatre-style conferences); the latter
have excellent facilities that include a remarkable state-of-the-art auditorium
with a battery of translating booths along the back. Next to Killarney Golf and
Fishing Club. Sister hotel to *Hotel Ard-na-Sidhe* (Caragh Lake) and *Dunloe Castle*
(Beaufort) – see entries. ***Rooms** 205. Garden, indoor swimming pool, gym,
solarium, sauna, spa bath, beauty salon, hair salon, tennis, games room, snooker
room, news kiosk, boutique, children's playroom and playground, riding, fishing,
helipad. Closed Nov-Mar. Amex, Diners, MasterCard,* **VISA**

KILLARNEY   Foley's Town House   £65

Tel 064 31217 Fax 064 34683   Map 2 A5   **RR**
23 High Street Killarney Co Kerry

A Killarney landmark since the late 40s, Foley's is another example of the
winning Kerry format – a front-of-house bar which gradually develops into a
fully-fledged restaurant further back – in this case a cosy bar with an open fire,
furnished to encourage lingering, backed by rather business-like rows of tables

indicating clearly the level of turnover which might be expected in high season. With Denis and Carol Harnett here since 1967, the well-established feel of Foley's is reassuringly disregarding of fashion and Carol Harnett's menus reflect this in both style and content. Fish is obviously a favourite and daily fresh offerings like crab claws in garlic butter, pan-fried swordfish provençale and fillets of sole véronique might appear under the heading 'specialities' on the menu. A quartet of soups includes 'cockles and mussels' and lobster and prawn bisque; oysters are served direct from their tank or grilled and served with a champagne sauce; smoked salmon is carved to order; and the likes of moules marinière and lamb kidneys in burgundy sauce complete the first-course picture. The main-course choice is eqully extensive, offering lobster, black sole with hollandaise, steaks and boneless roast duckling with blackcurrant and red wine sauce. Sweets from a trolley or a selection of five Irish farmhouse cheeses to finish. The wine list is outstanding and comprehensive (although half bottles are in short supply); house wines are well chosen and very fairly priced; classics feature many of the great houses. Families are made welcome. *Seats 95. Parties 20. Private Room 25. L (bar food only except in high season) 12.30-3 D 5-11. Closed 2 weeks Jan or Feb. L £8/£9.50 (Sun £12.50) D £25/£30. Amex, MasterCard, VISA*

Rooms   £82

Top-class accommodation is also provided in twelve rooms. Each is individually decorated to a high standard and much thought has gone into planning each room to maximise use of space and comfort, including double-glazing to reduce traffic/late-night noises. Special care was taken with the bathrooms which are all exceptionally well appointed with unusual colour schemes, quality tubs and wash basins, special tiles and all the touches more usually found in the better hotels. Guests use a separate entrance and public areas include a residents' lounge and a private dining-room. Banqueting/conference facilities for up to 95/25. No dogs. *Closed Nov-Mar.*

KILLARNEY   *Gaby's Seafood Restaurant*   **£60**

Tel 064 32519   Fax 064 32747   Map 2 A5
27 High Street Killarney Co Kerry   **R**

One of Ireland's longest-established seafood restaurants – Gert and Marie Maes will not only be celebrating running Gaby's for 21 years this year but also their winning of our Ireland Seafood Restaurant of the Year award for 1997. The Maes have sustained a consistent level of dedication, both in the kitchen and front of house, that has kept all their old friends coming back while also winning new ones all the time. The atmosphere is welcoming and informal, the set-up appealing, with a little bar and a cosy seating area beside an open fire just inside the door; up a few steps is the main dining area, cleverly broken up into several sections, with a window overlooking a little garden at the far end, making a bright area for summer dining. Menus are equally well designed, whether for a light (or long) lunch or a full dining experience in the evening. Lunch could be simply a choice of home-made soups with freshly-baked bread or open sandwiches, or one of a selection of around 15 main dishes that include house specialities like Gaby's 'famous' smoked salmon paté, fillet of beef Strogonoff or smoked haddock baked in a powerful Ardrahan cheese sauce; the leisurely luncher can also choose from the full range of the evening à la carte. Seafood is Gaby's speciality and absolute freshness is the priority: a note on the menu reminds diners that availability depends on daily landings, but there's usually a wide selection with steaks and local lamb as back-up. Start, perhaps, with a cassolette of prawns and monkfish – a shallow bowl of perfectly cooked Dublin Bay prawns (langoustine) and monkfish in a silky-textured, lightly gingered sauce – or wild Atlantic mussels in a fresh herb and garlic sauce. Main-course options include lobster salad, oak-smoked fillets of trout (smoked while you wait), brill fillets in a tomato and Pernod cream sauce and classics like sole meunière and grilled lobster; a whole page of specialities ranges from simply grilled wild Kerry salmon steak through Atlantic prawns with tagliatelle and a light garlic sauce to lobster Gaby with cognac, wine, cream and spices. Round off with lovely desserts – perhaps a striped light and dark chocolate mousse served on a cool crème anglaise or a trio of home-made ices in a crisp tuile basket with blackcurrant coulis. *Seats 60. L 12.30-2.30 D 6-10. Closed L Mon, all Sun, 10 days Christmas, mid Feb-mid Mar. Amex, Diners, MasterCard, VISA*

KILLARNEY   Great Southern   69%   £145

Tel 064 31262   Fax 064 35300   Map 2 A5   **H**
Killarney Co Kerry

Situated close to the town centre (3 minutes' walk), this former railway hotel dates back to 1854 and is a substantial building set in 36 acres of gardens that curve around the main building and bedroom extensions. The entrance hall is impressive, with Ionic columns, chandeliers and a large seating area. Bedrooms vary considerably in size and style; many have been recently refurbished (as have the main public areas). Leisure facilities are good and the hotel offers a variety of function facilities, taking conferences of up to 1400 theatre-style and banquets up to 650. The Punch Bowl cocktail bar overlooks the hotel gardens. Supervised children's events. 12½% service charge is added to all room prices. *Rooms 180. Garden, indoor swimming pool, plunge pool, children's pool, sauna, steam room, spa bath, gym, tennis, hair & beauty salon. Closed early Jan- mid Feb. Amex, Diners, MasterCard, VISA*

KILLARNEY   Kathleen's Country House   £75

Tel 064 32810   Fax 064 32340   Map 2 A5   **A**
Tralee Road Killarney Co Kerry

Just a mile from the centre of Killarney, this family-run establishment is peacefully set in well-maintained gardens and equally well-known for the warmth of Kathleen O'Regan-Sheppard's welcome and her scrupulous attention to detail. The last year has seen a new library created in one of the first-floor drawing rooms. Public areas are spacious and individually decorated bedrooms with views exceptionally well appointed, all with fully-tiled bath and shower en suite, direct-dial phone, trouser press, tea/coffee facilities, individually controlled central heating, radio alarm clock, orthopaedic beds, TV and hairdryer. Good breakfasts are cooked to order and served in an attractive dining-room overlooking the garden and unspoilt countryside. All rooms non-smoking. No children under 7. Low season tariff £59 Mar/Apr & Oct/Nov. *Rooms 17. Garden, croquet. Closed mid Nov-mid Mar. Amex, MasterCard, VISA*

KILLARNEY   Killarney Heights Hotel   62%   £90

Tel 064 31158   Fax 064 35198   Map 2 A5   **H**
Cork Road Killarney Co Kerry

Friendly staff and a relaxed atmosphere are the main characteristics of this recently re-built hotel situated prominently on a rise at the Killarney end of the Cork Road. Although functions, especially weddings, are the core business, the accommodation is good and reasonably priced. Pleasant, bright bedrooms are quite large and furnished with an unusual mixture of styles – combining, for example, modern pine with intricate gilded period pieces – that works surprisingly well. All rooms have the usual modern amenities neat en suite bathrooms; there's a residents' sitting-room on the first floor. Architectural salvage has played a major part in the reconstruction of this hotel, most obviously in the Old Mill Bar where a giant mill wheel is the main feature and the collection of milling memorabilia is growing all the time. A second phase of development was about start as we went to press, providing more bedrooms, a new function room and an Edwardian-style conservatory. Well-behaved pets are allowed. *Rooms 40. Patio. Closed 25 Dec. Diners, MasterCard, VISA*

KILLARNEY — Killarney Park Hotel — 71% — £150

Tel 064 35555   Fax 064 35266   Map 2 A5   **H**
Kenmare Place Killarney Co Kerry

In the same family ownership as the long-established Ross Hotel nearby, this stylish modern hotel is centrally located and immediately creates a good impression with its classic lines, yellow and white exterior paintwork, off-street parking and mature trees softening the approach. The reception area includes the main seating for the hotel and is scented by a welcoming open fire – the only real one, although there are gas ones through-out public areas, including the bar and a recently-added library. As we went to press there were plans to redesign the foyer and create a seating plan with more privacy. The overall design of the hotel is distinctly 'people-friendly' with an absence of straight lines and sharp corners that is unusual in modern hotels; bedrooms, which have nearly all been recently refurbished, are spacious and elegantly furnished in a modern classic style with generously-sized beds, thoughtfully designed en suite bathrooms with quality towels and toiletries and good amenities like multi-channel TV with a movie channel. Leisure facilities include an attractive indoor pool with access to a private patio where drinks and light food are served. No dogs. ***Rooms** 66. Terrace, indoor swimming pool, children's splash pool, gym, sauna, steam room, spa bath, news kiosk, library. Closed 24-26 Dec. Amex, Diners, MasterCard,* **VISA**

KILLARNEY — Killarney Ryan Hotel — 64% — £136

Tel 064 31555   Fax 064 32438   Map 2 A5   **H**
Cork Road Killarney Co Kerry

You don't have to have family in tow to enjoy a stay at the Killarney Ryan, but it helps: family-friendliness is the most striking characteristic of this modern low-rise hotel set in 20 acres of grounds on the edge of Killarney. In the summer holidays, especially, but also on holiday weekends and special breaks, the facilities and activities available for children from tiny tots to teenagers are exceptionally good with a supervised creche, children's entertainment (including a 'club' for older children), indoor and outdoor supervised sports and special menus and meal times. Most rooms have a double and single bed, ten are interconnecting and all are en suite and big enough for extra beds or cots for younger children. No dogs. ***Rooms** 168. Garden, terrace, tennis, crazy golf, indoor swimming pool, children's splash pool, sauna, steam room, spa bath, young children's playroom, children's playground, games room, sports hall, football, creche. Closed Jan. Amex, Diners, MasterCard,* **VISA**

KILLARNEY — Killarney Towers Hotel — 62% — £150

Tel 064 31038   Fax 064 31755   Map 2 A5   **H**
College Square Killarney Co Kerry

This large, modern, centrally-situated hotel is now even bigger, having added more (identical) rooms, a leisure centre and underground car park in its latest phase of development. While it may seem somewhat soulless, the location is extremely convenient and it provides guests (mainly groups) with everything they need on one site. Rooms are quite spacious and comfortably furnished with phones, multi-channel TV and rather standard (but neat) en suite bathrooms with over-bath showers. In addition to a lounge bar at the front of the hotel there is a large traditional-style bar, *Scruffy's*, next door (with an independent entrance from the street); live music is played in both bars nightly. Children welcome (free in parents' room up to 2 years). No dogs. **Rooms 180.** *Indoor swimming pool, sauna, steam room, sun beds. Amex, Diners, MasterCard,* **VISA**

KILLARNEY	Muckross Park Hotel	68%	£120

Tel 064 31938   Fax 064 31965   Map 2 A5   **H**
Muckross Village Killarney Co Kerry

Although probably best-known for *Molly's*, the large, traditional-style pub/restaurant that is part of it (but also accessible through an independent entrance from the car park), this hotel has a distinct character of its own and is well appointed and well furnished in what might be described as an 'urbanised' country-house style. A spacious reception area leads to public rooms that are of a good size but nevertheless have an intimate ambience: there's the Bluepool restaurant overlooking gardens towards the river, a residents' sitting-room and a dining-room suitable for private dinner parties and small conferences. Bedrooms are generous in size, with large double and single beds and quality furnishings including some one-off pieces (such as unusual locally-made ceramic lamps) and well-planned bathrooms. Back rooms have a pleasant outlook over the garden, while front ones are on the road side but look over to the trees in Muckross Park, where there are miles of woodland walks as well as the house itself to visit. Two fine suites are approached via their own staircase and have unusual features – a gallery sleeping area in one, for example, a bathroom with original stone walling and a corner bath in the other. In addition to rooms in the main building there are 48 2-bed apartments/suites in a new block just behind the hotel. No dogs. **Rooms 25.** *Garden. Closed Jan & Feb. Amex, Diners, MasterCard,* **VISA**

KILLARNEY	Randles Court Hotel	68%	£115

Tel 064 35333   Fax 064 35206   Map 2 A5   **H**
Muckross Road Killarney Co Kerry

Well situated – it is convenient for Muckross House and Killarney National Park but also within walking distance of the town centre – this attractive Edwardian house underwent extensive refurbishment before opening as an owner-run hotel in 1992. Period features including fireplaces and stained glass windows have been retained however and comfortably furnished public areas include a small bar, spacious drawing room with log fire, murals and antiques and an elegant restaurant opening on to a sheltered patio. Bedrooms have direct-dial telephones, satellite television, radio, hairdryer and well-appointed bathrooms; 24hr room service. No dogs. **Rooms 37.** *Garden. Closed 24-27 Dec & 6 Jan-17 Mar. Amex, MasterCard,* **VISA**

KILLARNEY	Ross Hotel	64%	£90

Tel 064 31855   Fax 064 31139   Map 2 A5   **H**
Kenmare Place Killarney Co Kerry

Older sister hotel to the *Killarney Park Hotel*, the cosy, comfortingly old-fashioned Ross Hotel has been under the management of the Treacy family for over 60 years. The scale of the hotel is very human and there is a well-polished quaintness about it, with its low ceilings, dark woods and front rooms with bow windows. The bedrooms have been refurbished to a high standard and, although they vary in size due to the age of the building, they are comfortably furnished with phone and multi-channel TV; well-finished bathrooms with built-in hairdryers and nice toiletries. Public areas have character as well as comfort, with dark wood, open fires and warm colour schemes; in addition, there's an attractive public bar that's popular with locals as well as residents (entrance from hotel and street). Hotel guest have use of the sister hotel's leisure facilities across the road. No dogs. **Rooms 32.** *Closed 20 Nov-Feb. Amex, Diners, MasterCard,* **VISA**

KILLARNEY — The Strawberry Tree — £70

Tel 064 32688
24 Plunkett Street Killarney Co Kerry

Map 2 A5

R

Evan Doyle's characterful little first-floor restaurant (over *Yer Man's Pub*) has become even smaller of late, as he has abandoned the second dining-room, deciding to convert it into a little sitting-room for aperitifs and after-dinner coffee. Evan's approach to food remains reassuringly constant, however, with the same emphasis on carefully sourced organic and wild local produce cooked in his much-praised modern Irish style. Established specialities to look out for include delicious starters like smoked wild salmon (home-smoked over oak and applewood, producing a pale, unusually subtle cure) and, a delightful variation on a traditional theme, corned beef and cabbage parcels (green cabbage leaves rolled up to enclose a stuffing of home-corned beef). Flavoursome soups – perhaps simple potato and leek – are served with a selection of freshly-baked breads, both traditional brown soda and more modern variations with fresh herbs and other flavourings. Game is always on the menu in season – typically in an old-fashioned game pie – and main courses also usually include local duck and meats such as imaginatively cooked Kerry lamb (with an 'Irish stew' sauce perhaps) and beef ('two ways' – fillet accompanied by traditional brisket). Tasty, lightly cooked side vegetables are served *en papillote* to preserve their natural flavours. Pudding choices are equally imaginative and may include a maize cake served with a fresh rosemary syrup or baked blackberry cheesecake; alternatively, a plated selection of Irish cheeses is served with dried apricots. Coffee, tea or infusions are served afterwards at the table or in the sitting-room. Wines are selected democratically each winter, when a tasting is held and regulars are invited to cast their votes for the next season's list. *Seats 20. Parties 12. D only 6.30-9.30. Closed Sun (also Mon Sep-Oct & Feb-May) & Dec-end Jan. Amex, Diners, MasterCard,* **VISA**

KILLARNEY — Torc Great Southern — 63% — £100

Tel 064 31611   Fax 064 31824
Park Road Killarney Co Kerry

Map 2 A5

H

A modern, low-rise hotel set in mature gardens half a mile from the town centre on the main Cork road, with views of the Kerry mountains. Well-run, it makes a good base for a family holiday in the area; free swimming lessons are given during July and August. Live music in the bar every night. Ask about special rates for two-night and longer stays. *Rooms 96. Garden, indoor swimming pool, sauna, table tennis, creche (Jul & Aug only), indoor playroom, tennis, bicycle hire. Closed Oct-end Mar. Amex, Diners, MasterCard,* **VISA**

KILLARNEY — West End House — £50

Tel 064 32271   Fax 064 35979
New Street Killarney Co Kerry

Map 2 A5

R

Situated opposite St Mary's church, this pleasant restaurant has a somewhat Tyrolean atmosphere and features an unusual open fire, built high into the wall of the bar end of the restaurant to cast warmth right across the room. Table settings are perhaps inappropriate for an otherwise upmarket restaurant: paper mats and foil-wrapped butter even at dinner. A starter such as pink grapefruit segments gratinated with brown sugar, a dash of rum and little balls of rum sorbet could equally well end a meal; presentation is attractive without ostentation and cooking of hearty dishes like soups (onion with port or leek and potato with country bacon) with home-made brown bread and rack of Kerry lamb is sound. *Seats 60. Parties 20. Private Room 25. L 12-2 D 6-10. Closed Mon. Set D £16.50. MasterCard,* **VISA**

KILLARNEY   Yer Man's Pub

Tel & Fax 064 32688   Map 2 A5   **P**
24 Plunkett Street Killarney Co Kerry

Underneath *The Strawberry Tree* restaurant and in common ownership, a
characterful, old-fashioned pub is to be found. The modern accoutrements
nowadays essential to a well-run bar have been skilfully disguised, while the
comforts of yesteryear are much in evidence – the long narrow bar has two
open turf fires, each with its own collection of mismatched but comfortable
seating, including an old leather-upholstered car seat and the top half of an
Edwardian armchair, easily set on a box. Plenty of shelf-height hooks for
outerwear and a small back bar with original black range add to the appeal.
Wholesome soups (perhaps chowder or vegetable), sandwiches, pie, quiche,
mussels and oysters from *The Strawberry Tree* kitchen are offered on a short bar
menu. Also home-made brown bread and ice creams plus tea and coffee. Live
music – usually traditional, but not necessarily organised – most nights in high
season. A new wine shop now sells a range of 150 wines plus chutneys and
preserves from the restaurant. *Open 12.30-1am (Sun & Mon to 11 in winter),
Sun 12.30-2, 4-11.* **Bar Food** *12-3 (no food Sun). Closed Good Friday & 25 Dec.
Amex, Diners, MasterCard,* **VISA**

KILLARNEY   Places of Interest

Tourist Information Tel 064 31633
Crag Cave Castle Island Tel 066 41244
Killarney Riding Stables Tel 064 31686
Killarney National Park & Muckross House Tel 064 31440
Muckross Riding Stables Tel 064 32238
Ross Castle Tel 064 35851 *May-Oct*

KILLEAGH   Ballymakeigh House   £50

Tel 024 95184   Fax 024 95370   Map 2 C6   **A**
Killeagh Youghal Co Cork

Set in the peaceful, lush countryside of east Cork at the heart of a working dairy
farm, this attractive 15th-century farmhouse is immaculately maintained and
run by Margaret Browne, who provides an exceptional standard of comfort and
hospitality in one of the most outstanding establishments of its type in Ireland.
Guests have comfort and space, both in the various public rooms – including
a lovely conservatory – and in all the individually decorated, thoughtfully
furnished, en suite bedrooms; two have recently been completely refurbished.
Dinners are £20 per head; children's B&B tariff 50%. No dogs. From the
Youghal-Midleton road, turn off at Old Thatch Tavern in Killeagh village.
*Rooms 5. Garden, terrace, patio, tennis, games room, snooker. Closed 5 Nov-end
Jan. MasterCard,* **VISA**

KILLINEY   Court Hotel   68%   £130

Tel 01 285 1622   Fax 01 285 2085   Map 2 D4   **H**
Killiney Bay Killiney Co Dublin

Half an hour from the city centre by car or DART railway, this extended
Victorian mansion looks over landscaped gardens to Killiney Bay. Public rooms
include a restructured Coast lounge, a cocktail bar and conservatory, and a modern
reception. Bedrooms, most with sea views, are spacious and pleasantly decorated
with darkwood furniture and co-ordinated fabrics; some rooms are in the old
part of the house, but the majority are a recent addition. Six rooms are 'bridal
suites'; these have canopied beds but are not suites in the true sense. Children
under 12 stay free in parents' room. The largest room in the international
conference centre can accomodate up to 300 delegates; permanent interpreting
facilities are offered. No dogs. *Rooms 86. Garden. Amex, Diners, MasterCard,* **VISA**

KILLINEY   Fitzpatrick's Castle   68%   £163

Tel 01 284 0700   Fax 01 285 0207   Map 2 D4   **H**
Killiney Co Dublin

Dating back to 1741 and converted by the present owners in 1974, this imposing castle hotel is half an hour's drive from Dublin city centre and, despite its size and style, has a surprisingly lived-in atmosphere. Extensive facilities include two large lounges, two restaurants, a basement disco and a conference suite for up to 560 delegates. Roomy bedrooms, including some mini-suites (£191), have darkwood furniture and draped curtains; 20 Standard rooms (£130) do not have balconies. Children's programme of events in school holidays and at Bank Holiday weekends. As we went to press building work was just starting on a new wing of bedrooms; 14 of the original bedrooms were also being revamped. *Rooms 90. Garden, indoor swimming pool, gym, sauna, steam room, hair & beauty salon. Amex, Diners, MasterCard, VISA*

KILLINEY   Places of Interest
Ayesha Castle Tel 01 285 2323

See the **County Listings** green tinted pages for details of all establishments listed in county order.

KILLORGLIN   Nick's Restaurant   £65

Tel 066 61219   Fax 066 61233   Map 2 A5   **R**
Lower Bridge Street Killorglin Co Kerry

Nick and Anne Foley's popular seafood restaurant always has a good buzz and Nick's cooking relies on daily catches for its seafood and local suppliers for lamb, beef and organically grown vegetables. From a wide seafood selection, boosted by daily specials, could come Kerry oysters, lobster in season, plaice, sole and salmon, plus a dish of grilled fillets of brill, John Dory and black sole served with lemon butter sauce. Elsewhere on the menu you might find smoked Westphalian ham and melon, fresh Cromane cockle and mussel soup, ballotine of duck with cherry relish, pork ribs with barbecue sauce, tournedos chasseur, deep-fried jumbo scampi, prawn and monkfish thermidor and various steaks. The wine list is splendid – note the extensive selection from the Loire particularly, but also Alsace and Burgundy. Even though Nick's is predominantly a seafood restaurant, red wine drinkers will not be disappointed, nor supporters of the New World. *Seats 70. Private Room 35. D only 6.30-10 Set D £23/£25. Closed all Nov, Mon & Tue Dec-Easter & 3 days Christmas. Amex, Diners, MasterCard, VISA*

KILMACANOGUE   Avoca Handweavers

Tel 01 286 7466   Fax 01 286 2367   Map 2 D4   **JaB**
Kilmacanogue Co Wicklow

Wholesome home-cooked food is the speciality at this informal restaurant adjoining one of the country's most famous craft shops. Baking is a strong point – freshly-baked breads and scones, quiches and other pastries are set out each day and a special cold food centre, offering the likes of a good selection of salads and farmhouse cheeses, reduces queueing at the hot food counter. Typical main courses – beef in Guinness with a baked potato and side salad or chicken Italian with pasta and a mixed-leaf salad – are around £3.95-£5.95. Outside eating area (20 tables). *Seats 110. Open 9.30-5. L 11-4. Closed 25 & 26 Dec. Amex, Diners, MasterCard, VISA*

KILMOON   The Snail Box

Tel 01 835 4277   Map 1 D3   **P**
Kilmoon Ashbourne Co Meath

Four miles north of Ashbourne on the N2, this pleasant local has a pool table bang in the middle of the friendly public bar and a comfortable lounge in rustic style, both with open fireplaces. But its curious name and the story of its origins are unique, going back to the early 1800s when the site was common land and a 'hedge' schoolmaster settled there for a while. Taking exception to this intrusion, the local landlord took him to court to get him evicted – but the justice of the day ruled that 'the snail and his box can settle where he chooses'. Live music every Friday. No food. *Open Mon-Fri 4.30-11.30, Sat 10.30am-11.30 (to 11 in winter), Sun 12.30-2, 4-11. Garden, outdoor tables. Closed Good Friday & 25 Dec. No credit cards.*

KILMORE QUAY   Kehoe's Pub & Parlour

Tel 053 29830   Map 2 C5   **P**
Kilmore Quay Co Wexford

In the Kehoe family for decades, this delightful pub is of interest for many reasons, but mainly because it houses what amounts to a nautical museum. Description cannot do it justice: it demands and deserves first-hand inspection. Also, although very light bar food –home-made soup and freshly-made sand-wiches, notably local crab – was the order of the day until very recently, the new marina has brought greatly increased demand for food, thus barman Eddie Dempsey (previously at *The Lobster Pot* in Carne – see entry) has made a brave move into the kitchen. More ambitious meals, mainly based on local seafood, will be available every day during the 1997 season – telephone ahead to ascertain exact hours if possible. Seating for 24 at garden tables. *Seats 50. Closed Good Friday & 25 Dec. No credit cards.*

KILMORE QUAY   The Silver Fox   £45

Tel 053 29888   Map 2 C5   **R**
Kilmore Quay Co Wexford

An unpretentious seafood restaurant, in the Cullen family since 1990, that, with the opening of the Kilmore Quay marina in 1996, is now very much on the map for visitors arriving by boat as well as by road. Absolute freshness is what chef Nicky Cullen stakes his reputation on and he knows his market well, offer-ing both popular, straightforward dishes as well as more ambitious seafood dishes that are his pride and joy. Expect to find starters that include everything from egg mayonnaise and stuffed garlic mushrooms to deep-fried (local) St Killian cheese as well as up to a dozen seafood options – Bannow Bay oysters (*au naturel* or hot buttered on toast), fresh Kilmore Quay crab or prawn cocktail and seafood hors d'oeuvre –then fish soups, 12 or 15 seafood main courses and salads, plus a sprinkling of poultry and meat dishes. Booking ahead is almost essential. *Seats 54. Parties 6. Meals served 12.30-9.30. L 12.30-2.30 D 6-9.30. Set L (Sun only) £7.95. Closed Good Friday & 25 Dec. Amex, MasterCard,* **VISA**

KILMUCKRIDGE Boggan's & Rafters Restaurant £55

Tel & Fax 053 30181
Kilmuckridge Co Wexford   Map 2 D5   **R/P**

In the family for 180 years and currently in the capable hands of Mary Boggan, who has instigated many sensitively handled improvements over the last few years, this attractive pub consists of a series of bars, each with its own special atmosphere but all equally welcoming. Thick stone walls, original flagstones and open fires have traditional appeal, especially in cold weather, whereas the two large courtyards provide seating for up to 200 when the 'sunny south-east' lives up to its name. In a sensitively renovated barn (complete with the open rafters that give the restaurant its name) there is a comfortably-appointed first-floor dining-room alongside one of the bars. Linen cloths and napkins, plain, generous wine glasses, candles in tall wrought-iron holders (even at lunch) and a welcoming basket of freshly baked-bread and scones on the table create a good impression that is quickly reinforced by friendly, efficient service from a young waiting team uniformed in long black aprons. Imaginative four-course dinner menus are priced by choice of main course (around £20) and might start with a terrine of quail and herb leads with a light veal 'jus', or fillets of John Dory on a bed of spinach with a light cream and mustard sauce. The well-balanced main-course selection includes choices such as marinated guinea fowl with roast beetroot and asparagus and seared scallops and Dublin Bay prawns with home-made pasta and star anise. Finish, perhaps, with chocolate bavarois or an unusual baked cheesecake on an amaretti biscuit base, served with apple sauce and a cafetière of aromatic coffee. Sunday lunch is treated as a more than usually serious gastronomic event, with a scaled-down version of the dinner menu offered à la carte. Bar food specialities include farmhouse cheeses – try the local goat's cheese with basil and plum tomatoes – and an unusual range of home-baked breads. There are blackboards and chalk for children to play with and even a children's theatre organised one evening a week in July and August. Disabled facilities in the bar only. No children in the bar after 9pm (but allowed in courtyard). *Pub open 11.30-11.30 (to 11 in winter), Sun 12-2, 4-11.* **Bar Food** *12.30-5pm (to 3pm in winter).* **Restaurant Meals** *L (Sun only) 12.30-3 D 7-9.30. Set D £16.90 (£22.90 Fri-Sun). Closed Good Friday & 25 Dec.* *Amex, MasterCard,* **VISA**

KINGSCOURT Cabra Castle Hotel 65% £80

Tel 042 67030 Fax 042 67039   Map 1 C3   **H**
Kingscourt Co Cavan

Attractively set in 100 acres of gardens and parkland, with views over the golf course to the lovely Cavan countryside beyond, this imposing castle is famous for its fishing and it is a spacious and welcoming place, elegantly furnished with antiques. Public rooms are interesting and comfortable, with unusual antiques and paintings everywhere and, especially from the first floor (notably the restaurant), a lovely outlook over trees and parkland. Functions are well catered for, with banqueting/conference facilities for up to 280/600, and the gracious setting and hospitable atmosphere make it a popular venue for weddings. Bedrooms vary somewhat in size and character due to the age of the building, although all have en suite bathrooms, phone and TV. The original building is most suited to guests who appreciate centrality while a newer section at the back, approached by a covered walkway, is often preferred by families. The latest development is in an imaginatively converted courtyard area behind the main building, where spacious suites have separate entrances; some are quite dramatic, with old beams and romantic furnishing – discussion of personal requirements at the time of booking is very worthwhile. Families welcome; children free in parents' room up to the age of 3. No dogs. Some ground-floor rooms are suitable for less able guests. *Rooms 46. Garden, terrace, patio, golf (9), fishing, snooker, gift shop. Closed several days at Christmas. Amex, Diners, MasterCard,* **VISA**

KINGSCOURT   Gartlans Pub

Tel 042 67003   Map 1 C3   **P**
Main Street Kingscourt Co Cavan

One of Ireland's great old bars, this pretty, thatched pub has been in the Gartlan family since 1911 and it's unlikely that anything very fundamental has changed in the intervening years. There's a little grocery section with a hatch, where basic provisions are available, and a simple little bar where the world is regularly put to rights. Unspoilt, with the genuine features of a real old country bar (low ceiling, bare floor, sparse seating), Gartlans is a proper local with an hospitable atmosphere, lots of news snippets – and John McKeon's poem *Saturday Night at Gartlans* – around the walls. *Open normal pub hours. Closed Good Friday & 25 Dec. No credit cards.*

KINGSTOWN   Kille House   £50

Tel & Fax 095 21849   Map 1 A3   **A**
Kingstown Clifden Co Galway

In a magnificently isolated location north of Clifden, this restored Victorian manor house provides a comfortable base to return to after a day walking the unspoilt Connemara hills or lonely beaches nearby. The spacious reception rooms have open fires and are elegantly furnished with antiques as are the pretty bedrooms; most have en suite facilities and all enjoy lovely views. Children are welcome (under-8s stay free in parents' rooms) as all rooms are large enough to accommodate extra beds (by arrangement) and cots (free of charge). A recently added family room sleeps four. There's also a high-chair available and children's teas can be served in the kitchen. Small conferences/private parties (14). No dogs. *Rooms 5. Garden. Closed Nov-Mar (except by arrangement). MasterCard, **VISA***

KINNEGAD   The Cottage

Tel 044 75284   Map 1 C3   **JaB**
Kinnegad Co Westmeath

Baking is a speciality at this neat, homely cottage restaurant, so afternoon tea is a good time to drop in for scones, cakes and preserves. Sandwiches, home-made quiche, salads and omelettes are popular orders for light meals, with the likes of home-made watercress soup, chicken vol-au-vent, lasagne and smoked salmon as more filling sustenance. *Seats 40. Private Room 26. Meals 8am-8pm (to 3pm Sat). Closed Sat (Nov-Mar), all Sun & Christmas week. No credit cards.*

Entries categorised as **JaB** are recommended for 'Just a Bite'.

KINNITY   Kinnity Castle   £120

Tel 0509 37318 Fax 0509 37284   Map 2 C4   **A**
Kinnity Birr Co Offaly

Set right in the middle of Ireland amid a very large estate (accessible to equestrian guests and for walking) with 650 acres of parkland and formal gardens, this distinctly theatrical establishment will have great appeal to guests of a romantic disposition. The entire castle -which has a colourful history of serial destruction and resurrection – has been refurbished to make it suitable for its present use and public areas are mainly furnished as might be expected. However, in the spacious bedrooms (which have views over the estate), the main distinguishing feature is a high sense of drama throughout the decorative schemes. A new conference/banqueting centre, built in medieval style, can accommodate up to 200 guests. *Rooms 18. Equestrian centre, shooting, clay-pigeon shooting, game & coarse fishing. Closed first 2 weeks Jan. Amex, MasterCard, **VISA***

KINSALE	**Actons Hotel**	60%	£100

Tel 021 772135 Fax 021 772231   Map 2 B6   **H**
Pier Road Kinsale Co Cork

Previously a Forte hotel but now under the ownership of the Stafford Hotel group. Overlooking the harbour, this attractive quayside hotel was created from several substantial period houses and the bedrooms within are priced at two levels: 33 with a sea view are charged at the higher tariff that we quote. Out-of-season tariff reductions; top-of-the range is a spacious Bridal Suite with canopied bed. 24hr room service. All rooms are due to be refurbished and plans are to add a further 14 bedrooms. A health and fitness centre and Ship's Tavern bar, where live music is played most weekends, are other attractions. Conference/banqueting facilities for up to 400. Children up to 14 stay free in parents' room. No dogs. *Rooms 56. Garden, indoor swimming pool, gym, sauna, solarium. Amex, Diners, MasterCard, VISA*

KINSALE	**Restaurant Annelie's**		£75

Tel 021 773074 Fax 021 773075   Map 2 B6   **R**
18/19 Lr O'Connell Street Kinsale Co Cork

No expense has been spared on the decor at this striking new restaurant, which is designed to a nautical theme with a bar/reception 'bridge' overhanging one end of the lower ground floor dining area and custom-made carpeting in deep blue with the restaurant motif in gold; the same design is repeated on plates, and waiters wear nautical-style uniforms with gold braid. Head chef Michael Benjamin produced an outstanding meal on a recent visit, although extremely slow service seriously marred the experience. Nevertheless, the standard of cooking was exceptional throughout and it is to be hoped that service difficulties will be overcome. An appetiser – perhaps a superb bisque served in tiny cups – starts the meal, along with a fine basket of freshly-baked breads. Then, from a tempting à la carte, five starters might include a light, tasty little tomato tart with black olives and basil, a fish soup (totally different from the bisque) with herbs, tomato and croutons or warm oysters on a bed of champ. Typical main courses, from a choice of seven, may include several seafood dishes – grilled wild salmon with herb butter or roasted lobster with herbs and baby vegetables – and red meats like fillet of beef with creamed potatoes, a pinot noir sauce, lardons and mushrooms or best end of lamb with roasted garlic and a thyme sauce. Each dish is individually garnished with appropriate vegetables and a gratin of potatoes may be served separately. Dramatic desserts – confit of orange and chocolate with cocoa sorbet, perhaps, or vanilla crème brulée with confit pineapple – are followed by an outstanding selection of petits fours served with freshly-brewed tea or coffee. *Seats 50. Parties 20. L (Sun only) 12.30-3 D 5-10.30 (Sun 7-10). Set Sun L £15. Closed Mon & 22 Dec-7 Jan. Diners, MasterCard, VISA*

KINSALE	**Blue Haven Hotel**	69%	£130

Tel 021 772209 Fax 021 774268   Map 2 B6   **HR**
Kinsale Co Cork

After ambitious extensions and refurbishment The Blue Haven is an inspiring example of what a small owner-run hotel can be. It's a great credit to the tireless efforts of owners Brian and Anne Cronin who keep improving standards regardless of the (not inconsiderable) inconvenience. Public areas include an attractive reception/sitting area next to the restaurant and a cosy bar that has an open fire, and there's also a bright cane-furnished conservatory area which leads on to a patio for fine days. Well-appointed bedrooms have all been upgraded and double-glazing offsets the street noise that is inevitable with the central location. Both the rooms and their neatly-fitted en suite bathrooms make up in thoughtful planning anything they may lack in space – many a room twice the size of these lacks their level of convenience. Children are made welcome;

under-3s may stay free in parents' room, extra beds and cots available. No dogs. An admirably shopper-friendly wine shop and delicatessen opens off the lobby and makes an enjoyable place to browse for picnics or presents. Most of all, however, it's the personal dedication of the owners and their admirable staff that makes The Blue Haven special – there isn't much going on in the area that Brian Cronin doesn't know about and he's always delighted to advise. The bar serves a wide choice of imaginative food, from a choice of soups and sandwiches to good seafood. Winner of our Ireland Hotel of the Year Award in 1996. *Rooms 18. Bar & conservatory (10.30am-9.30pm), teas and light snacks (3-5pm). Terrace, sea fishing. Closed 2 weeks Jan, 24 & 25 Dec. Amex, Diners, MasterCard,* **VISA**

Restaurant   £70

Recently refurbished with a strong maritime theme, a rounded conservatory area at the end of the restaurant looks – as if from the bridge of the ship – on to a small, floodlit garden complete with tumbling waterfall. Well-appointed tables with crisp linen, fresh flowers and fine glasses have comfortable, well-upholstered chairs and some striking decorative touches; good lighting, helpful and discreet service and a particularly good pianist add to the atmosphere, which is more restaurant than hotel dining room – an appropriate setting for some of the best food in town. While seafood is clearly the speciality, the extensive à la carte and set 'gourmet' menus are well balanced to provide a good cross-section of local produce that includes poultry, red meats, farmhouse cheeses and game in season. Specialities include starters such as Jack Barry's lamb kidneys (Jack's the local butcher – the chopped kidneys are sauteed with garlic and bacon and served with a mixed-leaf salad garnish and delicious wholegrain mustard dressing), smoked chicken and duck salad, Kinsale fish chowder and seafood platter (oysters, prawns, cockles, mussels, clams and crab). Diverse main-course specialities kick off with hot wood-smoked salmon with stir-fried vegetables and embrace the likes of seafood Kashmiri, monkfish with bacon and saffron cream sauce, roast pheasant and a vegetarian dish of the day. Pretty desserts or farmhouse cheeses follow; freshly-ground coffee is served in unlimited quantities and there is a choice of at least nine cognacs. The new wine list salutes the Irish Wine Geese, found as far afield as Chile and Australia, though better associated with Bordeaux. The list is thoroughly comprehensive and fairly priced, with really interesting historical and tasting notes. Note the wine shop off the hotel lobby where prices are even more reasonable! 10% service charge is added to the final bill. *Seats 90 (+ 30 on patio). Parties 18. Private Room 50. L 12.30-3 D 7-10.30. Set D £27.50.*

KINSALE	The Bulman Bar	
Tel 021 772131	Map 2 B6	**P**
Summercove Kinsale Co Cork		

Maritime local interests are reflected in the decor of this smashing little waterside pub about a mile along the harbour out of Kinsale towards Charles Fort; note the unusual 'boat table' to the right of the door. Its primary function is definitely as a bar, so it can be busy and quite smoky sometimes and, in fine weather, the crowd spills out on to the car park across the road. But the bar is quite well set up for eating in comfort and, under Chris and Laurie Ager's enthusiastic ownership – and the interested helpfulness of their of their attentive staff – the food and service continues to improve. In summer they have a printed menu but there are also two daily blackboard selections that lay an understandable emphasis on local seafood, although there are plenty of alternatives. Everything is freshly made on the premises by Chris and Laurie. Try, for example, their home-made scampi or a big plate of clams cooked marinière-style and served in the shell with a basket of crusty, fresh baguette and butter – simple enough, but surprisingly unusual. Or, perhaps, a lovely home-made burger – lean and meaty, cooked to order and served with a delicious mixed salad and a big pile of crisp, golden-brown chips. Finish off with real coffee, by the cup, or tea served on a little tray with an individual milk jug and sugar bowl, all served with a smile. New wheelchair toilet facilities and a 40-seater restaurant upstairs, with views across the harbour to Kinsale. *Pub open 10.30am-11.30pm (to 11 in winter), Sun 12-2, 4-11.* **Bar Food** *12.30-3, 6-9 (not Sun). Closed Good Friday & 25 Dec. MasterCard,* **VISA**

KINSALE   **Chez Jean-Marc**   **£55**

Tel 021 774625   Fax 021 774680   Map 2 B6   **R**
Lower O'Connell Street Kinsale Co Cork

Jean-Marc Tsai's low-ceilinged, green-walled back street restaurant has great charm, and an open fire, well-appointed tables with warm red cloths and a display of old plates on the walls create a cosy, cottagey atmosphere. In the past year the style of dining has changed to a more casual (bistro-style) approach, with no distinction between the upstairs former brasserie and main dining-room. Food has also changed somewhat in style with classic French cooking now dominating à la carte menus that previously demonstrated a unique and lively interaction between Oriental and French traditions. However, on Sunday evenings (May-Oct), Jean-Marc's flair for Oriental cooking comes to the fore with a special Chinese à la carte menu. Local produce features strongly – particularly seafood, including Rossmore oysters, fresh lobster from the tank and wild salmon pan-fried with noilly prat, shallots, cream and herbs. Further menu choices include various 'salades', home-made pasta and meat dishes such as grilled duck breast with stir-fried vegetables and a rich Madeira and soya sauce, or beef fillet with a peppercorn, brandy and cream sauce. Classic desserts might include apple tart served with good home-made vanilla ice cream. **Seats** *120. Parties 50. Private Room 60. D only 7-10. Closed Mon (except Jun-Sep), mid Feb-mid Mar & 24-26 Dec. Amex, Diners, MasterCard,* **VISA**

KINSALE   **The Dock Bar**

Tel 021 772522   Map 2 B6   **P**
Castle Park Kinsale Co Cork

Well situated between the marina at Castle Park and one of the few south-facing sandy beaches in the area (a few hundred yards across the peninsula), this traditional (and often very smoky) black and white pub looks over towards Kinsale and, although the town is very near, it feels like a world apart. The patio, where tables have a choice of sun or leafy shade, has a slightly Continental atmosphere and the interior is comfortable in the modern Irish idiom – quarry tiles, varnished tables, upholstered benches and photographs of some of landlord Michael Vance's winning horses to remind him of his years as a trainer. *Open 12-11.30 (4-11 Mon-Fri, Sat 12-11 in winter), Sun 12.30-2, 4-11. Garden, outdoor eating area. No credit cards.*

KINSALE   **Man Friday**   **£55**

Tel 021 772260 Fax 021 772262   Map 2 B6   **R**
Scilly Kinsale Co Cork

A popular and convivial restaurant housed in a series of little rooms high above the harbour. Seafood is the natural speciality, with oysters cold or poached, crab au gratin, sweet and sour scampi, black sole (grilled or Colbert) and monkfish with a prawn sauce among the wide choice. That choice extends outside the fishy realms to the likes of Robinson Crusoe's warm salad (mixed leaves,

croutons and bacon), deep-fried brie with a plum and port sauce, Swiss-style
veal escalope and roast rack of lamb with rosemary and a red wine sauce.
Strawberry crème brulée, chocolate terrine, grape pudding or home-made ice
creams round things off. Consistency is a keynote here, and it's owner-chef
Philip Horgan (here since 1978) who maintains it. *Seats 100. Private Room 40.
L (Sun only) 12.30-2,45 D 6.30-10.30. Closed Good Friday & 24-26 Dec.
Set L Sun £12.50. Amex, Diners, MasterCard,* **VISA**

KINSALE	Max's Wine Bar	£50

Tel 021 772443   Map 2 B6   **R**
Main Street Kinsale Co Cork

Wendy Tisdall has been at her charming little restaurant for over 20 years now.
You'll find highly varnished tabletops reflecting fresh flowers and plants, and
light and tempting menus. Wild smoked salmon, fresh clams in white wine,
cream and herbs, or roasted vegetables with black bean dressing could start a
meal, or there are some speciality salads like spinach with blue cheese, bacon
and croutons. Next might come the day's fish catch (up to five fresh fish dishes
daily), venison with juniper berries and red wine, roast duck with orange and
ginger sauce, or herb-roasted rack of lamb with plum and port sauce, with
home-made ice cream, chocolate rum mousse or ginger crème brulée to finish.
The early bird menu offers particularly good value for money (6.30-8pm £12)
and there are 50 bins on the wine list. No smoking in the conservatory (10 seats).
*Seats 40. L 12.30-3 D 6.30-10.30. Closed Nov-end Feb. Set L & D £12.
MasterCard,* **VISA**

KINSALE	The Moorings	£90

Tel 021 772376   Fax 021 772675   Map 2 B6   **A**
Scilly Kinsale Co Cork

Overlooking the marina in a unique waterside location, Pat and Irene Jones's
thoughtfully designed guesthouse was purpose-built to maximise views across the
harbour from a large conservatory (used for breakfast if guests prefer not to take
it in their rooms, as well as for lounging) and most bedrooms. Spacious rooms
have well-appointed bathrooms, TV, phone and tea/coffee facilities and are
comfortably furnished to a high standard, including balconies with seating in
some cases. There is a bedroom equipped for disabled guests. No children under
12 (or dogs). *Rooms 8. Garden. Closed Christmas week. Diners, MasterCard,* **VISA**

KINSALE	The Old Bank House	£90

Tel 021 774075   Fax 021 774296   Map 2 B6   **A**
11 Pearse Street Kinsale Co Cork

A Georgian building of some character, formerly a branch of the Munster
and Leinster Bank. Individually furnished bedrooms are spacious, elegant and
comfortable, with good antiques and well-appointed bathrooms. Public areas,
including breakfast room and sitting-room, are non-smoking. Babies are
accommodated, but 2-10 year-olds are not encouraged. No dogs. *Rooms 9.
Patio. Closed 3 days Christmas. Amex, MasterCard,* **VISA**

KINSALE	Old Presbytery	£50

Tel 021 772027   Map 2 B6   **A**
Cork Street Kinsale Co Cork

Philip McEvoy has made all the rooms en suite, one with bathroom, five
with shower and one with a Victorian private bathroom. The seven bedrooms
are decorated in traditional style, with big beds and Irish linen, and there's a
comfortable, redecorated sitting room with an open fire. Lower tariff applies for
the smaller rooms and out of season (£40). No evening meals. *Rooms 7. Garden.
Closed 1 week Christmas. No credit cards.*

KINSALE   Scilly House   65%   £100

Tel 021 772413 Fax 021 774629   Map 2 B6   **H**
Scilly Kinsale Co Cork

An old house of great charm and character overlooking the harbour and Kinsale Bay. The style is American country, with old pine furniture, antiques, traditional American quilts, floral prints and folk art. Public rooms include a bar/library with grand piano, a cosy sitting room and a dining-room with views over the garden down to the sea. There are views, too, from most of the individually appointed bedrooms, which include one honeymoon suite with a large bathroom that features a double tub. A cottage has a sitting-room, large bathroom and its own garden. No children under 12. *Rooms 7. Garden. Closed Nov-end Mar. Amex, MasterCard,* **VISA**

KINSALE   1601

Tel 021 772529   Map 2 B6   **P**
Pearse Street Kinsale Co Cork

Named after the year of the battle of Kinsale, details of which form an interesting and decorative presentation in the front lounge, this centrally located pub has earned a reputation for good bar food and is popular with locals and visitors alike. Their well-priced, freshly home-made food is worth waiting for; the menu changes daily. There's always a choice of chowder and another soup of the day and a short, well-balanced menu offers starters/light main courses such as a warm salad of goat's cheese, crabmeat cocktail, several local seafood dishes, traditional Irish fare like boiled bacon and cabbage with parsley sauce and Irish stew and the house special, '1601 Battle Burger', a home-made burger served with chips, salad and a choice of piquant dipping sauces such as chili, ketchup and chutney. The rear of the Lounge Bar is the Art Gallery restaurant, where food is served all day when it's busy. Food also served all day in summer. Live traditional Irish music five nights a week in summer, two nights in winter. *Open 10.30-11.30, Sun 12.30-11.* **Bar Food** *12.30-3, 6.30-9 (to 8 Sun). Closed Good Friday & 25 Dec. Amex, MasterCard,* **VISA**

KINSALE   The Spaniard Inn

Tel 021 772436   Map 2 B6   **P**
Scilly Kinsale Co Cork

High above the harbour near the *Man Friday* restaurant, the Spaniard dispenses good cheer, good food and good music. Mary O'Toole's bar food is plain and simple, running from salads, soups (thick vegetable), open sandwiches (try one with smoked Kinsale wild salmon) and fresh fish and seafood (monkfish, sole, mussels) to old favourites like Irish stew or bacon and cabbage; also cheese platter with home-made relish and soda bread, home-made apple pie and ice cream. Lunch can be taken on the terrace when the sun shines. Traditional Irish music sessions. The inn comprises several low-beamed rooms with stone floors, country furniture and assorted items of local interest – notably a 35lb salmon caught in 1912 at Little Island, Ardfinnan. *Open 11am-11.30pm (to 11 in winter), Sun 12.30-2.30 & 4-11.* **Bar Food** *12.30-3, 6-9.30 Tue-Sat. Patio, outdoor eating. Closed Good Friday & 25 Dec. MasterCard,* **VISA**

We only recommend the food in hotels categorised as **HR** and **AR**.
However, the food in many **A** establishments throughout
Ireland is often very acceptable
(but the restaurant may not be open to non-residents).

KINSALE — The Vintage Restaurant — £80

Tel 021 772502 Fax 021 774828   Map 2 B6   **R**
50 Main Street Kinsale Co Cork

After 'retiring' from one of Switzerland's greatest hotels, Raoul de Gendre and his delightful wife Seiko bought this legendary restaurant in July 1994 and have now established it in their unique way as a haven of discreet elegance and exciting culinary development. Much has gone into refurbishment of the premises, yet it has been done so sympathetically that there is no major change of atmosphere; they have put a lot of themselves into the restaurant, however – not least many of Raoul's own excellent paintings – and their professionalism and commitment, along with an irresistible gentle charm, seems to have won them many admirers. An adventurous style of cooking emanates from an unusually democratic kitchen where a number of chefs of equal standing take turns here and also in other kitchens (Raoul's networks of contacts in Europe permits some exceptional arrangements); the best of Irish ingredients are used with pride in dishes that tend towards classical cuisine yet frequently have a special, spicy twist. From a wide-ranging seasonal à la carte, for example, speciality starters may include a hors d'oeuvre of Kinsale seafood and 'develish angels on horseback' (hot fresh oysters wrapped in bacon and served with a piquant garlic sauce). In the same vein, seafood main courses might offer sautéed goujons of black sole with wild rice and a mustard seed sauce, while herb-crusted wild salmon comes surrounded with truffle butter. On the other hand, a cold starter of rabbit and pistachio terrine is served with home-made chutney and roast guinea fowl is accompanied by a light mushroom and Madeira sauce. Finish with a classic dessert, perhaps bread-and-butter pudding or crème brulée, or Irish farmhouse cheeses. With such confident cooking and general professionalism The Vintage has firmly established a special niche at the top end of the market in Kinsale. *Seats 52. Parties 12. Private Room 25. D only 6.30-midnight. Closed Sun (15 Oct-Easter, except Bank Holiday weekends) & mid Jan-end Feb. Amex, Diners, MasterCard, VISA*

KINSALE — White Lady Inn — 62% — £50

Tel 021 772737 Fax 021 774641   Map 2 B6   **H**
Lower O'Connell Street Kinsale Co Cork

Unpretentious family-run hotel in a back street near the marina, with co-ordinated furnishing schemes, TV and phone; all the bedrooms have neatly-tiled well-planned en suite bathrooms with efficient, user-friendly showers. Public areas include a bar used by locals and a franchised informal restaurant, where breakfast is served. The White Lady night club (Fri-Sun & Wed in Jul/Aug) is at the back of the building, but thoughtful staff ensure that rooms which might be affected by noise are only let to guests attending functions there. *Rooms 10. Amex, MasterCard, VISA*

KINSALE   Places of Interest
Tourist Information Tel 021 772234
Charles Fort Tel 021 772263
Desmond Castle Tel 021 774855
Kinsale Gourmet Festival October annually

We do not recommend the food in pubs where
there is no mention of Bar Food in the statistics.
A restaurant within a pub is only specifically recommended
where its separate opening times are given.

KINVARA   Tully's

Tel 091 637146
Kinvara Co Galway   Map 2 B4   **P**

A real local pub in the old tradition, with a little grocery shop at the front and stone-floored bar at the back, Tully's has a small enclosed garden with a few parasoled tables for fine weather but, better still, a fine old stove in the bar for cosy winter sessions. Not a food place – although sandwiches and tea or coffee are always available – but, as the old photographs and newspaper cuttings around the walls proclaim, definitely a spot for traditional music. *Open 10.30am-11.30pm (11 in winter), Sun 12.30-2, 4-11. Closed Good Friday & 25 Dec. No credit cards.*

KINVARA   Places of Interest
Coole Park Gort Tel 091 31804 *Summer Season only*

KYLEMORE ABBEY   Kylemore Abbey Restaurant

Tel 095 41146
Kylemore Connemara Co Galway   Map 1 D2   **JaB**

A neatly self-contained modern building in the grounds of Kylemore Abbey, run by the Benedictine nuns in conjunction with an excellent craft shop, everything at this daytime self-service restaurant is made on the premises and the range of wholesome offerings includes a good selection of hot (Irish stew, Guinness and beef casserole) and cold savoury dishes, including several vegetarian options, typically ratatouille or cauliflower crumble, and a choice of soups; home baking is a special strength and big bowls of the nuns' renowned home-made jams for the freshly-baked bread and scones beside the till, for visitors to help themselves. Reinforcing the appeal while the mood is on you, the next thing to catch your eye is a big display of neatly labelled jars, so the chances are you will buy some to take home too. (The abbey itself, a neo-Gothic crenellated mansion now used as a convent school, is dramatically situated on the lake shore near the restaurant car park and a short walk further along the wooded shore leads to the beautiful Gothic church (built in 1868), a miniature replica of Norwich cathedral – recently reopened after restoration). A high-chair, baby-changing and disabled facilities are all provided. Car parking for 150. *Seats 240. Open 9.30-5.30 (to 5pm off-season Apr & Oct). Closed Nov-mid Mar. Amex, MasterCard,* **VISA**

If you encounter bad service don't wait to write to us but make your feelings known to the management at the time of your visit. Instant compensation can often resolve any problem that might otherwise leave a bad taste.

LAHINCH   Aberdeen Arms Hotel   66%   £92

Tel 065 81100 Fax 065 81228   Map 2 B4   **H**
Lahinch Co Clare

Established in 1850, the Aberdeen Arms is the oldest golf links hotel in Ireland and has recently undergone a major refurbishment and extension programme. This included the construction of a health centre, renovation of public areas and the addition of banqueting facilities for 180 and a conference centre for up to 250 delegates. Public areas include a spacious, comfortably furnished lounge/foyer, a choice of bars – the lively Klondyke Bar (named after Lahinch's famous 5th hole) or the quieter residents' lounge – and an all-day grill room. Most of the good-sized bedrooms command views over Lahinch's long sandy beach and the golf links. *Rooms 55. Gym, sauna, spa bath, snooker. Amex, Diners, MasterCard,* **VISA**

LAHINCH   Barrtra Seafood Restaurant   £55

Tel 065 81280   Map 2 B4   **R**
Lahinch Co Clare

Paul and Theresa O'Brien's tiny two-room clifftop restaurant (the smaller room, without the view, is for smokers) is in an attractive, traditionally whitewashed house a mile or so outside Lahinch and has window tables overlooking Liscannor Bay. The decor is simple and the atmosphere French-goes-Maritime, with promising wine glasses plus a view of recycled wine bottles used to retain raised beds in the garden as a reminder of good times had by many. Paul is an attentive but unobtrusive host and Theresa makes the most of local produce in her strong, simple cooking; seafood majors but there's always an attractively wide choice that includes a vegetarian dinner menu. Start off with steamed clams with Thai sauce, Liscannor Bay chowder or grilled St Tola goat's cheese, all accompanied by good home-made brown bread. Main courses might include scallops au citron, brill with sun-dried tomatoes, Burren lamb with thyme or spinach pancakes filled with spinach and pine kernels. Delicious desserts include lemon tart, pecan pie or rhubarb crumble. Good cafetière coffee to finish.
Seats 35. Private Room 10. L 12.30-2 D 6-10. Set D £21. Closed L Mon, all Sun (except Bank Holidays) & Oct-end Feb (except D Thu-Sat Oct-end Dec).
Amex, Diners, MasterCard, **VISA**

LAHINCH   Mr Eamon's Restaurant   £60

Tel 065 81050   Fax 065 81810   Map 2 B4   **R**
Kettle Street Lahinch Co Clare

Eamon and Rita Vaughan's long-established restaurant is cosy and welcoming, with pretty lamps and books through which to browse. Choose from a well-balanced menu with the emphasis on seafood (but with plenty of other choices) and nibble at Eamon's excellent home-baked breads – dark nutty brown soda, fennel seed and, perhaps, tomato and basil bread too, all served with a generous bowl of little butter chunks – before tucking into starters such as a salad of calf's tongue with tomato chutney or perhaps chicken liver paté or fresh crab salad with herb mayonnaise. At dinner, a sorbet or good soups like well-flavoured chowder or a vegetable combination such as courgette and lettuce follow. Main courses might include some big, juicy, flavoursome Aran poached scallops, complete with the lovely orange roe, served with a vermouth sauce, or hot buttered lobster (surcharge £8) or chicken breast stuffed with Brie and spinach. Exceptionally good accompanying vegetables. To finish, choose between farmhouse cheeses (served plated with chutney and crackers) or quite simple but nicely presented desserts: dark chocolate marquise with blackberry coulis and sauce anglaise, or bread-and-butter pudding. *Seats 30. D 7-9.30 (till 10 in summer). Closed Mon-Fri Nov & Dec & mid Jan-mid Mar. Set D £17/£22.50.*
Amex, Diners, MasterCard, **VISA**

LARAGH   Derrybawn House   £50

Tel 0404 45134   Fax 0404 45109   Map 2 D4   **A**
Laragh Glendalough Co Wicklow

Surrounded by 90 acres of tranquil parkland in the heart of the scenic Wicklow Hills, this period country house is in the style of an Italianate villa. It's very much a family home, albeit a very large one, and combines gracious proportions with a pleasantly unstuffy atmosphere and roomy comfort. Public rooms include a choice of sitting-rooms with log fires and a lovely dining-room. Most of the bedrooms have parkland views and are large and comfortably furnished with antiques; some rooms have only en suite shower rooms. Some of the back rooms are considerably smaller, but have their own charm. No children under 11 (or dogs – kennels provided). *Rooms 6. Garden, snooker. Closed Christmas week. No credit cards.*

LARAGH   Mitchell's of Laragh   £45

Tel & Fax 0404 45302   Map 2 D4   **RR**
The Old Schoolhouse Laragh Co Wicklow

Jerry and Margaret Mitchell's lovingly restored old cutgranite schoolhouse, with leaded window panes, open fires and country pine furniture, provides adults not only with a tranquil haven from the crowds which nearby Glendalough tends to attract but also very good home cooking to boot. "All types of food are served all day to our visitors from all around the world", says Margaret, so one can eat quiche for breakfast or a fryup for dinner if it takes one's fancy. A daytime memu, served until 6.30, encompasses soused herring with fennel sauce, crab rémoulade with Melba toast, broccoli and seafood filo pie, steak and kidney pie, pasta, coffee cream meringues and lemon drizzle cake. In the evening one might be tempted by spiced pickled pears with blue cheese sauce, a Greek salad, home-smoked salmon, Cajun-style salmon with red pepper coulis and rouille, lanb's sweetbreads with Marsala, parmesan and oregano, beef Wellington and tempting home-made desserts. Popuolar Sunday lunch sees both a good choice and good value. Margaret's home baking is a great strength and, not surprisingly perhaps, afternoon tea is a speciality. Winner of our Best Presentation of Bread and Butter Award for 1997. Accommodation is offered in eight neat, ensuite twin rooms (£37) with a pleasant rural outlook; guest sitting room. Breakfast offers a fine choice, from kippers, kedgeree and smoked trout to a fry up with black and white pudding or egg florentine. Not suitable for children. No dogs.
*Seats 30. Private Room 20. Meals 9am-9.30pm (Sun 9pm). Set Sun L (to 5pm) £11.95 Set D £16.95. Closed from 5pm Sun to Wed lunchtime Oct-mid Mar, 4 weeks Jan, Good Friday, 25 & 26 Dec. Amex, MasterCard, **VISA***

LECANVEY   Staunton's

Tel 098 64850   Map 1 A3   **P**
Lecanvey Westport Co Mayo

In the same family ownership for about two hundred years, the current landlord of this roadside pub (it is on a shallow bend and hard to miss when driving from Louisburgh to Westport) is a charming young lady, Thérèse Staunton. It's a 'real' pub, traditional but not hide-bound by age and custom, with a good atmosphere. Thérèse currently offers just soup and sandwiches. *Open 10.30am-11.30pm (from 1pm-11pm Oct-Easter), Sun 12.30-2, 4-11. Closed Good Friday & 25 Dec. No credit cards.*

LEENANE   Delphi Lodge   £78

Tel 095 42211   Fax 095 42296   Map 1 A3   **A**
Leenane Co Galway

Set in a spectacular, unspoilt valley and surrounded by Connacht's highest mountains, this early 19th-century sporting lodge was built by the Marquis of Sligo in one of the most beautiful (and wettest) parts of Ireland. The current owners, Peter and Jane Mantle, have restored and sensitively extended the house which now has eleven guest bedrooms, which vary considerably in size and layout in keeping with the age of the house, but all are en suite, with lovely views over the lake, woodlands or mountains (six rooms with lake view £110). A comfortable family atmosphere prevails and, although quite grandly furnished with antiques, sporting paraphernalia and abundant reading matter everywhere ensure the relaxed comfort of guests. Dinner (£25), for residents only, is served at a long mahogany table, presided over by the captor of the day's biggest salmon. Just across the road, four restored cottages offer self-catering accommodation. ***Rooms** 11. Garden, fishing, snooker. Closed 10 days Christmas/New Year. MasterCard, **VISA***

| LEENANE | **Killary Lodge** | 59% | **£62** |

Tel 095 42276   Fax 095 42314   Map 1 A3   **H**
Leenane Co Galway

Superbly located in woodland with beautiful views through to Killary Harbour,
this unusual hotel is owned by Jamie and Mary Young, who also run the
renowned Little Killary Adventure Centre nearby, and provides the best of both
worlds for people attracted to the idea of a healthy outdoor activity holiday but
also willing to pay for the comfort of a hotel rather than returning to a bleak
hostel at the end of a long day in the fresh air. Rooms, mostly twin but also
some singles and doubles, all with shower or bath en suite, are comfortably
furnished and have phones but no television (as a matter of policy). Children
up to 12 stay free in parents' room. Activities such as scuba diving, canoeing,
orienteering, archery, sailing and tennis are available; no experience is necessary,
as trained guides will ease guests into new activities to suit their individual pace.
Relaxation is the aim. No dogs. *Rooms 20. Garden, tennis, sauna, bicycle hire,
shop. Closed Dec & Jan. MasterCard,* **VISA**

| LEENANE | **Portfinn Lodge** | | **£60** |

Tel 095 42265   Fax 095 42315   Map 1 A3   **RR**
Leenane Co Galway

Rory and Maeve Daly have been running this seafood restaurant at the head of
Killary Harbour since 1988 and the dining area is shared between a room of the
main house and an adjoining conservatory, both with western window tables
(on a good evening) offering views of the sun sinking behind the mountains.
Very good moist brown soda bread with sunflower seeds is on the table to
welcome guests; thereafter seafood takes pride of place although the menu
actually offers quite a wide choice. A typical meal might start with a roulade
of stuffed smoked salmon, or a seafood bisque followed, perhaps, by scallops
in cheese, dill, champagne and cream sauce, pan-fried plaice with lemon, caper,
almond and herb butter, or sirloin steak with garlic and herb butter. Finish
with something like 'Dad's gooey meringue pudding', or stay safe with an
Irish cheeseboard. 10% service charge added to total bill. *Seats 36. Parties 10.
D only 5.30-9 (flexible). Closed Oct-Easter. Set D £18.50. Diners, MasterCard,* **VISA**

Rooms   **£44**
Eight neat purpose-built en suite rooms, all sleeping three and one with four
beds; accessible (but not specially equipped) for disabled guests.

| LEIGHLINBRIDGE | **The Lord Bagenal Inn** | | **£45** |

Tel & Fax 0503 21668   Map 2 C4   **R/P**
Leighlinbridge Co Carlow

Food, wine and hospitality are all dispensed in good measure at this renowned
old inn just off the main M9 Waterford-Carlow road. The style of cooking
continuously evolves and more modern dishes are joining old favourites on the
large, long menu that features extensive suggestions on matching wines to food.
This is, of course, all for the best as the Lord Bagenal's wine list is one of
Ireland's most impressive wine lists – an extensive choice, copious notes, all laid
out in compendium style in country order (complete with maps of growing
areas) and more food cross-referencing. Game is served in season (Nov-Feb:
wild duck, pheasant, snipe, woodcock and more) and there are good pasta and
vegetarian choices. Fresh Dunmore East prawns, monkfish à la dieppoise (with
prawns, mussels and mushrooms), fillets of sole, and scallops with a fresh ginger
sauce sit happily alongside steaks, lamb, traditional Irish stew and chicken curry.
A good bar menu offers pasta, steaks, sandwiches and filling puds. The whole

family is made very welcome and there's a special children's menu; outside the front door is a play area and there's also a play room inside. Booking is advised for Sunday lunch. *Seats 90. Parties 25. Private Room 40. L 12.30-2.30 D 6-10.30 (bar food 12.30-10.30). Closed Good Friday & 25 Dec. Diners, MasterCard,* **VISA**

LEIGHLINBRIDGE   Places of Interest
Altamont by Tullow Tel 0503 59128

LETTERFRACK Rosleague Manor	72%	£120

Tel 095 41101 Fax 095 41168   Map 1 A3   **HR**
Letterfrack Connemara Co Galway

"Tranquil, invigorating, refreshing, magical Connemara – the last truly civilised place on earth" says the no-holds-barred brochure; however, it is true, Connemara can be truly delightful and Rosleague Manor is a tranquil base from which to explore its magic. Owned and managed by the brother and sister team of Anne and Patrick Foyle, this Regency manor stands in 30 acres of gardens overlooking sheltered Ballinakill Bay, seven miles north of Clifden. A path through the hotel's gardens leads down to the ocean's edge. Character and comfort are in generous supply within the hotel, the former including carefully chosen antiques and paintings, the latter assisted by central heating and peat fires. Bedrooms are nearly all of a very good size (with separate seating areas or mini-suites) and all have good bathrooms; mini suites (£140) attract only a small supplement. Children under 8 stay free in parents' room. There are two drawing rooms and a conservatory bar. A reduced tariff (£90) applies during Apr, May & Oct; special break rates during September. Boats leave nearby Cleggan harbour for trips to the island of Inishbofin. *Rooms 20. Garden, sauna, tennis, billiards, fishing. Closed Nov-Easter. Amex, MasterCard,* **VISA**

Restaurant   £70

Nigel Rush's four-course dinner menus are served at round antique tables under chandeliers in a delightfully civilised room. A daily-changing table d'hote with four or five choices at each course might encompass steamed mussels in white wine, garlic and cream and roast pork ribs with ginger, aniseed and sweet chili sauce among the starters, then a cream of brocolli soup or blackcurrant sorbet as a second course, following with lamb kebabs with a light peanut cream, grilled lobster with garlic or roast ray wings with crispy capers and balsamic vinegar. Fresh strawberry tart, chocolate mousse and Irish farmhouse cheeses await those who make it to the end of the fixed-price dinner menu. Only cold dishes at lunchtime. Teas and coffees are served in the drawing rooms. No smoking in the dining-room. *Seats 60. Parties 8. Private Room 10. D 8-9.30 (till 9 Sun). Set D from £25.*

LETTERFRACK   Places of Interest
Connemara National Park Tel 095 41054
Kylemore Abbey Connemara Tel 095 41146

Many hotels offer reduced rates for weekend or out-of-season bookings. Our guide price indicates high-season rates. Always ask about special deals for longer stays.

LETTERKENNY   Castle Grove Country House   £80

Tel 074 51118   **Fax 074 51134**   Map 1 C1   **AR**
Ballymaleel Letterkenny Co Donegal

Just outside Letterkenny, Mary Sweeney's lovely 17th-century house overlooking Lough Swilly is set in well-tended gardens and parkland, with ample parking space discreetly arranged to be practical without spoiling the outlook from public rooms. An impressive entrance hall promises well and the house does not disappoint, especially in well-proportioned, elegantly furnished reception rooms with welcoming fires. More recent additions include a large conservatory and a new drawing-room, which takes the place of the previous dining-room. Bedrooms (four reserved for non-smokers) vary in size and outlook due to the age and nature of the house, but are generally spacious and furnished to a high standard; all have en suite shower and/or bathroom; a trouser press on the landing is available for all guests' use. An extra seven bedrooms were at the planning stage when we went to press and may be ready for the 1997 season. Delicious breakfasts include a choice of fish as well as traditional grills, home-made breads and preserves. Mary Sweeney's good management is reflected in a high standard of housekeeping and the helpful attitude of friendly staff. Two boats belonging to the house are available for fishing on Lough Swilly. No dogs. ***Rooms** 8. Garden, terrace, fishing, shooting. Closed 22-27 Dec & 9 Jan-1 Feb. Amex, Diners, MasterCard,* **VISA**

Restaurant   £60

Sean Roche, previously at *Drimcong House* with Gerry Galvin, has now been head chef at Castle Grove for over a year and, during that time, a completely new dining-room has been built. Six-course dinner menus start off with a choice of three starters – a confit of duck, perhaps, with a seasonal salad – then soup of the day or sorbet, served with freshly-baked breads. A selection of five main courses might include two or three seafood choices (with risotto or Provençal vegetables) and, perhaps, local Donegal lamb or something like chicken piccata with caper and balsamic dressing. Tempting desserts range from the homely – bread-and-butter pudding with caramel sauce – to more sophisticated offerings such as a white chocolate mousse with Cointreau. Finish off with Irish farmhouse cheeses, then freshly-brewed coffee and home-made petits fours. ***Seats** 60. Parties 8. D only 6.30-9.30. Set D £25. Closed 22-27 Dec & 9 Jan-1 Feb.*

LIMERICK   Castletroy Park Hotel   74%   £143

Tel 061 335566   **Fax 061 331117**   Map 2 B5   **HR**
Dublin Road Limerick Co Limerick

Located on the Dublin road on the outskirts of town, this well-designed red-brick hotel meets every business need. The university concert hall and foundation building, just three minutes' walk away, has greatly enhanced Limerick's growing reputation as a major conference centre, and with its own state-of-the-art conference and leisure facilities the hotel is ideally situated to benefit. Within the hotel, a welcoming atmosphere warms the wood-floored entrance hall and conservatory, while the 'Merry Pedlar' pubby bar offers traditional Irish hospitality and a decent pint. Bedrooms are large with plenty of writing space, good lighting and up-to-date features – satellite TV, fax and computer points, two phones, minibar and trouser press; bathrooms are on the small side. 25 Executive rooms offer more extras including king-size bed, bathrobe and turn-down service plus several other complimentary items. Two Presidential suites (£300) are top of the range and there are further Junior suites (£180); two rooms are equipped for disabled guests. Whether you need facilities for a conference (the Barrington Suite holds up to 300 and there's an elegant ballroom) or a private boardroom, the hotel can cater for both admirably and also provides a fully-equipped business centre; the hotel won our Business Hotel of the Year in 1995. Note the amenities available in the superbly equipped leisure centre. Good buffet breakfast served in the restaurant. 24hr room service and lounge service. No dogs. *Rooms 107. Garden, patio, indoor swimming pool, children's splash pool, gym, keep-fit equipment, solarium, sauna, spa bath, steam room, beauty salon, jogging track. Closed 24 & 25 Dec. Amex, Diners, MasterCard,* **VISA**

McLaughlin's Restaurant   £65

Named after the man who first brought electricity to Ireland, McLaughlin's retaurant tries hard to be cosy, with candlelight and shelves of old books to soften the surroundings, but the atmosphere is still rather business-like. The four-course dinner menu presents reliable *cuisine moderne* starting, perhaps, with a tasty *amuse-bouche* followed by crab and salmon cannelloni with a ginger and corainder veloute, or chicken and marinated duck terrine with grilled aubergines, then a choice of soups or sorbet. Main-course choices might offer roulade of black sole with a salmon and pepper mousse and lobster sauce, roast loin of lamb wrapped in a chicken and Parma ham mousse, or pan-fried pork chop with braised leeks and a mustard sauce. Puddings may include rhubarb and orange parfait with orange sauce or white chocolate mousse with a dark chocolate shell and forest fruit compote. Informal lunch and evening meals are also available from an international bar menu at the hotel's Merry Pedlar 'pub'. *Seats 70. Parties 30. L (Sun only) 12.30-2 D 7-9.30. Set L Sun £15.50 Set D £26. Closed L Mon-Sat, D Sun.*

LIMERICK	Freddy's Bistro	£60

Tel 061 418749 Fax 061 316141   Map 2 B5   **R**
Theatre Lane Lower Glenworth Street Limerick

Neat premises in a city-centre laneway conceal an attractively informal two-storey restaurant; on the ground floor there is just room for a few tables, a leather sofa and some chairs near the bar, while the main restaurant is upstairs. Open brickwork creates a warm tone and skylights provide natural light on summer evenings, although candles are also set on the simple, oilcloth-covered tables. The food (deep-fried farmhouse cheese filo pastry 'moneybags' with a small salad garnish, chicken breast au poivre or seafood tagliatelle) is well cooked and tasty but portions are decidedly dainty, so don't underestimate the side orders required. On a recent visit the unsatisfactory state of the Ladies let the side down. *Seats 60. D only 5.30-10.30. Closed Sun, Mon, Good Friday & 24-26 Dec. MasterCard,* **VISA**

LIMERICK	Greenhills Hotel	62%	£90

Tel 061 453033 Fax 061 453307   Map 2 B5   **H**
Ennis Road Limerick Co Limerick

A family-run hotel where some of the bedrooms have a pleasant outlook over the garden or tennis court and all are well equipped, with telephone, tea/coffee-making facilities, trouser press and TV. Nine De Luxe rooms (£100) are larger and more comfortable, with well-finished, fully-tiled bathrooms. Public areas include a leisure centre with an 18m swimming pool, spacious lobby and a pleasant Jockey Club bar. No dogs. *Rooms 60. Garden, indoor swimming pool, children's pool, gym, sauna, steam room, solarium, beauty salon, tennis. Closed 25 Dec. Amex, Diners, MasterCard,* **VISA**

LIMERICK   Jasmine Palace   £55

Tel 061 42484   Fax 061 410201   Map 2 B5   **R**
O'Connell Mall O'Connell Street Limerick Co Limerick

A large first-floor restaurant on Limerick's main street, this well-appointed
Chinese restaurant offers inexpensive weekday lunches, but really shows its paces
in the evening, when there is a choice of five set menus and a wide-ranging
à la carte menu featuring specialities such as Jasmine Palace roast duck pot (sliced
roast duck and king prawns combined with Chinese vegetables in a spicy sauce),
steamed fish – brill, sole or even sea bass depending on the catch – with ginger
and spring onions, several lobster dishes and a selection of vegetarian options.
Sunday lunch is understandably a high point of the week for family outings –
the Jasmine Palace runs an 'Eat as much as you can' buffet with a choice of over
20 dishes. *Seats 120. Parties 26. L 12.30-2.30 (Sun 1-3) D 5.30-11. Closed 25 & 26
Dec. Set L (Sun only) £10.50 Set D from £15.50. Amex, Diners, MasterCard,* **VISA**

We do not recommend the food in pubs where
there is no mention of Bar Food in the statistics.
A restaurant within a pub is only specifically recommended
where its separate opening times are given.

LIMERICK   Jurys Hotel   68%   £145

Tel 061 327777   Fax 061 326400   Map 2 B5   **H**
Ennis Road Limerick Co Limerick

Centrally situated just across the bridge from Limerick's main shopping and
business area, the low-lying Jurys hotel is set in a five-acre site by the river.
A good impression is created in the spacious lobby area and carried through
the public areas, including the pleasant Limericks Bar (which features the history
of the famous rhyming verse), two restaurants and extensive leisure facilities.
Friendly staff provide 24hr room service. Newer bedrooms are larger and more
stylishly decorated with smarter bathrooms but older rooms are equally well
equipped (including trouser press and multi-channel TV; tea/coffee-making
facilities available on request). Families are welcome; under-12s stay free in
parents' room. Entertainment in high-season summer months. Conference
facilities for up to 200 theatre-style. No dogs. *Rooms 95. Garden, indoor
swimming pool, children's splash pool, gym, sauna, steam room, spa bath, tennis,
coffee shop (7am-10.30pm). Closed 24-28 Dec. Amex, Diners, MasterCard,* **VISA**

LIMERICK   Limerick Inn Hotel   68%   £120

Tel 061 326666   Fax 061 326281   Map 2 B5   **H**
Ennis Road Limerick Co Limerick

The helipad in front of this low-rise modern hotel attracts considerable attention
from passing traffic and there is usually a bit of a buzz around the large, airy
reception area and public rooms. Good-sized rooms at the back of the hotel
have a pleasant outlook over countryside; they have well-designed bathrooms
and are equipped with trouser press, iron and ironing board, hairdryer, phone,
tea/coffee-making facilities and multi-channel TV. Superior rooms and suites
also have mini-bars. Conference and business facilities for up to 600 delegates
include secretarial services. Good health and leisure facilities; resident hair stylist
and beautician. *Rooms 153. Garden, indoor swimming pool, gym, sauna, solarium,
steam room, whirlpool bath, tennis, putting, snooker, coffee shop (7.30-2.30 & 6-
10.30). Closed 25 Dec. Amex, Diners, MasterCard,* **VISA**

LIMERICK   Limerick Ryan Hotel   62%   £90

Tel 061 453922 Fax 061 326333   Map 2 B5   **H**
Ardhu House Ennis Road Limerick Co Limerick

On the outskirts of Limerick city, a Ryan Group hotel with a mixture of building styles and ages: an elegantly proportioned 18th-century mansion provides its period front and entrance, while the large 1960s wing is most obvious from the road. In the original section, public areas have a pleasing feeling of spaciousness with attractive features such as fine plasterwork, imposing fireplaces and crystal chandeliers, while the newer wing provides en suite bedrooms and the facilities expected of a modern hotel that include laundry service and 24hr room service. Familes are welcome and children up to 12 may stay free in their parents' room. One bedroom is suitable for disabled guests. Banqueting/conference facilities for up to 240/130; 24hr business centre. Complimentary use of a nearby fitness centre. No dogs. *Rooms 181. Garden. Amex, Diners, MasterCard, **VISA***

LIMERICK   Mortells   £30

Tel & Fax 061 415457   Map 2 B5   **R**
49 Roches Street Limerick

This unpretentious, inexpensive daytime restaurant and shop will please those who value freshness and respect chefs like Brian Mortell who have the confidence to keep it simple. 'Wonderful fresh mussels' it says on the menu, and they are – definitely an experience not to be missed. Mortell's breaded fillets of fresh haddock or deep-fried cod will restore the most battered faith in deep-fried fish, or you could try a pan-fried fillet of plaice or peppered lemon sole – it all depends on the catch, but freshness is guaranteed. Big, traditional breakfasts kick off each day and steaks and roasts are an additional lunchtime feature. Homely desserts like apple, rhubarb or lemon meringue pie, but seafood is the real star of the show. *Seats 60. Meals 8.30am-5.30pm (carvery 12.30-2.30). Closed Sun, Bank Holidays, 25 & 26 Dec. No credit cards.*

LIMERICK   Quenelle's Restaurant   £70

Tel 061 411111 Fax 061 400111   Map 2 B5   **R**
Corner of Mallow & Henry Street Limerick Co Limerick

Kieran and Sindy Magner-Pollard have run their interesting little three-level city-centre restaurant overlooking the river since 1993. Kieran's confident, adventurous cooking can be sampled on a 5-course dinner menu that, typically, might include duck and red onion terrine with pumpkin and nutmeg brioche or local spiced beef salad with honey and lime vinaigrette; a choice of soups and also an unusual, amusingly presented sorbet and a full range of local produce in the main-course choices, including beef sirloin with Guinness and mustard sauce, medallions of pork with sweet red wine and apple chutney or peppered rack of lamb, perhaps an interesting vegetarian option such as poached figs and curried lentils and, of course, a selection of local seafood. Imaginative desserts and a good selection of farmhouse cheeses. Attention to detail is outstanding throughout, from the presentation of little *amuse-bouche* on arrival, through garnishing side vegetables with a dainty filo moneybag parcel filled with a julienne of vegetables, to the minted truffles served with coffee. *Seats 35. D only 7-9. Closed all Sun & Mon, Good Friday & 24-26 Dec. Set D £24.50. MasterCard, **VISA***

LIMERICK   Two Mile Inn Hotel   63%   £95

Tel 061 326255   **Fax 061 453783**   Map 2 B5   **H**
Ennis Road Limerick Co Limerick

Three miles from the centre of Limerick, this striking modern hotel features an enormous lobby with a large seating area, rather like an airport lounge, but the hotel as a whole is imaginatively laid out and other areas are surprisingly intimate. Bedrooms are attractively arranged in single-storey buildings around garden areas that afford a feeling of quietness and privacy and are furnished with deck chairs and sun shades in summer. Conference/banqueting facilities for 300/350. Musical entertainment in the bar during the summer. Good-value low season tariff (Nov-Apr). No dogs. *Rooms 123. Garden, shop. Amex, Diners, MasterCard, **VISA***

LIMERICK   Places of Interest

Tourist Information Tel 061 317522
City Gallery of Art Upper Mallow Street Tel 061 310663
City Museum John Square Tel 061 417826
King John's Castle Tel 061 411201
Hunt Museum at Limerick University Tel 061 333644
St John's Cathedral Tel 061 414624
St Mary's Cathedral Tel 061 310293 *Nightly sound and light show in summer*
Limerick Racecourse Tel 061 29377
Cratloe Woods House Cratloe Tel 061 327028 *5 miles*
Lough Gur Interpretative Centre Lough Gur Tel 061 85186 *6 miles*

LISDOONVARNA   Ballinalacken Castle Hotel   63%   £70

Tel & Fax 065 74025   Map 2 B4   **H**
Lisdoonvarna Co Clare

Beautifully situated on the lovely scenic coastal road between Ballyvaughan and Lahinch, Ballinalacken is just a few minutes' drive from Doolin (where the ferries operate to the Aran Islands) and has uninterrupted views of the islands, the Cliffs of Moher and the distant hills of Connemara. The hotel, which is set in 100 acres of grounds, is an attractive, well-proportioned house built as a private residence in 1840 and its history is intertwined with that of the 15th-century O'Brien stronghold beside it. The atmosphere is more country house than hotel – a welcoming fire in the spacious entrance hall sets the tone of relaxed hospitality which is a feature of the place – especially in public rooms that include an elegant drawing-room furnished with antiques and command sweeping sea views. The dining-room, which is the corresponding room across the hall (and shares similar views), is to be extended for the 1997 season to allow space required for non-residents; a small residents' bar is also planned. Most of the bedrooms have a sea view, with comfortable chairs and tables arranged to make the most of it; all are all en suite (some with shower only) and are generous in both size and furnishings. No dogs. *Rooms 13. Garden. Closed mid Oct-Easter. MasterCard, **VISA***

LISDOONVARNA   Sheedy's Spa Hotel   66%   £55

Tel 065 74026   **Fax 065 74555**   Map 2 B4   **HR**
Lisdoonvarna Co Clare

Under the management of the current owners, Frank and Patsy Sheedy, since 1971, this welcoming and immaculately maintained small hotel has been in family ownership for generations. A good first impression, created by a well-tended approach and the warm ambience of a sunny foyer with polished wooden floor, open fire and soft country colours, is carried through all the public areas, including a cosy night-time bar just off the foyer. Simple bedrooms vary in size, but are all en suite, neatly decorated and well equipped. *Rooms 11. Croquet, tennis. Closed Oct-Apr. Amex, Diners, MasterCard, **VISA***

Orchid Restaurant   £50

🍵 🫖 📷 V 🍽

Chef Frankie Sheedy deserves the enviable reputation of the little restaurant at
the Spa. Orders are taken in the foyer seating area, or in the little bar and, once
seated at rather closely packed tables, waitress service is speedy and friendly. The
à la carte menu offers a wide choice of dishes with a tendency towards exotic
flavours; these are augmented by daily specials (perhaps Liscannor lobster).
Regular starters might include a not-to-be-missed dish of pan-fried scallops and
black pudding on a bed of champ with pesto (an unusual but successful mixture)
or a crispy duck confit served Oriental-style with Chinese spices and a star anise
and ginger dressing. Middle courses include interesting soups (smoked haddock
and red lentil) and refreshing salads, followed by a well-balanced choice of main
courses which will usually include Burren lamb (maybe a rack served with a
courgette and tomato gateau on a rosemary and thyme jus), although the main
thrust is towards local seafood. Lovely desserts – poached peach in champagne
syrup on a ring of whiskey and honey ice cream or chocolate marquise with
Tia Maria on a fresh coffee bean and strawberry coulis – or farmhouse cheeses.
No smoking. *Seats 36. D only 6.30-8.45.*

LISMORE	**Buggy's Glencairn Inn**		**£36**
Tel 058 56232		Map 2 C5	
Glencairn nr Lismore Co Waterford			

🍵 🫖 📷 🥗 🛏 V 🍽

Ken and Cathleen Buggy's new venture is very much in keeping with the
style that won them so much praise at their previous establishment, *The Old
Presbytery* in Kinsale. Here they have constructed the perfect home for Ken's
collection of agricultural memorabilia in an olde worlde bar which, like the little
dining-room across the hall, looks as if it has been there for ever – but they have
'before and after' photographs to prove the transformation. The whole place
is charming and the food (all 'made on the day'), especially, is very good.
Wonderful breads, home-made soups, ploughman's lunches with big chunks of
farmhouse cheese and home-made chutneys. Everything's up on a blackboard
just inside the door – look out for an unusual cockles and mussels paté and hot
specials like poached local salmon with salad and boiled potatoes. Puddings are
simple but successful – apple crumble and custard, strawberries and cream – and
freshly-made cafetière coffee is generously served. A delight. Accommodation
is available in three delightful en suite rooms, with old-fashioned high brass
and iron beds, crisp white bedlinen and big puffy pillows. Bathrooms are also
heavy on the charm, with big freestanding claw-foot baths and oodles of style.
*Bar Food 12.30-2, 5-9. Closed L Sun & Tue, Good Friday & 25 Dec.
Accommodation 3 bedrooms, all en suite, £36. No credit cards.*

LISPOLE	**Churchfield**		**£62***
Tel 066 51843	**Fax 066 51067**	Map 2 A5	**A**
Lispole Co Kerry			

'Country house accommodation and French cuisine' is how Chris and Joelle
Johnson describe the hospitality of their Dingle peninsula home – and that just
about sums up Churchfield. Food – a no-choice menu reflecting a different
region of France each night – is so much an integral part of a visit that the rate
they quote is demi-pension, although (like most of what they do) any other
preferred arrangement is open to negotiation. 'By arrangement' is the catch-all
phrase here and applies to the (otherwise) set menu, including vegetarian option,
dinner times, breakfast times – even whether smoking (which is not allowed
upstairs) is permitted in the dining-room: if all the guests agree to it that's OK,
otherwise not. Guests gather in the drawing-room for a drink beside the fire,
consult the brief, set menu and order wine from a short, carefully selected list,
then drift through the kitchen to the dining-room, where a communal table is

laid. Joelle serves food as it is ready; if it is a night for the Loire (Joelle's home territory), dinner might begin with a warm *salade aux lardons*, followed by a simple *saumon beurre blanc* with potatoes and seasonal vegetables, finishing with a hot *brochette de fruits* – simple and delicious. Coffee is served with mints in the drawing-room and then guests chat, watch one of a library of videos, listen to music, read one of the thousands of books around the house, go to one of the Dingle pubs or drift off to bed. Bedrooms are not large, but are charming, with characterful traditional furnishings, comfortable beds and wash basins; by the 1997 season each room will have its own private bathroom (although not en suite). A stay of more than one night is recommended at Churchfield, as there is so much to do in the house as well as in the area around it. The appeal is mainly adult, but children over 12 are welcome. Non-residents are welcome to dine if there is room. Themed gourmet weekends are organised throughout the year. **Rooms** 4. *Garden. MasterCard,* **VISA**

LISTOWEL	Allo's Bar & Bistro	£60

Tel 068 22880   Map 2 A5   **P/R**
41 Church Street Listowel Co Kerry

Visitors to Caherdaniel who have been bewailing the loss of Armel Whyte's and Helen Mullane's renowned restaurant *Loaves & Fishes* should hasten to Listowel, where they have taken over Allo's Bar & Bistro. Named after the previous owner ('Alphonsus, known as Allo') Armel and Helen are working the same old magic in their new premises, which seems much older than it is – they have reconstructed the whole interior with salvaged materials (the flooring was once in the London Stock Exchange), but it is sensitively done and surprisingly convincing. The long, narrow bar is divided up in the traditional way and, bar the lobster tank in the window, it's pretty authentic – and stylish, true to the Mullane flair. Likewise Armel's food, which is lively, modern and based on the best local ingredients – typically in daytime starters or 'tasty bits' like seafood chowder (creamy, with chunky pieces of fish) served with freshly-baked bread, Caesar salad or a hot parcel of farmhouse cheese, with blackcurrant sauce. Main courses could include warm salad of duck confit or potted crab, mousseline of chicken and apple with a calvados cream or a pan-fried 4oz fillet steak with wild mushroom sauce, followed by classic desserts like tangy lemon tart or Bakewell tart with home-made custard. Evening menus incoporate many of the daytime dishes into a more formal menu structure and broaden the choice to include the likes of hot lobster with lemon and herb butter and rack of Kerry Lamb with a honey and port jus. Finish in the best of all possible ways with Allo's assorted dessert plate – or a platter of Irish cheeses with a glass of port. At the time of going to press plans were afoot for a new *Loaves & Fishes* close to Allo's. **Seats** 34. *Parties 8. Meals L 12-3 Bistro Menu L 3-7, D 7-8.30. Closed all Sun, D Mon, Good Friday & 25 Dec. Access, Amex,* **VISA**

MACROOM	Castle Hotel	63%	£60

Tel 026 41074   Fax 026 41505   Map 2 B6   **H**
Macroom Co Cork

The neat frontage of this hotel on the main street of Macroom creates a positive impression that is reinforced by many details throughout the premises. It has been in the Buckley family since 1952 and is currently under management of Don and Gerard Buckley; the warm and helpful attitude of both the Buckleys and their staff go a long way towards explaining the charm of the place. The hotel itself is quite modest, but imagination and hard work are maximising its potential through thoughtful refurbishment (and now a new phase of recon-struction). Public areas gleam welcomingly and the bar and dining room, especially, are most attractive. Bedrooms have all been refurbished recently but are on the small side with unexceptional bathrooms; there are slight variations, with some older rooms having just a shower, and newer ones including trouser presses. At the time of going to press there were plans to demolish the back of the building (currently occupied by leisure facilities, notably an under-used squash court, and replace it with a two-storey extension to include a new leisure centre (with swimming pool and up-to-date gym) on the ground floor and new bedrooms above it – all due to be completed in time for the 1997 season. *Rooms 26. Gym, steam room, sun bed. Closed 24-26 Dec. Amex, Diners, MasterCard,* **VISA**

| **MADDOXTOWN** | **Blanchville House** | **£60** |

Tel 056 27197
Dunbell Maddoxtown Co Kilkenny

Map 2 C5

A

Easily recognised by the folly in its grounds, this elegant Georgian house is on a working farm and, while conveniently close to the crafts and culture of Kilkenny city, has all the advantages of peace and restfulness associated with the country – and similarly Tim and Monica Phelan aim to provide guests with 20th-century comfort to balance 19th-century style. The house has a lovely, airy atmosphere, with matching, well-proportioned dining- and drawing-rooms on either side of the hall and pleasant, comfortably furnished bedrooms (all are now en suite and overlook lovely countryside). Dinner (five courses £20) is available to residents by arrangement and, like the next morning's excellent breakfast, is taken at the communal mahogany dining table. *Rooms 6. Garden. Closed Nov-end Feb. MasterCard,* **VISA**

| **MALAHIDE** | **Bon Appétit** | **£75** |

Tel & Fax 01 845 0314
9 St James Terrace Malahide Co Dublin

Map 1 D3

R

Patsy McGuirk's well-known basement restaurant in a Georgian terrace near the marina underwent a total transformation in 1996. It's now all cool dark blue and creamy yellow, making a lovely soothing background for a growing collection of local watercolours; elegant drapes are slung simply from a wooden pole while high-back chairs and air-conditioning provide real comfort. A shortish well-balanced lunch menu is deservedly popular and there's a five-course dinner menu plus a few daily specials and 'chef's recommendations' in addition to a full à la carte. Typical starters include a tian of crab meat mixed with avocado pear and roasted red peppers in a garlic mayonnaise, a sauté of duck livers with a timbale of saffron rice plus specials like Gigas oysters or Kilmore crab claws – but don't miss the fresh prawn bisque with cognac. Well-balanced main-course choices include popular dishes like steak Diane, wiener schnitzel and roast rack of Wicklow lamb, but fish is the real strength of the menu. A long-established house speciality is *sole création McGuirk* (a whole boned black sole filled with turbot and prawns in a beurre blanc sauce); sole on the bone may be presented whole at the table then re-presented bone-free and neatly reassembled. Baked hake fillet with a red pepper coulis, garden peas and a herb sauce is an exceptional dish (our Seafood Dish of the Year – see Awards pages) – a thick square of fillet, seared skin side up, set in a pattern reminiscent of the Irish flag, in sections of red pepper sauce, creamy herb sauce and lovely fresh garden peas – and the simple but stylish presentation is followed through with perfect cooking and well-balanced flavours. Details are good throughout, including freshly-baked breads and vegetables selected to complement each dish. Lively desserts, dramatically presented on huge black plates with a 'spoon and fork' left clear in a dusting of icing sugar, might include fresh strawberries in a crisp filo basket, sliced and sprinkled with Grand Marnier, or a smooth, tangy lemon torte served with crème anglaise. Or you could finish with an Irish cheese platter, then good coffee. Though half bottles may be in short supply on the wine list, there can be no complaints about the selection from France, which includes many superb clarets and burgundies; other European countries are represented and the New World also gets a look-in; helpful tasting notes. *Seats 55. Parties 20. Private Room 24. L 12.30-2.30 D 7-10.30. Closed L Sat, all Sun & Bank Holidays. Set L £10.50/£15 Set D £23.50. Amex, Diners, MasterCard,* **VISA**

MALAHIDE   Eastern Tandoori   £40

Tel 01 845 4154/5   Fax 01 677 9232   Map 1 D3   **R**
1 New Street Malahide Co Dublin

Although it's on the first floor, overlooking the Malahide marina development, the atmosphere at this out-of-town branch of the well-known, grander city-centre restaurant is distinctly other-worldly, with an all-Indian staff, authentic furnishings and sound effects. Choose from four set menus at varying prices, or from the à la carte: between them they offer a wide, well-balanced choice of dishes ranging from gently aromatic to fiery hot, suiting the novice without offending old hands. Old favourites are there in mild onion bhaji, served with a small salad, various tandoori dishes – chicken tikka, mackerel, even quail and crab claws – and several jalfrezi dishes such as beef, lamb or chicken, hot with chili, fresh ginger and coriander. Chef's recommendations are more interesting, some desserts garnished with the classic silver leaf, and side dishes like tarka dal (lentils with fresh coriander) and aloo jeera (dry potatoes with cumin seed) are good. Wine is pricy, but Cobra Indian beer probably suits the food better anyway. 12½% sevice charge added to final bill. Branches also in central Dublin (34-35 South William Street Tel 01 671 0428 open 7 days, closed L Sat), Blackrock (Old Parish Hall, Kill Lane, Deansgrange Tel 01 289 2856) and Cork (Emmet Place Tel 021 272 020). *Seats 64. Parties 20. L 1-4 (Sun only) D only 6-11.30. Closed Good Friday, 25 & 26 Dec. Set L Sun £7.95. Amex, Diners, MasterCard, VISA*

MALAHIDE   Giovanni's

Tel 01 845 1733   Map 1 D3   **JaB**
Townyard Lane Malahide Co Dublin

This buzzy little pizza place and family restaurant in a laneway near the new marina complex is run by two friendly, unflappable North Africans and is so popular that it has had to double in size since they opened in 1991. The menu reads much like many other pizza places, with some pasta, a few chicken dishes and even some steaks, but everything is unpretentiously nice and wholesome and fresh, including the grated parmesan on the table – which must be the secret of their success. They still keep the flasks of chianti hanging from the ceiling as part of the decor – corny, but kids love it. Swift service. *Seats 70. Open 12.30pm-midnight (Sun from 2pm). Closed Good Friday, 25 & 26 Dec & 1 Jan. MasterCard, VISA*

Entries categorised as **JaB** are recommended for 'Just a Bite'.

MALAHIDE   Grand Hotel   66%   £120

Tel 01 845 0000   Fax 01 845 0987   Map 1 D3   **H**
Malahide Co Dublin

Polished double doors in the splendid cream-painted frontage lead into a pillared entrance hall resplendent with fine crystal chandeliers, marble fireplace, comfortable, well-spaced settees and winged armchairs. At the rear of the ground floor is Matt Ryan's bar, a split-level room decorated in a distinctive 20s' Mackintosh style, while to the left of the entrance is the Griffin bar (open evenings only). Bedrooms have smart pickled-pine furniture and a host of amenities as well as double-glazing and bright, well-equipped bathrooms; 24hr room service. No dogs. Conference/banqueting (900/600). A leisure centre, complete with indoor swimming pool, mini-gym, sauna and steam room, is due to open in July 1997. *Rooms 100. Garden. Closed 25 & 26 Dec. Amex, Diners, MasterCard, VISA*

MALAHIDE   Siam Thai Restaurant   £50

Tel 01 845 4698 Fax 01 478 4798   Map 1 D3   **R**
Gas Lane Malahide Co Dublin

Thai food is unusual in Ireland and this neat restaurant close to the marina development has proved a winner; head chef Yupa Onsroi previously worked at *The Oriental Hotel* in Bangkok, so he brings an authentic touch to the subtleties of this popular Oriental cuisine. From a little bar in the reception area a pianist draws diners through into the quite large, impressively furnished, comfortable restaurant. 'Siam Combinations' includes a good choice of well-balanced, light starters: chicken satay with a crunchy peanut dip, whole prawns in a crisp, spicy coating, fresh and juicy spring rolls and crisp little deep-fried 'money-bags with a seafood filling, all with a spicy dip. The hotter side of Thai food can be experienced in *Thai tom yum gung*, a clear soup with whole prawns and a shock of chili providing a striking contrast to other dishes characterised by gentler, more aromatic flavours such as peanut, coconut or lemon grass. Green curry, a Thai signature dish, *(gaeng kiew wan nua)* is based on green curry paste, with coconut milk, peas and Thai herbs; this might mix well with *praew wan mu*, a sweet and sour pork dish with mixed vegetables, and *pla muak phad nam prik paow*, a spicy dish of stir-fried squid with onion, chilis and spring onion in chili oil. Thai noodles, fragrant rice and jasmine tea are the traditional accompaniments. Set menus are good examples of how to balance a Thai meal but tend to stick to the most popular dishes. The main impression is one of great freshness – the vegetables, for example, are all cooked to be just tender, but retaining plenty of bite. Desserts are never a high point, but Siam custard (rather like very sweet semolina) is a more authentic choice than the selection of bought-in ice creams and desserts on an illustrated menu. 10% service charge is added to the bill. *Seats 95. Parties 60. D only 6-12 (till 10 Sun). Set D from £17. Closed 25 & 26 Dec. Amex, Diners, MasterCard,* **VISA**

If you encounter bad service don't wait to write to us but make your feelings known to the management at the time of your visit. Instant compensation can often resolve any problem that might otherwise leave a bad taste.

MALAHIDE   Silks Restaurant   £45

Tel 01 845 3331   Map 1 D3   **R**
5 The Mall Malahide Co Dublin

Situated within smart premises – that include a floodlit miniature garden, with stream and bridge – this Chinese restaurant has become increasingly popular. Menus, including the special menus for given numbers in a group, give little away although one or two of the chef's specials look more than usually promising – but it's the sheer quality of the cooking, teamed with seamless service from charming staff, that explain this restaurant's great succcess. Taking an ordinary set menu, chicken or crabmeat sweetcorn soup, barbecued ribs, chicken satay, cantonese spring rolls with barbecue sauce all sound quite ordinary, yet chef Derek Sung breathes new life into these familiar dishes, a reminder of the reasons they are now so well known. Garlic prawns, Cantonese duck, beef with green pepper all tell the same story and, although certainly not Chinese, even desserts merit more than a casual glance. *Seats 90. Private Room 20. D only 6-12.30 (Sun 5-11). Closed Good Friday & 25-27 Dec. Set D from £19. Amex, Diners, MasterCard,* **VISA**

MALAHIDE   Places of Interest
Malahide Castle Tel 01 846 2516

MALLOW   **Longueville House**   78%   £144

Tel 022 47156   Fax 022 47459   Map 2 B5   **HR**
Mallow Co Cork

This imposing Georgian mansion was built in 1720 by ancestors of the O'Callaghan family who have run it with commendable warmth and informality as a country house hotel since 1969. It enjoys splendid views across the Blackwater Valley to the ruins of the original riverside castle below. Beautifully proportioned public rooms have fine plasterwork, antiques, gilt-framed portraits and mirrors yet somehow, despite the grandeur, still retain the relaxed atmosphere of a family home. A recently added wing has now mellowed enough to blend inconspicuously with the original building and, with the opening of The Oriental Room, a private dining-room richly decorated to an eastern theme, that phase of development was successfully completed in 1996. Some of the bedrooms in the new wing are very large, with two king-size beds for example, or a dressing room with space for an extra single bed for a child. Top-quality furnishings in classic country-house style are complemented by nice touches like bowls of fruit and bottles of local mineral water, all enhanced by impeccable housekeeping. Marbled bathrooms are finished to the highest standards – details vary according to the size and shape of the room, but the largest ones have twin basins and a separate shower as well as an over-bath shower; all are enhanced by outstanding attention to detail and there is generosity in quality and quantity of towels and toiletries. *Rooms 21. Garden, fishing, games room, snooker. Closed 22 Dec-late Feb. Amex, Diners, MasterCard,* **VISA**

Presidents' Restaurant   ★   £75

Decorated in a warm salmon shade that is equally suited to soft evening lighting or morning sunshine, details like the bright-hued ceiling lighten the rather serious atmosphere created by the restaurant's unique array of specially commissioned portraits of past presidents of Ireland. Elegantly appointed, the room – which has an original Turner conservatory for summer use at one end and a smaller 'smoking' dining-room at the other – provides a fitting setting for some of the finest food in Ireland (winner of our Irish Food Award for 1997). The recently-added wing has provided William O'Callaghan with a new and much larger kitchen, which is clearly inspirational. The outstanding quality of his ingredients gives this talented and dedicated young chef a head start: all are carefully sourced and many, including the lamb, beef, vegetables, fruit and salmon, are from their own farm, garden and river which, like the famous little vineyard, are the domaine of William's father, Michael. William's confidence and flair are clearly evident in both the seven-course Surprise Tasting Menu and the extensive dinner menu. The number of house specialities is growing by the season: first courses are still likely to include sveral of William's favourites like a dashing tian of crab and tomato with a horseradish cream sauce or a luscious ravioli of Castletownbere prawns with julienne of leek and an aromatic tomato sauce; their own very lightly home-smoked wild Blackwater river salmon, layered with a salad of leaves and herbs from their own garden and topped with crunchy deep-fried shredded potato, is a superb dish. Middle courses include outstanding soups -perhaps a light, clear chicken consommé with perfectly balanced spicing of ginger, chili and fresh coriander – or beautifully simple green salads with fresh herb vinaigrette. Main courses always include Longueville lamb, although the style is frequently varied and could equally well be roast leg with a gratin of turnips or roasted noisettes wrapped in herb stuffing and served with couscous; local Kilbrack pork also features along with fresh Blackwater salmon, free-range duck – perhaps with a ginger, tea and cinnamon sauce – and a catch of the day such as escalope of sea bass filled with a scallop and lemon balm mousse served with a spicy tomato sauce. Excellent desserts range from the sophistication of a long-established house speciality such as pyramid of chocolate with an orange sauce to the simplicity of apple tart with calvados ice cream. Proximity to the many cheese producers of west Cork means that farmhouse cheeses are especially dear to William's heart. Round all this off with teas or coffee and home-made petits fours served by the fireside in the drawing-room – but bear in mind that breakfast is another unmissable gastronomic occasion at Longueville, with a whole cooked ham and farmhouse cheeses on the buffet along with the likes of gooseberry compote fresh from the garden, freshly-baked scones and breads, home-made preserves, fresh fish or a traditional fry with home-made sausages, good bacon and black and white puddings made by the local butcher. Faultless service under the watchful eye of William's mother Jane or his wife Aisling is a perfect match for his fine food. *Seats 50. Parties 8. Private Room 14. D only 7-9. Set D £29. Light bar lunches 12.30-2.*

MALLOW   Places of Interest

Annes Grove Gardens Castletownroche Tel 022 26145
Doneraile Wildlife Park Tel 022 24244
Mallow Racecourse Mount Ruby Tel 062 51357

MAYNOOTH	Moyglare Manor	75%	£150

Tel 01 628 6351   Fax 01 628 5405   Map 2 C4   **HR**
Moyglare Maynooth Co Kildare

'Keep right at the church' is the instruction to visitors heading west through Maynooth and, a couple of miles further on, the neat hedges of the Manor appear on cue, followed by a pleasing tree-lined avenue leading up to this imposing Georgian house. Set in lovely gardens that give way to extensive parkland, with views of the Wicklow hills beyond, the interior is of a suitably grand scale to house owner Norah Devlin's ever-growing collection of antiques; a practical bonus is that no guest is likely to go unseated, no matter how busy the house may be – so if you relish a snooze in front of one of the numerous log fires you are unlikely to be disappointed. Spacious bedrooms are lavishly furnished in period style, some with four-poster or half-tester beds, and include a ground-floor suite; all have well-appointed bathrooms with quality appointments and good attention to detail. Television is only available in rooms on request, as peacefulness is the aim at Moyglare. No children under 12 (or dogs). *Rooms 16. Garden. Closed 24-27 Dec. Amex, Diners, MasterCard,* **VISA**

Restaurant   £80

Hotel manager Shay Curran personally supervises the formally appointed restaurant, which spreads through several interconnecting rooms; the middle rooms are nice and cosy for winter, while those overlooking the garden and countryside are particularly pleasant in fine weather. The grand and romantic setting is just the place for a special occasion, with traditional deep red walls providing a rich background for gilt-framed pictures and gleaming chandeliers. A nicely balanced combination of traditional favourites and sophisticated fare is attractively presented, with an emphasis on seafood and game in season. Starters range from chilled tomato soup and deep-fried Brie with tomato chutney to crab claws and shrimps in a Pernod and cream sauce. Dark, moist home-made bread is replenished automatically as required. In addition to a wide selection of fish – typically including poached sea bass with a shrimp and white wine sauce or fillet of brill with hollandaise – main courses include the likes of duckling (crisp-skinned and succulent, served off the bone with a classic orange sauce) and a brace of quail with Dijon mustard and cider vinaigrette. Pretty desserts (or farmhouse cheeses) are followed by plentiful cafetière coffee and home-made petit fours. Lunch menus offer less choice than dinner but are nevertheless quite formal and convey a sense of occasion. Very fine wine list. No smoking. *Seats 100. Parties 20. Private Room 50. L 12.30-2.15 D 7-9.30. Set D £27.50.*

MAYNOOTH   Places of Interest

Castletown House Celbridge Tel 01 628 8252.

Entries categorised as **JaB** are recommended for 'Just a Bite'.

MIDLETON	**Farmgate**	**£50**

Tel & Fax 021 632771   Map 2 B6   **R**
The Coolbawn Midleton Co Cork

Maróg O'Brien and Kay Harte have been delighting visitors to their lovely food shop and restaurant since 1984. Delicious home-baked breads, cakes and biscuits are served with morning coffee and afternoon tea, while more substantial snacks and main dishes are to be found on the lunch menu – open crab sandwich, perhaps, oysters, smoked bacon and mushroom baguette, or lamb burger with minted yoghurt and redcurrant sauce. More sophisticated offerings on weekend dinner menus might include warm salad of marinated chicken and chargrilled peppers, chili crabcakes with hollandaise and roast monkfish with rosemary, garlic and red pepper coulis. Kay Harte also runs a restaurant above the English Market in Cork. Outside seating for 20. *Seats 60. Meals 9am-5.30pm. L 12-4 D (Fri & Sat only) 7-9.45. Closed Sun, Bank Holidays, Good Friday & 25 Dec. MasterCard, **VISA***

MIDLETON	**Glenview House**	**£60**

Tel & Fax 021 631680   Map 2 B6   **A**
Ballinaclasha Midleton Co Cork

When Ken and Beth Sherrard bought their lovely Georgian house near Midleton in 1963 it was virtually derelict. Two years later, long before architectural salvage was the buzz word on every restoration job in the country, Ken bought the entire contents of the Dublin Georgian buildings infamously demolished to make way for the new ESB offices – and much of the interior of Glenview House, including the front door and bannisters which look as if they were made for the stairs, is the richer for that act of courage. Today it is hard to imagine it any other way than the well tended, comfortable and elegantly furnished house it now is, with a welcoming fire in the hall and two well-proportioned reception rooms on either side. Off the hall there is a bedroom suitable for wheelchair-users, with its own specially adapted bathroom and a door that provides access to a parking space directly outside. The other bedrooms are on the first floor, all comfortably furnished with en suite bathrooms (one has an old bath with a highly original and practical shower arrangement built in). Dinner (£18) for guests at this hospitable house is cooked by Beth and served at a communal table. For the 1997 season it is hoped to have a conservatory and barbecue area on a terraced lawn, where guests can make their own lunch. Picnic lunches (£5) provided on request. *Rooms 4. Garden, croquet, lawn tennis, forest walks. MasterCard, **VISA***

MIDLETON   Jameson Heritage Centre

Tel 021 613594 Fax 021 613642   Map 2 B6   **JaB**
Midleton Co Cork

This pleasant little restaurant area in the Jameson Heritage Centre offers
a sensibly restricted choice of simple home-made food – soups, salads,
ploughman's and a hot dish of the day (Irish stew, bacon and cabbage, chicken
and mushroom pie). Tempting home-made cakes, scones and jam with tea or
coffee. *Seats 60 (+12 outside). Food served 10am-5.30pm. Closed mid Oct-mid Apr
except for private parties (check for details). Amex, Diners, MasterCard,* **VISA**

MIDLETON   Midleton Park Hotel   68%   £80

Tel 021 631767 Fax 021 631605   Map 2 B6   **H**
Midleton Co Cork

This low-rise modern hotel close to the Jameson Heritage Centre has spacious
public areas and good facilities for exhibitions, conferences and functions of all
kinds. Bedrooms are all en suite, with TV, video, phone, hairdryer and trouser
press and include a 'presidential suite' for VIP guests; two rooms reserved for
non-smokers and one equipped for disabled guests. Banqueting/conferences 300.
Bistro 10am-10pm. Ample free parking. Children welcome – under-8s stay free
in parents' room (four family rooms); cots, extra beds, high-chairs, early evening
meal available by arrangement. ***Rooms** 40. Closed 25 Dec. Amex, Diners,
MasterCard,* **VISA**

MIDLETON   Places of Interest
Jameson Heritage Centre Tel 021 613594 *See entry above*

MONAGHAN   Andy's Bar & Restaurant

Tel 047 82277   Map 1 C2   **P/R**
12 Market Street Monaghan Co Monaghan

A strong local following underlines the merits of owner-chef Ciaran Redmond's
delightfully well-run bar in Monaghan town centre. In traditional Victorian
style, it's high-ceilinged with plenty of fine mahogany, comfortable high-backed
bar seats as well as stools and acres of bottles lined up against the mirror behind
the bar. Substantial bar meals include a range of midday specials on a blackboard:
soup of the day (hearty home-made vegetable broth), crisp, deep-fried breaded
fillets of plaice or lemon sole and tortelloni with a crunchy cheese topping.
Evening menus include the likes of home made paté with hot toast and salad,
chicken Kiev, steaks and a short children's menu. The upstairs restaurant offers
a more extensive range of Ciaran Redmond's good home cooking. Traditional
desserts like pavlova, lemon cheesecake, fresh fruit salad and home-made ices
are served from a trolley; look out for something comforting like a hot treacle
sponge pudding in cold weather. No food served on Sunday. *Seats 100 (Bar)
52 (Restaurant).* **Bar Food** *L 12-3.30 D 6-10.30. No food L Sun & D Mon. Set D £15.
Closed Good Friday, first 2 weeks July, 25 Dec. MasterCard,* **VISA**

We only recommend the food in hotels categorised as **HR** and **AR**.
However, the food in many **A** establishments throughout
Ireland is often very acceptable
(but the restaurant may not be open to non-residents).

MONAGHAN   Hillgrove Hotel   66%   £80

Tel 047 81288   Fax 047 84951   Map 1 C2   **H**
Old Armagh Road Monaghan Co Monaghan

Poised high on a hill on the edge of (and overlooking) Monaghan town, this very pleasant modern hotel was carefully planned to make the most of its location. A large foyer doubles as a lounge and reception area for the weddings and functions that form a major part of the hotel's business, while public rooms on the town side, including the bar, open on to their own terraces, creating a stylish, bright and airy atmosphere as well as capitalising on the view. Major refurbishment throughout has been undertaken since the hotel was taken over by the Quinn Group in 1994 and, although the overall effect is quite striking, the decor is not overpowering. Bedrooms include four suites and two designed for disabled guests as well as a rather splendid bridal suite complete with traditional four-poster, mini-bar and double jacuzzi bath. All rooms are en suite with above-average bathrooms and a good range of the usual modern facilities. De luxe rooms and suites are very spacious. Nice, helpful staff. Banqueting/conference facilities for up to 700/800. No dogs.
Rooms 44. Terrace, patio, disco. Amex, Diners, MasterCard, **VISA**

MONKSTOWN   The Bosun Bar & Restaurant   £55

Tel 021 842172   Fax 021 842008   Map 2 B6   **R/P**
Monkstown Co Cork

Handy to the Cobh car ferry, Nicky Moynihan's bright and cheerful waterside pub has a pleasantly nautical atmoshere that is only partly due to the decor – it also serves as a place of sustenance for teachers at the sailing school nearby and acts as an unofficial clubhouse to the local sailing fraternity after racing, so the maritime attributes are real enough. They take pride in the bar food here and a chef is available to cook fresh food at any time; seafood is the speciality – anything from chowder or crab claws through to real scampi and chips, but they'll also run to a good steak. Next to the bar there's a neat, comfortably furnished restaurant where dinner is served and also Sunday lunch, which is a big draw (booking essential). The choices, from a three-course set dinner or a full à la carte menu, are wide and include popular starters like crab claws in garlic butter, a really fresh prawn cocktail with lemon mayonnaise and glazed oak-smoked salmon with fresh chives and capers, all served with home-baked bread (although foil-wrapped butter portions are a let-down). Main courses include steaks, local duckling, baked pork tenderloin with Clonakilty black pudding and an apple and calvados cream, and a selection of seafood ranging from pan-fried brill with spinach, garlic and herb cream sauce, through exceptionally good fresh scampi with home-made tartare sauce to unusual options like marinated Atlantic Porbeagle shark in lemon juice and white wine, with a light saffron and dill sauce. Abundant vegetables are imaginative, flavoursome and carefully cooked. Puddings might include refreshing strawberries 'splashed with Irish Mist' and home-made ices, or you could finish with a selection of Irish farmhouse cheeses, served plated and in good condition, then coffee with chocolate mints. *Seats 80. Bar Food 10.30am-11pm. Restaurant Meals L 12-2.30 D 6.30-9.30. Set L £11.50 Set D £20. Closed Good Friday & 25 Dec. Set D £20. Amex, Diners, MasterCard,* **VISA**

Please note there are two places named **Monkstown**,
one in Co Cork and one in Co Dublin

MONKSTOWN   Coopers Restaurant   £50

Tel 01 284 2037
8a The Crescent Monkstown Co Dublin

Map 4 D1

R

Well-established restaurant in a characterful old building with eating areas spread between an upstairs room, downstairs wine bar, new patio and no-smoking rear conservatory. Offerings include fresh mussels with garlic, white wine and cream, chicken liver parfait with Cumberland sauce, grilled sea trout with a citrus and pink peppercorn dressing, roast duck with orange and ginger sauce and tiramisu or home-made ice cream. Further branches at 62 Lower Leeson Street (Tel 01 676 8615) and in Ballsbridge (Tel 01 660 1525), plus two franchised outlets in Kilternan (Tel 01 295 9349) and Greystones (Tel 01 287 3914). *Seats 100 (+ 16 on patio). Parties 12. Open L (Sun only) 12.-5 D 5-11. Closed L Mon-Sat, Good Friday & 1 week Christmas. Sun L £9.95. Amex, MasterCard,* **VISA**

We publish annually, so make sure you use the current edition
– it's well worth being up-to-date!

MONKSTOWN   Empress Restaurant   £60

Tel 01 284 3200   Fax 01 284 3188
Clifton Avenue Monkstown Co Dublin

Map 4 D1

R

Brother and sister Anita and Burt Tsang have run this luxuriously appointed first-floor restaurant just off Monkstown Crescent since 1992. Burt is the power in the kitchen, producing a range of Chinese menus – Szechuan, Shantung (Shandong) and Beijing – and also Thai cuisine, in set dinners that follow the familiar Oriental format (menus for two, three and four or more) and quite an extensive à la carte. Specialities include Beijing duck, carved at the table and served with fresh vegetables and hoi sin sauce on pancakes (24 hours' notice). A fair sprinkling of vegetarian options includes Thai soup (*tom pag*), Thai curry (*masaman mansawirat*) and a Chinese mixed-flavour hors d'oeuvre selection. Charming service under the direction of Anita Tsang attracts an automatic 10% supplement. *Seats 100. Parties 10. Private Room 60. D only 6-11.30. Set D from £16.50. Amex, Diners, MasterCard,* **VISA**

MONKSTOWN   FXB's

Tel 01 284 6187   Fax 01 284 5713
3 The Crescent Monkstown Co Dublin

Map 4 D1

JaB

This large, middle-market restaurant is owned by F.X. Buckley, the highly regarded Dublin butchers, so red meat is the thing here, especially steaks. Short à la carte and set lunch menus are offered alongside a blackboard of daily-changing specials (tomato and herb soup, roast poussin with a wild mushroom and soya sauce, pan-fried turbot with mange tout and hollandaise), most of which are also on offer at a second restaurant in Pembroke Street (in the centre of Dublin), which is slightly smaller but run on the same lines and under a common executive chef. You can also tuck into a one-pound T-bone steak and there are even larger steaks 'available on request', or maybe choose beefburger with fries, or chargrilled marinated chicken with side salad. Families are welcome and they offer a children's menu. *Seats 150. Open 12.30-11 (L 12.30-6 D 6.30-11, Sun to 10.30). Set L £9.95. Closed Good Friday, 25 & 26 Dec.*
Also at:
Pembroke Street Dublin 2 Tel 01 676 4606   Map 6 G2

MONKSTOWN   Purty Kitchen

Tel 01 284 3576   Map 4 D1   **P**
Old Dunleary Road Monkstown Co Dublin

Passers-by might be forgiven for thinking that this is the kind of pub that looks too good to be true. It was established in 1728, which makes it the second oldest pub in Dublin (after *The Brazen Head*) and the oldest in Dun Laoghaire. A new owner took over towards the end of last year, but chef Sheenagh Toal remains in the kitchen. Soothingly cool and dark within, it has plenty of tables dotted around for the comfortable consumption of food from a tempting bar menu that ranges from the usual soups and nibbles – chowder, garlic mussels, prawns in filo pastry – to deep-fried goat's cheese with plum sauce, open seafood sandwiches served on home-made brown bread, steak and even duck sandwiches (on home-made white bread) to full main courses such as fillet steak with pebble mustard and Jameson sauce, or even hot buttered lobster. Also seafood specialities like baked cocotte – a combination of fresh and smoked cod in a mushroom cream sauce topped with breadcrumbs – and black sole on the bone. Desserts range from perennial favourites like apple crumble and tangy, light lemon tart to seasonal specialities such as a very moreish chocolate roulade with fresh strawberries and cream. *Open 11am-11.30pm Mon-Sat (Sun 12-11).* *Bar Food 12.30-10. Closed Good Friday & 25 Dec. Amex, MasterCard,* **VISA**

MOONE   Moone High Cross Inn

Tel 0507 24112   Map 2 C4   **P**
Bolton Hill Moone Co Kildare

The Clynch family are the most welcoming of hosts, and their rambling 18th-century pub is up among the front-runners in the hospitality and home cooking stakes. Morning coffee, lunch, afternoon tea and evening meals are all available, and the menus are based on the best of ingredients, simply cooked and generously served. The lounge service menu (lunch every day) announces that Jacob sheep roam freely in the 16 acres around the inn – at their peril, perhaps, because they also appear inside as roasts; other favourites on the various menus include brown bread sandwiches with home-cooked meats or local Cheddar, vegetable soup, steaks, traditional bacon and cabbage, Irish stew and the grandmother of apple pies. A few more fish dishes (mussels, catch of the day, monkfish, salmon) have been added to the menu in the last year. Sunday lunch is a particularly popular occasion. There is a proper dining-room (but it is the bar food that has our recommendation here), but many visitors opt for a seat by the fire in the back bar, or a spot in the new beer garden. Children are very welcome "if supervised". Simple, comfortable country accommodation is offered in five en suite rooms (£50) above the pub. *Open 11-11.30 (Sun 12-2, 4-11).* *Bar Meals 11-10. Garden, outdoor eating. Closed Good Friday & 25 Dec.* *Accommodation 5 bedrooms, all en suite, £50. MasterCard,* **VISA**

MOUNTRATH   Roundwood House   58%   £70

Tel 0502 32120 Fax 0502 32711   Map 2 C4   **HR**
Mountrath Co Laois

A 'love it or loathe it' kind of place, with some visitors objecting to the very air of eccentricity which makes the majority of guests love Frank and Rosemarie Kennan's small, early Georgian Palladian villa enough to keep coming back for more. Don't expect curtains at your bedroom windows, but the big wooden shutters (correct for a house of this period) will be snugly closed while you communally enjoy Rosemarie's unpretentious good home cooking around a large polished mahogany table in their lovely dining-room. Old-fashioned bathrooms have all that is needed, including towels that are mismatched but plentiful, and like the rest of the house, lovely and warm; there will also be a hot water bottle tucked into your bed when you finally make it there. Frank is the host, dispensing pre-dinner drinks in front of the huge drawing room fire and letting guests in on the local scene. In the morning, guests wake to a chorus of birdsong from the surrounding woods and children, especially, will enjoy visiting the yard to see if there are any chicks or kittens around, or perhaps to collect a warm egg for breakfast. The original 17th-century courtyard house has been restored and houses four more bedrooms. Children under 2 stay free whilst under-12s pay 50% of tariff when sharing with their parents. No dogs. Stabling available. *Rooms 10. Garden, croquet. fishing, children's playroom. Closed 25 Dec. Amex, Diners, MasterCard,* **VISA**

Restaurant   £50

Non-residents can book for Sunday lunch (when separate tables are laid), or dinner if there is room. Rosemarie's food continues to make friends – lovely home cooking, from the Aga, is the norm. Roasts with fresh herbs, simple, lightly-cooked vegetables, gratins of potato (with more than a hint of garlic), farmhouse cheeses and a choice of wickedly gooey or wholesome desserts. Finish with coffee by the fireside. No children under 12 at dinner. *Seats 26. Parties 16. L (Sun only) 1.30 D 8 for 8.30pm. Set L Sun £12 Set D £20.*

MOUNTRATH   Places of Interest
Ballaghmore Castle Tel 0505 21453 *10 miles*
Damer House Roscrea Heritage Centre Tel 0505 21850 *16 miles*

| MOYARD | Rose Cottage | £32 |

Tel 095 41082   Fax 095 41112   Map 1 A3
Rockfield Moyard Co Galway   **A**

Situated on a working farm in a scenic location surrounded by the Twelve Bens mountains, this neat, attractive, cottage-style farmhouse is a pleasing blend of the old and the new and very much a family affair. Expect a warm welcome from Mary Shanley O'Toole or one of her family, simple but comfortable accommodation and good home cooking (especially baking) and you won't be disappointed. There's a sitting-room with open turf fire and television to relax in, in front of a dining-room for guests (separate tables) and six bedrooms, all with showers en suite, tea/coffee-making trays and hairdryers. Not suitable for children. No dogs. Nearby attractions include sandy beaches, scenic walks, bird watching, fishing, island trips, traditional Irish music, horse riding and golf. *Rooms 6. Closed Oct-end Mar. Amex, Diners, MasterCard,* **VISA**

| MOYCULLEN | Cloonnabinnia House Hotel | 63% | £70 |

Tel 091 555555   Fax 091 555640   Map 2 B4
Ross Lake Moycullen Co Galway   **HR**

Although the building is typical of the 1960s, landscaping has helped soften its hard edges and the views over Ross Lake are magical – but it's the warmth and genuine hospitality of the Kavanagh family that make a visit to this unpretentious hotel a memorable experience. The bar is Tommie's domain, equally appealing to locals and guests for its relaxing chat about fishing or, perhaps, a quiet game of draughts, while Norah Anne presides over other public areas (comfortably furnished with a homely mixture of new and old), the recently refurbished en suite bedrooms (with lovely views) and the kitchen. Function rooms (conferences 200/banquets 250) are downstairs, well away from residents and with a separate entrance. Children are made very welcome with three family rooms, cots available at no extra charge, under-9s allowed to stay free in their parents' room and a children's menu/early evening meal. Angling is a big attraction, and Tommie runs a purpose-built Angling Centre on site, providing everything from bait and boat hire to maps and freezing facilities. Several self-catering cottages are also available, with full access to hotel facilities. 16 new bedrooms are due to be completed in May 1997. *Rooms 14. Garden, game and coarse fishing, walking. Closed Nov-Easter. MasterCard,* **VISA**

The Ross Restaurant   £50

Norah Anne, previously a fish cookery demonstrator with BIM (Irish Fisheries Board), oversees the restaurant with its wonderful sunset views over the lake and makes good use of local produce, including home-grown herbs, wild watercress and hedgerow fruits in unpretentious, wholesome meals. Start, perhaps, with pan-fried Atlantic prawns served with a colourful seasonal salad and home-made breads, followed by roast rack of local Connemara lamb with a red wine and rosemary sauce and maybe a stir-fry of local vegetables, all rounded off with luscious desserts – an Irish whiskey coffee gateau perhaps, or a light, crisp, fresh fruit tartlet or some farmhouse cheeses. *Seats 50. Parties 20. D only 7-9.30.*

MOYCULLEN	Drimcong House Restaurant ★	£60

Tel 091 555115 Fax 091 555836   Map 2 B4   **R**
Moycullen Co Galway

Gerry Galvin, and his wife Marie have been running their renowned restaurant just west of Moycullen on the Galway-Clifden road since 1984, and it is still one of the most remarkable establishments in the country. Gerry's classical skills are put to the test nightly in inventive cooking based firmly on the best local ingredients, with the menu (priced for three, four or five courses) and the à la carte changing regularly to make best use of produce at its peak. The choice, remarkable for a small restaurant, also includes a five-course vegetarian menu (£18.95), a limited-choice, three-course Budget menu (£17.50) and, unusually for any leading restaurant (but typical of a chef who has established a special reputation for encouraging the young), a special three-course menu "for pre-teenage people" (£9.50). There is ample time to inwardly digest the menus in the comfortable, book-strewn bar before moving through to the oak-polished formality of a dining-room that overlooks gardens on two sides. A typical evening's offerings might include game terrine with orange salad or Drimcong paella, followed by a choice of soup or sorbet, while main courses may include roast stuffed pork with rowanberry sauce or baked chicken breast with herb mousse and broccoli sauce – and fish of the day, fresh from the boat. A la carte options might extend to lobster sausage and peach chutney or baked scallops in shellfish cream to start, with main courses like grilled beef sirloin with savoury butter to follow. Tempting desserts like caramelised berry and lemon mousse or warm orange pudding with sweet geranium sauce. Always an excellent Irish farmhouse cheeseboard, served with home-baked biscuits. The manageable wine list that dips into countries not always represented (eg Hungary, Greece and Portugal), is fairly priced with several bottles under £15. *Seats 50. Private Room 32. D only 6.30-10.30. Closed Sun, Mon & 22 Dec-mid Mar. Set D £21/£23/£24. Amex, Diners, MasterCard,* **VISA**

MOYCULLEN   Moycullen House   £70

Tel & Fax 091 555566
Moycullen Co Galway

Map 2 B4

A

Originally a sporting lodge – built in the arts and crafts style at the beginning of the century and still featuring the original iron locks and latches on solid oak doors – Moycullen House is above the village (on the Moycullen-Spiddal road), overlooking Lough Corrib and set peacefully in 30 acres of rhododendrons and azaleas, with its own supply of pure spring water. Spacious, antique-furnished bedrooms all have private baths and the residents' sitting-room and dining-room have period fireplaces with cheering log fires. No children under 7 (or dogs). *Rooms 5 (2 large, suitable for families). Garden. Closed Nov-end Feb. Amex, MasterCard,* **VISA**

MOYCULLEN   White Gables Restaurant   £60

Tel 091 555744 Fax 091 556004
Moycullen Village Co Galway

Map 2 B4

R

Right on the main street of Moycullen, chef Kevin Dunne and his wife Anne have attracted a growing following since opening this attractive cottagey restaurant in 1991. Well-appointed, with thick walls providing cosy insulators from traffic noise as well as inclement weather, the open stonework, low lighting, candlelight (even at lunchtime) and soothing away-from-it-all atmosphere create a fitting setting for Kevin's well-balanced menus. Start, perhaps, with a clear beef consommé, fresh mussels steamed in white wine, both served with excellent home-made brown bread and scones. Main courses of John Dory with a lemon and leek sauce, escalopes of veal with marsala sauce, and fresh lobster from their tank (poached, grilled or thermidor) come with a generous and imaginative vegetable selection. Good ices, soft fruit in season, aromatic coffee. *Seats 45. Parties 12. L (Sun only) 12.30-3 D 7-10. Set L Sun £11.95 D £19.50. Closed Mon (end Sep-Jun) & 23 Dec-14 Feb. Amex, Diners, MasterCard,* **VISA**

MOYDOW   The Vintage   £45

Tel & Fax 043 22122
Moydow Co Longford

Map 1 C3

R

Former cookery teacher Regina Houlihan has developed The Vintage bar into quite a catering enterprise, looking after both local functions and serving Sunday lunch, and dinner four nights a week (nightly May-Sep). The four-course Sunday lunch may be a kiwi and melon cocktail followed by home-made soup, then roast rib of beef, and a pudding to follow. The dinner menu offers a reasonable choice, possibly including fresh crab salad, roast calf's sweetbreads, stuffed salmon with a prawn sauce, and scallops and monkfish with a lemon and dill sauce. A la carte dishes are also available: tempura of seafood with basil and garlic, roast rack of lamb with creamed leeks, and fresh vegetables in filo pastry with a tomato and basil sauce. Garden, outdoor eating. Children's menu and portions available. *Seats 40. Parties 10. L (Sun only) 1-5 D 7-10.30. Set Sun L £9.95 Set D £18.95. Closed Mon-Wed (Oct-Apr), Good Friday & 25 Dec. Amex, MasterCard,* **VISA**

MOYDOW   Places of Interest

Carriglass Manor Tel 043 45165 *6 miles*

MULLINGAR   Crookedwood House   £55

Tel 044 72165 Fax 044 72166   Map 1 C3   **RR**
Crookedwood Mullingar Co Westmeath

Noel and Julie Kenny's lovely Georgian rectory overlooking Lough Derravaragh continues to develop amd improve. Not only do we recommend the food in the characterful white-washed basement restaurant but also the excellent accommodation. A promising sense of confidence is immediately noticeable in the comfortable bar, where aperitifs are served by a fire; making a choice might well be hard as almost everything on Noel's strongly seasonal menus sounds irresistible. In addition to well-sourced local produce he uses wild food from the fields and woodlands around the house in dishes like grilled breast of wood pigeon with blackberry and port sauce. Local poultry, especially free-range duck, frequently features and their seafood is excellent (trio of salmon, sole and scallops with fresh basil, or monkfish on a bed of roasted peppers); vegetarians are always well looked after. However, it is Noel's meat cooking – notably using local Mullingar beef in dishes like pan-fried medallions of fillet steak with rösti and whiskey sauce or sirloin with traditional colcannon and a mead and tarragon sauce – that is probably most popular; for this reason Crookedwood House won our Irish Beef Award last year. Noel has been heard to remark that it would be more than his life is worth to open for Sunday lunch without roast beef on the menu. Game in season is also very much a speciality, particularly venison dishes (goulash is now almost a signature dish or grilled venison served with a compote of fruit and juniper berry sauce). Irish farmhouse cheeses or simple, yet lovely, desserts (caramel parfait, crème brulée) are followed by freshly-brewed coffee served with home-made petit fours. 3-course early bird menu (Tue-Fri 6.30-7.30). Service, under Julie's watchful eye, is prompt and friendly. *Seats 35. Parties 14. Private Room 25. L (Sun only) 12.30-2.30 D 6.30-10. Closed D Sun, all Mon, L Tue-Sat, 24-27 Dec. Set Sun L £13.50 Set D £13.95 (early bird) & £21. Amex, Diners, MasterCard, VISA*

Accommodation   £90
A carefully designed wing of the house provides excellent accommodation in eight spacious, individually designed en suite bedrooms, all with direct-dial telephone and TV. There are lovely country views from the rooms, three of which are non-smoking and one is suitable for disabled guests; some have doors leading on to a little fenced patio that overlooks the lough. Nice touches include complimentary mineral water and quality toiletries. Residents' parking is provided in an enclosed yard at the back of the house, beside a separate entrance that leads into a comfortable reception/lounge area with direct access to the restaurant. Good breakfasts include freshly-baked breads and home-made preserves. No dogs. *Rooms 8. Garden, croquet, tennis, basketball.*

MULLINGAR   Places of Interest
Tourist Information Tel 044 48650
Tullynally Castle and Gardens Castlepollard Tel 044 61159 *16 miles*

MULRANY   Rosturk Woods   £55

Tel & Fax 098 36264   Map 1 A3   **A**
Rosturk Mulrany Co Mayo

It is only on close examination that the first-time visitor realises that this attractive traditional house in a lovely shoreside location between Westport and Achill is recently built, so well does it fit into its snug wooded setting and so convincingly do the recycled building materials deceive. The result in this comfortable and welcoming family home is an ideal combination of new and old, an unusually successful marriage of convenience and style which pervades reception rooms and thoughtfully planned, imaginatively decorated bedrooms and en suite bathrooms alike. Children are welcome (free up to 4 in parents' room), there's a cot provided at no extra charge, high-chairs are available and children's early evening meals in the kitchen from 5-7pm. No dogs. *Rooms 4. Garden. Closed Christmas. No credit cards.*

NAAS   Fletcher's

Tel 045 897328   Map 2 C4   **P**
Commercial House Naas Co Kildare

A characterful pub that's well worth a visit just for the interest of being there. Opened in 1930 by Tom Fletcher's father, it's a very old-fashioned place, a long, narrow hall, broken up into sections in the traditional way with a mahogany divider complete with stained-glass panels. Having escaped the scourge of modernisation, Fletcher's remains somewhat austere and masculine: the plain wooden floor and very long mahogany bar with its full complement of built-in drawers and shelves behind is softened by the occasional aspidistra in an old cachepot. The back room was being done up as we went to press. Masculine – and adult, too: only well-supervised children in the bar. *Open 10.30-11.30 (Sunday 12.30-2, 4-11). Closed Good Friday & 25 Dec. No credit cards.*

NAAS   The Manor Inn

Tel 045 897471   Map 2 C4   **P**
Main Street Naas Co Kildare

The Manor Inn offers warmth, hospitality and good food within well modernised surroundings. Local interest is reflected in pictures and mementos connected with horses and the army base at the nearby Curragh, car racing at Mondello (note the clock in a racing helmet) and there's a clutter of notices giving due warning of upcoming local events. The menu available throughout both bar and restaurant offers a wide variety of familiar pub fare, from sandwiches, salads and omelettes to pasta, burgers, pies, grills, ribs, chicken wings and steaks. High-chairs and a menu of children's favourites are provided. *Open 12-11.30 (to 11 winter), Sun 12.30-11. Bar Food 12-10.30 (Sun from 12.30). Closed Good Friday & 25 Dec. Amex, Diners, MasterCard, VISA*

NAAS   Places of Interest
Naas Racecourse Tel 045 97391
Punchestown Racecourse Naas Tel 045 97704

NAVAN   Ardboyne Hotel   60%   £78

Tel 046 23119 Fax 046 22355   Map 1 C3   **HR**
Dublin Road Navan Co Meath

A friendly, well-run modern hotel standing in its own grounds on the outskirts of town. Bedrooms, all with compact tiled bathrooms, are simple and practical, with fitted furniture and good desk/dressing table space. There's a bright, comfortable lounge and a warm, convivial bar. All-day snacks are available in the bar/foyer area. Children are more than welcome, and under-12s can stay free in their parents' room. *Rooms 27. Garden, disco (Fri & Sat). Amex, Diners, MasterCard, VISA*

Terrace Restaurant   £55

Simple, straightforward dishes – prawns provençale, wiener schnitzel, shish kebab, sirloin steak – are the order of the day here. In addition to the à la carte and table d'hote menus there's a budget Tourist menu at night and, from 5.30 till about 7.30 (all evening on Sunday), there's an à la carte high tea menu. Sweets from the buffet. *Seats 97. Private Room 50. L 12.30-3 D 6.30-10.30 (Sun till 9). Set L £12.50 Set D £13.50 & £18.95.*

NAVAN — Hudson's Bistro — £50

Tel 046 29231   Map 1 C3   **R**
Railway Street Navan Co Meath

Richard and Tricia Hudson's lively little restaurant has attracted a strong local following. Stylish, informal decor provides just the right setting for Richard's modern magpie cooking style, which is offically described as Cal-Ital but other influences are also creeping in, with a Mexican dish here and a Thai one there. From an à la carte menu enlivened by daily blackboard specials, expect starters like gambas pil-pil ('shrimp fried in lotsa chili oil and garlic') alongside 'Mediterranean palate' (houmus, tapénade, pesto dips with tomato bread) and hot main dishes such as Cajun chicken, saffron fettuccine (with prawns or chick peas) and *gung chup bang tod* – deep-fried tiger prawns with chinese egg noodles, a rouille dip and a Thai hot and sour dip. Irish ingredients are also used to good advantage in daily-changing soups, pigeon salad, smoked mackerel paté (served traditionally with horseradish and lemon) and simple chargrilled steaks and salmon. Tricia heads up a willing waiting team, well able to cope with the crush and buzz. At the time of going to press plans were afoot to convert the first floor into a tapas/wine bar for lunches and evening overflow. *Seats 40. Parties 8. D only 6.30-10.45. Closed Mon (except Bank Holidays), Good Friday & 24-26 Dec. Amex, Diners, MasterCard,* **VISA**

NAVAN   Places of Interest
Hill of Tara Tel 046 25903
Navan Racecourse Tel 046 21350
Butterstream Garden Trim Tel 046 36017

NEW QUAY — Linnane's Bar

Tel 065 78120   Map 2 B4   **P**
New Quay Burrin Co Clare

This unassuming country pub has sliding doors at the back, which open virtually on to the rocks in summer and bring the magnificent seascape beyond right inside. In winter, it is inward-looking, as visitors (who may have had difficulty finding it if, as sometimes happens, gales have blown down local road signs) cluster round the peat fire. It has rightly attracted attention for the quality of its seafood: in addition to luxury lobster there's plenty (less in winter) of good but less expensive fare at Linnane's: a steaming bowl of chowder, perhaps, served with brown bread; steamed clams in garlic butter or a huge crab salad, the plate burgeoning with the white meat of a pair of crabs. *Open 12-11.30 (Sun to 11, Nov, Jan & Feb 5-11 and usual hours weekends).* **Bar Food** *12-9 (no food weekdays Nov-Mar except by arrangement). MasterCard,* **VISA**

NEWBAWN — Cedar Lodge — 62% — £78

Tel 051 428386   Fax 051 428222   Map 2 C5   **H**
Carrigbyrne Newbawn Co Wexford

14 miles from Wexford on the main Rosslare-Waterford road, this family-run hotel stands in lush countryside beneath the slopes of Carrigbyrne Forest. Redbrick walls, wooden ceilings and open fires create a warm and welcoming atmosphere in the public rooms and paintings and frescos by local artists provide interesting focal points. Bedrooms are practical and neatly appointed, featuring direct-dial telephones, TVs and spacious bathrooms. Conference/function suite for up to 100 in adjoining low-rise wing. No dogs. *Rooms 28. Garden. Closed Dec & Jan. MasterCard,* **VISA**

NEWBAWN   Places of Interest
John F Kennedy Arboretum Tel 051 388171

NEWBAY   Newbay Country House   £70

Tel 053 42779   Fax 053 46318   Map 2 D5
Newbay nr Wexford Co Wexford   **A**

A comfortable family-run country house dating from 1822 but incorporating
earlier outbuildings. The outside impression is a touch stern, but the atmosphere
within is very warm and relaxed. Day rooms are of imposing proportions, with
interesting antiques, amply-sized country furniture and displays of dried flowers
arranged by Mientje (Min) Drum. Bedrooms are spacious, comfortable and
individually furnished with four-poster beds but without TVs or phones. Paul
Drum's four-course £25 set dinners (for residents only) are served at one large
table for communal dining. The house is situated 2 miles from Wexford and not
far from the ferry port of Rosslare. No dogs. *Rooms 6. Garden. Closed 2 weeks
Christmas. Amex, Diners, MasterCard,* **VISA**

NEWBRIDGE   Hotel Keadeen   69%   £90

Tel 045 431666   Fax 045 434402   Map 2 C4
Curragh Road Newbridge Co Kildare   **H**

Just a mile from the Curragh racecourse and 25 miles from Dublin (leave the
M7 at exit 10, not before, and follow signs to Newbridge), the hotel is set in
eight acres of landscaped gardens. An indoor pool and health and fitness club
with a Grecian theme has just opened, complementing the existing conference
facilities (up to 600 for banqueting) and decent bedrooms; the latter are furnished
in a variety of styles and all offer up-to-date amenities including satellite TV.
No dogs. *Rooms 37. Garden, indoor swimming pool, children's splash pool, gym,
aerobics studio, sauna, steam room, spa bath, sun beds. Amex, Diners, MasterCard,*
VISA

> The Egon Ronay Guides are completely independent.
> We do not accept advertising, hospitality or payment
> from any of the establishments listed in this Guide.

NEWBRIDGE   The Red House Inn   £55

Tel 045 431516/431657   Fax 045 31934   Map 2 C4
Newbridge Co Kildare   **R**

Despite its location just off the Naas dual carriageway, this cosy inn has a
surprisingly away-from-it-all atmosphere, notably in the very pleasant olde-worlde
bar area and the conservatory and garden at the back. Long-serving staff include
restaurant manager Tom Tinsley and chef Willie Ryan who have been in tandem
here since 1980, presenting traditional food appropriate to the well-appointed
dining-room. From a balanced menu, a typical meal might begin with fresh
asparagus or black pudding dijonnaise among six or so starters, then two soups
or sorbets, followed by a good choice of fresh fish (perhaps monkfish Crécy or
brill bonne femme) and meat main courses. Vegetarian options are always given,
freshly-baked scones are on the table, simple vegetables are crisp and colourful,
and popular desserts include good home-made ices. *Seats 70. (+ 20 in garden).
Parties 14. Private Room 40. L (Sun only) 12.30-2.30 D 6.30-10.15. Closed D Sun,
all Mon & 1st 2 weeks Jan. Set L £12.50 Set D £21.50. Amex, Diners, MasterCard,*
VISA

NEWBRIDGE   Places of Interest

Emo Court and Gardens Emo Tel 0502 26110 *10 miles*
Irish National Stud Tully Tel 045 521251 *5 miles*
Japanese Gardens Tully Tel 045 521617 *5 miles*

NEWMARKET-ON-FERGUS   Clare Inn Hotel   64%   £100

Tel 061 368161   Fax 061 368622   Map 2 B4   **H**
Dromoland Newmarket-on-Fergus Co Clare

Outstanding leisure facilities are provided at the modern, low-rise Clare Hotel, which stands in the middle of Dromoland's 18-hole golf course (£17 green fee). The leisure centre (free to guests; children under 16 must be accompanied, no children after 6pm) includes a fully-equipped gym, and deep-sea fishing can be arranged from the hotel's catamaran, the *Liscannor Star*. The Castlefergus Bar, with weekend entertainment, is a good place to unwind, and there are residents' lounges, two restaurants and a children's playroom (Jun-Sep). Bedrooms are of a decent size, most of them suitable for family occupation. Children up to 4 are accommodated free (5-10s £13, 11-16s £16) prices include B&B and high tea. No dogs. Conference facilities for up to 400. Nine miles from Shannon Airport on the main Limerick/Galway road. ***Rooms 121. Garden, indoor swimming pool, children's splash pool, gym, sauna, steam room, solarium, tennis, pitch & putt, crazy golf, croquet, lawn bowling, outdoor draughts & chess, children's playroom. Amex, Diners, MasterCard, VISA***

NEWMARKET-ON-FERGUS Dromoland Castle Hotel 81%   £239

Tel 061 368144 Fax 061 363355   Map 2 B4   **HR**
Newmarket-on-Fergus Co Clare

Just a short distance from Shannon airport, this fairy-tale castle dates back to the 16th century and is set in 370 acres of beautifully maintained grounds and parkland that include a delightful walled garden and a championship golf course. Public rooms throughout the castle are notable for their height and grandeur, with fine plasterwork, crystal chandeliers and rich fabrics all contributing to an overall sense of majestic style. Yet, despite its undoubted grandeur, this magnificent place has a surprisingly relaxed and friendly atmosphere; far from intimidating, its magnificently broad, comfortably furnished corridors beckon the visitor to sit, admire the antiques, family portraits and old stonework and be charmed by the scent of woodsmoke wafting through the building. The castle was once part of the estate of the O'Briens, direct descendants of Brian Boru, High King of Ireland so it is appropriate that the conference centre, purpose-built to fit in with the castle and including a great hall, gallery, boardroom and business centre, should now be named after the king. Bedrooms inevitably vary in size and outlook due to the age and geography of the building but, although some rooms are approached down long corridors (and in some cases stairs as well), the refurbishment programme that has been in progress for some years is now complete and all rooms have now been brought up to the standard that would be expected of a hotel in this class. The best rooms are very impressive, with lovely views of the lake or grounds, and have magnificent marbled bathrooms; all are beautifully appointed, with the best of furniture and fabrics, quality bed linen and a host of extras including robes and slippers, mineral waters, a good range of toiletries and even complimentary miniature of Irish Mist liqueur. High standards of housekeeping and service are overseen by General Manager Mark Nolan, who is also closely involved in the next stage of development at Dromoland, namely the new leisure centre which was currently under construction as we went to press and expected to be in full swing in time for the 1997 season.

Children up to 12 may stay free in their parents' room. The off-season tariff is almost £100 less than the high-season rate that we quote. No dogs. *Rooms 73. Garden, croquet, tennis, golf (18), putting green, riding, fishing, hair salon, games room, boutique. Amex, Diners, MasterCard,* **VISA**

The Earl of Thomond Room ★ £95

Orders are taken in the library bar, which overlooks the eighth green of the golf course, then diners move through to the most beautiful room in the castle: The Earl of Thomond Room is high-ceilinged and elegant, with lovely plasterwork, rich fabrics and gold leaf against soft pastel walls, gilt-framed mirrors and pictures. All this plus crisp linen, fine china, gleaming crystal, fresh flowers and, in the evenings, gentle background music by a traditional Irish harpist, provide the perfect setting for meals with a real sense of occasion – and Head Chef David McCann is well up to providing food to match the surroundings. Previously at *The Connaught* hotel in London and now in his second season at Dromoland, David McCann is clearly heading up an outstanding team that is well supported by superb service under restaurant manager Tony Frisby. A range of evening menus includes a five-course table d'hote, a vegetarian menu, a special Taste of Ireland meal and an à la carte. Although the styling may be contemporary, David McCann's greatest strengths are classical: take a simple pork and chicken liver terrine, for example, served with a scrumptious little apple and prune chutney – it will not only be beautifully presented, but have real depth of flavour and interest of texture to match; other typical starters might include cappuccino of west coast seafood with a leek and chive bouillon, a frothy-topped soup cup of delightful contrasts with pieces of fish (salmon, monkfish, hake, a large prawn and some mussels) in a deliciously light, green-flecked broth. Irresistible home-baked breads are offered. Main courses might include a pavé of salmon, seared skin uppermost, on a nage of vegetables or with a tomato and lemon 'beurre nantais' and grilled fillet of Irish beef with a confit of stuffed new potatoes and tomato salsa. Quite elaborate, carefully planned individual vegetable garnishes for each dish are balanced by simple, perfectly cooked side vegetables. But it's the desserts that steal the show: for example, a lovely chocolate and Baileys mousse, topped by a 'tortured willow' of spun sugar and surrounded by colourful fruit coulis 'teardrops' in chocolate frames; best of all is 'Dromoland's Assortment Dessert Plate' (winner of our Ireland 1997 Dessert of the Year award): a 'horn of plenty' tuile with jewel-like soft fruits (perhaps including wild strawberries) tumbling out, a pyramid of marbled chocolate concealing a surprise dark chocolate mousse within a white one, a creamy vanilla ice with dark chocolate pieces through it, all beautifully presented with a garnish of exotic fruits. A fine selection of Irish and Continental cheeses is also served, from a trolley; aromatic freshly-brewed coffee or tea and home-made petits fours to finish. There are some rather naughty prices on the predominantly French wine list, though there is a nod to the New World with some new arrivals from Australia and New Zealand. No children under 12 after 8pm. No smoking. At lunchtime there is a more limited à la carte and a three-course 'chef's suggested lunch'; at the time of going to press it was expected that lunch would be served in the new leisure centre restaurant (The Fig Tree, closed Nov-Jan). 15% service charge is added to all food and beverage (except inclusive Sun lunch £16.50). *Seats 100. Parties 10. Private Rooms 24 & 60. L 12.30-2 D 7.30-9.30. Set L £16.50 Set D £29.50/£34 & £45.*

NEWPORT   Newport House   67%   £138

Tel 098 41222   Fax 098 41613   Map 1 A3   **HR**
Newport Co Mayo

A creeper-clad Georgian house stands in large gardens adjoining the town and overlooking the Newport river and quay – an unusual location for one of the most attractive and hospitable country houses in Ireland, run by Kieran and Thelma Thompson. Fishing is the major attraction, with salmon and sea trout fishing on the river and nearby loughs. Golf, riding and pony trekking are also available locally, but the appeal of the house itself with its beautiful central hall and sweeping staircase (clad in a hand-woven McMurray carpet from Connemara) and gracious drawing room is enough to draw guests without sporting interests. Bedrooms, like the rest of the house, are furnished in style with antiques and fine paintings and come with bathrooms which can be eccentric but work well; most of the rooms are in the main house, a few are around the courtyard. No dogs. The day's catch is weighed and displayed in the hall and a cosy fisherman's bar provides the perfect venue for reliving the day's sport. *Rooms 18. Garden, sea & game fishing, snooker. Closed 7 Oct-18 Mar. Amex, Diners, MasterCard,* **VISA**

Restaurant   £75

A high-ceilinged dining-room overlooking the gardens and decorated in restrained period style provides an elegant setting for John Gavin's confident cooking, based on the best of local produce, much of it coming from the organically-worked walled kitchen garden. courgette flower stuffed with mousseline of sole with a tomato and basil sauce makes a perfect starter on the six-course dinner menu, followed by soup (cold summer fruit or cream of mushroom) and, perhaps, steamed fillet of turbot with julienne of vegetables and a saffron sauce or noisettes of lamb with garlic, rosemary, shallots and red wine sauce. Oysters (either *au naturel* or baked Rockefeller) are usually offered as an additional course (£5-£6 extra). Vegetables and salads are as fresh as it is possible to be and there's a choice of farmhouse cheeses or a fine dessert menu (rhubarb tartlet with fruit coulis and vanilla sauce, frozen lemon cream) to finish. Fabulous French wines, including many exceptional vintage clarets, on the list, and a little bit of this and that from elsewhere. Prices are pretty fair throughout, and there's a good selection of house recommendations. No smoking in the dining-room. *Seats 38. Parties 10. D only 7.30-9.30. Set D £30.*

OUGHTERARD   Connemara Gateway Hotel   66%   £110

Tel 091 552328   Fax 091 552332   Map 1 B3   **H**
Oughterard Co Galway

Originally a typical 60s' motel, the Connemara Gateway has been cleverly extended and developed to make the discreetly stylish modern building it is today. Warmth, comfort and a relaxed atmosphere are the keynotes and, although the decor is generally low-key, the work of local artists, including impressive wallhangings on Celtic themes in the reception area, create a nice feeling of continuity – an idea successfuly developed in the cosy bar, which is based on a rural agricultural theme and has a welcoming turf fire – definitely a cut above the average modern hotel bar. Rooms vary considerably in age and appointments, but local tweed is used to advantage in most and the emphasis is on homely comforts such as properly organised tea and coffee facilities; similarly, bathrooms, although variable, have nice touches like hanging space for guests' hand laundry. Family facilities include an indoor swimming pool, children's entertainment in high season, and high teas (5.30pm) and videos (7pm) every evening. Bicycle hire, golf and riding nearby. Banqueting/conference facilities for up to 150. No dogs. *Rooms 62. Garden, croquet, indoor swimming pool, sauna, solarium, tennis, children's playroom & playground, games room, snooker. Closed Dec-17 Feb (except 29 Dec-2 Jan). Amex, Diners, MasterCard, VISA*

OUGHTERARD   Currarevagh House   65%   £103

Tel 091 552313   Fax 091 552731   Map 1 B3   **AR**
Oughterard Co Galway

Harry and June Hodgson, the fifth generation of Hodgsons at Currarevagh have for nearly 30 years been practising the art of the old-fashioned hospitality at their Victorian manor house set in parkland, woods and gardens by Lough Corrib. Day rooms are homely and traditional, and the drawing room is a perfect setting for afternoon tea. Bedrooms are peaceful, with no phones or TV. The hotel has sporting rights over 5000 acres and fishing facilities that include boats and ghillies. *Rooms 15. Garden, croquet, tennis, fishing, mooring, swimming in the lake, hotel boats. Closed Nov-Mar (except for parties by arrangement). No credit cards.*

Restaurant   £50

A succulent meat dish is the centrepiece of no-choice, six-course dinners prepared by June Hodgson from the pick of local produce. That dish might be confit of duck with cassis sauce, haunch of venison with cranberry sauce or roast Irish beef with Yorkshire pudding and horseradish sauce. Preceding it could be poached Corrib trout and tomato and orange soup, with a pears in lime custard or baked Alaska, Irish cheeses (with home-made biscuits, the bread is home-baked too) and coffee to complete a really satisfying meal. No smoking. Snack lunches. 10% service charge added to final bill. *Seats 28. D only at 8. Set D £19.50.*

OUGHTERARD   Powers

Tel 091 552712   Map 1 B3   **P**
The Square Oughterard Co Galway

Despite its picturesque exterior, unchanged for 180 years, this little thatched pub in the middle of Oughterard is a genuine 'local'. The previous owners had it in the family for a century and a half and, when Frank O'Meara took over in 1990 after it had been disused for a decade, he was determined that the oldest pub in the town should retain its character. There's a big open fire in the original front bar in winter and traditional Irish music at weekends. Children are welcome if supervised. No food. *Pub open 10.30-11.30 (to 11 in winter), Sun 12.30-2.30, 4-11 all year). Closed Good Friday & 25 Dec. No credit cards.*

OUGHTERARD   Sweeney's Oughterard House   59%   £116

Tel 091 552207   Fax 091 552161   Map 1 B3   **H**
Oughterard Co Galway

Unobtrusive newer extensions do not detract from the old-fashioned charm of this 200-year-old hotel just across the road from a particularly pretty stretch of the Owenriff River. The cottagey impression extends to cosy public rooms, furnished with antiques, and well manicured lawns providing a perfect setting for tea on sunny afternoons. Bedrooms, where under-12s may stay free with their parents, vary considerably in size and appointments. *Rooms 20. Garden. Closed 22 Dec-15 Jan. Amex, Diners, MasterCard, VISA*

OUGHTERARD   Places of Interest

Tourist Information Tel 091 82808
Aughnanure Castle Tel 091 82214

OYSTERHAVEN   Finders Inn   £70

Tel & Fax 021 770737   Map 2 B6   **R**
Nohoval Oysterhaven Co Cork

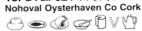

Situated snugly in a row of converted stone cottages, this attractive family-run
restaurant has an easy charm with its quirkily decorated bar and series of antique-
filled dining-rooms – an ambience many would find irresistible without a pick
of food. But food there is, in plenty – chef Rory McDonnell, together with his
brother Cormac, offers generous, traditional menus, made special through the
quality of ingredients – seafood comes straight from the fishing boats and all of
the vegetables are organically grown. Local seafood takes pride of place in dishes
like seafood chowder, warm oysters with a hot cucumber and butter sauce, fresh
lobster, and plaice stuffed with crab with a Chablis sauce, but carnivores take
consolation in rack of lamb with tarragon sauce or succulent roast duckling with
sage sauce. Finish with a plate of local farmhouse cheeses, perhaps, or a simply-
presented dessert (home-made ices are good) and an aromatic cup of coffee.
*Seats 40. Private Rooms 10/16/34. D only 7-9.30 (Sat to 10). Closed Sun (except
July & Aug & Bank Holiday weekends), 25 Dec & Bank Holidays. Amex, Diners,
MasterCard, **VISA***

Set menu prices may not include service or wine.
Our guide price for two diners includes wine and service.

OYSTERHAVEN   The Oystercatcher   £65

Tel & Fax 021 770822   Map 2 B6   **R**
Oysterhaven Belgooly nr Kinsale Co Cork

Established in 1989, Bill and Sylvia Patterson's delightful, antique-filled waterside
cottage restaurant has much to recommend it. Although the cooking style is
perhaps a little less flamboyant than it was in the earlier days, it is none the
worse for that – if anything, the food is even better these days and the place has
certainly lost none of its considerable charm. There are no fundamental changes
on a menu that offers generous choices for all courses and reflects Bill's classical
tendencies. Pheasant breast is flambéed with calvados and served with roast
apples, lamb fillet is presented with a sauce of cepes and Puy lentils, and
increasing respect is paid to local ingredients: the celebrated 'Ummera' smoked
products are credited in a dish of wild oak-smoked salmon with lemon buttered
oysters. House specialities include 'The Oystercatcher Celebrated Oyster Sausage'
– a single, large sausage that tastes of the sea and is served on a pool of saffron
sauce – and fresh local lobster flambéed in cognac and served on a bed of pasta
with a garlic, tomato and tarragon sauce. Main courses on the seasonally-
changing menus kick off with seafood choice, perhaps monkfish tempura with
lime kumquat chutney, and include old favourites such as Gressingham duck
with wild damson sauce as well as the more predictable modern fish and meat
dishes. Irish cheeses, selected at the table, follow, then a choice of classic desserts
(don't miss the prunes in armagnac) or, a rarity these days, savouries such as
Scotch woodcock, angels and devils on horseback or grilled goat's cheese.
A good all-round wine list has plenty of excellent drinking under £20.
*Seats 26. Parties 14. Private Room 20. D only 7.30-9.30 (bookings only in winter).
Closed Jan-Easter – phone for details. Set D £25.95. Amex, MasterCard, **VISA***

See the **County Listings** green tinted pages for
details of all establishments listed in county order.

PARKNASILLA   Parknasilla Great Southern   72%   £189

Tel 064 45122   Fax 064 45323   Map 2 A6   **H**
Parknasilla Sneem Co Kerry

Set in 300 acres of private woodland and gardens with magnificent views over Kenmare Bay, this late-Victorian waterside hotel enjoys one of the loveliest locations in Ireland – and has excellent facilities to match. A uniformed porter is always on hand to greet arriving guests and keep an eye on the needs of those sitting out on the terrace over the swimming pool, and the spacious foyer with its antiques and fresh flowers, sets a tone of quiet luxury that is totally in keeping with the surroundings. Whether the guest is in need of energetic activity or restful relaxation, leisure activities of all kinds are very well catered for, including the simple pleasures of a quiet read or afternoon tea. Extensive, comfortably furnished lounge and bar areas take up most of the front ground floor of the hotel and include a no-smoking drawing-room that is normally used in conjunction with the large, impressively furnished restaurant. Public rooms now include a first-floor library, added in 1995 in celebration of the hotel's centenary, which is ideal for meetings and small conferences. Bedrooms, which vary somewhat in size and outlook, may sometimes seem a little dated and access can involve long walks down corridors. However, all rooms have en suite bathrooms with bath and shower, and all the usual modern amenities including TVs with an in-house movie channel. Children are welcome (free in parents' room up to the age of 3); baby-sitting by arrangement, children's high tea, creche in school holidays. Banqueting/conference facilities for up to 150/80. 24hr room service. No dogs. *Rooms 85. Garden, croquet, pétanque, tennis, golf (9), riding, woodland walks, cycling, clay pigeon shooting, archery, water skiing, pleasure cruises, fishing (inshore and deep sea), indoor swimming pool, sauna, steam room, spa bath, outdoor Canadian hot tub, outdoor children's playground, games room, snooker, table tennis, news kiosk, small golf shop. Closed early Jan-mid Feb. Amex, Diners, MasterCard,* **VISA**

PARKNASILLA   Places of Interest
Derrynane National Historic Park Caherdaniel Tel 066 75113

PONTOON   Healy's Hotel   60%   £55

Tel 094 56443   Fax 094 56572   Map 1 B3   **HR**
Pontoon Co Mayo

An attractive creeper-clad hotel overlooking Lough Cullen (popular for fishing). Healy's has provided a home-from-home to generations of fisherfolk who prefer things not to change too much, so expect traditional comforts without undue concern for fashion – while not smart, the piano and dancing area in the bar suggest many a good night had by all, for instance. Bedrooms, while not large, are individually decorated and overlook the lake (rooms to the rear of the hotel are £40). All have direct-dial phone and en suite facilities and televisions available on request. Children are welcome (and may stay free in their parents' room up to 5) with cots and extra beds, children's menu, high-chairs, and early evening meal. Conferences/banqueting 60/70. No dogs. *Rooms 10. Garden, fishing. Closed Oct-Apr. MasterCard,* **VISA**

See over

The Lough Cullen Room Restaurant   £50

Attractively-appointed, comfortable restaurant providing wholesome food, nicely
cooked without unnecessary frills. Good home cooking is the aim, fresh fish
from nearby lakes and seafood (hot seafood platter with creamy dill sauce, fish
chowder) from Clew Bay the specialities. Local girls provide friendly service and
family connections with Australia are reflected in the wine list. *Seats 70. L (Sun
only) 1-3 D 7-9. Set Sun L £9.95 Set D £19.50. Bar food available in lounge 1-3pm
and 6.30-9pm.*

PORTMAGEE   Fisherman's Bar

Tel 066 77103   Map 2 A6   **P**
Portmagee Co Kerry

Just beside the bridge over to Valentia Island, this comfortable, well-run pub
has tables on a sunny site overlooking the water for fine days and a good choice
on the all-day bar menu. Local seafood is a natural choice – chowder, perhaps,
or hot crab claws with garlic butter, both with home-made brown bread. More
substantial dishes include a wide range of seafood platters, from smoked mackerel
to Portmagee lobster. Irish stew and a range of grills and hot snacks –
from steaks to pizzas. *Open 10.30-11.30 (to 11 in winter), Sun 12.30-2, 4-11.
Bar Food served throughout opening hours from Easter-end Sep only. No food
in winter except by arrangement. Closed Good Friday & 25 Dec. VISA*

PORTMAGEE   Places of Interest
Skellig Heritage Centre Tel 0667 6306

RAMELTON   The Manse   £40

Tel 074 51047   Map 1 C1   **A**
Ramelton Co Donegal

Expect little in the way of modern conveniences at Mrs Scott's remarkable
house, as she has made few changes since setting up home as a bride in 1930.
In compensation for the lack of en suite facilities, however, there is the pleasure
of using a genuinely old bathroom (complete with canopy shower and original
fittings), sharing the family library, sleeping in a room untouched by fashion and
the pleasure of Mrs Scott's inimitable company. No room service, but all are
welcome to help themselves to tea and coffee from the kitchen; breakfast is
served at 9 o'clock, when a bell is rung. Not suitable for children (because of
the large number of breakable treasures on display), but do make a point of seeing
the 'children's room'. *Rooms 3. Garden. Closed mid Sep-Easter (except by
arrangement). No credit cards.*

RAMELTON   Places of Interest
Old Meeting House Ramelton Tel 074 51266

RATHCOOLE   An Poitín Stil

Tel 01 458 9205/9244
Rathcoole (off Naas Road dual carriageway) Co Dublin

Map 2 D4

P

Established in 1643, this famous thatched inn has grown considerably in recent years. Divided up into a number of bars, each with its own individual character a surprising degree of intimacy has been retained. Note the fine old copper still, from which the pub takes its name, and abundance of original Arkle memorabilia – it's very much a sporting house and frequently packed with punters from the nearby racecourses, often with a good sprinkling of famous faces. Although best known for the carvery, which offers a wide range of hot food through a three-hour lunchtime period every day (with a selection of about seven main courses, including a vegetarian choice), there's a limited bar food menu available throughout normal opening hours. Traditional Irish music is a big draw four nights a week (Wed-Sun). *Bar Food 10.30am-11.30pm (to 11pm in winter). Carvery 12.30-3.30. Closed Good Fri & 25 Dec. Amex, Diners, MasterCard,* **VISA**

Many hotels offer reduced rates for weekend or out-of-season bookings. Our guide price indicates high-season rates. Always ask about special deals for longer stays.

RATHMULLAN   Rathmullan House   62%   £110

Tel 074 58188 Fax 074 58200

Map 1 C1

Rathmullan nr Letterkenny Co Donegal

HR

For more than 30 years Bob and Robin Wheeler have been welcoming guests to their extended Georgian mansion which stands in lovely tranquil gardens that run down to the shore of Lough Swilly. Open fires warm the antique-furnished day rooms, which include a period drawing room, library and cellar bar. Not the least of the distinctive features here is the unique pool complex with Egyptian Baths. Accommodation ranges from eight well-appointed mini-suites to superior doubles and budget/family rooms (some without en suite bathrooms). No dogs. Outstanding breakfasts. *Rooms 20. Garden, croquet, indoor swimming pool, sauna, steam room, tennis. Closed Nov-mid Mar. Amex, Diners, MasterCard,* **VISA**

The Pavilion   £65

The famous tented Pavilion restaurant makes a delightful setting for one of the best hors d'oeuvre buffet displays in the country (a speciality on Sundays) although the temptation is to try too many things from a selection that includes fishy starters like smoked salmon and various terrines (both sliced to order) and eels, lots of salads and vegetarian options. Main-course choices, like the hors d'oeuvre, are strong on seafood; duo of monkfish and lobster in a brandy cream sauce with mixed rice, pan-fried guinea fowl with roasted garlic and a shallot sauce, and chicken marinated with yoghurt and Tandoori spices show the style. Good soups (carrot and orange, chicken and sweetcorn), interesting sauces and accompaniments. Desserts may include apricot flan with sauce anglaise, lemon and lime soufflé with raspberry ice cream, or warm date pudding with butterscotch sauce; coffee with petits fours is served in the drawing room. No smoking in the dining-room. Booking essential. 10% service charge is added to the final bill. *Seats 60. L (Sun only) 1-1.45. D 7.30-8.45. Set Sun L £13.50 Set D £22.50.*

RATHMULLAN   Places of Interest

Flight of the Earls Heritage Centre Tel 074 58178
Glebe House and Gallery Church Hill Letterkenny Tel 074 37071
Glenveagh National Park Tel 074 37088

RATHNEW   Hunter's Hotel   63%   £95

Tel 0404 40106 Fax 0404 40338   Map 2 D4   **HR**
Newrath Bridge Rathnew Co Wicklow

Now in its fifth generation of family ownership, this delightful old coaching inn is one of Ireland's best-loved small hotels. Close enough to the main Dublin-Wicklow road for convenience yet far enough away to have a peaceful rural atmosphere, a feeling that is enhanced by the lovely garden (where afternoon teas are served in summer), with its famous herbaceous borders and little river running along the edge. The hotel itself is on an almost cottagey scale, with polished floor tiles, old rugs and dark antique furniture brightened by cosy chintzes and an open fire in the bar. Although the Gelletlie family take care to ensure a feeling of unchanging traditions at Hunter's, there have in fact been major, if discreetly accomplished, changes recently: the older bedrooms (which were previously charmingly 1950s in atmosphere, but without private bathrooms) have been redesigned, with remarkably little loss of character, to provide en suite facilities, and incorporated into a new wing built in place of demolished outbuildings, in a style so faithful to the old building that it will soon be indistinguishable. The new accommodation includes a junior suite as well as upgraded bedrooms, while extra space on the ground floor has been designed to provide a small conference facility. No dogs. *Rooms 16. Garden. Closed 24-26 Dec.*
Amex, Diners, MasterCard, VISA

Restaurant   £55

Looking over the herbaceous border towards the river, the dining-room seems to take a step back in time with its slightly domestic atmosphere, fresh flowers from the garden in big, generous arrrangements around the room. These are echoed by little arrangements on the tables that are neatly appointed in a slightly old-fashioned style, totally in keeping with everything that is Hunter's. A new chef, Christopher Renton, took up the reins in the kitchen last year but he is already well schooled in the house style and there has been little obvious change. Local produce, especially Wicklow lamb, is still very much the order of the day, and there will be fish from nearby Greystones harbour (poached fillet of codling stuffed with a salmon mousse or simple plaice meunière) along with traditional roasts such as stuffed chicken served with ham. Fruit from the garden features in homely puddings like stewed rhubarb or apple and tayberry tart, dishes which sit easily on the menu alongside classics such as peach Melba, crème caramel and chocolate soufflé. Good cafetière coffee is served in the garden in fine weather or by the fire in the bar in winter. *Seats 54. Parties 10. Private Parties 20. L 1-3 D 7.30-9. Set L £15 Set D £20.*

RATHNEW   Tinakilly House   76%   £132

Tel 0404 69274 Fax 0404 67806   Map 2 D4   **HR**
Rathnew Co Wicklow

Set in extensive gardens overlooking a bird sanctuary, this substantial mansion was built in the 1870s by Captain Halpin, commander of *The Great Eastern*, which laid the first telegraph cable linking Europe and America. Since 1983 it has been run as a hotel by William and Bee Power, who have been responsible for extensive renovations and the additon of a period-style wing. Today it is as well known for William Power's excellent management and discreet hospitality as for its fine surroundings, with antiques, good pictures, an interesting collection of Halpin memorabilia and, perhaps most of all, fresh flowers and an ever-burning fire in the hall, all contributing to the lovely atmosphere.

All this, plus a lovely location convenient to Dublin, a consistently high standard of service and an excellent reputation for food make Tinakilly a suitable venue for prestigious meetings and conferences as well as a delightful place for a private break. Period bedrooms in the main house are spacious and inevitably vary somewhat, but all are elegantly furnished for comfort; the best have four-posters, one with a wonderful original Halpin bathroom (everything works perfectly, due to careful modernisation, but its 19th-century nautical flavour is undiminished) and most with lovely sea views. Top of the range are three suites. Fifteen newer bedrooms are in the 1991 wing, which also has conference facilities for up to 150 and banqueting for 80. Very good breakfasts. No dogs. **Rooms** 29. *Garden, tennis, croquet. Amex, Diners, MasterCard,* **VISA**

Restaurant   £80

Although it is in the new wing, the restaurant is sensitively designed to harmonise with the original house and overlooks well-tended grounds towards the sea; a spacious, elegant room, with classically appointed tables and comfortable carver chairs, makes a a very fitting setting for John Moloney's fine food. Local ingredients provide the starting point for a repertoire of imaginatively updated classics seasoned with some fashionable fare, both in light lunch menus offered in the bar and five-course dinner menus that change daily. Details are good throughout, notably Bee's brown bread (a traditional family recipe and one of the first to become famous in the current revival), excellent soups based on really good stocks and the various starters and side dishes using vegetables and herbs from the garden. Starters might include pan-fried duck livers − perhaps on an aubergine mousse − or crispy little tartlets of Mediterranean vegetables with lightly cooked spinach and a hazelnut dressing − typical of the imaginative vegetarian dishes available. Roast loin of lamb is almost a signature dish, cooked perfectly pink and served with courgettes provençale and a light port and rosemary jus; look out also for wild Wicklow venison with crisp, bright green, buttered cabbage, braised shallots and carrots. Desserts might include an amusing lemon tart with gin and tonic sorbet or wicked honey ice cream served in a brandysnap basket with toasted almonds and butterscotch sauce. Good cafetière coffee and home-made petits fours are served at the table or drawing-room bar. The wine list offers a wide choice, from champagne by the glass through a viognier house wine to a good choice of claret vintages, lots of New World and over twenty interesting half-bottles. Friendly, efficient service from well-trained staff. **Seats** 70. Parties 10. Private Room 20. Morning coffee 10-12 L 12.30-2 afternoon tea 2.30-5 D 7.30-9. Set L £18.50 Set D £32.

RATHPEACON   Country Squire Inn

Tel 021 301812   Map 2 B6   **P**
Mallow Road Rathpeacon Co Cork

A couple of miles out of Cork on the N20 towards Mallow, Pat McSweeney's immaculate roadside pub is very much geared up to eating. The small bar has not only old 'sewing machine' tables but also some of the original cast-iron 'Singer' stools, now comfortably matched to match the banquette seating. Bar lunches are a blackboard affair (minimum charge of a main course) with the likes of grilled garlic-stuffed mussels, salmon and crab salad, tripe and onions and venison casserole. The home-cooked food is generously portioned, so bring a healthy appetite. In the evenings, a cosy, 28-seat candle-lit restaurant offers similar fare with meals from around £20 − priced according to one's choice of main course − perhaps sirloin steak with garlic butter or pepper sauce, lemon sole stuffed with crab, or monkfish in a Chablis sauce. No children under 8. *Open 12.30-2.30 (not Sun) & 5-11.* **Bar Food** 12.30-2.30 (not Sun) & 6.30-9.30 (not Sun or Mon). **Restaurant** D only 7.30-10 Tue-Sat. Closed L Sun, Good Friday, 24 & 25 Dec & 1 week Jan. MasterCard, **VISA**

RECESS   Ballynahinch Castle   71%   £132

Tel 095 31006 Fax 095 31085   Map 1 A3   **H**
Ballynahinch Lake Recess Co Galway

You don't have to be a fisher-person to enjoy Ballynahinch, but it must help – for, while the wonderful setting may attract the first-time visitor, it is as a fishing hotel that this crenellated Victorian mansion is renowned. Both the building and its lovely romantic views down through ancient woodland to the Ballynahinch River below are wonderfully impressive, but first-time guests usually find it more relaxed than anticipated and it's the unstuffy atmosphere combined with a high level of comfort, friendliness and an invigorating mixture of residents and locals in the Fisherman's Pub bar at night that brings people back. Recent renovations and extensions have been completed with unusual attention to period detail, a policy also generally carried through successfully in furnishing both public areas and bedrooms. Most bedrooms and some reception rooms – notably the dining-room – have river views. Public areas are lofty, with a lot of stonework, old oak and wood smoke creating a real castle atmosphere – something to relish over afternoon tea by a huge log fire in the hall or later in the bar. A limited range of carefully-prepared and well-presented food is served in the Fisherman's Pub; everything from a freshly-made sandwich with soup of the day to avocado and crabmeat salad, a fresh seafood platter or a plate of Irish farmhouse cheeses is prepared and served with the same care. Children are not encouraged and surprisingly, given the otherwise relaxed atmosphere, no dogs are allowed inside (although kennels are provided). The 350-acre estate offers miles of walks, and five woodcock shoots a year are arranged in the 13,000 acres of surrounding woodlands; fly-casting tutorials and winter fly-tying weekends complete the list of sporting pursuits. *Rooms 28. Garden, croquet, fishing, shooting, tennis. Bar meals served 12-3 & 7-9 daily. Closed 20-26 Dec & all Feb. Amex, Diners, MasterCard,* **VISA**

RECESS   Lough Inagh Lodge   68%   £132

Tel 095 34706 Fax 095 34708   Map 1 A3   **H**
Inagh Valley Recess Connemara Co Galway

Former sporting lodge set in spectacular scenery on the shores of Lough Inagh,

42 miles from Galway. Opened by the present owners as a hotel in 1990, it combines the advantages of the old and the new with interesting period detail balanced by modern comfort and practicality. Public areas include two drawing rooms, each with an open fire, a lovely dining-room with deep-green walls and graceful spoonback Victorian mahogany chairs and a very appealing bar, with a big turf fire and its own back door and tiled floor for dripping fisherfolk. Bedrooms, some with four-posters, are all well appointed and unusually spacious with views of lake and countryside and with walk-in dressing rooms leading to well-planned bathrooms. While it has special appeal to sportsmen, Lough Inagh is a good base for touring Connemara and there is golf and pony trekking nearby. Children up to 12 stay free in parents' room. *Rooms 12. Garden, fishing, bicycles. Closed end Oct-Easter. Amex, Diners, MasterCard,* **VISA**

RENVYLE   Renvyle House   63%   £184

Tel 095 43511   Fax 095 43515   Map 1 A3   **H**
Renvyle Co Galway

Once owned by Oliver St John Gogarty, this famous Lutyens-esque house is approached via a stunning scenic drive along a mountain road with views down into a blue-green sea of unparalleled clarity. However, once reached, the hotel itself seems to be snuggling down for shelter and has only limited views. Public areas celebrate the house's glorious past, when it was visited by the rich and famous including Sir Winston Churchill; the bar, which is the scene of many a late-night revel, has a particularly poignant atmosphere and also a memory-laden back corridor, lined with photographs and press cuttings. There's a pleasant lounge/sun room leading on to a sunny verandah near the swimming pool and an interesting, well-appointed dining-room (Lutyens-style furniture still casts its spell over much of the house). Bedrooms are very variable and include two pleasant suites with little balconies overlooking the pool, and a number of other good-sized rooms of character. Refurbishment of the 20 older-style bedrooms has recently been completed and, hopefully, they are now more in keeping with the illustrious history of the place. Children are welcome; high summer activities, playroom and free accommodation for under-2s, with under-12s half-price. Conference facilities for up to 120, banqueting for 150. *Rooms 65. Garden, croquet, bowling, outdoor swimming pool, tennis, golf (9), putting, bowling green, riding, fishing, snooker, bicycles, children's playground & playroom. Closed midweek Dec, all Jan & Feb. Amex, Diners, MasterCard,* **VISA**

We only recommend the food in hotels categorised as **HR** and **AR**. However, the food in many **A** establishments throughout Ireland is often very acceptable (but the restaurant may not be open to non-residents).

RIVERSTOWN   Coopershill House   69%   £95

Tel 071 65108   Fax 071 65466   Map 1 B3   **AR**
Coopershill Riverstown Co Sligo

Standing at the centre of a 500-acre estate, this immaculate Georgian mansion has been home to seven generations of the O'Hara family since it was built in 1774 and now successfully combines the spaciousness and elegance of the past with modern amenities and the warmest of welcomes. The rooms retain their original regal dimensions and are furnished in period style with family portraits and antiques. Spacious bedrooms all have en suite bathrooms and most have four-poster or canopy beds; no smoking in the bedrooms. Peace and tranquillity sum up the atmosphere: no TVs or radios, but books and personal touches like fresh flowers and mineral water. A splendid breakfast starts the day at this most hospitable of country hotels. No dogs in the house. *Rooms 8. Garden, croquet, tennis, coarse and game fishing, boating. Closed Nov-mid Mar. Amex, Diners, MasterCard,* **VISA**

Restaurant   £60

Polished antique tables, silver candelabra and a log fire in the white marble fireplace provide a fitting setting for Lindy O'Hara's good home cooking. A no-choice five-course menu might include crab tart; carrot and fennel soup; roast stuffed quail with mushroom and port sauce, a good choice of nine farmhouse cheeses and, perhaps, pears in a fudge sauce. No smoking. *Seats 16. D only 8-9.30. Set D £24.*

ROSSES POINT   Austie's

Tel 071 77111   Map 1 B2   **P**
Rosses Point Co Sligo

Named after a previous owner, Austie Gillen, and close to the house where
Yeats and his brother used to stay on summer holidays (now neglected and in
disrepair), this 200-year-old pub overlooking Sligo Bay is a nautical place – not
a 'theme' pub but one that has always been associated with a seafaring family and
is crammed full of nautical paraphernalia which is both decorative and fascinating
to anyone with an interest in maritime history. The simple bar menu is strong
on local seafood – chowder, garlic mussels, open sandwiches or salads with crab,
prawns and salmon. *Open 12-11.30 (to 11 in winter) Sun 12.30-2, 4-11.* **Bar Food**
*12-10, winter from 6. Pub closed until 4pm in winter. Waterside terrace. Closed
Good Friday & 25 Dec. Amex, MasterCard,* **VISA**

ROSSES POINT   The Moorings   £55

Tel 071 77112   Map 1 B2   **R**
Rosses Point Co Sligo

With an almost waterside location (there's a road between it and the sea), views
over Sligo Bay and cosy dining-rooms (one non-smoking) with open beams and
traditional furniture, The Moorings makes an attractive venue and Sunday lunch
is a speciality. Local seafood predominates in old favourites – warm smoked
salmon with cucumber and dill, seafood chowder, lobster thermidor, sweet and
sour prawns and monkfish Mediterranean style. Popular food, freshly cooked
at reasonable prices. *Seats 80. Parties 40. L (Sun only) 12.30-2.30 D 5.30-9.30.
Set Sun L £9. Closed Mon in winter & 3 weeks Jan. Amex, MasterCard,* **VISA**

ROSSLARE   Great Southern   62%   £94

Tel 053 33233   Fax 053 33543   Map 2 D5   **H**
Rosslare Co Wexford

Its position overlooking Rosslare harbour makes this modern hotel a useful
stopover for ferry users and there's plenty to keep children happy with a creche,
playground and their own restaurant. Public rooms are light and spacious, with
ample seating; many of the simply-furnished bedrooms are suitable for family
occupation. Up to 150 conference delegates can be accommodated theatre-style,
100 for a banquet. Ask for their helpful golfer's guide to local courses and about
special rates for two-night and longer stays. No dogs. *Rooms 100. Terrace, indoor
swimming pool, mini-gym, tennis, sauna, steam room, games room, snooker,
hairdressing, indoor and outdoor children's play areas. Closed Jan & Feb.
Amex, Diners, MasterCard,* **VISA**

ROSSLARE — Kelly's Resort Hotel — 76% — £132

Tel 053 32114   Fax 053 32222
Rosslare Co Wexford

Map 2 C5

HR

Total relaxation is the aim at Kelly's, family-run for four generations and often referred to as "the hotelier's hotel" because so many in the business find its professionalism and hospitality offers the perfect switch-off; 24hr room service. Constant renovation and refurbishment have resulted in a very high standard of comfort throughout, from the many seating areas and two bars through elegant, spacious and thoughtfully furnished bedrooms – all with excellent bathrooms and some with balconies or direct access to garden or patio – to exceptional leisure facilities (including two swimming pools) and a wide range of health and beauty treatments such as aromatherapy and underwater massage. Various activity and theme breaks out of season. Children welcome (14 family rooms); playroom, outdoor play area, children's entertainment, high chairs, early evening meal. One room is equipped for disabled guests. No dogs. Winner of our Ireland Hotel of the Year award in 1995. **Rooms** *99. Garden, croquet, crazy golf, badminton, bowls, squash, tennis, indoor driving and putting range, indoor swimming pools, sauna, spa bath, steam room, solarium, gym, games room, snooker, beauty & hair salon. Closed 8 Dec-end Feb.* Amex, Diners, MasterCard, **VISA**

Restaurant £55

An L-shaped room, cleverly designed to have a surprisingly intimate atmosphere for its size, the restaurant is elegantly appointed and smoothly run, with some striking examples of the hotel's well-known art collection providing a special background for confident cooking under the direction of Jim Aherne, chef de cuisine since 1973. Menus reflect respect for local ingredients – Bannow mussels, Kilmore scallops, Rosslare lamb, St Helen's crab meat and lobster, Wexford strawberries, game in season, farmhouse cheeses – mainly in traditional dishes: terrine of guinea fowl and ham with cranberry coulis, veal mignon with calvados and apple sabayon, whole lemon sole with garden herb butter, oak smoked salmon and herb omelette with tossed salad. Sunday lunch is always a sell-out and dinner ends with a sing-song at the piano in the aptly-named Carmen Bar. No children under 10 in the restaurant after 7.30. 10% service charge is added to the final bill. **Seats** *220. Private Room 40. L 1-2 D 7.30-9. Set L £12.50 Set D £20.95.*

ROSSLARE   Places of Interest

Ferry Terminal Tourist Information Tel 053 33622
Stena Sealink Tel 053 33115
Windsurfing Centre Tel 053 3210

We endeavour to be as up-to-date as possible but inevitably some changes to owners, chefs and other key staff occur after this Guide has gone to press.

ROSSNOWLAGH Sand House Hotel   69%   £99

Tel 072 51777   Fax 072 52100   Map 1 B2   **HR**
Rossnowlagh Co Donegal

The crenellated Sand House hotel sits right by a long sandy beach looking out to Donegal Bay and the Atlantic Ocean. The Atlantic conservatory lounge takes full advantage of views that are also enjoyed by many of the bedrooms (those with the very best views attract a small supplement). Mary Britton and her son Brian, together with their staff, extend a warm welcome, reinforced by a fire in the Victorian-style lobby. En suite bedrooms, immaculate like the rest of the hotel, are individually decorated with expensive, stylish fabrics; furniture varies from antiques to fairly modest fitted units, and superior rooms have chaises longues. Six new antique-furnished bedrooms were added last year. A delightful, peaceful hotel, as the many regular guests will testify. Conference facilities for 75. Good golf and riding facilities nearby. *Rooms 45. Garden, tennis, mini-golf, putting green, croquet, surfing, canoeing, board sailing, sea fishing, games room, snooker, table tennis. Closed Nov-Easter. Amex, Diners, MasterCard,* **VISA**

Restaurant   £60

Although it is at the front of the hotel and therefore misses out on the sea view, the dining-room is well appointed, in keeping with the rest of the hotel. Comfortable chairs are set at generously-spaced tables and there is solicitous attention from hospitable staff. Daily-changed five-course dinner menus are based on local ingredients, notably seafood, and the best choices are the simplest – typical in starters like Donegal Bay oysters on a bed of ice, perhaps, or fresh crab and spinach roulade. Main courses include old favourites such as beef Wellington and roast lamb with rosemary and garlic; some dishes tend to be a bit over-complicated. It may come as a surprise to be offered a mixed salad, complete with egg mayonnaise, along with their selection of hot vegetables. The wholesome fare is rounded off with a choice of Irish cheeses and nice fruit pies among the desserts. 10% service charge. *Seats 70. L 1-2.30 D 7-9. Set L Sun £12.50 D £22.50.*

ROSSNOWLAGH Smugglers Creek Inn   £49

Tel 072 52366   Map 1 B2   **IR**
Rossnowlagh Co Donegal

Conor Britton's imaginatively restored pub and restaurant is perched high on the cliffs overlooking the wonderful golden strand at Rossnowlagh. Visitors have the endless fascination of watching the powerful Atlantic rollers come in from afar to spend themselves on the beach far below – and all this while sitting in considerable comfort, with open fires and delicious bar food. Accommodation is offered in five rooms, all en suite, interestingly decorated and with sea views. Rooms vary considerably and most are on the small side – one corner room, with windows in two walls, is slightly larger than average and has even better views. Children are well catered for; under-5s accommodated free in parents' room. Traditional Irish music Friday and Saturday evenings and summer Sunday afternoons. *Rooms 5. Garden. Closed Good Friday (bar only), 20 Nov-25 Dec & Mon & Tue Nov-Easter. MasterCard,* **VISA**

Restaurant £45

Across the corridor from the bar, the rustic/nautical atmosphere is continued in the stone-floored restaurant, furnished with pleasing informality using stripped-pine dressers and old country kitchen furniture to advantage and lots of plants. Tables near the window have splendid sea views, while those at the back are in a cosy non-smoking area. All share cheerful service and a wide menu that works the 'smugglers' theme to death. There's a predictable emphasis on seafood in dishes like fish soup, Donegal Bay seafood platter, wild Irish salmon hollandaise and baked hake in white wine. Simple meat dishes cater for carnivorous tastes and there are always vegetarian options. No children under 10 after 9pm. **Seats** 50. Parties 10. Private Room 24. L (Restaurant Sun only, bar snacks daily from 12-6pm) 12.30-2.30 D 6.30-9.30. Set Sun L £10.50.

ROUNDSTONE   O'Dowd's Seafood Bar and Restaurant

Tel 095 35809
Roundwood Co Galway   Map 2 A4   **P**

A reassuringly unchanging traditional pub and seafood bar overlooking the harbour. It's an oasis of calm where regular summer visitors – notably Dublin lawyers and doctors, plus the odd politician – come to recharge their batteries. The simple, old-fashioned bar is a relaxing place to renew old friendships over a pint and a bite from the reasonably-priced bar menu, which includes a good range of seafood – chowder (a speciality), Mannin Bay oysters, crab claws in garlic, stuffed mussels, crab salad, smoked salmon pasta and an unusually named salmon burger with spicy tomato sauce – plus old favourites like shepherd's pie and sirloin steak and with vegetarian specialities such as bean burgers. Salmon is smoked or cured for gravlax locally; herbs and lettuce come from their own garden. Lobster, grilled oysters, game (mallard, quail, venison and pheasant) and blackberry and apple pie are always popular in the restaurant; a roast goose is the traditional offering on New Year's Eve. Open 11am-11.30pm (Sun 12.30-2, 4-11). **Bar Food** 12.30-9.30 (Sun 12.30-2, 4-9.30). **Restaurant Meals** 12.30-9.30. Restaurant closed mid Oct-Christmas & 2nd week Jan-Easter, Good Friday & 25 Dec. Amex, MasterCard, **VISA**

ROUNDWOOD   Roundwood Inn £60

Tel 01 281 8107
Roundwood Co Wicklow   Map 2 D4   **R/P**

Set amid spectacular scenery in the highest village in the Wicklow Hills, Jürgen and Áine Schwalm's 17th-century inn is in traditional style with wooden floors, darkwood furniture and huge log fires throughout. Chef Paul Taube's restaurant menu leans towards dishes like rack of Wicklow lamb, roast wild Wicklow venison (a speciality) and other game in season. German influences are evident in long-established specialities like wiener schnitzel, blueberry pancake and a feather-light fresh cream gateau which is not to be missed. Booking is advisable for Sunday lunch (three-courses £15.50), when roast suckling pig is a long-standing attraction. A mainly European wine list, strongest in France and Germany, starts at under £10 for the house selection and ascends to 40 times that for a 1967 Pauillac. The Roundwood Inn also has a unique reputation for excellent, varied bar food, which is served swiftly and efficiently by friendly staff at big sturdy tables in front of the ever-burning log fire. Specialities on the bar menu range from nourishing home-made soups (vegetable, lobster bisque) and enormous bowls of Irish stew (an established favourite, especially with hill walkers) through smoked eel and hearty venison ragout served with red cabbage and potatoes boiled in their jackets to the refinement of local smoked Wicklow trout and lobster salads, served with home-baked brown bread. Blackboard specials broaden the range and, with one or two desserts added from the restaurant menu, a wonderful value, balanced three-course meal can be enjoyed informally (but in considerable comfort) in the bar throughout the day and evening. No children after 7.30pm. Winner of our Bar Food of the Year award in 1995. *Seats 45 Restaurant. Parties 35. Private Room 30. L 1-2.15 D 7.30-9.30 (Sat to 10). Bar open 12-11.30, (Sun 12-2, 4-11). Bar food served 12 noon-10 pm (Sun 12-2, 4-10). Restaurant closed D Sun & all Mon & Tue. Inn closed Good Friday & 25 Dec. Amex, MasterCard,* **VISA**

SANDYCOVE	Bistro Vino	£45

Tel & Fax 01 280 6097   Map 2 D4   **R**
56 Glasthule Road Sandycove Co Dublin

A buzzy little first-floor restaurant near the seafront at Sandycove and clearly a big hit with the locals who appreciate the moderate prices, unpretentiously good food with an Italian emphasis and an informal atmosphere. A not over-ambitious (and all the better for it) à la carte menu is offered, plus an early evening set menu. Typical starters include grilled garlic mussels with camembert and a herb crust, Mediterranean fish soup and marinated roast vegetables with basil and sun-dried tomato pesto. Main-course options range from good pasta dishes to more substantial dishes such as Italian fish and shellfish stew, monkfish pepperonata and roast stuffed duck with honey, orange and ginger sauce. Nice, homely puds on the blackboard dessert menu. Beware the steep stairs as you leave. No children under 12. Sister restaurant in Dublin (1 Upper Rathmines Road, Dublin 6 − 01 497 1566) − see entry. *Seats 45. Parties 35. D only 5-11.30. Closed Good Friday & 25 Dec. Set D Early Bird £10.95 (5-7pm). Amex, Diners, MasterCard,* **VISA**

SANDYCOVE	Cavistons Seafood Restaurant	£35

Tel 01 280 9120   Map 2 D4   **R**
59 Glasthule Road Sandycove Co Dublin

The Caviston family have been running their famous Food Emporium here for 40 years and, in 1996, Peter and Stephen Caviston realised a long-held ambition to start a restaurant (albeit a tiny one) on the premises. With simple decor (tiled floor and cheerful murals), friendly service and a good buzz, noise can be a problem but it is no real deterrent. Chef Noel Cusack's menus are almost exclusively devoted to the freshest of seafood, the only exception being one or two imaginative vegetarian dishes, changed daily − penne with a spicy tomato sauce, perhaps, or a roast red pepper, onion and spinach flan. Dishes that were already set to become specialities of the house after the first few months include a homely seafood pie made with whatever fish is best value each day, and wonderful seared scallops, either served in their shells with olive oil, chili and lime or shelled and mixed with monkfish. Tempting desserts include the likes of bread-and-butter pudding with crème anglaise or a rich chocolate torte; Irish farmhouse cheeses are always represented in a cheese of the day (a nutty mature Doolin, perhaps) and there's a choice of coffees as well as a surprisingly good selection of wines for such a tiny place. At the time of going to press a reservations policy was in the shake-down phase (12, 1.30 and 3pm, plus a possible extra sitting at about 4 pm) and evening opening was under consideration for 1997. No smoking is allowed in the restaurant; tables are set up on the pavement in fine summer weather. *Seats 24. Parties 5. L only 12-4. Closed Sun, Mon, Bank Holidays & 3/4 days Christmas. MasterCard,* **VISA**

SANDYCOVE   Morels Bistro   ⬆   £70

Tel 01 230 0210   Fax 01 230 0466   Map 2 D4   **R**
18 Glasthule Road Sandycove Dun Laoghaire Co Dublin

〰️ 🛏️ 🍽️ 🎫 👓 📖 V 👏

Alan O'Reilly's Morels occupies a very visible position on the first floor of the
Eagle House pub, which is so well illuminated at night that it is virtually
impossible to miss. When you climb the stairs to the dining-room the decor hits
you with its dazzlingly contrasting summery Mediterranean hues. Curvaceous
metal and rattan chairs contrast with tables simply but formally appointed with
white linen and fresh flowers. Bright sunshine yellow is the dominant colour of
the decor along with the richest terracotta, deepest blues and brilliantly coloured
modern artwork from American artist Emer Diamond and Irish artist Killian
Rory. The food mirrors this colourful, lively environment perfectly with an
eclectic selection of dishes that are well thought out: a starter of meaty baked
crabcakes sit on a bed of diced peppers surrounded by a drizzle of lemon oil
with coriander pesto. In a similarly interesting vein, one could choose salad
of confit duck with tapenade or terrine of leeks, chicken and red pepper with
balsamic vinegar. For a main course one might choose a very tender, grilled,
aged beef sirloin set amid a selection of crisply-cooked root vegetables,
chargrilled wood pigeon with crispy bacon, roast shallots and mushrooms,
tempura of monkfish with lime and coriander dressing or spiced Thai chicken
with sesame and chili aoili. Finish with a dark chocolate terrine with espresso
sauce, autumn fruit pudding or date, pecan and toffee pudding. The three-course
Early Evening Special menu (£12.50) and Sunday lunch offer exceptional value
for money. A separate selection of wines at £10 a bottle represents excellent
value. The cheerful staff are the icing on the cake of this highly recommended
restaurant. *Seats 75. Parties 15. L (Sun only) 12.30-2.45 D 6-10.30. Set Sun L £12.50.
Closed 1 week Christmas. Amex, MasterCard,* **VISA**

We welcome bona fide complaints and recommendations on
the tear-out Readers' Comments pages at the back of the Guide.
They are followed up by our professional team.

SCHULL   Adèle's

Tel 028 28459   Map 2 A6   **JaB**
Main Street Schull Co Cork

🛏️ V 👏

The aroma of Adèle Connor's endeavours waft through from her bakery at the
back of this popular little café-restaurant; the display of home-made foods at the
counter is well-nigh irresistible at any time of day – all the cakes and bread are
made on the premises, from ciabatta for sandwiches to Chelsea buns. Evening
menus bring a shift of emphasis, with Simon Connor cooking a short menu for
the informal first-floor dining-room. You might find roasted peppers or a chilled
mint and pea soup followed by a choice of pasta dishes (perhaps fusilli with
artichokes and olives and tomato sauce or tagliatelle with crab meat in a fennel
and cream sauce). Finish with tiramisu or petit pot au chocolat – try a glass
of the unusual French red dessert wine from Banyuls. Interesting wine list.
*Seats 40. Meals 9.30-6.30 D 7-10.30 (Sun to 9.30). Closed all Mon (except Jul
& Aug), Nov-mid Dec, early Jan-Easter. No credit cards.*

The Egon Ronay Guides are completely independent.
We do not accept advertising, hospitality or payment
from any of the establishments listed in this Guide.

SCHULL   Bunratty Inn

Tel 028 28341   Fax 028 28702   Map 2 A6   **P**
Schull Co Cork

Val and Vera Duffy have a well-deserved reputation for bar food in their
comfortably appointed pub. Since 1986 they have concentrated on providing
an interesting menu that features seafood. Look out for seafood chowder served
with Vera's excellent home-made brown bread, seafood pie, garlic mussels and
oysters alongside lasagne, shepherd's pie, chicken curry and a ploughman's platter
of local West Cork cheeses (perhaps Milleens and Durrus); a toasted smoked
salmon and Gubbeen cheese is described as a 'mini masterpiece'. Crab is a
favourite and may appear in an open sandwich with smoked salmon, in a salad
or hot, either as sizzlingly hot, garlicky claws or as a cheese-topped baked dish
with peppers, onions and chilis. Ask about their free-range 'recycled pork'.
Leave room for the likes of home-made ice creams, fresh strawberry cheesecake
or individual pavlovas with chocolate sauce. *Open 11am-11pm Mon-Sat (to 11pm
in winter), Sun 12.30-2, 4-11. **Bar Food** 12-5 (Jun-Sep till 7). No food Sundays.
Closed Good Fri & 25 Dec. Garden, patio, outdoor eating. MasterCard,* **VISA**

Many hotels offer reduced rates for weekend or out-of-season
bookings. Our guide price indicates high-season rates.
Always ask about special deals for longer stays.

SCHULL   La Coquille   £55

Tel 028 28642   Map 2 A6   **R**
Schull Co Cork

Jean-Michel Cahier's chic little restaurant is situated in the main street and
convenient to the harbour but, in contrast to the majority of restaurants in the
area, sets seafood in context on a wide-ranging menu including typically Gallic
offerings such as frogs' legs as well as red meat and poultry. Competently
handled classics are the main feature in starters like prawns or scallops in garlic
butter, smoked salmon and crab mayonnaise, well-made soups and main courses
such as guinea fowl with redcurrant and port sauce, scallops in cream and brandy
sauce, fillet of pork with cider sauce and ray with black butter and, while
desserts include an excellent tarte tatin, M Cahier's cheese selection concedes the
quality of local produce. Facilities for the disabled. Professional service by French
staff. 10% service charge added to the final bill. *Seats 35. L 12.30-2.30 (Jul & Aug
only) D 7-10. Closed Sun in summer (except Bank Holiday weekends) & all Feb.
Set L Sun £12 Set D £22. MasterCard,* **VISA**

SCHULL   Corthna Lodge   £40

Tel & Fax 028 28517   Map 2 A6   **A**
Schull Co Cork

Set in large, well-designed gardens overlooking the islands of Roaring Water
Bay, this spacious modern house has a suntrap patio with sweeping sea views
where residents may relax on fine days and a cosy sitting room with an open
fire for cooler weather. Good-sized, individually-decorated bedrooms are
comfortably furnished, all with en suite showers but no phones or TV – the aim
is to provide a peaceful retreat (although there is a small television in the sitting
room). Excellent standard of housekeeping. Breakfast options include the local
Gubbeen cheese, plain or smoked, served with freshly-baked brown bread.
Children welcome (cots available). Parking (10 spaces). No dogs. *Rooms 6.
Garden. Closed Nov-end Mar. No credit cards.*

SCHULL   East End Hotel   60%   £50

Tel 028 28101
Schull Co Cork

Map 2 A6

H

Situated on the main street near the harbour, continuing improvements and renovations at Derry and Dorothy Roche's friendly family hotel – smartly painted in yellow and navy blue – reflect the steady interest of the owners. Bedrooms are modest but some have harbour views, others overlook the garden and hills behind – and most are now en suite, although there are plenty of extra bathrooms (also available to sailing folk). Family-friendliness is central to the hotel, expressed in a generally relaxed attitude: most rooms can sleep at least three, children under three may stay free in their parents' room, there are cots, extra beds, and lots of high-chairs. Public areas include a streetside bar/lounge and refurbished dining-room. Banqueting for 120. No private parking, but ample free public parking nearby. No dogs. *Rooms 17. Garden. Closed 5 days Christmas. Amex, MasterCard,* **VISA**

We only recommend the food in hotels categorised as **HR** and **AR**.

SCHULL   Restaurant in Blue   £60

Tel 028 28305
Crookhaven Road Schull Co Cork

Map 2 A6

R

Since they opened in 1992, Burvill Evans and Christine Crabtree have been building up a loyal following at their charming little restaurant near Schull. A dingly-dell garden, thick walls, small windows and homely antique furnishings create a relaxed cottagey atmosphere in which to enjoy Burvill's splendid food. Start, perhaps with crab parcels with red pepper mousse, or mussel and orange soup with wonderful, warm home-baked yeast breads, typically followed by an imaginative fish dish like monkfish baked with chives and ginger with a basil sauce, or herb-crusted local lamb with a red wine sauce, served with delicious organic vegetables. Finish with local cheeses or the quartet of desserts – small servings of four daily desserts, served in ramekins on a large plate – and lovely aromatic cafetière coffee. Separate vegetarian menu. Reduced menu out of season. No children under 8. *Seats 40. Parties 12. D only 7-9.45. Closed Mon, Sun-Tue low season, unless by arrangement; 1-18 Dec, 25 Dec & 6 Jan-mid Feb. Set D £22.50. Amex, Diners, MasterCard,* **VISA**

SCHULL   T J Newman's

Tel 028 28223
Corner House Main Street Schull Co Cork

Map 2 A6

P

Situated close to the harbour, where the main street joins the road down to the quay, this characterful little bar is especially popular with sailing people. Old-fashioned decor features turquoise paintwork. *Open 10.30am-11.30pm, Sun 12.30-2, 4-11 (winter 6-11 only). Garden. No credit cards.*

SCOTSHOUSE   Hilton Park   £111

See entry under Clones, Co Monaghan

If you encounter bad service don't wait to write to us but make your feelings known to the management at the time of your visit. Instant compensation can often resolve any problem that might otherwise leave a bad taste.

SHANAGARRY   Ballymaloe House   66%   £140

Tel 021 652531 Fax 021 652021   Map 2 B6   **AR**
Shanagarry Midleton Co Cork

Part of an old castle that became a farmhouse, modernised through the centuries, but with the 14th-century keep remaining in its original form. The hotel is situated in the middle of a 400-acre farm, both owned and run by Ivan and Myrtle Allen, and part of a group of family enterprises that includes a cookery school, craft shop and the *Crawford Gallery Café* in Cork (see entry). Two miles from the coast, near the small fishing village of Ballycotton, the main house provides the day rooms – a large drawing room with open fire and a TV room, complete with video recorder. Throughout, there's an interesting collection of modern Irish paintings with works by Jack B Yeats in the dining-room. Thirteen bedrooms in the main building are traditionally furnished, and a further five modern, garden rooms open on to a lawn. Another eleven rooms, more cottagey in character, surround the old coachyard, with some on ground level suitable for wheelchairs. Teenagers especially will appreciate the self-contained 16th-century Gatehouse which has its own small entrance hall and a twin-bedded room with its bathroom up a steep wooden staircase. Ballymaloe is a warm and comfortable family home, especially welcoming to children of all ages (high tea is served at 5.30pm), who can rely on the Allen grandchildren to relay the latest news from the farm or share the sandpit and pool. For the delightful breakfasts, all the ingredients are local or home-made, with even the oatmeal used for porridge ground in an old stone mill down the road. No dogs in rooms (but kennels provided). ***Rooms** 30. Garden, croquet, outdoor swimming pool, tennis, golf (5), children's outdoor play area. Closed 24-26 Dec. Access, Amex, Diners,* **VISA**

Restaurant   ★   £80

Head chef Rory O'Connell is doing a great job in the kitchen, having sharpened up the style of cooking and presentation without losing sight of the great Ballymaloe philosophy in which the quality ingredient is king. The system is the same as ever: guests gather in the conservatory or drawing-room for aperitifs – or even at tables out at the front in fine summer weather (a real treat) – then proceed to a table in one of a sequence of dining-rooms (some for non-smokers). Although Myrtle Allen may not be in the kitchen herself these days, she and her husband, Ivan, are very much present – Ivan gamely queueing up with other guests for the Friday evening seafood buffet or the huge selection that is put up for Sunday lunch, while Myrtle keeps a sharp eye on proceedings and moves around the tables to talk to everyone. The whole family works together in a most remarkable way, seemingly tireless in their pursuit of perfect hospitality. And the food on the plate is better than ever – just as flavoursome, but with a slightly more professional edge. A five-course dinner menu (with vegetarian dishes given a leaf symbol) starts with a choice of soups, sorbet and a salad – Ballycotton fish soup, for example, is deep-flavoured in classic Breton style, and the salad will be something interesting such as globe artichokes, courgettes and tomatoes à la vinaigrette. Next, the choice of second courses might include a delicate fish mousse prettily presented in a 'flower' of carrots and courgettes, decorated with fennel leaves, a fashionable dish like Rory's 'refined' fish and chips, a millefeuille of lamb's kidneys – a superb, richly-flavoured mixture topped with crunchy pastry and served with spinach and garlic – or perhaps a dashing dish of goat's cheese with roast peppers and Puy lentils. To follow, half a dozen main courses like grilled cod with herb butter and lobster served with cucumbers and fennel, or succulent crisp-skinned roast duck with a Madeira sauce and wonderful fresh peas, a pretty and unusual dish of escalopes of beef served with glazed onions, garlic mayonnaise and tarragon, and a strong vegetarian choice like spiced aubergine and potato sandwich with a parsley and coriander pesto. Lovely, simple side dishes – new potatoes, sugar snap peas, young carrots and a green salad – accompany. A cheese course follows – Irish farmhouse cheeses, of course, in excellent condition – and then the famous dessert trolley is wheeled to the table. You can expect it to be laden with irresistible things like lemon soufflé, fresh raspberries, chocolate hazelnut tart and praline ice cream (served from the ice bowl that was their invention). Coffee and home-made petits fours served in the drawing-room are a fine end to a perfectly wonderful meal. The wine list is not long but is one of quality, featuring top French growers and a few wines from around the world. *Seats 40. Private Room 45. L 12.30-2 D 7-9.30 (Sun buffet 7.30). Set Sun L £17 Set D £30.*

SHANAGARRY   Places of Interest
Stephen Pearse's Pottery Emporium

SHANNON	Oak Wood Arms Hotel	63%	£96

Tel 061 361500   Fax 061 361414   Map 2 B4   **H**
Shannon Co Clare

A family-owned, redbrick hotel (opened in 1991) that creates a good first impression with its neatly laid-out flower beds. If the mock-Tudor style of the hotel is somewhat surprising in this setting, its aviation theme is less so: the lounge bar and function room both honour the memory of the pioneer female pilot Sophie Pearse, who came from the area, and the restaurant is named after Howard Hughes's famous flying boat, *The Spruce Goose*. Public areas are quite spacious and comfortably furnished and, although not individually decorated, bedrooms have all the necessary comforts and are double-glazed. No dogs. In the past year a further 30 bedrooms, including six suites (not inspected), and a new gym have been added to the hotel. Facilities have also been improved for banquets (350) and conferences (400). *Rooms 75. Patio, gym. Closed 25 Dec. Amex, Diners, MasterCard,* **VISA**

SHANNON AIRPORT	Great Southern	64%	£110

Tel 061 471122   Fax 061 471982   Map 2 B4   **H**
Shannon Airport Shannon Co Clare

Situated directly opposite the main terminal building, this modern airport hotel was totally refurbished a few years ago. Soundproofed bedrooms include 11 Executive rooms and three suites; all with direct-dial phones, multi-channel TV, tea-maker, hairdryer, trouser press and en suite bath/shower room. Fourteen rooms are designated non-smoking. Conference facilities for up to 200 (fully-equipped business centre), banqueting for 150. Ask about special rates for two-night and longer stays. No dogs. *Rooms 115. Garden. Amex, Diners, MasterCard,* **VISA**

SHANNON   Places of Interest
Airport Tourist Information Tel 061 471664
Airport Arrivals Hall Tel 061 471644
Cratloe Woods House Tel 061 327028

SKERRIES   Red Bank Restaurant   £60

Tel 01 849 1005   Fax 01 849 1598   Map 1 D3   **R**
7 Church Street Skerries Co Dublin

The original safe is now the wine cellar at Terry & Margaret McCoy's converted
bank, which is well appointed in a pleasingly restrained style – a comfortable
bar/reception for aperitifs, well-spaced tables, fresh flowers and promising wine
glasses – and its close proximity to the other Red Bank (well known to the local
fishing fleet) is reflected on Terry's colourful, imaginative menus. Dishes range
from the day's soup (cockle and mussel consommé), served with delicious
home-baked bread (made with locally-milled flour), Rossmore rock oysters,
monkfish with a smoked bacon and leek sauce, herb-crusted cod through classics
like sole on the bone and a carefully balanced short choice (rack of lamb with
rosemary, fillet steak and duck) for carnivores and there's a thoughtful system of
symbols to assist vegetarian choices. Follow with farmhouse cheeses or tempting
desserts from the trolley plus a choice of coffees. Not suitable for children under
6. Winner of our Ireland Seafood Restaurant of the Year in 1995. The McCoy's
have recently acquired and revamped an adjacent guesthouse (Redbank Lodge)
and now offers accommodation in five en suite bedrooms (£40 double – not yet
inspected). *Seats 45. Parties 14. Private Room 10. L (Sun only) 12.30-2.15 D 7-10.
Closed D Sun, all Mon & Christmas week. Set Sun L £14.75 Set D £21 & £23.
Amex, Diners, MasterCard,* **VISA**

SKERRIES   Places of Interest
Ardgillan Castle   Balbriggan Tel 01 849 2212

SKIBBEREEN   Liss Ard Lake Lodge   77%   £242

Tel 028 22365   Fax 028 22839   Map 2 B6   **AR**
Skibbereen Co Cork

Set in extensive gardens (open to the public)
overlooking Lough Abisdealy, this imaginatively
renovated and extended Victorian lodge opened as a
small luxury hotel in 1994. Furnished and decorated
with the emphasis on design, the minimalist, oriental
style is carefully judged to distract as little as possible
from the garden and water views that are framed by
every window. Black and white are the dominant
colours, with lacquer red accents in some places,
softer shades in others and an overall feeling of great
tranquillity and other-worldliness. Rooms – all suites
except one double – are designed to maximise views
and combine clean-lined simplicity with luxury: mini-bars, TV units with video
and hi-fi and equally unusual bathrooms finished to a very high standard.
Helpful staff provide 24hr room service. Excellent breakfasts. Well-behaved
children welcome (under-6s stay free in parents' room; cot and high-chair
available). Suitable for small conferences of up to 20. No dogs. *Rooms 10.
Garden, fishing. Closed 17 Jan-12 Feb. Amex, Diners, MasterCard,* **VISA**

Restaurant   £85

Although decorated in keeping with the rest of the hotel, an open fire and
slightly gentler lines create a warmer tone in the restaurant where elegantly
appointed tables provide a fitting setting for Claudia Meister's and Stephen
Walsh's imaginative (non-dairy) limited-choice five-course menus. Freshly-baked
breads are served with little bowls of seasoned olive oil and accompany, perhaps,
oysters with lime scented hollandaise or roasted langoustine and crab filled

cherry tomatoes, followed by vichyssoise or lemon balm sorbet. Typical main courses are grilled Liss Ard lamb cutlets on a fine ratatouille risotto and pan-fried black sole with baby spinach and lemon-crushed potatoes. Accompanying vegetables are good, as are desserts such as orange and thyme scented crème brulée or chocolate hazelnut soufflé with caramelised peach. Good choice of teas and coffee. 10% service charge added to bill. *Seats 20. Parties 8. D only (except for residents) 7-9.30. Closed Tue (except for residents). Set D £29.*

SKIBBEREEN   Places of Interest
Tourist Information Tel 028 21766
Liss Ard Experience Tel 028 22368

SKRYNE   O'Connell's

Tel 046 25122
Skryne nr Tara Co Meath   Map 1 C3   **P**

The old castle on top of the hill is your marker for this delightfully unspoilt old country pub whose main attraction is a good pint pulled by charming landlady Mary O'Connell (she has held the reins for over 10 years, but the pub has been in her husband's family for three generations). The two simple bars contain friendly locals, records of sporting endeavours and a history of the nearby monastery. *Open 10.30-11.30 (Sun 12.30-2.30, 4-11.30). Closed Good Friday & 25 Dec. No credit cards.*

SLIGO   Bistro Bianconi   £35

Tel & Fax 071 41744
44 O'Connel Street Sligo Co Sligo   Map 1 B2   **R**

Decor at this attractive middle-market restaurant is in the currently popular Roman revival style, with frescos and whatnot in terracottas and soft sandy tones all gently lit with cleverly designed wall lights and brought to life with large leafy plants. The food is unpretentious, simple fare – a wide range of pizzas and some good pastas, all based on fresh, lively ingredients and cooked to order. Vegetarians are well catered for and 'healthy options' (low in calories, fat and cholesterol) are highlighted on the menu. *Seats 85. Parties 25. D only 5.30-12. Closed Good Friday, 25 & 26 Dec. Amex, Diners, MasterCard,* **VISA**

SLIGO   Hargadon's

Tel 071 70933
O'Connell Street Sligo Co Sligo   Map 1 B2   **P**

Hargadon's is one of the great legendary pubs of Ireland: bought by a British MP in 1868, it passed into the hands of the Hargadon family in 1908 and has been maintained by them, unspoilt, ever since. Bar food includes soup and sandwiches served all day plus one or two hot dishes like black-eyed bean casserole, Russian-style lamb casserole or chicken breast with leek and smoked bacon sauce at lunchtime; country-theme dinners are served Thursday-Saturday in a room at the back where it will not interfere with the real business of running a bar. Otherwise it is as it was – the snugs, the pot-belly stove, the wooden benches and the shelves which used to hold groceries. Children allowed in the bar during the daytime only. Go and enjoy. Beer garden. *Open 10.30-11.30 (to 11 in winter), Sun 12.30-2, 5-11.* **Bar Food** *10.30-5 Mon-Wed (to 9 Thu-Sat). No food Sun. Closed Good Friday & 25 Dec. Garden, outdoor eating. MasterCard,* **VISA**

We only recommend the food in hotels categorised as **HR** and **AR**.

SLIGO   McGettigan's (An Cruiscín Lán/Cruskeen Lawn)

Tel 071 62857   Map 1 B2   **P**
Connolly Street Sligo Co Sligo

Liam and Geraldine McGettigan's comfortable, unselfconscious pub is well
supported by locals and visitors alike. Its reputation is based on serving good,
plain food at a very fair price; the emphasis throughout is on old-fashioned
courtesy and service rather than on quaintness of decor or tradition. Expect simply
presented, middle-of-the-road food in generous portions, with value for money
firmly in mind. Good-value lunches offer the likes of plaice and chips, burgers
and chips, home-made lasagne and roast chicken; bar snacks, including children's
favourites (high-chair provided), are served all day every day. Leave room for
home-made apple tart and cream. Accommodation is also offered in 10 modest
rooms (B&B £31 double – two en suite and not yet inspected). *Open 10.30-11.30
(Sun 12.30-2, 4-11), closed 3-5 in winter months. **Bar Food** 12.30-2.30 (no food Sat
& Sun except in high season). Closed Good Friday & 25 Dec. No credit cards.*

SLIGO   Sligo Park   58%   £99

Tel 071 60291   Fax 071 69556   Map 1 B2   **H**
Pearse Road Sligo Co Sligo

In the absence of any real competition, this modern hotel set in seven acres of
parkland on the southern edge of town attracts a high proportion of the area's
business. Bedrooms are adequate and children up to four may stay free in their
parents' room; 4-12s pay £20 (with dinner) when sharing; ask for one of the
refurbished bedrooms when booking. No dogs. The hotel's main strengths are
its conference and banqueting facilities, which can cater for up to 400 (theatre-
style conferences), and a particularly good leisure centre. The *Mespil Hotel* in
Dublin is a sister hotel. *Rooms 90. Garden, tennis, indoor swimming pool &
children's pool, gym, solarium, sauna, spa bath, steam room, snooker. Amex, Diners,
MasterCard, **VISA***

SLIGO   The Tower Hotel   64%   £76

Tel 071 44000   Fax 071 46888   Map 1 B2   **H**
Quay Street Sligo Co Sligo

Centrally located, this striking redbrick hotel presents a neat modern exterior
and warm, bright interior. The lobby incorporates well-spaced seating areas in
light woods with contemporary upholstery in bold checks and lots of greens and
soft terracottas, creating a good first impression; interior design throughout the
public areas (particularly the restaurant) is a positive feature. Bedrooms, which
include one designed for disabled guests, are not very spacious but they are
pleasant, with fairly neutral decor and above-average facilities. En suite bathrooms
are not large either, but are fully tiled, well lit and quite stylish, with over-bath
power shower, ample shelf space and heated towel rail (but only adequate towels
and minimal toiletries are provided). Pleasant, helpful staff. Banqueting/conferences
for 180/200. *Rooms 58. Amex, Diners, MasterCard, **VISA***

SLIGO   Places of Interest
Tourist Information Tel 071 61201
Lissadell House Drumcliffe Tel 071 63150
Parkes Castle Tel 071 64149
Sligo Racecourse Cleveragh Tel 071 62484/83342

We publish annually, so make sure you use the current edition
– it's well worth being up-to-date!

SPIDDAL   Boluisce Seafood Bar

Tel 091 553286   Fax 091 553285
Spiddal Connemara Co Galway

Map 2 B4   **JaB**

Seafood is the star of the show in Kevin and Monica MacGabhann's first-floor restaurant and the downstairs bar: seafood chowder, mussels in cream sauce, oysters natural or baked, Atlantic black sole, Galway Bay salmon, lobster thermidor. Also good steaks and stir-fries in the bar; children's portions. *Seats 60. Parties 30. Meals 12-10 (Sun 12.30-10). Closed Good Friday & 24-26 Dec.* MasterCard, **VISA**

SPIDDAL   Bridge House Hotel   59%   £70

Tel 091 553118   Fax 091 553435
Spiddal Connemara Co Galway

Map 2 B4   **H**

The relaxed atmosphere of this comfortable, unpretentious family-run hotel has been attracting a loyal clientele since 1959. En suite bedrooms are neat and homely. French windows open on to the back garden from the bar and dining-room. The Stirrup Room grill is open all day for informal food. No dogs. *Rooms 14. Garden. Closed Christmas-end Feb. Amex, MasterCard,* **VISA**

We do not recommend the food in pubs where
there is no mention of Bar Food in the statistics.
A restaurant within a pub is only specifically recommended
where its separate opening times are given.

STILLORGAN   Beaufield Mews Restaurant   £55

Tel 01 288 0375   Fax 01 288 6945
Woodlands Avenue Stillorgan Co Dublin

Map 4 C1   **R**

The Cox family's Beaufield Mews (Dublin's oldest restaurant) has been charming guests with its lovely garden setting and olde-worlde atmosphere since 1959, when it all started with refreshments provided for people visiting the Coach House antique shop. Antiques are still an active side of the enterprise and are part of the fun of a visit as much of the furniture (including, perhaps, the very chair on which you sit and enjoy an aperitif) is for sale and comparing price tags with similar items known to guests invariably provides great entertainment. The influence of head chef Derval Hooper's young kitchen team is to be seen in some trendier dishes – a starter of Louisiana crab cakes with tomato and coriander salsa, perhaps, angel hair pasta with chicken consommé, or a main course of chargrilled Cajun kebabs with a satay sauce – but the main style of food is very traditional. Standards can vary somewhat: a salmon roulade may delight with its freshness of flavour and delicately creamy lemon and dill sauce, while prawn salad could turn out to be somewhat different from the 'fresh Dublin Bay prawns' promised, a fault compounded by dated presentation on a bed of mixed salad squeezed on to a tiny side plate. Yet, taken overall, menus are balanced and the cooking wholesome and in keeping with the surroundings; roast duckling is a speciality, perhaps cooked with walnuts and apple then finished with orange and black grapes. Exceptionally friendly and helpful staff also add greatly to the pleasure of a visit. Fragrant Java coffee rounds it all off nicely. *Seats 120. Parties 14. Private Rooms 40/60. L (Sun only) 12.30-2 D 6.30-10.30. Closed L Tue-Sat, D Sun, all Mon, Bank Holidays & 24-27 Dec. Sun L £11.90 Set D £17.60. Amex, Diners, MasterCard,* **VISA**

STILLORGAN   China-Sichuan Restaurant   £50

Tel 01 288 4817   Fax 01 288 0882   Map 4 C1   **R**
4 Lower Kilmacud Road Stillorgan Co Dublin

Established in 1986 by David and Julie Hui in co-operation with the China
Sichuan Food Authority, this smart, civilised and authentic Chinese restaurant
is situated five miles south of Dublin city centre. Sichuan-style cooking is
renowned for its chili-hot and spicy dishes (denoted on the menu by an asterisk)
but there is a careful balance of dishes on the shortish menu that includes
smoked duckling, ma-po tofu (with minced pork) in a hot and spicy sauce, fried
lamb shreds in aromatic sauce, sizzling dishes and almond bean curd. Fish dishes
(black sole with ginger, fried prawns in garlic sauce) obviously benefit from the
availability of good local produce. Wines include Great Wall white and red from
China. Winner of our Ireland Oriental Restaurant of the Year Award last year.
Seats 46. L 12.30-2.30 D 6-11. Closed Good Friday & 25-27 Dec. Set L from £8
Set D £18. Amex, Diners, MasterCard, **VISA**

STILLORGAN   The Millhouse

Tel 01 288 8672   Fax 01 283 6353   Map 2 D4   **P**
Lower Kilmacud Road Stillorgan Co Dublin

The Mill House is hard to miss with its coat of bright pink and shiny gold
paintwork. Inside, once past the rather off-putting porch/hall area, the interior
is surprisingly calm and peaceful, broken up into a number of small semi-snug
areas with plenty of gas coal-effect fires. The large, irregular mahogany bar is
pleasingly solid and there's a lot of dark wood in the traditional style, successfully
offset by mirrors, pictures and plants in old china cachepots. Daily carvery in
the Lounge (12.30-2.30 Mon-Fri); standard bar food menu (steak sandwiches,
chicken Kiev and so on) from 2.30pm. Pepper Cannister Restaurant open
Mon-Sat from 6pm, Sun 12.30-9pm; also open for lunch before Christmas.
Open 10.30-11.30 (Sun 12-11). **Bar Food** *12.30-9.30. Patio. Amex, Diners,*
MasterCard, **VISA**

STILLORGAN   The Stillorgan Orchard

Tel 01 288 8470   Map 2 D4   **P**
The Hill Stillorgan Co Dublin

Despite its slightly incongruous situation close to a large suburban shopping
centre, the Orchard's main claim to fame is 'the largest thatched roof in Ireland'.
Inside, there's a surprisingly genuine country cottage atmosphere with low
ceilings, small windows, lots of tapestry style and chintzy seating in snugs and
alcoves and all the traditional clutter of brass, copper and old plates on the walls.
Open 10.30-11.30am (to 12 Thu-Sat, Sun from 12.30). Garden. Closed Good Friday
& 25 Dec. Amex, Diners, MasterCard, **VISA**

STRAFFAN   Barberstown Castle   70%   £121

Tel 01 628 8157   Fax 01 627 7027   Map 2 C4   **HR**
Straffan Co Kildare

Next door to the Kildare Hotel &
Country Club (with whom they
share golf and leisure facilities),
Barberstown Castle is historically
fascinating with parts dating back to
the early 13th century. Under the
present ownership since 1987, the
castle has been thoroughly renovated
and refurbished in keeping with its
age and style and now offers very
comfortable accommodation in well-
appointed, individually decorated,

en suite rooms – some in the oldest part, the Castle Keep, others in the 'new' Victorian wing. 24hr room service. Four rooms have been added in the mews, and a new wing of 12 rooms and a 40-seat conference room completed last year. Public areas, including two drawing rooms and an elegant bar, have been renovated with the same care and there are big log fires everywhere. A separate function room in converted stables has banqueting facilities for 160 No children under 12 (or dogs). *Rooms 26. Garden. Closed 24-26 Dec. Amex, Diners, MasterCard,* **VISA**

Castle Restaurant   £70

A series of whitewashed rooms in the semi-basement of the old Castle Keep, with a great atmosphere heightened by fires, candles in alcoves and on tables, and wall lighting; the table style is appropriately simple: plain white cloths and ladderback oak chairs. Starters, all served with excellent dark, moist wholemeal soda bread could be cream of fennel soup, roast quail with rosemary and thyme sauce, and mussels with white wine and garlic. Main courses might include black sole with vermouth and dill, beef Wellington and rack of lamb with roasted beetroot and garlic. A good selection of simply prepared vegetables is left on the table for guests to help themselves. Desserts and farmhouse cheeses which are served with home-made biscuits and big, juicy grapes. Lovely cafetière coffee to finish. In addition to the dinner and à la carte menus, a special tasting menu is available to complete parties. Bar meals at weekday lunchtimes. Smoking discouraged. 10% service charge. *Seats 55. Parties 15. Private Room 35. L 1-2.30 (Sun only) D 7.30-9.30 (Sun 7-8.30). Set Sun L £18.50 (£11.50 children) Set D £25 & £27.50.*

STRAFFAN	Kildare Hotel	89%	£288

Tel 01 627 3333   Fax 01 627 3312   Map 2 C4   **HR**
Straffan Co Kildare

Opened in 1991, the Kildare is known worldwide as The K Club since it is not only a hotel but also a major resort and golfing venue, with a course designed by Arnold Palmer; the Smurfit European Open returns here in 1997. The hotel is best reached from Dublin via the N7, taking a right at Kill and following the signs. Previous owners of the original house were reputedly jinxed by bad luck, not something you can level at the current owners, who have spent a small fortune in making this one of the great hotels of the world, let alone in Ireland, and a worthy winner of our 1997 Ireland Hotel of the Year Award. Everything about the place has matured gracefully in a very short time and General Manager Ray Carroll, one of the most astute and committed hoteliers in the business, combines with his team of dedicated staff to offer levels of service rarely seen elsewhere. Set in 330 acres of beautifully landscaped gardens with several lakes (coarse fishing) and the River Liffey (trout and salmon) running through the grounds, the main house, the new buildings and the country club all blend in tastefully; there's much opulence in the day rooms, sumptuous furnishings and fine period antiques as well as a splendid collection of paintings (including several by Jack B Yeats). Each of the spacious bedrooms has been individually designed and all are lavishly and handsomely furnished; in addition, flowers, a bowl of fruit, chocolates and mineral water greet guests on arrival. Marble bathrooms, most with separate walk-in shower and each with a different *trompe l'oeil* design, are particularly grand – note the monogrammed bathrobes, luxury toiletries, all-enveloping towels, slippers and toy duck. Standard amenites in bedrooms include satellite TV, VCR, CD music system, mini-bar, personal safe and handily-placed telephones. Housekeeping and maintenance are quite exemplary and the nightly turn-down service includes the provision of a linen bedside mat. There are several meeting rooms, ranging from the elegant Tower Room to the ornate John Jefferson Smurfit Room and the Arnold Palmer Room located in the Golf Clubhouse. Due for completion in summer 1997 are further self-contained courtyard apartments to go alongside the existing ones and a three-bedroomed lodge overlooking the 7th fairway. *Rooms 45. Garden, tennis, golf (18), putting green, bicycles, coarse & game fishing, clay-pigeon shooting, indoor swimming pool, spa bath, gym, squash, sauna, solarium, hair & beauty salons, snooker, gift shop. Amex, Diners, MasterCard,* **VISA**

The Byerley Turk   ★   £120

Fine pictures of racehorses (the restaurant's name derives from one of the three Arab stallions in the male line of every thoroughbred horse in the world) are a feature in the imposing dining-room, which is cleverly shaped to offer semi-private areas. Marble columns and draped windows create a luxurious ambience; tables are grandly set up and there are even handbag stools. At night a pianist plays (little piano-shaped cards enable you to request your favourite tune!). French chef Michel Flamme presents a classical à la carte menu as well as a *menu du jour* with choices at both lunch and dinner. Additionally, the 'Dining Experience' allows an entire table to choose 'blind' with dishes reflecting 'the market, the garden, the sea and the season'. Local ingredients bring a national slant to the menus, as in starters such as terrine of Irish stew with a confit of garden vegetables, pan-fried Clonakilty black and white pudding with colcannon potato and parsley jus, or Irish salmon gravad lax with a deep-fried oyster. Follow with roast rib of Tipperary beef or tournedos of silver hake stuffed with bone marrow and served with pearl barley risotto and red wine sauce. Pastry chef Derek O'Brien's desserts (Baileys and praline chocolate mousse with a port sabayon, plum gratiné served with a passion fruit sorbet) will tempt, or else choose from a fine cheese trolley. More casual eating is available at *The Legends Restaurant* in the Golf Clubhouse, open from 12.30 through to 9.45pm (Nov-Mar till 8pm except at weekends). *Seats 70. Parties 8. Private Room 44. L 12.30-2 D 7-9.45. Closed L Mon-Sat mid Oct-end Apr. Set L £22 (Sun £26) Set D £39 & £55.*

Sᴛʀᴀꜰꜰᴀɴ   Places of Interest
Steam Museum Tel 01 627 3155
Castletown House Celbridge Tel 01 628 8252
Irish National Stud Tully Tel 045 521251 *15 miles*
Japanese Gardens Tully Tel 045 521617 *15 miles*

Sᴛʀᴀɴᴅʜɪʟʟ   The Strand   £50

Tel 071 68140   Fax 071 68593   Map 1 B2   **R/P**
Strandhill Co Sligo

Just outside Sligo, beside the airport and one of Europe's most magnificent surfing beaches, this welcoming bar charms quickly with its big turf fire, cosy snugs, friendly bar staff – and the smell of good food wafting through from the kitchen. Well set up for eating and drinking in the bar as well as the restaurant (which has a separate entrance as well as access directly from the bar), this is a family-friendly place where local parents (and grandparents) bring little ones for a bar meal or an early dinner; there is a pool room behind the bar to keep teenagers happily occupied. The bar and restaurant meals overlap considerably at certain times, especially off-season when local business takes over from tourists and anything ordered from the à la carte is cheerfully served in the bar if preferred. This might include a choice of several excellent soups (French onion or superb, creamy chowder) served with a big basket of brown soda bread and a pottery bowl of butter, and a rich game paté served with green tomato chutney and melba toast. Main courses include steaks, roast herb-crusted rack of lamb, pork fillet with apple and calvados sauce and seafood dishes such as scallops and crab claws with herb butter and pasta. Vegetarian dishes change daily and there's a good choice of both popular and more unusual desserts ranging from caramel profiteroles to crème brulée ratafia. *Seats 50. Bar meals served 12-10 (to 6 Oct-May). L 12.30-2.30 (Sun only) D 6-9. Set Sun L £11.50. Set D £18. Closed Good Friday, 25 Dec & Tue, Wed in winter. MasterCard,* **VISA**

SWORDS   Lukas   £45

Tel & Fax 01 840 9080   Map 1 D3   **R**
River Mall Main Street Swords Co Dublin

Denis Murnane, formerly of Dublin's popular *Pasta Fresca*, is heading up the kitchen at this atmospheric little modern restaurant close to the airport. It will come as no surprise that a choice of home-made pastas takes pride of place on the menu; typically there might be a choice of spaghetti, penne or tagliatelle served with a wide selection of sauces. In addition, there are warm salads, pizzas a handful of spicy Mexican and Cajun dishes like beef enchiladas with refried beans and chicken, shrimp and smoked bacon jambalaya. Live music Thursday and Friday nights. No children after 8pm. *Seats 60 (+ 10 on terrace). L 12.30-2.30 D 5.30-11.30. Closed L Sat & Sun, Good Friday, 24 & 25 Dec. MasterCard,* **VISA**

SWORDS   The Old Schoolhouse   £60

Tel 01 840 4160   Fax 01 840 5060   **R**
Coolbanagher Swords Co Dublin   Map 1 D3

Set in a quiet backwater away from the main road, this old stone building has been sympathetically restored and converted to make a delightful restaurant. Good fish from nearby harbours Skerries and Howth highlight the à la carte and set menu choices. Typical à la carte dishes might be a warm smoked duck salad with balsamic vinaigrette, crab claws in garlic butter, a choice of up to four home-made soups, pigeon with chestnuts and red wine, venison with prune and cognac sauce, tandoori baked brill, medallions of pepper-crusted monkfish with mustard sauce and a couple of vegetarian options. Steaks are served with a choice of sauces. Desserts like home-made ice creams, Austrian apple strudel, and ginger and honey cheesecake. Early Bird 3-course menu (6.30-7.30 Monday-Friday). Plans for 1997 include adding upmarket accommodation. *Seats 70 (+ 20 outside). Parties 20. Private Rooms 10/20. L 12.30-2.30 D 6.30-10.30. Closed L Sat, all Sun, 1 week Christmas & Bank Holidays. Set L £11.95/£13.95 Set D £13.50 & £22.95. Amex, Diners, MasterCard,* **VISA**

SWORDS   Travelodge   £48

Tel 01 840 9233   Map 1 D3   **L**
N1 Dublin/Belfast Road Swords Bypass nr Dublin Co Dublin

On the southbound carriageway of the Swords bypass at Swords roundabout, 1½ miles north of Dublin airport, 16 miles north of Dublin city centre. The room rate of £36.50 (without breakfast) could include up to three adults, a child under 12 and a baby in a cot. Reception is only staffed between noon and 7am. *Rooms 40. Amex, Diners, MasterCard,* **VISA**

SWORDS   Places of Interest

Newbridge House Donabate Tel 01 843 6534 *4 miles*

TAHILLA — Tahilla Cove Country House — £72

Tel 064 45204   Fax 064 45104   Map 2 A6   **A**
Tahilla Sneem Co Kerry

One of the few truly waterside establishments in the area, this architecturally unremarkable house is nothing less than a little bit of heaven for the many regulars who return again and again. In the family since 1948, it has been run with great warmth and charm by James and Deirdre Waterhouse since 1987. Comfort and relaxation are their priorities. All the public rooms have sea views, including the dining-room and a large sitting-room with plenty of armchairs and sofas; the latter opens on to a terrace where there are patio tables and chairs overlooking the garden and the cove with its little stone jetty. Accommodation is divided between the main house and another close by; rooms vary considerably but all except two have sea views, many have private balconies and all are en suite, with bathrooms of varying sizes and appointments (one single has a shower only). The bar is open to non-residents and flat-capped sheep farmers down from the hills often drop in at weekends. *Rooms 9. Garden, croquet, fishing (pier). Closed 10 Oct-Easter. Amex, Diners, MasterCard,* **VISA**

We do not accept free meals or hospitality – our inspectors pay their own bills and **never** book in the name of Egon Ronay's Guides.

TERMONFECKIN — Triple House Restaurant — £60

Tel & Fax 041 22616   Map 1 D3   **R**
Termonfeckin Co Louth

On cold evenings a welcoming log fire in the reception area (an alternative to the conservatory used for aperitifs in the summer) sets the tone at Pat Fox's attractive restaurant in the pretty village of Termonfeckin. The hearty "Celebration Dinner Menu" is supplemented by a blackboard of seafood from nearby Clogherhead. Typical first courses might include mushroom risotto with fresh parmesan and pigeon breast sautéed with cepes and garlic butter. A choice of soup (red onion with cider) or well-dressed salad follows, with freshly baked bread accompanying, then a wide choice of main courses with the emphasis on fish (haddock au gratin), but plenty else beside, including an imaginative vegetarian option and red meats such as breast of guinea fowl with Madeira sauce and roast loin of lamb with a tomato and herb sauce. Finish with a speciality dessert, a dacquoise that varies with the season's fruits, home-made ice creams or a plated selection of farmhouse cheeses. Early evening 3-course dinner (7-7.30) £10. *Seats 40. L 1-2.30 (Sun only) D 7-9.30. Closed all Mon, Good Friday & 1 week Christmas. Set L Sun £11 Set D £15.50. MasterCard,* **VISA**

THOMASTOWN   Mount Juliet Hotel   84%   £235

Tel 056 24455   Fax 056 24522   Map 2 C5   **HR**
Thomastown Co Kilkenny

Some 75 miles south of Dublin and signposted from the main N9 Waterford road, Mount Juliet is in fact an estate of around 1500 acres of parkland and formal gardens through which flow the rivers Kings and Nore. It is also home to the Ballylinch stud (where the four-bedroomed house, complete with personal housekeeper, can be rented), the David Leadbetter Golf Academy, the Jack Nicklaus-designed golf course, and the Iris Kellett Equestrian Centre. Add to these facilities a self-contained spa and leisure centre, tennis, archery, hunting, fishing and shooting and you have the complete sporting estate. It's a long and picturesque drive to reach the main house, built in the 18th-century, where you'll encounter elegant and handsome public rooms with fine fireplaces and historical pictures all commanding splendid views of the river and estate. The walls of the club-like Tetrarch Bar list home winners of major horse races through the years. Most (32) of the spacious bedrooms are in the main house, each individually and charmingly designed with good furniture and seating, and with fine bathrooms to match. On arrival you will be welcomed by a box of chocolates and a bowl of seasonal fruit and among the host of extras, there's a decent hairdryer and luxurious bathrobes. Housekeeping is exemplary and, there's a full turn-down service at night. Room service is available only in the main house. More rustic accommodation is available in the Courtyard rooms (£140) and Rose Garden suites at the Hunters Yard, converted from the old stableyard. A short club away from the 1st tee, this is also the site of the golf shop, spa, bars and the Loft restaurant. Children under 12 stay free in their parents' room. Banqueting for up to 140, theatre-style conferences 50. *Rooms 54. Garden, croquet, indoor swimming pool, spa bath, sauna, steam room, exercise room, beauty salon, tennis, snooker, game fishing, golf (18), putting green, archery, clay-target shooting, riding, bicycles, helipad. Amex, Diners, MasterCard, **VISA***

Lady Helen McCalmont Dining Room   £80
👑 ☕ 🍷 🎴 V 🧤

An elegant room decorated in Wedgwood style, with all the trappings of luxury from crisp Irish linen and fine crystal to gleaming silver and the regimental lifting of cloches. The four-course set menu offers a wide choice which could include a warm terrine of fresh and smoked salmon with spring onions and horseradish cream, a middle course of soup (vegetable with roasted almond) or sorbet followed by roasted loin of veal with wild mushrooms and asparagus speared ragout. Pear and almond tart with honey sauce and pear sorbet or a selection of Irish cheese to finish. Staff are professional and correct in every manner. The Jinks Restaurant, open from 7am-10pm (12-7pm Nov-Feb), serves more traditional and hearty dishes (grilled black pudding, Irish stew, apple strudel) and is suitable for families. *Seats 50. Private Room 30. L (Sun only) 12.30-2.30 D 7-9.30. Set L Sun £16.50 D £38.*

Set menu prices may not include service or wine.
Our guide price for two diners includes wine and service.

THURLES   Inch House   £50

Tel & Fax 0504 51348   Map 2 C4   **AR**
Bouladuff nr Thurles Co Tipperary

Approached by a long drive winding through fields cultivated right to the edge
of the road, Inch House makes a striking image as it suddenly looms ahead,
like the ghost it almost became. John and Nora Egan have done a remarkable
restoration job on this 1720s' house since they acquired it in derelict condition
in the mid-80s; it may have taken nearly a decade to complete but it is now a
comfortable and very welcoming place. There are some fine public rooms that
include a William Morris drawing room and adjoining library (now a little bar),
boldly decorated in the original bright blue and white colour scheme. Big log
fires in the drawing-room and dining-room augment central heating which
(winter guests will be pleased to know) is used generously throughout. An elegant,
shallow-stepped double staircase leads up to thoughtfully furnished rooms with
comfortable beds (some of which are half-tester) and electric blankets. Hospitable
gestures include fresh flowers, hairdryer, tissues, Tipperary mineral water and
complimentary fruit, but don't expect amenities such as a phone or TV.
Bathrooms are all en suite but vary according to the space available; smaller
ones are quite cramped, with just a shower. Two rooms for families; under-5s
accommodated free in parents' room, bed and cot provided. No dogs – kennel
provided. *Rooms 5. Garden. Closed 1 week Christmas. MasterCard, VISA*

Restaurant   £55

Across the hall from the drawing-room, the restaurant occupies a large, well-
proportioned room; its focal point is a big fire burning in a fireplace surrounded
by a traditional club fender. Promisingly well-appointed tables set with white
linen cloths and napkins, fine modern glasses and silverware, plain white porcelain,
fresh flowers and candles provide a fine setting for the sound cooking of chef
Keiran O'Dwyer. Set five-course dinner menus are changed fortnightly and
begin with a selection of freshly-baked breads and soup, followed by fish terrine,
duck salad with pink peppercorn dressing, or timbale of smoked salmon stuffed
with cream cheese, chives and garlic. Main-course choices are strong on red
meat – juicy fillet steak with red wine and shallot sauce, perhaps, or roast quail
with berry game sauce – but balanced by poultry and fish options, and accompanied by a generous selection of vegetables. Classic desserts from the trolley
might include warm chocolate sponge with crème anglaise and home-made ice
cream with apricot coulis, all served on colourful Portuguese ware. Coffee, served
perhaps with home-made shortbread crescents, is taken in the drawing room.
Good breakfasts, too. No children under 10; an early evening meal is provided
for them in library. *Seats 40. D only 7-9.30. Closed Sun & Mon. Set D £22.50.*

TIMOLEAGUE   Dillon's

Tel 023 46390   Map 2 B6   **P**
Mill Street Timoleague Co Cork

That one can see in through the plant-filled clear shop window immediately
distinguishes Dillon's from the usual Irish town bar; their description of
themselves as a café-styled bar is very apt. There's a conventional bar counter
down one side of the single room, a mixture of furniture that includes a few
Lloyd Loom chairs around eating-height tables and postcards of the owner's
native Brittany. It's run by Isabelle Dillon who offers good bar food like seafood
pasta, home-made soups, mussels, stuffed pancakes, couscous, chili, steaks, and
tarte tatin or chocolate marquise. Good cafetière coffee and pots of tea are
served alongside the pints of stout. The nearby Franciscan Friary in Timoleague
Abbey is of great historical interest and dates back to 1230 AD. *Open 12-11.30
(Sun 12.30-2, 4-11) mid Mar-Oct (Fri-Mon only in Oct). Bar Food 12-9.30.
Closed Tue-Thu in Oct & all Nov-mid Mar. No credit cards.*

TIMOLEAGUE   Lettercollum House   £55

Tel 023 46251   Fax 023 46270   Map 2 B6   **R**
Timoleague Co Cork

Unusually situated in a period house which was once a convent and now
operates as an independent hostel. Organic produce grown on the premises in
a walled kitchen garden forms the basis for some unexpectedly sophisticated fare
served in a well-proportioned, high-ceilinged dining-room with some striking
modern paintings and tall windows overlooking the garden. 'Innovative country
cooking' is a fair description of the style: warm duck confit with raspberry
vinegar, braised rabbit with red wine and rosemary, seafood casserole with fennel
and chives – all served with flavoursome vegetables on the side. Vegetarian
options might include tortellini of four cheeses with tomato butter and basil
sauce. Delicious desserts – chocolate and rum mousse cake, plum crème brulée
or a selection of West Cork cheeses. *Seats 40. Parties 12. Private Room 16.*
L (Sun & daily Jul & Aug only) 1-3 D 7-9.30. Closed all Mon (except Jul & Aug)
D Sun-Thu mid Oct-mid Mar (call to check details). Set Sun L £12. Amex, Diners,
MasterCard, **VISA**

TOORMORE   The Altar   £65

Tel 028 35254   Map 2 A6   **RR**
Toormore nr Goleen Skibbereen Co Cork

Michael and Peggy Ryan have been running this attractive cottage restaurant
since 1978; it is named in honour of a local church and carries the clerical
association through to the dramatic black decor in the restaurant. Seafood is
the speciality, especially at lunchtime when they like to serve chowders and big
platters of local fish and shellfish with baskets of freshly-baked bread and perhaps
a generous selection of the many local cheeses, including some lesser-known
ones as well as famous names like Gubbeen and Milleens. Evening menus are
more varied, with the likes of spiced chicken wings and smoked chicken salad
alongside a wide selection of seafood starters and then fillet steak, roast local
ducking with plum sauce, a daily vegetarian dish, Toormore Bay lobster (grilled
with butter and pepper), Kenmare Bay mussels and an evening version of the
Altar's seafood platter. Simple home-made puddings and good, freshly-brewed
coffee. Seven tables are outside in the Garden Room. *Seats 32. Parties 10.*
Private Room 16. Morning coffee from 10 am, L 12-3, Tea 3-6, D 6-10.30.
Closed 10 days at Christmas; ring to check off-season opening from late September.
Amex, Diners, MasterCard, **VISA**

Rooms   £30

Accommodation is available in four en suite rooms, two of them wheelchair-
accessible. Garden and three acres of grounds, private foreshore.

TOORMORE   Fortview House   £40

Tel 028 35324   Map 2 A6   **A**
Gurtyowen Toormore nr Goleen Skibbereen Co Cork

Slightly off the beaten track, Violet and Richard Connell's delightful stone
farmhouse (on a working dairy farm in the hills just up behind Goleen) is well
worth seeking out. The house is immaculate and beautifully furnished with
country pine and antiques including brass and iron beds in en suite bedrooms
that are all individually decorated and have all sorts of thoughtful little details
to surprise and delight. Violet loves cooking ("I really put my heart and soul
into it") and not only provides guests with a remarkable choice at breakfast but
also a proper dinner menu (£14) served, by arrangement, in the dining-room at
8pm around a communal table. Dinner starts with a little appetiser followed by
a daily soup served with home-made bread, then a choice of about eight main

courses that might include local seafood and duck as well as their own beef. There's a speciality cheese course – Tom and Giana Ferguson's Gubbeen is made down the road – a dessert that changes each day and a 'bottomless pot' of tea or coffee. Now that's hospitality! *Rooms 5. Garden, bicycles. Closed Nov-end Feb. No credit cards.*

TORY ISLAND   Óstan Thóraíg (Hotel Tory)   £45

Tel 074 35920   Fax 074 35613   Map 1 B1   **H**
Tory Island Co Donegal

Tory, a Gaeltacht (Irish-speaking) island off the north-west corner of Donegal, derives its name from its 'high pinnacle cliffs eroded by the battering swells of the Atlantic' and, despite its exposed position, has been inhabited for four thousand years by fiercely independent people who, even today, refer to the mainland as 'the country'. A surprising place in many ways – not only does this small island have a varied and fascinating history but it also boasts a recognised primitive school of art (founded with the support of well-known artist Derek Hill of nearby Glebe House and Gallery, Church Hill) and even a king as a founder member of the group: the present King of the Tory is Patsy Dan Rogers, who has exhibited his colourful primitive paintings of the island throughout the British Isles and in America. A tiny gallery on Tory provides ongoing exhibition space for the current group of island artists and is of fascination to visitors. Hotel Tory is close by, right at the harbour, and, although simple by mainland standards, it provides comfortable en suite accommodation in pleasantly decorated rooms with both double and single beds and also telephone and TV – and guests are sure of being right at the centre of the island's social activities, which centre on The People's Bar in the hotel. Tory is accessible by ferry from several mainland ports (Donegal Coastal Cruises Tel 075 31991 for details). *Rooms 14. Closed Oct-Mar. Amex, MasterCard,* **VISA**

If you encounter bad service don't wait to write to us but make your feelings known to the management at the time of your visit. Instant compensation can often resolve any problem that might otherwise leave a bad taste.

TRALEE   Abbey Gate Hotel   64%   £80

Tel 066 29888   Fax 066 29821   Map 2 A5   **H**
Maine Street Tralee Co Kerry

Central yet just off the beaten track, this big new hotel would make a good base for touring north Kerry – spacious, well equipped and with a certain style, it is also offers good value for the level of comfort provided. A large marble-floored foyer sets the tone, with nice little seating areas built in to the design; off the foyer are the more formal Vineyard Restaurant and a small bar to one side and the enormous traditional-style Market Place pub, where bar food is served all day, on the other. Broken up into snugs and mini-pubs with their own fireplaces, this area seems smaller than it is, but it has a public entrance from the street and must get very busy at times. Accommodation areas are more serene, however, and bedrooms are quite large, with fairly standard modern decor, comfortable furnishings, good amenities including well-finished en suite bathrooms. Children under 4 stay free in their parents' room – many of the bedrooms have three beds; there's an outdoor playground, a children's menu (6-9 at the Market Place buffet) and Tralee's Aquadome is nearby. Five rooms are equipped for disabled guests. Banqueting/conference facilities for 250/350. 24hr room service. *Rooms 100. Closed 25 Dec. Amex, Diners, MasterCard,* **VISA**

TRALEE — Ballyseede Castle Hotel — 60% — £100

Tel 066 25799   Fax 066 25287
Tralee Co Kerry

Map 2 A5

H

Just off the Killarney road, this 15th-century castle was once the chief garrison of the Fitzgeralds, Earls of Desmond. Granite pillars and wrought-iron gates stand at the entrance and impressive public rooms include a lobby with Doric columns, two drawing rooms with fine plasterwork and a dining-room overlooking ancient oaks. Bedrooms are spacious and comfortable; bathrooms vary considerably. Conference/banqueting for 170/80. Golf, fishing, riding and shooting available nearby. Children up to the age of 4 stay free in their parents' room. No dogs. *Rooms 14. Garden. Diners, MasterCard,* **VISA**

TRALEE — Brandon Hotel — 61% — £90

Tel 066 23333   Fax 066 25019
Princes Street Tralee Co Kerry

Map 2 A5

H

This pleasantly-situated, modern hotel is in the heart of medieval Tralee, overlooking a park and the famous Siamsa Tire folk theatre. Public areas are impressively roomy and bedrooms, although some are on the small side, are all comfortably furnished and have neat, fully-tiled bathrooms with plenty of shelf space and thermostatically-controlled bath taps. The well-equipped leisure centre includes a beauty salon and there are conference and banqueting facilities for 1100/550. Parking for 500 cars. No dogs. 24 new de luxe bedrooms (including suites) were added last year. A complete new frontage, revamped reception area/lobby and new cocktail bar were due for completion by May 1997. The 49-room budget hotel *Brandon Court* is 100 yards away and under the same ownership. *Rooms 186. Indoor swimming pool, gym, solarium, sauna, steam room, beauty salon, night club. Amex, Diners, MasterCard,* **VISA**

TRALEE — Larkins — £50

Tel 066 21300   Fax 066 21363
14 Princes Street Co Kerry

Map 2 A5

R

Just beside the *Brandon Hotel* (see entry), a striking restaurant with a small bar/reception room that leads through to a balconied main dining area where an open fire and Mediterranean yellow walls provide a cheerful background for well-appointed tables. A wide-ranging à la carte offers plenty of choice: from a choice of two soups and seven starters, for example, Clonakilty black pudding on a bed of sweet red onion with Pommery mustard, seafood chowder and warm goat's cheese salad; all accompanied by fresh brown soda bread. Typical dishes from a choice of about ten main courses could be rack of lamb with mint béarnaise; pan-fried monkfish with a green pepper and tomato salsa; seafood tagliatelle with garlic cream sauce; or chargrilled sirloin steak with cognac butter. Cheese is deliberately restricted to a choice of three — Cashel Blue Inagh goat's cheese and Wilmas Gouda — each supplied directly by the producers in prime condition. Tempting desserts like crème brulée or white chocolate mousse in a chocolate tulip cup. Good, strong coffee to finish. Short, good-value early evening menu (6-7pm) Excellent service supervised by proprietor Michael Fitzgibbon and characterised by a genuine desire to please guests and send them home happy. *Seats 70. Parties 8. Private Room 26. L 12.30-2 D 6-9.30. Closed L Sat, all Sun (from end Sep) & Mon (end Oct-Jun) & 1 week Christmas. Set D £13.50 (6-7pm). Amex, Diners, MasterCard,* **VISA**

We only recommend the food in hotels categorised as **HR** and **AR**.

TRALEE   The Oyster Tavern   £55

Tel 066 36102   Fax 066 36047   Map 2 A5   **R**
The Spa Tralee Co Kerry

This large informal, family-friendly restaurant and bar is easily spotted on the
landward side of the Spa Road. Window tables have views across Tralee Bay
and there are some good local photographs to compensate other tables, some of
them in a smaller, semi 'snug' area near the bar. Wholesome, unpretentious fare
with family appeal is served by pleasant easy-going staff. Expect popular starters
like Cromane mussels cooked in white wine and cream, home-made paté with
Cumberland sauce or Greek salad with feta cheese; main courses lean towards
seafood, typically baked Portmagee scallops with cheese sauce, Kerry Head
lobster, grilled Brandon Bay black sole and baked turbot with seafood and white
wine sauce; but red meats and poultry are also fairly represented. Finish off with
classic desserts. Sunday lunch is an especially popular family outing, with a
separate children's menu; no children under 5 after 7.30pm. Disabled toilet
facilities. *Seats 120. L 12-3 (Oct-Easter Sun only 12-2.30) D 6-10 (Oct-Easter
to 9.30). Closed Good Friday & 25 Dec. Set Sun L £8.50. Amex, Diners,
MasterCard,* **VISA**

TRALEE   Places of Interest
Aqua Dome Tel 066 28899
Blennerville Windmill Tel 066 21064
Bus Eireann Tel 066 23566
Fenit Seaworld Fenit Pier Tel 066 36544
Kerry The Kingdom Tel 066 27777
Listowel Racecourse Tel 068 21144
Siamsa Tire National Folk Theatre of Ireland Tel 066 23055
Tralee & Dingle Railway Tel 066 28888
Tralee Racecourse Tel 066 26188

TUAM   Cré na Cille   £50

Tel & Fax 093 28232   Map 1 B3   **R**
High Street Tuam Co Galway

Venetian blinds, darkwood tables with place mats, simple cutlery and paper
napkins create quite a businesslike lunchtime atmosphere that is emphasised by
the crush of people coming in from the street – perhaps more Toulouse than
Tuam. Evenings are more formal and the setting softer, but the common link
is owner-chef Cathal Reynolds's confident use of local ingredients in generously
portioned dishes served at remarkably keen prices. Typical dishes include pan-
fried Irish Brie with white wine and vermouth sauce, baked oysters with a herb
crust, wild salmon with cream and dill, roast duck with a sherry and orange
sauce, and a vegetarian dish of the day. Good baked desserts: strawberry charlotte
with a summer berry sauce, hot apple tart with sauce anglaise. Light supper
menu (6-7pm). Commendable list of 12 house wines at £10; all available by the
glass. *Seats 45. Private Room 30. L 12.30-2.45 D 6-10. Closed L Sat, all Sun, 24-27
Dec & Bank Holidays. Amex, Diners, MasterCard,* **VISA**

TUAM   Places of Interest
Tourist Information and Little Mill Museum Tel 093 24463

We do not recommend the food in pubs where
there is no mention of Bar Food in the statistics.
A restaurant within a pub is only specifically recommended
where its separate opening times are given.

TUBBERCURRY   Killoran's Traditional Restaurant & Lounge

Tel 071 85679   Fax 071 85111   Map 1 B2   **P**
Main Street Tubbercurry Co Sligo

"The welcome doesn't die on the doormat" is the motto at Tommy and Anne Killoran's whale of a place; no-nonsense, reliably-priced food and authentic entertainment are the draws. On Thursday nights from Jun-Sep its 60-seater bar/restaurant/lounge (call it what you will) is crammed to the gunwales, with all and sundry tucking into boxty, potato cakes, crubeens and cali – a local name for hot potato, spring onion and melted butter, better known as champ – to help along the traditional music and Irish dancing. Visitors can even try their hand at butter-churning in the middle of it all. Organic vegetables, local goat's cheese and home-made brown bread are regulars on the menu, alongside more everyday fare. In season, the salmon comes from the river right on the doorstep. There's nowhere else quite like it in Ireland – Killoran's is an original. Not elegant, not folksy, but definitely different. "Children are welcome at any time." *Open 10.30-11.30 (Sun from 12.30).* **Bar Food** *9-9 (bar snacks only winter eves). Garden. Closed Good Friday & 25 Dec. Amex, Diners, MasterCard,* **VISA**

VIRGINIA   Sharkey's Hotel   60%   £78

Tel 049 47561   Fax 049 47761   Map 1 C3   **H**
Main Street Virginia Co Cavan

Situated in the centre of this attractive, large lakeside village and run by the Sharkey family since 1990, this bustling little hotel works hard at pleasing a cross-section of guests, both private and business. Public areas include a large street-side bar where wholesome traditional bar food is served (lunchtime carvery and evening bar menu 3-9.30pm), a small evening dining-room and an attractive function room that opens on to a pretty garden with a river at the end (predictably popular for wedding photographs). Rooms are quite modest and tend to be on the small side, but are pleasant and recently refurbished, with phone, TV and en suite shower and/or bath. Banqueting/conferences for up to 400/250. No dogs. **Rooms** *11. Garden, fishing. Closed 24 & 25 Dec. Amex, MasterCard.*

WATERFORD   Dwyer's Restaurant   £60

Tel 051 77478   Map 2 C5   **R**
8 Mary Street Waterford Co Waterford

Situated in a quiet back street close to the bridge, Martin Dwyer's fine restaurant is in an old police barracks and, although the thickness of the walls might give a hint to its previous use, the gentle decor and soothing classical background music immediately create a relaxed mood for the best enjoyment of his excellent cooking. While not at all flamboyant, this is stylish food characterised by interesting combinations and a sure touch with complementary flavours. Typical starters are prawns and Jerusalem artichokes baked in filo parcels or a warm salad of pheasant sausage with apple and horseradish dressing, followed by gutsy cabbage soup with bacon or a passion fruit sorbet. Equally interesting main courses offer a wide range of tempting main ingredients: duck, steak, pork and several fish/seafood choices. Roast duck breast might be marinated in calvados and served with an apple and calvados sauce, pork fillet cooked 'liégeoise' with bacon, cream, juniper and gin, or salmon stuffed with mushrooms, cooked in filo pastry and served with a herbed hollandaise. Details are good throughout, with lovely home-baked breads and generous, wholesome vegetables. Finish with good Irish cheeses and gorgeous puddings that range from a homely apple and almond crumble served hot with crème anglaise to irresistible brown sugar meringues with walnut and caramel sauce or the sophistication of a marquise of three chocolates. **Seats** *30. Parties 12. Private Room 8. D only 6-10. Set D (6-7.30 only) £14. Closed Sun & 1 week at Christmas. Amex, Diners, MasterCard,* **VISA**

WATERFORD   Foxmount Farm   £45

Tel 051 74308   Fax 051 54906   Map 2 C5   **A**
Passage East Road Waterford Co Waterford

At the heart of a working farm just outside Waterford, this lovely 17th-century house is run by Margaret Kent with a well-judged balance of warmth and professionalism that cossets guests yet leaves them free to come and go – suiting families and lone travellers equally well. Furnished traditionally with grace and style throughout and meticulously maintained, Foxmount offers a rare degree of comfort in reception rooms and bedrooms that vary in size and outlook but are all – including one exceptionally large family room – thoughtfully furnished, with views over well-tended gardens and farmland. Children welcome – cots, baby-sitting, high chair and early evening meal by arrangement. No dogs. Golf and fishing nearby. *Rooms 6 (4 en suite). Garden, tennis, table tennis. Closed Nov-mid Mar. No credit cards.*

WATERFORD   Granville Hotel   69%   £90

Tel 051 855111   Fax 051 870307   Map 2 C5   **H**
Meagher Quay Waterford Co Waterford

On the quay by the River Suir, the Granville is kept in tip-top condition by owners Liam and Ann Cusack and their staff. The style throughout the day rooms is traditional, and there are many reminders of the hotel's history: the Thomas Francis Meaghar bar honours an early owner, the Bianconi restaurant salutes another owner (the man who started Ireland's first formal transport system) and the Parnell meeting room remembers where Charles Stewart Parnell made many famous speeches. Stylishly decorated bedrooms of various sizes all have good bathrooms. Children under 4 stay free in parents' room. No dogs. Facilities for functions (200) and conferences (300). *Rooms 74. Closed 25 & 26 Dec. Amex, Diners, MasterCard, VISA*

WATERFORD   Henry Downes

Tel 051 874118   Map 2 C5   **P**
10 Thomas Street Waterford Co Waterford

It is easy to miss this legendary pub so modestly unpubby is the exterior yet, once visited, it will not be forgotten – the pub celebrates being in the same family for 200 years in 1997, and is one of the few remaining houses to bottle their own whiskey, this place is a one-off. Large, dark and cavernous, it incorporates a series of bars of various temperaments each with its own particular following, effortlessly achieving what modern pubs are spending fortunes to copy. The friendly bar staff enjoy filling customers in on the pub's proud history – and will sell you a bottle of Henry Downes' No 9 to take away. No food. *Open 11-11.30 (Sun 12.30-2, 4-11). Closed Good Friday & 25 Dec. No credit cards.*

WATERFORD   Jack Meade's Bar

Tel 051 50950   Map 2 C5   **P**
Cheekpoint Road Halfway House Waterford Co Waterford

This delightful early 18th-century pub has been in the Hartley family for nearly 150 years and owners Carmel and Willie continue to retain its essential character and remarkable charm. The building, which is well kept and cottagey, has not been altered or extended and they make the most of its sun-trap position, with flower tubs at the door and climbing plants up the walls contrasting with the cool, dark, low-ceilinged interior with its two small traditional bars complete with pictures and photographs of local interest and open fires for cold weather; in summer there's traditional music in the open and barbecues at weekends. An agricultural museum of farm machinery and (across the bridge) an old limekiln (for making fertiliser) and ice house (for preserving fish) are among the things to look at. Outdoor toilet with facilities for the disabled and mothers with babies. The northern end of the car park is a reeded area that has recently been declared a bird sanctuary. Only in Ireland? *Open 10-11.30 (Sun 12-2, 4-11). **Bar Food** 12-9 (Easter-end Oct). Children's playground with slide, swing and basketball. MasterCard, **VISA***

WATERFORD	Jurys Hotel	61%	£135

Tel 051 832111   Fax 051 832863   Map 2 C5   **H**
Ferrybank Waterford Co Waterford

Large modern hotel dominating a hillside on the opposite side of the River Suir to Waterford town. The spacious lobby/lounge features a long white marble reception desk, a pair of fine Waterford crystal chandeliers and a comfortable sitting area. There are five floors of bedrooms (half recently refurbished), all of which share the same fine view over the city, with darkwood furniture, matching floral curtains, polycotton duvets and smart bathrooms with white marble vanity units providing good shelf space. Up to two children under 12 stay free in parents' room; 20 rooms have both a double and single bed. 24hr room service. Activity club and playroom for children June to September and Bank Holiday weekends. 38 acres of garden. Banqueting for 600, conference facilities for 700. No dogs. *Rooms 98. Garden, indoor swimming pool, plunge pool, gym, solarium, sauna, spa bath, steam room, beauty salon, hair salon, tennis, children's indoor playroom. Closed 24-27 Dec. Amex, Diners, MasterCard, **VISA***

WATERFORD	Prendiville's Restaurant & Guesthouse	£55

Tel 051 78851   Fax 051 74062   Map 2 C5   **RR**
Cork Road Waterford Co Waterford

Peter and Paula Prendiville serve imaginative food at reasonable prices and with professionalism at their converted gate lodge, which is just out of the centre and a short drive from the crystal factory. Paula plans her menus around the best of fresh local ingredients, and her dishes show a deal of controlled creativity: chicken parfait with tangy Cumberland sauce, warm monkfish and orange salad with pine nuts, roast sea bass with tomato, garlic and wine, pan-fried venison on a bed of savoury cabbage with creamy rosemary sauce, fresh fish of the day. Irish farmhouse cheeses and tempting desserts such as passion fruit and raspberry terrine or rhubarb crumble with vanilla custard. No children under 5 after 7.30pm. No smoking. *Seats 50. Private Room 20. L 12.15-2.15 D 6.30-9.45. Closed L Sat, all Sun, Good Friday & 23-30 Dec. Set L £12.95 Set D (till 8pm) £14.95. Amex, Diners, MasterCard, **VISA***

Rooms   **£49**
Nine simply-furnished rooms are available, all with en suite facilities and phones. Some have crochet bedspreads and TVs are available on request. No dogs.

WATERFORD	Tower Hotel	59%	£132

Tel 051 75801   Fax 051 70129   Map 2 C5   **H**
The Mall Waterford Co Waterford

Opposite, and taking its name from, an ancient Viking tower, the hotel has been extended and refurbished in recent years. The spacious lobby copes well with tour groups and a large plush bar overlooks the River Suir. Apart from a couple of singles, bedrooms are of good size and similarly decorated and furnished with plain walls and simple darkwood furniture whether in the old or new part of the building. All have good easy chairs and modern bathrooms. 24hr room service. Banqueting for 400, conference facilities for 600. *Rooms 141. Indoor swimming pool, children's splash pool, gym, solarium, sauna, spa bath, steam room. Closed 25-28 Dec. Amex, Diners, MasterCard, **VISA***

| WATERFORD | Waterford Castle | 74% | £240 |

Tel 051 78203   Fax 051 79316   Map 2 C5   **HR**
The Island Ballinakill Waterford Co Waterford

From the town centre, head for Dunmore East and follow the signs to the hotel, which is situated on its own island. A small chain car ferry transports you across the water to the imposing 18th-century castle with carved granite arch entrance and studded oak doors. The great hall has a roped-off coat of arms hand-woven into the carpet, a cavernous fireplace, again with the Fitzgerald coat of arms on the chimney breast, old panelling, a fine ribbon plaster ceiling and antique leather chairs, as well as many portraits on the walls. The stylish drawing-room has several comfortable sofas and genuine antiques, which also feature in some bedrooms, notably the suites. Others are a combination of the old and the new, but nearly all command fine views of the surrounding parkland and water. Bathrooms, offering good toiletries and bathrobes, have freestanding Victorian bath tubs with gold fittings (but no shower curtains), painted washbasins and loos with wooden seats and overhead cisterns and chains! First-rate breakfast includes fresh orange juice and leaf tea. Two conference rooms can accommodate up to 25. The indoor swimming pool is housed separately, a few hundred yards from the hotel. Dogs in kennels only. *Rooms 19. Garden, indoor swimming pool, tennis, golf (18), bicycles. Amex, Diners, MasterCard,* **VISA**

Restaurant   **£80**

The dining-room setting is spectacular – old oak panelling, plaster ceiling, oil paintings and Regency-striped chairs. Cathal O'Hehir has been promoted to head chef having been at the castle for three years, and produces daily-changing lunch and dinner menus, the latter is twice the price of the former, with only a soup or sorbet in addition. A typical offering might consist of sautéed quail with a rich brandy and raisin sauce, cream of celery and apple soup or apple and cinnamon sorbet followed by herb-crusted monkfish with a tomato and basil sauce and pecan and raisin cheesecake with a raspberry coulis. The bread is good and the coffee strong. The wine list is safe without being particularly outstanding. *Seats 70. Private Room 24. L 12.30-2 D 7-10 (Sun & Bank Holidays to 9). Set L £16 Set D £33.*

| WATERFORD | The Wine Vault | £55 |

Tel & Fax 051 853444   Map 2 C5   **R**
High Street Waterford Co Waterford

Wine man David Dennison opened this busy, buzzy bistro in the oldest part of town in 1993 and the ground-floor restaurant (situated in the remains of an Elizabethan townhouse) has proved the perfect partner for his wine shop in the vaults below, (where customers are free to browse and wine tastings and courses are held). Food, under head chef Paul Brady, is informal, bistro style with an emphasis on seafood – oysters (natural or baked with Venetian pepper sauce), chargrilled monkfish with mussels, spinach and ginger – and strong vegetarian options, such as baked goat's cheese soufflé with stuffed artichoke. Steak and chicken features strongly – also game in season, notably venison. Finish with dessert (rhubarb and ginger compote, bread-and-butter pudding) or some plated farmhouse cheeses served with water biscuits and big fat black grapes. Our 1997 Cellar of the Year demonstrates that a wine list does not necessarily have to be that long. This one is refined and informative, comprehensive and titillating, but, above all, fairly priced. Spend as little as £10 for a decent bottle or as much as £165 for a classic '82 claret. *Seats 38. Parties 10. Meals 10.30am-midnight (L 12.30-2.30 D 5-11). Closed L (Bank Holiday Mon only), all Sun, Good Friday & 25 Dec. Set D £12.95/£15.95 (5-7.30). Amex, MasterCard,* **VISA**

WATERFORD   Places of Interest

Tourist Information Tel 051 75788
Waterford Cathedral Tel 051 74757
Waterford Crystal Glass Factory Kilbarry Tel 051 73311
Waterford Mussel Festival (Passage East) Tel 051 382677 *September*
Waterford Racecourse Tramore Tel 051 381574

WATERVILLE	Butler Arms Hotel	68%	£110

Tel 066 74144   Fax 066 74520   Map 2 A6   **H**
Waterville Co Kerry

Once one of Charlie Chaplin's favourite haunts, this landmark hotel still dominates the seafront and much has remained unchanged – notably a reputation for hospitality and service – notwithstanding the many improvements that have been made in recent years. Public areas, including two sitting rooms, a sun lounge and a cocktail bar, are spacious and comfortably furnished for relaxation and peace, while the characterful, beamed Fishermen's Bar (which also has a separate entrance from the street) offers contrasting buzz. Bedrooms vary from distinctly non-standard rooms in the old part of the hotel (which many regular guests prefer) to smartly decorated, spacious rooms with neat en suite bathrooms and uninterrupted sea views in a reconstructed wing opened in 1992, but the standard of comfort is high throughout. Under-12s may stay free in their parents' room. 24hr room service. Conference facilites for up to 25.
Rooms 31. Garden, fishing, tennis, games room, snooker. Closed mid Oct-mid Apr (private shooting parties, Nov-Jan). Amex, Diners, MasterCard, **VISA**

WATERVILLE	The Huntsman		£50

Tel 066 74124   Fax 066 74560   Map 2 A6   **R/P**
Waterville Co Kerry

Raymond and Deirdre Hunt's modern-design building has become a landmark since they came here in 1978 and many a chef has been trained by Raymond along the way. Classic French seafood cookery is the speciality and tables are set up in both bar and restaurant to maximise enjoyment of classic Kerry sea and mountain views while you eat. Service runs on well-oiled wheels with uniformed waiters greeting and seating guests on arrival, whether for restaurant or bar meals – the distinction between bar and restaurant is blurred at the edges, as table settings and service in the bar are on a par with the restaurant and the full à la carte menu is also available for more informal meals in the bar. A welcoming turf fire burns in the bar and the decor is warm and cosy, making for a relaxing meal even on cooler days. The bar menu is quite extensive and includes popular dishes like deep-fried fish and fries, Irish stew, omelettes and pasta as well as classics like grilled black sole and sea and shellfish in garlic butter. Set dinner menus range from a relatively limited tourist menu to the discerning diner's four-course menu which offers a wide range of seafood, plus a few meat/vegetarian choices on each course. Start, perhaps, with cockles and mussels marinière or oysters Hunstman (served hot with a delicious herby cream sauce), followed by a bisque or salad, then any one of 14 main courses, including lobster from their own tank (for a supplement), all served with simply-cooked side vegetables that complement the rich sauces. Classic desserts – crème caramel, raspberry crème brulée, meringues and chocolate sauce –are followed by good coffee. Modest accommodation is available (£40-50, but not specifically recommended). At the time of going to press plans were in place for a major leisure/accommodation development to be completed during 1997. *Seats 90 (+ 4 patio tables). Parties 20. Private Room 20. Bar open 10.30-11.30, Sun 12.30-11. Meals L 12-3 D 6-10. Closed 24-27 Dec & all Feb. Set D £15.95 & £22.95. Amex, Diners, MasterCard,* **VISA**

WATERVILLE   The Smugglers Inn   £70

Tel 066 74330   Fax 066 74422   Map 2 A6   IR
Waterville Co Kerry

Right beside Waterville's championship golf course, in a clifftop position with
sweeping Atlantic views over a long golden beach, this 100-year-old former
farmhouse is indeed blessed in its location. Harry and Lucille Hunt converted
it into its present form and, since 1980, have run it as a hospitable bar and
restaurant with unpretentious, comfortable family-friendly accommodation. Bar
food is served all day and ranges from soup and sandwiches through patés, Irish
cheese plates and salads to seafood dishes, their speciality. Kerry cream teas are
also served. Bedrooms, which are all en suite (some with shower only) are quite
spacious and now include a large front bedroom with its own corner conservatory
balcony and superior bathroom. A comfortably furnished residents' sitting/TV
room has magnificent sea views. *Rooms 17. Garden, sea fishing. Closed Nov-end
Feb. Amex, Diners, MasterCard,* **VISA**

Restaurant   £65

Situated on the sea side of the cosy bar to make the most of the view, the
restaurant is just right for a seaside inn – well set up but not too formal. Good-
value lunch menus offer a choice of seven starters and main courses – typically
seafood cocktail Marie Rose, soup or paté (chicken liver or an excellent version
with smoked salmon, served with hot, crisp toast), then perhaps grilled lemon
sole with garlic butter, a steak or sautéed chicken in white wine sauce, all served
with hearty portions of seasonal vegetables and followed by homely puddings
like apple pie or ice cream with chocolate sauce. Harry Hunt's dinners are a
more serious affair, offering a wide choice of seafood on both the dinner and à
la carte menu – starters like squid in garlic butter or lobster cocktail are typical,
then perhaps cream of seafood soup and main courses like pan-fried John Dory
provençale, wild salmon with béarnaise sauce, grilled whole black sole and lobster,
grilled or boiled. Kerry lamb, steaks and local duckling widen the choice, and
there's a full vegetarian menu (£15) available. Waitress service is pleasant and
friendly. *Seats 60. Bar Food 11.30am-10pm. Restaurant Meals L 12-3 D 6.30-10.
Set L £12.95 Set D £22.50.*

WESTPORT   Asgard Tavern & Restaurant   £55

Tel 098 25319   Fax 098 26523   Map 1 A3   R
The Quay Westport Co Mayo

Named after the sail training ship *Coiste Asgard* (a well-loved visitor to the port),
Michael and Mary Cadden's famous quayside bar is appropriately decorated with
nautical artefacts. Upstairs, over the well-run bar, the Caddens run a relaxingly
unpretentious family-friendly restaurant with an old-fashioned emphasis on
quality ingredients and good value. A keenly-priced à la carte menu offers a
choice of about ten starters ranging from soups and well-made favourites like
paté maison with Cumberland sauce and hot buttered toast to an excellent and
unusual peppered beef fillet on a warm salad. Fish takes pride of place, from
lobster in brandy cream sauce with mushrooms and shallots through poached
salmon hollandaise to baked turbot with Chardonnay and dill sauce, with
steaks a close second. Vegetarians are not forgotten, with two specials such as
ratatouille omelette or a seasonal vegetarian platter always on offer. Finish with a
cheese plate or popular desserts. Good-value table d'hote menu. The bar menu,
served daily in the lounge and Captain's Deck, also underlines links with the sea
in a varied seafood selection that includes favourites such as chowder, Clew Bay
oysters and main dishes like fisherman's platter and prawn salad. For meat-eaters

there's traditional Irish lamb stew, lasagne and burgers. Live music Fridays and Saturdays (more often in high season). *Bar: open 12-11.30 (to 11 in winter), Sun 12.30-2, 4-11.* **Bar Food** *12-3, 6-9. Garden. Restaurant: Seats 40. Private Room 14. D only 6.30-9.45. Restaurant closed Mon & Sun in low season. Closed Good Friday & 24-26 Dec. Set D £17.50. Amex, Diners, MasterCard,* **VISA**

WESTPORT   Matt Molloy's Bar

Tel 098 26655   Map 1 A3   **P**
Bridge Street Westport Co Mayo

Owned by *the* Matt Molloy, of The Chieftans, this is a pleasingly dark, atmospheric pub which feels much smaller than its real extent and has some admirable features, such as a no-TV policy and no children after 9pm. Unsurprisingly, there's a lot of musical memorabilia, including plenty on The Chieftans themselves, but groceries of yesteryear, displayed on high shelves, also pay tribute to the places earlier role as a traditional grocer-pub. Traditional music is a big draw here – either in the back room or out at the back in fine weather. *Open 4-11 (Fri from 2, Sat & Sun from 12.30). Closed Good Friday & 25 Dec. No credit cards.*

WESTPORT   The Olde Railway Hotel   63%   £70

Tel 098 25166   Fax 098 25090   Map 1 A3   **H**
The Mall Westport Co Mayo

Beautifully situated alongside the tree-lined Carrowbeg River on the Mall in the centre of Westport, the Olde Railway Hotel is the real McCoy. Once described by William Thackeray as "one of the prettiest, comfortablist hotels in Ireland", it was built in 1780 as a coaching inn for guests of Lord Sligo. Now, in the hands of Mr and Mrs Rosenkranz (who have owned it since 1983), it retains considerable character and is well known for its antique furniture and a pleasing atmosphere of slight eccentricity, although concessions to the present generation of traveller have been made in the form of en suite bathrooms, satellite television and private car parking, also a secretarial service including use of fax machine and computer. 'Superior' rooms attract a tariff of £90 (£70 in low season) including service; there are six suites. Public areas include a conservatory dining-room quietly situated at the back of the hotel and a rather splendid function room with original stone walls. The large bar is the public face of an essentially private hotel and the main entrance is from the mall. Children are welcome; half-price if sharing parents' room; extra bed or cot provided; three family bedrooms; high-chairs provided. No dogs. **Rooms** *24. Garden. Closed 23-27 Dec. Amex, Diners, MasterCard,* **VISA**

WESTPORT   Quay Cottage Restaurant   £50

Tel 098 26412   Fax 098 28120   Map 1 A3   **R**
The Harbour Westport Co Mayo

A strong maritime theme pervades this cosy, informal, stone-built waterside cottage and there is much of interest to observe once settled at a scrubbed pine table and contemplating the meal ahead. Not surprisingly, seafood predominates on the menu – although other tastes are catered for with lamb chops and steaks, plus imaginative vegetarian options (tagliatelle with blue cheese sauce). Typically, start with thick vegetable and mussel chowder, mussels with garlic and deep-fried Irish Brie with seasonal fruit coulis; all accompanied by plenty of lovely home-baked brown soda bread. Main courses might include lobster from the tank, or wild salmon with wholegrain mustard crust and mustard sabayon, or sirloin steak with Gaelic sauce. Nice homely desserts – nutty apple crunch, perhaps – and freshly-brewed coffee by the cup. As from March 1997 there will be two dining-rooms; one no-smoking. **Seats** *60 (+ 20 on terrace). Parties 20. Private Room 65. D only 6-10pm. Closed 24 & 25 Dec & all Jan. Amex, MasterCard,* **VISA**

WESTPORT   Towers Bar

Tel 098 26534   Fax 098 27017   Map 1 A3   **P**
The Harbour The Quay Westport Co Mayo

A pair of ancient towers (now preserved buildings) inspired the name of this characterful, family-friendly pub. In addition to a range of seafood – typically crab or prawn cocktail, fish pie, baked stuffed mussels, mixed seafood salad (crab, mussels, prawns and smoked fish) – there's simple fare like ploughman's lunches, home-made burger, beef in Guinness, filled baked potatoes with salad and a vegetarian salad option. As we went to press a restaurant (separate menu) was about to open. Although on the harbour side of the road, there is a walled garden with a safe play area for children that includes a tree house and a sand pit. *Open 12-11.30pm (till 11 in winter), Sun 12-2, 4-11. **Bar Food** 12-9 (Sun 12.30-2, 4-8.30). Garden, outdoor eating. Closed Good Friday & 25 Dec. MasterCard,* **VISA**

WESTPORT   The West Bar

Tel 098 25886   Map 1 A3   **P**
Lower Bridge Street Westport Co Mayo

Just across the bridge from The Olde Railway Hotel (*qv*) on a good corner site beside the river, the West Bar is a well-run pub of some character and, being divided up into several sections, intimacy too. There's a restaurant operating separately in the evenings, but bar food is available at lunchtime. *Open 10.30-11.30 (to 11 winter). **Bar Food** 12.30-2.30 Mon-Fri. Closed Good Friday & 25 Dec. No credit cards.*

WESTPORT   Westport Woods Hotel   62%   £96

Tel 098 25811   Fax 098 26212   Map 1 A3   **H**
Louisburgh Road Westport Co Mayo

A low-rise 1970s' building set in trees and within walking distance of Westport House and the harbour pubs and restaurants. First impressions of Westport Woods are mildly positive but improvements in the past year have seen the once dated public areas and function room completely refurbished. Medium-sized rooms have dated decor but are comfortable, with good amenities including a double and a single bed, TV, direct-dial phone, hairdryer and trouser press, well-placed lights and mirrors and bathrooms which, although small and in need of refurbishing, have all that is necessary, including ample shelf space. 38 new, up-to-the-minute bedrooms, including one suite, were added last year; 24hr room service. Children are exceptionally well catered for: family rooms, cots, extra beds, indoor/outdoor play areas, supervised activities organised by age group in school holidays, high-chairs and booster seats, and early evening meal are all provided. Off-season the focus moves to an older age group and equally well-designed activities for 4-5 day Golden Holidays. Banqueting/conferences 200/250. No dogs. *Rooms 95. Garden, tennis, crazy golf, indoor bowling, pétanque, children's indoor playroom. Closed 5-31 Jan. Amex, Diners, MasterCard,* **VISA**

WESTPORT   Places of Interest
Tourist Information Tel 098 25711
Ballintubber Abbey Tel 094 30934 *8 miles*
Clare Island Safaris Tel 098 25048
Salmon World Visitor Centre Newport Tel 098 41107
Westport House & Children's Zoo Tel 098 25430

WEXFORD   Archer's

Tel 053 22316 Fax 053 22087
Redmond Square Wexford Co Wexford

Map 2 D5

P

Just around the corner from *The Granary* restaurant (*qv*), this very pleasant pub is warm and cosy with a comfortably semi-rustic atmosphere. There's an eating area with proper tables (and a high chair) just off the main bar for consumption of appealing bar meals: roast of the day, beef stew, chili, cod in cheese sauce, vegetable lasagne. Sandwiches, soup, salads and a daily special are available throughout opening hours. *Open 10.30-11.30 (Sun 12.30-2, 4-11).* **Bar Food** *12-7 (carvery lunch 12-3) Mon-Sat. Closed Good Friday & 25 Dec. MasterCard,* **VISA**

WEXFORD   Clonard House   £40

Tel & Fax 053 43141
Clonard Great Wexford Co Wexford

Map 2 D5

A

John and Kathleen Hayes offer a warm welcome at their large Georgian farmhouse on a dairy farm overlooking Wexford town and harbour – an Irish coffee at the drawing room fireside before bed is *de rigueur* and ensures guests get to know each other. Rooms vary somewhat but all have en suite shower and TV and three have (modern) four-posters. Children welcome (under-3s stay free in parents' room, 50% reduction for under-12s); cots, high-chairs, outdoor play area. Limited room service. No dogs. **Rooms** *9. Garden, games room. Closed Nov-Easter. Amex, Diners, MasterCard,* **VISA**

WEXFORD   White's Hotel   60%   £82

Tel 053 22311   Fax 053 45000
George Street Wexford Co Wexford

Map 2 D5

H

Although appearing to be modern, much of the original interior of this famous hotel is old but skilfully integrated to provide maximum comfort and a wide range of services without any great loss of character. Public rooms furnished to a high standard include a popular bar (heart of the Opera Festival social scene, late Oct/early Nov), choice of sitting rooms, an elegantly appointed dining-room and cosy informality at the red and white check clothed Country Kitchen grill which has direct access from the street. Comfortable bedrooms vary considerably according to age and situation, but all have neat en suite bathrooms, phone, tea/coffee facilities and satellite TV. Attractive function rooms include an atmospheric converted barn – lofty, with exposed stonework and a huge fireplace – and Mr White's, the conference and banqueting centre. Leisure facilities are in the basement where a singularly sybaritic health and fitness club has been installed – and there's even an imaginative night club and bar, Hunters, next door. Banqueting/conferences (600). Parking (35 spaces + 100 adjacent to the hotel). Children welcome (two family rooms): under-3s stay free in their parents' room, under-12s half price; cots £2, baby-sitting, high-chairs. No dogs. **Rooms** *82. Gym, spa bath, steam room, sauna, solarium, beauty salon. Closed 25 Dec. Amex, Diners, MasterCard,* **VISA**

WEXFORD   Places of Interest

Tourist Information Tel 053 23111
Irish National Heritage Park Ferrycarrig Tel 053 41733
Johnstown Castle Demesne and Agricultural Museum Tel 053 42888
Westgate Heritage Centre Tel 053 46506
Wexford Racecourse Tel 053 23102

WICKLOW · The Bakery Café & Restaurant · £60

Tel 0404 66770
Church Street Wicklow Co Wicklow

Map 2 D4

R

When Sally Stevens opened this delightful restaurant as chef/proprietor in spring 1996 it was an immediate hit. The original bakery had been closed since 1962, but it was a fine stone building, the ovens were still intact and, sensitively restored, the two-storey premises has made a characterful setting for the enjoyment of her good food. Downstairs, where the ovens and other baking paraphernalia provide a pleasing mixture of educational and decorative background for the café, there is an attractive bar/reception area and informal seating for 25, while the more serious dining takes place upstairs. The standard of cooking is high and both menus offer plenty of interest – the café has starters like chicken satay, boxty salmon (potato cake with smoked salmon) or garlic mushrooms tempura, for example, and substantial main courses include traditional dishes like Irish Stew and beef in Guinness, served with champ and imaginative vegetarian dishes that are clearly marked on the menu. Upstairs, there is more emphasis on seafood, in first courses like crab salad and fresh prawns in olive oil with garlic and main dishes such as seafood risotto and escalope of wild salmon with saffron sabayon; there will always be a good choice of meat dishes, too, including Wicklow lamb. Delectable desserts common to both café and restaurant tend to be classical – crème brulée, strawberry sablé, chocolate and Cointreau mousse; perhaps the best solution is to try the Bakery tasting plate on a first visit. Good choice of coffees, friendly service. Children welcome in café (downstairs), but not after 8pm in the restaurant. *Seats 70. Parties 10. Private Room 25. L 1-6 D 6-10 (till 11 Fri & Sat, till 9 Sun). Set L £13 (Sun only). Closed L Mon-Sat & 10 Jan-10 Feb. MasterCard,* **VISA**

WICKLOW · Old Rectory · 69% · £92

Tel 0404 67048   Fax 0404 69181

Map 2 D4

AR

Wicklow Co Wicklow

Since 1977 Paul and Linda Saunders have been welcoming hosts at their immaculately maintained early-Victorian rectory on the edge of town, near the famous Mount Usher gardens (2 miles away). It's decorated with great care and individuality throughout; the cosy sitting-room has a white marble fireplace and traditional furnishings are brought to life by some unusual collections, notably ex-fireman Paul's display of helmets and related paraphernalia. Colourfully decorated bedrooms, including four new rooms in a sympathetically designed extension, feature spotless en suite bathrooms (plentiful towels), antique furnishings and many homely extras including fresh flowers. Keep-fit equipment and a sauna are also housed in the new wing. There's an outstanding choice at breakfast (Irish, Scottish or Swiss menus). No dogs. *Rooms 8. Garden, keep-fit equipment, sauna. Closed 27 Dec-end Feb. Amex, Diners, MasterCard,* **VISA**

Restaurant

£60

Linda Saunders and Richard Doyle present a blend of Victorian and modern, French and Irish in the Orangery dining-room. Most guests choose the special gourmet menu, a no-choice meal which might typically comprise herb-stuffed baked mushrooms for canapes, crab and leek ravioli with avocado and lime sauce, hot grapefruit with Irish whiskey, herb and lavender-crusted rack of Wicklow lamb with blueberry and liqueur sauce and rich home-made cheesecake with frosted pansies. A particularly unusual and imaginative feature is a floral dinner menu (served only during the Co. Wicklow Garden Festival, May-Jun) containing such delights as fresh herb consommé with spicy pheasant sausage and chive flowers, sole and wild salmon with marigold sauce, and champagne ice cream with crystalized primrose biscuits. No smoking and no children under 5. Winner of our Happy Heart Eat Out Award 1997. *Seats 16. Parties 6. D only at 8. Set D £27.*

WICKLOW   Places of Interest
Tourist Information Tel 0404 69117
Mount Usher Gardens Ashford Tel 0404 40116

YOUGHAL	Aherne's Seafood Restaurant	£70

Tel 024 92424   Fax 024 93633   Map 2 C6
163 North Main Street Youghal Co Cork   **RR**

Local seafood is the major attraction at this long-established bar and restaurant on the main street of historic Youghal town. In the FitzGibbon family for three generations now, the current team – brothers John (managing) and David (head chef), with their wives – has held the reins since 1979 and their combined talent and hard work produce high standards of food, service and hospitality. The list of seafood choices on both bar and restaurant menus includes many a house speciality – the renowned chowder (served with an equally famous brown bread), *moules marinière*, oysters (served *au naturel* or in a white wine cream sauce), a hot seafood selection with two sauces, traditional seafood platter with salads, prawns in garlic butter, lobster (thermidor or with butter sauce), grilled black sole on the bone, pan-fried monkfish – all these and many more; the list goes on and on. There are other specialities too – desserts, for example, that include an excellent tasting plate. The all-day bar menu features some of the above, plus other specialities such as Aherne's gratin of hot potato and smoked salmon with salad, their seafood pie and a comprehensive range of lighter, snackier items like their very special open and toasted sandwiches; there are even a few popular foods that have never seen salt water such as lamb burgers, sirloin steak, warm chicken salad and some zippy vegetarian dishes (perhaps tagliatelle with chilis, peppers, sun-dried tomatoes with basil pesto and tomato sauce). Try their freshly-squeezed orange juice and a really delicious local speciality: fresh, farm-pressed Cappoquin apple juice. *Seats 60. Parties 15. Private Room 20. L 12.30-2.15 D 6.30-9.30. Bar Food 10.30am-10.30pm. Set L £17 Set D £27.50. Closed 5 days Christmas. Amex, Diners, MasterCard,* **VISA**

Rooms   £120
The energy of the FitzGibbon family knows no bounds, it seems – their latest venture involved buying a house next door, which has now been converted to provide extra accommodation bringing the total number of luxurious rooms to 12. The latest ones are very special indeed and are equipped to give the option of self-catering if required; they have a separate entrance from the street as well as direct access from the main building. Patio. Own parking (12 spaces). No dogs.

We only recommend the food in hotels categorised as **HR** and **AR**.

YOUGHAL   The Earl of Orrery   £50

Tel 024 93208   Map 2 C6   **R**
140 North Main Street Youghal Co Cork

After working for Myrtle Allen at *Ballymaloe House* and then with Antony
Worral Thompson in London, young Colm Falvey was certainly well qualified
to run his own restaurant; The Earl of Orrery (named after the first earl, Roger
Boyle, 1621-1679) duly opened its doors in March 1996. It's a snazzy little place
on minimalist lines (maybe less so as the decor develops) with modern black
chairs, black and neutral striped oilcloths, lovely fresh flowers, well-presented
bread and butter and quality modern cutlery and glasses, all creating a positive
first impression. Open all hours and successfully conveying a casual atmosphere
which belies the seriousness of the kitchen, this is a place that attracts all age
groups and is all the better for that. Friendly staff put everyone at their ease with
no pressure to eat more than one course (there's even a remarkably generous
'minimum order £3.50' note on the sensibly-priced lunch menu) but menus
are very tempting indeed. The style is bright and modern and ingredients are
very good in starters like salade tiède of goat's cheese, walnuts and pesto, for
instance, or fresh local prawns tossed in garlic butter. Main courses might
include chargrilled breast of chicken with a red pepper sauce, seafood paella and
a strong vegetarian choice (penne with peppers, goat's cheese, pesto and black
olives). Round off with particularly good desserts – an irresistible meringue
roulade with soft summer fruits, perhaps, or a wonderfully refreshing orange
jelly with Grand Marnier – whole orange segments in an individual jelly on a
Grand Marnier syrup flecked with fresh mint – simply delicious. Freshly-brewed
cafetière coffee rounds it all off nicely. No children after 8pm. *Seats 38. Parties 12.
L 12.3-3 D 6-10 (7-10 Oct-Apr). Closed 26-27 Dec. Telephone for Jan opening
times. MasterCard,* **VISA**

YOUGHAL   Places of Interest
Lismore Castle Gardens Lismore Tel 058 54424 *17 miles*
Myrtle Grove Tel 024 92274

Northern Ireland

The addresses of establishments in the following
former **Counties** now include their new
Counties/Unitary Authorities

Co Antrim
Antrim, Ballymena, Ballymoney, Belfast City
Carrickfergus, Larne, Moyle, Newtonabbey

Co Armagh
Armagh, Craigavon, Newry & Mourne (part)

Co Down
Ards, Banbridge, Castlereagh, Down
Lisburn, Newry & Mourne (part), North Down

Co Fermanagh
Fermanagh

Co Londonderry
Coleraine, Derry City, Limavady, Magherafelt

Co Tyrone
Cookstown, Dungannon, Omagh, Strabane

AGHADOWEY   Brown Trout Golf & Country Inn   £80

Tel 01265 868209 Fax 01265 868878   Map 1 C1   IR
209 Agivey Road Aghadowey Coleraine BT51 4AD

Although golf is the major attraction (both the 9-hole course on the premises – green fees £4 Mon-Fri, £6 Sat, Sun & BH – and the nearby Portrush Golf Club), non-golfers will also warm to the relaxed atmosphere and friendly staff at Bill O'Hara's big-hearted country inn. Comfortable public areas have a convivial bar as the focal point, and bedrooms are all on the ground floor, arranged around a garden courtyard. Spacious and pleasantly decorated, with two (small) double beds, TV, phone and hospitality tray, all rooms are en suite with bath and separate shower. Although they may fall down on details such as placing of lights and the quality of towels and bedding, the overall level of comfort is more than adequate and there is plenty of room for golfing paraphernalia. One room is equipped for disabled guests. Leisure facilities include a mini-gym, a putting green, fishing in the grounds and riding stables half a mile away. The Brown Trout is in the townland of Aghadowey on the A54 Coleraine-Kilrea road, 7 miles north of Kilrea and 5 miles south of Coleraine; ask for directions when booking. **Rooms** *17. Garden, golf (9), putting green, riding, fishing, mini-gym, games room. Amex, Diners, MasterCard,* **VISA**

Restaurant   £35

Up a steep staircase (with chair lift for the less able), the restaurant commands a pleasant view of a magnificent tree and the garden end of the golf course. Good home cooking of fresh foods characterises meals that are not over-ambitious and all the better for it. There's an early high tea (5-7pm) followed by an à la carte dinner menu offering excellent versions of favourites such as chicken liver paté with Cumberland sauce and fresh scampi. Weekly specials such as tender fillet of pork with a white wine sauce and desserts like Jamaican bananas baked with rum ensure variety. Sandwiches, home-made 'pubby' dishes and children's favourites are served all day in the bar. **Seats** *42. Parties 15. Private Room 50. (Sun only) 12.30-2 High Tea 5-7 D 7-10 (till 9.30 in winter). Set Sun L £9 (children £5).*

AGHADOWEY   Greenhill House   £48

Tel 01265 868241 Fax 01265 868365   Map 1 C1   PH
24 Greenhill Road Aghadowey Coleraine BT51 4EU

James and Elizabeth Hegarty bought their pleasant Georgian farmhouse in 1969 because they wanted the land and, although graciously framed by mature trees and lovely countryside views, it is still very much the centre of a working farm. Elizabeth greets arrivals at her guest house with an afternoon tea in the drawing-room that includes such an array of home-made tea breads, cakes and biscuits that dinner plans may well waver. Rooms, including a large family room with a cot, are unostentatious but individually decorated, with colour co-ordinated towels and linen; good planning makes them exceptionally comfortable and there are many thoughtful touches – fresh flowers, fruit basket, chocolate mints, tea/coffee-making facilities, hairdryer, bathrobe, proper clothes hangers, even a torch. All rooms now have en suite bathroom facilities. A 5-course set dinner is available (by arrangement) to residents (£30 for two) at 6.30pm, except on Sundays; unlicensed (and guests are asked not to bring their own either). No dogs. **Rooms** *6. Garden. Closed Nov-Feb. MasterCard,* **VISA**

AGHADOWEY   Places of Interest

Causeway Safari Park Tel 01265 741474 *12 miles*
Leslie Hill Heritage Farm Park Ballymoney Tel 01265 666803 *6 miles*
Mountsandel Fort Nr Coleraine

ANNALONG   Glassdrumman Lodge   69%   £110

Tel 01396 768451   Fax 01396 767041   Map 1 D2
85 Mill Road Annalong Down BT34 4RH   **HR**

Situated just off the A2 coast road, with lovely views over the sea or back into the Mournes, this former farmhouse has luxurious bedrooms with fresh flowers, fruit, mineral water and exceptionally well-appointed bathrooms. Superior rooms (£125) and two Executive suites (£135) are also offered. Service is a high priority, including 24hr room service, overnight laundry and a secretarial service, and breakfast a speciality – you can even go and choose your own newly-laid egg if you like. Beaches, walking, climbing, and fishing available locally. No tariff reductions for children. No dogs, but kennels are provided.
Rooms 10. Garden, tennis. Amex, Diners, MasterCard, **VISA**

Restaurant   £60

For the French-style restaurant chef Stephen Webb makes good use of organically-grown vegetables and naturally-reared beef and pork from the hotel farm and seafood from local ports. A typical four-course, fixed-price dinner might include a choice of four soups (among them perhaps oyster and prawn bisque), then salmon fishcakes, bangers and mash, grilled pigeon with redcurrant sauce, braised shank of lamb, peppered pineapple flamed with peach schnapps and lemon cream custard tart. No smoking in the dining-room. *Seats 40. Parties 20. Private Room 20. L by reservation only to residents D at 8. Set D £27.50.*

ANNALONG   Places of Interest

Burren Heritage Centre Tel 01693 773378 *8 miles*
Newry Museum Newry Tel 01693 66232
Silent Valley Visitor Centre Tel 01232 746581

BALLYCASTLE   House of McDonnell

Tel 01265 762975   Map 1 D1
71 Castle Street Ballycastle Moyle BT64 6AS   **P**

Unusually, even for a characterful old pub, McDonnell's is a listed building and as such no changes are allowed inside or out. Not that change is much on the cards anyway, as it has been in the family since the 18th century and is clearly much loved – as visitors soon discover from the landlady Eileen O'Neill. She enjoys nothing better than sharing the history of the long, narrow, mahogany-countered bar which was once a traditional grocery-bar. Alas, no food is now offered, but The Open Door, a good traditional Northern Ireland bakery across the road, has hot snacks and a wide range of fresh sandwiches to order. Inside the pub is a fine collection of original etched mirrors. Traditional Irish music on Friday nights (and Wednesday during the summer) and folk music on Saturday nights throughout the year. "In every sense, a real, traditional Irish pub." *Open 11.30-11 (Sun 12.30-2.30 & 7-10 – but 7-11 only Oct-Easter except Bank Holidays). No credit cards.*

BALLYCASTLE   The Marine Hotel   63%   £70

Tel 01265 762222   Fax 01265 769507   Map 1 D1
1-3 North Street Ballycastle Moyle BT64 6BN   **H**

A substantial building on the seafront (where ferries depart for Rathlin Island), The Marine caters equally to private and business guests, with activities such as golf, tennis, fishing, pony-trekking and bowling nearby, good leisure facilities on site plus conference capacity for over 300 delegates and banqueting for 450. Rooms are fairly modest, but many have sea views and all are en suite with phone and TV. Two rooms are equipped for disabled guests. Families are welcome: there are several family/interconnecting rooms, children under 4 stay free in their parents' room and there are creche facilities at the leisure centre as well as children's early evening meal from 5.30-7pm. Self-catering appartments for 2-6 are also available. No dogs. *Rooms 32. Indoor swimming pool, children's splash pool, gym, sauna, steam room, spa bath. Amex, Diners, MasterCard, VISA*

BALLYCASTLE   Places of Interest

Tourist Information Tel 01265 762024
Ballycastle Museum Tel 01265 762024
Carrick-A-Rede Rope Bridge Larrybane Tel 01265 731159
Rathlin Island Bird Sanctuary Tel 01265 763935

BALLYMENA	Adair Arms Hotel	62%	£78

Tel 01266 653674   Fax 01266 40436   Map 1 D1   **H**
Ballymoney Road Ballymena BT43 5BS

Taken over from the Hastings Group in 1995, this attractive, creeper-clad town-centre hotel is now run by the McLarnon family, who are taking a hands-on approach to management. Spacious public areas on the ground floor and comfortable en-suite bedrooms with satellite TV and trouser press as well as phone, tea/coffee tray and hairdryer make for a pleasant base – the hotel is conveniently situated next to the shopping centre and opposite the cinema with golf (including the new Galgorm Castle Golf Club), fishing and riding all nearby. Children up to 12 may stay free in their parents' room and 'small, friendly dogs' are allowed. Banqueting for 200 and conference facilities for 250 delegates. *Rooms 40. Closed 25 Dec. Amex, Diners, MasterCard, VISA*

BALLYMENA	Galgorm Manor	71%	£125

Tel 01266 881001   Fax 01266 880080   Map 1 D1   **HR**
136 Fenaghy Road Ballymena BT42 1EA

Next to a natural weir on the River Maine, which runs through the 85 acres of grounds, this Georgian manor house has splendid public areas where rich fabrics, warm colour schemes and a scattering of antiques create an unashamedly luxurious atmosphere. The 'designer-rustic' Gillies Bar in a converted outbuilding offers a change of mood and lunchtime snacks. A couple of Executive bedrooms are stylishly decorated and furnished with antiques but the remainder, although spacious, comfortable and well equipped, do not quite manage to match the style of the public areas; there are five suites. Bathrooms all have separate shower cubicles in addition to the tub. There are also six self-catering cottages in the grounds that are available on daily or weekly terms. 24hr room service. An equestrian centre to the rear of the house includes a show-jumping course, eventing cross-country practice area, specially constructed gallops and numerous rides through the estate. The splendid Great Hall conference (for up to 500) and banqueting (up to 450) centre (quite separate from the hotel) is most impressive, with huge Waterford crystal chandeliers and quality decor to match. Considerably reduced tariff at weekends (from £80 Fri-Sun). No dogs. Located to the west of town halfway between Galgorm and Cullybackey. *Rooms 23. Garden, riding, fishing. Closed 25 & 26 Dec. Amex, Diners, MasterCard, VISA*

Restaurant   **£70**

A fine room with glittering chandeliers, elaborately draped curtains and Arcadian murals depicting the four seasons. Chef Charles O'Neill offers both table d'hote and à la carte dinner menus, the latter proposes a good choice with starters like breast of pigeon on truffle-oil mashed potato or pan-fried monkfish with spinach and tomato timbales; main courses encompass a good range of meats (some may be offered from a chargrill and there's a daily evening roast) and game as well as a few fish dishes. The Irish farmhouse cheese trolley is a popular alternative to the half-dozen desserts. A shorter, fixed-price lunch menu has 4 or choices at each stage. Toilet facilities for disabled diners. *Seats 73. Parties 24. Private Rooms 14/60. L 12-2.30 D 7-9.30 (Sun 6-8.30). Set L £9.95/£12.90 (Sun £14.50) Set D £19.95.*

BALLYMENA   Tullyglass House Hotel   67%   £100

Tel 01266 652639   Fax 01266 46938   Map 1 D1   **H**
Galgorm Road Ballymena BT42 1HJ

Set in well-kept grounds on the edge of Ballymena town, Tullyglass House has
been imaginatively renovated by the McConville family to make a pleasing hotel
with some striking features. In keeping with the original building, Victorian-
style conservatories have been added to extend and brighten public areas. All
rooms have been recently refurbished and accommodation – whch ranges from
a bridal suite with four-poster through executive suites with jacuzzis to good-
value family rooms sleeping up to five – is of a high standard throughout; all
rooms have generously-sized orthopaedic beds, comfortable armchairs, marbled
en suite bathrooms and satellite TV. One bedroom is equipped for disabled
guests. Attractive banqueting facilities can take separate groups of 600 and 300;
conference suites for up to 600 delegates. 24hr room service. Only small dogs
are allowed. The new Galgorm Castle Golf Club is nearby. *Rooms 32. Garden,
terrace. Closed 25 Dec. Amex, Diners, MasterCard,* **VISA**

We endeavour to be as up-to-date as possible but
inevitably some changes to owners, chefs and other
key staff occur after this Guide has gone to press.

BALLYMONEY   Old Bank House

Tel 01265 663924   Map 1 C1   **P/R**
9 Church Street Ballymoney BT53 6HS

Joey and Margaret Erwin enjoyed only the briefest of 'retirements' after leaving
the celebrated *Blackheath House*, near Coleraine. Their new baby is a converted
Victorian bank, an impressive building in the centre of Ballymoney town with
an extraordinary interior that they have changed as little as possible, so that
original details such as the magnificent moulding in the soaring banking hall may
be enjoyed to the full. The bar/restaurant food operation – à la carte menus
under Margaret's personal supervision with help from some of their old staff –
was running smoothly by the end of their first season and the style of cooking
will be reassuringly familiar to anyone who had enjoyed MacDuff's Restaurant
at Blackheath House. Margaret's wide-ranging interest in food can be seen in the
modern dishes on her menus – warm salad of chicken breast marinated with
rosemary and basil, served on bruschetta with a mixed-leaf salad and light pesto
dressing – but her strong country roots also come through in excellent home-
baked breads (served with wonderful soups such as apple and celery or courgette
and Brie) and hearty bakes such as fish pie or steak, ale and mushroom pie.
Vegetarians are well looked after (vegetable and pasta bake, perhaps) and there
are always daily specials on the board to augment the written lunch and evening
menus. In line with local custom, portions are generous and side dishes – of
sautéed potatoes, herb or garlic fries, jacket potatoes or salad – also substantial.
Friendly service under Joey's direction, and an unusually good choice of wines
served by the glass or bottle, also available from his wine shop next door.
Children allowed, but preferably not under 10 after 7.30 pm. *Seats 40.
Private Room 16. L 12.30-3 D 5-8 (Sat till 8.30). Closed all Sun, D Mon & Tue,
25 & 26 Dec. MasterCard,* **VISA**

BALLYMONEY   Places of Interest

Benvarden House & Gardens Tel 01265 741331 Jun-Aug 2-6pm (not Mon)
Leslie Hill Heritage Farm Park Ballymoney Tel 01265 666803 *6 miles*

BANGOR   Clandeboye Lodge Hotel   65%   £98

Tel 01247 852500   Fax 01247 852772   Map 1 D2   **H**
10 Estate Road Clandeboye Bangor North Down BT19 1UR

Set in woodland on the edge of the Clandeboye estate, the design – which is modern but echoes traditional themes – and country colours used in this pleasant low-rise hotel ensure that it blends comfortably into its rural surroundings. Good impressions are continued in the spacious foyer with its welcoming fire, warm-toned decor and plentiful seating areas and in the high-ceilinged Lodge Restaurant with its Gothic-style windows and furnishings. Good-sized bedrooms are accessible by lift and pleasingly decorated in subtle shades; quality furnishings include orthopaedic mattresses, practical features such as open wardrobes and phones with voice mail and fax/modem points, while extras supplied as standard include robes, mineral water, turn-down service and a complimentary morning newspaper. Compact, well-planned bathrooms have over-bath showers, ample shelf space and quality towels and toiletries. There are two suites (with whirlpool baths) and also two wheelchair-friendly rooms. The Poacher's Arms, a country-style pub, is in an original Victorian building beside the hotel. Conference and banqueting suites can accommodate groups of up to 350. Significantly reduced tariff Fri-Sun. *Rooms 43. Golf, bikes, riding, walking. Closed 3 days Christmas.* Amex, Diners, MasterCard, **VISA**

BANGOR   Marine Court Hotel   64%   £85

Tel 01247 451100   Fax 01247 451200   Map 1 D2   **H**
18-20 Quay Street Bangor North Down BT20 5ED

Although theoretically 'harbourside', this modern hotel actually overlooks a large public car park and even larger marina area beyond it; the first-floor restaurant is the only public room with a long view and only a small proportion of bedrooms are on the front – most overlook uninspiring but tidy service areas. Decor has been improved somewhat recently, although overall impressions are still of a somewhat institutional style, with unimaginatively decorated corridors, few pictures and – a noticeable fault in bedrooms as well as public areas – cold and sometimes inadequate lighting. On the plus side, rooms are of quite a good size and amenities are above-average, with king-size beds, orthopaedic mattresses (but very large, hard pillows) and plenty of shelf/desk space. Otherwise well-planned bathrooms have taps with an awkward revolving lever mechanism, but quality toiletries and towels. Noise from a disco at the back of the hotel can be a problem on certain nights. Excellent leisure facilities at the hotel's Oceanis Health and Fitness Club include an 18m pool, steam room, whirlpool and sunbeds as well as a well-equipped, professionally staffed gym. 24hr room service, but only Continental breakfast is served in the rooms (at an extra charge of £3 per person). Informal eating in the Upper Deck coffee shop/bistro and the nautically-themed Calico Jack's bar. Banqueting facilities for 250, conference facilities in four areas for up to 450 delegates. No dogs. *Rooms 51.*
Indoor swimming pool, gym, solarium, steam room, whirlpool bath, sunbeds, coffee shop (10am-10pm). Closed 25 Dec. Amex, Diners, MasterCard, **VISA**

BANGOR   Shanks   ★   £75

Chef Robbie Millar and his team
have made real impact on the
Northern Ireland dining scene at this
Conran-designed restaurant in the
Blackwood Golf Centre, on the
Clandeboye Estate just outside
Bangor. Since opening in 1994
Robbie and his wife Shirley, who
heads up a fine, well-trained front-
of-house team, have gradually
achieved a softening of the original
hard-edged decor, most noticeably in
the lofty first-floor bar, which opens on to a wide balcony (where tables are set
up in summer). One half of the bar has now been transformed into a comfortable
and stylish seating area with the arrival of funky modern sofas and chairs in
bright colours; in the other half a set of modern paintings provides a striking
background for half a dozen tables used as overflow from the main restaurant on
busy nights. The addition of blinds, generous flower arrangements and a carpeting
of deep blue forms a strong link between the floors. The downstairs restaurant
is brightly lit, determinedly minimalist and quite low-ceilinged, which makes
it seem smaller than it is and sometimes uncomfortably hot and airless, especially
as cigarette smoking is allowed. A mixture of simple banquette seating and
comfortable lightwood chairs, classic white cloths and napkins and largely
unadorned sunshine yellow walls all ensure that the focus of attention is the large
kitchen window at one end of the room and the activity going on beyond it,
in the engine room of this sweetly-tuned food factory. Robbie's carefully
constructed fixed-price dinner menus offer a choice of seven dishes for each
course and his great achievement lies in being able to create each one as a complete
entity without repetition of flavours, textures or garnishes, while also conveying
a strongly identifiable house style in a modern idiom that clearly draws on
influences much closer to home as well as those of Italy, France and the Pacific
Rim. Carefully sourced ingredients are often local, including venison, pheasant
and guinea fowl raised on the Clandeboye Estate and organic fruit and vegetables grown nearby. Attention to detail is evident throughout, starting with
the selection of home-made breads and tapénade that provide the first welcome,
followed by a complimentary amuse-bouche – a little coffee cup of harissa-spiced
sweet potato soup with a surprise smoked chicken and coriander dumpling
at the bottom, perhaps – then, at sensibly measured intervals, the meal itself.
Starters might include seared diver-caught scallops (from Portavogie) arranged
around a little tower of spicy smoked chili creamed orzo, with basil and tomato
concassé, and a more delicate dish of wontons filled with chicken and foie gras,
enlivened with a ginger and fresh mango salsa; or beetroot and goat's cheese
fritters – a colourful concoction of golden-brown crisply-fried balls that open up
to reveal deep-pink interiors – topped with a frill of deep-fried beetroot and
contrasting, bright green frisée, encircled with finely-diced beetroot, chopped
walnuts and a dressing of lemon oil. Dishes have large white plates and a
repeated circular motif in common, yet each is a distinctive, original creation.
Equally imaginative and varied main courses might include quite a complex yet
clear-flavoured 'layered' dish of steamed brill and Dublin Bay prawns with
stacked spinach and potatoes, surrounded by a dill-flavoured grain mustard sauce
or tender venison cooked juicily medium-rare then topped with a 'hat' of crispy
noodles and served with a spinach and shiitake custard mould. Such care is taken
to balance flavours and adjust seasonings that the salt and pepper mills provided

are rarely needed. Excellent but not overdressed desserts include a chef's special – a rich, creamy, thin crusted warm chocolate tart, perhaps, with a contrasting 'pool' of jewel-like autumn berry compote, a ball of creamy vanilla ice cream and a tiny glass of raspberry wine – and six others, or a stunning selection of around two dozen or so Irish and Continental cheeses. Coffee and home-made petits fours provide the perfect finale. Two- and three-course lunch menus are somewhat simpler, but true to the philosophy of this talented young chef. *Seats 70. Parties 16. Private Room. L 12.30-2.30 D 7-10. Set L £10.95/£14.95 Set D £28.50. Closed L Sat, all Sun & Mon, 1 week July, 25 & 26 Dec, 1 Jan. Amex, MasterCard, VISA*

BANGOR	Villa Toscana	£40

Tel 01247 473737 Fax 01247 460062   Map 1 D2   **R**
Toscana Park West Circular Road Bangor North Down BT19 1FH

Large bistro/pizzeria with an extensive à la carte of familiar Italian dishes, from *calzone* folded pizza through *prosciutto e melone*, lightly-battered vegetables with a garlic dip (*misto di vegetali*), a variety of popular pasta dishes, and chicken six ways (at least!). Grilled swordfish is served with a pesto dressing and saffron rice; fillet of pork is filled with ham, cheese and sage and accompanied by an apricot sauce. To finish, try filo pastry parcels filled with sticky toffee, banana custard, honey and sponge. Sister restaurant to *Speranza* in Belfast. *Seats 200. L (Sun only) 12-3 D 5-11.30 (Sun to 10.30). Closed 25, 26 & 31 Dec. Amex, MasterCard, VISA*

BANGOR   Places of Interest

Tourist Information Tel 01247 270069
Abbey of Bangor
Bangor Marina
Museum of Childhood Tel 01247 471915
North Down Heritage Centre Tel 01247 271200
Pickie Family Fun Park Tel 01247 274430
Ulster Folk & Transport Museum Cultra Tel 01232 428428 *5 miles*

BELFAST	Antica Roma	£65

Tel 01232 311121 Fax 01232 310787   Map 1 D2   **R**
67 Botanic Avenue Belfast BT7 1JL

Impressive decor based on ancient Rome – mosaic floor, classical murals, columns, distressed stucco – combines with sophisticated Italian cooking at this fashionable restaurant in the University district. The evening-only à la carte includes the likes of *aragosta al cognac* (vine-wrapped lobster mousse with a prawn and cognac sauce), *fegatini d'anatra* (pan-fried duck livers layered with corn biscuits) and *salsicce alla mostarda* (home-made, chargrilled lamb sausages with a grain mustard and basil sauce) among the starters; follow these with fresh pasta (black, red or green – perhaps according to one's mood), daily fresh fish (maybe monkfish, turbot with zucchini, thyme and cream or *misto con finocchio* – a selection baked with fennel, served with pepper tapénade and deep-fried anchovies) or traditional dishes like *vitello alla parmigiana* or *pollo al prosciutto*. An *assortito* gives a taster of desserts such as coconut cheesecake with pistachio nut and Malibu sauce, spiced Arborio rice pudding with tutti frutti ice cream or chocolate, ginger and pear cake served with 'vanilla milkshake sauce'. Only a good-value fixed-price menu (offering a choice of around four main dishes) is served at lunchtime. Particularly good Italian wines, as one might expect. Sister restaurant *Villa Italia* (see entry below). *Seats 170. Parties 25. Private Room 70. L 12-3 D 6-11.30. Set L £9.95/£12.95. Closed L Sat, all Sun, Easter Monday, 12 July, 25 & 26 Dec. Amex, MasterCard, VISA*

BELFAST — Bengal Brasserie — £35

Tel 01232 640099
339 Ormeau Road Belfast BT7 3GL

Map 1 D2   **R**

About a mile south of the city centre, this Indian restaurant is situated in a modern shopping arcade. Sound Bengali cooking includes daily blackboard specials such as scampi masala, tandoori duck and Indian river fish as well as a wide choice on the main menu with lamb and chicken dishes jostling for space beside prawns, lobster, tandoori crayfish and 'European dishes' (steaks with sauces, omelettes, chicken Kiev). Vegetarian options revolve mainly around paneer cheese. Friendly, helpful staff. *Seats 46. L 12-1.45 D 5.30-11.15 (Sun till 10.15). Closed 25 Dec. Set menu £16.95. Diners, MasterCard,* **VISA**

BELFAST — Crown Liquor Saloon

Tel 01232 325368
44 Great Victoria Street Belfast BT2 7BA

Map 1 D2   **P**

Belfast's most famous and best-preserved bar, High Victorian and wonderful in its exuberant opulence. 'Gaslight glints on painted windows, vivid in amber and carmine, on gilded glass and on highly-patterned tiles which abound everywhere. It reflects from shining brass, from ornate mirrors, and glows against the burnished ceiling embossed with entwining curves. Richly-carved wood, a granite-topped bar, bright panels of plasterwork – and a floor laid in a myriad of mosaics completes the picture of relentless decoration' – we couldn't put it better as it truly is an architectural fantasy. The building belongs to the National Trust and is run by Bass Taverns. Every visitor to Belfast should experience the joy of a pint in one of the delightful 'snugs' – if snugs could talk there would be many a tale to tell from these clandestine retreats! Upstairs, The Britannic Lounge, with an Edwardian feel, is fitted out with original timbers from the SS Britannic, sister ship to the Titanic. *Open 11.30-11.30, Sun 12.30-2.30, 7-10. MasterCard,* **VISA**

BELFAST — Dukes Hotel — 67% — £100

Tel 01232 236666 Fax 01232 237177
65 University Street Belfast BT7 1HL

Map 1 D2   **H**

A Victorian facade covers a bright modern hotel in a residential area close to Queen's University and the Botanic Gardens. Black leather and chrome feature in the foyer seating. There are function facilities for up to 140 and a health club with separate men's and women's saunas. Pastel decor and impressionist prints set the tone in the bedrooms, all of which are double-glazed. 24hr room service. Children up to 12 stay free in parents' room. No dogs. *Rooms 21. Mini-gym, sauna. Amex, Diners, MasterCard,* **VISA**

BELFAST — Europa Hotel — 71% — £148

Tel 01232 327000 Fax 01232 327800
Great Victoria Street Belfast BT2 7AP

Map 1 D2   **H**

A 70s' high-rise, Belfast's best-known hotel has an impressive facade. Smart public areas cater for all moods, from an all-day brasserie and lively public bar on the ground floor (off the large lobby) to a more relaxed and comfortable split-level cocktail bar-cum-lounge on the first floor where a pianist plays nightly. For the really energetic a disco/night club operates four or five nights a week. Double-glazed bedrooms feature darkwood furniture and matching bedcovers and curtains in stylish floral fabrics. Two twin-bedded rooms are well equipped for disabled guests. 24hr room service. There is 50% concessionary parking at a nearby multi-storey for which friendly, efficient porters also offer a valet parking service (ask before checking out if you want the cost added to your hotel account). Extensive conference and function facilities (for up to 1200) include an air-conditioned Eurobusiness Centre with its own reception area and full secretarial services. Afternoon tea is served in The Gallery Lounge between 2.30 and 5 to the soothing sounds of a resident pianist. Substantial weekend tariff reductions. Ulster Dinner Cabaret Fri-Sun Jul-Sep. Hastings Hotels. *Rooms 184. Beauty & hair salon, brasserie (24hrs). Closed 24-26 Dec. Amex, Diners, MasterCard,* **VISA**

BELFAST   Holiday Inn Garden Court   64%   £85

Tel 01232 333555   Fax 01232 232999   Map 1 D2   **H**
15 Brunswick Street Belfast BT2 7GE

Ultra-modern city-centre business hotel with well-equipped bedrooms, all with satellite TV, hairdryer and trouser press as standard, and five conference suites (capacity 70 theatre-style, 100 restaurant-style). Children and young adults up to the age of 19 stay free in their parents' room; four rooms have extra beds. Lower tariff (£55) Fri-Sun subject to availability. No dogs. The hotel has undergone extensive refurbishment since being renamed from the Plaza Hotel early in 1996. *Rooms 76. Amex, Diners, MasterCard,* **VISA**

BELFAST   Kelly's Cellars

Tel 01232 324835   Map 1 D2   **P**
30/32 Bank Street Belfast BT1 1HL

A protected building, this characterful bar boasts the oldest cellars in Ireland, dating back to 1720. Friday and Saturday nights alternate a folk group with a blues or rock band (if the folk is on Friday one week it will be on Saturday the next). Some times there is also live traditional Irish music. *Open 11.30-11 (till 1am Thu-Sat). Closed Sun & some Bank Holidays. MasterCard,* **VISA**

BELFAST   Manor House Cantonese Cuisine   £45

Tel & Fax 01232 238755   Map 1 D2   **R**
43-47 Donegall Pass Belfast BT7 1DQ

Owned and managed by Joe Wong and his family since 1982, this family-run Cantonese restaurant offers a long menu that runs to more than 300 items. Alongside ubquitous items like barbecued spare ribs, paper-wrapped prawns, crispy duck, char siu, beef in oyster sauce and sizzling dishes you'll also find a dozen soups (try beef with hot pickle), stuffed scallops, stewed eel with roast belly pork, braised fish head with bean curd and beef with preserved mustard plant. The menu is fascinating and deserves careful consideration and the pastel decor and air-conditioning provide a comfortable setting in which to make your choice. Baked lobster and crab, roast duck in 'open oven Cantonese style' and deep-fried, Cantonese-style crispy chicken are specialities. Set menus for two to six diners; in addition there are vegetarian and Peking-style set menus – the latter features Peking duck and hot pickle turnips with shredded pork (for a minimum of four diners). Sound cooking over the whole range. *Seats 80. Private Room 50. L 12-2.30 D 5.30-11.30 (Sun 12.30-11). Closed 25 & 26 Dec, 12 & 13 Jul. Set L from £5.50 Set D from £14.50. Diners, MasterCard,* **VISA**

We publish annually, so make sure you use the current edition
– it's well worth being up-to-date!

BELFAST   Mizuna   £45

Tel 01232 230063   Map 1 D2   **R**
99 Botanic Avenue Belfast BT7 1JN

Deep rust-red walls, hessian-draped windows, wooden floors, simply set marble-topped wrought-iron tables and eclectic menus combine to give this opened up traditional red-brick house a thoroughly modern feel. Paul Clarke's no-choice 3-course menu – typically an organic leaf and walnut salad, then wild salmon with a spiced crab and ginger broth, finishing with poached meringue with white chocolate sauce – changes once or twice a week and is backed by shortish but imaginative à la carte menus with a slightly wider choice offered in the evening. Presentation, on plain white plates, is strikingly simple and flavours carefully considered for maximum impact. Typical starters might include a white onion soup with mature Cheddar and croutons, a smoked bacon salad with pine nuts and caponata and a (surprisingly hot) celery root rémoulade with slivers of cured beef and roasted peppers; these may be followed by tender slices of pigeon breast served with wild mushrooms, fillet of hake with tomato fondue and pistachio butter, or old-fashioned fish and chips with mushy peas. Old favourites also feature on the dessert menu where hot creamed rice pudding with sultanas and vanilla may be found rubbing shoulders with Sauternes and olive oil cake with plum compote or deliciously refreshing caramelised oranges with crème fraiche. Freshly-brewed coffee to finish, served with mints in the evening. Good service from friendly staff. *Seats 64. L 12.30-2.30 D 6-10. Closed Sun, Mon, 12 & 13 July, 25 & 26 Dec. Set L & D £13.95. MasterCard,* **VISA**

We do not recommend the food in pubs where
there is no mention of Bar Food in the statistics.
A restaurant within a pub is only specifically recommended
where its separate opening times are given.

BELFAST   Nick's Warehouse   £45

Tel 01232 439690   Fax 01232 230514   Map 1 D2   **R**
35-39 Hill Street Belfast BT1 2LB

Nick and Kathy Price's popular and lively 'bar with wine and restaurant' is on two floors and offers a mix of menus with a fair range of tasty, straightforward dishes. At lunch you may find Jerusalem artichoke and orange soup, beef and Guinness with oyster mushrooms, tuna and pasta salad with mustard vinaigrette and French bread sandwiches on the wine bar menu, with more involved dishes like black and white pudding with a balsamic onion compote and sauced meat and fish dishes on the restaurant side. From an evening table d'hote (available on both floors) could come Thai chicken with a ginger lentil salad, fillet of brill with a watercress sauce, courgette and tomato risotto, and orange and Grand Marnier marquise. Cheeses are always interesting and include good Irish varieties. Live music Fri and Sat nights. No children in the wine bar. *Seats 90. Private Room 45. Wine bar open for drinks 11.30-11. Meals L 12-3 D 6-9. Closed L Sat, D Mon, all Sun, Bank Holidays, 12 & 13 Jul & 25-27 Dec. Set D £14.95/£17.95 Tue-Sat. Amex, Diners, MasterCard,* **VISA**

If you encounter bad service don't wait to write to us but make
your feelings known to the management at the time of your visit.
Instant compensation can often resolve any problem that
might otherwise leave a bad taste.

BELFAST   **Roscoff**   ★   **£80**

Tel 01232 331532   Fax 01232 312093   Map 1 D2   **R**
Lesley House Shaftesbury Square Belfast BT2 7DB

Although commitments in the media and other areas of enterprise keep Paul and Jeanne Rankin from their dashing city-centre restaurant more often than many of their guests might perhaps like, it is a tribute to the quality of their training and the dedication of their staff that the quality of cooking seldom, if ever, falters – and that Roscoff-trained staff continue to make an impact wherever they establish themselves. Fixed-price menus offer great value for the standard of both food and service – the atmosphere (distinctly 'waiting room' in the reception area) and hard-edged modern decor may not be to everyone's taste but, once seated in the restaurant, sheer professionalism takes over and it would take a rare diner indeed who could fail to be impressed by the machine that is Roscoff. The style continues in its successful 'eclectic Cal-Ital' pattern, in a fixed-price dinner menu (£28.95 for three courses, with side orders an extra £1.20-£2.75) that offers seven choices at each course, plus the option of a selection of Irish and British cheeses. Start, perhaps, with a wonderful fresh asparagus soup with crunchy buttery croutons or crispy duck confit with sliced new potatoes and a small salad of rocket – both helped along by constantly topped-up iced water and the repeated offering of a selection of irresistible home-made breads, both traditional and modern, served with the best unsalted butter. This may be followed by the likes of sauté of chicken with Thai spices and a crispy noodle cake or seared scallops with black pasta and saffron butter, all served with individual garnishes and elegant insouciance on over-sized white plates. Desserts combine the light and modern – exotic fruit sorbets – with must-haves like chocolate millefeuille, dark chocolate sorbet and white chocolate ice cream or almost-classic caramel crème brulée with a gingered plum compote. A choice of coffees or tea and home-made petits fours rounds off an exceptional dining experience. The 3-course business lunch menu offers less choice but a similar standard of cooking at a very reasonable price. The wine list features good New World wines and extends to a few grand clarets but some helpful tasting notes wouldn't go amiss; prices are generally fair. *Seats 70. L 12.15-2.15 D 6.30-10.30. Set L £16.50 Set D £28.95. Closed L Sat, all Sun, 11-13 July, 25, 26 Dec & 1 Jan. Amex, Diners, MasterCard, VISA*

We do not accept free meals or hospitality – our inspectors pay their own bills and **never** book in the name of Egon Ronay's Guides.

BELFAST   **Speranza**   **£40**

Tel 01232 230213   Fax 01232 236752   Map 1 D2   **R**
16 Shaftesbury Square Belfast BT2 7DB

Large, bustling pizzeria/restaurant on two floors with red check tablecloths and rustic chalet-style decor. The menu offers a range of huge crisp-based pizzas and about a dozen pasta dishes plus a few chicken and other meat dishes. Attentive service from boys and girls smartly kitted out in bright red cummerbunds with matching bow ties. For children there are high-chairs and a special menu written on colouring mats (crayons supplied). In the same ownership as *Villa Toscana* (see entry under Bangor). *Seats 170. D only 5-11.30. Closed Sun, 3 days Christmas, 11 & 12 Jul. Amex, MasterCard, VISA*

BELFAST   Stormont Hotel   69%   £133

Tel 01232 658621   Fax 01232 480240   Map 1 D2   **H**
587 Upper Newtownards Road Stormont Belfast BT4 3LP

Way out of town on the Newtownards Road, opposite Stormont Castle, this
modern hotel is always busy and bustling, having various function rooms in
addition to the Confex Centre with its ten purpose-built trade and exhibition
rooms; conference facilities are provided for up to 100 and banqueting for up
to 300 (plus parking for 400 cars). Public areas centre around a sunken lounge
(sometimes used as a conference 'break-out' area) off which is a cosy cocktail
bar. A mezzanine lounge has huge windows overlooking the castle grounds.
The majority of bedrooms are spacious, comfortable and practical, with good,
well-lit work space, satellite TV and modern easy chairs. Good bathrooms feature
marble tiling. One room is fully equipped for disabled guests. Top of the range
are two suites (£178). Smart, helpful staff offer attentive lounge service and
there's a 24hr room-service menu. All-day brasserie. Hastings Hotels.
Rooms 106. Closed 25 Dec. Amex, Diners, MasterCard, **VISA**

The Egon Ronay Guides are completely independent.
We do not accept advertising, hospitality or payment
from any of the establishments listed in this Guide.

BELFAST   Villa Italia   £45

Tel 01232 328356   Fax 01232 234978   Map 1 D2   **R**
39 University Road Belfast BT7 1ND

Sister restaurant to *Antica Roma* (see entry above) but with a little less emphasis
on pizzas and more on pasta and other Italian dishes. Chef's specials change
fortnightly and might include the likes of *anatra con lenticchie* (grilled breast
and roasted duck leg stuffed with garlic, mshrooms and bacon, served with
Puy lentil sauce); from the main menu *pollo Villa Italia* (pan-fried chicken breast
topped with ham and finished with a cheese sauce) is a popular dish. A shade
more upmarket too, although still informal in style, with quieter background
music, a new Italian courtyard theme in one section and a no-smoking area.
When the pizza chef is not too busy children may make their own pizzas;
colouring pages and crayons are also provided. Service is equally friendly and
efficient. Disabled toilet and baby-changing facilities. *Seats 180. D only 5-11.30
(Sat from 4, Sun 4-10.30). Closed 24-26 & 31 Dec, 12 July & Easter Sun & Mon.
Amex, MasterCard,* **VISA**

BELFAST   Welcome Restaurant   £50

Tel 01232 381359   Fax 01232 664607   Map 1 D2   **R**
22 Stranmillis Road Belfast BT9 5AA

The entrance to San Wong's welcoming emporium is topped by a pagoda roof,
and inside dragons, screens and lanterns establish that this is indeed a Chinese
restaurant. The menu runs to over 100 items, mainly familiar, popular dishes,
and there are special menus for both individuals and small parties. Good vegetarian
dishes, a choice of over 25 hot pots and a few 'English' dishes complete the
picture. A bargain set lunch offers chicken and sweetcorn soup, spare ribs or
melon followed by a choice of ten main dishes. Toilet facilities for disabled diners.
*Seats 60. Parties 20. Private Room 30. L 12-1.45 D 5-10.30. Closed L Sat & Sun,
24-26 Dec. Set L £4.95 Set D £14 & £19 (for 1), £27-£40 (for 2). Amex, Diners,
MasterCard,* **VISA**

BELFAST   Wellington Park   £110

Tel 01232 381111   Fax 01232 665410   Map 1 D2   **H**
21 Malone Road Belfast BT9 6RU

Redesigned public areas and bedroom upgrades have kept the Wellington Park up to date in recent years; however, as we went to press the first phase of further improvements was getting underway. Due for completion by May 1997 was a new wing of 25 bedrooms (two for disabled guests), extended conference facilities for up to 300, and a new themed bistro. The locality and a thriving conference business ensure a lively atmosphere here, but one of the bars is kept exclusively for residents. Children up to 12 stay free in parents' room. Residents have free use of Queens University's sports centre, 5 minutes from the hotel. Graded at 59% in last year's guide. No dogs. Sister hotel to *Dunadry Inn* (see entry under Dunadry). *Rooms 50. Closed 25 & 26 Dec. Amex, Diners, MasterCard, **VISA***

BELFAST   Places of Interest

Tourist Information Tel 01232 246609
City Airport Tel 01232 457745
International Airport Tel 01849 422888
Helicopter Tours Tel 01849 453663
Belfast Zoo Tel 01232 776277 *5 miles north*
Down Royal Racecourse Lisburn Tel 01846 621256 *6 miles*
Malone House Art Gallery and Gardens Upper Malone Rd Tel 01232 681246
Mount Stewart House and Gardens (NT) Greyabbey Tel 01247 788387 *17 miles*
Sir Thomas & Lady Dixon Park Upper Malone Rd Tel 01232 611506
Transport Museum Tel 01232 451519
Ulster Museum and Botanic Gardens Tel 01232 381251

Theatres and Concert Halls

Grand Opera House Great Victoria St Tel 01232 241919
Group Theatre Bradford St Tel 01232 329685
Lyric Theatre Ridgeway St Tel 01232 381081
Ulster Hall Bedford St Tel 01232 323900

BELFAST AIRPORT   Aldergrove Airport Hotel   62%   £87

Tel 01849 422033   Fax 01849 423500   Map 1 D2   **H**
Belfast Airport Antrim BT29 4AB

The only hotel actually at the international airport, which is about 17 miles south of the city centre. Good, practical accommodation with all rooms having plenty of work space and, with families in mind, a sofa bed with additional truckle bed underneath; three rooms are equipped for disabled guests. Children under 16 may stay free in their parents' room. Multi-channel TV includes flight information. 24hr room service; breakfast is served from 6am. Banqueting/conference facilities for 180/250. No dogs. *Rooms 108. Garden, gym, sauna, play area. Amex, Diners, MasterCard, **VISA***

BELLANALECK   The Sheelin

Tel 01365 348232   Map 1 C2   **JaB**
Bellanaleck nr Enniskillen Fermanagh

A pretty, thatched bar and restaurant, The Sheelin provides hearty country dinners for the local community and makes a useful stopping point for travellers – Sunday lunch is worth stopping for. Friendly, honest waitresses and clean facilities make rather a contrast to the scruffy garage opposite. *Seats 50. Meals 10.30-9.30 (till 6.30 Mon), till 10.30 (Fri & Sat). Closed Mon & Tue in winter & 25 Dec. MasterCard, **VISA***

CARNLOUGH · Londonderry Arms Hotel · £70

Tel 01574 885255   Fax 01574 885263   Map 1 D1
20 Harbour Road Carnlough Glens of Antrim Larne BT44 0EU

Attractive old inn situated close to the pretty little harbour and enjoying good views over Carnlough Bay towards the Antrim Mountains beyond. Owned by the O'Neill family for 25 years, they have gradually extended and upgraded the building and it makes a useful overnight stop or refreshment stop on the famous scenic coastal route. Well known locally for 'good plain food', with a satisfying range of bar snacks (home-made vegetable soup with wheaten bread, open prawn sandwiches, paté with Cumberland sauce, chef's home-made pie) served in both the pubby bar and hotel lounge. Seventeen spacious and comfortable new bedrooms have just been completed (the total is now 35), each furnished and decorated to a modern, superior standard with co-ordinating fabrics, king-size beds, attractive wall coverings and well-appointed en suite bathrooms with power showers over the tubs. Original bedrooms, most due for a revamp, feature individual pieces of furniture (many of them antique) and a more traditional style of decor; top rooms enjoy views across the bay. *Open 11.30-11 (Sun 12-10.30).* **Bar Food** *12-3 only. Garden, disabled facilities.* **Accommodation** *35 bedrooms, all en suite, £70 (single £45). Children welcome overnight (under-3s stay free, 3-12s £15 in parents' room). Amex, Diners, MasterCard,* **VISA**

CARRICKFERGUS · Wind-Rose Bar

Tel 01960 364192   Fax 01960 351164   Map 1 D2   **JaB**
The Marina Carrickfergus BT38 8BE

Forming part of a marina complex on the edge of town, this popular wine bar overlooks a yacht-filled basin and Belfast Lough beyond. A strong nautical theme fills the bar and comfortable raised dining area, where good light lunches and evening meals are served. A varied printed menu satisfies all tastes, from speciality sandwiches and burgers to lasagne, filled pittas, beef stroganoff and fillet steak au poivre. Daily specials may include stir-fried pork with pitta bread, home-made pizza and a hearty home-made soup (typically carrot and tarragon or lentil and bacon). Vegetarian dishes are always available. Function room upstairs seating 60. *Seats 46. Open 12-2.30, 5.30-9 (Sat 12-9, Sun 12-2.30, 5.30-8.15). Closed 25 Dec. MasterCard,* **VISA**

CARRICKFERGUS   Places of Interest

Tourist Information Tel 01960 366455
Ballylumford Dolmen Island Magee *10 miles*
Carrickfergus Castle Tel 01960 351273
Ford Farm Park Museum Ballystrudder, Island Magee Tel 01960 353264 *8 miles*
Larne Historical Centre Tel 01574 279482
Larne Tourist Information Tel 01574 260088

COLERAINE · The Salmon Leap

Tel 01265 52992   Fax 01265 43390   Map 1 C1   **JaB**
53 Castleroe Road Coleraine BT51 3RL

Stylish riverside premises, hands-on management by owner Brian McGinnis, a characterful front bar, lively modern food from head chef Eamon Cosgrove's kitchen, and friendly, interested staff make a winning combination at *The Salmon Leap*. Functions and special music events such as jazz brunches are a regular part of the scene here and the 'Bailiff's Watch' bar has a late licence to 1am Mon-Sat. On the food side, the 'Poacher's Hide' bistro provides smart, informal meals, typically in fashionable, flavoursome dishes such as chargrilled ginger chicken (soaked in ginger, lemon, thyme and soy sauce, chargrilled and served with a garlic mayonnaise) or marinated beef kebabs (diced steak, threaded with onion and peppers, chargrilled and served with a tangy Szechuan sauce dip), both served with garlic potatoes or chunky chips in their skins. The layout and decor has been thoughtfully achieved, producing an unusual establishment that works well on a number of levels. A Sunday lunch carvery is offered in The Lennox Suite. The Still Water restaurant is open for dinner only from 6.30-9.30 Tue-Sat (but it is the bar food that we specifically recommend here). *Seats 60. Open 11.30-11 (Sun 11.30-3, 7-10). Meals 12-10.30 (Sun carvery 12.30-3, 3.30-9.30). Closed 25 Dec. Amex, Diners, MasterCard, VISA*

COMBER	La Mon House	59%	£85

Tel 01232 448631   Fax 01232 448026   Map 1 D2   **H**
The Mills 41 Gransha Road Comber Ards BT23 5RF

Public areas in this low-rise modern hotel include a bar featuring copper-topped tables, a small residents' lounge (which may be in private use), carvery restaurant and a fun bar with lots of entertainment that includes a Friday night disco. Practical bedrooms have simple fitted furniture; several larger rooms have balconies (£95) and there are eight small singles with shower only. Families will enjoy the country health spa and outdoor areas. Banqueting facilities for 450, conferences up to 1100 theatre-style. Reduced weekend tariff (from £50) with regular Saturday night dinner dances. In the countryside, 5 miles from Belfast city centre. No dogs. *Rooms 38. Garden, indoor swimming pool, gym, sauna, solarium, spa bath, games room. Amex, MasterCard, VISA*

COMBER   Places of Interest

Ballycopeland Windmill *8 miles*
Castle Espie Tel 01247 874146
Down Country Museum Downpatrick Tel 01396 615218
Downpatrick Racecourse Downpatrick Tel 01396 612054
Grey Abbey *10 miles*
Mount Stewart House and Gardens Newtownards Tel 01247 788387
Nendrum Monastery Mahee Island
Newtownards Priory *3 miles*
Northern Ireland Aquarium Portaferry Tel 01247 728062 *26 miles*
Rowallane Gardens Saintfield Tel 01238 510131 *6 miles*
Wildfowl and Wetlands Centre Castle Espie Tel 01247 874146 *3 miles*

COOKSTOWN	Tullylagan Country House	64%	£70

Tel 01648 765100   Fax 01648 761715   Map 1 C2   **H**
40b Tullylagan Road Cookstown BT80 8UP

Tucked away off the Cookstown to Dungannon road (A54), down a pleasant tree-lined drive on a 30-acre estate, is Tullylagan House – a rather grand-looking, white-painted building that, surprisingly, was only built three years ago. It's tastefully decorated throughout in country-house style with quality co-ordinating fabrics, notably in the comfortable lounge-cum-bar, which is filled with relaxing sofas and easy chairs. Beyond the sweeping staircase are fifteen well-appointed bedrooms, all sporting TVs, direct-dial telephones, tea-making facilities and smart, marble-floored bathrooms with bidets. Children under 5 may share their parents' room at no charge; extra beds and cot are available. The master bedroom and suite are particularly spacious. 24hr room service. A panelled library doubles as a meeting room seating 30. 20% discount for over-55s. No dogs. *Rooms 15. Garden. Closed 25 Dec. MasterCard, VISA*

Raisi 660620,

~~Jenni~~ 260 5889

CRAWFORDSBURN   Old Inn   £85

Tel 01247 853255   Fax 01247 852775   Map 1 D2   **I**
15 Main Street Crawfordsburn North Down BT19 1JH

Located off the main Belfast to Bangor road, this 17th-century inn is in a pretty village setting and is supposed to be the oldest in continuous use in all Ireland. Its location is conveniently close to Belfast and its City Airport. Oak beams, antiques and gas lighting emphasise the natural character of the building, an attractive venue for business people (conference facilities for 150, banqueting for 90) and private guests alike. Individually decorated bedrooms vary in size and style, most have antiques, some four-posters and a few have private sitting rooms; all are non-smoking. Romantics and newly-weds should head for the honeymoon cottage (£135). Tariff Fri-Sun £65 (single £45). Free private car parking for overnight guests. No dogs. *Rooms 33. Garden. Closed 24-26 Dec. Amex, Diners, MasterCard,* **VISA**

CRAWFORDSBURN   Places of Interest

Bird of Prey Centre Tel 01247 853397
Crawfordsburn Country Park Tel 01247 853621
Somme Heritage Centre Tel 01247 823202

CUSHENDALL   P J McCollam

No Telephone   Map 1 D1
23 Mill Street Cushendall Moyle BT4 0RR   **P**

Currently run by Joe and Sheila Blaney (Joe is the nephew of Joe McCollam), McCollam's has been in the family for 300 years. It's a magical place with a tiny front bar complete with a patchwork of photographs of local characters, many of them sheep farmers (and great fiddle players) who come down from the glens at weekends. The range in the old family kitchen behind the bar is lit on cold evenings and a converted 'cottage' barn across the yard makes a perfect setting for the famous traditional music sessions. Hospitable and full of character. *Open 4-11 in summer (August 12.30-11, winter: Mon-Thu 8-11, Fri & Sat 4-11). Closed Sunday lunchtime. No credit cards.*

DUNADRY   Dunadry Inn   64%   £115

Tel 01849 432474   Fax 01849 433389   Map 1 D2
2 Islandreagh Drive Dunadry Antrim BT41 2HA   **H**

Originally a paper mill founded early in the 18th century, later a linen mill, now a well-known riverside hotel 15 minutes from Belfast city centre and 10 from the airport. Best bedrooms are on the ground floor, with access to the gardens. Executive rooms (£140) feature computer points and fax machines. The Copper Bar under the main staircase is a popular spot for a drink and the lunchtime buffet. Extensive conference facilities for up to 350 delegates (banqueting for 300). Children up to 5 stay free in parents' room. No dogs. Breakfast may be charged additionally to the tariff quoted above. Sister hotel to *Wellington Park* (see entry under Belfast). *Rooms 67. Garden, croquet, crazy golf, game fishing, bicycles, indoor swimming pool, keep-fit equipment, spa bath, steam room, solarium. Closed 24-26 Dec. Amex, Diners, MasterCard,* **VISA**

DUNADRY   Places of Interest

Antrim Round Tower
Antrim Castle Gardens Tel 01849 428000

DUNDRUM   Buck's Head Inn

Tel 01396 751868   Fax 01396 751898   Map 1 D2   **P**
77 Main Street Dundrum nr Newcastle Down BT33 0LU

Situated on the main Belfast-Newcastle road, this attractive, welcoming
family-run pub offers fairly traditional bar food from a blackboard menu which
changes daily. The decor is traditional in a comfortably understated way, creating
a warm, relaxed atmosphere. The restaurant is in a conservatory extension at
the back of the pub, looking out on to a walled garden where tables are set
up in summer. Light, bright and pleasantly furnished with cane chairs and
well-appointed tables, the bar offers a blackboard menu that always features
lasagne, home-made burgers, Dundrum mussels and oysters; in addition, you
might find bang bang chicken, deep-fried Brie, pepper-crusted salmon, poached
plaice with salmon mousse or lamb shank with champ. Three-course Sunday
lunch. *Open 11.30-10.30 (Sun 12-2.30, 5.30-10).* **Bar Food** *12.30-2.30, high tea
5.30-7, 7-9.30 (Sun to 8.30, all day Jun-Aug). Garden, outdoor eating. Closed 25 Dec.
Amex, MasterCard,* **VISA**

DUNGANNON   Grange Lodge   £65

Tel 01868 784212   Fax 01868 723891   Map 1 C2   **PH**
7 Grange Road Dungannon BT71 1EJ

Just outside Dungannon, a mile or so from the M1 on the A29 to Armagh,
Nora and Ralph Brown's pleasing creeper-clad house is set on a rise in about 20
acres of grounds, which are not only well kept but produce a bountiful supply of
food for the table and fresh flowers for the house. The earliest part of the house
is late 17th-century and well-proportioned additions are sympathetic in style and
furnished with antiques throughout. The five bedrooms are all no-smoking.
Good breakfasts. Local activities include golf, swimming, boating, angling (game
and coarse), squash and horse-riding. Not really suitable for children. No dogs.
Rooms 5. Garden. MasterCard, **VISA**

DUNMURRY   Forte Posthouse Belfast   67%   £99

Tel 01232 612101   Fax 01232 626546   Map 1 D2   **H**
300 Kingsway Dunmurry Belfast BT17 9ES

This business-oriented hotel is a short drive from Belfast city centre and airport,
and was until recently a Forte Crest. Accommodation includes no-smoking
rooms and three rooms with an additional sofa bed for families; the 'room only'
price (excluding breakfast) is £79; Fri-Sun tariff £49, subject to availability.
Children up to 16 stay free in parents' room. Conference/meeting facilities
for up to 400. *Rooms 82. Amex, Diners, MasterCard,* **VISA**

ENNISKILLEN   Blakes of the Hollow

Tel 01365 322143   Map 1 C2   **P**
6 Church Street Enniskillen Fermanagh BT74 7JE

The Blake family have reigned supreme over this wonderfully characterful pub
in the centre of Enniskillen since 1929 (Donal himself has been here since 1953).
It presents a double image, with its gleaming black and red shop-front brightening
up an otherwise ordinary street and, from the riverside through-road, an
immaculate (if, for first-time visitors, somewhat mysterious) alleyway and stairs
straight up into a bar that has remained unchanged since 1875. Owners and
regulars alike are rightly proud of their haven and delight in introducing visitors
to it, through photographs and the story of the robin behind the bar. Pints of
Guinness are the thing here (with a shamrock on top if you like) but, although
food is not the reason for coming, they do home-made soup and a fresh,
fatly-packed sandwich all the same (Mon-Fri 12.30-2.30 only). No children.
Open 11.30-11 (Sun 7-10 only). Closed lunch Sun. No credit cards.

ENNISKILLEN   Places of Interest
Tourist Information Tel 01365 323110
Castle Coole Tel 01365 322690
Carrothers Family Heritage Museum Lisbellaw Tel 01365 387278
Cole Monument Tel 01365 323110
Enniskillen Castle Tel 01365 325000
Florence Court House Tel 01365 348249

FIVEMILETOWN   Blessingbourne   £90
Tel 01365 521221   Map 1 C2   **PH**
Fivemiletown Dungannon BT75 0QS

Built in 1874 in the Elizabethan style and immaculately maintained by its
hospitable owners, Robert and Angela Lowry, Blessingbourne is a delightfully
fairytale house of great character with mullioned windows, beautiful grounds
that include a private lake and lovely views across the estate to the mountains
beyond. Furnished in style and comfort with family antiques, the reception
rooms are elegant yet relaxed and the four bedrooms (one with a four-poster
bed) are very comfortably furnished and share two bathrooms. An unusual
attraction is the Blessingbourne carriage and household museum, a collection
which guests are free to browse around and which is open to the public by
arrangement (admission £1.50). Woodland walks are an added attraction.
No children under 10. No dogs. On the outskirts of Fivemiletown on the B122
Fintona/Omagh road. ***Rooms 4. Garden, tennis, rowing, fishing. Closed 1 week at
Christmas. No credit cards.***

FIVEMILETOWN   Places of Interest
Coach and Carriage Museum Tel 01365 521221
Fivemiletown Display Centre Tel 01365 521409

HELEN'S BAY   Deane's on the Square   †   £75
Tel 01247 852841   Map 1 D2   **R**
7 Station Square Helen's Bay North Down BT19 1TN

Built in 1863 in the style of a Scottish Baronial castle, the first Marquis of
Dufferin and Ava's own railway station is the unlikely setting for some of the
best food in Ireland – not least because it is still a fully operational station. This
can be somewhat disconcerting on a first visit if you are shown straight to one
of the tables for two in the long, narrow 'corridor' near the platform! However,
the building is sympathetically converted, immaculately maintained inside and
out and has an open kitchen and a great deal of atmosphere in all areas, including a small basement bar. Pleasingly understated table settings – white cloths,
white china and simple modern cutlery and glasses – are complemented by
comfortable chairs. Chef-proprietor Michael Deane's main menus, priced for
two or three courses with some of the dishes (tatin of potatoes and foie gras with
caramelised apples or roast fillet of beef with cabbage and pepper) attracting a
supplement, is amplified by both a separate two-course vegetarian menu (£16)
with nine dishes and a seven-course Tasting Menu. Michael's appealing, modern
style is evident as soon as you pick up the menu: tomato and couscous soup
with cumin brioche, confit of quail with mushy peas, roast snails and mushrooms,
terrine of rabbit with pistachio, roast pigeon and truffle – and that's just for
starters. Thai-style haddock with crab wonton and a coriander and chili oil
continues in the same vein for main courses alongside pork bourguignon with
onion sauce, or roast cod with a mustard crust, deep-fried celery and a lemon
and basil dressing; accompanying herb or celeriac and lemon grass mash show
that much thought goes into balancing each dish and creating genuinely interesting
and original dishes. Five dessert wines are offered to accompany wonderful
desserts like pan-fried pineapple with vanilla syrup and white pepper ice cream,

espresso tart with mocha cheesecake and cappuccino ice cream, or millefeuille of roast pears. Ten or so cheeses include some of the very best that Ireland has to offer. The wine list is clearly laid out and covers a range wide enough to complement the superb cooking with such a diverse range of ingredients. *Seats 40. L (Sun only) 12.30-2 D 7-9.30. Set Sun L £15 Set D £19.95/£24.95 & £36. Closed D Sun, all Mon, 1 week Jul, 3 days Christmas & 2 weeks Jan. Amex, Diners, MasterCard, **VISA***

HILLSBOROUGH   The Hillside Bar

Tel 01846 682765   Fax 01846 682557   Map 1 D2   **P/R**
21 Main Street Hillsborough Lisburn BT26 6AE

A delightful, well-run establishment, The Hillside '1777' is easily found in the centre of this pretty little town – and very well worth finding it is, too. The atmosphere is warm and cosy in both the main bar, where a real fire burns all year, and a smaller one to the side. Throughout, the atmosphere is gently rustic – dark green paint and soft country browns and greys in natural materials – and comfortably set up for eating. The new Refectory Bar and a separate kitchen for bar food have alleviated much of the pressure on the bar food system that has recently arisen. Now, the bar menu is served throughout the day (with only a short break after lunch before cream teas are served in the afternoon) by charming young staff. Typical fare from the bar menu might include tempura of cod with roast pepper pesto, open ciabatta sandwiches, smoked haddock and leek tart with crispy bacon and herb aïoli, deep-dish lasagne plus daily specials like confit of duck with plum sauce or salmon escalope with puff pastry and a lemon sauce; home-baked fruit pie, tangy lemon meringue and Hillside banoffee among the puddings; in the evening, flame-grilled home-made burgers and steaks extend the range. The whole operation is overseen by Diane Shields and her family and a new chef, Albert Neilly, had just taken over as we went to press. His new restaurant menus promise good things: wild mushroom and rosemary soup finished with a light sabayon and poppy seeds, goujons of pan-fried salmon marinated in dill and yoghurt with sautéed spinach, wild rice and a tarragon and white wine sauce, and petit tarte tatin with a Grand Marnier crème anglaise – tempting stuff! Bar manager Randall Brennan offers Northern Ireland's best range of real ales: try the new White Water ale, brewed in nearby Kilkeel, one of Hilden's ales (also brewed locally) or seek out Morland's Old Speckled Hen; you can even get a pint of Guinness at either cool room temperature or chilled, and the wine list offers around 12 wines by the glass. Outside seating on the recently-extended (and cobbled) beer garden. New disabled loo (access for bar food only). Our Ireland Pub of the Year in 1995. *Open 11.30-11 (Sun 12.30-2.30, 7.30-10.30).* **Bar Food** *12-2.30, 3.30-8. Restaurant 7-9.30 (not Sun eve). Closed Good Friday & 25 Dec. Beer garden. Amex, Diners, MasterCard, **VISA***

HILLSBOROUGH   The Plough Inn

Tel 01846 682985   Fax 01846 682472   Map 1 D2   **P**
The Square Hillsborough Lisburn BT26 6AG

Former coaching inn, dating back to the 18th century, overlooking the Market Court House and the Secretary of State for Ireland's residence at the top of the main street. Since purchasing the establishment in 1990 the hard-working Patterson family, especially the enthusiastic head chef Derek Patterson, have created a popular dining pub, famous for its seafood restaurant, warm hospitality and for hosting the Hillsborough Oyster Festival in September. In fact, the Plough is to be commended for successfully running three distinct food operations each day, which, as a result, attracts a varied clientele, from a good lunchtime business trade to discerning evening diners. Derek Patterson's style of cooking on an assortment of menus has been influenced by his travels worldwide, with classical French blending with traditional Irish, ethnic and Oriental styles. Home-cooked 'pub' meals (open prawn sandwich, chicken, mushroom and bacon pie, Malaysian beef curry, summer salads, fresh fish of the day) are served in the comfortable front bar, complete with open fire, beams, memorabilia-adorned walls and well-kept Theakston Bitter, at lunchtime only. Served at the same time (and in the early evening 5-7pm) in the upstairs wine bar and bistro, is a more select range of dishes aimed at the business market. Here, Thai seafood kebab, pan-blackened cod fillet with chargrilled vegtables, and rib-eye steak can be accompanied by one of at least twenty wines available by the glass, or a bottle from the interesting list of wines with good tasting notes. After 7pm both the wine bar and main bar fill up with a young drinking clientele, while the kitchen shifts up a gear in preparation for the serious diners who eagerly await their table in the 'evening-only' rear restaurant – booking essential. Housed in the old stables with the atmosphere of a Scottish Baronial undercroft, this is where Derek Patterson excels in preparing the excellent choice of seafood dishes (Galway oysters Thai-style, fresh lobster, roast ray wing with crushed pepper-corns, Donegal mussel and saffron scented soup, Cajun-spiced shark steak, pan-blackened Glenarm salmon with mushrooms and ginger soya) listed on the short, hand-written and daily-changing menu. Meat-eaters should not be disappointed with calf's liver, onion compote and lime jus, Oriental duck breast and deep-fried noodles, or a prime Angus sirloin steak. Well-executed dishes are carefully presented and service is efficient from young, keen staff. The Pattersons also find time to organise seasonal gourmet evenings, summer barbecues and a beer festival (October). No children in the pub. Winner of the Northern Ireland Regional Award for our 1997 Seafood Pub of the Year. *Open 11.30-11.30 (Sun 12-3, 7-10.30).* **Meals:** *Bar 12-2.15 only (from 12.30 Sun), Wine Bar/Bistro Tue-Sat 12-2.15, 5-7 & Restaurant Tue-Sat 6-9 only. Wine Bar/Bistro & Restaurant closed Sun & Mon. Garden, outdoor eating, barbecue. Amex, Diners, MasterCard,* **VISA**

We welcome bona fide complaints and recommendations on the tear-out Readers' Comments pages at the back of the Guide. They are followed up by our professional team.

HILLSBOROUGH **White Gables Hotel**	**60%**	**£101**

Tel 01846 682755   Fax 01846 689532   Map 1 D2   **H**
14 Dromore Road Hillsborough Lisburn BT26 6HS

Modern, purpose-built hotel conveniently located just off the main Belfast-Dublin road (A1), 10 miles south of Belfast, on the edge of Hillsborough, which is famous for its Georgian architecture and castle. Designed specifically with the business traveller in mind, both the smart public areas and the 31 uniformly decorated bedrooms are generally busy on weekdays with a corporate clientele; special weekend rates tempt visitors to stay overnight in this historic village. The functional bedrooms are clean and well appointed, each featuring the usual modern facilities and clean bathrooms. Conference/banqueting facilities for 150. Coffee shop 9.30am-4.30pm. *Rooms 31. Amex, Diners, MasterCard,* **VISA**

HILLSBOROUGH   Places of Interest

Tourist Information Tel 01846 660038
Hillsborough Fort Tel 01846 683285
Irish Linen Centre Lisburn Tel 01846 663377
Moira Station Tel 01846 611439

HOLYWOOD   Bay Tree

Tel 01232 421419   Map 1 D2   **JaB**
Audley Court 118 High Street Holywood North Down BT18 9HW

Reached via an archway opposite the police station in the main street (one can
also drive through to a small car par at the rear), the Bay Tree is part pottery
shop, with the work of over 30 Irish potters on show, and part small coffee
shop, where Sue Farmer's delicious cooking is the big attraction. Throughout
the day there are various cakes – carrot, chocolate, fresh pineapple crunch,
chocolate chantilly tart and Sue's cinnamon scones – while lunchtime brings
soup (carrot and parsnip, vegetable and haricot bean), cheesy broccoli and
cauliflower croustade, and spicy coconut chicken. Open for dinner on the first
and last Friday of each month, but booking is essential. There are a couple of
tables on a small patio. No smoking. *Seats 34. Open 10-4.30 (D first & last Fri
of month only 7.30-11). Closed Sun, 3 days Christmas, 3 days Easter & 2 or 3 days
around 12 July. No credit cards.*

HOLYWOOD   Culloden Hotel   78%   £160

Tel 01232 425223   Fax 01232 426777   Map 1 D2   **H**
142 Bangor Road Craigavad Holywood North Down BT18 0EX

Standing in 12 glorious acres of
gardens and woodland overlooking
Belfast Lough and the Antrim coast,
this impressive 19th-century building
was originally a palace for the Bishops
of Down and is a splendid example
of Scottish Baronial architecture.
    The Culloden is the flagship of
the Hastings Hotel Group, who are
gradually refurbishing and upgrading
every facet of the hotel, which may
well live up to their brochure motto
'Built for a Bishop, Fit for a King' on completion. Considerable improvements
have already been made to the day rooms, where antiques, stained glass, fine
plasterwork and paintings succeed in giving the place an air of elegance. A side
extension houses most of the bedrooms, all of which are spacious, tastefully
decorated and well equipped, with writing desk, easy chairs, telephone, satellite
TV, hairdryer and trouser press, as well as thoughtful extras like fresh fruit and
biscuits. Good toiletries and bathrobes feature in the bathrooms, all of which
have both baths and power showers. The vast and luxurious Palace Suite –
'Fit for a President' – enjoys the best Lough views, along with the Mitre
restaurant (the food was disappointing on our last visit) and elevated main-
building rooms, the latter requiring the most updating and investment. There is
a well-appointed health and fitness suite, an inn in the grounds, various function
rooms (conference facilities for up to 500, banqueting 450) and 24hr room service.
Good, attentive service from well-attired staff. No dogs. *Rooms 87. Garden,
pitch & putt, indoor swimming pool, gym, squash, sauna, steam room, spa bath,
sun beds, tennis, snooker, hair & beauty salon. Closed 24 & 25 Dec. Amex, Diners,
MasterCard,* **VISA**

HOLYWOOD   Sullivans   £60

Tel 01232 421000   Map 1 D2   **R**
Sullivan Place Holywood North Down BT18 9JF

Bright and cheerful, with sunny yellow walls and colourfully upholstered chairs,
Sullivans operates as a coffee shop during the day (Devon scones, double chocolate
truffle cake from 10-12 and 2.30-4, then lunchtime dishes like a choice of soups,

seafood terrine and Mexican chili tacos from 12-2.30) before turning into a fully-fledged restaurant in the evening when young chef-patron Simon Shaw steps up a gear or two with both a short, fixed-price menu and an à la carte. The former might see three choices at each stage, perhaps leek and potato soup with a dash of olive oil, hot goat's cheese salad with garlic croutons or roast cod with parsley and nut brown butter to start, followed by salmon with tomato relish and herb oil, peppered duck confit with red onion marmalade or pork loin with wild mushroom risotto. More involved dishes on the carte might be seafood puff pastry with a herb cream sauce or duck breast with five spice, roast pears and apple. The cooking is accomplished and portions are substantial. Desserts range from glazed lemon tart, summer berry pudding and Sullivans Alaska on the table d'hote to individual rhubarb meringue tart, caramelised pear and apple crepes with rum and raisin ice cream, a choice of three savouries or an Irish cheeseboard à la carte. Unlicensed, but there are a couple of wine merchants nearby. Booking advisable at weekends. It says on the menu that 'Sullivans closes at 1am'. *Seats 40. L 10-2.30 D 7-10.30. Set D £19.95. Closed Sun, 25 & 26 Dec. MasterCard, VISA*

HOLYWOOD   Places of Interest

Ulster Folk and Transport Museum Cultra Tel 01232 428428

IRVINESTOWN   The Hollander

Tel 01365 621231

Map 1 C2 **P**

5 Main Street Townhill Irvinestown nr Eniskillen Fermanagh BT94 1GJ

The Holland family – Jim and Margaret plus their son Stephen – run a tidy ship at this long-established town-centre eatery. Jim, the manager, is usually to be found in the bar (which has a fascinating array of aeronautical memorabilia spanning two World Wars) while Margaret and head chef Stephen look after the food side. Both family and formula work well together, producing a unique combination of food, drink and hospitality that draws locals and visitors alike, whether for popular bar food dishes like freshly-made burgers or seafood bakes with a special 'home-made' touch. House specialities are always on the evening menus but can be produced by arrangement at lunchtime for a group of four or more – all it takes is a phone call and the à la carte menu will be produced. Try the popular stuffed duck, a whole fresh duck, de-boned and stuffed, or the salmon en croute (shaped by Stephen to look like a fish). Hard-working and hospitable, Jim will even run boating visitors back to the local marina after dinner. Separate no-smoking room. Toilet facilities for the disabled. *Open 12-2, 5.30-11 (Sun 6.30-9.30). Bar Food 12-2, 5.30-7. Restaurant Meals 5.30-9.30 (Sun 6.30-9). Closed L Sun, all Mon & Tue (except Jul & Aug), 24-26 Dec. Amex, MasterCard, VISA*

KESH   Lough Erne Hotel   60%   £59

Tel 01365 631275   Fax 01365 631921

Map 1 C2

Main Street Kesh Fermanagh BT93 1TF

H

Located in the town centre but making the most of its position on the banks of the Glendurragh River, a friendly family hotel offering homely accommodation in rooms that tend to be on the small side, with en suite bath/shower rooms, TV and tea/coffee facilities. The downstairs bar and function rooms are particularly attractive, with direct access to a paved riverside walkway and garden. Banqueting and conference facilities for 200/250. Cot, high-chair and early evening meals provided for children (50% tariff reductions for children). Four self-catering studio apartments (by the side of the river) are available on weekly terms. *Rooms 12. Garden, fishing. Closed 24 & 25 Dec. Amex, Diners, MasterCard, VISA*

KESH — Lusty Beg Island

Tel 01365 632032 Fax 01365 632033   Map 1 C2   **P**
Kesh Fermanagh BT93 8AD

Bought by the Cadden family four years ago, Lusty Beg Island has been imaginatively developed to create a self-contained facility satisfying a number of different markets. As soon as guests enter the isolated phone box to call the little ferry that will spirit them across to the island they know this is going to be something different. The ferry (which is free) might just take two (very small) cars but it is mostly intended for foot passengers and their luggage, as self-catering cottages are the most obvious attraction on the island. But wait, is this a friendly inn we spy? – Indeed it is and very nice, too, serving good bar snacks (home-baked bread, wild Irish smoked salmon, garlic mussels, pizzas and baked potatoes). As we were going to press Lusty Beg was entering its penultimate stage of development (the final one is a swimming pool and leisure centre, to be ready in time for the 1997 season), with a bed and breakfast operation in village-style little houses (no dogs) and banqueting/conference facilities coming on stream in addition to the established self-catering chalets. Two rooms for the disabled. Ned's Cottage, a thatched tea room, is open for snacks in the summer only from 9am-7pm. *Bar open 10-11.30. **Bar Food** 12-9. Restaurant 6.30-9.30. Garden, croquet, tennis, putting green, fishing, children's playroom & playground, games room, snooker, shop, mountain bikes, nature trail, canoeing. **Accommodation** 18 bedrooms, all with shower en suite, £45 (single £28.50). Children welcome overnight (under-2s free if sharing, 2-8 25% of tariff, 8-14 50%). No dogs. MasterCard,* **VISA**

KESH   Places of Interest

Castle Archdale Country Park Tel 01365 621333
White Island Tel 01365 621731

LIMAVADY — Radisson Roe Park Hotel   74%   £110

Tel 01504 722212 Fax 01504 722313   Map 1 C1   **H**
Roe Park Limavady BT49 9LB

Self-styled as 'Northern Ireland's premier golf, leisure and conference resort', this large, purpose-built hotel and golf course complex occupies a 150-acre estate on the west bank of the River Roe. Perfectly positioned adjacent to the beautiful Roe Valley Country Park (good walking) and close to the spectacular Antrim coast, Donegal and the thriving business centre of Londonderry, Roe Park is attracting good corporate business through its provision of seven conference, syndicate, seminar and banqueting rooms, which accommodate up to 440 in theatre-style conference or 280 for dinner seated around tables. The hotel's appeal extends to keen golfers (challenging 18-hole course, floodlit driving range, resident professional) and visitors wishing to explore the surrounding area from a comfortable and relaxing base. Beyond the modern, spacious and pristine lounge/foyer are 64 equally spacious and uniformly decorated bedrooms. All have a king-size bed, telephone, trouser press, iron and ironing board, satellite TV, well-equipped bathroom with power shower over the tub, and 24hr room service. De luxe rooms afford even more space and are ideal for families as they have extra beds (under-5s free and under-15s £15 if sharing their parents' room), while those seeking more comfort can book one of the five suites. Non-golfers may satisfy their exercise needs in the Fairways Leisure Club. A notable buffet-style breakfast is served in the Courtyard Restaurant. Just off the A2 Limavady-Londonderry road. *Rooms 64. Golf (18), indoor swimming pool, jacuzzi, steam room, sauna, fitness studio, health & beauty salon, play area, games room. Amex, Diners, MasterCard,* **VISA**

LIMAVADY — Streeve Hill £90

Tel 01504 766563 Fax 01504 768285   Map 1 C1   **PH**
Limavady BT49 OHP

Having handed their magnificent Drenagh on to the next generation, Peter and June Welsh are now welcoming guests to the delightful Dower House of the estate, a lovely, well-proportioned house with a rose-pink brick facade and unusually wide windows framing views of parkland and distant hills. A year-round log fire in the hall, where tea is taken at comfortable sofas, sets the tone, and all who enter are cast under the spell of Streeve. Dining-room, drawing-room and June's walled garden were receiving the finishing touches as we went to press but already it was a place guests urgently wished to return to – the Welshes have great style and this, combined with their choice of antiques and memorabilia from a far bigger house, creates a very special atmosphere. One senses a joyous feeling of 'playing house' here, in a house which is large but of comfortably human proportions; while comfort is the main priority, informality and a sense of fun in the decor have not been overlooked. *Rooms 5. Garden, patio, woodland walks. Closed Dec-Mar. MasterCard,* **VISA**

LONDONDERRY — Beech Hill House Hotel 59% £75

Tel 01504 49279 Fax 01504 45366   Map 1 C1   **HR**
32 Ardmore Road Londonderry Derry City BT47 3QP

Dating from 1729, Beech Hill is a substantial house set in 36 acres of mature parkland in the rural hinterland two miles south of the city centre; the hotel is signposted off the main A6 as you approach Londonderry from the Belfast direction. Very much centred around its restaurant and three function/meeting rooms (for up to 100) the only day room is a comfortable bar/lounge with unusual 'cattle head' frieze under the ceiling. Attractive, individually decorated bedrooms vary in shape and size and boast a variety of antique pieces along with a well-lit desk or work space. Telephones are standard, as are remote-control TVs (the latter with set-top aerials so reception is not always perfect). 13 of the bathrooms have shower and WC only. An antique-furnished Executive Suite (£100) overlooks the gardens, as does the honeymoon suite with its delightful four-poster bed. No dogs. *Rooms 17. Garden, croquet, tennis. Closed 24 & 25 Dec. Amex, MasterCard,* **VISA**

Ardmore Restaurant £65

The dining-room is a former billiard room where green Regency-striped wallpaper, brass 'oil lamp' lights and views over the gardens set the scene for generously-portioned, enthusiastic cooking. In addition to the à la carte there is also a daily-changing, fixed-price menu for both lunch and dinner as well as an interesting vegetarian menu. A new chef recently took over. *Seats 40. Parties 8. Private Room 30. L 12-2.30 D 7-9.30. Set L £13.95/£15.95 (Sun £14.95) Set D £21.95.*

LONDONDERRY   Everglades Hotel   59%   £86

Tel 01504 46722   Fax 01504 49200   Map 1 C1   **H**
Prehen Road Londonderry Derry City BT47 2PA

South of the town on the banks of the River Foyle, this modern low-rise hotel
is a popular venue for conferences and banqueting (550/350) besides providing
bright, practical accommodation. Top of the bedroom range are two suites
(£150) with jacuzzis and turbo showers. Eleven new bedrooms were recently
added and a major refurbishment programme underway. Children up to 12 stay
free in parents' room. Hastings Hotels. *Rooms 63. Garden. Closed 24 & 25 Dec.*
Amex, Diners, MasterCard, **VISA**

LONDONDERRY   Places of Interest

Tourist Information Tel 01504 267284
Brachmore Stone Circus nr Cookstown
Derry's Walls Guided Walks Tel 01504 267284
Fort Duncree Military Museum Buncrana Tel 00 353 74 21160
Harbour Museum Tel 01504 365151
Heritage Library and Genealogy Centre Butcher St Tel 01504 373177
Ness Wood Country Park Tel 01504 722074
O'Doherty World Museum Inch Island Tel 00 353 77 61052
Sperrin Heritage Centre Strabane Tel 01662 648142
St Eugene's Cathedral Tel 01504 262894
St Columb's Cathedral off London St Tel 01504 267313
Tower Museum Magazine St Tel 01504 372411
Tullyarvan Mill Buncrana Tel 00 353 77 61613
Ulster-American Folk Park Omagh Tel 01662 243292 *15 miles*
Woodrow Wilson's Cottage Tel 01504 883735

NEWCASTLE   Slieve Donard Hotel   63%   £110

Tel 01396 721006   Fax 01396 724830   Map 1 D2   **H**
Downs Road Newcastle Down BT33 OAG

Imposing redbrick Victorian railway hotel facing the Irish Sea (next to the Royal
County Down Golf Club) with the Mountains of Mourne in the background,
'The Slieve' caters mainly to conferences in winter and holidaymakers, tour
groups and weddings in the summer. A grand, galleried entrance hall sets the
tone for public areas, which include a large elegant lounge with conservatory
extension (sometimes used for functions), cosy library sitting-room and a bar
named after Charlie Chaplin, who once stayed here. Bedrooms vary in shape
and size but share the same blue and peach colour scheme, polycotton duvets
and dark mahogany furniture; eight suites start at £135. Good leisure centre.
Major conference and banqueting facilities can cater for up to 1000 conference
delegates theatre-style and 500 for sit-down banqueting; parking for 400 cars.
An indoor playroom is provided for children during school holidays. The pubby
Percy French inn is situated at the entrance to the hotel. 27 rooms were recently
added and the Elysium health spa was extended with a new dance studio
and changing rooms. Hastings Hotels. No dogs. *Rooms 126. Garden,*
indoor swimming pool, gym, sun beds, steam room, spa bath, beauty salon, shop.
Amex, Diners, MasterCard, **VISA**

NEWCASTLE   Places of Interest

Tourist Information Tel 01396 722222
Butterfly House Seaforde Tel 01396 811225
Castle Ward Strangford Tel 01396 881204 *7 miles*
Castlewellan and Arboretum Tel 01396 615218
Dundrum Castle
Helicopter Tours Tel 01849 453663
Mourne Countryside Centre Tel 01396 778664
Murlough National Nature Reserve Tel 01396 751467
Route 66 American Automobile Collection Tel 01396 725223
Seaforde Gardens Tel 01396 87225 *5 miles*

PORTAFERRY   The Narrows   £58

Tel 01247 728148   Fax 01247 728105   Map 1 D2   **PH**
8 Shore Road Portaferry Ards BT22 1JY

Brothers Will and James Brown returned to their birth place in 1992 to restore
and extend their father's family home, creating accommodation and conference
facilities designed to make the most of both the building and its location; they
opened for business in May 1996. An archway in the middle of the soft primrose
yellow facade draws the eye, attracting visitors into an 18th-century courtyard
that is central to the development. The ground floor includes a cosy sitting-
room with an open fire and a spacious restaurant (that was just coming fully on
stream as we went to press). A talented young team, under the direction of head
chef Stephen McCullough and Will's wife Sara Brown (who specialises in baking,
making all the breads herself and also tutoring a breadmaking course on their
programme of off-season workshops), promises well for this side of the venture.
The style throughout is light and bright with natural materials a strong feature –
hessian and jute floor coverings, warm-toned light wood, soft furnishings in
cotton and walls painted in gentle tones of primrose, sea blues and greens. The
bedrooms are all different and almost spartan, but their simplicity emphasises the
beauty of lough views; they have a serene, almost Oriental atmosphere and all
are en suite (only three with baths). Especially sympathetic to guests with special
needs, all the shower rooms are wheelchair-friendly, eight are specially designed
and there is a lift. Families are welcome: there are two interconnecting rooms,
two family rooms (children under 2 may stay free in their parents' room), high-
chairs are available and children's tea is available at 5pm. Banqueting/conference
facilities are provided for 40/50 in a fine room over the archway, which opens
on to a private balcony. *Rooms 13. Garden, playroom, fishing, sauna.*
Amex, MasterCard, **VISA**

PORTAFERRY   Portaferry Hotel   64%   £90

Tel 01247 728231   Fax 01247 728999   Map 1 D2   **HR**
10 The Strand Portaferry Ards BT22 1PE

Formed out of an 18th-century terrace on the seafront, where the ferry crosses
the neck of Strangford Lough, the Portaferry has been substantially remodelled
over recent years to create a delightful small hotel run with a winning combination
of charm and professionalism by John and Marie Herlihy. Public areas include a
tweedy bar and several tastefully decorated little lounges sporting pictures of the
surrounding area by local artists. Light, airy bedrooms come with lightwood
furniture and matching floral bedcovers and curtains, neat bathrooms with huge
bath sheets. All bedrooms are the same price but only some have the lough
views. Particularly busy around the time of the Castleward Opera Festival in
June. No dogs. *Rooms 14. Closed 24 & 25 Dec. Amex, Diners, MasterCard,* **VISA**

Restaurant   £55

Recently refurbished but retaining a slightly cottage style, the restaurant
itself establishes the tone for food that is setting the pace locally but avoids
pretentiousness. Donal Keane (previously at *Sheen Falls Lodge*, Kenmare), head
chef since January 1996, presents a well-balanced table d'hote dinner menu
(with a two- or three-course option) plus a short carte with plenty of choice:
seafood, much of it from Strangford or nearby Portavogie, stars in starters like
crab and prawn salad (served with Galia melon and an orange mayonnaise) and
main courses such as baked Strangford lobster with hollandaise, pan-fried scallops
with bacon and garlic on leeks with a balsamic dressing, or roast fillet of monkfish served on a bed of spinach with a saffron butter sauce or in an original and
rather dramatic presentation of a globe artichoke with a tomato and chive butter.
Fish from further afield sometimes features, too, as in a delicious red mullet salad
with chargrilled vegetables and garlic lemon dressing, and Oriental influences

may be seen in a spiced starter of crisp duck pieces served like a stir-fry with spring onions and quince. Look for roast rack of Mourne lamb, perhaps with a herb crust and ratatouille, medallions of pork wrapped in smoked ham with fresh pasta and pickled chanterelles, or the more traditional peppered rib-eye steak with crisp fried onions and herb butter. Delightful desserts taste as good as they look – a striped dark and white chocolate terrine may be balanced by a fresh orange sauce, a moulded pannacotta looks serenely pale against a compote of berries – or there's a plated selection of Irish farmhouse cheeses. Lunch menus offer a simpler choice of about five dishes for each course – seafood pancake, roast loin of pork with apple sauce, hazelnut meringues with caramel sauce are all typical – and there's an excellent lunchtime bar menu (including 'children's choice') available every day except Sunday. *Seats 80. Parties 14. L 12.30-2.30 D 7-9. Set L £11.50/£14.50 Set D £19.50-£22.50. Amex, Diners, MasterCard,* **VISA**

PORTAFERRY   Places of Interest

Exploris Aquarium Tel 01247 728062
Castleward House (NT) Opera Festival Tel 01232 661090 June

PORTBALLINTRAE	Bayview Hotel	58%	£70

Tel 01265 731453   Fax 01265 732360   Map 1 C1   **H**
2 Bayhead Road Portballintrae nr Bushmills Moyle BT57 8RZ

Overlooking the tiny harbour and the bay, the long pebbledash hotel building stands half a mile from the main A2 coastal route. Functions and conferences (up to 300) are quite big business, but residents have their own sitting-room, and there's also a convivial bar. Bedrooms include one semi-suite with a small sitting-room area; they generally have modern bathrooms. No dogs. *Rooms 16. Indoor swimming pool, sauna, snooker. MasterCard,* **VISA**

PORTBALLINTRAE	Sweeney's

Tel 01265 732404   Fax 01265 731279   Map 1 C1   **P**
6 Seaport Avenue Portballintrae Moyle BT57 8SB

On the sea side of the road, this attractive stone building has its origins in the 18th century when it was built as coaching stables for the nearby Leslie estate. It has now been pleasingly renovated and converted by the current owner, Seymour Sweeney, into a stylish bar and comfortable, informal restaurant. Although the main building is cut off from the view from another similar one on the seaward side (used for accommodation), a conservatory addition gets around the problem for daytime use and the main interior has a cosy open fire and generally welcoming atmosphere (except for pervasive background music in all areas except the conservatory). While gourmet food is not the aim, the kitchen produces a fairly extensive range of snappy modern dishes that should appeal to most age groups – typically, good soup, baked potatoes with various fillings, chicken kebab in pitta bread, confit of duck with creamed lentils or vegetarian leek and mustard crumble. No bookings taken, except for parties. Live music is a regular feature (Mon, Wed, Fri & Sat in summer, Fri & Sat in winter) and there's a late licence until 12.30am when it's playing. Toilet facilities for the disabled. No-smoking area. *Open 11.30-11, Sun 12.30-2.30, 7-10). Bar Food 12-9.30 summer & holidays (12-2.30, 5-9.30 winter), Sun 12.30-2.30, 7-10. Garden, outdoor eating. Closed 25 Dec. No credit cards.*

PORTBALLINTRAE   Places of Interest

Dunluce Castle Tel 01265 731938
Giant's Causeway Tourist Information Tel 01265 731855/31582
The Old Bushmills Distillery Tel 01265 731521

PORTGLENONE   Crosskeys Inn

Tel 01648 50694   Map 1 D2   **P**
nr Portglenone Ballymena BT42

Follow signs for Randalstown on leaving Portglenone, then lookout for the
signs to Crosskeys to find this charming, 17th-century stone-and-thatch rural
inn, which enjoys an isolated position at a country crossroads. Formerly an old
coaching inn and, until recently, the local post office and general stores, it
remains truly unspoilt and one of the best pub venues for traditional Irish music
in Antrim. Eamonn Stinson is in charge behind the bar, just as his father was
before the war, serving a loyal band of locals and thirsty tourists who track this
gem down. The bar is simply adorned and the adjacent 'kitchen' has a huge
fireplace and rustic tables and chairs; the basic back room is where the musicians
gather and the 'impromptu' sessions begin (Wed, Fri, Sat & Sun eve). No food
available. *Open 11-11.30 (Sun 12.30-3, 7-10.30). Patio. No credit cards.*

Many hotels offer reduced rates for weekend or out-of-season
bookings. Our guide price indicates high-season rates.
Always ask about special deals for longer stays.

PORTRUSH   Causeway Coast Hotel   £80

Tel 01265 822435   Fax 01265 824495   Map 1 C1   **H**
36 Ballyreagh Road Portrush Coleraine BT56 8LR

Owned by the O'Neill family for the last five years, this modest 1960s-style
hotel on the edge of Portrush is in the midst of redevelopment, which will soon
see it totally redesigned, with a new wing incorporating a leisure centre, new
rooms with sea views and balconies (including five rooms designed for disabled
guests) and much more – even including a special railway halt right at the back
door that will enable guests travelling from Dublin to arrive direct in just three
hours. There are also changes taking place in the main building but, despite the
upheaval, this remains a convenient, comfortable hotel for holidaymakers, golfers
and conferences (banqueting/conference facilities for 300). Bedrooms vary, all
with satellite TV and hospitality tray and some with fridges; others have a balcony
with sea views and a few have breakfast kitchenettes. There are also 20 self-
catering apartments. *Rooms 21. Garden, snooker. Amex, Diners, MasterCard,* **VISA**

PORTRUSH   Maddybenny Farm House   £50

Tel & Fax 01265 823394   Map 1 C1   **PH**
18 Maddybenny Park off Loguestown Road Portrush Coleraine BT52 2PT

Exceptional breakfasts are just part of the attraction of Rosemary White's
farmhouse just outside Portrush as the accommodation is just as successful in
matching guests' required comforts. The bedrooms are all en suite and there are
all sorts of nice touches – electric blankets on the bed, a comfortable armchair
for reading, hospitality tray complete with tea cosy, a torch and alarm clock
beside the bed, nailbrush (and even indigestion tablets!) beside the washbasin,
trouser press, hairdryer – and, on the landing, an ironing board, fridge and pay
phone for use by guests. Across the yard there are six self-catering cottages
(one suitable for those in wheelchairs), open all year. There's a riding school on
the farm and youngsters are well catered for, with a football lawn provided; golf,
fishing, tennis and pitch and putt are all nearby. To find, look for the sign 'to
Maddybenny Riding Centre' off the A29 Coleraine-Portrush road. No dogs.
Rooms 3. Garden, croquet, games room, children's playroom, riding. MasterCard,
VISA

PORTRUSH   Ramore   ★   £65

Tel 01265 824313   Map 1 C1   **R**
The Harbour Portrush Coleraine BT56 8BN

Sole ownership of this renowned north-coast restaurant has now passed into the hands of chef George McAlpin and his wife Jane, who plan to buid a new 'inbetween' restaurant in addition to their current restaurant and Wine Bar below (open 12.15-2.15 & 5.15-9.15 Mon-Sat) over the 1997/8 winter. The exceptionally professional operation runs smoothly on well-oiled wheels, constantly reinforcing its reputation as one of the country's premier modern restaurants – its sleek, chic, black-and-chrome decor is right up-to-date. The bustle and buzz never fail to amaze and delight first-time visitors – the floor staff move around like dancers under the expert supervision of Hilda and Sam Stephenson and the sense of drama conveyed by George's open kitchen always thrills. The tension just as the second wave of diners arrives and orders start to come in is palpable, making first-sitting types feel like staying on just for the show. The à la carte menu offers a good choice of about eight dishes at each course – starters mostly under £5, main courses up to around £12 – augmented by a number of daily specials on the blackboard that usually include several starters designed to double as vegetarian main courses. The cooking style is vibrant and the presentation of dishes dramatic without unnecessary posing: any flourishes add to the enjoyment of the meal rather than distracting from the kitchen's excellent standard. Mediterranean influences remain strong in dishes tempered by the strength of Irish ingredients, especially seafood such as Dublin Bay prawn croissants with garlic cream sauce or a main course of brill with Mediterranean vegetables and tomato butter. Where there are weaknesses they are minor – small, old potatoes presented as 'new' for example (and, perhaps, the queue in the Ladies) – but attention to detail in other areas, like the superb range of home-baked breads and Irish farmhouse cheeses (a selection of five, all served in perfect condition with salad and fresh fruit), more than compensates and the overall experience is rewarding. Don't forget to leave room for the wonderful desserts – hot soufflés in particular are a speciality and not to be missed – before finishing off with lovely aromatic coffee and petits fours. The wine list has something for everyone, from a handful of fancy clarets, New World reds and ubiquitous French whites to a dozen half bottles.
Seats 80. D only 6.30-10.30. Closed Sun, Mon (except Easter Monday) & 24-26 Dec. MasterCard, **VISA**

PORTRUSH   Royal Court Hotel   64%   £100

Tel 01265 822236   Fax 01265 823176   Map 1 C1   **H**
Whiterocks Portrush Coleraine BT56 8NF

Exceptionally well located in a scenic cliff-top position just outside Portrush, this new hotel has a dining-room and bar that take full advantage of uninterrupted sea views; balconies on four of the front bedrooms (being completed as we went to press) will also benefit from the coastal setting. Bedrooms, which include a bridal suite with four-poster, vary in size and outlook and have a consistent decorative style with co-ordinated schemes throughout. Some of the back rooms are smaller but all are comfortable and include a large-screen satellite TV. Bathrooms are particularly pleasant, some with corner baths. 24hr room service. No dogs. **Rooms** 18. Garden. MasterCard, **VISA**

We only recommend the food in hotels categorised as **HR** and **AR**.

PORTRUSH — Places of Interest

Dunluce Castle Tel 01265 731938 *3 miles*
Giant's Causeway Tourist Information Tel 01265 731855/31582
Hezlett House Tel 01265 848567
Mussenden Temple Downhill Tel 01265 848728
The Old Bushmills Distillery Tel 01265 731521

TEMPLEPATRICK   Templeton Hotel   66%   £110

Tel 01849 432984   Fax 01849 433406   Map 1 D2   **H**
882 Antrim Road Templepatrick Ballyclare Newtownabbey BT39 0AH

An eye-catching modern hotel a mile from the M2 and handy for Belfast airport.
Spacious bedrooms are equipped with the expected up-to-date amenities; four
Executive rooms have mini-bars and jacuzzi baths. Day rooms take various
decorative themes – sleek black and gold for the cocktail bar, Scandinavian for
the banqueting hall (catering for up to 350), echoes of medieval knights in the
restaurant. 24hr room service. Conference facilities for up to 300. Weekend
tariff reductions (£60 Fri-Sun). *Rooms 24. Garden. Closed 25 & 26 Dec.*
Amex, Diners, MasterCard, **VISA**

TEMPLEPATRICK   Places of Interest

Castle Lipton Tel 01849 433470

TEMPO   Tempo Manor   £100

Tel 01365 541450   Fax 01365 541202   Map 1 C2   **PH**
Tempo Fermanagh BT94 3PA

An impressive Victorian manor house of considerable charm, surrounded
by 11 acres of lakes and gardens, established in 1869 by the Langham family.
Tempo is in the capable hands of John and Sarah Langham whose recent
restoration, modernisation (including the installation of central heating) and
redecoration is in sympathy with the style of the house. Many original features
and furniture, including three four-poster beds, have been retained and all of
the spacious bedrooms have lovely views of the surrounding gardens and en
suite bathrooms – an ideal combination of the interesting old and convenient
new. Reception rooms are impressive yet welcoming, with crackling log fires,
and dinner is served in the beautiful dining-room overlooking the lake and
garden. The meal is served communally or at separate tables, as preferred.
Children under 5 may stay free in their parents' room. Woodland walks
and fishing are big attractions. No dogs. *Rooms 5. Garden, croquet, fishing.*
Closed Nov-end Feb. MasterCard, **VISA**

UPPERLANDS   Ardtara Country House   £100

Tel 01648 44490   Fax 01648 45080   Map 1 C1   **AR**
Upperlands near Maghera Magherafelt BT46 5SA

Set in well-maintained gardens and woodland, this graciously-proportioned
Victorian country house has much to offer: elegant decor, warmth and comfort
and, under the watchful management of Mary Breslin, a genuinely hospitable
atmosphere. The hall sets the tone: it's spacious, with inherited tapestries,
interesting artefacts and new furnishings that have been carefully selected to tone
with the old; fresh flowers from the garden add a welcoming touch. Decorated
throughout in period style and with considerable verve, both the public rooms
(which include a dining-room converted from its previous use as a snooker
room, with full Victorian skylight and original friezes) and all the individually
decorated bedrooms have soothing views and a pleasing sense of homogeneity
with the surrounding countryside. The decor is nicely judged to lighten
Victorian features and please modern tastes, new additions blending well with

the antiques that are used extensively throughout. Bedrooms are luxurious (king-size beds and original fireplaces) and the bathrooms combine practicality with period details, some including freestanding baths and fireplaces. Not really suitable for children. No dogs. Allow time in the morning to make the most of the excellent breakfasts. Banqueting facilities for small weddings/private parties (45) and small conferences (20). To find: take the A29 to Maghera/Coleraine; follow the sign to Kilrea until reaching Upperlands. *Rooms 8. Garden, tennis, woodland walk, golf practice tee. Amex, MasterCard,* **VISA**

Restaurant   £60

The former snooker room, complete with Victorian skylight and an original hunting frieze, is decorated to echo the snooker theme in subtle ways, with dark Victorian furniture, rich green leather upholstery and dark green undercloths topped by crisp white linen, making a cosy and characterful setting for Patrick McLarnen's fine, strongly seasonal cooking. Based firmly on the best of local ingredients, tempting evening menus offer a choice of around seven or eight at each course, with game well represented in season. Typical dishes might include starters such as seafood chowder, an unusual salmon dish – hot-smoked and served on a warm tomato, bean and olive salad – and roast snipe with a thyme jus alongside a speciality wild boar sausage, served with a lime-pickled banana chutney. Main courses will usually include Sperrin lamb – a rack, perhaps, on a confit of aubergine with roasted tomato and garlic sauce – beef, such as pan-fried fillet on garlic mash with a lively smoked chili sauce, game – maybe roast wigeon with glazed apple on a blackberry sauce – and several fish dishes. The latter might be steamed salmon served on a mussel butter sauce finished with Rathlin dulse or monkfish roasted with saffron and served with a pepper and beansprout salad. Imaginative, well-judged dishes are presented without gimmicks and accompanied by simple, perfectly cooked side vegetables. Tasty desserts might include a hot spiced apple tart, contrasting nicely with a ball of creamy prune and armagnac ice cream; otherwise, finish with plated Irish cheeses and water biscuits before taking freshly-brewed coffee and home-made petits fours beside the drawing-room fire. *Seats 45. Parties 10. Private Room 12. L 12.30-2 D 7-9. Closed L Sat, 25 & 26 Dec. Set L £12.50.*

Establishments listed in County Order

Republic of Ireland entries listed in County order

HR = Hotel with a recommended Restaurant open to the public **H** = Hotel **RR** = Restaurant with Rooms **L** = Lodge **R** = Restaurant **I** = Inn

P = Pub (see entries for details of food recommendations) **A** = Accommodation (classified by Bord Fáilte, the Irish Tourist Board, as a Private House or Irish Home)

AR = A but with a recommended restaurant open to the public **PH** = Private House hotel (Northern Ireland only)

See Starred Restaurants & De Luxe hotels lists and map on page 13 for Ireland's highest-graded hotels, **R★** and **R†** restaurant listings. **P★** indicates starred **bar** food (not restaurant food) in pubs. Some hotels are ungraded due to their categorisation as a Private House Hotel (**A** or **PH**) or as an Inn without public rooms (**I**); the former are usually de luxe B&B establishments and, generally, their restaurants may not be open to non-residents (thus the food is not specifically recommended – although it is often prepared to a good standard for residents).

Restaurants with Rooms are also ungraded.

Restaurants without prices are generally of an informal, snackier nature and categorised as **JaB** (Just a Bite). Food is only recommended in pubs where the statistics at the end of a gazetteer entry include Bar Food times.

Swimming pool refers to an indoor pool (a few places have outdoor pool only – see Sporting Facilities quick reference list)

Location	Telephone	Establishment	Food Price	Category	Room Price	Hotel %	No. of Rooms	Beautifully Situated	Family Friendly	Swimming Pool	Golf	Address
Co Carlow												
Bagenalstown	0503 75282	Lorum Old Rectory		A	£55		5	▲				Kilgreaney Bagenalstown
Carlow	0503 43324	Barrowville Townhouse		A	£42		7					Kilkenny Rd Carlow
Carlow	0503 31824	The Beans Restaurant	£60	R								59 Dublin St Carlow
Carlow	0503 43307	Buzz's Bar		P								7 Tullow St Carlow
Carlow	0503 40817	Danette's Feast	£65	R								Urglin Glebe Bennekerry
Carlow	0503 31621	Royal Hotel		H	£58	60%	34					Dublin St Carlow
Carlow	0503 31862	Tully's		P								149 Tullow St Carlow
Fighting Cocks	0503 48744	Fighting Cocks		P								Fighting Cocks
Leighlinbridge	0503 21668	Lord Bagenal Inn	£45	R/P★				▲				Leighlinbridge

Co Cavan

Location	Phone	Name		Type		%			Address
Ballyconnell	049 26444	Slieve Russell Hotel	£45	H	£130	71%	151	▲	Ballyconnell
Belturbet	049 22616	International Fishing Centre		R					Loughdooley Belturbet
Blacklion	072 53022	Mac Nean House & Bistro	£60	RR†	£40		10		Blacklion
Butlersbridge	049 31003	Derragarra Inn		P					Butlersbridge
Kingscourt	042 67030	Cabra Castle Hotel		H	£80	65%	46		Kingscourt
Kingscourt	042 67003	Gartlans Pub		P					Main St Kingscourt
Virginia	049 47561	Sharkey's Hotel		H	£78	60%	11		Virginia

Co Clare

Location	Phone	Name		Type		%			Address
Ballyvaughan	065 77023	An Féar Gorta		JaB					Ballyvaughan
Ballyvaughan	065 77005	Gregans Castle Hotel	£84	HR	£120	73%	22	▲	Ballyvaughan
Ballyvaughan	065 77037	Hyland's Hotel		H	£64	65%	20		Ballyvaughan
Ballyvaughan	065 77059	Monks Bar		P				▲	The Quay Ballyvaughan
Ballyvaughan	065 77044	Whitethorn Restaurant	£50	R				▲	Ballyvaughan
Bunratty	061 357352	Bunratty View		A	£34		7		Cratloe Bunratty
Bunratty	061 364861	Durty Nelly's	£60	R/P					Bunratty
Bunratty	061 361177	Fitzpatrick Bunratty Shamrock		H	£121	63%	115	▲	Bunratty
Bunratty	061 364082	MacCloskey's Restaurant	£70	R					Bunratty Mews House
Clarecastle	065 28442	Carnelly House		A	£156		5		Clarecastle
Doolin	065 74061	Aran View House Hotel		H	£70	60%	19		Doolin
Doolin	065 74390	The Lazy Lobster	£45	R					Doolin
Doolin	065 74168	O'Connor's Pub		P	£34		4		Doolin
Ennis	065 21247	Auburn Lodge Hotel		H	£80	64%	100	▲	Galway Rd Ennis
Ennis	065 29521	The Cloister		P					Abbey St Ennis
Ennis	065 41800	Cruise's Pub		P					Abbey St Ennis
Ennis	065 28127	Old Ground Hotel		H	£108	67%	82		Ennis
Ennis	065 23300	Temple Gate Hotel		H	£70	64%	34		The Square Ennis

Location	Telephone	Establishment	Food Price	Category	Room Price	Hotel %	No. of Rooms	Beautifully Situated	Family Friendly	Swimming Pool	Golf	Address
Ennis	065 28421	West County Hotel		H	£100	66%	110		▲			Clare Rd Ennis
Kilfenora	065 88004	Vaughan's Pub		P								Kilfenora
Kilkee	065 56032	Halpin's Hotel		H	£75	63%	12				▲	Erin St Kilkee
Killaloe	061 376000	Kincora Hall	£60	HR	£80	60%	25					Killaloe
Lahinch	065 81100	Aberdeen Arms Hotel		H	£92	66%	55					Lahinch
Lahinch	065 81280	Barrtra Seafood Restaurant	£55	R				▲				Lahinch
Lahinch	065 81050	Mr Eamon's Restaurant	£60	R								Kettle St Lahinch
Lisdoonvarna	065 74025	Ballinalacken Castle Hotel		H	£70	63%	13	▲				Ballinalacken Lisdoonvarna
Lisdoonvarna	065 74026	Sheedy's Spa View Hotel	£50	HR	£55	66%	11					Lisdoonvarna
New Quay	065 78120	Linnane's Bar		P				▲				New Quay Burrin
Newmarket-on-Fergus	061 368161	Clare Inn Hotel		H	£99	64%	121		▲	▲	▲	Newmarket-on-Fergus
Newmarket-on-Fergus	061 368144	Dromoland Castle	£95	HR★	£239	81%	73	▲		▲	▲	Newmarket-on-Fergus
Shannon	061 361500	Oak Wood Arms Hotel		H	£96	63%	75					Shannon
Shannon Airport	061 471122	Great Southern		H	£110	64%	115					Shannon Airport Shannon

Co Cork

Location	Telephone	Establishment	Food Price	Category	Room Price	Hotel %	No. of Rooms	Beautifully Situated	Family Friendly	Swimming Pool	Golf	Address
Ahakista	none	Ahakista Bar		P				▲				Ahakista Bantry
Ahakista	027 67045	Hillcrest House		A	£35		4	▲				Ahakista nr Durrus
Ahakista	027 67030	Shiro	£110	R★								Ahakista nr Bantry
Ballinadee	021 778294	Glebe Country House		A	£50		4					Ballinadee Bandon
Ballycotton	021 646746	Bayview Hotel	£65	HR ↑	£110	67%	35					Ballycotton
Ballydehob	028 37292	Annie's Bookshop/Café		JaB								Main St Ballydehob
Ballydehob	028 37292	Annie's Restaurant	£60	R								Main St Ballydehob
Ballydehob	028 37118	Levis Bar		P								Main St Ballydehob
Ballylickey	027 50071	Ballylickey Manor House	£75	AR	£185	67%	5	▲				Ballylickey nr Bantry

Location	Tel	Establishment	£	RR	£	%	No.	Symbols	Address
Ballylickey	027 66181	Larchwood House	£60	HR	£44		4	▲▲	Pearsons Bridge Ballylickey
Ballylickey	027 50462	Seaview House Hotel	£60	H	£90	70%	17	▲▲	Ballylickey nr Bantry
Ballyvourney	026 45237	Mills Inn		I	£44		12		Ballyvourney
Baltimore	028 20361	Baltimore Harbour Hotel		H	£74	64%	35		Baltimore
Baltimore	028 20125	Bushe's Bar		P	£30		3		Baltimore
Baltimore	028 20197	Casey's Cabin		P				▲	Baltimore
Baltimore	028 20136	Chez Youen	£70	R					The Pier Baltimore
Baltimore	028 20441	La Jolie Brise		JaB					The Square Baltimore
Baltimore	028 20390	The Mews	£55	R					Baltimore
Bandon	023 41562	Munster Arms Hotel		H	£60	63%	34	▲	Oliver Plunkett St Bandon
Bantry	027 50012	Anchor Tavern		P				▲▲	New St Bantry
Bantry	027 50360	Westlodge Hotel	£60	H	£105	66%	90	▲▲	Bantry
Bere Island	027 75063	Laurence Cove House		R				▲	Bere Island nr Bantry
Blarney	021 385281	Blarney Park Hotel	£60	H	£80	63%	76	▲	Blarney
Butlerstown	023 40115	Atlantic Sunset		A	£34		4	▲	Butlerstown nr Bandon
Butlerstown	023 40314	Dunworley Cottage	£60	R				▲▲	Dunworley nr Butlerstown
Butlerstown	023 40228	O'Neill's		P					Butlerstown Bandon
Butlerstown	023 40151	Sea Court		A	£45		6		Bandon nr Butlerstown
Carrigaline	021 373878	Glenwood House		A	£55		8		Ballinrea Rd Carrigaline
Carrigaline	021 371512	Gregory's	£50	R				▲	Main St Carrigaline
Castlelyons	025 36349	Ballyvolane House		A	£80		7	▲	Castlelyons
Castletownbere	027 70014	MacCarthy's		P					Town Square Castletownbere
Castletownshend	028 36114	Bow Hall	£50	A	£60		3	▲	Castletownshend
Castletownshend	028 36146	Mary Ann's Bar/Restaurant		R/P★					Castletownshend
Clonakilty	023 33498	An Sugan	£50	R/P					41 Strand Rd Clonakilty
Clonakilty	023 343555	Fionnuala's	£35	R					30 Ashe St Clonakilty
Clonakilty	023 33384	Kicki's Cabin	£35	R					53 Pearse St Clonakilty
Clonakilty	023 33498	Strand House		A	£40		7		Sand Quay Clonakilty
Cobh	021 811965	Mansworth's		P					Midleton St Cobh

Location	Telephone	Establishment	Food Price	Category	Room Price	Hotel %	No. of Rooms	Beautifully Situated	Family Friendly	Swimming Pool	Golf	Address
Cork	021 277949	An Spailpin Fanac		P				▲				28-29 South Main St Cork
Cork	021 501237	Arbutus Lodge	£80	HR★	£90	70%	20					Montenotte Cork
Cork	021 273555	Bully's	£25	R								40 Paul St Cork
Cork	021 274415	Crawford Gallery Café	£45	R								Emmet Place Cork
Cork	021 505071	Dan Lowrey's		P								13 MacCurtain St Cork
Cork	021 278134	Farmgate Café		JaB								English Market Princes St Cork
Cork	021 507533	Fitzpatrick Silver Springs		H	£112	65%	109	▲	▲		▲	Tivoli Cork
Cork	021 821621	Flemings	£55	RR	£85		4					Silver Grange House Tivoli
Cork	021 275411	Gingerbread House		JaB								Paul St Plaza Cork
Cork	021 361613	Harolds Restaurant	£55	R								Douglas Cork
Cork	021 315600	Hayfield Manor Hotel		H	£175	75%	53					Cork
Cork	021 354354	Holiday Inn Express		L	£57		100					Lee Tunnel R'bout Dunkettle
Cork	021 274040	Imperial Hotel		H	£110	66%	100					South Mall Cork
Cork	021 503805	Isaacs	£40	R								48 MacCurtain St Cork
Cork	021 274665	Ivory Tower Restaurant	£65	R								35 Princes St Cork
Cork	021 277387	Jacques	£55	R								9 Phoenix St Cork
Cork	021 276444	Jurys Cork Inn		H	£65	60%	133					Anderson's Quay Cork
Cork	021 276622	Jurys Hotel		H	£152	66%	185		▲			Western Rd Cork
Cork	021 822344	Lotamore House		A	£50	60%	21					Tivoli Cork
Cork	021 294909	Lovetts	£72	R								off Well Rd Douglas
Cork	021 508122	Metropole Hotel		H	£95	60%	108		▲			Maccurtain St Cork
Cork	021 275858	Morrisons Island Hotel		H	£110	68%	40					Morrisons Quay Cork
Cork	021 316531	Proby's Bistro	£40	RR	£40							Probys Quay Crosses Green
Cork	021 317660	Quay Co-Op		JaB								24 Sullivan's Quay Cork
Cork	021 275751	Reidy's Wine Vaults		P★								Lancaster Quay Western Rd
Cork	021 892233	Rochestown Park Hotel		H	£101	67%	63		▲			Rochestown Rd Douglas

Town	Phone	Establishment	£	Code	Price	%	No				Address
Cork	021 397191	Seven North Mall		A	£60		5				7 North Mall Cork
Cork	021 310722	Travelodge		L	£48		40				Cork Airport Blackash
Courtmacsharry	023 46198	Courtmacsharry Hotel		H	£63	60%	11		▲		Courtmacsharry
Crookhaven	028 35183	Journey's End	£70	R							Crookhaven
Crookhaven	028 35200	O'Sullivan's		P					▲		Crookhaven
Crosshaven	021 831207	Cronin's Bar		P					▲		Crosshaven
Durrus	027 61187	Blairs Cove House Restaurant	£65	R						▲	Blairs Cove Durrus nr Bantry
East Ferry	021 813390	Marlogue Inn		P					▲		E Ferry Marina E Ferry Cobh
Glandore	028 33214	Hayes' Bar		P★							Glandore
Glandore	028 33366	Marine Hotel		H	£64	60%	16		▲		Glandore
Glandore	028 33079	Pier House Bistro	£50	R							Glandore
Glandore	028 33072	The Rectory	£70	R						▲	Glandore
Glanmire	021 866211	The Barn Restaurant	£60	R						▲	Glanmire
Glengarriff	027 63167	The Blue Loo		P							Main St Glengarriff
Goleen	028 35225	The Heron's Cove	£45	RR	£37		5			▲	The Harbour nr Skibbereen
Gougane Barra	026 47069	Gougane Barra Hotel		H	£66	60%	27			▲	Gougane Barra Ballingeary
Innishannon	021 775121	Innishannon House Hotel		H	£110	63%	14			▲	Innishannon
Kanturk	029 50171	Alley Bar		P							Strand St Kanturk
Kanturk	029 50015	Assolas Country House	£75	AR★	£120	72%	9			▲	Kanturk
Kanturk	029 50549	The Vintage		P							O'Brien St Kanturk
Kilbrittain	023 49944	Casino House	£50	R							Coolmain Bay Kilbrittain
Killeagh	024 95184	Ballymakeigh House		A	£50		5				Killeagh
Kinsale	021 772135	Actons Hotel		H	£100	60%	56	▲			Pier Rd Kinsale
Kinsale	021 772209	Blue Haven Hotel	£70	HR	£130	69%	18		▲		Pearse St Kinsale
Kinsale	021 772131	The Bulman Bar		P							Summer Cove Kinsale
Kinsale	021 774625	Chez Jean-Marc	£55	R							Lower O'Connell St Kinsale
Kinsale	021 772522	The Dock Bar		P					▲		Castlepark Kinsale
Kinsale	021 772260	Man Friday	£55	R							Scilly Kinsale

Location	Telephone	Establishment	Food Price	Category	Room Price	Hotel %	No. of Rooms	Beautifully Situated	Family Friendly	Swimming Pool	Golf	Address
Kinsale	021 772443	Max's Wine Bar	£50	R								Main St Kinsale
Kinsale	021 772376	The Moorings		A	£90		8					Scilly Kinsale
Kinsale	021 774075	The Old Bank House		A	£90		9					Pearse St Kinsale
Kinsale	021 772027	Old Presbytery		A	£50		7					Cork St Kinsale
Kinsale	021 773074	Restaurant Annelie's	£75	R								Lower O'Connel St Kinsale
Kinsale	021 772413	Scilly House		A	£100	65%	7	▲				Scilly Kinsale
Kinsale	021 772529	1601		P					▲			Pearse St Kinsale
Kinsale	021 772436	The Spaniard Inn		P								Scilly Kinsale
Kinsale	021 722502	Vintage Restaurant	£80	R								Main St Kinsale
Kinsale	021 772737	The White Lady Inn		H	£50	62%	10					Lower O'Connell St Kinsale
Macroom	026 41074	Castle Hotel		H	£60	63%	26					Macroom
Mallow	022 47156	Longueville House	£75	HR*	£144	78%	21	▲				Mallow
Midleton	021 632771	Farmgate	£50	R								The Coolbawn Midleton
Midleton	021 631680	Glenview House		A	£60		4	▲				Ballinaclasha Midleton
Midleton	021 613594	Jameson Heritage Centre		JaB								Midleton
Midleton	021 631767	Midleton Park Hotel		H	£80	68%	40		▲			Midleton
Monkstown	021 842172	The Bosun Bar & Restaurant	£55	R/P								Monkstown
Oysterhaven	021 770737	Finders Inn	£70	R								Nohoval Oysterhaven
Oysterhaven	021 770822	The Oystercatcher	£65	R				▲				Oysterhaven Belgooly
Rathpeacon	021 301812	Country Squire Inn		P								Mallow Rd Rathpeacon
Schull	028 28459	Adele's		JaB								Main St Schull
Schull	028 28341	Bunratty Inn		P								Schull
Schull	028 28642	La Coquille	£55	R								Schull
Schull	028 28517	Corthna Lodge		A	£40		6	▲				Schull
Schull	028 28101	East End Hotel		H	£50	60%	17	▲				Schull
Schull	028 28305	Restaurant in Blue	£60	R				▲	▲			Crookhaven Rd Schull

Town	Tel	Establishment	£	Class	P	£	%	No.				Address
Schull	028 28223	TJ Newman's			P							Main St Schull
Shanagarry	021 652531	Ballymaloe House	£80	AR★	P	£130	66%	30	✓	✓	✓	Shanagarry
Skibbereen	028 22365	Liss Ard Lake Lodge	£85	AR		£242	77%	10	✓	✓		Skibbereen
Timoleague	023 46390	Dillon's			P				✓	✓		Mill St Timoleague
Timoleague	023 46251	Lettercollum House	£55	R								Timoleague
Toormore	028 35254	The Altar	£65	RR		£30		4				Toormore Skibbereen
Toormore	028 35324	Fortview House		A		£40		5				Gurtyowen Toormore
Youghal	024 92424	Aherne's Seafood Restaurant	£70	RR		£120		12				North Main St Youghal
Youghal	024 93208	The Earl of Orrery	£50	R								North Main St Youghal

Co Donegal

Town	Tel	Establishment	£	Class	P	£	%	No.				Address
Annagarry	075 48201	Danny Minnie's Restaurant	£75	R								Killindarragh The Rosses
Ardara	075 41187	Nancy's			P							Ardara
Ballybofey	074 31018	Kee's Hotel	£55	HR↑		£72	64%	36			✓	Stranolar Ballybofey
Bruckless	073 37071	Bruckless House		A		£50		4		✓	✓	Bruckless
Bunbeg	075 31177	Ostan Gweedore		H		£75	65%	39	✓	✓	✓	Bunbeg
Bundoran	072 42160	Le Chateaubrianne	£55	R							✓	Sligo Rd Bundoran
Culdaff	077 79116	McGuinness's			P					✓		Culdaff Inishowen
Donegal	073 21065	St Ernan's House Hotel	£65	HR		£124	70%	12	✓	✓		St Ernans Island Donegal
Donegal Town	073 22650	Ardnamona House		A		£90		5	✓			Lough Eske Donegal Town
Donegal Town	073 22208	Harvey's Point Country Hotel	£60	HR		£99	63%	20	✓	✓		Lough Eske nr Donegal
Dunkineely	073 37022	Castle Murray House	£55	HR		£68	64%	10	✓	✓		Dunkineely
Fahan	077 60289	Restaurant St John's	£55	R					✓			Fahan Inishowen
Greencastle	077 81010	Kealys Seafood Bar	£50	R								The Harbour Greencastle
Letterkenny	077 51118	Castle Grove Country House	£60	AR		£80		8	✓			Letterkenny
Ramelton	074 51047	The Manse		A		£40		3				Ramelton
Rathmullan	074 58188	Rathmullan House	£65	HR		£110	62%	20	✓	✓	✓	Rathmullan nr Letterkenny
Rossnowlagh	072 51777	Sand House Hotel	£60	HR		£99	69%	45	✓	✓	✓	Rossnowlagh

Location	Telephone	Establishment	Food Price	Category	Room Price	Hotel %	No. of Rooms	Beautifully Situated	Family Friendly	Swimming Pool	Golf	Address
Rossnowlagh	072 52366	Smugglers Creek Inn	£45	IR/P★	£49		5	▲				Rossnowlagh
Tory Island	074 35920	Óstan Thóraig (Hotel Tory)		H	£45		14		▲			Tory Island
Co Dublin												
Blackrock	01 283 1767	Ayumi-Ya	£40	R								Newtownpark Ave Blackrock
Booterstown	01 283 5101	La Tavola	£45	R								Rock Rd Booterstown
Clondalkin	01 459 2428	Kingswood Country House	£60	RR	£80		7					Naas Rd Clondalkin
Dalkey	01 285 4569	The Queens		P								Castle St Dalkey
Dublin (Central)	– see below											
Dublin Airport	01 844 4211	Forte Posthouse		H	£135	57%	189					Dublin Airport
Dun Laoghaire	01 280 0509	Brasserie na Mara	£50	R								Harbour Rd Dun Laoghaire
Dun Laoghaire	01 280 7860	Chestnut Lodge		A	£60		4					Monkstown Dun Laoghaire
Dun Laoghaire	01 284 1761	de Selby's Restaurant	£45	R								Patrick St Dun Laoghaire
Dun Laoghaire	01 280 1911	Royal Marine Hotel		H	£135	64%	104					Marine Rd Dun Laoghaire
Dun Laoghaire	01 280 8788	The South Bank	£50	R								Martello Terrace
Glencullen	01 295 5647	Johnnie Fox's Pub		P				▲				Glencullen
Howth	01 839 0307	Abbey Tavern		P								Howth
Howth	01 839 1696	Adrian's	£50	R								Abbey St Howth
Howth	01 839 3823	Casa Pasta		JaB								Harbour Rd Howth
Howth	01 832 2624	Deer Park Hotel	£50	HR	£96	64%	51	▲		▲		Howth
Howth	01 832 1010	Howth Lodge Hotel	£55	HR	£130	65%	46		▲			Howth
Howth	01 832 6729	King Sitric	£70	R								East Pier Harbour Rd Howth
Killiney	01 285 1622	Court Hotel		H	£130	68%	86					Killiney Bay Killiney
Killiney	01 284 0700	Fitzpatrick's Castle		H	£163	68%	90		▲			Killiney
Malahide	01 845 0314	Bon Appétit	£75	R								James Terrace Malahide
Malahide	01 845 4154	Eastern Tandoori	£40	R								New St Malahide

Town	Phone	Name	£		£	%	No.		Address
Malahide	01 845 1733	Giovanni's		JaB					Townyard Lane Malahide
Malahide	01 845 0000	Grand Hotel	£50	H	£120	66%	100		Malahide
Malahide	01 845 4698	Siam Thai Restaurant	£45	R					Gas Lane Malahide
Malahide	01 845 3331	Silks Restaurant	£50	R					The Mall Malahide
Monkstown	01 284 2037	Coopers Restaurant	£60	R					The Crescent Monkstown
Monkstown	01 284 3200	Empress Restaurant		R					Clifton Ave Monkstown
Monkstown	01 284 6187	FXB's		JaB				▲	The Crescent Monkstown
Monkstown	01 284 3576	Purty Kitchen		P					Old Dunleary Rd
Rathcoole	01 458 9205	An Poitin Stil		P					Rathcoole
Sandycove	01 280 6097	Bistro Vino	£45	R					Glasmile Rd Sandycove
Sandycove	01 280 9120	Cavistons Seafood Restaurant	£35	R					Glasthule Rd Sandycove
Sandycove	01 230 0068	Morels Bistro	£70	R↑					Glasthule Rd Sandycove
Skerries	01 849 1005	Red Bank Restaurant	£60	R					Church St Skerries
Stillorgan	01 288 0375	Beaufield Mews Restaurant	£55	R					Woodlands Ave Stillorgan
Stillorgan	01 288 4817	China-Sichuan Restaurant	£50	R					Lower Kilmacud Rd
Stillorgan	01 288 8672	The Millhouse		P					Lower Kilmacud Rd
Stillorgan	01 288 8470	Stillorgan Orchard		P					Stillorgan
Swords	01 840 9080	Lukas	£45	R					River Mall Main St Swords
Swords	01 840 4160	Old Schoolhouse	£60	R					Coolbanagher Swords
Swords	01 840 9233	Travelodge		L	£48		40		Swords Bypass nr Dublin

Dublin (Central)

Town	Phone	Name	£		£	%	No.		Address
Dublin 1	01 855 2424	Le Café	£35	R					5 Beresford Place
Dublin 1	01 873 2266	Chapter One	£70	R					18/19 Parnell Square
Dublin 1	01 874 6881	Gresham Hotel		H	£236	64%	202		Upper O'Connell St
Dublin 1	01 670 1699	The Harbourmaster		JaB					Custom House Docks
Dublin 1	01 607 5000	Jurys Custom House Inn		H	£55	60%	234		Custom House Quay
Dublin 1	01 874 5011	101 Talbot	£30	R				▲	101 Talbot St
Dublin 1	01 873 3666	Royal Dublin Hotel		H	£120	63%	117		40 Upper O'Connell St
Dublin 2	01 670 7100	Adams Trinity Hotel		H	£120	62%	28		28 Dame St

Location	Telephone	Establishment	Food Price	Category	Room Price	Hotel %	No. of Rooms	Beautifully Situated	Family Friendly	Swimming Pool	Golf	Address
Dublin 2	01 475 1092	Albany House		A	£90		29					84 Harcourt St
Dublin 2	01 622 0233	Ayumi-Ya Japanese Steakhouse	£40	R								132 Lower Baggot St
Dublin 2	01 475 2705	Bleeding Horse		P								24 Upper Camden St
Dublin 2	01 671 5622	Blooms Hotel		H	£87	60%	97					Anglesea St Temple Bar
Dublin 2	01 677 4369	Café en Seine		P								40 Dawson St
Dublin 2	01 679 7302	Central Hotel		H	£140	57%	70					1-5 Exchequer St
Dublin 2	01 671 0362	The Chameleon	£45	R								Fownes St Lwr Temple Bar
Dublin 2	01 478 1233	Chicago Pizza Pie Factory		JaB					▲			St Stephen's Green
Dublin 2	01 677 3721	The Chili Club	£45	R								Anne's Lane Sth Anne St
Dublin 2	01 670 9000	The Clarence	£75	HR↑	£191	80%	50					6 Wellington Quay
Dublin 2	01 475 2597	The Commons Restaurant	£90	R↑								St Stephen's Green
Dublin 2	01 676 5555	Conrad International		H	£259	78%	191					Earlsfort Terrace
Dublin 2	01 679 0536	Cooke's Café	£70	R								14 South William St
Dublin 2	01 661 6800	Davenport Hotel		H	£201	76%	116	▲	▲			Merrion Square
Dublin 2	01 677 5217	Davy Byrnes		P								21 Duke St
Dublin 2	01 676 4679	Dobbins Wine Bistro	£75	R								15 St Stephen's Lane
Dublin 2	01 676 2945	Doheny & Nesbitt		P								5 Lower Baggot St
Dublin 2	01 679 0100	Eamonn Doran		P								Crown Alley Temple Bar
Dublin 2	01 671 0428	Eastern Tandoori	£60	R								34 South William St
Dublin 2	01 661 1919	L'Ecrivain	£80	R↑								109 Lower Baggot St
Dublin 2	01 679 1399	Elephant & Castle	£50	R								18 Temple Bar
Dublin 2	01 679 4555	Les Freres Jacques	£80	R								74 Dame St
Dublin 2	01 679 7000	George's Bistro	£70	R								29 South Frederick St
Dublin 2	01 661 8832	Georgian House		H	£88	56%	47					18 Lower Baggot St
Dublin 2	01 679 7699	Girolles	£60	R								64 South William St
Dublin 2	01 677 5373	Good World	£40	R								Sth Great George's St

Area	Phone	Name		Type							Address
Dublin 2	01 679 5266	Gotham Café	£45	R							8 South Anne St
Dublin 2	01 475 0888	Grafton Plaza Hotel		H	£110	64%	75				Johnsons Place
Dublin 2	01 676 3286	Grey Door	£65	RR	£104		7				22 Upper Pembroke St
Dublin 2	01 679 6500	Harding Hotel		A	£61		53				Copper Alley Fishamble St
Dublin 2	01 677 1060	Harvey's Coffee House		JaB							14/15 Trinity St
Dublin 2	01 677 2580	Imperial Chinese	£40	R							13 Wicklow St
Dublin 2	01 475 1235	Kapriol	£65	R							45 Lower Camden St
Dublin 2	01 677 7066	Kilkenny Kitchen		JaB				◀			Nassau St
Dublin 2	01 671 8714	Little Caesar's Pizza		JaB							Chatham House Balfe St
Dublin 2	01 676 1367	Longfield's Hotel	£65	HR	£123	61%	26				Fitzwilliam St Lower
Dublin 2	01 679 0522	The Mercantile		P							27-28 Dame St
Dublin 2	01 661 6669	La Mere Zou	£45	R							St Stephen's Green
Dublin 2	01 670 8236	Mermaid Café	£55	R					◀		69/70 Dame St
Dublin 2	01 667 1222	Mespil Hotel	£35	H	£86	65%	153				Mespil Rd
Dublin 2	01 662 4724	Mitchell's Cellars		R							21 Kildare St
Dublin 2	01 661 6799	Mont Clare Hotel		H	£172	66%	74			◀	Merrion Square
Dublin 2	01 662 1269	National Museum Café		JaB							Kildare St
Dublin 2	01 676 5011	Number 31		A	£75		18				off Lower Leeson St
Dublin 2	01 676 2807	O'Donohue's		P							15 Merrion Row
Dublin 2	01 676 3574	O'Dwyer's		P							Mount St
Dublin 2	01 677 7220	The Old Stand		P							37 Exchequer St
Dublin 2	01 679 2402	Pasta Fresca		JaB							2-4 Chatham St
Dublin 2	01 676 4192	Patrick Guilbaud	£115	R★†							21 Upper Merrion St
Dublin 2	01 662 0760	Peacock Alley	£90	R†							47 South William St
Dublin 2	01 679 4203	Periwinkle Seafood Bar		JaB							South William St
Dublin 2	01 676 1494	Pier 32	£55	R							23 Upper Pembroke St
Dublin 2	01 671 1248	Pierre's	£30	R							2 Crow St Temple Bar
Dublin 2	01 679 9847	Porter House		P							16-18 Parliament St
Dublin 2	01 478 3373	Il Primo	£45	R							16 Montague St

Location	Telephone	Establishment	Food Price	Category	Room Price	Hotel %	No. of Rooms	Beautifully Situated	Family Friendly	Swimming Pool	Golf	Address
Dublin 2	01 679 4274	Rajdoot	£50	R								Clarendon St
Dublin 2	01 475 5060	Saagar	£50	R								16 Harcourt St
Dublin 2	01 671 0738	Shalimar	£50	R								17 South Great George's St
Dublin 2	01 676 6471	Shelbourne Meridien	£55	HR	£240	74%	164					St Stephen's Green
Dublin 2	01 679 3701	Stag's Head	£60	P								1 Dame Court
Dublin 2	01 677 8611	La Stampa	£60	R↑								35 Dawson St
Dublin 2	01 478 2300	Stauntons on the Green		A	£94		33					83 St Stephen's Green South
Dublin 2	01 661 0585	Stephen's Hall & Morels	£60	HR	£157	65%	37					Lwr Leeson St
Dublin 2	01 677 3333	Temple Bar Hotel		H	£120	66%	108					Fleet St Temple Bar
Dublin 2	01 677 1487	Thomas Read		P								1-2 Parliament St Temple Bar
Dublin 2	01 676 3090	Toners Pub		P								139 Lower Baggot St
Dublin 2	01 679 6744	Tosca		JaB								20 Suffolk St
Dublin 2	01 679 1122	The Westbury	£90	HR	£226	79%	203					Off Grafton St
Dublin 3	01 833 4400	Wong's	£60	R								436 Clontarf Rd
Dublin 4	01 283 8155	Aberdeen Lodge		A	£83		16					53/55 Park Ave Ailesbury Rd
Dublin 4	01 668 3877	Anglesea Town House		A	£90		7					63 Anglesea Rd
Dublin 4	01 668 5512	Ariel House		A	£99		28					52 Lansdowne Rd Ballsbridge
Dublin 4	01 660 0363	Bats Restaurant	£45	R								10 Baggot Lane
Dublin 4	01 660 1711	Berkeley Court		H	£235	76%	188					Lansdowne Rd
Dublin 4	01 660 5222	Burlington Hotel		H	£177	70%	450					Upper Leeson St
Dublin 4	01 454 0306	Canaletto's	£35	R								69 Mespil Rd
Dublin 4	01 668 9070	Le Coq Hardi	£100	R★								35 Pembroke Rd Ballsbridge
Dublin 4	01 283 8815	The Courtyard	£45	R								1 Belmont Ave Donnybrook
Dublin 4	01 269 3311	Doyle Montrose Hotel		H	£133	65%	179					Stillorgan Rd
Dublin 4	01 269 4666	Doyle Tara Hotel		H	£133	61%	114					Merrion Rd
Dublin 4	01 269 3260	Ernie's	£80	R								Mulberry Gdns Donnybroook

Location	Phone	Name	£	Code	£	%	No			Address
Dublin 4	01 667 1301	Fitzers Café Ballsbridge	£65	R						RDS Merrion Rd
Dublin 4	01 283 0522	Furama Chinese	£60	R						88 Donnybrook Rd
Dublin 4	01 668 4612	Glenveagh Town House		A	£80		10			Northumberland Rd Ballsbridge
Dublin 4	01 668 7666	Hibernian Hotel	£70	HR	£145	70%	40			Eastmoreland Place Ballsbridge
Dublin 4	01 667 0033	Jurys Hotel Dublin		H	£178	69%	290	▲		Pembroke Rd Ballsbridge
Dublin 4	01 283 0209	Kielys		P						Donnybrook Rd
Dublin 4	01 660 8050	Kitty O'Shea's Bar		P						23–25 Upper Grand Canal St
Dublin 4	01 668 2760	Langkawi Malaysian	£40	R						46 Upper Baggot St
Dublin 4	01 668 0025	Lobster Pot	£70	R						9 Ballsbridge Terrace
Dublin 4	01 660 5539	Marrakesh Restaurant	£60	R						11 Ballsbridge Terrace
Dublin 4	01 269 3816	McCormack's Merrion Inn		P						188 Merrion Rd
Dublin 4	01 668 1426	Merrion Hall		A	£65		15			54–56 Merrion Rd
Dublin 4	01 660 0277	No 88		A	£72		50			88 Pembroke Rd Ballsbridge
Dublin 4	01 660 6697	Raglan Lodge		A	£80		7			10 Raglan Rd Ballsbridge
Dublin 4	01 668 2611	Roly's Bistro	£50	R†						7 Ballsbridge Terrace
Dublin 4	01 668 0995	Sachs Hotel		H	£118	62%	20			Morehampton Rd Donnybrook
Dublin 4	01 668 4544	Senor Sassi's	£60	R						146 Upper Leeson St
Dublin 4	01 667 0633	The Towers at Lansdowne Rd		H	£240	76%	104	▲		Lansdowne Road
Dublin 5	01 831 3772	The Station House		P					▲	3–5 Station Rd Raheny
Dublin 6	01 283 0045	Ashtons		P						Clonskeagh
Dublin 6	01 497 1566	Bistro Vino	£45	R						1 Upper Rathmone's Rd
Dublin 6	01 492 0633	Ivy Court	£55	R						88 Rathgar Rd
Dublin 6	01 492 9346	Popjoys	£45	R						4 Ratufarnham Rd Terenure
Dublin 6	01 497 9428	Zen	£50	R†						89 Upper Rathmines Rd
Dublin 7	01 838 6633	Charleville Lodge		A	£65		22			268/272 North Circular Rd
Dublin 7	01 838 3218	Halfway House		P					▲	Ashtown

Location	Telephone	Establishment	Food Price	Category	Room Price	Hotel %	No. of Rooms	Beautifully Situated	Family Friendly	Swimming Pool	Golf	Address
Dublin 7	01 679 8138	Ta Se Mohogani Gaspipes	£45	R								17 Manor St Stoneybatter
Dublin 8	01 677 9549	Brazen Head		P								20 Lower Bridge St
Dublin 8	01 454 0000	Jurys Christchurch Inn	£85	H	£67	60%	182					Christchurch Place
Dublin 8	01 454 3391	Locks Restaurant	£60	R								1 Windsor Terrace Portobello
Dublin 8	01 454 2420	The Lord Edward	£65	R								23 Christchurch Place
Dublin 8	01 454 2028	Old Dublin Restaurant		R								90–91 Francis St
Dublin 8	01 671 9352	Ryan's of Parkgate Street	£55	R/P								28 Parkgate St
Dublin 8	01 454 9067	Thornton's	£90	R★								1 Portobello Rd
Dublin 9	01 830 8514	P Hedigan: The Brian Boru		P								5 Prospect Rd Glasnevin
Dublin 9	none	Kavanagh's		P								Prospect Square Glasnevin
Dublin 13	01 839 0000	Marine Hotel		H	£120	64%	26		▲			Sutton Cross
Dublin 14	01 298 4145	The Goat		P				▲				Goatstown
Dublin 14	01 493 2994	Yellow House		P								Willbrook Rd Rathfarnham
Dublin 24	01 464 0140	Bewley's Hotel	£65	H	£57	60%	126					Newlands Cross

Co Galway

Location	Telephone	Establishment	Food Price	Category	Room Price	Hotel %	No. of Rooms	Beautifully Situated	Family Friendly	Swimming Pool	Golf	Address
Ballinasloe	0905 42347	Hayden's Hotel		H	£63	63%	48					Ballinasloe
Ballyconneely	095 23553	Erriseask House	£65	HR★	£77	66%	13	▲	▲			Ballyconneely Clifden
Barna	091 592487	Donnelly's of Barna		P								Barna
Barna	091 592223	Ty Ar Mor	£60	R				▲				The Pier Barna
Cashel	095 31001	Cashel House	£80	HR	£152	76%	32	▲				Cashel
Cashel	095 31111	Zetland House	£70	HR	£118	68%	20	▲				Cashel Bay Connemara
Clarenbridge	091 796226	Paddy Burke's		P								Clarenbridge Clarenbridge
Clifden	095 21201	Abbeyglen Castle		H	£110	60%	33	▲				Sky Rd Clifden
Clifden	095 21384	Ardagh Hotel	£65	HR	£95	67%	21	▲				Ballyconneely Rd Clifden

Location	Phone	Name	Price	Type	Rate	%	No.	●	●	●	Address
Clifden	095 21722	Destry Rides Again	£50	R							Clifden
Clifden	095 21330	E J King's		P					▲		The Square Clifden
Clifden	095 21801	Foyles Hotel		H	£68	61%	30				The Square Clifden
Clifden	095 21849	Kille House		A	£50		4			▲	Clifden
Clifden	095 21450	O'Grady's Seafood Restaurant	£50	R	£50		11				Market St Clifden
Clifden	095 21369	The Quay House	£55	AR	£80		10			▲	Beach Rd Clifden
Clifden	095 21035	Rock Glen Manor	£60	HR	£110	67%	29			▲	Balconneely Rd Clifden
Furbo	091 592108	Connemara Coast Hotel		H	£135	71%	112			▲	Furbo nr Galway
Galway	091 21433	Ardilaun House		H	£110	66%	89			▲	Taylors Hill Galway
Galway	091 568166	Brennans Yard		H	£95	64%	24		▲		Lwr Merchants Rd Galway
Galway	091 566 231	Bridge Mills Restaurant		JaB							O'Brien's Bridge Galway
Galway	091 755281	Corrib Great Southern Hotel		H	£142	68%	180	▲	▲	▲	Dublin Rd Galway
Galway	091 753181	Galway Ryan Hotel		H	£136	63%	96	▲	▲	▲	Dublin Rd Galway
Galway	091 526666	Glenlo Abbey Hotel	£70	HR	£175	75%	45			▲	Bushypark Galway
Galway	091 564041	Great Southern		H	£155	68%	114			▲	Eyre Square Galway
Galway	091 771166	Holiday Inn Express		L	£62		100				Headford Rd Galway
Galway	091 568351	Hooker Jimmy's		JaB							Fishmarket Spanish Arch
Galway	091 566444	Jurys Galway Inn		H	£56	60%	128				Quay St Galway
Galway	091 565001	McDonagh's	£35	R							22 Quay St Galway
Galway	091 569600	Hotel Spanish Arch		H	£150	65%	20				Quay St Galway
Galway	091 568820	Tigh Neachtain		P							Cross St Galway
Galway	091 521442	Westwood Bistro	£60	R							Dangan Upper Newcastle
Inishbofin Island	095 45829	Day's Bar		P							Inishbofin Island
Inishbofin Island	095 45809	Day's Hotel		H	£55	61%	14				Inishbofin Island
Kilcolgan	091 96113	Moran's Oyster Cottage		P★				▲			The Weir Kilcolgan
Kingstown	095 21849	Kille House		A	£50		5				Kingstown Clifden
Kinvara	091 637146	Tully's		P				▲			Kinvara
Kylemore Abbey	095 41146	Kylemore Abbey Restaurant		JaB				▲			Kylemore

Location	Telephone	Establishment	Food Price	Category	Room Price	Hotel %	No. of Rooms	Beautifully Situated	Family Friendly	Swimming Pool	Golf	Address
Leenane	095 42211	Delphi Lodge		A	£75		11	▲				Leenane
Leenane	095 42276	Killary Lodge		H	£62	59%	20	▲				Leenane
Leenane	095 42265	Portfinn Lodge	£60	RR	£44		8	▲				Leenane
Letterfrack	095 41101	Rosleague Manor	£70	HR	£120	72%	20	▲				Letterfrack
Moyard	095 41082	Rose Cottage		A	£32		6					Rockfield Moyard
Moycullen	091 555555	Cloonabinnia House Hotel	£50	HR	£70	63%	14	▲	▲			Ross Lake Moycullen
Moycullen	091 555115	Drimcong House Restaurant	£60	R★					▲			Moycullen
Moycullen	091 555566	Moycullen House		A	£70		5	▲				Moycullen
Moycullen	091 555744	White Gables Restaurant	£60	R								Moycullen
Oughterard	091 552328	Connemara Gateway Hotel		H	£110	66%	62	▲	▲	▲		Oughterard
Oughterard	091 552312	Currarevagh House	£50	AR	£103	65%	15	▲				Oughterard
Oughterard	091 82712	Powers		P								Oughterard
Oughterard	091 82207	Sweeney's Oughterard House		H	£116	59%	20					Oughterard
Recess	095 31006	Ballynahinch Castle		H	£132	71%	28	▲				Recess
Recess	095 34706	Lough Inagh Lodge		H	£132	68%	12	▲				Inagh Valley Recess
Renvyle	095 43511	Renvyle House		H	£184	63%	65	▲	▲		▲	Renvyle
Roundstone	095 35809	O'Dowd's Seafood Bar		P								Roundstone
Spiddal	091 553286	Boluisce Seafood Bar		JaB								Spiddal
Spiddal	091 553118	Bridge House Hotel		H	£70	59%	14					Spiddal
Tuam	093 28232	Cré na Cille	£50	R								High St Tuam

Co Kerry

Location	Phone	Name	£	Code	£	%	No.			Address
Aghadoe	064 31711	Killeen House Hotel	£60	HR	£88	64%	19			Aghadoe
Annascaul	066 57252	Dan Foley's		P						Annascaul
Ballybunion	068 27522	Marine Links Hotel		H	£66	60%	10			Ballybunion
Ballyferriter	066 56344	Tigh an t-Saorsaigh		P	£32		4			Ballyferriter
Beaufort	064 44111	Hotel Dunloe Castle		H	£110	72%	120	▲	▲	Beaufort nr Killarney
Caherciveen	066 72021	Brennan's Restaurant	£55	R						13 Main St Caherciveen
Caherciveen	066 73426	Old Schoolhouse Restaurant	£55	R						Caherciveen
Caherciveen	066 72165	The Point Bar		P						Renard Point Caherciveen
Caherdaniel	066 75136	Derrynane Hotel	£45	HR	£77	62%	75	▲	▲	Caherdaniel
Caherdaniel	066 75273	Loaves & Fishes	£55	R				▲	▲	Caherdaniel nr Derrynane
Caragh Lake	066 69105	Hotel Ard-na-Sidhe		H	£120	71%	20	▲		Caragh Lake nr Killorglin
Caragh Lake	066 69115	Caragh Lodge		A	£88	65%	10	▲		Caragh Lake nr Killorglin
Dingle	066 51244	Bambury's Guest House		A	£40		12			Mail Rd Dingle
Dingle	066 51588	Beginish Restaurant	£58	R†						Green St Dingle
Dingle	066 51108	Cleevaun Country House		A	£43		9	▲		Lady's Cross Milltown
Dingle	none	Dick Mack's		P						Green Lane Dingle
Dingle	066 51144	Dingle Skellig Hotel	£65	H	£115	61%	115	▲	▲	Dingle
Dingle	066 51174	Doyle's Seafood Bar		RR	£72		8			John St Dingle
Dingle	066 51414	Greenmount House		A	£60		12			Greenmount Dingle
Dingle	066 51600	Half Door	£55	R						John St Dingle
Dingle	066 51634	James Flahive		P						The Quay Dingle
Dingle	066 51277	Lord Baker's Bar & Restaurant	£65	R/P						Main St Dingle
Dingle	066 51372	Milltown House		A	£60		10			Dingle
Dingle	066 51461	O'Flaherty's		P						Bridge St Dingle
Dingle	066 51458	The Old Merchant		JaB						The Harbour Dingle
Dingle	066 51215	Tigh Mhaire de Barra		P						The Pier Head Dingle
Dingle	066 51458	The Waterside	£60	R						Dingle

Location	Telephone	Establishment	Food Price	Category	Room Price	Hotel %	No. of Rooms	Beautifully Situated	Family Friendly	Swimming Pool	Golf	Address
Fenit	066 36164	The Tankard Restaurant	£65	R				▲				Kilfenora Fenit nr Tralee
Glencar	066 60101	Climbers' Inn		I	£46		8	▲				Glencar
Kenmare	064 41589	d'Arcy's	£60	R								Main St Kenmare
Kenmare	064 41657	Dronquinna Manor Hotel		H	£90	60%	28	▲				Blackwater Bridge
Kenmare	064 41553	The Horseshoe	£45	R								Main St Kenmare
Kenmare	064 41225	The Lime Tree	£60	R								Shelbourne St Kenmare
Kenmare	064 41508	Packie's	£50	R								Henry St Kenmare
Kenmare	064 41200	Park Hotel Kenmare	£100	HR★	£230	87%	49	▲			▲	Kenmare
Kenmare	064 41016	Purple Heather		P	£70							Henry St Kenmare
Kenmare	064 42066	Sallyport House		A	£70		5					Glengarriff Rd Kenmare
Kenmare	064 41600	Sheen Falls Lodge	£100	HR★	£266	87%	40	▲			▲	Kenmare
Kenmare	064 41013	Shelburne Lodge		A	£70		7					Killowen Cork Rd Kenmare
Killarney	064 31766	Aghadoe Heights Hotel	£100	HR↑	£155	70%	60	▲	▲			Aghadoe Killarney
Killarney	064 31555	Beaufield House		A	£42		14					Cork Rd Killarney
Killarney	064 31895	Cahernane Hotel	£80	HR	£130	65%	48	▲				Muckross Rd Killarney
Killarney	064 31144	Castlerosse Hotel		H	£106	63%	110					Killarney
Killarney	064 31079	Dingles Restauraunt	£55	R								40 New St Killarney
Killarney	064 34009	Earls Court Guesthouse		A	£60		11					Muckross Rd Killarney
Killarney	064 31900	Hotel Europe		H	£110	74%	205	▲		▲		Killorglin Rd Fossa Killarney
Killarney	064 31217	Foley's Town House	£65	RR	£82		12		▲			23 High St Killarney
Killarney	064 32519	Gaby's Seafood Restaurant	£60	R								27 High St Killarney
Killarney	064 31262	Great Southern		H	£145	69%	180		▲			Killarney
Killarney	064 32810	Kathleen's Country House		A	£75		17					Tralee Rd Killarney
Killarney	064 31158	Killarney Heights Hotel		H	£90	62%	40					Cork Rd Killarney
Killarney	064 35555	Killarney Park Hotel		H	£150	71%	66		▲			Kenmare Place Killarney

Location	Phone	Name	Single	Type	Double	Occ	Rooms			Address
Killarney	064 31555	Killarney Ryan Hotel		H	£136	64%	168	▲		Cork Rd Killarney
Killarney	064 31038	Killarney Towers Hotel		H	£150	62%	180			College Square Killarney
Killarney	064 31938	Muckross Park Hotel		H	£120	68%	25			Muckross Village Killarney
Killarney	064 35333	Randles Court Hotel		H	£115	68%	37			Muckross Rd Killarney
Killarney	064 31855	Ross Hotel		H	£90	64%	32			Kenmare Place Killarney
Killarney	064 32688	The Strawberry Tree	£70	R						24 Plunkett St Killarney
Killarney	064 31611	Torc Great Southern		H	£100	63%	96	▲		Park Rd Killarney
Killarney	064 32271	West End House	£50	R						New St Killarney
Killarney	064 32688	Yer Man's Pub		P						24 Plunkett St Killarney
Killorglin	066 61219	Nick's Restaurant	£65	R						Lower Bridge St Killorglin
Lispole	066 51843	Churchfield		A	£62★		4			Lispole
Listowel	068 22880	Allo's Bar & Bistro	£60	R/P						41 Church St Listowel
Parknasilla	064 45122	Parknasilla Great Southern		H	£189	72%	85	▲	▲	Parknasilla Sneem
Portmagee	066 77103	Fisherman's Bar		P						Portmagee
Tahilla	064 45204	Tahilla Cove Country House		A	£72		9	▲		Tahilla Sneem
Tralee	066 29888	Abbey Gate Hotel		H	£80	64%				Maine St Tralee
Tralee	066 25799	Ballyseede Castle Hotel		H	£100	60%	14			Tralee
Tralee	066 23333	Brandon Hotel		H	£90	61%	186	▲	▲	Princes St Tralee
Tralee	066 21300	Larkins Restaurant	£50	R						14 Princes St Tralee
Tralee	066 36102	The Oyster Tavern	£55	R						The Spa Tralee
Waterville	066 74144	Butler Arms Hotel		H	£110	68%	31			Waterville
Waterville	066 74124	The Huntsman	£50	R/P						Waterville
Waterville	066 74330	The Smugglers Inn	£65	IR	£70		17	▲		Waterville

Co Kildare

Location	Phone	Name	Single	Type	Double	Occ	Rooms			Address
Athy	0507 31473	Tonlegee House	£55	R/R	£60		9			Athy
Ballymore Eustace	045 864585	The Ballymore Inn		P★						Ballymore Eustace
Castledermot	0503 45156	Kilkea Castle	£80	HR	£186	70%	36	▲		Kilkea Castledermot

Location	Telephone	Establishment	Food Price	Category	Room Price	Hotel %	No. of Rooms	Beautifully Situated	Family Friendly	Swimming Pool	Golf	Address
Kilcullen	045 481260	Berney's Bar & Restaurant	£60	R								Kilcullen
Maynooth	01 628 6351	Moyglare Manor	£80	HR	£135	75%	17	▲				Moyglare Maynooth
Moone	0507 24112	Moone High Cross Inn		P★	£50		5		▲			Bolton Hill Moone
Naas	045 897328	Fletcher's		P								Commercial House Naas
Naas	045 897471	Manor Inn		P					▲			Main St Naas
Newbridge	045 431666	Hotel Keadeen		H	£110	68%	37		▲			Curragh Rd Newbridge
Newbridge	045 831516	Red House Inn	£55	R								Newbridge
Straffan	01 628 8157	Barberstown Castle	£70	HR	£121	70%	26					Straffan
Straffan	01 627 3333	Kildare Hotel	£120	HR★	£288	89%	45	▲	▲	▲	▲	Straffan

Co Kilkenny

Location	Telephone	Establishment	Food Price	Category	Room Price	Hotel %	No. of Rooms	Beautifully Situated	Family Friendly	Swimming Pool	Golf	Address
Bennettsbridge	056 27644	Mosse's Mill Café	£50	R								Bennettsbridge nr Kilkenny
Castlewarren	0503 26123	Langton's		P								Castlewarren
Inistioge	056 58655	The Motte	£60	R				▲				Plas Newydd Lodge Inistioge
Kilkenny	056 64987	Café Sol	£50	R								Kilkenny
Kilkenny	056 65406	An Caislean Ui Cuain		P								2 High St Kilkenny
Kilkenny	056 22118	Kilkenny Kitchen		JaB								Design Centre Castle St
Kilkenny	056 61085	Lacken House	£65	RR	£60		9		▲			Dublin Rd Kilkenny
Kilkenny	056 65133	Langton's		P	£90		10		▲			69 John St Kilkenny
Kilkenny	056 22122	Newpark Hotel		H	£102	58%	84		▲			Castlecomer Rd Kilkenny
Kilkenny	056 21543	Shem's		P								61 John St Kilkenny
Kilkenny	056 61828	Tynan's Bridge House Bar		P								Bridge House 2 Johns Bridge
Maddoxtown	056 27197	Blanchville House		A	£60		6	▲				Dunbell Maddoxtown
Thomastown	056 24455	Mount Juliet Hotel	£80	HR	£235	84%	54	▲	▲		▲	Mount Juliet Thomastown

Co Laois

Town	Phone	Name	£	Cat	£	%	No				Address
Abbeyleix	0502 31233	Morrisseys	£70	P							Main St Abbeyleix
Abbeyleix	0502 31432	Preston House Café		RR	£50		4				Main St Abbeyleix
Mountrath	0502 32120	Roundwood House	£50	HR	£70	58%	10		▲		Mountrath

Co Leitrim

Town	Phone	Name	£	Cat	£	%	No				Address
Carrick-on-Shannon	078 21124	Hollywell House		A	£56		4				Liberty Hill
Dromahair	071 64140	Stanford's Village Inn		P	£30		5		▲		Dromahair
Keshcarrigan	078 42056	Canal View House	£55	AR	£40		6				Keshcarrigan

Co Limerick

Town	Phone	Name	£	Cat	£	%	No				Address
Abbeyfeale	068 31085	The Cellar	£90	P							The Square Abbeyfeale
Adare	061 396566	Adare Manor	£55	HR	£250	79%	64	▲		▲	Adare
Adare	061 396633	Dunraven Arms	£55	HR	£124	72%	66	▲		▲	Adare
Adare	061 396633	The Inn Between	£45	R							Adare
Adare	061 396451	The Wild Geese	£75	R↑							Rose Cottage Adare
Adare	061 396118	Woodlands House Hotel	£70	H	£66	60%	57				Adare
Ballingarry	069 68508	Mustard Seed at Echo Lodge	£70	AR↑	£150		12				Ballingarry
Ballyneety	061 351881	Croker's Bistro	£55	R							Limerick County G & C Club
Castleconnell	061 377724	Bradshaw's Bar		P							Castleconnell
Castleconnell	061 377666	Castle Oaks House Hotel		H	£99	65%	20			▲	Castleconnell
Croom	061 397130	The Mill Race	£50	R							Croom Mills Croom
Glin	068 34173	Glin Castle		A	£210		6		▲		Glin
Limerick	061 335566	Castletroy Park Hotel	£65	HR	£143	74%	107	▲		▲	Dublin Rd Limerick
Limerick	061 418789	Freddy's Bistro	£60	R							Theatre Lane nr Glenworth St
Limerick	061 453033	Greenhills Hotel		H	£90	62%	60			▲	Ennis Rd Limerick
Limerick	061 42484	Jasmine Palace	£55	R							O'Connell Mall O'Connell St

Location	Telephone	Establishment	Food Price	Category	Room Price	Hotel %	No. of Rooms	Beautifully Situated	Family Friendly	Swimming Pool	Golf	Address
Limerick	061 327777	Jurys Hotel		H	£145	68%	95		▲	▲		Ennis Rd Limerick
Limerick	061 326666	Limerick Inn Hotel		H	£120	68%	153		▲	▲		Ennis Rd Limerick
Limerick	061 453922	Limerick Ryan Hotel		H	£90	62%	181					Ardhu House Ennis Rd
Limerick	061 415457	Mortells	£30	R								49 Roches St Limerick
Limerick	061 411111	Quenelle's Restaurant	£70	R								Upper Henry St Limerick
Limerick	061 326255	Two Mile Inn		H	£95	63%	123					Ennis Rd Limerick

Co Longford

Location	Telephone	Establishment	Food Price	Category	Room Price	Hotel %	No. of Rooms	Beautifully Situated	Family Friendly	Swimming Pool	Golf	Address
Moydow	043 22122	The Vintage	£45	R					▲			Moydow

Co Louth

Location	Telephone	Establishment	Food Price	Category	Room Price	Hotel %	No. of Rooms	Beautifully Situated	Family Friendly	Swimming Pool	Golf	Address
Ardee	041 53523	Red House		A	£65							Ardee
Blackrock	042 21393	Brake Tavern		P			3					Blackrock nr Dundalk
Carlingford	042 73118	Carlingford House		A	£35		5	▲				Carlingford
Carlingford	042 73223	Jordan's Townhouse	£60	RR	£75		5					Carlingford
Carlingford	042 73751	Magee's Bistro	£35	R								D'Arcy Magee Centre
Carlingford	042 73116	McKevitt's Village Hotel		H	£60	59%	13	▲				Carlingford
Carlingford	042 73106	The Anchor Bar		P								Carlingford
Collon	041 26272	Forge Gallery Restaurant	£65	R								Collon
Drogheda	041 37737	Boyne Valley Hotel		H	£84	65%	38					Drogheda
Dundalk	042 71124	Ballymascanlon House		H	£80	62%	55		▲	▲		Ballymascanlon Dundalk
Dundalk	042 38567	Quaglino's	£60	R								Clanbrassil St Dundalk
Termonfeckin	041 22616	Triple House Restaurant	£60	R								Termonfeckin

Co Mayo

Location	Phone	Name		Type		%	No				Address
Ballina	096 21033	Downhill Hotel	£55	H	£119	65%	50		▲		Ballina
Ballina	096 70811	Mount Falcon Castle		AR	£98	60%	10	▲	▲		Ballina
Cong	092 46003	Ashford Castle/Connaught Room	£100	HR ↑	£275	89%	83	▲		▲	Cong
Crossmolina	096 31112	Enniscoe House		A	£96		6	▲			Castlehill nr Crossmolina
Dugort	098 43244	Gray's Guest House		A	£40		15				Dugort Achill Island
Keel	098 43134	The Beehive		JaB							Keel Achill Island
Lecanvey	098 64850	Staunton's		P							Lecanvey Westport
Mulraney	098 36264	Rosturk Woods		A	£55		4	▲			Rosturk Mulrany
Newport	098 41222	Newport House	£75	HR	£138	67%	18				Newport
Pontoon	094 56443	Healy's Hotel	£50	HR	£55	60%	10				Pontoon
Westport	098 25319	Asgard Tavern & Restaurant	£55	R/P							The Quay Westport
Westport	098 26655	Matt Molloy's Bar		P							Bridge St Westport
Westport	098 25166	The Olde Railway Hotel		H	£70	63%	24				The Mall Westport
Westport	098 26412	Quay Cottage Restaurant	£50	R				▲			The Quay Westport
Westport	098 26534	Towers Bar		P						▲	The Quay Westport
Westport	098 25886	West Bar		P							Lower Bridge St Westport
Westport	098 25811	Westport Woods Hotel		H	£96	62%	95				Louisburgh Rd Westport

Co Meath

Location	Phone	Name		Type		%	No				Address
Ceanannas Mor (Kells)	046 41110	O'Shaughnessy's		P							Market St Ceanannas Mor
Kilmoon	01 835 4277	Snail Box		P							Kilmoon
Navan	046 23119	Ardboyne Hotel	£55	HR	£78	60%	27				Dublin Rd Navan
Navan	046 29231	Hudson's Bistro	£50	R							30 Railway St Navan
Skryne	046 25122	O'Connell's		P							Skryne nr Tara

Co Monaghan

Location	Telephone	Establishment	Food Price	Category	Room Price	Hotel %	No. of Rooms	Beautifully Situated	Family Friendly	Swimming Pool	Golf	Address
Carrickmacross	042 61438	Nuremore Hotel		H	£120	72%	69		▲		▲	Carrickmacross
Castleblayney	042 46666	Glencam Hotel		H	£65	62%	30		▲			Castleblayney
Clones	047 56007	Hilton Park		A	£135		6					Scotshouse Clones
Monaghan	047 82277	Andy's Bar & Restaurant		R/P								Monaghan
Monaghan	047 81288	Hillgrove Hotel		H	£80	66%	44					Old Armagh Rd Monaghan
Scotshouse	047 56007	Hilton Park		A	£111		5	▲			▲	Scotshouse nr Clones

Co Offaly

Location	Telephone	Establishment	Food Price	Category	Room Price	Hotel %	No. of Rooms	Beautifully Situated	Family Friendly	Swimming Pool	Golf	Address
Banagher	0509 51350	Brosna Lodge Hotel		H	£52	56%	14					Banagher
Banagher	0509 51893	JJ Hough's		P								Main St Banagher
Banagher	0509 51463	The Vine House		P								Westend Banagher
Birr	0509 20032	Dooly's Hotel		H	£60	60%	18					Birr
Birr	0509 20572	Tullanisk		A	£90		7	▲				Birr
Crinkle	0509 20682	The Thatch	£50	R/P					▲			Crinkle Birr
Dunkerrin	0505 45377	Dunkerrin Arms		P	£37		6					Dunkerrin Birr
Kinnity	0509 37318	Kinnitty Castle		A	£120		18	▲				Kinnitty Birr

Co Roscommon

Location	Telephone	Establishment	Food Price	Category	Room Price	Hotel %	No. of Rooms	Beautifully Situated	Family Friendly	Swimming Pool	Golf	Address
Athleague	0903 63383	Gilligan's Olde Worlde Tavern		P								Athleague

Co Sligo

Location	Telephone	Establishment	Food Price	Category	Room Price	Hotel %	No. of Rooms	Beautifully Situated	Family Friendly	Swimming Pool	Golf	Address
Ballisodare	071 67288	The Thatch		P								Ballisodare
Ballymote	071 83329	Temple House		A	£80		5					Ballymote
Castlebaldwin	071 65155	Cromleach Lodge	£80	HR★	£130	78%	10	▲				Castlebaldwin via Boyle

Town	Phone	Establishment	£	Code	£	%	No.				Address
Collooney	071 67787	Glebe House	£45				5	▲			Collooney
Collooney	071 67800	Markree Castle	£55	HR	£108	66%	30	▲			Collooney
Drumcliff	071 63117	Yeats Tavern & Davis's Pub		P					▲		Drumcliff
Riverstown	071 65108	Coopershill House	£60	AR	£95	69%	8	▲			Riverstown
Rosses Point	071 77111	Austie's		P							Rosses Point
Rosses Point	071 77112	The Moorings	£55	R				▲	▲		Rosses Point
Sligo	071 44226	Bistro Bianconi	£35	R							The Mall Sligo
Sligo	071 70933	Hargadon's		P							O'Connell St Sligo
Sligo	071 62857	McGettigan's		P	£31		10	▲	▲		Connolly St Sligo
Sligo	071 60291	Sligo Park		H	£99	58%	90		▲		Pearse Rd Sligo
Sligo	071 44000	The Tower Hotel		H	£76	64%	58				Quay St Sligo
Strandhill	071 68140	The Strand	£50	R/P							Strandhill
Tubbercurry	071 85679	Killoran's		P				▲	▲		Main St Tubbercurry

Co Tipperary

Town	Phone	Establishment	£	Code	£	%	No.				Address
Birdhill	061 379227	Matt the Thresher		P							Birdhill
Borrisokane	067 21129	Ballycormac House		A	£60		5				Aglish Borrisokane
Cashel	062 61177	Chez Hans	£70	R							Rockside Cashel
Cashel	062 62130	Dowling's		P							Cashel
Cashel	062 61143	The Spearman	£50	R							Main St Cashel
Clonmel	052 21233	Clonmel Arms		H	£85	61%	31				Sarsfield St Clonmel
Clonmel	052 38353	Knocklofty House	£60	HR	£120	67%	14	▲	▲		Knocklofty nr Clonmel
Dundrum	062 71116	Dundrum House		H	£97	66%	60	▲			Dundrum
Glen of Aherlow	062 56153	Aherlow House		H	£70	63%	30	▲		▲	Glen of Aherlow nr Tipperary
Killaloe	061 376792	Goosers		P*							Killaloe Ballina
Thurles	0504 51261	Inch House	£55	AR	£50		5				Bouldaduff nr Thurles

Co Waterford

Location	Telephone	Establishment	Food Price	Category	Room Price	Hotel %	No. of Rooms	beautifully Situated	Family Friendly	Swimming Pool	Golf	Address
Ardmore	024 94106	Cliff House Hotel		H	£80	59%	20	▲				Ardmore
Checkpoint	051 382119	McAlpin's Suir Inn		P								Checkpoint
Dunmore East	051 383141	The Ship		R/P								Dunmore East
Lismore	058 56232	Buggy's Glencairn Inn	£60	I	£36		3					Glencairn nr Lismore
Waterford	051 77478	Dwyer's Restaurant		R								8 Mary St Waterford
Waterford	051 74308	Foxmount Farm		A	£45		6					off Passage Rd East
Waterford	051 855111	Granville Hotel		H	£90	69%	74					1 Meagher Quay Waterford
Waterford	051 874118	Henry Downes		P								10 Thomas St Waterford
Waterford	051 73187	Jack Meade's Bar		P				▲				Cheekpoint Rd Halfway Hse
Waterford	051 832111	Jurys Hotel		H	£135	61%	98	▲	▲			Ferrybank Waterford
Waterford	051 78851	Prendiville's Restaurant	£55	RR	£49		9					Cork Rd Waterford
Waterford	051 75801	Tower Hotel		H	£132	59%	141		▲	▲		The Mall Waterford
Waterford	051 78203	Waterford Castle	£80	HR	£240	74%	19	▲	▲	▲	▲	The Island Ballinakill
Waterford	051 853444	The Wine Vault	£55	R								High St Waterford

Co Westmeath

Location	Telephone	Establishment	Food Price	Category	Room Price	Hotel %	No. of Rooms	beautifully Situated	Family Friendly	Swimming Pool	Golf	Address
Athlone	0902 94517	Restaurant Le Chateau	£55	R								Abbey Lane Athlone
Athlone	0902 92519	Higgins's		P	£32		4					2 Pearce St Athlone
Athlone	0902 92444	Hodson Bay Hotel		H	£105	66%	100	▲		▲	▲	Hodson Bay nr Athlone
Athlone	0902 94446	Left Bank Bistro	£55	R								Bastion St Athlone
Athlone	0902 92358	Sean's Bar		P								13 Main St Athlone
Glasson	0902 85001	Glasson Village Restaurant	£50	R								Glasson nr Athlone
Glasson	0902 85158	Grogan's & Nannie Murph's		P				▲				Glasson nr Athlone
Glasson	0902 85466	Wineport Restaurant	£55	R				▲				Glasson nr Athlone

Town	Phone	Name	Single	Type	Double	%	No.					Address
Kinnegad	044 75284	The Cottage										Kinnegad
Mullingar	044 72165	Crookedwood House	£55	RR	£90		8	▲				Crookedwood Mullingar

Co Wexford

Town	Phone	Name	Single	Type	Double	%	No.					Address
Ballyhack	051 389284	Neptune Restaurant	£50	R								Ballyhack New Ross
Ballymurn	053 38105	Ballinkeele House		A	£70		5					Enniscorthy Ballymurn
Bunclody	054 77253	Clohamon House		A	£90		4		▲			Bunclody
Carne	053 31110	Lobster Pot	£50	R/P*					▲	▲		Carne
Ferrycarrig Bridge	053 20999	Ferrycarrig Hotel	£65	HR	£100	61%	40		▲	▲	▲	Ferrycarrig Bridge
Foulksmills	051 565771	Horetown House	£50	R						▲		Foulksmills
Gorey	055 21124	Marlfield House	£80	HR	£160	81%	19		▲			Gorey
Kilmore Quay	053 29830	Kehoe's Pub & Parlour		P								Kilmore Quay
Kilmore Quay	053 29888	The Silver Fox	£45	R								Kilmore Quay
Kilmuckridge	053 30181	Boggan's & Rafters Restaurant	£55	R/P								Kilmuckridge
Newbawn	051 428386	Cedar Lodge		H	£78	62%	28					Carrigbyrne Newbawn
Newbay	053 42779	Newbay Country House		A	£70	62%	6	▲				Newbay nr Wexford
Rosslare	053 33233	Great Southern		H	£94	62%	100			▲	▲	Rosslare
Rosslare	053 32114	Kelly's Resort Hotel	£55	HR	£132	76%	99			▲	▲	Rosslare
Wexford	053 22316	Archer's		P								Redmond Square Wexford
Wexford	053 43141	Clonard House	£40	A			9					Clonard Great Wexford
Wexford	053 22311	White's Hotel	£55	H	£82	60%	82				▲	George St Wexford

Co Wicklow

Town	Phone	Name	Single	Type	Double	%	No.					Address
Blessington	045 865199	Downshire House	£60	H	£77	59%	25				▲	Blessington
Bray	01 286 3498	The Tree of Idleness	£40	R								Seafront Bray
Delgany	01 287 5701	Delgany Inn		IR	£50		12					Delgany
Delgany	01 287 3399	Glenview Hotel		H	£125	65%	43			▲	▲	Glen of the Downs
Dunlavin	045 403112	Rathsallagh House	£70	AR	£140	72%	17	▲		▲	▲	Dunlavin

Location	Telephone	Establishment	Food Price	Category	Room Price	Hotel %	No. of Rooms	Beautifully Situated	Family Friendly	Swimming Pool	Golf	Address
Enniskerry	01 286 3542	Enniscree Lodge	£60	HR	£80	59%	10	▲				Glencree Valley
Greystones	01 287 5759	The Hungry Monk	£60	R								Greystones
Kilmacanogue	01 286 7466	Avoca Handweavers		JaB								Kilmacanogue
Laragh	0404 45134	Derrybawn House		A	£50		6	▲				Laragh Glendalough
Laragh	0404 45302	Mitchell's of Laragh	£45	RR	£37		8	▲				Old Schoolhouse Laragh
Rathnew	0404 40106	Hunter's Hotel	£55	HR	£95	63%	16	▲				Newrath Bridge Rathnew
Rathnew	0404 69274	Tinakilly House	£80	HR	£132	76%	29					Rathnew Wicklow
Roundwood	01 281 8107	Roundwood Inn	£60	R/P★								Roundwood
Wicklow	0404 66770	The Bakery Café & Restaurant	£60	R								Church St Wicklow
Wicklow	0404 67048	Old Rectory	£60	AR	£92	69%	8	▲				Wicklow

Northern Ireland entries listed in County order

HR = Hotel with a recommended Restaurant open to the public H = Hotel RR = Restaurant with Rooms L = Lodge R = Restaurant I = Inn
P = Pub (see entries for details of food recommendations) A = Accommodation (classified by Bord Fáilte, the Irish Tourist Board, as a Private House or Irish Home)
AR = as A but with a recommended restaurant open to the public PH = Private House hotel (Northern Ireland only)

See Starred Restaurants & De Luxe hotels lists and map on page 13 for Ireland's highest-graded hotels. R* and R‡ restaurant listings. P* indicates starred **bar** food (not restaurant food) in pubs. Some hotels are upgraded due to their categorisation as a Private House (A or PH) or as an Inn without public rooms (I); the former are usually de luxe B&B establishments and, generally, their restaurants may not be open to non-residents (thus the food is not specifically recommended – although it is often prepared to a good standard for residents). Restaurants with Rooms are also ungraded.

Restaurants without prices are generally of an informal, snackier nature and categorised as **JaB** (Just a Bite). Food is only recommended in pubs where the statistics at the end of a gazetteer entry include Bar Food times.

Swimming pool refers to an indoor pool (a few places have outdoor pool only – see Sporting Facilities quick reference list)

Location	Telephone	Establishment	Food Price	Category	Room Price	Hotel %	No. of Rooms	Beautifully Situated	Family Friendly	Swimming Pool	Golf	Address
Antrim												
Ballycastle	01265 762975	House of McDonnell		P								71 Castle St Ballycastle
Ballycastle	01265 762222	The Marine Hotel		H	£70	63%						1-3 North St Ballycastle
Ballymena	01266 653674	Adair Arms Hotel		H	£78	62%		▲				Ballymoney Rd
Ballymena	01266 881001	Galgorm Manor	£70	HR	£125	71%	23	▲				136 Fenaghy Rd
Ballymena	01266 652639	Tullyglass House Hotel		H	£100	67%						Galgorm Rd
Ballymoney	01265 663924	Old Bank House		R/P				▲				9 Church St
Belfast	01232 311121	Antica Roma	£65	R								67 Botanic Ave
Belfast	01232 640099	Bengal Brasserie	£35	R								339 Ormeau Rd
Belfast	01232 249476	Crown Liquor Saloon		P								46 Great Victoria St
Belfast	01232 236666	Dukes Hotel	£100	H	£100	67%	21					65 University St
Belfast	01232 327000	Europa Hotel	£148	H	£148	71%	184					Great Victoria St

Location	Telephone	Establishment	Food Price	Category	Room Price	Hotel %	No. of Rooms	Beautifully Situated	Family Friendly	Swimming Pool	Golf	Address
Belfast	01232 333555	Holiday Inn Garden Court		H	£85	64%	76					15 Brunswick St
Belfast	01232 324835	Kelly's Cellars		P								30/32 Bank St
Belfast	01232 238755	Manor House Cantonese	£45	R								43-47 Donegall Pass
Belfast	01232 230063	Mizuna	£45	R								99 Botanic Ave
Belfast	01232 439690	Nick's Warehouse	£45	R								35-39 Hill St
Belfast	01232 331532	Roscoff	£80	R*								Lesley Hse Shaftesbury Sq
Belfast	01232 230213	Speranza	£40	R				▲				16 Shaftesbury Square
Belfast	01232 658621	Stormont Hotel		H	£133	69%	106					Upper Newtownards Rd
Belfast	01232 328356	Villa Italia	£45	R				▲				39 University Rd
Belfast	01232 381359	Welcome Restaurant	£50	R								22 Stranmillis Rd
Belfast	01232 381111	Wellington Park		H	£110		50					21 Malone Rd
Belfast Airport	01849 422033	Aldergrove Airport Hotel		H	£87	62%	108	▲				Belfast Airport
Carnlough	01574 885255	Londonderry Arms Hotel		I	£70		▲					20 Harbour Rd Carnlough
Carrickfergus	01960 364192	Wind-Rose Bar		JaB								The Marina
Cushendall	none	PJ McCollam		P								23 Mill St Cushendall
Dunadry	01849 432474	Dunadry Inn		H	£115	64%	67	▲	▲			2 Islandreagh Drive
Portballintrae	01265 731453	Bayview Hotel		H	£70	58%	16	▲	▲			Bayhead Rd Portballintrae
Portballintrae	01265 732404	Sweeney's		R/P								6 Seaport Ave
Portglenone	01648 50694	Crosskeys Inn		P								Portglenone
Templepatrick	01849 432984	Templeton Hotel		H	£110	66%	24					882 Antrim Rd Ballyclare

Down

Town	Phone	Establishment	£	Type	Rate	%	No.					Address
Annalong	01396 768451	Glassdrumman Lodge	£60	HR	£110	69%	10			◄	◄	85 Mill Rd Annalong
Bangor	01247 852500	Clandeboye Lodge Hotel		H	£98	65%	43	◄		◄	◄	10 Estate Rd Clandeboye
Bangor	01247 451100	Marine Court Hotel		H	£85	64%	51		◄			18-20 Quay St Bangor
Bangor	01247 853313	Shanks	£75	R★								Blackwood Golf Centre
Bangor	01247 473737	Villa Toscana	£40	R					◄			Toscana Park Waste Circle Rd
Comber	01232 448631	La Mon House		H	£85	59%	38	◄		◄		The Mills 41 Gransha Rd
Crawfordsburn	01247 853255	Old Inn		I	£85		33					15 Main St Crawfordsburn
Dundrum	01396 751868	Buck's Head Inn		P								77 Main St Dundrum
Dunmurry	01232 612101	Forte Posthouse Belfast		H	£99	67%	82		◄			300 Kingsway Dunmurry
Helen's Bay	01247 852841	Deane's on the Square	£75	R↑								7 Station Square
Hillsborough	01846 682765	The Hillside Bar		P★								21 Main St
Hillsborough	01846 682985	The Plough Inn		P								The Square
Hillsborough	01846 682755	White Gables Hotel		H	£101	60%	31					14 Dromore Rd
Holywood	01232 426414	Bay Tree		JaB								High St Audley Court
Holywood	01232 425223	Culloden Hotel		H	£160	78%	92		◄			Bangor Rd Craigavad
Holywood	01232 421000	Sullivans	£60	R								Sullivan Place Holywood
Newcastle	01396 721006	Slieve Donard Hotel		H	£110	63%	126		◄			Downs Rd Newcastle
Portaferry	01247 728148	The Narrows		PH	£58		13			◄		8 Shore Rd Portaferry
Portaferry	01247 728231	Portaferry Hotel	£55	HR	£90	64%	14				◄	10 The Strand Portaferry

Fermanagh

Town	Phone	Establishment	£	Type	Rate	%	No.					Address
Bellanaleck	01365 348232	The Sheelin		JaB								Bellanaleck nr Enniskillen
Enniskillen	01365 322143	Blakes of the Hollow		P								6 Church St Enniskillen
Irvinestown	01365 621231	The Hollander		P								5 Main St Enniskillen
Kesh	01365 631275	Lough Erne Hotel		H	£59	60%	12			◄		Main St Kesh
Kesh	01365 632032	Lusty Beg Island		P	£45					◄	◄	Kesh
Tempo	01365 541450	Tempo Manor		PH	£100		5				◄	Tempo

Londonderry

Location	Telephone	Establishment	Food Price	Category	Room Price	Hotel %	No. of Rooms	Beautifully Situated	Family Friendly	Swimming Pool	Golf	Address
Aghadowey	01265 868209	Brown Trout Golf & Country Inn	£35	IR	£80			▲			▲	209 Agivey Rd
Aghadowey	01265 868241	Greenhill House		PH	£48		6	▲				24 Greenhill Rd
Coleraine	01265 52992	The Salmon Leap		JaB								53 Castleroe Rd
Limavady	01504 722212	Radisson Roe Park		H	£110	74%	64		▲		▲	Roe Park
Limavady	01504 766563	Streeve Hill		PH	£90							Limavady
Londonderry	01504 49279	Beech Hill House Hotel	£65	HR	£75	59%	17					32 Ardmore Rd
Londonderry	01504 46722	Everglades Hotel		H	£86	59%	63					Prehen Rd
Portrush	01265 822435	Causeway Coast Hotel		H	£80		21					36 Ballyreagh Rd
Portrush	01265 823394	Maddybenny Farmhouse		PH	£50			▲				Maddybenny Park
Portrush	01265 824313	Ramore	£65	R★								The Harbour Portrush
Portrush	01265 822236	Royal Court Hotel		H	£100	64%						Whiterocks Portrush
Upperlands	01648 44490	Ardtara House	£60	AR	£100		8	▲				Upperlands nr Maghera

Tyrone

Location	Telephone	Establishment	Food Price	Category	Room Price	Hotel %	No. of Rooms	Beautifully Situated	Family Friendly	Swimming Pool	Golf	Address
Cookstown	01648 765100	Tullylagan Country House		H	£70	64%	15					40b Tullylagan Rd
Dungannon	01868 784212	Grange Lodge		PH	£65							7 Grange Rd
Fivemiletown	01365 521221	Blessingbourne		PH	£90		4	▲				Fivemiletown

Hotels with Sporting Facilities

Hotels with Sporting Facilities

Certain facilities may not necessarily be owned by the hotels listed, but they are a major attraction of the establishment; many hotels arrange reduced green fees for golf or have an arrangement, say, with a local angling club. For example, *Halpin's Hotel* in Kilkee, Co Clare is popular with golfers (due to its proximity to a superb golf course); other hotels like *The Davenport* and *Mont Clare* hotels in Dublin offer an arrangement for their guests to have members' rates at the Riverview Racquets and Fitness Club (see entries for further details).

Location	Establishment	Category	Indoor Pool	Outdoor Pool	Squash	Tennis	Golf	Fishing	Riding	Croquet
REPUBLIC OF IRELAND										
Co Cavan										
Ballyconnell	Slieve Russell Hotel	H	▲			▲	▲	▲		
Co Clare										
Ballyvaughan	Gregans Castle Hotel	HR								▲
Bunratty	Fitzpatrick Bunratty Shamrock Hotel	H	▲							
Ennis	Auburn Lodge Hotel	H				▲				
Ennis	West County Hotel	H	▲			▲				
Kilkee	Halpin's Hotel	H					▲			
Lahinch	Aberdeen Arms Hotel	H				▲				
Lisdoonvarna	Sheedy's Spa View Hotel	HR				▲				
Newmarket-on-Fergus	Clare Inn Hotel	H	▲			▲	▲		▲	▲
Newmarket-on-Fergus	Dromoland Castle	HR				▲	▲	▲	▲	▲
Co Cork										
Ballinadee	Glebe Country House	A				▲				▲
Ballylickey	Ballylickey Manor House	AR		▲				▲		▲
Bantry	Westlodge Hotel	H	▲		▲	▲				
Castlelyons	Ballyvolane House	A						▲		▲
Cork	Arbutus Lodge	HR				▲				
Cork	Fitzpatrick Silver Springs	H	▲		▲	▲	▲			
Cork	Hayfield Manor Hotel	H	▲							
Cork	Jurys Hotel	H	▲	▲	▲					
Cork	Metropole Hotel	H	▲							
Cork	Rochestown Park Hotel	H	▲							
Innishannon	Innishannon House Hotel	H						▲		
Kanturk	Assolas Country House	AR				▲		▲		
Kinsale	Actons Hotel	H	▲							
Kinsale	Blue Haven Hotel	HR						▲		
Mallow	Longueville House	HR						▲		
Midleton	Glenview House	A					▲			▲
Shanagarry	Ballymaloe House	AR		▲		▲	▲			▲

Location	Establishment	Category	Indoor Pool	Outdoor Pool	Squash	Tennis	Golf	Fishing	Riding	Croquet
Co Donegal										
Ballybofey	Kee's Hotel	HR	▲							
Bunbeg	Ostan Gweedore	H	▲			▲				
Donegal Town	Ardnamona House	A						▲		
Donegal Town	Harvey's Point Country Hotel	HR				▲		▲		
Letterkenny	Castle Grove Country House	AR				▲		▲		▲
Rathmullan	Rathmullan House	HR	▲			▲				
Rossnowlagh	Sand House Hotel	HR				▲		▲		
Co Dublin										
Dublin 4	Jurys Hotel Dublin	H	▲	▲						
Dublin 4	The Towers at Lansdowne Road	H	▲	▲						
Dublin 13	Marine Hotel	H	▲							
Howth	Deer Park Hotel	HR					▲			
Howth	Howth Lodge Hotel	HR	▲							
Killiney	Court Hotel	H						▲		
Killiney	Fitzpatrick's Castle	H	▲		▲	▲				
Co Galway										
Cashel	Cashel House	HR				▲		▲	▲	
Cashel	Zetland House	HR				▲		▲		▲
Clifden	Abbeyglen Castle	H		▲		▲				
Clifden	Rock Glen Manor	HR				▲				▲
Furbo	Connemara Coast Hotel	H	▲			▲				
Galway	Corrib Great Southern Hotel	H	▲							
Galway	Galway Ryan Hotel	H	▲							
Galway	Glenlo Abbey Hotel	HR					▲			
Galway	Great Southern	H	▲							
Leenane	Delphi Lodge	A						▲		
Leenane	Killary Lodge	H				▲				
Letterfrack	Rosleague Manor	HR						▲		
Moycullen	Cloonnabinnia House Hotel	HR						▲		
Oughterard	Connemara Gateway Hotel	H	▲			▲				▲
Oughterard	Currarevagh House	AR				▲		▲		
Recess	Ballynahinch Castle	H				▲		▲		▲
Recess	Lough Inagh Lodge	H						▲		
Renvyle	Renvyle House	H		▲		▲	▲	▲	▲	▲
Co Kerry										
Beaufort	Hotel Dunloe Castle	H	▲			▲		▲	▲	
Caherdaniel	Derrynane Hotel	HR		▲						
Caragh Lake	Hotel Ard-na-Sidhe	H						▲		
Caragh Lake	Caragh Lodge	A				▲		▲		
Dingle	Dingle Skellig Hotel	H	▲			▲				
Dingle	Milltown House	A							▲	
Kenmare	Dromquinna Manor Hotel	H				▲		▲		
Kenmare	Park Hotel Kenmare	HR				▲	▲			▲
Kenmare	Sheen Falls Lodge	HR				▲	▲	▲	▲	

Location	Establishment	Category	Indoor Pool	Outdoor Pool	Squash	Tennis	Golf	Fishing	Riding	Croquet
Co Kerry (continued)										
Killarney	Aghadoe Heights Hotel	HR	▲			▲		▲		
Killarney	Cahernane Hotel	HR				▲		▲		
Killarney	Hotel Europe	H	▲			▲		▲	▲	
Killarney	Great Southern	H	▲			▲				
Killarney	Kathleen's Country House	A								▲
Killarney	Killarney Park Hotel	H	▲							
Killarney	Killarney Ryan Hotel	H	▲							
Killarney	Torc Great Southern	H	▲							
Parknasilla	Parknasilla Great Southern	H	▲			▲	▲	▲	▲	
Tahilla	Tahilla Cove Country House	A								▲
Tralee	Brandon Hotel	H	▲							
Co Kildare										
Castledermot	Kilkea Castle	HR	▲			▲	▲	▲		
Maynooth	Moyglare Manor	HR				▲				
Newbridge	Hotel Keadeen	H	▲							
Straffan	Kildare Hotel	HR	▲		▲	▲	▲	▲		
Co Kilkenny										
Kilkenny	Newpark Hotel	H	▲			▲				
Thomastown	Mount Juliet Hotel	HR	▲			▲	▲	▲	▲	▲
Co Laois										
Abbeyleix	Morrisseys	P								▲
Mountrath	Roundwood House	HR						▲		▲
Co Leitrim										
Carrick-on-Shannon	Hollywell House	A						▲		
Co Limerick										
Adare	Adare Manor	HR	▲				▲	▲	▲	
Adare	Dunraven Arms	HR	▲			▲				
Castleconnell	Castle Oaks House Hotel	H	▲			▲		▲		
Glin	Glin Castle	A				▲				▲
Limerick	Castletroy Park Hotel	HR	▲			▲				
Limerick	Greenhills Hotel	H	▲			▲				
Limerick	Jurys Hotel	H	▲			▲				
Limerick	Limerick Inn Hotel	H	▲			▲				
Co Louth										
Dundalk	Ballymascanlon House	H	▲		▲	▲	▲			
Co Mayo										
Ballina	Downhill Hotel	H	▲		▲	▲				
Ballina	Mount Falcon Castle	AR				▲		▲		
Cong	Ashford Castle	HR				▲	▲	▲	▲	▲
Crossmolina	Enniscoe House	A						▲		
Newport	Newport House	HR						▲		
Westport	The Olde Railway Hotel	H						▲		

Location	Establishment	Category	Indoor Pool	Outdoor Pool	Squash	Tennis	Golf	Fishing	Riding	Croquet
Co Monaghan										
Carrickmacross	Nuremore Hotel	H	▲		▲	▲	▲			
Castleblayney	Glencarn Hotel	H	▲							
Scotshouse	Hilton Park	A					▲	▲		
Co Offaly										
Birr	Dooly's Hotel	H						▲		
Birr	Tullanisk	A								▲
Kinnitty	Kinnitty Castle	A						▲	▲	
Co Sligo										
Ballymote	Temple House	A						▲		▲
Castlebaldwin	Cromleach Lodge	HR						▲		
Collooney	Markree Castle	HR						▲		
Riverstown	Coopershill House	AR				▲		▲		▲
Sligo	Sligo Park	H	▲			▲				
Co Tipperary										
Clonmel	Knocklofty House	HR	▲		▲	▲		▲	▲	
Dundrum	Dundrum House	H			▲	▲	▲	▲		
Glen of Aherlow	Aherlow House	H							▲	
Co Waterford										
Waterford	Jurys Hotel	H	▲			▲				
Waterford	Tower Hotel	H	▲							
Waterford	Waterford Castle	HR	▲			▲	▲			
Co Westmeath										
Athlone	Hodson Bay Hotel	H	▲			▲	▲	▲		
Co Wexford										
Bunclody	Clohamon House	A						▲	▲	
Ferrycarrig Bridge	Ferrycarrig Hotel	HR	▲							
Foulksmills	Horetown House	R							▲	
Gorey	Marlfield House	HR				▲				
Rosslare	Great Southern	H	▲			▲				
Rosslare	Kelly's Resort Hotel	HR	▲	▲	▲	▲				▲
Co Wicklow										
Blessington	Downshire House	H				▲				▲
Delgany	Glenview Hotel	H	▲							
Dunlavin	Rathsallagh House	AR	▲			▲	▲			▲
Rathnew	Tinakilly House	HR				▲				▲

Location	Establishment	Category	Indoor Pool	Outdoor Pool	Squash	Tennis	Golf	Fishing	Riding	Croquet
NORTHERN IRELAND										
Antrim										
Ballymena	Galgorm Manor	HR						▲	▲	
Dunadry	Dunadry Inn	H	▲					▲		▲
Portballintrae	Bayview Hotel	H	▲							
Templepatrick	Templeton Hotel	H		▲						▲
Coleraine										
Portrush	Maddybenny Farmhouse	A							▲	▲
Down										
Annalong	Glassdrumman Lodge	HR				▲				
Bangor	Clandeboye Lodge Hotel	H					▲		▲	
Bangor	Marine Court Hotel	H	▲							
Comber	La Mon House	H	▲							
Holywood	Culloden Hotel	HR	▲		▲	▲				
Newcastle	Slieve Donard Hotel	H	▲							
Fermanagh										
Kesh	Lough Erne Hotel	H						▲		
Kesh	Lusty Beg Island	A				▲		▲		▲
Tempo	Tempo Manor	PH						▲		▲
Londonderry										
Aghadowey	Brown Trout Golf & Country Inn	IR					▲	▲	▲	
Limavady	Radisson Roe Park	H	▲				▲			
Londonderry	Beech Hill House Hotel	HR				▲				▲
Upperlands	Ardtara House	AR				▲				
Tyrone										
Fivemiletown	Blessingbourne	PH				▲			▲	

Maps

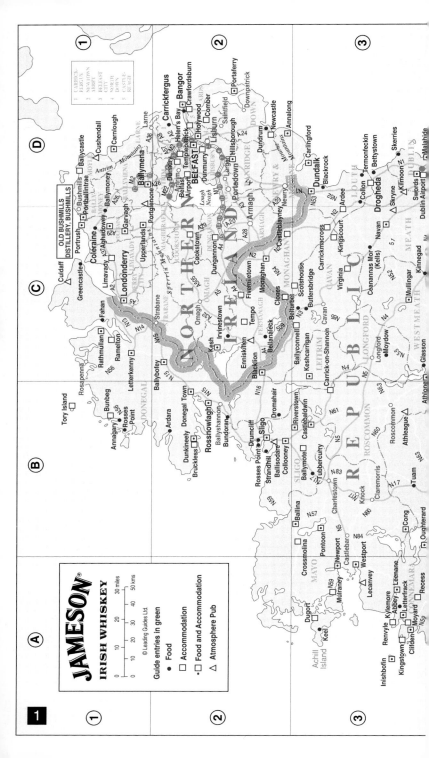

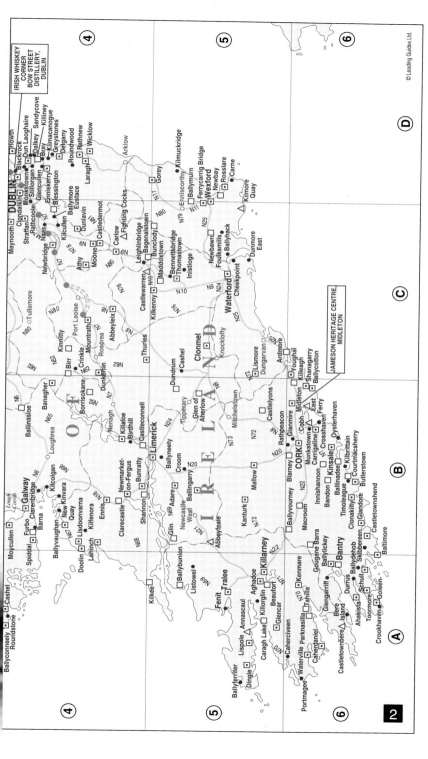

IRISH WHISKEY CORNER
BOW STREET
DISTILLERY,
DUBLIN

JAMESON HERITAGE CENTRE,
MIDLETON

© Leading Guides Ltd.

2

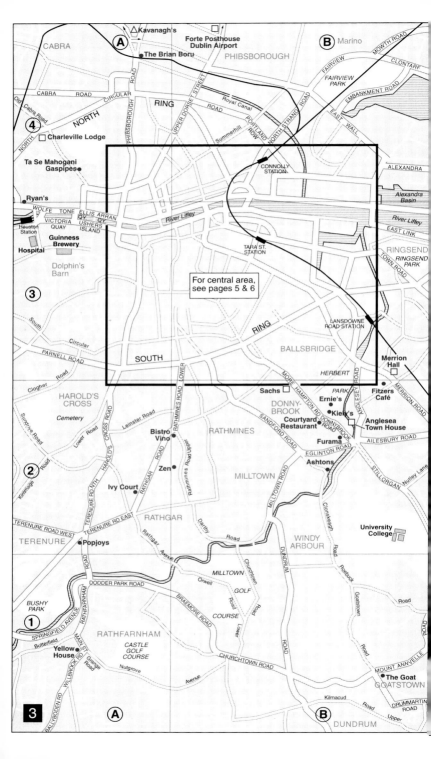

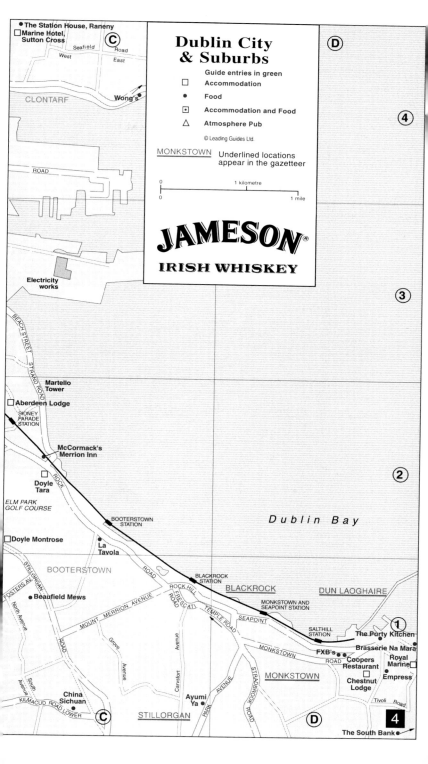

Dublin City & Suburbs

Guide entries in green

☐ Accommodation

● Food

⊡ Accommodation and Food

△ Atmosphere Pub

© Leading Guides Ltd.

<u>MONKSTOWN</u> Underlined locations appear in the gazetteer

0   1 kilometre
0   1 mile

JAMESON®
IRISH WHISKEY

Ⓒ   Ⓓ

④   ③   ②   ①

● The Station House, Raheny
☐ Marine Hotel, Sutton Cross

Seafield Road
West   East

CLONTARF

Wong's ●

ROAD

Electricity works

BEACH STREET   STRAND ROAD

Martello Tower

☐ Aberdeen Lodge

SIDNEY PARADE STATION

McCormack's Merrion Inn

☐ Doyle Tara

ROCK ROAD

ELM PARK GOLF COURSE

☐ Doyle Montrose

BOOTERSTOWN STATION

Dublin Bay

La Tavola

BOOTERSTOWN

FOSTERS AVENUE

STILLORGAN ROAD

● Beaufield Mews

North Avenue

MOUNT MERRION AVENUE

Grove Avenue

Carysfort Avenue

ROCK HILL

FRESCATI ROAD

TEMPLE ROAD

SEAPOINT

BLACKROCK STATION

BLACKROCK

DUN LAOGHAIRE

MONKSTOWN AND SEAPOINT STATION

SALTHILL STATION

① The Purty Kitchen

MONKSTOWN ROAD

FXB's ● ●

Brasserie Na Mara

Coopers Restaurant

Royal Marine ☐

Empress

☐ Chestnut Lodge

Tivoli Road

South Avenue

KILMACUD ROAD LOWER

China Sichuan ●

Ⓒ

STILLORGAN

Ayumi Ya ●

STRADBROOK ROAD

PARK AVENUE

<u>MONKSTOWN</u>

Ⓓ

The South Bank ●

4

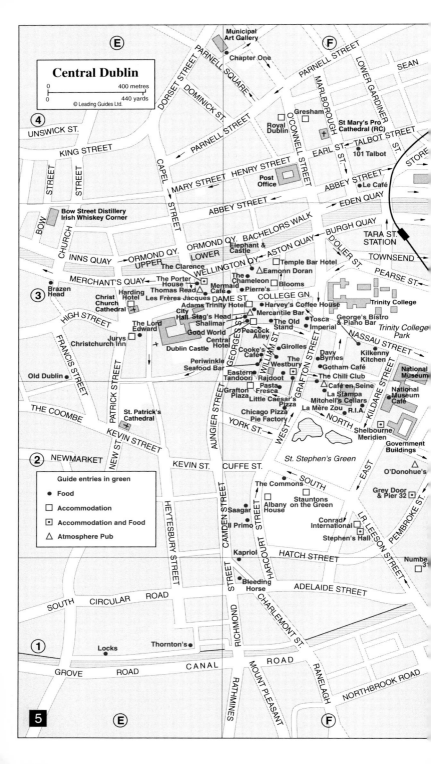

Central Dublin

0	400 metres
0	440 yards

© Leading Guides Ltd.

E **F**

4

Municipal Art Gallery
Chapter One
PARNELL SQUARE
PARNELL STREET
SEAN
DORSET STREET
DOMINICK ST.
MARLBOROUGH
LOWER GARDINER STREET
Gresham
Royal Dublin
O'CONNELL STREET
St Mary's Pro Cathedral (RC)
UNSWICK ST.
KING STREET
CAPEL STREET
PARNELL STREET
EARL ST.
TALBOT STREET
STREET
STREET
MARY STREET
HENRY STREET
101 Talbot
ST.
STORE
Post Office
ABBEY STREET
Le Café
BOW
CHURCH
Bow Street Distillery Irish Whiskey Corner
STREET
ABBEY STREET
EDEN QUAY
BURGH QUAY
INNS QUAY
ORMOND QY. BACHELORS WALK
ORMOND QY. LOWER
TARA ST. STATION
Elephant & Castle
ASTON QUAY
D'OLIER ST.
TOWNSEND
ORMOND QY. UPPER
WELLINGTON QY.
Temple Bar Hotel
PEARSE ST.
MERCHANT'S QUAY
The Clarence
Eamonn Doran
3
Brazen Head
The Porter House
The Chameleon
Blooms
Trinity College
Thomas Read
Mermaid Café
Pierre's
Christ Church Cathedral
Harding Hotel
Les Frères Jacques
Adams Trinity Hotel
Harvey's Coffee House
HIGH STREET
City Hall
Stag's Head
Mercantile Bar
George's Bistro & Piano Bar
The Lord Edward
Good World
The Old Stand
Tosca
Trinity College Park
Jurys Christchurch Inn
Peacock Alley
Imperial
NASSAU STREET
FRANCIS STREET
Dublin Castle
Central Hotel
Cooke's Café
Girolles
Davy Byrnes
Kilkenny Kitchen
Old Dublin
Periwinkle Seafood Bar
The Westbury
Gotham Café
National Museum
Eastern Tandoori
Rajdoot
The Chili Club
Café en Seine
National Museum Café
THE COOMBE
PATRICK STREET
St. Patrick's Cathedral
Grafton Plaza
Pasta Fresca
Little Caesar's Pizza
La Stampa
Mitchell's Cellars
La Mère Zou
R.I.A.
KEVIN ST.
Chicago Pizza Pie Factory
YORK ST.
Shelbourne Meridien
2
NEWMARKET
NEW STREET
KEVIN ST.
CUFFE ST.
St. Stephen's Green
Government Buildings
O'Donohue's
SOUTH
The Commons
EAST
Grey Door & Pier 32
PEMBROKE ST.
HEYTESBURY STREET
Albany House
Stauntons on the Green
CAMDEN STREET
Saagar
Il Primo
Conrad International
LR. LEESON STREET
Numbe 3
HARCOURT STREET
Kapriol
Stephen's Hall
HATCH STREET
STREET
Bleeding Horse
ADELAIDE STREET
SOUTH CIRCULAR ROAD
RICHMOND
CHARLEMONT ST.
1
Locks
Thornton's
GROVE ROAD
CANAL
RATHMINES
MOUNT PLEASANT
NORTHBROOK ROAD
RANELAGH

Guide entries in green

- **●** Food
- **□** Accommodation
- **⊡** Accommodation and Food
- **△** Atmosphere Pub

5

E **F**

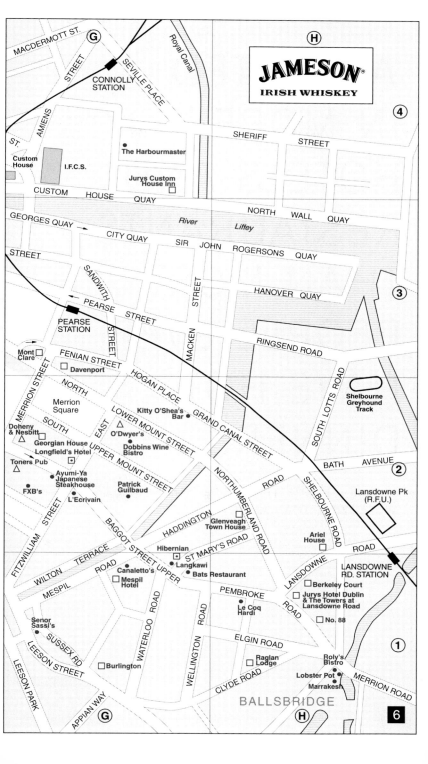

ACCEPTED IN MORE HOTELS AND RESTAURANTS THAN MOST PEOPLE EVER HAVE HOT DINNERS.

VISA IS ACCEPTED FOR MORE TRANSACTIONS WORLDWIDE THAN ANY OTHER CARD.

MAKING LIFE EASIER

Index

Advertisers' Index

Acknowledgements

Egon Ronay's Guides would particularly like to thank Georgina Campbell, our Ireland consultant, for her invaluable assistance in the writing and production of this Guide. We also wish to thank the following for their assistance in supplying photographs:

Reference

Shanks, Bangor
Jurys Hotel Group

Credit

Nick Cann
Frank Fennell Photography

Egon Ronay's Guides would also like to thank all those unnamed persons who kindly supplied photographs to assist in the compilation of this Guide.

ACCEPTED IN MORE HOTELS AND RESTAURANTS THAN MOST PEOPLE EVER HAVE HOT DINNERS.

VISA IS ACCEPTED FOR MORE TRANSACTIONS WORLDWIDE THAN ANY OTHER CARD.

MAKING LIFE EASIER

READERS' COMMENTS

Please use this sheet, and the continuation overleaf, to recommend establishments of **really outstanding quality** and to comment on existing entries.
Complaints about any of the Guide's entries will be treated seriously and passed on to our inspectorate, but we would like to remind you always to take up your complaint with the management at the time. We regret that owing to the volume of readers' communications received each year we will be unable to acknowledge these forms, but your comments will certainly be seriously considered.

Please post to:
Egon Ronay's Guides, 77 St John Street, London EC1M 4AN

Please use an up-to-date Guide. We publish annually. (Ireland 1997)

Name and address of establishment

Your recommendation or complaint

Name and address of establishment   **Your recommendation or complaint**

_____   _____

_____   _____

_____   _____

_____   _____

_____   _____

_____   _____

_____   _____

_____   _____

_____   _____

_____   _____

_____   _____

_____   _____

_____   _____

_____   _____

_____   _____

_____   _____

_____   _____

_____   _____

Your name and address _(BLOCK CAPITALS PLEASE)_

_____

_____

_____

_____

_____

_____

READERS' COMMENTS

Please use this sheet, and the continuation overleaf, to recommend establishments of **really outstanding quality** and to comment on existing entries.
Complaints about any of the Guide's entries will be treated seriously and passed on to our inspectorate, but we would like to remind you always to take up your complaint with the management at the time. We regret that owing to the volume of readers' communications received each year we will be unable to acknowledge these forms, but your comments will certainly be seriously considered.

Please post to:
Egon Ronay's Guides, 77 St John Street, London EC1M 4AN

Please use an up-to-date Guide. We publish annually. (Ireland 1997)

Name and address of establishment

Your recommendation or complaint

480

Name and address of establishment   **Your recommendation or complaint**

_____   _____

_____   _____

_____   _____

_____   _____

_____   _____

_____   _____

_____   _____

_____   _____

_____   _____

_____   _____

_____   _____

_____   _____

_____   _____

_____   _____

_____   _____

_____   _____

_____   _____

Your name and address *(BLOCK CAPITALS PLEASE)*

_____

_____

_____

_____

_____